D0948215

Speculum Spinozanum
1677–1977

1 Pictorial Tribute by Perle Hessing

199.492
Sp31

Speculum
Spinozanum
1677–1977

Edited by
Siegfried Hessing

with a foreword by
Huston Smith

Routledge & Kegan Paul
London, Henley and Boston

KIRTLEY LIBRARY
COLUMBIA COLLEGE
COLUMBIA, MO 65216

By the same author

Spinoza – Festschift 1632–1932
Spinoza – Dreihundert Jahre Ewigkeit (2nd edn)

First published in 1977
by Routledge & Kegan Paul Ltd
39 Store Street,
London WC1E 7DD,
Broadway House,
Newtown Road,
Henley-on-Thames,
Oxon RG9 1EN and
9 Park Street,
Boston, Mass. 02108, USA
Set in Monotype Times
and printed in Great Britain by
The Camelot Press Ltd, Southampton

© Routledge & Kegan Paul Ltd, 1977
No part of this book may be reproduced in
any form without permission from the
publisher, except for the quotation of brief
passages in criticism

British Library Cataloguing in Publication Data

Speculum Spinozanum, 1677–1977.

1. Spinoza, Benedictus de
I. Hessing, Siegfried. II. Spinoza, Benedictus de
199'.492   B3998   77-30214

SBN 0 7100 8716 0

*To my beloved Perle, a Sagittarius accompanying
with affinity her Capricorn as a pilgrim on the
path pointing to the very same otherlessness not
only to know but to become and to be it: the self
via the deifying pair-concept of all-oneness*

A PROSAIC HOMAGE TO PARALLEL
THE UNPROSAIC CHALLENGE
Royalties from this book and all its
future transactions (translation, etc.)
will go to the Vereniging Het
Spinozahuis which has been 'housing'
for a timeless while the quasi-embodied
Baruch de Spinoza. Now the quasi-
bodiless memory will continue to live as
if it had started from 21 February 1677
via perennial ideas not 'as dumb
pictures on a tablet' but to dwell
wherever and whenever the mind is
'housed' with that unforgettable innate
immemorial nostalgia: a challenge for
man and mankind alike . . .

Contents

Contents

Illustrations

Foreword

Huston Smith, Syracuse

Benedict Spinoza died in 1677; these essays are being published in 1977. Obviously they are a tribute. The book is a way for philosophers to say, on the occasion of this tricentennial, that they remember. They remember a man who continues to live vigorously in their classrooms and on the pages of their journals, a man no history of human thought would dream of omitting.

The book is a tribute, but for philosophers the highest tribute is not praise but engagement: engagement with the thought of the person being honoured. So it should be added that this collection constitutes a *philosophical* tribute. Each of the essays in the volume attests to that fact. Together, they test and probe, winnow and knead, and try once again to extract meaning from what is obscure, all in the interests of keeping alive and virile in man's ongoing consciousness the mind that was Spinoza's.

I should like for my Foreword, too, to conform to this pattern, so I shall touch on a substantive issue. As Forewords are not the place for details, I choose a topic that is global and inclusive. I shall call it 'the Spinoza anomaly', and formulate it, simply, as follows: Why is Spinoza so loved and respected, yet so little followed?

The love and respect need scarcely be argued. What teacher, in introducing Spinoza to his students by way of the epithet 'the Blessed Spinoza', sees himself as merely translating 'Benedict', the latinized equivalent of the Hebrew *Baruch*, meaning blessing or benediction? He lingers over the name-turned-epithet because the grounds for doing so are overwhelming; it fits the man as if it had been preordained. Bertrand Russell comes close to speaking for all of us when he wrote in *A History of Western Philosophy* 'Spinoza is the noblest and most lovable of the great philosophers.' But this only accentuates the paradox: Why then is he so little followed? Thomists, Kantians, and Wittgensteinians abound, but how often does one run across a Spinozist?

There is an easy way to resolve this anomaly, which I shall note only to put it behind us. According to this superficial resolution, Spinoza is loved because his life was so exemplary, or alternatively because his system is architectonically so impressive; he is not followed because he was mistaken. If he was not mistaken in trying to construct a metaphysical system in the first place, as many philosophers today would contend, he was clearly mistaken in the way he went about building it. Given the excitement attending the birth of modern science in the seventeenth century we can understand why the geometrical method excited him, but too much has happened in the three hundred years that have intervened to allow us to take it seriously. Geometries have become multiple, logic turns out to be wedded to paradox,[1] and all efforts to find bed-rock foundations on which logic's ladder might be planted unshakably have led to quicksand. Percepts shift with their contexts (Gestalt psychology), facts reflect the theories that sponsor them (science, and cognition generally), and there appear not to *be* any elementary particles from which nature is constructed (particle physics).

I call the foregoing resolution of the Spinoza anomaly superficial because it trivializes the truth component in what we esteem, a move that is particularly unseemly for philosophers. It assumes that the not-less-than-holy life Spinoza lived[2] was unrelated to the truth he saw. Or if we prefer to hew to the cognitive grounds for our admiration, it assumes that coherence alone suffices to win our respect, whereas outside the formal sciences we know that it does not suffice – if it did we would applaud paranoids, for as a rule there is nothing wrong with their logic, its only flaw being that it is out of touch with reality. To reduce metaphysics to a game well played is to rob it, and ultimately all philosophy, of its basis and importance. The mind that is fed 'wholly with joy . . . unmingled with sadness' (*On the Improvement of the Understanding*) is not a mind applauding a logical joust. We need an explanation of the Spinoza anomaly that avoids the travesty of disjoining the respect we accord a philosopher from the question of whether he was right.

I suggest the following: we sense that Spinoza was right,[3] but we don't follow him – don't consider ourselves Spinozists or think of ourselves as his followers – because we don't see how he got where he did. The argument that carried him to conclusions we sense to be true don't carry *us* there; we don't find them compelling. This way of putting the matter may seem as paradoxical as the anomaly it is introduced to resolve, but of course it isn't. Right and left our instincts for truth outstrip the reasons we adduce to justify them – in Michael Polanyi's formula, we know more than we can tell. In so far as we claim (or would like to claim) the opposite, we exhibit 'the European mistake'; the mistake of thinking that it is the role of the sage to explain things from zero, whereas in fact his vocation is first to 'see' and then to 'cause to see'; that is, to provide a key. The classic error of Western rationalism is to assume that metaphysical conclusions are no stronger than the arguments adduced to support them and that they collapse the moment weaknesses in those arguments are exposed, an exposure that is easily accomplished because the premises of metaphysical proofs invariably elude everyday (which is to say unanimous) experience. The truth is the reverse. Rather than being the causes of certainty, metaphysical arguments are their results. This makes the certainty in one sense subjective, but at the same time it is objective if it is in fact a prolongation of realities that are independent of our minds.

In calling the mistake just cited 'Western' I mean, of course, that it is the recent Western mistake; our very word 'theory' derives, as we know, from *theoria*, a term originally drawn from the theatre and implying vision. Like Plato, Spinoza saw something. Had his mysticism been ecstatic we might be inclined to say that he experienced something, but because it was in fact immaculately intellective – gnostic, or *jnanic* as the Vedantists would say – it is better to say he saw, or perhaps sensed, something. ('Saw' captures the *clarity* of his controlling insight, 'sensed' its *intuitive character* – the difficulty of conveying it to persons who have had no direct contact with it.) A moment ago we were citing Gestalt psychology and particle physics to document the mind's inability to arrive at ultimates. For the phenomenal world this is plain fact, awash as that world is in relativity and change – in *maya*, to reach again for a Vedantic term. But beneath this remorseless flux Spinoza discerned something permanent. This is not a place to try again to say what it was, or rather what it is. It is enough to say that he saw as clearly as man ever has what Substance is and what is its relationship to accident, grasping at the same time that every single thing participates in both while being always accident in relation to the one and only Substance that empowers it. In doing so he understood in principle the meaning, not only of all religion, but of all metaphysics in the true and etymological sense of that word. As for ourselves, we sense that he had hold of that meaning, however little we may be able to follow his approach to it or blaze an alternative route.

This is my suggestion regarding the Spinoza anomaly. We do not call ourselves Spinozists because the way he articulated his insight is, for the most part, not the way we would do so; it is too coloured by thought patterns of a period that is not our own. But metaphysical systems are not mirror-images of reality; they are symbols – fingers point at the moon, as Ch'an Buddhists would say.[4] And Spinoza's finger, we sense – many, many of us do, at least – was precisely and accurately angled. That is why we honour him. He points us toward truth of a mode which, to the degree that we succeed in encompassing it, can free us as it freed him.

I speak of degree, and this is important, for truth that is as existential as the kind Spinoza was involved with is not simply accepted or rejected; it is appropriated incrementally. Sufis liken three stages in the acquisition of gnosis to hearing about fire, seeing fire, and being burned by fire. Comparably one can respond affirmatively to Spinoza by assenting to what he says, seeing what he says, and being consumed by what he says – George Eliot seems to have been on to something like these distinctions when she wrote that 'Spinoza says from his own soul what all the world is saying by rote.' Not many reach the last stage (being consumed by Spinoza), for it involves recognizing one's individuality as a 'cosmic accident'. But Spinoza was himself living proof that it is possible to catch sight of something majestic – a Good beyond all goods – that at the mere sight of it one loses personal desires completely, forgets oneself in its contemplation, and adds a new dimension to the treasures of the soul. Spinoza has been faulted because his *Deus sive Natura* is impersonal. His audience is a different breed; persons whose taste is for the Absolute, for that cold, remote, emotionless beyond where nothing stirs, where there is no agitation, there is just that immaculate, almost unreachable height of the aloneness of God.

In writing what I have I may have presumed on the invitation accorded me to enter this Foreword, for the points I have made are personal ones and are not to be charged against the book's contributors. So let me close by turning to the book itself.

It is at once a work of insight, devotion, and extraordinary range.

I feel as if its authors – and especially its editor, Siegfried Hessing, who has poured the latter years of his life into this project (actually the third tributary Spinoza project he has effected), first into conceiving it and then seeing it through to completion – have, as I suggested in my opening paragraph, performed a service for us all, the entire philosophical community and in larger sense its surrounding intellectual community.[5] By virtue of their labours we can all feel better about 1977.

NOTES

1 Bertrand Russell admitted that the Theory of Types, concocted to deal with self-referential paradoxes ('This sentence is false') was not really a theory but a stop-gap. 'Similar self-referential paradoxes . . . are considered quite acceptable in the ordinary theory of equations' (G. Spencer Brown, *Laws of Form*, p. ix).

2 By birth a man of exile, by temperament a recluse, he showed not the slightest bitterness in spite of his excommunication and his inherited memories of centuries of persecution and fanaticism. Whatever his subject, he always brought to it a mind free of attachment to self, party, or nation.

3 Not all of us sense this, of course, and among those who do there is a significant difference in degree. To the latter point I shall return in a moment.

4 This association of Spinoza with an oriental outlook is not fortuitous. A contributor to this volume, Paul Wienpahl, has called my attention to the fact that Pierre Bayle in the article on Spinoza in his dictionary said that there was nothing new in this man's philosophy, comparing it to that of a certain sect of Chinese theologians. Wienpahl feels certain that he was referring to Ch'an Buddhism and details the parallelism as follows: What, according to Spinoza, we erroneously take to be a plurality of substances corresponds in Ch'an to the deluding fabrications of the ego; Spinoza's imagination is Ch'an's bifurcating intellect; Spinoza's understanding or intuitive knowing is Ch'an's enlightenment, and Spinoza's Substance is Ch'an's non-dual *sunyata*. Siegfried Hessing touches on Wienpahl's

point in his Prologue to this book while adding other Eurasian parallels.
5 Poets are the only writers Spinoza quotes, and it was poets and novelists, in turn, who first appreciated him. Among them were Wordsworth, Schelling, and above all Goethe, who on completing his second reading of the Ethics reported: 'I have never seen things so clearly, or been so much at peace!' George Eliot's tribute I have already quoted; to her name can now be added, among others, those of: Gustave Flaubert, Romain Rolland, Renan, Novalis, Lessing, Jacobi, Schiller, Schlegel, Schleiermacher, L. Feuerbach, Grillparzer, Heine, Nietzsche, Brandes, Dehmel, F. Mauthner, Fritz Droop, Jakob Wassermann, Arnold Zweig.

Pathfinders pointing the rare way for pathseekers

Arranged and adapted by Siegfried Hessing

If the way, which I have shown leads hither, seems very difficult, it can nevertheless be found. It must indeed be difficult since it is so seldom discovered, for if salvation lay ready at hand and could be discovered without great labour, how could it be possible that it should be neglected by everybody? But all noble things are as difficult as they are rare.

Baruch de Spinoza

It is a great joy to realize that the path to freedom which all Buddhas have trodden is ever existent, ever unchanged and ever open to those who are prepared to enter upon it.

Precepts of the Gurus

When the pupil is ready, then the Master will appear before him.

Light on the Path

Thou canst not travel on the path before thou hast become the path itself.

The Voice of Silence

When this path is beheld . . . without moving, is the travelling on this road. In this path to whatever place one would go, that place one's self becomes.

Jnaneshvari

The path is one for all, the means to reach the goal must vary with the pilgrims. As there is neither any traversing nor any traverser of the path, the expression 'PATH' is merely figurative.

Precepts of the Gurus

'PATH' is merely a metaphor descriptive of the method of realizing spiritual growth of progress.

W. Y. Evans-Wentz

On this path we have to find our own touchstone of truth, independent of academic or theological approval. What we want is one's own perception of the truth, not one taken on ready made.

Sri Madhava Ashish

Anyone who so desires can move into the vitalizing study [of the path] and dig in his own mind indefinitively making his own discoveries and can be a point of consciousness to which revelation comes.

Carlo Suares

'I am' [is] that 'I am' – 'I am' [is] the God of thy father, the God of Abraham, the God of Isaac and the God of Jacob. (I and the father are one!)

Exod. 3: 6, 14

. . . that ye may know that 'I am' [is] the LORD! Ezek. 6: 7

'I am' [is] unique: every-thing and no-thing. Ani = Ayin. Aham = Maha. *Causa sive ratio: vel sui vel alius* . . . the indeterminate. Meta-Esoterics

If 'I' am 'I' *because* 'you' are 'you' and if 'you' are 'you' *because* 'I' am 'I' – then: I am not [really] I and you are not [really] you. Hassidic Saying

I am not only I, I am also you, he, she and it. – *Ego = id = idem*. Then: how to learn to reidentify with the seemingly or para-other (the so-called 'parallel' meeting each other otherless in the infinite according to Euclid!)? How: with that Tat twam asi? Siegfried Hessing

'I am' [is] because 'I think' [of] 'I am': *cogito ergo sum*. René Descartes

The uni-verse is a play: as if an empty shell wherein 'your' mind [as 'I am'] frolics infinitely. – As (I-less) waves come with water and (I-less) flames with fire, so uni-versal waves come with 'us' [as 'I am' – awareness] – I (am) can toss [one-sided] attachment for body aside realizing 'I am' (is) every 'where' [and every 'when']. One who is every 'whereness' is joyous ('everness'). [Conclusion: he is not *alone* but all-one or one-all as 'I am' via omni-awareness.] Lakshamanjoo revitalizes Tantra

'I am' [is] the Way, the Truth and Life. John 14: 6

The way up and the way down is the very same way! [to thy own otherless self.] Heraclitus

The undefinable omni-present is the '*way*' called *Tao*. *Tao* is that which lets now the dark, now the light. Lao-Tse

To know (other) men: is to be wise. To know one's self is to be illumined. To con-quer (other) men: is to have strength. To con-quer one's self is to be stronger . . . and to know when you have enough [of having and of knowing – ed.]. Lao-Tse
[Conclusion: The goal is to re-verse the omni-versal habit and co-habit, namely: *know thy neighbour*! and *love thyself*! by transmuting into: *know thyself*! and into: *love thy neighbour*!]

Know therefore this day and consider it in thine heart that Yahweh is the Elohim in heaven above and upon earth beneath: there is none else. Thus hear, o Israel: Yahweh is our Elohim! Yahweh (and Elohim are not two but) is *one*! Deut. 4: 39

The sole object with which the Holy, blessed be He, sends man into this world is: to know that Yahweh is the Elohim! [That is man's WAY.]   Zohar Pt. II

There are [apart from the One Way] three ways which are too wonderful for me, yea, four which I know not: the way of an eagle in the air; the way of a serpent upon the rock; the way of a ship in the midst of the sea, and the way of a man with a maid.   Prov. 30: 18, 19

Philo-sophia abducit et reducit.   Bacon of Verulam

Philosophy is the dis-ease for which it should be the cure.... No-thing empirical is knowable.   Ludwig Wittgenstein

Let your mind be re-made and your whole nature thus trans-formed: meta-noiete [not: para-noiete – ed.]!   Rom. 12: 2

Renew a right spirit in me!   Ps. 51: 12

A revulsion or re-volution must take place by self-realization in the deepest recess of your being: paravrittasraya.   Lankavatara Sutra

Scriptura non docet sed experientia. Ergo doctissima ignorantia et arrogantia.
Ego experientia: vivos voco, mortuos plango, fulgura frango. Sic.!   Dixi

Experience is the bald man's comb [Never able to be used].

Chinese Saying

Apart from the experience of the subjects there is nothing, no-thing, bare nothingness.   Alfred North Whitehead

There is simply experience. There is not 'some*thing*' or 'some*one*' experiencing experience. You never were aware of being aware.   Alan Watts

Experience is like self-alchemization. The enlightening ex-perience is the self-'X'-perience of your own otherless and 'ex'-less unknown, the mysterious 'X': *causa sive ratio vel sui vel alius*: the indeterminacy!   Siegfried Hessing

Alchemy is not armchair philosophy or speculative science. It is the *practice* of inner unity on all levels of consciousness: separately and conjoined.

Ralph Metzner

The essence of life and nature, the secret of immortality cannot be found by dry intellectual work and selfish desire: but *only* by touch of undiluted life in spontaneity of in-tuition.   Lama Anagarika Govinda

Let him who seeks [the path] not cease seeking until he finds and when he finds, he will be troubled, and when he has been troubled, he will marvel.

Gospel of Thomas

Siegfried Hessing

SUMMUM BONUM

Yes, let us all marvel:
>   lonely or all-onely-together!
Whitehead points to the importance of
>   what man does with his aloneness!
How to escape from self-separation?
>   How to attain self-unification and be
>   again back in Eden with access to the
>   Tree of Life?
Yes, let us marvel
>   at the enigma of life!
Although unknowable, because unknowable,
>   it remains for ever so marvellous!
In messianic expansion of consciousness
>   exoteric knowledge, *cognitio alius*, will
>   turn into esoteric one, *cognitio sui*.
In messianic urge life and knowledge,
>   like self and other are not two, but a
>   pair-concept for the twoless self-same ONE!
Kabbalists convince us:
>   it is the very same tree in the center of Eden.
>   Only for those in exile it seems split:
Life versus knowledge or self against other.
>   Readmitted from Diaspora in the gathering
>   of longing re-turn home,
Pseudo-twoness, para-otherness becomes:
>   quasi-twoness, pseudo-otherness and quasiness
>   is revealing the salvation of Advaita.
>   Twolessness, otherlessness, one-allness, all-oneness!
One not a number but the countless indeterminate:
>   *ratio sive causa vel sui vel alius*!
'Vel' is a velum to veil the ECHAD . . . !
>   Yahweh and the Elohim (are not two but)
>   is the very self-same, otherless ECHAD!
Le Chayim! To life or to Eden with nostalgia!
Le Daath! To knowledge or to death of deadening dichotomy:
>   of quasi-knower versus quasi-known.
Knowledge expelled us from Eden, keeps us in exile . . .
>   is lifeless and never self-experienceable.
Life although unknowable is experience of omniality, with oceanic
>   feeling of the bubbling oceanic drop and
>   re-aware with cosmic-divine orgasm the ex-less
>   mystery of our 'X':

XX

to marvel at, to wonder and then
to ponder only in order to marvel again,
to wonder again and again back in Eden . . .

IN SPINOZA'S OWN WORDS:
forma sive essentia . . .
essendi fruitio (percipiendi fruitio?) omnia animata (sumus) . . .
sentimus experimurque nos – omnes – aeternos esse.
Deus sive Veritas sive Natura:
vel naturans vel naturata. vel deificans vel deificatus.
Amor Dei sive Naturae intellectualis!
Causa sive ratio vel sui vel alius!
Perseitas non est de-monstrabilis: Q.E.D.!
Spinozistic pegs, makeshifts, expedient means to express the
inexpressible . . . *sive, vel, quatenus*
quamvis,
In symbols also serving as pegs, makeshifts and expedient means:

$$0^0 - 0^x - 0^\infty - 0^{\maltese} = \sqrt[0]{0} - \sqrt[0]{x} - \sqrt[0]{\infty} - \sqrt[0]{\maltese}$$

$$x^0 - x^x - x^\infty - x^{\maltese} = \sqrt[x]{0} - \sqrt[x]{x} - \sqrt[x]{\infty} - \sqrt[x]{\maltese}$$

$$\infty^0 - \infty^x - \infty^\infty - \infty^{\maltese} = \sqrt[\infty]{0} - \sqrt[\infty]{x} - \sqrt[\infty]{\infty} - \sqrt[\infty]{\maltese}$$

CABBALAH
NUGATORES CABBALISTAE = NUGATORES PHILOSOPHICI!
MAGNUM ARCANUM:

$$\maltese^0 - \maltese^x - \maltese^\infty - \maltese^{\maltese} = \sqrt[\maltese]{0} - \sqrt[\maltese]{x} - \sqrt[\maltese]{\infty} - \sqrt[\maltese]{\maltese}$$

יְיָ הוּא הָאֱלֹהִים

INVITA LATINITATE
INVITA LINGUA
INVITA COGITATIONE

Idea vera cum suo ideato con-venire debet . . .
Ordo et connexio idearum idem est ac ordo et connexio rerum . . .
ego = id = idem
e(r)go identificabilis sum via omnia animata . . .
omnia naturata . . . omnia deificata . . .

$$\sqrt[\maltese]{x}: \sqrt[x]{\maltese} = \infty^\infty$$

Prologue with Spinozana - parallels via East and West

Siegfried Hessing, London

> Scriptura non docet sed experientia, ergo doctissima ignorantia et
> arrogantia. Sic: ego, experientia, vivos voco, mortuos plango, fulgura
> frango. Dixi.

Not to study the scriptures, not to expound them, not to explain them while
the plain message eludes us but rather to experience them plainly 'in' us and
'as' us. Experience thus is not reduced to word-experience as a lifeless spirit
of the letter in a paper existence. The word was the beginning of life: to
speak out what is in the unspeakable.

> What God was, was the word. . . . The Lord gave the word and great
> was the company of those who made it public.

The word naming a thing and the thing named are the very same. This
identity is demonstrated in Biblical language where 'dawar' means: word,
matter and thing. Job was capable of 'seeing that the root of matter (word,
thing) is found in me', and therefore 'me' and 'everything' involving experience leads to one's root-awareness. Experience, the magic of life, 'happens'
only in the instant *now* and *here* as 'instasis' or 'enstasis' and cannot be
understood but has to be *lived*, bringing one back to the Tree of Life as if into
the midst of the Garden of Eden. There the Etz Chayim impartially stands
and withstands the grand trial and dilemma arriving from the Tree of
Knowledge always in relation to it. Knowledge tries to separate with discrimination and dichotomy a quasi-knower from a quasi-known via knowing,
as though they were two separate entities *per se*, while life unites and reunites
again via experience those with a longing for the otherless self-realization.

> I am fully conscious that not being a literary man, certain presumptuous
> persons will think they may reasonably blame me; alleging that I am not
> a man of letters. Foolish folks! Do they not know that I might retort
> as Marius did to the Roman Patricians by saying: that they who deck
> themselves out in the labour of others will not allow me my own.
> They will say that I, having no literary skill, cannot properly express
> that which I desire to treat; but they do not know that my subjects are

1

to be dealt with by *experience* rather than by words. And (experience) has been the mistress of those who wrote well. And so as mistress, I will cite her in all cases.[1]

The experience, and especially the experience of Spinoza's teaching as essential to life, cannot be the exclusive property only of academic scriptural studies remote from real life, which often declare the timeless and unfashionable as occult, only to find it later hailed by posterity. Experience remains the one and only challenge. A challenge to attract to Spinoza exceptional men above the prosaic average such as the Geheimrat von Weimar, Jacobi, Lessing, Herder, Novalis, Heine and all those sharing alike the god-thirsty and god-intoxicated Apollonian mission. From the very early days of my youth and my thinking[2] I admired Spinoza with an innate lyrical affinity. And like Spinoza I despised the fading myth of the graduate with a fading craving for life and life-experience using the *philosophia perennis* as a guide. While trying to follow Spinoza's footsteps I discovered that he rejected for himself any academic umbrella as a legal protection for his (illegal) philosophy and refused an invitation to take a chair of philosophy at the University of Heidelberg, knowing only too well that he would never ever be able to sit comfortably in such a chair; to think only for thinking's sake: *causa sui sive ratio sui!* And now as I happily bask in Spinoza's radiant sunshine, I am sure I also need no umbrella as protection against the sunlike splendour of his teaching, especially now as I try again to testify in the witness-box for the third time during my life. Spinoza's path, so rare and so difficult, remains a challenge indeed only for those who have the urge and surge of vocation; and is very seldom accessible to that craving profession whose only aim is a brilliant mediocrity.

Once I discovered with great satisfaction that an international journal *Art and Science, Leonardo*,[3] dealing mostly with scholarly approaches to the conceptualization of grasping art and creativity alike, had found it necessary to claim a controversial motto by Leonardo da Vinci himself. I then admired da Vinci much more than before for so well defending his non-academic status, and I felt proud indeed as only a successful partisan of Spinoza could feel towards an army ready to grade ranks for the majority of platitudes they uttered under the dictatorship of regimentation. It was just this that Charles Luk warned me to be aware of, when he told me to 'redouble my efforts to make Spinoza's philosophy known in the West' in my own way; unbiased and free from any 'isms', as it were. And I felt proud indeed when I saw others joining me again in my Spinoza-quest – me, an outsider concerned with the inside and in-sight of man and mankind as the very mission in life.

Even in the very early stages of my adolescence the *Ethics* was like a Bible to me, and at that time I did not dream that one day the first verse of Bereshit would become as significant to me as the first axiom in Spinoza's *Ethics*; to grasp genesis via gnosis and gnosis via genesis. Sic! To study such a book as the *Ethics*, sealed with concealed mysteries, for me was as if I looked beyond myself; i.e. beyond my I-mindedness into my own unknown: circumscribed best with *causa sive ratio sui* or the indeterminate.

Now, how to find the door, that magic door of direct perception or intuition bypassing quasi-otherness *per se* via ex-tuition? How? Otherness is only quasi-otherness, para-otherness soon becoming pseudo-otherness when quasiness is not intuited and when one is ready to divide a quasi-perceiver and quasi-perceived as though *per se* evolving into a double *perseitas*. Sic! I was too eager and ready then to enter that door and face there my faceless face, the egoless (and otherless) Self. Paul Reps[4] has introduced an immanent experience via Zen flesh and bones and presents an odd and old text with 112 ways to open the invisible door of consciousness for direct self-experience. And such doors are like gateless gates to marvel at.

As a rule, with such rare and marvellous exceptions, academics and priests, both commanding 'ism'-infested keywords for fossilized dogmas can very seldom provide a real key to such a real invisible door leading into such real beyondness. Lacking self-experience, they cannot have any empirical approach, save only with a dia-'lectic' access to that door, while they themselves are banned and exiled into the 'otherness' of words to disguise their failure with dignity. They can never even attract true followers, apart from quoters of their dogma, unless they show how they themselves were attracted to accept self-confrontation with the riddle of the own, otherless unknown; because they dare not avoid the deviations, via quasiness, of quasi-otherness *per se* as salvation. One can only feel the challenge to become a follower, a disciple, when seeing before oneself exemplary self-discipline driven by unceasing fervour, inspiring an equal fervour to self-commitment and to self-involvement. Not a teacher himself, seeking refuge in the asylum of imperatives: *you* (the 'other') should! Always you, but never I, never I, that unique co(s)mic exception which so freely accepts the universal exception as the rule.

And now we are witnessing the spiritual revival of the Cabbala and alchemy alike, it becomes so convincingly clear when we see how all the misty patchwork (which the lazy multitude takes for the real *work*, the *magnum opus*) has been swept aside so that the basic essence could be heard and the re-affirmation of every basic equal essence of teaching recognized. Fulcanelli, the last living alchemist of our present time, has something to add to this message. I was very glad that I was able to meet his pupil, Eugène Canseliet, who not only published his master's manuscripts but continues to follow him in his way. I was also glad to find here, on the same (p-)latitude that I live on, the living commentator of *Le Mystère des Cathédrales*, Walter Lang in alchemical disguise so to speak. A strong personality trying through his universality to help diffuse the perennial hidden meaning of alchemy better than the specialists, who in their overzeal confuse us so often. The old occult message of alchemy – unfortunately presented to Spinoza himself only in the crass exoteric meaning then – was not to transmute common base metal into common gold, but rather to point to such uncommon transmutation of dualistically seen layers of consciousness. This becomes clear only when the revivalists of alchemy dare to point openly to the oneness of experimenter and the quasi-object of experimentation, which is the very same quasi-otherness of self. *Em-peiron* means 'in the trial', i.e. of the self-committed with the *a-peiron*. The worker identified with the work.

In my own contributions to this book I further expound how I was already attracted via my own unknown or unconscious side to that famous text in Spinoza's *Ethics*, namely to that

> truth which some of the Hebrews appear to have seen as if through a cloud, since they say that *God, the Intellect, and the things which are the objects of that Intellect are one and the same thing* (2P7) (my italics).

Further, Spinoza finishes his *Ethics* with the dawn of liberation from self-bondage when he points to the wise man who, when he becomes conscious of himself, of God, and the world (of things: *omnia animata*) just crowns this glorious *leitmotif* which has inspired Cabbalists and alchemists alike to (otherless) self-experience. It is the self-realization of the all-oneness of God, God's intellect and God's intellected world of quasi-otherness *per se*, i.e. things or objects, so to speak. It took me years and years of seeking, and seconds of enlightenment to discover the very same signposts pointing to that occult or mysterious all-oneness or one-allness via quasi-otherness *per se* which leads to the verification of that same: Know Thyself! *Tat twam asi!* Such verification includes the self-identification with the 'ordo et connectio idearum sive rerum' = 'causa sive ratio (vel sui vel alius)'. And you? You are not only you, but me, him, her, and it as well – but regrettably you do not know it. You are not aware, self-aware of it 'as' you and 'in' you until self-realization begins to dawn. Such signposts are to be found in the various teachings of the East, but also in the Esoterics of the Cabbala, such as Moses Cordovero, to whom Spinoza makes some allusions as quoted above. Among so many and often repetitive themes about Spinoza only a single paper by David Kahana is to be found in Jean Préposiet's *Bibliographie Spinoziste* (Paris, 1973), namely Moshe Qordobhero u Barukh Shpinoza, Ha Shiloa, 1897, in Hebrew. No one would have thought then that Cordovero had found re-affirmation via alchemy and the Cabbala and also via Eastern doctrines of that magic all-oneness or one-allness to which I propose to return later, in my own papers.

And Carlo Suares, in his revision of the *Qabala* using the newly discovered key, points to the direct perception or identity of knower, known and knowing, and thus continues the rare way of Cordovero indeed with the main aim in mind elucidating otherless self-experience. In my own paper (Proton Axioma kai Proton Pseudos) I consider it as my own homage, to the primordial message of Spinoza (abolishing quasi-otherness *per se* and accepting quasiness instead) to approach the discriminative, binary, alternating view of multi-dimensionality of cosmic consciousness from the amoeba via man to the galaxies. . . .

And while still on the subject of the contemporary revival of alchemy let us hear what Fulcanelli has to say when appealing to man to prepare for the self-experience of such divine-cosmic all-oneness which seems as odd as the transformation of base metal into noble gold.[5]

> The mysterious science requires: no one may aspire to possess the great secret, if he does not *direct* his life in accordance with the research he has undertaken. . . . It is not enough to be studious, active and persevering, if one has not firm principles, no solid basis, if immoderate enthusiasm blinds one to reason, if pride overrules judgement, if greed expands before the prospect of a golden future. The mysterious science requires: great precision, accuracy and perspicacity in observing facts, a healthy, logical and reflexive mind, a lively but not overexcitable imagination, a warm and pure heart. It also demands the greatest simplicity and complete indifference with regard to *theories, systems and hypotheses*, which are generally accepted without question on the *testimony of books or the reputation of their authors*. It requires the candidates to learn to *think more with their own brains and less with those of others*. Finally, it insists that they should check the truth of its principles, the knowledge of its doctrines and the practice of its operations from nature: the mother of us all (my italics).

If such a stern warning cannot bring about the dawn of one's aim and endeavour, then this door of direct perception via self-confrontation is closed and blocked by oneself. If it is to be re-opened and unblocked, then the stumbling-block must be removed by no 'other' than oneself. *Ergo*: Know Thyself! Although you might think you already know everything or 'almost' everything, you will still have to learn to know thyself as the quasi-knower of the quasi-unknowable (otherless) self. Such knowledge does not know the so-called 'known' via a heterological method of separating quasi-knower from quasi-known via knowing though they were two (*entia per se*). Self-knowledge comes via an auto-logical (or 'illogical' *sine causa sive ratione*) method of in-tuition: re-uniting or rather re-identifying ego and id as idem again. These quasi-two are actually a 'pair-concept' impressing and expressing wholeness, and they could be likened to parallels (never known by grammar as singular but only as dual or an extended dual, and therefore as plural), or para-others with quasiness endowed: as coming from no-'where' and going to no-'where', i.e. to the very same unknown: *causa sive ratio sui*, or the indeterminate (a better word for void or no-'thingness'). And you, the quasi-knowable (to others or quasi-others) and unquasi to yourself, you are always in the no-man's land of no-'where', no-'when', no-'why', as if on a universal island called *here and now*. As an islander in the great ocean (with individualized drops and waves *per se* or *quasi-se*) you as you could be tempted to think that your unknowable must be known once at least, and therefore becomes 'knowable' to match your 'wishful' expectations. This can 'happen' only when you become 'it' or when you become aware that you 'are' it and have overlooked or disregarded the cosmic identity which occurs on the 'way' of 'I am'. Of every 'I am' it is said that it is the Way, the Truth and the Life. 'I am' [is] the Way and no other, and this waits for you when you experience for yourself such otherless-self-identity as self-realization. Then you 'know' *that* you live in the oneness of 'I am' = Way = Truth = Life! Sic!

The mind is the author of all work and the body the sufferer of all ills.
Do not blame 'others' plaintively for what properly belongs to you!

So did Yoka Daishi attain enlightenment with such sudden in-sight in the quasi-in-side of that 'I am', the otherless self, which is beyond any partisanship. When you suddenly realize 'no otherness *per se*', then the dilemma of the body-mind as a pair-concept is solved and dissolves the quasi-twoness into oneness and indeed it becomes possible to live the indivisible wholeness of life with no dichotomy whatever under the rule of *causa sive ratio (alius)*. In such a silence of self-awareness then the 'Voice of Silence' reveals to you, 'that the mind is the great slayer of the real. Let the disciple slay the slayer! The Psalmist tried in the very same way to captivate his own captivity (of such discriminative thinking). One of the contributors to this third symposium, Jon Wetlesen, remarkable in his field for his scholarly admiration of Spinoza, nevertheless dares to point to the Achilles heel of reason and rational approach of that which *per se vel praeter causam sive rationem est*, which is still so fashionable in academic circles. I will come back to it later; but I must say it reminds me of Martin Luther calling reason the 'great whore' perhaps in rhyme with 'treason', betraying itself when absolutizing otherness *per se*. What has Wetlesen to say?[6]

It seems to me that when we approach the philosophy of Spinoza there is always a certain danger of becoming overinvolved in the technical apparatus of definitions, axioms, propositions, demonstrations, and so forth. Our approach may easily become *more intellectualistic or academic than was intended by Spinoza himself.*

Wetlesen will be glad to see how he echoes Lama Anagarika Govinda:[7]

The use of logic in thought is as necessary and justified as the use of perspective in painting – but only as a medium of expression, not as a criterion of reality. If, therefore, we use logical definitions, as far as possible, in the description of meditative *experiences* and of centres of consciousness, with which they are connected, we must regard the understanding of the dimensions of consciousness of a different nature, in which the various impressions and experiences of different planes or levels are combined into an organic whole. . . . Intuitive feeling as well as intellectual understanding are transformed in to *living reality through direct experience.* Thus intellectual conviction grows into spiritual certainty, into a knowing in which *the knower is one with the known.*

And earlier Eastern witnesses for 'experience' add their voices, for example, Dih Ping Tsze, when commenting on a note by the Dhyana Master Hui An to the famous Sutra of Hui-Neng, feels that this is the moment to hint and hit at the Pandits.[8]

Scholastic Buddhist scholars can never give an explanation as satisfactory as this. For this reason Dhyana Masters are superior to the so-called Scriptural Expounders. . . . The most important point in the teaching of the Dhyana School lies in 'introspection', which means the turning of one's own 'light' to reflect inwardly.

This corresponds fully with Spinoza's aspiration to let the mind reflect on itself, contemplate on itself excluding all fake-otherness *per se.* And in our day Joe Miller[9] continues to expound in our own language with exceptional skill and verve this precious and rare tradition for us to marvel at. A tradition exerting, in our disillusioned and frustrated world of Western writers and readers, an impact never to be forgotten again, namely to look to the East and to the Eastern Way of thinking. There man's bondage and salvation can find a solution not in explanations (which is our strong monopoly in weakness) explaining away quasi what seems to be an obstacle or stumbling-block in man's way to himself with no witness to his stress and no feelings of distress. And not allowed to confess to anybody any inferiority nor able to run away from himself in despair:[10]

What is it that Buddha wished to teach? Was it sagacity, was it *brilliant academic understanding*? Was his aim to encourage the reading of the scriptures, or asceticism, or austerities? In reality it was none of these. He simply wished to show all living beings how to set in order body and mind. The method of doing this is given in the classic on meditation called *Zazengi*: 'Think of not thinking of anything at all. How is one *to think of not thinking of anything at all*? Be without thoughts – this is the secret of meditation.

To be without a single, singularizing self-existing thought is to be without duality and plurality as well which every 'I am' in his I-mindedness projects via *cogitandi*. It is to be without any-'thing', any single, dual or plural view of quasi-thingness *per se*. With Spinoza *ideae singulares sive res singulares, particulares* in the very same *ordo et connectio idearum sive rerum sive causarum*. I asked Edward Conze, the well-known Buddhist scholar, who thinks and writes about such paradox-like thoughtless thinking, to contribute to this volume as I was eager to learn about his connection with Spinoza since I had already learned about his connection with Buddha. David Ben-Gurion was another man I knew also attracted alike to Buddha and Spinoza – he was among the pioneers (and joined me 1962 in *Spinoza – 300 Jahre Ewigkeit*, my former and second symposium about Spinoza under the aegis of M. Nijhoff, The Hague) to 'right the wrong (doing) against Spinoza'. Conze now responded to my invitation as he desired to show me – and via me – my readers here how his Western academic teacher estranged him from Spinoza by forming a very final opinion (long before having had a very final beginning one!) on Spinoza and Spinozism:

> In my youth Spinoza was my favourite philosopher. In 1925 I suggested a thesis on him to Prof. Heinrich Scholz in Kiel. He said that *everything possible had been said about Spinoza so far . . .* and offered instead the dusty folio of F. Suarez' *Disputationes Metaphysicae* which he had that very morning fetched from the cellar of the library. This led to my 1928 doctoral thesis: 'Der Begriff der Metaphysik bei F. Suarez S. J.' and a lifelong interest in the perennial philosophy which took concrete form first as Aristotelianism, then as dialectical materialism and then as the Wisdom Philosophy of Buddhism. In doing a great deal of work in connection with all this I have now become exhausted and suffer from serious heart disease. My writing days are over, and I have no longer the energy, at the age of 71, to say, or even to know, what I think of Spinoza's place in perennial philosophy. I still prize him greatly as one of the few European philosophers *who lived like one*, and have often gone to the Spinozahuis as to a kind of shrine. But as for the intellectual effort involved in looking at his ideas once again in the light of what I have learned over the past 50 years, I just cannot do it! I do therefore hope that I will one day be able to read what all these interesting people you mention have contributed to your Speculum Spinozanum, but as for myself you have come too late in the day. I have shot my bolt and cannot be of any use to you. With my best wishes, I am, etc.

Now, how does one attain (intentionally) the realm of non-thought, to which Conze helps to point the way, which leads to enlightenment? How, if not by first removing the dust, not from the cellar of old libraries (The Mecca for Scriptural Expounders), but of old dusty concepts of thinking without self-experience? Yes! – What I am just doing here, is to remove the old and new dust from Spinoza during the perennial *scriptural* approach, with no self-approach as sincerely as Spinoza himself did it to himself.

Perhaps Saraha, the ancient poet, has the prosaic answer and remedy in unprosaic capsules when he says: 'The world is enslaved by thought and no one has known this non-thought.'[11] No one has known this non-form and non-thought (form). It is the sub-stant, instant which is the basis of every standing and every understanding of I and I-mindedness. The world is enslaved by purely *intellectualistic or academic approaches* (puzzling my friend Wetlesen), excluding self-experience while including *per se* or *per quasi-se* via singular and dualistic discrimination of the indivisible wholeness. Life demands the full surrender to direct experience of indiscrimination of *causa sive ratio sui sed non alius.* . . .

And here, John Blofeld, another expert in Buddhism and Taoism (with no bondage to any Western 'ism' involved) speaks along the very same lines:

I feel at once honoured and puzzled by your kind invitation to contribute to a work on Spinoza. The truth is that I know nothing whatever about him, beyond what the average schoolboy might be expected to know. I have never read one of his works, having seldom taken much interest in Western philosophy, which seems dry to me because confined to speculations, usually based on certain assumptions and logical processes derived from the Greek, which I believe to be invalid. Any philosophy I may have acquired comes from living among Taoists and Buddhists with but limited respect for the written word, who make of their *philosophy a way of life*, so that it permeates not just their thought but also their activities. In all I know, Spinoza may have been such a man and thus *a rare exception among philosophers reared in the European tradition.* So please accept my thanks for the honour you have done to me and permit me to decline. I wish you all success with the book. . . .

And when pointing to Spinoza as 'a rare exception among philosophers reared in the European tradition', I ought to mention here the thoughts of Lu K'uan Yü (also known as Charles Luk) who 'devotes himself to presenting as many Chinese texts as possible so that Buddhism can be preserved in the West'.[12]

I have not read the works of Spinoza but I have found in a book of references this: 'Spinoza formulates one sole and infinite substance of which extension and mind are attributes, all individual beings being changing forms.' Larousse says this: 'Spinozisme: Système panthéisme de Spinoza suivant lequel Dieu est une substance constituée par une infinité d'attributs dont nous ne connaissons que deux: la pensée et l'étendue. Le monde est l'ensemble des modes de ces deux attributs. L'homme est une collection de modes de l'étendue et de la pensée. Il n'y a entre Dieu et le monde qu'une différence de point de vue.' Spinoza was, therefore, a great man, and you will find consolation in Ch'an master Lin Chi's words which say: 'Since olden times, my predecessors were expelled everywhere they went because people did not believe them; for this hostility alone, they were held in great honour. As to one who is accepted everywhere, what is he worth? Hence the ancient saying: "A lion's roar can burst the brain of a wild dog." ' [Cf. Luk, *Ch'an and Zen Teaching*, 2nd series (San Francisco, Shambhala, 1971), p. 121]. I am only a small fry as you know, but I have been viciously criticized, ridiculed, attacked, humiliated and insulted by some reviewers of my books, but I have never paid attention to their stupidity. You should redouble your efforts to make Spinoza's philosophy well known in the West if you want to put an end to the platitude of ignorance and its regimentation. Assuring you of my deepest sympathy for the last Spinoza symposium of yours, Yours etc.

I also find it of some value to add here Lama Anagarika Govinda's thoughts on Spinoza as he, too, comes from the East. For many years I have held a rich correspondence with him as we have the same affinity for the East, and he recommended me to Tibetan centres in England when I arrived there from Australia. Among other interesting topics he had this to say about Spinoza:

I admire Spinoza so to say from the afar like a mighty mountain giant. Philosophical abstractions leave me as cold as snow on icy mountain tops. I am interested only in that which is *experienceable* and here I do agree with Alan Watts, whose *Wisdom of Insecurity* and *Way of Zen* I hold in high esteem. . . .

Because of a lack of written evidence about mystic experience, no such experience could be ascribed to Spinoza, although he might have followed a certain tradition and trend which forbids any disclosure of self-experience of inwardness. In this book there is an article by a Western man pointing to the 'Logical and Experiental Roots of Spinoza's Mysticism', H. G. Hubbeling, who is so deeply and sincerely involved with Spinoza. I give him a special place of honour as he is my esteemed friend through Spinoza. I was very moved when he recognized my own efforts focusing on Spinoza:

I consider it a great honour to cooperate with a great representative of an older generation of Spinoza scholars. I hope that you will consider the work of my colleagues and myself as a continuation of your scholarly work on Spinoza so that generations may pass Spinoza's wisdom through the centuries. . . .

I will go on to quote from others who come from the East or who speak of the East with reference to Spinoza. Herbert V. Guenther, a new shining star on the Tibetan academic horizon, expresses his feelings about Spinoza thus:

It is true that there are points of contact between Spinoza and the little known (up to now) and yet most influential rdzogs-chen teaching which in certain respects resembles Spinoza's *sub specie aeternitatis*. I must admit *I do not know of any other work in Western Philosophy that can come up to Spinoza's Ethics*. After all, as Bertrand Russell said, Spinoza is supreme in his *Ethics*. I do hope that with so much inhumanity around its (i.e. your former *Festschrift's*) fate will be happier and certainly some, and if they only be a few, will take renewed interest in one of the *greatest philosophers*. . . .

Similar encouragement came from other contributors and non-contributors, all admirers of Spinoza. Erich Fromm, although he was among the very first of those willing and eager to join the ranks in offering their common homage to Spinoza, unfortunately had to withdraw later because of a sudden and serious illness, which prevented him against his own wish from fulfilling certain commitments involving physical activity. I, nevertheless feel, I must mention how he replied to my invitation with such great enthusiasm:

I appreciate your invitation to join the other authors in homage to Spinoza, since my own thinking is to a considerable extent influenced by Spinoza. Nothing could be more welcome than to honour him. . . .

Then from Huston Smith came the jubilant message about another Paul, this time an apostle of Spinoza, who 'is bursting with enthusiasm for Spinoza by way of having, he is convinced, unearthed new insights into the man by going back to the Latin. 'The full name of this apostle is Paul Wienpahl from Santa Barbara and he hopes to finish the apostolic task: 'to translate the entire writings of Spinoza and commenting on them' by 1977. Indeed only such great enthusiasm can save Spinoza from great fossilization of those who think they do him full justice by storing him with other curious antiquities, covered with archaeo'logical' dust and dirt instead of re-storing his timeless validity. And these are the people who as co-witnesses will try to testify in the same witness-box with me. The very same thing happened with the Cabbala when Baron Spedalieri in 1884 (at a time when Cabbalist teaching was so fashionable among scholars, Christian more than Jewish) declared boldly with scholastic ignorance and arrogance alike, in accordance with the ancient proverbial *doctissima ignorantia*[13]

I consider that from henceforth the study of the Cabbala will be considered but an object of curiosity and erudition like that of Hebrew Antiquities.

I hope this book will be a break with the merely scholastic (school-) master-approach to the letter and the spirit of the letter rather than to the spirit itself: for both the Cabbala and for Spinoza. The spirit needs from time to time a breakthrough and not a breakdown to remove the barriers which divide the out-siders, keeping them for ever outsiders, even when 'speaking' and commenting as if on the inside which they reach via verbalization. Finally I must mention a man about whom Spedalieri had to wait so long to hear and then via posterity. And there are also many among our contemporaries who will have to wait, together with Spedalieri, for one only hears perfectly such a message via posterity, when distance returns to the stars their starlike splendour. I invited Carlo Suares to write a foreword to this collective homage to Spinoza, because he already knew from our close proximity, how I have learned through introspection and retrospection to see Spinoza via Suares and Suares via Spinoza. Unfortunately due to his advanced age (well into his eighties) his physical strength does not permit any stress, which is very regrettable indeed. But I am happily able to quote here from a letter of his on some revolutionizing hints on a new and quasi-apocalyptic approach to Spinoza via Cabbala *rediviva* with the new key Suares has discovered. So here he can say in his own words, much better, what I as his ambassador in my enthusiasm might only hint at:

My dear Siegfried, many thanks for having gone through such a job as writing your very long letter of Nov. 2, 75. I am grateful and honoured. And if you do mention my contribution to the Principle of Indeterminacy, yes, that would point in the direction of one of my 'openings'. It would be valuable if you could say that that view results *directly* from the original code of the letter-numbers (that came to be used as a simple alphabet) as I discovered it. Because that is the original code, without which the Bible, and particularly Genesis, is erroneously read. The vernacular Hebrew is just mistaken as any other idiom. Whereas the science of the structure of cosmic energy, as revealed by that original Qabala, is a factor of enlightenment of what Spinoza tried to say without knowledge of that code. With that code, when we come to read such combination of letter-numbers as *Elohim and Yahweh*, for what they are: *equations* of different aspects and processes of the one and double cosmic energy, we throw a light on Spinoza that such abstract metaphysicians as Jean Lacroix and other contributors will only dim with their mental and very complicated approach. Dear Siegfried, I do not feel qualified to join your learned contributors. Any text I would attempt to give you would first of all take me weeks of hard work, or *months* – and my brain is exhausted beyond repair when such a job is considered. And I must candidly tell you that Spinoza did what was possible 300 years ago with the scientific method of that time. We are far beyond it today and Spinoza will appear obsolete when treated by metaphysicians and philosophers. I see that you have scientists in a flow of metaphysics. But whatever you could say in the way of modern scientific approach of Spinoza, based on the *revival* of Qabala, as I am trying to expose, would appeal to a number of physicists, especially American. Spinoza's vocabulary would need to be translated into modern scientific terms. What a job! I have too clear a view of what to do, to imagine that I could, even in a modest way, help. Yours with much affection.

Now I will try to condense the essentials of Suares's teaching, and the advanced Spinoza scholar will have to find parallels with Suares's message, together with the intuitive affinity for the unbiased mind. I myself will, in my own paper, focus on the first verse of Genesis and on the first axiom of Spinoza's gnosis, as it were. As we have had a wrong image of the imageless unknown when seeing it via the quasi-known, so Suares encounters it as the very indeterminate or say, self-determinate principle *via causa sive ratio sui*:[14]

> The Qabala is always in touch with the unknown, the Great Unknown: as a presence. . . . The unknowable unknown is a presence. The knowing of that presence *is* the unknown. There is no other revelation . . . . We have to allow the unknown to operate *directly* in our minds. . . . As long as we are not in *direct* contact with that which transcends the human mind, the fundamental significance of life escapes us. The revelation is always there but for its being witnessed. There is no other transcendence than our intimacy with the unknown *as* the unknown. Seeking it is avoiding it. It is an everlasting present in an ever present Genesis. . . . The other key is for the mind, the contained, the human and cosmic germ of life, unconditioned which can only 'be' when it is indeterminate: the Qabala . . . for therein lies the prodigious mystery of all that is determined by indetermination. . . . We live and do not *know* what life is [we know with Spinoza 'that' it is; it as 'us' and 'in' us the same]. The principle of indeterminacy is at stake which allows all that can be to become. And complete awareness is the fact that anything at all exists (and) is a total mystery (my italics).

Here, in the Cabbala, you find awestruck ordinary life as your own plain, unexplainable, unknown, and you become aware or re-aware of it by being it (yourself) via your otherless self: *causa sive ratio sui*. With Suares came the epoch-making breakthrough. With him came the key to the Cabbala and via the Cabbala the key to self-salvation. He did not try to replace old 'isms' by new more odd and fashionable ones in order to rob the plain enigma of life of its plainness; explaining away the unexplainable, the ex-less 'X' indeed. Sic!

> the interplay of those energies in the Universe and in Man, we are then subjected to an amazing mental exercise which can modify our way of thinking to the extent of uniting us with those energies . . . and that, that only is revelation. (*ibid*)

The very same revelation is attained by self-alchemization and spiritual transmutation of which Spinoza speaks at the end of the *Ethics* as the grandeur of expansion of (the otherwise so narrow I-minded isolation in an omni-verse as uni-verse!) consciousness, namely of God, of self and of things as the very same oneness and all-oneness.

Suares, like Spinoza, does not promise a new word-salvation with a paper existence, but he reveals a magic innerness as a revelation in omni- or self-awareness of *omnia animata sumus* in that substant, constant, instant *now* and *here* with *instasis* or *enstasis* to enlighten us. With no 'before', with no 'after' and thus with no 'when' to ask for, no instant 'once' of indeterminacy missed as in a cosmic-divine tale in the style of the Garden of Eden. You will never ever resurrect the missed and lost 'once' and its constant 'onceness' so unique and so magic. Missed and lost for ever on a cemetery of fossilized yesterdays and yesteryears. No coming and no be-coming of any 'other' now, except that very same instant *now* which has no knowledge of knowing but has knowledge of life. Not knowing *what* it is, but living *that* it is indiscriminate *causa sive ratio sui*: with so much quasiness of eitherness or otherness (as if) *per se* to puzzle us and then to marvel at. Now we understand why all divine commandments in the Bible refer to the constant, instant, today. Today, or 'this day', this very day is a special signpost to trans-understand (with *metanoia*) *'sine causa sive ratione alius sed sui. Vivat suitas'*! Today has its own existence – it is not just a day 'between' yesterday and tomorrow. *'Dies per se sive dies sui'* like *'causa sui'*! The day of 'between' (quasi-otherness and other quasi-otherness) in the midst of quasiness *per se* to marvel at the present, ever-present, omni-present unknown. *This* is the day when the Messiah will come. Any day can be for Him 'this' day. He does not discriminate like us between this or that, good or evil, as sinning worshippers of knowledge do with the negative legacy from paradise. The Messiah remains untouched by knowledge (of quasi-otherness *per se*) and attracts us to the unknowable life. *Le Chayim!* When you hear His voice – as a revelation during the 'other' quasi-unrevealed days – *then one* day will become for you *this* day, when you see Him coming, after 'hearing His voice today'. Our sages say I should go and meet Him half-way, some say I should run all the way to meet Him sooner, still in 'my' life as quasi last incarnation (i.e. last discrimina-tion between carnate and discarnate). So I have the first insight into the divine commandment:

> to know today and to take it to your heart, that Yahweh is Elohim in the heaven above and on earth below and no-'thing' else [no otherness of Acher *per se*].

I then realize through the *Zohar* why 'God has sent man into this world to understand (that what stands 'under' or sub-stands) that Yahweh is Elohim! *Deus sive Natura. Deus sive Veritas. Deus sive Amor.* Such revealable understanding can only and only suddenly take place today or 'this' day as if coming with the Messiah (or you be-coming Him as not 'you' anymore). This day will help to remove causal or rational borders of a quasi-beginning and quasi-ending; i.e. of quasi-birth and quasi-death, which is not an expression of 'otherness *per se*', otherwise Echad *per se* would not deserve the name of Echad. Not as a number but as the indeterminate, indefinite the unknown, the ex-less 'X' = life.[15] Yes. Revelation reveals the magic of quasiness and opens the vista of the so-called First Days, the same as the so-called Last Days, when the prophet Elijah[16] shall come to

'turn the heart of the fathers to the children and the heart of the
children to their fathers, lest I come and smite the earth with a curse.'
(At the 'beginning' I said: 'My spirit shall not always dwell with man
because (in their body) it is only flesh' (and not spirit as in Me).

God speaks of turning the 'beginning' to reconnect it with the 'end' and vice versa, and universa. He speaks of re-turning home to the original state of indiscriminative thinking as before, or as beyond good and/or evil, which means beyond eitherness = otherness, to let the human mind cling to the alternating binary dichotomy which splits the whole into quasi-knower and (another?) quasi-known via knowing.[17]

The essence of mind belongs neither to death nor to rebirth; it is
uncreated and eternal. If the mind could be kept free from *discriminative*
thinking, there would be no more arbitrary thoughts to give raise to
appearance of forms, existences and conditions.

The divine spirit – in Biblical language – will continue to dwell 'in' the human mind and not become 'flesh' or body *per se* divided from mind *per se* as if two *per se*: Yahweh *per se* and Elohim *per se*. 'Natura naturans *per se* and natura naturata *per se*', to use Spinoza's wording for it. *Idea per se* and *ideatum per se* or 'knower' *per se* and 'known' *per se* divided and separated by he pseudo-assumption of otherness (*per se*).[18]

Omnia sunt Deus. Deus est omnia. Creator et creatura idem. Ideae
creant et creantur. Deus ideo dicitur finis omnium, quod omnia
reversura sunt in ipsum, ut in Deo immutabiliter conquiescant, et unum
individuum atque incommutabile permanebunt. Et sicut alterius naturae
non est Abraham, alterius Isac, sed unius atque ejusdem: sic dixit:
omnia esse unum et omnia esse deum. Dixit enim, Deum esse essentiam
omnium creaturarum.

In the newly found Spinoza letter one finds for the very first time Spinoza speaking of the identity of father and son, in order to ponder on it and on its connecting link via the Cabbala.

Among Spinozists, I found the enthusiastic Paul Wienpahl was attracted like myself equally to Spinoza and Zen-Buddhism, while referring to Peter Bayle's article, 'Spinoza'. 'You will be amazed to hear from Bayle 'what his (Spinoza's) new method had in common with other ancient and modern philosophers, European and Oriental', when mentioning one particular Chinese sect. This – Wienpahl is quite right – has 'gone unnoticed in the literature on Ch'an Buddhism', but also unnoticed in the literature on Spinozism – such parallel thinking is amazing. I myself would like to emphasize this – as I have already by quoting – in order to see Spinoza better seeable indeed. The same applies when seeing him via Cordovero and especially such laconic allusion in the *Ethics* 2PVII which I will discuss in more detail in my own paper. The mainstream of my urge and affinity cannot wait until then, it demands its right to flow with spontaneity and indeterminacy of *causa sui*. . . . Sic! Only to pick out one sentence: 'Ideae creant et creantur.' This is another version for 'ideae et ideata' of which Spinoza demanded: 'convenire debent,' although it is not so convenient for the discriminative quasi-otherness *per se* which attracts us and divides 'us' from 'it'. But still more is to say that this sentence stems from: *natura naturans* and *natura naturata* which, in accordance with the equation of *Deus = Natura*, would mean also: *Deus deificans = Deus deificatus*. Only for the serious indiscriminative mind the copula 'et' or 'and' should be replaced by 'sive = or' in order to show better the binary, alternating way of thinking.

In our own time Carlo Suares with his new revelation as revolutionizing as those I mentioned before and to which Spinoza made so many magic hints, as it were, contributes to salvation quasi via self-alchemization when observer and observed via self-observation are both serving the same work. They have to abandon their quasi-otherness and then bring illumination, samadhi, satori. Surface-existence has surface-problems and dilemmas and is often happy with surface-solutions of pseudo-salvation via words and explanations by other words and by other explanations again. This does the opposite of helping man to turn from discrimination (to *convenire debent!*) and to re-turn to the primordial state of indiscrimination, i.e. of life *per se* via living (not via thinking of living instead as a substitute). Man returning will become himself again, the very otherless, causeless, reasonless *same* in his knowable and unknowable aspect, level or dimension of self-awareness into omni-self-awareness. Man is whole and when self-aware of wholeness, he cannot be half-me and half-it, but whole, otherless himself. And this as if a quasi-knower of a quasi-known is always on the via knowing in order not to know otherness *per se*, but himself. To know himself *per* quasiness, as it were, so that on the 'via knowing' he becomes the via himself – knowing only for knowing sake, with no division of me or it, of knower or of known as (if) two. Western thinkers sometimes feel attracted by parallels between East and West, but only seldom can hints be seen which point to common affinities between East and Spinoza (as Wienpahl does) or between East and Cabbala while there are still voices to be heard or re-heard with fresh and unnoticed attraction between Spinoza and Cabbala. When speaking of 'Kabbalah To-day' I must mention Herbert Weiner.[19] He brings Rav Kook's teaching nearer to us and connects us also with Rabbi Nachman's message, not only to transcend man's ephemeral existence and existential awareness (just at a time when Transcendental Meditation entered the scene of man's need for help!), he also re-opened the (closed or blocked) door to perception: to man's direct (otherless) perception of his own unknown while ignoring or not knowing of Suares. While Timothy Leary tried to 'turn' on from outside that closed door, Jewish Esotericism had the key to safe 're-turn' as if coming home safely from cosmic orbit when traversing the same path of the quasi-universe or inner multi-verse with multi-dimensional consciousness. . . .

'That burning thirst for inner substance' that matters so much when followed by the 'vision that transcends [in Kook's words] the sur-face of existence'. All that waits to be experienced as yearning for salvation, not by brooding over scholastic scholarly definitions with dangerous dialectic acrobatics talking one 'in' or 'out' of an itching problem with no remedy at all against itching other than by scratching, and scratching with the consolation of healing. This yearning is such longing to expand innerness and its self-awareness of the many mansions of the Lord, now called multi-dimensionality and by Spinoza called infinite attributes self-attributing infinite or absolute infinity leading to 'essendi fruitio' and 'experientia essendi sive aeternitatis'. . . . Sic! That is to express our own absolute infinity as ∞^∞. . . . Such longing becomes stronger when men are disappointed with lifeless philo-sophizing, called by Spinoza *Cabbalistae nugatores*[20] and it provoked Rabbi Moses of Bourgos to exclaim about *nugatores philosophici*:

> where you philosophers are at an end, there we (the true Cabbalists) are only to begin,

namely to begin to point the way (of direct otherless perception) in order to experience that otherless riddle of: Know Thyself! Transcending egomorphous limitations must lead to the expansion of consciousness as predicted by Spinoza for the wise man, not only

> to be conscious of himself, but also of God and of the world [of a multiplicity of things].

The grand cosmic-divine consciousness is equated with a quasi-co-consciousness on three levels, aspects or dimensions. This in accordance with Cordovero does point to the experienceable identity of God, God's Intellect and (the quasi-intellected) objects. Thus the infinite intellect is the infinite quasi-knower identical with the infinite quasi-known via infinite knowing. *Ergo intellectus sui* or *causa sui* like *ratio sui*, like *existentia sui* (equal with eternity!) *sine alio*. Here we would recognize Cordovero, Cabbala and Spinoza, all of them blending with and paralleled by the East.

In such prologue to a Spinoza Symposium I think I have to mention, as Jean Préposiet did, a pleasant coincidence when two contemporary Spinozists have both found that Spinoza could offer the key (not only as key-word!) to salvation. F. H. Hallett, who soon became my personal friend via Spinoza, has not only been with me in my former witness-box: *Spinoza - 300 Jahre Ewigkeit*,[21] but has also published at the same time and with the same publisher his own work: *Creation, Emanation and Salvation*. A forerunner in his inspiring mission for Spinoza, he anticipated some new insight, and I am sure Spinozists have only started to quote him again so often.

Salvation always involves bondage as a bipolar concept with relational meaning and significance. Hallett brings the whole dilemma into the lime-light and within the graspable anecdotal framework so handy to everyone's understanding in 'vulgar phrasing':

> The 'natural' man like Sancho Panza, *must scratch where it itches*, the 'civilized' man, like Kai Lung, *learns to itch where he can scratch*, the morally 'obedient' man, like Goethe's 'gentleman' *refrains from scratching where it itches*, and the 'enlightened' man has so far *ceased to itch*.[22]

'Even such words (about itching and scratching) are like raising waves in a windless sea or performing an operation upon a healthy body. If one clings to what "others" have said and tries to understand (Zen) by explanation, he is like a dunce who thinks he can beat the moon with a pole or *scratch an itching foot from outside of a shoe*. It will be impossible after all.'[23] Thus the causal or rational relationship between itching and scratching has to be seen in the right light to know what relief could be expected at all. Should salvation apply to itching or to scratching to become effective? The Salvation Army for the masses is only concerned with the regi-mentation (of mentation!) of saving the ignorant man when his bondage is only seen under regimentation. Where there is no bondage to itching or scratching, there is no need for salvation to bring pseudo-relief. Man with his burning yearning confesses to his God: I have waited for Thy salvation! And in the waiting-room for salva-tion is revealed the urge, alertness and awareness as vital as life itself. It is in the very same *here* and *now* that every here-after (or before-here) shows its re-identification via quasi-otherness *per se* in the constant instant, or co-instant and substant 'it'. Standing 'in' it, being 'it' and not understanding 'it' as the very otherless self-same unknown (substance) standing 'under' every standing and under every under-standing also. . . . Yes! Why is salvation after all so rare and so difficult? Why? As even Spinoza, aiming all his life in one direction, confesses at the end of his life-work, the *Ethics*, when he has completed the whole path unwaveringly became the path himself: seeker and finder, you must confirm 'I am' (is) the Way, the Truth and Life! Because no rational and no causal approach can help to attain what one contains in his innermost unknown, but is regrettably so often unaware of it as him, himself.

Sudden illumination as Hui-Neng experienced and taught with no intention or bias, comes from the confidence in our unknowable, the indeterminacy of *causa sive ratio sui*. That is what both Spinoza and Suares speak about so convincingly to us. And this makes so many see indeterminacy as no-thingness (Ayin, shunya, void, i.e. devoid of human determinability, causality, rationality). This indeed is like a divine Grace, *chen* Adishtana. Spinoza holds such grace in esteem:

> sola revelatio doceat, id ex singulari Dei Gratia quam Ratione assequi non possumus fieri. . . . (*TTPXV*)

No calculation can work for it, nothing can work out what is not figurative, not calculable. No fathom can measure the unfathomable of our own unknowable, otherless self: life *per se sine ratione, sine causa, sine alio*. No eitherness = otherness *per se* is thinkable any more save via quasiness or in Spinoza's terms via *tamquam, quamvis, sive, quatenus*, etc. Yahweh = Elohim = Echad! Such oneness is assessed or re-assessed again and again when letting the mind contemplate on itself, re-flect itself and expand itself to grasp the arcanum of otherlessness. Thus have Gersonides and Cordovero condensed its challenging truth indeed. This is why Spinozists long for the revelations via true Cabbala and, vice versa, why Cabbalists sometimes crave to re-affirm the same truth via Spinoza. It is amazing to find how A. Jellinek, in his equal link with Cabbala and Spinoza, gave an enthusiastic emphasis to Spinoza's way of *mos geometricus*. And S. L. MacGregor Mathers was so much enchanted about it that he reprinted the whole text, which Christian D. Ginsburg has incorporated already in his 'Kabbalah',[24] namely the lucid analysis of the erudite A. Jellinek about the sephirotic ideas according to the *Ethics* of Spinoza, to mould the cabbalistic content into Definitions, Propositions, Proofs and Scholions as if to become more handy for Spinozists too. Sic! To make it more palatable for one's own taste one could see it in 'Kabbalah Unveiled' like another Euclidian veil.

I should also mention here Henry Walter Brann, who offered a theme for the common homage to Spinoza 'Spinoza and the Kabbalah', while reviving in such excellent manner the perennial approach of Gelbhaus as if this had gone unnoticed in the dusty libraries to herald again a renaissance of Cabbala and Mysticism via Eastern or via Western thinking on the very same path to the own unknowable, otherless Self.

At the end of the *Ethics* final freedom has been attained by Spinoza from one's own bondage (which stems from one's assumed quasi-otherness *per se*, that horrifying phantom appearing as other, other than me, namely as you, him, her or it) and three levels of consciousness of the wise man are pointed at. And 'the wise man thus is scarcely ever moved in his mind'. He is in *se ipso*: in his otherless self, and with Hui Neng he is 'realizing inwardly the imperturbability of the essence of mind'. If there is no real otherness *per se*, what then should or could actually ever perturb the mind of the wise man – 'scarcely ever moved in his mind'? Having thus realized no otherness *per se* (only quasiness but having experienced self-realization to testify the self-affirmed truth, the so-called self-consciousness must then mean: self-omni-consciousness or co-consciousness of self (introverting as) of God and (extroverting as) of the world of things called external or externalized: *omnia animata sumus*! Or in other words: aware of the way to identify with singularity, plurality and omniality as the self-sameness. And Spinoza then continues with his own words about such a wise man:

> being conscious by a certain eternal necessity of himself, of God
> (allself) and of things (quasi-other selves) and never ceases to be – and
> always enjoys true peace of soul.[25]

Necessity better contemplated not as coercion but as no-cessation of being, involves no beginning and no ending, thus must quiet or co-quiet the wise man to delight in his otherless self-realization as final salvation attained. '*Acquiescentia in se ipso vel in se ipsa means: in se ipso vel in Deo vel in mundo (rerum): ipse vera acquiescentia sui like causa sui like ratio sui. Vivat suitas!* The wise man never does think that he ceases to be, as he never ever thinks that he ever started once to be or to become, when already conscious of life as causeless, reasonless and plain: ex-less 'X'. So otherless self-reflection expands into God-reflection via world-reflection, in the way Cordovero is heralding the oneness of such apparently threefold reflection. Yes! The experience of cosmic divine universal self-reflection points to: *Deus sive Natura Sui*! *Suitas* is thus deifying or naturing itself via quasi-otherness with levels, aspects or dimensions of consciousness leading to enlightenment in the dark ignorance of otherlessness: *essendi fruitio, fiendi delectatio!* Non cognoscendi. . . . The wise man never believes in any 'before' nor 'after' nor 'when'. So Spinoza himself never believed it and so we believe him such now – belief as great relief from great grief. . . . The wise man – after Spinoza and Spinoza himself as an example of it – is not ignorant of God and things, of creator and creatures (as created world) as being otherless the very same. And *Amor Dei* or *beatitudo* – Spinoza equates both as the very same diviniza-tion or blessedness. The wise man always feels the blessing of the creator when not extro- nor when intro-verted but re-verted and re-turned to the root-source where he can experience the *Amor Dei* or *Amor Naturae* as universal self-love or self-blessing via infinite selves and quasi-non-selves until the quasiness is unmasked to reveal salvation. . . . And such *Amor Dei* is identi-fied by Spinoza with virtue, namely *ipsa virtus* or *virtus sui* like *causa sui*, like *ratio sui*. Everything tends to *suitas* although it in-tends *alteritas*. *Suitas* excludes *omnia alia*. So the wise man is not 'alien' to himself, not a stranger to God, nor alienated from the world (of things so strange and odd, to us in their at-homeness!). Everything belongs to the wholeness and when aware of it one as totalitarian is longing for such re-awareness again and again, to partake of totality as cosmic-divine co-consciousness. No 'mad obsession of introspection or extrospection' and no onesidedness for ex-tuition or in-tuition is there to split the wholeness into quasi in-side or out-side or into quasi in-sight or out-sight. It took me decades of wandering through many platitudes of books and latitudes of the globe: of wondering and wandering, of wondering and pondering until the *Ethics*, this wonder-book, suddenly became an open book for me. So I could then wander freely through this wonder-land of God, mind and human emotions either to see their superiority or their inferiority when man becomes wise and conscious of himself, of God and the world (of motions and emotions). My clouded mind in a flash of illumination became an open mind: vast like the ocean and the sky. Yes, the wonder, *tauma* for the Hellenes, was the very first step into the wonder-land of philo-sophia, of love for wisdom. To follow the wise man for wisdom and harvest, like him, the fruits described in the finale of the *Ethics*. Previously Spinoza dealt at the last stage of the path with the power of the intellect or with the human freedom as an inner strength. He tries first in the preceding stages to familiarize man as a thinking being not yet with his strength before confronted successfully with the strength of his e-motions as if not his own but others than his. This comes when thinking adequate and clear ideas to avoid such own puzzling bondage. Own freedom can only be attained, when unblocking the stumbling-blocks of his own ego-narrowed mind or I-mindedness in order to expand such narrow consciousness: from I-consciousness to God- or All-consciousness and to the quasi-plurality of things not as (if) three things different from each other, but as of different aspects of the otherless same, same oneness via quasi-otherness *per se*. From awareness of such oneness stems salvation and illumination as self-experience and never via dia'lectic' explanations of the unexplainable, of the exless 'X': our own unknown, *causa sive ratio sui*! For Spinoza and for those to follow him on such rare and difficult path, it means to learn about God or substance infinite in infinite ways, when having dissolved otherness and ab-solved the di-lemma of the indeterminate 'in' us and 'as' us but *quasi* as if 'non' us. . . . Then man has to learn about the nature and the origin of the mind with no beginning (nor end!) but only hypothetically supposed so for better self-reflection and self-contemplation, God and mind (*ens: mens*) the very same source: *causa sive ratio sui*. Mind for Spinoza therefore is auto-maton (i.e. self-learning, self-revolving) self-contemplating, self-reflecting self-obser-vations via quasi-otherness *per se* and accepting the mediation of quasiness as in Bible language the godlikeness of man or the manlikeness of God: 'Creator et creatura idem'! Then to learn about human emotions which could become a bondage when 'bound' by *causa sive ratio alius* or by otherness *per se* under the prey of pseudoness *per se*: the phantom of unidentifying quasi-ness: as if, *tamquam, quamvis, quatenus*, etc.

All these are like pegs or makeshifts as expedient means (upaya) to express the unexpressible of *causa-suitas*, or *ratio-suitas*. Yes! And at the end of such learning to reach initiation, the learner is not clinging to inadequacy deriving from causality or rationality and thus can be confronted with quasi-otherness of himself, the exless 'X': the divine cosmic Unknown, the universal totality as ocean with oceanic feeling to bestow. . . . This unknown is for the learner either he, himself, God, the all-self, the things around which sur-round quasi such narrow I-minded self in order to expand it by longing via the *Amor Dei sive Amor Naturae, Amor Veritatis*. Then one can witness as it were the divine Intellect in the very sameness as quasi-knower or as quasi-known: as God, the divine Intellect and the intellected objects, self-intellected by God, the All-self to become re-deified so to speak or re-naturalized as it were on the 'facies totius universi' facing the same *natura naturans* and/or *natura naturata*. Only human thought singularizes and separates, particularizes before illumination and before awareness of *omnia animata sumus* is experienced. The very same instrument discriminates or indiscriminates, separates or unites again and again when intellecting quasi-otherness as God does himself to co-experience divine quasiness in the light of the first axiom of the *Ethics*.

Thought bound brings bondage and re-leased brings release! Of that there is no doubt. By that with which fools are bound, the wise are quietly released.[26]

Saraha speaks like Spinoza of the same man: when ignorant and when not ignorant (or fool!) of God, himself or the things. Ignorance makes us exclaim after illumination: We thought it was a snake we saw on the road which terrified us from afar. When seen nearer it was only a rope looking quasi like a snake from the distance (of ignorance!). What fools we have been to have complained about stumbling-blocks on our path! We complained and ex-plained why we complained to feel unhappy. We failed to see into the very plain truth, that can shed light to let us avoid stumbling in the darkness (of ignorance), ignoring to see deeper and nearer than surface-existence and surface-awareness. To see into it via ourselves and into ourselves via it: as one and the same via. The via *per se*. Via *viae sive* via *sui*!

The other Spinozist pointing to Spinoza for 'salvation from despair' is Errol E. Harris and his work tends to be a 're-appraisal of Spinoza's philosophy'. Are these not two remarkable signposts: Hallett and Harris, both pointing with emphasis the way to the *path* where man suddenly discovers liberation from his self-imposed bondage after he has learned how to expose it as himself? While expanding the I-minded, singularizing consciousness, man no longer ignores the oneness and wholeness of God and the world: the very same own universal unknowable life. Le Chayim! 'Vivat vita sui!' Then extro-version or intra-version appear only as two versions of the same otherless self. Yes! Speaking of that *path* I have tried to voice a chorus of 'pathfinders' pointing at the rare and difficult way for pathseekers, with the intention of stimulating from the beginning of my homage for Spinoza in this book: urge, surge and yearning (for innerness and expanding re-awareness of it!) in order to reach salvation. Salvation is meant from the own unknown when dissolving quasi-otherness *per se* into instru-mental quasiness so helpful for *causa sive ratio sui* and the principle of indeterminacy. Pathfinders emphasize the very odd and strange sameness of 'us' when 'on' the path and of the path 'as' us ourselves.

> Thou canst not travel on the path before thou hast become the path itself (Voice of Silence). To whatever place one would go, that place one's own self becomes (Jnaneshvari). As there is neither any traversing nor any traverser of the path, the expression *'path'* is merely figurative (Precepts of the Gurus). *'Path'* is merely a metaphor descriptive of the method of realizing spiritual growth or progress (Evans-Wentz). On this path we have to find our own touch-stone of truth, independent of *academic or theological approval*. What we want is one's own perception of the truth, not one taken on ready made (Sri Madhava Ashish). Anyone who so desires, can move into the vitalizing study [of the path] and dig in his own mind indefinitively making his own discoveries – and can be a point of consciousness to which revelation comes (Carlo Suares).

Suares emphasizes that point of consciousness which I contemplated upon to expand on Spinoza's path with his finger-pointings, to cease to remain ignorant of multi-dimensionality of cosmic-divine consciousness which as co-consciousness means con-sciousness of all-oneness or one-allness indeed! Then also it is to understand quasiness which only the ignorant takes for otherness *per se*, while the wise man recognizes (again?) his own divine, cosmic legacy from the very Old Testament and the Old Garden of Eden. There man, God, things (*omnia animata*) were all together in co-essence and co-existence either inspiring and aspiring omni-self-consciousness of *omnia animata* (*sumus*)! The wise man is going to regain admittance into the Garden of Eden. Not without any co-incidence has the symbol of the garden captured thinkers when reaching salvation. Gan in Hebrew consisting only of two letters: G(imel) and N(un), is and stands for an abbreviation, namely for G(uf) and N(eshamah): body: soul, or in today's terminology, psychosomatic pair-concept. Garden or Pardess is also a symbol-word composed by the four abbreviated first letters PRDS (Pardes) and can be equated with four ways of knowledge or cognition. And there is also a story of four men: Ben Azzai, Ben Zoma, Akiba and Elisha Ben Abuya. They entered the (forbidden) Garden of Mysteries. Three of them were harmed and only Akiba was able to pass through such initiation and yet to return safely to everyday life from the own beyond as if from outerspace of otherness *per se*. Akiba, until his death and even with his death, was fully convinced of the otherless sameness to defy the phantom of ghostlike horror which cannot hurt the mature and wise man: to know himself via various quasi-otherness *per se* as temptations to deviate him from the *via viae*. The primordial state of indiscrimination as in the Garden of Eden does not dualize oneness as: heaven and earth, male and female, body and soul, but rather sees only quasi-twoness, quasi-otherness and in truth a pair-concept expressing wholeness and omni-awareness either as pairness or wholeness, the very same. The garden-simile as two or as four shows the squaring of the concept in accordance with the tetragrammaton, the tetraktys as if the quasi-two are lifted up to a higher level (of consciousness) of oneness via 2^2 or via se^{se}. Quaternity is often equated with divinity itself and the whole base of the numerical system as derived from Pythagoras. And all this 'happens' by self-experience when on the path and not by scriptural studies alone. One must have a key provided by a teacher who has experienced self-realization himself to unlock the locked words in scriptural teaching leading to the bare wordless path and its essence beyond the layers of form and formlessness to the very substance: to that which stands 'under' everything and 'under' every thought, and which nobody can understand or even stand unless by otherless self-experience. Then quasi-knower and quasi-known are re-united again on the via knowing to become that very via, that way, that path itself. Ex-per-iri = going through 'it' and as coming from some-where (indeterminate, acausal, irrational!) 'I' am going via 'me' through 'it' and via 'it' through 'me'. Then 'me' and 'it' are dissolving each other altogether with their discrepancy of pseudo-twoness, namely of experiencer and experienced: subject and object. The 'going' becomes intransitive as a self-alchemization in a sudden revelation to reveal the identity of me and it, of ego and id as idem. Knower and known are both (with reciprocal receptivity!) on the same via knowing with a two-way traffic. The via me *sive* via id transmutes me and id into the via of idem: via *viae sive* via *sui*, like *causa sui* like *ratio sui*. *Vivat suitas!* After experience wholeness and the omni-awareness of it knows no more quasi knower versus a quasi known, but only via of knowing. Ire is to go. Iri to be gone, the person trans-personalizes quasi. . . . Sic! Now I know myself: not me it or it me. No more half-knowledge of that pair-concept of wholeness which is that otherless Self. Yes! It is a re-formation by such reciprocal receptivity. A trans-mutation in the true alchemical sense. All my little life I heard the great, the wise man postulate: know thyself! Not this nor that. Not that nor this, but thyself! Which is neither-nor and appears as either-or (a pair-concept) via quasiness simulating quasi-otherness *per se*. Quasiness will soon vanish to make room for the ripe self-realization of the quasi-unreal, namely the otherless 'it'. And that (it) you are. *Tat twam asi!* Now I know myself. And I know that I know. And I know that there is no otherness to evolve or involve anymore when speaking of quasi-knower and quasi-known. To know thyself is equal to know the unknowable – as a presence, omni-presence co-present as you – and without expecting that it ever become knowable. Its presence is convincing after Suares brought such message to us of our non-us. Us is 'what' we know of it 'as' us and 'it' is 'that' we know of it as it: itself. Yes. In the same way Maimonides and Spinoza speak both of knowing 'that' God is and 'what' God is. This is more in line with Sepher Yetzirah which rejects any anthropomorphous 'what' as whatness, *quidditas* and describes such undescribable rather beli-mah = without 'what', i.e. without dichotomy or discrepancy of me and not-me. As 'object' I am so used to object it (objectify) to my standing and under-standing but disregarding the *omni* sub-stant instant and co-instant, that despotically I make it 'subject' to my outsidedness as quasi-other. Thatness implies rather indiscrimination and self-reflection inflecting quasi-otherness belonging to the pair-concept self-other or other-self. The ultimate step on the path to know thyself! Then every-thing is like no-thing and no-'thing' is no longer absolute negativity *per se*, as negative-positive is again the very same pair-concept. Now I recognize it under any dis-guise. 'I am' (is) life to live (not to know). I know is to know: quasiness as knower *vis-à-vis* known until the identification with the via knowing dawns with transcendental magic. Then 'I am' (is) the via, the Way, *tao* and the Truth. *Ergo* life again. Spinoza does not express life like Descartes – so over-ego-conscious – he does not remain in the domain of egohood via ego-consciousness. He expands the ego into God (as trans-ego) via God-consciousness and into the world via world-consciousness: 'omnia animata sive omnia animantia sumus'! Descartes would have said: 'animatus sum' and said: 'ego sum'. 'Ego cogito.' Spinoza used the universalized ego: *sumus* pointing to omniality, totality. And totality has no discrimination between knower versus known. Spinoza leant on 'Idea creant et creantur'. Not 'ego con-scius sum sed omnia animata' (not *animatos* personalized). Here is manifest *natura naturans* and *naturata* as idem. 'Participium presentis sive participium perfecti' via omni-presence of omni-consciousness which is timeless, causeless or synchronic with Jung (speaking and pointing at acausality). Ex-per-iri = as if coming from somewhere equal with no-where with no determinable 'whatness' but with indeterminable 'thatness' is allowed to speak out the whole truth: 'veritas sui sine alio' with no pseudoness but quasiness. This is in accordance with the structure of multidimensionality of omni-consciousness. Experience makes self-realization self-experienceable of the unknowable 'thatness', namely 'that' I experience 'experiencing' . . . with no elseness any more. . . . The ob*server* becomes con-scious of 'serving' and not of looking, on-looking as an out-sider. Out-side or in-side have lost their loosable meaning as pair-concept, and lost any leaning via ex-per-iri i.e. via trans-ire which is encapsulated in the in-transitive verb and thus experience becomes a 'happening' of which never can be said: 'I' happen but only 'it' and I am always 'in' it and 'as' it: The pair-concept: acausal, irrational coming to the end of divisibility and becoming the indivisible wholeness as wholeness: 'omnia animata sumus' with no '*sumus*' sive egos, with no '*animata*', with no '*omnia*', with no sayability of the Ayn, the Void, Shunya: the indeterminable, *causa sui.* . . .

Personally I consider it a divine boon like that of Nachiketas as described in the Kathopanishad. And just this special Upanishad became so dear and near to me via Sri Krishna Prem and his commentary. Further, Prem himself became a challenge to me with his person and personality pointing in his letters always to salvation 'while in the body' while re-assuring me as 'being on the path'. . . . After his death I continued the pleasant contact with his successor, Sri Madhava Ashish, who finished Prem's last book and later added another one of his own on the same lines. That boon I mentioned before came to me not only for being so privileged to enter the witness-box three times in the cause of 'Spinoza', but also claim and proclaim the urge for salvation as a challenge. This time I feel immensely enriched with valid experiences of self-cultivation leading to self-realization quasi-permeated with the parallel teaching of the East. And this to such an extent that I often ponder about showing 'Spinoza in the Light of the East' while also revealing striking parallels pointing to 'the East in the Light of Spinoza'. Especially, when so familiar with the basic vital and vitalizing essence of Spinoza's message leading to *essendi fruitio* or to *fiendi delectatio* (if I may paraphrase . . .) but not to cognoscendi fruitio, delectatio. . . .

Spinozists would feel like at home in the 'essentials of Buddhism' and vice versa. Buddhists would like to re-experience at-homeness via Spinoza like everywhere when man is estranged from his own unknown self (and its 'thatness'!) and is longing and craving to turn the mind to its own roots (and not to the branches!) and re-turn to one's root-awareness of being a home-comer from one's own 'quasi-afar' via quasi-otherness *per se* (and its 'whatness'!).

Jewish prophets, as self-appointed missionaries, feel the very same challenge to re-awake the nostalgia of home-coming by longing and by the odd feeling of be-longing to such longing. . . . To return to Yahweh and to experience after the Zohar why man has been sent into this world to understand this day that Yahweh is (no 'other' but the very same) Elohim. To 'under-stand' that there is no-thing to understand as some-'thing' other than me, a 'what', but rather to reverse it into 'stand under'. . . . Then to know is not to know, but to now, ever to now the own unknown instant, sub-stant, con-stant (*being*) as otherless, timeless and placeless: *causa sive ratio sui (non alius!)*. Echad! *Vivat suitas*!

Not only was such prophetic home-calling valid and a comfort when the Jews had no land anymore on earth, and for their God no house to 'house' the invisible, indivisible, exless 'X' since the destruction of the second temple by Titus Vespasian. Historians record that he had the shock of his life (similar to Alexander the Great on a similar occasion!) when, with the rioting army, he penetrated the sanctuary of the devastated temple to be 'puzzled' by the invisible 'holiness' while an odd awe shook his being. . . . For the first time the magic of invisible holiness penetrated into the recess of his mind as it did with the prophet to make him exclaim: Holy, holy, holy is Yahweh Tsebaoth! Full is the whole earth with His (heavenly) Glory! And Vespasian, did he feel such Glory which could not be destroyed together with the temple (made by man to house God in his godlikeness and to remember Eden and the togetherness with God the gardener of that Garden of Mankind!)? Did he feel that such Glory was not housed only within walls and could not be destroyed, together with the ruins to remain an exile, but that the 'wailing wall' was wailing because of the quasi-exile of the quasi invisible, indivisible glory filling all the quasi-emptiness of the earth? Yes. The Jews now defend the wailing wall together with the few walls of their 'miniaturized' former homeland of their fathers given to them by the God of their fathers, the fathers of Israel to the Children of Israel, not only as a Biblical promise with testimonies in heaven and on earth – and now Spinoza's quasi-Messianic expectation and pseudo-contradictory but pre-dictory words of such re-turn become true in our days and before our eyes.

> I would *absolutely* believe that they, the Jews, once at a given *chance*, as things are submitted to *change* [*and:* chance] will again build their land and that God will s-elect them again.[27]

In this word 'chance' or opportunity, the latent indeterminist in Spinoza, so hidden and occult for Spinozists, comes through not via *causa sive ratio alius, sed via causa sive ratio sui,* i.e. via *indeterminationis.* . . . Sic! With no be-cause to ex-plain the plain ex-less being, while chance involves change and vice-versa or uni-versa. We have to think of it here and pause with reflection, contemplation, namely how Spinoza sometimes disclosed (against his former rationalized intention and attention) such deeper links with Israel and with the God of Israel, of whom he expects a second selection in 'time and space' so to speak. Was it perhaps to over-compensate in the deep recess of his (omni-) consciousness while always conscious of himself as conscious or co-conscious of God and co-conscious of the world (of *omnia animata sumus*)?

Was it perhaps to over-compensate the surface-disconnection, namely when saying that I would *dare* to say that I also agree with the *ancient Hebrews*? It shows that he did not so often 'dare' so. Sic! He saw already in his life and lifetime what he fore-saw for posterity, that a certain wishful re-Judaization would take place as a renaissance and as a nostalgia with the same charm as the 'second birth' of enlightenment described as experienced in his work of God, Man and His well-being. But let me first 'pause' with a little intermezzo of Spinoza's prediction of the rebuilding of Israel.

INTERMEZZO I

Gerschom Scholem let us relive again that tense period in history when the messianic fire of Sabbatai Sevi swept through the whole world and soon reached Holland. But there Spinoza was in his hermitage, quite unharmed, and immune from the events. . . . Some of his friends did ask him about his opinion, but unfortunately his answer has not yet been found. Yet the way to posterity as the newly discovered Spinoza letter had. Nevertheless, certain remarks of Spinoza are ascribed to the echo of this messianic movement, and Jewish Historic salvation was on the agenda as it were. . . . Such agenda is in our days again and again under scrutiny, especially with the focus on oil to make it an imperative to give more light and for some more lime-light to see the world-scenery of history biased by oil as an excellent turm-oil 'oiling' much better wishful shaping and shaking of history indeed.

> As for the fact that they have survived their dispersion and the loss of their state for so many years, there is nothing miraculous – as a consequence – we must admit – no other election peculiar to Jews! And – since they have incurred hatred by cutting themselves off completely from all other people: and not only by practising a form of worship opposed to the rest, but also by preserving the mark of circumcision with devoutness. That their survival is largely due to the hatred of the Gentiles, has already been shown by experience [slavery in Egypt, exile in Babylon, Autodafé, pogroms, gas-chambers, etc.]. The mark of circumcision is also, I think, of great importance in this connexion: so much that in my view it alone will preserve the Jewish people for all time. Indeed did not the principles of their religion make them *effeminate*, I should be quite convinced, that some day when the opportunity arises – so mutable are human affairs – they will establish their state once more, and that *God will choose them afresh*. . . . [*Fiat voluntas Sua!*]

One must not be guided by hate against the Benedictus, as Hermann Cohen was with the purpose of exposing such crass self-contradiction of a second Balaam to bene-'dict' (as a Benedictus himself!) and to pre-'dict' some opportunity which was unpredictable and uncalculable under the ruling of *causa sive ratio* (*alius sed SUI!*), i.e. by chance not seen *sub specie humana*, *ergo* not anthropomorphously but rather theomorphously . . . by *Deus sive Veritas, Deus sive Amor, Deus sive Natura:* Yahweh = Elohim! And admittedly Spinoza had perhaps written the words at the beginning of my quotation by impulse (tricky, itchy and provocative for the prickly Jewish neighbour, whom he was always so ready to love after the Decalogue of Moses, his teacher). Such re-election meant re-eligible again in time as it had meant before in timeless history with the very same chance! And when we re-read this sentence before ontrusting the whole text ripe for us, his posterity, we find Spinoza has had time enough to ponder and to reconsider in order to wipe out (or not!) any trace of rebukeable self-contradiction. In doing it, Spinoza would have had then to ostracize (in his own eyes with no outside witness at all to interfere . . . !) his own former ostracizing attitude towards his people. But Spinoza did not do it. He stuck to what he once said. His diction was no accusable contra-diction but laudable pre-diction instead, which in our days (A.D. 1948) – after the calendar started with one of Israel's and God's sons – became true history and which some will try in vain to distort or revert or pervert again, Sic!

My pores and cells still tremble with awe remembering the event which I have been so especially privileged to witness (as I witness now for Spinoza again!) under a special insular hospitable barbed wire . . . until only much later I was found ripe for initiation to continue and to follow history and its course on the new-old soil. Now, when in the witness-box for Spinoza, I feel I have to mention my testimony to hail Spinoza's prophecy which some still intend to trivialize. I cannot be persuaded that universality must be seen and shown as a noble compensation for the loss of statehood. Such talk was a farce, disguised by friend and foe as well, especially disguised as a consolation for the dispersion of Jews. And just at the time when new small states are springing up everywhere, claiming independence under the approval of the (Dis-)United Nations with a numerical approval of the multitude as it were which only Israel has never sought or found . . . some day had to come when the opportunity arose (in Spinoza's prediction!) for Jews to establish or re-establish their state once more. This is not only to say that they, the Jews, were able to survive where others (of their size!) would have vanished for good on our beautiful globe, but to demonstrate that global or universal significance cannot become a consolating substitute. And it is also to demonstrate that 'the principles of their religion were not meant to make them *effeminate* Sic! It is to demonstrate again that their mission includes to become like other states with their statehood recognized again and to preserve unlike others their striking universality *vis-à-vis* other states and their statehood as well, only because God Himself willed to choose them afresh. One of my co-workers, Sylvain Zac, has a theme: Spinoza and the State of the Hebrews, and he likes to point to the quintessence and its focus on the 'Hebrews as the Chosen People'. He continues:

> this is one of the propositions of the Tractatus Theologico-Politicus and
> does not have a spiritual meaning. It is rather a historical and political
> meaning. What are the foundations and the institutions of the Hebrew
> State? What was, in spite of its excellence, the primary cause of its
> decline and fall? In answering these questions, Spinoza draws lessons
> which throw a new light on the aims he pursues in his political works.

Now to return to G. Scholem. After the flames of the messianic fire of
Sabbatai Sevi have been extinguished in the cremation place of history, one
still wonders, especially when connected with Spinoza then and now as now
and then with no discrepancy of 'before' or 'after', one wonders why Scholem
analyses and also trivializes Spinoza's remarks regarding 're-election of
Jews'.

> It matters *little* [says Herr Prof. Scholem – with more retrospection than
> introspection] for *our* purpose whether Spinoza meant his words
> regarding a renewed election of Israel by God to be taken *literally* or as
> a *figure of speech* only.

As self-appointed ambassador for Spinoza I am certain that Spinoza has
never been attracted by or submitted to the tricks of verbalizations with the
sole purpose of hiding the true thoughts of his true philosophy, which he
emphasized was not the best, but the *true* one.

Joseph Klausner supports Spinoza against Gerschom Scholem and backs
his sincerity, especially when pointing to Joseph Albo, a pupil of Crescas.
Spinoza has been too familiar with both of them and with their writings.
Klausner is able to show how Spinoza leaned fully and with intention on
Albo (Ikkarim, IV, 45 at the end) and then adds his own words: 'The connexion between circumcision and continuance of the nation and its salvation, a wonderful similarity of Albo and Spinoza, and it is difficult to
assume that such similarity is only accidental.' [Not a figure of speech, but of
thought instead!] J. Klausner: 'Der Jüdische Charakter der Lehre Spinozas',
my Spinoza Festschrift (Heidelberg, Carl Winter, 1933) and again 2nd edn.
(The Hague, Martinus Nijhoff, 1962). Now – I give due honour to a non-Jew,
A. E. Waite, in 'his own lineage in the spirit' as he calls it, in order to show
how he thinks with inner sympathy of this cardinal theme of circumcision
with regard to Jews leading to their 'divine election'.

> The Kabbalistic Jew, dreaming of liberation and of union under the
> grievous yoke of his law [to avoid the danger of 'effemination' which
> Spinoza feared so much] giving it the wings of interpretation and rising
> himself thereon, *is of my own lineage in the spirit*, of my kinship in the
> heart of quest. The Jew's covenant in the flesh is assuredly in Zoharic
> understanding, one of God's most true covenants. The Master Who seals
> us within does often seal us without, whence peers and co-heirs have always
> known one another in every place of the world, and every sign-manual of
> heaven is honourable and worshipful, since it sets apart to His service
> (*The Holy Kabbalah*, N.J. Univ. Books, 1970, p. 598.)

In our time, after new successful excavations with the Key for Qabala into
our own unknown, Carlo Suares points again to that very meaning of

circumcision as if to join Spinoza in order to vindicate his prediction. He discloses the special significance of Jewish circumcision versus any other application of it, be it at the age of 13 years or be it for any other reason whatsoever. Such a seal when applied only a few days after birth gives quasi a special entry into the world. Everything turns to seem only (as if) flesh *per se* against the spirit (as if) fleshless *per se*. King Midas was cursed and could not enjoy the horrible boon granted to him: that every thing touched by him became gold, noble gold, without he himself becoming noble in nature. . . . So man in his trend of siding with one-sided dichotomizing mind turns everything into (one-sided) flesh only. With circumcision such seal is then pointing to the very same mission of the prophet Jeremiah: 'to change the (fleshy) heart into a new (fleshless) one and to serve afresh the *Lord* Who dwells in the heart. The *Lord* Who fills the whole empty earth as the whole void body with His Glory'!

I am glad to have these witnesses to back the foresight and insight Spinoza gave to such fleshy symbol as allegiance to the fleshless spirit in connexion with the re-election of the nation of Israel and the re-establishment of their lost homeland: now again a controversy which will have no say whatsoever before the *Lord*, Yahweh: Elohim (*Deus sive Natura*), the *Lord who chooses them afresh*!

On the other hand only with much regret I finish this intermezzo on circumcision as viewed and previewed by Spinoza, while I have to mention on such historical occasion as this homage to Baruch de Spinoza, that a contemporary pupil of Spinoza, although so eager to revive his spiritual legacy, could not face and endure such dilemma and discrepancy. . . . Constantin Brunner did back and support Spinoza with much enthusiasm in his essential basic teaching save only when it came to such a super-delicate crux latent in Spinoza's prediction of the re-establishment of the lost Jewish homeland. He rather seems to stick to the opinion that they, the Jews, are not and have not been elected at all. How then to speak of any re-election here?

Now when again in the witness-box for Baruch de Spinoza I have to prove his prediction and its validity for Spinoza's sake and for the dignity of truth involved. Let me thus compare Spinoza's statement about the Jews and the other statement of his ardent pupil, Constantin Brunner (formerly Leo Wertheimer) in order to ponder on the truth transcending any like or dislike, while avoiding any siding with deviations of the truth. Spinoza had still in his memory the historical destruction of the Jewish homeland with the dispersion among the nations on earth. He could still listen to the reverberating echo from the autodafé. . . . And on top of this, his own excommunication was a stigma for him and for his nation. But he did not feel excommunicated from the Ancient Hebrews when he leaned on them in the essentials of his doctrine. In spite of all this Spinoza did not stumble over the many stumbling-blocks in his way. He did not crumble in his sincere faith and inner link with the latent mission of his people to awaken his deeper identity to predict their re-election not by Man and Mankind, but by God Himself; Yahweh = Elohim. He was convinced that such a divine promise was not an empty word. As it could create the world, it could re-create the Jewish world in their former homeland as a fulfilment to be expected 'in our days' as 'our daily prayers' remind us during the dispersion in all the days of longing. . . .

Now I have to quote Brunner's statement from 1918 as promised. It was just soon after the First World War and the coming of Adolf the Great has not begun yet to forecast the foretaste of the historical (and hysterical) mission of the Third Reich: with that new *gloria in excelsis* (*et profundis*) *dei*.

Spinoza's statement:

As for the fact that they have survived their dispersion and the loss of their state for so many years, there is nothing miraculous – as a consequence – we must admit – no other election peculiar to Jews! And – since they have incurred hatred by cutting themselves off completely from all other people: and not only by practising a form of worship opposed to the rest, but also preserving the mark of circumcision with devoutness. That their survival is largely due to the hatred of the Gentiles has already been shown by experience [slavery in Egypt, exile in Babylon, Autodafé, pogroms and gas-chambers]. The mark of circumcision is also, I think of great importance in this connexion: so much that in my view it alone will preserve the Jewish people for all time. Indeed did not the principles of their religion make them effeminate, I should be quite convinced, that some day when the

Brunner's statement:

Those devout-pious, visionary-devout Jews with their faith in the promises, with their Bible, 'that scriptural fatherland of God's Children', they indeed are not waiting for their political Reich but for a miracle, which the Zionists never ever will make to become a reality. It could be said rather of these *meshichim en masse* enticing to a false historical fact: 'Your comforters are misleading you and they destroy the way you have to go – they are servants for cutting to pieces' – and Zionism is rather to be called Anti-Messiah than Messiah! The Jews a nation? In the various houses in the city pieces of roast cut on plates, these I would rather call a living ox than the Jews a nation! But admittedly they were thousand times a nation, could therefore such a nation be set into Palestine? A nail sticks in the wall, but once taken out, it is no use to put it back into the old hole: it will not stay there anymore!

opportunity arises – so mutable are human affairs – they will establish their state once more, and that God will choose them afresh!
[*Fiat voluntas Sua!*]
(transl. A. G. Wernham, Clarendon, Oxford 1958.)

(Constantin Brunner, *Der Judenhass und die Juden,* Oesterheld Co., Berlin, 1918, p. 113.)

Now, after 1948 – only thirty years after such a negative prophecy – Brunner's words make life for his pupils in Israel somehow awkward and they try (in vain it seems) to revoke them when read against the words of Baruch de Spinoza which after three hundred years have reached their fulfilment.

It should be left to the unbiased researcher of Spinoza to ponder again and again what he has said and foresaid, sounding at the beginning like a contradiction but later turned into a pre-diction. Such words in the mouth of Spinoza as:

chance, change, mutable human affairs and . . . God's will of a fresh choice regarding Jews . . .

quasi outside *causa sive ratio vel determinatio.*
Then, one can give a second and more thorough thought to such quasiness which has 'puzzled' one of Spinoza's pupils to such extreme like Constantin Brunner. . . .

INTERMEZZO II

Man is so often baffled by oddities. Already his divine creation appears so odd: 'So God created man in his own image: male *and* female, he created them.' How odd, while we are used to: male *or* female as alternative to such quasi-twoness. More odd when God himself could say of man that he 'is become as one of us!' 'Adam knew Eve' (not as quasi-two: one another but a pair-concept!): flesh of his flesh and bones of his bones. To attain such 'knowledge' 'man shall leave his father and mother [with their quasi-twoness] and shall cleave unto his wife!' They shall be not quasi-two anymore but one in the flesh. The two parents procreated man: male *or* female (not male *and* female as God created him) with the innate craving to cleave to each other reciprocally – and they shall be again one: flesh and bones. Adam and Eve, in every male and female, 'know' such oneness from creation still to be remembered and they always look to restore again oneness in the flesh via quasi-twoness by two para-others. A quasi-knower versus a quasi-known until they become (aware or re-aware of being) not dui-versus but uni-versus: to realize and uni-versalize all-oneness or one-allness in the flesh which reveals for a timeless moment fleshless, endless life.

To attain such odd knowledge man must leave everything and every thought

33

(of quasi-twoness, para-otherness), and also leave the quasiness of knower *per se* or known *per se*, but rather try to identify or re-identify both as other-less same-self. *Know thyself*! Man must leave everything, c-leave to no-thing or all-oneness, otherless sameness! And then they shall be one *mind* (to mind everything!): one as created and quasi-two as procreated. Then – then God's image in man and man's imagination will be restored to remember that God has made and still makes him yet a 'little lower' than God, and also that 'God has crowned him with glory and honour'. A 'little lower', quasi-lower only, when in God and in God's image and imagination there is no-thing low or high in itself. 'Full is the whole earth with his glory!' With that glory with which man on that earth has been crowned. A crown of thorns? Or rather a bush of thorns? 'Out of the midst of the bush the angel of the Lord appeared in a flame of fire which burned and the bush was not consumed by it.' We will ask with Moses: How odd? And with William Norman Ewer[28]: 'How odd of God to choose the Jews?' How odd? The odd and Old Testament left such odd legacy which only an emissary of the New Testament came to confess and understand in front of Spinoza and Spinoza admirers A.D. 1977. It was then Blaise Pascal, a contemporary of Baruch de Spinoza and now a witness in posterity, who 'recorded Monday, the 23rd of Nov. 1654, from about half past ten evening until half past midnight, on a piece of parchment this decisive experience, found sewn into his clothing after death and it seems that he carried it with him at all time![29] Fire . . . God of Abraham, God of Isaac, God of Jacob, not of philosophers and scholars!' – What fire? Still from that eternal burning bush: burning in front of Moses and in Moses, as in the Baal Shem, the founder of Hassidism. How odd of Pascal to feel it burning in himself! How odd of Spinoza to feel it and its oddity linked with the divine selection of Jews via his diagnosis becoming a true prognosis! Do you agree, Baruch, how I approached with no re-proach such magic oddity which you enjoyed and for which you suffered like all of us: from the first days to the last days of mankind . . . ? Pascal seconds Spinoza with the same utterance. 'We know of the quasi-two, (the pair of) attributes ex-tension and mind (in-tension) what they are, but of the (quasi-other) unknowable only that they are.' Pascal about God: 'we may well know that God exists without knowing what he is'! (From his '*Wager*' which was found among his private papers – hidden?)[29]

To 'know' such unknowable oddities is to know life by 'living it' not by knowing of it. This is divine selection, karmic longing of the drop in the fathomless ocean to self-realize omniality and to identify with the uni-verse as self uni-versus and not versus. Entification of mens or mentification of ens is to parallel quasiness of man and God as of the same otherless sameness. . . . Pascal's 'Wager' is supposed to be a work started by a mathematician and continued by a mystic. I could say this also about Spinoza's *Ethics* to justify his trans-retional and trans-causal words in accordance with his first axiom and its axiomatic truth of 'I am' [is] the way, truth and life! Which words? *Sentimus experimurque (non cognoscimus) nos aeternos esse! Essendi (non cognoscendi!) fruitio!* This is life itself, no more knowledge of life as knowing some quasi-otherness *per se* than knowing as knowing without knower *per se* nor known *per se*.

Now let me return to the main theme after the intermezzo and reconnect the thread with Spinoza's saying: 'that I would *dare* to say that I also agree with *ancient hebrews*.' Was this meant perhaps to over-compensate his surface-disconnexion from the Jewish mainstream of thought in order to please superficial one-sided Spinoza admirers? It shows that Spinoza did not often 'dare' so. He saw already in his own lifetime and foresaw it for posterity and us during our lifetime: that a certain wishful re-Judaization will try to replace former proud over-Christianizations of his work. Gebhardt, when editing Spinoza's works in 1925 gave them not the title of Benedict de Spinoza, but rather Baruch de Spinoza. And so it will soon be reprinted as such. Could this be deciphered as a renaissance of the 're-elected' Jews and their re-established homeland after God's choice? And then could it be compared perhaps with the charming nostalgia of the enlightened man as 'his second birth', so appealingly described by Spinoza in his early work: Of God, Man and His Well-being?

Today, for instance, when reading Jean Lacroix's: *Le Christ selon Spinoza*[30] one should not wonder if next time the title is *Spinoza selon Christ!* remnants of traces from over-Christianization! The Geheimrat, for example, called Spinoza *'theissimus'*, but this seemed not *'theos'* enough and perhaps too much Jewish-theissimus, so he then felt he had to add *theissimus et christianissimus*. Sic! Here you have it – the over-Christianization of Spinoza and the over-paganization of Jesus, that Jew from Nazareth, with no good reputation. Good Christians, like Arnold Toynbee, are already aware of something grafted and labelled 'Christian' but not being 'Christian' in fact. When he passed away ripe in knowledge – in Eastern parlance – some of his letters were published where he suggests to a Jewish friend and scholar, that they should reclaim their Jew Jeshu, estranged by pagans and by over-paganized Judaism disguised as Christianity. The clever Romans after their secular exit from the world scene, returned soon wisely disguised as Roman-Catholics (i.e. universalized Romans!) to intermingle over-worldly and this-worldly in human affairs with much skill, named after Jesu, namely Jesuits. And Spinozists not too successful in their Christianizing trend, behave today as in Spinoza's days they did, although he made it then unequivocally clear: 'that I hold an opinion about God and Nature [etc.] *very different* from that which *Modern Christians are wont to defend. . . .*'

And 'Modern Christians' today still 'are wont to defend' the preserved and reserved evidence of monopolized Christian Mysticism in order to apply it with much overzeal to Spinoza's mystical experience, of which with (or rather *with no*) regret to say only very rare and bare traces of evident revelation are to be found. And when *not* found, they are sometimes grafted onto or read 'between' the words of those disappointed to have looked in vain for something to compare with recorded confessions in the mausoleum of history for a mausoleum-admiring posterity.

Spinoza uses the words *fruitio*, *essendi fruitio* and perhaps not as a simile only. This word could have been known as a phrase or phase of enlightenment and as such we find the Psalmist using it:

O, taste and see the *Lord* is good! (Ps. 34: 8)

In the *Korte Verhandeling*, the very same words: 'te mogen smaaken (German: schmecken) de vereniging met God'[31] focuses on the very same context and essence of meaning. When later using the way of self-contemplation or self-reflection and when on the way to meditate on God as Spinoza did in the expanded consciousness as omni-consciousness or self-consciousness of *omnia animata* (*sumus*), we then must discover with spontaneous in-tuition rather than via *causa sive ratio* (*alius*!) that such a word, *fruitio*, had to convey introspection and mystical insight. To wonder why such insight cannot be converted or extroverted into out-sight or ex-tuition for the out-sider to witness as if (simulating) a co-insider himself: equal to equal quasi . . . this remains much better unasked than answered at all, because it is only 'self'-evident and not allo-vident!

As a re-affirming coincidence, I learned about a contemporary of Spinoza, called Johann George Gichtel, from Regensburg (1638–1710). He was a follower of Jacob Boehme and published a booklet in 1696, 'Theosophia Practica', with the fuller subtitle

Eine kurze Eröffnung und Anweisung der dreyen Principien und Welten *im* Menschen in unterschiedlichen Figuren vorstellet: wie und wo eigentlich ihre Centra im innern Menschen stehen; gleich sie der Autor *selbst* im Göttlichen Schauen in sich gefunden und gegenwärtig in sich empfindet, *schmecket* und fühlet.[32]

Gichtel laid the foundation stone for a sect of 'Engelsbrüder' in Holland and Northern Germany. I cannot say for sure if Spinoza had any knowledge of these angelic brethren when coming in such close contact with the Collegiantes and other contemporaries bursting with such craving for mystical self-cultivation leading to mystical experience, but the similar wording like '*fruitio*' and '*smaaken*' does not seem to serve only as an unobliging metaphor for orna-mentation. Evidence only exists when the conceptual dichotomy into self and other (than self) as if observer versus observed is preserved at any price. A few written hints (with the intention to remain hints only!) disclose for hungry curiosity hunters that a thinker like Spinoza, *homo solitarius aut Deus aut bestia*, must avoid vulgarizing publicity for the out-sider who never ever can side with an insider as equal (co-insider) unless when himself 'realizing inwardly the (quasi irreal) imperturbability of one's own essence of mind': via *meditandi*. Spinoza pointed to it at the apex of his teaching: to reflect on one's mind, to contemplate on one's self in a way of being conscious of self, God and the world (of things) not as three but as threeless *one*. . . . Evidence is only e-vidence as allo-(e)vidence: seen by others either as witnesses or when relying on written confession recorded for posterity with super-modest or super-immodest exaggerations to describe, *test* and *taste* of such mystical experience of one's (i.e. every-one's!) otherless self. Mystical experience can seldom be co-experienced, and so we read how the vision 'visionable' to Daniel remained unwitnessed by his bystanders. We have to ponder on it. . . . Heraclitus reminds us 'how nature likes to hide' and so also likes the nature of the mystic. René Descartes, although hiding behind a screen of his motto *bene vivit qui bene latuit*, had a remarkable fiasco with his 'discovery of the pineal gland', because he left the door open too wide for 'others' to ascribe to him what he never attained himself in any expansion of consciousness (of his own unknowable being!), while we can find some traces in Spinoza's writings before the end of his 'difficult and rare path'. Descartes simulated happiness in his narrowed consciousness (or *ego sum* only *quia ego cogito*) when Spinoza experiences not *ego animor sed omnia animata* (*sumus*) via omni-consciousness or cosmic-divine identity! Some researchers digging in Descartes' dream could not excavate treasures to make him afterwards retrospectively more introspective than he actually was to be so proud of. From a member of the Rosicrucian Order one actually might expect some mystical insight and experience with hints left about such mental states (instances) leading to illumination. His unsuccessful discovery of that pineal gland was so quickly unmasked by Spinoza via the nearness of contemporary media which did not oblige a philosopher to see another thinker via a pre-liminary, dim anticipated (or precipitated) posterity. Spinoza never considered him a rival in the true quest for trust involving zest eager to communicate. . . . If the Spinoza of that time could have had a chance (as we have it now 300 years later, namely to read ancient Eastern texts in Western language with commentaries as well!) to familiarize himself with Eastern tradition (now paralleled with Western advancement in biology) describing the 'third eye', then he would have accepted such axiomatic truth quasi as re-affirmation of mystical insight or self-experience. The 'third eye' has no retina with the inbuilt scope of our 'two eyes' to see twolessness via the projection of the retina's otherness and thus, free from that discrepancy between quasi seer versus a quasi-seen via seeing. And this would have had confirmed Spinoza's equation:

forma sive essentia – Natura sive Deus – idea et ideatum – natura naturans et naturata, etc.

Descartes instead 'rätselte an der Funktion der Zirbeldrüse herum, in der er den "Verbindungsort" von Körper und Seele vermutete',[33] while sticking so clumsily to assertions too vague to please Spinoza or any thinker of his calibre. We have to thank an admirer of Spinoza, John Bleibtreu,[34] who pays open tribute and attention to Spinoza as to the great unique thinker of mankind, when it comes to disclosing marvellous secrets of science, unearthed for the first time while guided by a motto from Spinoza: 'nobody has known yet the frame of the body so thoroughly as to explain all its operations'. And mystical experience quasi self-explanatory and unquestionable tends to point to such plain revelations. Among other important findings, Bleibtreu has the merit to show via Eastern and Western research and viewing the very true nature of this 'third eye' which once was the privilege of ancient seers, rishis, sages ... to reveal beyond discriminiation and binary dichotomy a quasi-otherness *per se*. Tibetans and Indians alike were both well occupied with this delicate instru-mentality of the body to point to quasi-bodiless experience (of *sentimus experimurque nos (aeternos) esse: omnia animata!*). Nobody can fully explain the plain materiality of the musical instrument in order to see 'materializations or realizations' quasi as immaterial or irreal (acausal?) delight and enlightenment deriving 'from the frame of the body so thoroughly as to explain all its operations. ...' Spinoza claims for the extension of substance to be quite compatible with the dignity of its divine nature! The very same dignity as for the 'thinking level' of substance as this is substantially standing 'under' *extensio sive cogitatio (sive in-tensio!)* or standing 'under' any understanding (of understanding itself) as well! There is no place for God, no place for godlike or divine = natural beyondness, namely beyond *ratio sive causa vel sui vel alius*, i.e. beyond *determinatio* or *indeterminatio*, it is the very same con-stant, in-stant, or co-instant, sub-stant *now* and *here* on the brink of *essendi fruitio* when not lacking receptivity for such insight and self-experience. Beyond me and my I-mindedness: outside of me to become inside ripe for insight. Thus disegotized, I cannot understand 'it', as not-me but rather standing 'under' me and 'under' my quasiness to appear as 'otherness' *vis-à-vis* me. Finally everything and no-thing become equal and *id idem* to identify or re-identify with in order to become re-aware of *omnia animata (sumus) omnia animata*, i.e. *nos omnes*, not *ego persona singularis, peculiaris quasi maxima exceptio universi!*

Spinoza thus does not speak: *ego sentio experiorque*. Why? Because disegotizing his ego, this super-certain *ani* is to reverse into the super-uncertain *ayin*: the void de-void of singularizations, dualizations, pluralizations, etc., is the void or the omni-indeterminacy in Spinozanic and Cabbalistic parlance alike: *causa sive ratio sui*. This, yes this must lead to illumination and salvation. Spinoza's confession is not expected to be a singular one: an individual salvation *sui generis* but universalized indeed.

when the only end that I endeavour to attain is, to be able to taste of union with God, and to bring forth true ideas, and to make these things known also to my neighbours; for we can all participate equally in this happiness, as happens when it creates in them the same desire that I have, thus causing their will and mine to be one and the same, constituting one and the same nature, agreeing always in all things. I beseech you that you should not hasten at once to refute it, before you have pondered it *long enough* and *thoughtfully enough* – and if you do this, I feel sure that you will attain to the enjoyment of the fruits of this tree which you promise yourselves!

Now you can better feel the invitation to universality or omniality of the words: 'sentimus experimurque (nos omnes!) aeternos esse et delectamus essendi fruitionem . . .! Spinoza, I am sure, knew of Abot de Rabbi Natan (ARN) with such talmudic omni-revelation: 'this thou doest learn that one man's life is equal to all the work of creation', and he also knew of the more daring identity: *creator et creatura idem*. Or 'Omnia essentialiter esse Deum, et formas esse accidentia imaginata. Omnia sunt Deus. Deus est Omnia. Omnia esse unum et esse Deum. . . .' Now how can I, in the darkness of egohood, discover that which I ascribe to the quasi-other who always thinks and lives as if between: self and/or otherness or between no-where and no-where? I can say only positively 'No' to my own beyond which is egoless. How then to uncover the non-I and still remain the yes-I unless mystical (acausal, irrational, undetermined!) or alchemical identification takes place as divine/cosmic orgasm? So I have to dare to describe the undescribable and marvellous experience of *causa sive ratio sui* and via such *suitas* to reach salvation! This 'happens' only *now* and *here*: present as ever-presence; i.e. every-where *here* and every-when *now* as instant self-co-awareness of *omnia animata*. Hence illumination comes from that in-tuition that there is no here *per se*. There is no there *per se*. And also no 'no *per se*' either. And no yes *per se*.

Everything is '*se*' and nothing is '*se*'. Yes = No. Only when I can accept your claim and his claim and their all claim within the very same limits of (universal) I-mindedness, then I would be able to transcend such self-limitation to crave instead for self-liberation (from self-bondage). Until then one recognizes no when, no where, no why and no asking at all in that hunt and fear for quasi-otherness *per se* (as cosmic phantoms among natural phenomena). To ask is to remain within the boundaries of discrimination, of *causa sive ratio alius*. For the pathseekers I have compiled at the beginning of this book many finger-pointings of pathfinders together with Spinoza, who interests us here with his findings and revelations on that path to one's self when conscious not only of himself, but also (identical) of God and the world (of things, *omnia animata*) not as three *entia per se*, but as three aspects, levels or dimensions to become omni-conscious of the in-di-visible wholeness: *omnia animata sumus*. To record mystical self-experience as self-realization would stain the person with sin as if changing otherlessness into quasi-otherness *per se*: idolatry in the most crass sense of the word. Sin which stems from the taste of the tree of knowledge, while knowledge always wants to mean knowing otherness *per se* as a quasi-knower versus a quasi-known on the via knowing. The so-called known then would have to remain for ever separated from the knower stigmatized with dichotomy! And mystical experience thus will 'taste of the tree of life with no otherness *per se*' involved: when considering my life, then only I will have to live it as undivided and you could only know it (lifeless) as divided by dividing knowledge. Such is the *taste* they speak of when pointing to revelation. A sudden taste of something so very near and dear. The language of the Bible has all this in mind to bring our own far nearness and near farness to marvel. . . .

> For this commandment which I command thee this day, it is not hidden
> from thee, neither is it far off: it is not in heaven that thou shouldest
> say: who shall go up for us to heaven and bring it to us, that we may
> hear it and do it? Neither is it beyond the sea, that thou shouldest say:
> who shall go over the sea for us and bring it unto us, that we may
> hear it and do it? But the *word* [matter, thing] is very nigh unto thee,
> in thy mouth, and in thy heart, that thou mayest do it.[35]

Far be it for me to try to locate – as Descartes assumed it – a place for the placeless unknown, the void or undeterminable *causa sive ratio sui*. And still far be it for me to speak of the function of its awareness to voice living life but happy of only 'knowing' it. We all only can know 'that' life is (unknowable *per se*), but never 'what' it is, as it would then not be life anymore and unwitnessable: as know thyself the old-new mystery of our own unknown 'X'. Suares thus points (in his Cipher of Genesis and Gnosis) to an 'interfertilization (between quasi-twoness and para-otherness dichotomizing between me and it) which happens in the moment seeing it'. The very same phenomenon happened to Elisha when saying farewell to his Master, the prophet Elijah. I will cite him as a crown-witness, as the Lord Himself will cite him before the coming of the Messiah. Elijah asked Elisha what was his wish before they parted: 'A double portion of your spirit!' was the immodest reply of the pupil. 'You asked for a hard thing,' said Elijah, 'but when you will see 'it', then it will be!' [as you: yourself!].[36] It was like transference of an untransferable power of self-realization which only Grace could grant. And, it was granted to Elisha the very moment when the words were spoken and a driver-less chariot came from heaven to separate the two, Elijah and Elisha, while the inside power has shifted to the quasi-other container with the very same content of insideness: as if an instant reincarnation with no discarnation to witness for the quasi-other from out-side and from out-sight. Elisha cried loudly in ecstatic enlightenment of such 'seeing': pure seeing with no quasi-seer *vis-à-vis* quasi-seen as if two. He then lifted the mantel the prophet had left behind as a legacy to his worthy successor. Suares reminds us: 'There is no other transcendence than our intimacy with the [very same] unknown as the unknown' to enable us to see it not as 'it' *vis-à-vis* 'us', but to become aware of it 'in' us and 'as' us or 'it': our otherless self. This is the core of experience, of mystical experience in the Bible style recording non-duality and otherlessness: the very essence of acausal or irrational and indeterminable mysticism indeed, metabolized when conscious of *omnia animata sumus cum essendi fruitione!* When myself involved with such craving for self-experience via self-approach I was often helped by non-flirting commitments to Eastern doctrines in order to reach a better intimacy with Spinoza via the East and with the East via Spinoza: both culminating in a marvellous common affinity and awesome urge for one's own unknown. I would call such unknown the infinity or eternity or *existentia sui* as exless 'X'. In Eastern jargon this would come nearer on the path (to the otherless self!) as to become aware of one's own birthless (and deathless) state (of mind). Such state equates with the state of thinking 'no thoughts' to discriminate by singularization, dualization and pluralization the very same holy wholeness. According to the Great Maggid of Mesritch, it is 'as if' becoming aware of our thoughts *before* we think them (as our thoughts). It is like *tohuwabohu!* the formlessness of thought or thing; it is the indeterminate of *causa sive ratio sui* always in constant instant, substant *now* and *here*. And the last among the pathfinders cited as witness for the grand occasion, with the last Messianic finger-pointing in accordance to the Gospel of Thomas:

> when seeking the path, not to cease seeking it until finding. And when finding it, not to worry about when being troubled, and finally when being troubled, suddenly to marvel.

To marvel in illumination and enlightenment. To marvel and to wonder, especially when needing no cause, no reason, no otherness to wonder. Just to wonder for wonder's sake: wonder *per se*. *Admiratio sui?* And with no otherness *per se* as a stumbling block, to wonder again and again as with a sunrise after a long dark night: so natural and so divine to wonder! *Deus sive Natura. Natura sive Deus.* That is the wonder. Yahweh = Elohim = Echad! That is the wonder to be aware 'that' we are and awareness identical with being. We do not want anymore to know 'what' we are, 'what' is being, 'what' awareness. Whatness has no wonder and wonder-inspiring magic while always bringing otherness *per se* into play and dis-play as it were. Whatness always splits the wholeness of the uni-verse into a dui-verse: me and not-me, the old arch-enemy! Only with the belief in quasiness you can reach and attain your own otherless state of mind as your 'I am' (is) the Way the Truth and Life. And whatever has been said, has been pointed at in the whole Bible is 'that ye may know that 'I am' (is) the Lord, Yahweh and then that Yahweh is Elohim: Echad!

Self-cause or self-reason is a wonder to marvel at. And so is the wonder 'that' one exists: factual and actual with no reference to anything else. Existence with no elseness is divine as essence is divine to marvel at both as the same and only quasi-unsame. . . . The mystery of the totality, the omniality of the grand ocean with oceanic feeling for the drop always used to drop-feeling versus wave-feeling but rarely uni-versus! The drop expands to the ocean as the ocean can withdraw to the drop to co-awareness in *co-quiescentia in se ipso* or *in se ipsa*; to ponder and to wonder. To wonder and to marvel. And when just paving the way and the mood prepared for it, to celebrate Spinoza via a collective homage in my prologue here, there are two voices to be mentioned with the same urge of joining me. One, Jon Wetlesen, speaks of the 'Body as Gateway to Eternity' as a 'Note on Spinoza's Mysticism' and the other is H. G. Hubbeling, who speaks of the 'Logical and Experiential Roots of Spinoza's Mysticism' as 'Answer to Jon Wetlesen'.

Some like to approach Spinoza as the Master and not the Slave of *ratio*. They, like G. A. A. Balz,[37] put most emphasis on the 'rational mysticism' and 'immanentism'. And Spinoza can accept with no partiality witnesses for *causa sive ratio alius* and *sui*. The '*sive*': *alius sive sui quasi* divides the first axiom and every axiomatic self-evident truth: 'Everything which is, is either in itself or in another (itself).' I will try to stand as witness for this axiom in connexion with the first Bible verse in Bereshit as Genesis via Gnosis or as Gnosis via Genesis later in my own paper as my *casus sui*!

Here I only would like to repeat, how it is already only too well known and accepted in Jewish esoteric tradition which does not *permit to show or record any personal experience of mystical insight* (while impersonal!). Looking for evidence is looking for so-called allo-evidence or 'vidence' when something is self-evident and axiomatically true, and this must sound so odd and paradoxical. There can be no witness for acausal or irrational insight and inside to make it outsight and outside for quasi-otherness *per se*, and thus to convert *seitas* into *alteritas*. No proxy, no substitute for the one substance. To record it is to become an object for a subject and to loose its own subjectivity, while in self-experience the object has to loose also its own objectivity to become 'self'. E-vidence needs no 'vidence' for seer and seen via seeing, which is not mystical. 'Faith gives substance to our hopes and makes us always certain of realities we do not see'[38] with eye-sight as quasi-others to witness otherness *per se*, but with eyeless insight to witness otherlessness as the mystery of self-realization, self-experience. The inside is the very same inside of the universal immanent and permanent instant, substant and constant *now* and *here* as *enstasis*. This I would like rather to call in-vidence than evidence, to differentiate between ecstatic and instatic and to diversify the meaning better. I would then equate better in-vidence with *in-tuitio sui* to parallel it with *causa sive ratio sui*. It is unquestionable and unanswerable. You can describe the indescribable to make the otherless in you transcend insideness only in order that I as outsider can testify from outsight what I should like you from insight and inside as a quasi co-insider so to speak: an equal to an equal. In the acausal or irrational experience I am not only I and you are not only you. No one is divided from each other but is indivisible the very same otherless universal *individuum* (indivisible wholeness!) in all-inclusiveness. *Omnia animata sumus*. How then could you need evidence to help in the absence of co-awareness via omni-awareness? How? Only when partaking of the cosmic/ divine collective orgasm of self-experience with all-togetherness of omniality of *essendi fruitio!* When you from 'your' inside recognize my and every-one's inside and insight as same in accordance with the universal *know thyself*!, then you will only marvel with no I-mind with no You-mind but with all-mind or omni-consciousness including: self, God and the world as self-identic sameness with infinite *extensio* and *intensio*: *substantia per se*!

It is like the *tao* 'which lets now the dark, now the light!' And only then our godlikeness with Elohim and via Elohim with Yahweh reciprocates the manlikeness of God: *Deus sive Natura. Natura sive Deus* with or without '*quatenus, tamquam, quamvis, sive*, etc.' Only then divine revelation of the divine word and 'in' the wording 'Let "it" be light' can be seen by us, not versus it, but reversus or universus: *creator et creatura idem!* Let it be light on the path of quasi-otherness *per se* so the light can become my delight and enlightenment coming to light and be-coming it, itself. This mystical acausal or irrational experience with no evidence but co-invidence. Then 'I am' [is] Light, Way, Truth and Life.

Hence that wonder to wonder and to ponder, and to marvel with the mystical seer seeing no otherness *per se* only quasiness, no duality, no plurality but omniality or indeterminability of *causa sive ratio sui. Vivat suitas!* Le Chayim! *Essendi fruitio. Miraculum non est demonstrandum sed propositiones, suppositiones!* The student of the scriptural Spinoza studies only infinity via de-finitions of the indefinable, indefinitive as if to study otherness from another attribute beyond those of *extensio sive intensio (cogitatio)*. And what about those pegs of *tamquam, quamvis, quatenus*, etc.? Do they help such students not to study otherness *per se* but *per* quasiness and turning to *meta-noia* or re-turning the mind to study itself via the own root-awareness? This leads via self-reflection and self-contemplation to self-realization to a better understanding that *studeo* in Latin means 'to endeavour' only through books and craving for scriptural enlightenment! 'Self-realization is the key-note and transmitted from mind to mind [not from book to book-writers and book-readers] a special transmission[39] *outside the scriptural teaching*.' This just means inside the mind.

What is performed by scriptural teaching is to point for you what you have *within yourself*. A special transmission outside the Scriptures, not depending upon the letter [nor upon the spirit of the letter], but pointing *directly* to the mind. And leading us to 'see' into the nature itself, thereby making us to attain Buddhahood.[40]

'There is no transference from master to discipline. Teaching is not difficult, listening is not difficult either, but what is truly difficult is to become conscious of what you have in yourself and be able to use it as your own. This "self-realization" is known as "seeing into one's own being," which is satori. Satori is an awakening from a dream.'[41] Suzuki is challenging us 'to become conscious' of our insideness, Spinoza challenges us to expand this insideness of our self, to God and to the world as all-oneness or one-allness. Suzuki supports this with the ancient teaching as valid today as then: the perennial life-wisdom not to be known as lifeless knowledge.

> The self is not to be known through *study of the scriptures*, nor through subtlety of the intellect, nor through much learning. But by him, who longs, for him is he known – to be filled with joy [*fruitio*?]! Blessed are they tranquil of mind, free from passions.[42]

In those days a more extra-scriptural, extra-perceptional and extra-sensorial approach to oneself and to the magic own unknown via oral communications from Guru or Lama to Chela transmitted nothing, but lifted the cosmic veil, demisted the veiled illusion of quasi-otherness *per se*. We have to analyse how quasified the mind likes to be in its *causa suitas, ratio suitas* and its indeterminacy. Spirit *per se* points to directness, often bypassing scriptural expounders and hinters with the sole aim of self-liberation. Very few can use the lenses Spinoza ground for himself, untinted when looking into that puzzling mirror reflecting the *facies totius universi vel Dei vel Naturae*. Those attracted to the letter, the men of letters, want to demonstrate by the dematerialized and spiritualized letter the 'monster' of quasi-schismatic life: split into observer and observed as if two. There are still witnesses discovering such identity of the quasi-unsame and only sembling: of quasi seer and quasi seen via seeing and they are craving to testify with the experienceable and undemonstrable identity of seer and/or seen re-transferring or retransforming each other with reciprocal receptivity to become otherless the very same via of seeing. On this via seer *per se* and seen *per se* are vanishing with their *seitas* to discover they are really the via, the way. 'I am' (is) the Way, the Truth, the Life! Then there are no outside witnesses for the via save the via itself: the *via sui* or *via viae* as *vita vitae* or *vita sui*! Only this can count for self-realization to co-testify co-self-realization of all-self or all-oneness: *omnia animata sumus*! 'He who is being in the sun and at the same time in the eye, resides in the heart and is the doer and experiencer – him I meditate upon. . . .'[43]

Had the Geheimrat von Weimar this in mind?

Wär' unser Aug nicht sonnenhaft,
Nie könnt'es die Sonne blicken!

Does Master Eckhart refer to this state of mind (*per se* with *inseitas*)?

The eye with which I see God is the same with which God sees me. . . .
Simple people conceive that we are to see God as if He stood on that
side and we on this side. It is not so. God and I are (not two but) *one* in
the act of my perceiving Him.[44]

I and the Father are one. Yahweh = Elohim. *Deus sive Natura.* One and the
same and quasified as a quasi-perceiver (*per se*) and (another) quasi perceived
(*per se*) on the unique way of perceiving. Then the pseudo-two would give up
their pseudoness and re-awaken from a dream into the reality of a pair-
concept expressing omniality and wholeness.

It is like God seeing Himself. And as Himself He saw the *via creandi* 'it was
good'! How? *Creator et creatura idem. Idem ipsa via creandi, via veritatis, via
viae, via vitae.* God seeing Himself as seeing seeing (subjectless and objectless)
as divine light. Be it light! Let it be light! It happens to be light, delight and
enlightenment as light. God sees Himself via my eyes, via all eyes and via
eyelessness: as if facing His own face. . . . It is like God loving Himself via
all loving ones *vis-à-vis* all beloved ones with the *Amor Dei sive Amor Naturae
sive Amor Veritatis sive Amor sui. Vivat Suitas!*

To call one's own nameless unknowable being 'mystical' and such self-
experience 'mystical' only because there is no 'otherness' as otherness *per se*,
depends on the sincerity of non-faky self-observation. We all like attraction
with promises to let us know 'what' we are rather than a revelation to know
no-thing, nothingness, i.e. no 'whatness' save 'that' we are: a self-reflection
to marvel at . . . to reflect our acausal, irrational exless 'X' as salvation of
'thatness'. This is then divine self-affirmation of ephemeral existence in a
quasiness. Thatness reveals: *omnia animata* (*sumus*) with instant enstasis.
'What' we are, we are in the way of discrimination, namely as if body *per se*
and as if mind *per se*, while we aim to learn from Spinoza to be intellected
(self-intellected, self-reflected) *per attributum percipiendi sive intelligendi.*
And even at that point we are still too far from Cordovero to welcome his
hints which Spinoza accepted: that 'God, God's Intellect and the objects
intellected by Him are one and the same', the same as *idea divina: natura
naturans* and/or its *ideatum divinum: natura naturata*, i.e. *convenire debent.*
God, God's seeing and the objects seen by Him are one and the same as the
seer: on the only *via videndi sine evidentia* (*ex alio!*).

And Job, the great witness in mystical self-experience on his path may
guide other witnesses too shy to come out and forward from their citadel (of
flesh and bones):

I uttered that I understood not, things too *wonderful* for me which I
knew not – I have heard of Thee by the hearing of the ear [hearing only

quasi-otherness] but now mine eye seeth Thee [seeing seeing itself as otherless all-self, as you].[45]

Ashvagosha asks for permission to join the witnesses of that mysterious own unknown and exless 'X', this 'Thatness' which contains the mystery 'of' and 'in' all containers, the mystery 'that' we exist at all while quasi-confronted with luring quasiness as if quasi-otherness *per se*. To existence no 'what' and on 'whatever', etc., as explanation of the unexplainable 'plain' can fit, only the wonder of being to marvel at. . . .

Although all things from eternity are neither matter nor mind, neither infinite wisdom, nor finite knowledge, neither existing, nor non-existing, but are all inexpressible, we nevertheless use words. . . . When men consider and realize that the Absolute Mind has no need of thoughts like men, they are then following the right way to reach the Infinite.[46]

And in this way we learn how to think not thinking (single, singularizing) thoughts at all. On this way Infinity is revealed in a grain of sand, in a speck of dust on earth or dust on stars – Yes, this grain of infinity is the point of infinity which Euclid defines as 'with no dimensions' to show im-mensity 'in' it and 'as' it. The East explains 'plain' infinity as otherless 'self-same' to fit better and to recognize the disguise of pseudo-otherness. It must fascinate the true divine seeker of *Deus* (*sive Natura*) via Spinoza and via his own unknowable nature, when finding no object for seeking as apart from the seeker himself, and later no trace of the subject either as apart from the object, but only the via seeking, i.e. seeking no otherness, but seeking itself with the mystery of otherless quasiness. 'What' he finds, is himself, the seeker. And he finds in his findings, 'that' he seeks for seeking and revealing otherlessness to marvel at. . . . And later he finds: I am (is) the Way. I am (is) the Truth. I am (is) Life. So no-thing only I am as I am ... so 'that ye may know that "I am" (is) the Lord!' And to Moses the Lord revealed His 'I am' as 'I am that I am: the Self'.

Where one sees no-thing but the *one*, hears no-thing but the *one*, knows no-thing but the *one*, *there* is the Infinite. Where one sees an *other*, hears another, knows another, there is the finite. The infinite is below, above, behind, before, to the right, to the left. *I am* (is) *all this*. One who knows, meditates upon and realizes the truth of the *self*, such a one delights [*fruitio?*] in the *self*, rejoices the *self*.[47]

Realizing one's *own* otherless Self, one can attain self-realization and dismantle as it were quasiness or pseudoness of so-called birth or so-called death *per se* while always (mis-)guided by *ratio sive causa alius*. One always can see only the quasi-other dying or being born, but never himself as his own *vis-à-vis* of otherness. No evidence (as vidence) for mystical experience is available and also not for one's own quasi-birth or quasi-death. How is one to reconcile oneself then with one's horror *vacui* (of otherness *per se* as a vacuum!) or with one's horror *alius* in order to overcome the sting of death and birth alike when *perseitas* is assumed for both? The stumbling block is 'in' the flesh to stumble over the discovery of the fleshless 'as if' only flesh (and of the flesh 'as if' only fleshlessness!) when on the path to self-realization. It does 'happen' as a self-creation after the chaos of otherness that the identity of a re-creation dawns: *creator et creatura idem*. . . . It is an oceanic feeling of the former self-isolated (assumed self-isolated) drop to expand his (drop-)consciousness into omniality from singularity, duality and plurality. *Omnia animata sumus et omnia animantia sumus: tamquam Deus sive Natura.*

Is this not mystical experience and not mystical enough to ask for e-vidence instead of obliging in-vidence and in-tuition?

It would be puzzling for Spinoza students, to study Spinoza on school-benches, as he never intended to teach for 'benches' and never craved for a 'chair' to sit in front of such benches for philosophy. Maurice Bucke in his 'Cosmic Consciousness' lists Spinoza (although among the 'additional', i.e. lesser, imperfect and doubtful) instances of cosmic consciousness, while Walter I. Stace did not dare to include Spinoza among the few instances of Western cases in his 'Teaching of the Mystics'. Bucke therefore excuses himself, 'of not being in a position to have the necessary details' of his (Spinoza's) illumination as he so abundantly had in other cases. Nevertheless, Bucke feels mesmerized when reading and citing Spinoza: 'The union of the soul with God is its second birth and therein consists man's immortality and freedom.'[48] What Spinoza calls 'second birth' is for him experienceable self-creation or self-awareness of no beginning and *ergo* no ending. It is known in Buddhist teaching as awakening of the uncreate, the birthless state (of mind as *causa sive ratio sui!*) and involving the deathless as well (as same state of mind in omni-awareness: *omnia animata sumus* via self-reflection or self-contemplation). Hui Neng asks his pupil to 'show him his true face before birth' in order to point at his own beyond or at his own unknowable 'thatness' of being. When following Bucke's traces, I discovered more material than he did, which testifies better for Spinoza's illumination or mystical self-experience when in the witness-box for such mission. I feel tempted to say for and with Spinoza:

The only end I endeavour to attain, is to be able to *taste* [smaak] of union with God. And to make these things known also to my neighbours; for we can all participate *equally* in this happiness, as happens when it creates in them the same desire that I have, (re-?)constituting one and the same nature.[49] (My italics)

Spinoza thinks we can 'all participate equally in this happiness,' but can we all participate in such co-awareness or co-omni-consciousness? Can we co-witness each-other's inside insight and 'mystical' experience? And what about such quasi 'second birth'? The first birth seemed as if: *ab alio* as allo-evidence can demonstrate it, while the second is quasi a re-assessment of the thought I think about 'my' quasi birth from quasi-otherness so to speak excluding self-experience and self-awareness. When including such, then, it is as if freshly born with fresh awareness quasi *ab se ipso: causa sui, ratio sui.* . . . No more heterophobia, horror *causae sive rationis* (*alius*) either. Omni-awareness has created or re-created a new feeling, not separated I-mindedness as before, but oceanic feeling including all-oneness and one-allness as self-realization of *omnia animata sumus, ergo etiam ego sum.* Sic! We are all sentient beings: *omnia animata* and therefore we have to enforce '*sentimus*' by adding '*experimurque*', i.e. it is a lofty elated feeling with an awareness of it and our self-identity as well. Are there still some looking for more, for the ultimate (explanation) of the unexplainable, exless 'X' in Spinoza but without his longing for expanded omni-consciousness to 'constitute one and the same nature' or divinity? And when so looking for evidence instead for in-vidence or intuition, they overlook what they actually expect. It is not what experience has to reveal for us, the 'others' as witnesses, but 'that' it has to reveal otherlessness for the equal otherless. . . . Here it is to wonder and to marvel at for the equal but never for the unequal who feels doomed for outsided ex-tuition never ever to intrude where the equals are accepted 'to constitute the whole one and the same nature!' Then the equal and those with the same nature are all alike 'conscious of self, God and the world' with omni-self-identification of the same nature: *Natura sive Deus.* . . .

Is therein not to be found expansion from I-mindedness into All-mindedness via various levels, aspects or dimensions? Is this not illumination enlightenment, satori, nirvana to nirvanize, satorise, alchemize the quasi-otherness and to unmask the discriminative dichotomy of twoness into twoless, otherless self-same Echad, Advaita?

We remember how Spinoza speaks of the body: it exists as 'we' perceive 'it', namely as our own sensation via quasi-otherness or togetherness. In the earlier work better suitable for Bucke's admission as instance of 'cosmic consciousness', Spinoza says:

> for even the knowledge that we have of the body is not such, *that we know it as it is* or perfectly and yet – what a union [I would prefer 'sameness']. What a love!

This invites to ponder and wonder again, namely that we know not the body just 'as' it is (or perfect = beyond perception, knowledge!) but rather reversed: the body is (for us) as we know it, perceive it (to be *inside* perception = imperfect). When disegotizing the ego means to become identified with our own egoless 'id', then this equals to *thatness* versus *whatness* via a quasi-somatic or a quasi-mental self-awareness of the otherless, attributeless sub-stans *per se*. We then know properly 'that' we are via our self-awareness: the unknowable beyond a quasi knower *vis-à-vis* a quasi-known as the quasifiable via knowing of knowing *per se*. On the path to liberation one attains salvation (from a known *per se* and from a knower *per se*, i.e. from duality *per se*!), and we experience oneness, all-oneness as one-allness happy with and on the via knowing in order to become (what we cannot know) the via itself: *ego via sum, via mei ad viam sui. Vivat suitas!* William James, who knows to tackle the 'dilemma of determinism', has consecrated his whole life for the research in expanded consciousness as cosmic omni-consciousness and his self-experience is pointing to the very same path all the pathfinders pointed to, and especially one in accordance with the gospel of Thomas.

> Out of my *experience*, such as it is (and it is limited enough) one fixed conclusion dogmatically emerges, and that is, that we with our lives are like islands in the sea, or like trees in the forest. The maple and the pine may whisper to each other with their leaves, and Conanicut and Newport hear each other's foghorns. But the trees also commingle their roots in the dark underground, and the islands also hang together through the ocean's bottom. Just so there is a continuum of cosmic consciousness against which our indivi-duality builds but accidental fences and into which our several minds plunge as into a mother-sea or reservoir.[50]

Should the philosopher who formulated that: *omnia animata (sumus)* not have experienced himself such omniality as oceanic feeling expanding the drop into the own unknowable oceanic infinity to test and taste *essendi fruitio*? And could we thus frivolously deny to Spinoza mystical experience only be-cause there is no cause or reason for it in a thinker who thought and taught to think the best thinkable thought ever thought, namely: the thought of *causa sive ratio sui* animated by *Amor Dei sive Amor Naturae* to reflect or re-reflect cosmic consciousness or co-consciousness?

In the language of the Sutras, especially the Lankavatara, we must think of that store-consciousness called Alayavijnana as if a cosmic womb enwombing all collective universal unknown and also entombing all our knowable knowledge of quasi-yesterdays, yester-years and yester-life *vis-à-vis* a quasi-tomorrow. Then we will suddenly discover that we live life as *now* and *here per se* not *per* otherness of a quasi 'before' or a quasi 'after'. Nowledge not knowledge encapsulates life and its self-revelations: today as if on morrow's eve heralding as on New Year's Eve the dawning wholeness of the quasi-newness with messianic joy. . . . Some of us will compare James's simile with Spinoza's *omnia animata (sumus)* as pan-psychism to ruminate better an old truth. Truth with a hard crust already. . . . Those from the school of Jung will think of the 'collective unconsciousness' thus assuming to know the un-knowable, namely *that we are* and not *what we are*. To be conscious 'that' we are and that we are conscious (of being conscious) is evolving universality or omni-versality via omni-consciousness called, cosmic, divine or natural after Spinoza. Then the micro- or macro-cosmic identification of ego and id or of id and ego as *idem via vitae* leads to become aware or re-aware of such 'order or connection' of an indivisible cord to re-cord as it were via our root-awareness alive as in a forest or a garden (of Eden?) with forest-like and ocean-like feeling of all-togetherness. This reminds us of the first garden where God and Man lived together in a godlikeness compatible with manlikeness which only paradise can grant without discrimination and where only man can despise and defy such divine grant to prefer discriminative knowledge to life itself. Paradise also has included in such grant the abolition and invalidity of any 'before', of any 'after' and any 'when' at all. This one can discover on the end of the road, of the rare and difficult path. Rare and difficult to follow . . . and when not following not to believe in its way, truth and life! I wonder if Spinoza admirers have ever pondered and wondered at the same time when connecting Spinoza's denial of the notion 'before *per se*' and 'after *per se*' with the very denial of the present *now* and *here* itself.

Few of us had a chance to look for philosophical support from grammar, especially when such grammar has been written by a philosopher like Spinoza. Sic!

> The Hebrews usually refer actions to no other time that to the past and
> to the future. The reason for this seems to be that they acknowledge
> only these two divisions of time, and that they consider the present
> tense only as a point, that is as the end of the past and the beginning of
> the future. I say, they viewed time to be like a line consisting of many
> points each of which they considered the end of one part and the
> beginning of another.[51]

In Hebrew one cannot properly say: I am as *ego sum* and that first encounter of God with Moses when sending him to Pharaoh with the special mission of freeing his people is always distorted in translation as: I am that I am and standing for Ehjeh Asher Ehjeh. But this is not a present tense as we use in accordance with sacrosanct grammatical rules, ruling schoolmasters and pupils alike on hard schoolbenches, but it is a future tense, 'I shall be that I shall be'. It sounds like a self-confident experience of the fleeting 'I' and its 'life-span' confronting a bodiless I with an I-less body so to speak. I and I-s duration while pointing to itself, is fleeting and makes such pointing fleeting too. Both have already passed, passed away from that only mo(ve)ment to give way to another fleeting moment on the same point to become a so-called 'past', past *now*. A past tense is quasi offering a better chance than before to ponder upon as if stopping such fleeting when seeing it seeking asylum (in our quasi-static mind: the foreign out-sighting and out-siding observer!) with the hope to pre-serve or mummify that 'moment': a dead past as more welcome than the living mo(ve)ment fleeting and so attracting with the delight of a present in-stant *causa sui*. What is actually called future that *must* really be the 'real' acting as the real fleeting moment (a great para-doxon) in his coming and be-coming a quasi-present (for our mind the observer), as if avoiding for a moment instant present to appear as omni-instant and omni-present and omni-aware of it 'in' us and 'as' us via self-experience and revelation disregarding dichotomy, discrimination of quasi-otherness *per se*. I repeat Spinoza: 'In eternity there is no when, no after and no before.' In eternity, i.e. *in ipsa existentia vel in existentia sui*, there is no 'when' at all, as timelessness cannot admit it. And cannot permit artificial divisions (of time-conception) into 'before' or 'after' which refer to past or future. No 'when' refers to any presentable time or time-unit and refutes its question-ability at all. The great paranoetic way dimensioning in our consciousness something which appears 'as if' in a quasi-simulating confrontation with a fake-beyond of a *vis-à-vis* so to speak. To become free from it and free from stupid questioning is only to discover that there is no 'other *per se*' in any disguise of time or space. While our consciousness has its levels, aspects or dimensions to become conscious of the totality quasi slicing it in order to swallow better such 'sliced totality'. . . . We discover, then, to our amazement that quasi-real *no* which is so fleeting. This is a further mile-stone into no-man's-land with no-egohood and *ergo* with no *causa sive ratio alius* to captivate us with enticing quasifying discrimination for a quasi better confrontation with the very same unchanged fleeting: *panta rei* of Heraclitus. When I do re-verse the Ani(ego) then the uni-verse of Ayin (void or indetermin-able!) reveals the unavoidable indeterminacy of *causa sive ratio sui* to marvel at. . . . To marvel at in the cosmic store-house of thoughtlessness and form-lessness, when some-where = some-when, and also no-where = no-when. Then in no-when ego can easily become no-ego and restore its indivisible wholeness (man and universe as *one*): *omnia animata sumus*, including *nos egos, omnes ego*. Then as no-then or timeless the exless 'X', our own unknown responds or corresponds to indeterminacy and drops any claim of time and space. No more claim for explainable plainness or for questionable questions of life. *Vivat vita et suitas!* Then – the instant *now* appears the only stimulus and impetus for self-revelation, self-experience (of the quasi-real as irreal and vice-versa: one *omnis* instant as enstasis). Then the quasi fleeting grasps its quasiness (and means: Know Thyself!) and the present is not a present *per se*, but a present *per futurum*, an ante-future like today is morrow's eve.

Here in the messianic expectation of the indeterminate revelation of *causa sive ratio sui* one can marvel at with alchemizing, mesmerizing, nirvanizing magic of the own unknown of otherless *suitas*. One marvels at one's own omni-indeterminacy identifying with omniality of *omnia animata sumus*. In the quasi-fleeting the quasi-coming appears as a becoming. *Natura* stems from *nascor* (*nosco?*) to lead from genesis to gnosis and vice versa as uni-versa. And this via quasiness so lively of living *suitas* via quasi-otherness (but not *per se!*). In order to second Spinoza when he has no present tense to present, but only future (presentation), I have to let him have more light from the East and more high-light from Jewish Esotericism. 'When the Messiah will come today.' Today is already messianized like every *now* and *here* with the totality of time and space, namely with the morrow as on every morrow's eve. On the foregoing 'eve' does the 'day of creation' start, not afterwards to please wishful despotic thinking of watch and calendar via *causa sive ratio alius*. We follow the heavenly sun and its cosmic clock. Messianization is so helpful for salvation – to expect and experience the indeterminate of which the fleeting does not rob anything so to speak. Sic! The future via the messianized present tense is most suitable for the timelessness worthy of our egolessness. Then the 'Last Days' will have to come with the Messiah, to restore the 'First Days' from Eden. To re-instate the A and O, the A and Z, the Aleph and Taw as the whole, holy life. Le Chayim! Suares has brought more light and enlightenment into the dim, dark waiting-room for salvation: waiting here and now for the own unknowable and livable redeemer, the Messiah. In the evening of morrow the new morning is latently dawning and heralding already the messianic message: 'He who in the evening of his life would find the freshness of newly lived morning that man would be a man of Qabala.' This message comes via Suares and his Cipher of Genesis which aims to decipher Gnosis better then before, namely gnosis of *causa sive ratio sui sine alio*. We do not need to understand any so-called cause or reason of eternal pacific indeterminate, the own unknowable life, but we have to stand receptive of Cabbalistic with Suares: 'in the way of blessing of maturation' [i.e. of completion]. Age is maturation for Hassidic Teaching when it can reveal that 'winter is old age for the unlearned. For the learned it is the season of harvest.' It can 'season' dull life with its mechanics and habits of mummifications and ossifications. The best season is Erev Machar, on Morrow's Eve for the coming Dawn of Magic Morrow. Finally, let Master Hui-Hai witness for Spinoza and Cabbalah with his own findings:

How may we perceive our own nature? – That which perceives is your own nature. The monk still asked: Just as a bubble having burst can never re-form, so can a man once dead never be reborn, for nothing remains of him. Where will the nature of his mind be 'then'? The master: Do you believe there will be a morrow? – Yes, said the monk, certainly. – The master: Bring it forth and show 'it' to 'me'! The monk: There will be surely a morrow, but not just 'now'. The master: Yes, but its *not* being *just now* does not mean that there will be *no* morrow. You personally do not perceive your own nature [The perceiver cannot perceive his perceiving] but this does not mean that your nature does not exist. Just now, there is before you that which wears a robe, takes food, stands, sits or reclines, but you do not recognize it for 'what' it is. You may well be called a stupid and deluded person. If you discriminate between today and tomorrow, that is like using your own nature to search for your own nature. You will not perceive 'it' even after myriads of aeons. Yours is the case of *not seeing* the sun, not of there *being no sun*.[52]

Causa sive ratio sui or the indeterminable can be likened to 'negative existence', negative while latent and not 'open' yet for the narrow and close mind, until it expands and becomes the oceanic all-mind, the cosmic/divine consciousness of *omnia animata sumus*. Such negative existence as a sub-stans quasi in the in-stans to express via quasiness the wholeness with no siding, this is always true aim of all esoteric teaching, especially the Cabbala. 'The wisdom of not being, the wisdom of the void (Ayin) – cannot be realized. It is not something but it makes all some-things possible. . . . There is no way to realize the void before the future is come to be now.'[53] Here Nachman of Bratslav seconds Spinoza's *futurum pro presente* and also means the sub-stans morrow in the 'stans' today as the messianic trend. . . . Messianic faith is in the unseeable being more than in the seeable non-being as fleeting. Messianic challenge is urge to *live* now and not to *know* it while knowing can be only a knowing better a dead past after now or an unborn (or stillborn!) future before.

Everyone is invited and lured to come to heap knowledge on knowledge: mountains like pyramids in the great desert of the chaos with dead kings of the past inside. Life as already in Eden after the 'fall', is always guarded as the Tree of Life by the Angel with the whirling sword not to allow hunters for knowledge, for lifeless knowledge to have access to unknowable life as self-revelation of *causa sive ratio sui*. . . .

Life comes not from knowledge, not from scriptures and scriptural teaching for scriptural living only: life on schoolbenches with schoolmastership mastering the 'other ones' (never the otherless own self!) and mustering them if ripe enough for postulates in life from outside life.

Scriptura non docet sed experientia, ergo doctissima ignorantia et arrogantia. Sic: ego, experientia vivos voco, mortuos plango, fulgura frango. Dixi.

INTERMEZZO III

Just at the moment when I was ready to let the flowing thoughts for this prologue come to a quasi-ending and then to shift them to another scene, that of my own paper with the same inner urge – just at that moment the dispute between Wetlesen and Hubbeling took a certain 'turn'. I then observed a turning-point in my own mind re-volving again and again in a pseudo-dilemma and I waited for a miracle to unmask such pseudoness. The miracle suddenly appeared at such uncertain, undetermined, acausal or irrational moment (*per se ?*) presenting a crown-witness for the truth (not for the defence nor for the offence of the prosecutor!). The witness offered his good offices in a friendly way and hoped for a happy ending. I have no need to introduce here Mircea Eliade and his *opus* as *magnum opus* called: 'Immortality and Freedom,' in order to accept with great satisfaction and welcome an unbiased and unfaltering viewpoint. A point to pacify as it were that (op-)position of knowledge versus life or rational against mystical experience. Sic!

Since time immemorial the exoteric tradition has liked to speak of two trees in the midst of the Garden of Eden: the Tree of Knowledge and the the Tree of Life, while the rare and cryptic esoteric tradition points to the very same one and unique tree. It is offering knowledge of lifeless quasi-otherness *per se*, namely a quasi-knower versus a quasi-known for some and for others knowledge of the otherless self, namely as unknowable life. It has been said of the tree of knowledge in Biblical language to be 'good for food and pleasant for the eyes to be desired to make one wise. . . .' Such description reads like a propaganda trap for attractive promising sight of something pleasant to the eyes of the seer awakening his desire to become only wise when able to reach and possess 'it', the 'seen' *per se*, together with its otherness, and to quench thus his own obsession by it. But there is a trapdoor: *ratio sive causa alius* can have no better handmaiden to appear pleasant so that the senses of the eyes can make a 'sense' or a 'reason' for its quasi-otherness to attract us. From thence had to come wisdom and that from oneself: so they argue, while presumably lacking a chance to incorporate the quasi-corporeal otherness *per se*, so to speak. Cause or reason makes us easily believe in otherness and also wise with such belief in the quasi-unbelievable reality of justified otherness which my reason 'reasons' out for me as a monopoly indeed. Wise – in their sense – would thus mean to dichotomize the via knowing into knower versus known and never to experience the useless and reasonless via the Way itself. The way which seems to go in a quasi-two-way traffic which they do not see as reciprocal receptivity transmuting knower into known or known into knower and both into the same via: 'I am' (is) the Way, the Truth and Life! *Vita = veritas, via = ego sum: omnia animata sumus!* Three important stages, levels, aspects of self-awareness with no real discrepancy between them: me, the way, the truth and life. All this . . . that ye may know 'I am' (is) the Lord, Yahweh! And that Yahweh is Elohim, for such mission man has been sent to earth. . . . Is it not to ponder on those stages when being conscious of self, God and world in Spinoza's finger-pointings? To be conscious in three ways of the very same identity and to re-identify again the des-identified oneself, as also to expand one's narrow I-consciousness into cosmic divine and world consciousness of *omnia animata sumus!*

I must apologize for not having yet called into the witness-box the above-mentioned important crown-witness, who came from so far away with such far-away depth-observations of the way as path with pathfinders attached to one-way traffic while some attached to another way-traffic on the same path to the same goal. Eliade has now the word:

> The two trends, that of the 'experimentalists' (the jhains) and that of the 'speculatives' (the dhammayogas) – are the two constants of Buddhism. This brings us to the problem of 'gnosis" and of the 'mystical' experience, a problem that was destined to play a fundamental role. . . . 'The monks who devote themselves to ecstasy (the jhains) blame the monks who are attached to doctrine (the dhammayogas) and vice versa. On the contrary, they should esteem one another. Few, verily, are those who pass the immortal element (amata dhatu, i.e. nirvana). Few, too, are they who see deep reality (arthapada), penetrating it by prajna, by intellect.' The text emphasizes the extreme difficulty of the two 'ways': *gnosis* and *experience* through meditation. . . . According to the Anguttara-nikaya (III, 355) the two methods: experimentalists and speculatives are equally indispensable for obtaining arhatship. According to the abidharma doctrine, for example the prajna-vimukti, the 'dry saint', he who is liberated by wisdom (prajna), gains nirvana in exactly the *same way* as does he who has had the experience of the nirodhasama-patti.[54]

The temptation to rationalize is much greater than to irrationalize, so that some incline even to rationalize 'mystical experience' to make it more palatable. Sic! Spinoza would have accepted such identification of ratio = ex-tuitio with in-tuitio which Suzuki equates with prajna as scientia intuitiva. When retranslating Buddhist phrasing into Spinozistic terminology, both Wetlesen and Hubbeling can be pacified. It is not a question of 'right' and/or 'wrong' for which sophistic approach claims too anxiously a dualistic existence of *'perseitas'*.

Hu-Shih (Peking) presenting his contribution here: Spinoza and Chuang-Tzu also can act as a witness in the so-called controversy. He dislikes Spinoza's discrimination between right and wrong and likes Chuang-Tzu's immune indifference against 'either-or'. In the meantime Hu-Shih seems to overlook that Spinoza's first axiom in the *Ethics* with self-evident truth and way for the seeker of truth, points to *causa sive ratio: vel sui vel alius*. And such *'vel'* with its magic quasiness takes no sides and does not put aside anything at all. . . . When truth is not isolated as if an abstract 'theme' outside of 'me' the expounder of truth, beyond my 'way', then I must take care that I, the Way and the Truth and Life, that all this to be 'as' me and 'in' me as myself. Then I can understand what it means to: Know Thyself! And when taking such

55

care then I am sure, I have learned the lesson of otherless self on the path to becoming myself. I have learned the lesson via self-discipline: as teacher and disciple with no otherness in between to separate me from *omnia animata sumus*. I am now conscious of the self-identical omniality as conscious of self, God, world (of quasi plurality).

Having this in mind and being the mind itself, I have seen Wetlesen in his Spinoza and Hubbeling in his Spinoza and Spinoza in himself, when still always on the way to be:
The Way, the Truth and the Life. Le Chayim!

Now, before introducing all the witnesses offering, like myself, the common homage to Spinoza, and who appear in alphabetical order with the theme of choice, I have to point out that I myself have already entered the witness-box twice before to testify my loyalty to him. The *Speculum Spinozanum* as a Kaleidoscopic Homage for 1677–1977 has a very odd story and ill-fated history indeed.

Now, for the third time during my life I enter again such witness-box to justify as it were, the perennial validity of Spinoza's teaching as translated to our everyday's stress, distress and frustrations. . . .

In 1932 I published a Spinoza Festschrift in Heidelberg to honour the tricentenary of the birth of this great thinker of mankind, and these prominent writers joined me in such endeavour: I. Brucar, Martin Buber, Fritz Droop, Simon Dubnow, Albert Einstein, Sigmund Freud, Carl Gebhardt, Vasile Gherasim, Max Grunwald, Jakob Klatzkin, Joseph Klausner, Marc Marcianu, Ignacy Myslicki, I. Niemirower, Ion Petrovici,R omain Rolland, Karl Sass, Carl Siegel, Nahum Sokolow, Jakob Wassermann and Arnold Zweig. At that time nobody was wise enough – which afterwisdom so seldom can provide *a priori* – to foresee or foresay the events which by force intended to change the face and surface of world and history alike. As soon as they found in the Third Reich of Adolf the Great, that Spinoza, the editor and many contributors to the book belonged to the (ostracized!) nation of the Saviour then – the fate of such book was doomed to failure. Sic! And there, as a historic co-incidence, Heidelberg played for me the same role as it played for Spinoza in his lifetime. In 1672 Karl Ludwig, then Kurfürst of the Pfalz, wanted someone as successor for the deceased famous French savant, Tannequil Lefevre, and someone with a greater world reputation. Without consulting the Senate of the University of Heidelberg, he entrusted his private adviser, Johann Ludwig Fabricius, then professor of divinity, to invite Spinoza in 1673 for the vacant chair of philosophy. The text of the letter was so tricky and not in the liberal spirit of the Kurfürst, but rather full with diabolic divine transparent diplomacy, so that Spinoza not only would have had to reject such invitation *ad personam* but also *ad rem*, namely not to seek any academic umbrella for the protection of his own philosophy: the philosophia *vera sed non optima*. For us, as Spinoza's posterity, it seems now afterwards too obvious how such rejection was very justified once again to be repeated history. In A.D. 1933, when the very same Heidelberg under Adolf the Great or – what is the same – under great historical or hysterical pressure behaved in a similar way to my first Festschrift as if to look for a quite new pre-text for the quite old and unchanged text: of hate . . . I myself was so lucky to survive, sometimes even against my own wish. Thus, I escaped that grand holocaust of the Second World War, actually this time meant as a Jewish-World War, and I waited for another, better, Josephus Flavius to record those events for unbiased history to come. Via various metamorphoses, some adorned with visible, some with invisible barbed wire, I finally settled in Australia. Then, in 1962, Spinoza admirers encouraged me to replace the former lost(?) symposium by an enlarged edition published by Martinus Nijhoff, The Hague, with fresh inspirations from Ben-Gurion, Constantin Brunner and F. H. Hallett. It seems now that the former trend for writers and readers interested in Spinoza and Spinozana has shifted from the German to the English sphere of language. I thus hope to get more compensation for the lost and dim echo in the past by another team of thinkers, anxious like myself to express a common urge for such homage to Baruch de Spinoza. My initial intention was to make the content of the former German text accessible to the English reader with new additional material in English, but in the spirit of the coming Pan-Europe, German, French and English are equally read and understood these days. Having all this in mind, I finally embarked with quite fresh pulse and enthusiastic impulse on entirely new material, mainly in English. Such gigantic task I may compare with a conductor playing his own solo part and at the same time conducting the whole orchestra with the sole leitmotif as guidance. I have been thus assisted by:

Walter Bernard, New York; Lothar Bickel, Toronto; Emilia Giancotti Boscherini, Rome; Henry Walter Brann, Takoma Park; James Collins, St Louis; Edwin E. Curley, Canberra; Will Durant, Los Angeles; Paul E. Eisenberg, Indiana; Guttorm Fløistad, Oslo; German Seminar, Peking; Joaquim Cerqueira Goncalves, Lisbon; Klaus Hammacher, Aachen; Errol E. Harris, Milwaukee; Roger Henrard, Liège; H. G. Hubbeling, Groningen; Hu-Shih, Peking; George L. Kline, Bryn Mawr; Kisaku Kudo, Kanagawa; Alexandre Matheron, Paris; Robert Misrahi, Paris; Arne Naess, Oslo; A. K. Offenberg, Amsterdam; Jean Préposiet, Besançon; Hiroshi Saito, Kanagawa; Reiku Shimizu, Tokyo; Guido van Suchtelen, Amsterdam; Jon Wetlesen, Oslo; Paul Wienpahl, Santa Barbara; Colin Wilson, Cornwall; Sylvain Zac, Paris, and also by Huston Smith, Syracuse, with his foreword. Perle Hessing, my wife, gives a pictorial tribute to parallel in a magnificent manner such collective homage.

I feel bound to express my gratitude for having been encouraged in my daring venture to: the Calouste Gulbenkian Foundation, Lisbon; Magdalena Kasch, the living soul of the International Constantin Brunner Institute, The Hague; Svetoslav Bouzeskoul, Paris; my wife Perle, for useful prosaic and unprosaic suggestions. Especially to my instant, constant Master and Guru: Baruch de Spinoza not only for new exoteric explanations but rather for esoteric revelations and illuminations to keep awake the deepest layer of urge and alertness for experienceable self-realization. . . .

Now: witnesses for Baruch de Spinoza, please come forward and enter the witness-box to say the truth and nothing but the truth for a man who identified the truth with God and Nature alike, always with the intention to make it divine-natural indeed: *Deus sive Veritas; Deus sive Natura*. The very same truth to be loved like God, like Nature: *Deus sive Amor* as *causa sive ratio vel sui vel alius*. Hence it follows: not to causalize or to rationalize but to omnialize or universalize the self-exclusive arrogant and ignorant phantom of egohood while stopping brooding and inbreeding quasi-otherness *per se*! In this witness-box you will find me for the third time to present again together with all of you a common homage matched only by our all collective affinity to this monumental thinker of mankind. And matched by his own affinity to the all-infinity of the uni-verse or omni-verse appearing as an oceanic inside with a quasi-outside and with the challenge for the deep insight and quasi wide outsight: namely that very otherless secondless self-sameness: *causa sive ratio vel sui vel alius* veiled in quasiness (*tamquam, quamvis, sive*. . . .) And then to wonder and to ponder in order to ponder again and – to wonder again. To wonder what seems 'as if' behind or beyond the enigmatic di-'lemma' of chance and necessity.

London, 21 February 1977 in memory of The Hague, 21 February 1677
Siegfried Hessing

NOTES

1 Jean Paul Richter, *The Literary Works of Leonardo da Vinci*, 2nd edn. (Oxford University Press, 1939), p. 116.
2 Zeidler and Castles, *Österreichische Literaturgeschichte*, Vienna, introduced me to posterity with such an epithet, as lyric directing me to Spinoza.
3 Art and Science, 'Leonardo', *International Journal of the Contemporary Artist*, vol. 6, No. 1, Winter 1973.
4 Paul Reps, *Zen Flesh – Zen Bones*. A Collection of Zen and Pre-Zen Writings. (N.Y. Doubleday Anchor Books, 1961).
5 Fulcanelli, Master Alchemist: *Le Mystère des Cathédrales* (London, Neville Spearman, 1971), p. 176.

6 Jon Wetlesen: 'The Body as a Gateway to Eternity – A Note on the Mysticism of Spinoza and its Affinity to Buddhist Meditation'. Although this book is in alphabetical order of author's names, he has to be read first and later G. H. Hubbeling's contribution as an answer to him. The book is still unpublished.

7 Lama Anagarika Govinda, *Foundations of Tibetan Mysticism* (London, Rider, 1959), pp. 125, 137.

8 *The Sutra of Hui-Neng*. The Clear Light Series (Berkeley, Shambala, 1969), p. 22. To illustrate, let us take the analogy of a lamp. We know that the light of a lamp when surrounded by a shade will reflect inwardly with its radiance centring on itself, whereas the rays of a naked flame will diffuse and shine outwardly. Now when engrossed with criticizing others, as is our wont, we hardly turn our thoughts on ourselves, and hence scarcely know everything about ourselves. Contrary to this, the followers of the Dhyana School turn their attention completely within and reflect exclusively on their own 'real nature' known in Chinese as one's 'original face'. . . . It would be rewarding for Spinoza admirers to see how Spinoza himself speaks so strongly: that the mind has to reflect on itself, has to contemplate on itself etc. in order to re-assess one's own root-awareness of *omnia animata* (*sumus*), *ergo: sentimus experimurque nos aeternos* (*sive animata vel animatos et sive vanos*) *esse*. Sic! Spinoza admirers with more self-involvement and urge for self-realization when familiarizing themselves with the quasi-alternating (outward or inward) reflection as analysed by MacGregor Mathers based on the very same principle as Spinoza's aforementioned first axiom of 'either: or'. The one as indeterminate becomes quasi one as the (determinate) number when 'added' its reflection as ens *per se* (the great pseudo-reality for the senses: Maya). The de-finition (of the undefinable) forms an *eidolon* which 'duplicates' as it were, the thing defined. Spinoza warns so well that *omnis definitio, determinatio est negatio*. His warning is in vain. . . . The duplication forms a duad of 'one and its reflection'. Would man seeing himself in the mirror call the 'seer and the seen' *two* or rather *one and* the *other* . . . ? So reflection seduces man to think of otherness or eitherness *per se* rather than of otherless or eitherless self-reflection disregarding the quasi-alternating role of thinking. This then leads after Spinoza to *causa sive ratio: vel sui vel alius*. (See also (7) to my own contribution Proton Axioma kai Proton Pseudos.)

9 Joe Miller's Foreword to the *Sutra of Hui-Neng*, p. 3.

10 Edward Conze, *Buddhist Scriptures* (Penguin, 1959), p. 138 (my italics). Spinoza (in letter 37) gives precisely a similar method to empty the content of our memory consisting of single, singularizing thoughts assuming singular things (as *ideata*). To reach freedom of mind is to stop atomizing or itemizing the wholeness of the omni-verse as the identity of man: uni-verse . . . Too many trees bar us from seeing the forest and too many drops and waves from seeing the ocean with the taste of oceanic feeling of at-one-ment and all-oneness indeed. The famous Diamond Sutra condensed Eastern teaching to 'keep the mind independent of any (single) thoughts which arise within' and by hearing this recited on the highway, the (illiterate) Hui-Neng attained sudden enlightenment. Later, as the Sixth Patriarch, he pointed to the urge of path-seekers to 'realize inwardly the imperturbability of the essence of mind' (i.e. by singular intruding thoughts).

Many followed his footsteps for illumination, perhaps more than Patanjali with similar trends. . . .

11 *Buddhist Texts Through the Ages* (Oxford, Bruno Cassirer, 1954), p. 234.

12 From a bookjacket of his many books (all Rider, London) with biographical data as; 'Lu K'uan Yü (Charles Luk) was born in Canton in 1898. His first Master was the Hutuktu of Sikang, and enlighted Great Lama. His second Master was the Venerable Ch'an Master of Hsu Yun, the Dharma Successor of all five Ch'an Sects in China. Lu K'uan Yü now lives in Hongkong and devotes himself to presenting as many Chinese Texts as possible so that Buddhism can be preserved at least in the West, should it be fated to disappear in the East as it seems to be.'

13 Edward Maitland, *Anna Kingsford – Her Life, Letters, Diary and Work* (London, G. Redway, 1896), p. 178.

14 Carlo Suares, *Cipher of Genesis – The Original Code of the Qabala as Applied to the Scriptures* (London, Stuart & Watkins, 1970).

15 Gerschom Scholem (*Sabbatai Sevi: the Mystical Messiah*, Routledge & Kegan Paul, 1973, p. 11) re-emphasizes the importance of Ra'Ya Mehemna, often so much overlooked. Namely that the Torah manifests itself on its esoteric level via the tree of life *or* on its exoteric level via the tree of knowledge (i.e. of good and/or evil, which equates with death). In the spirit of sephirotic symbolism the 'two' trees in Eden are not really two as a number, but as a pair-concept (like the 'two' attributes of Spinoza). There are some unmistakable hints that it is the very same tree only seen from two aspects, levels of awareness or dimensions of consciousness: life and knowledge, or now-ledge and knowledge (m-ens: Sein – Bewusstsein). These are pair-concepts with no dualistic validity of entities *per se*. . . . In accordance with the cardinal first axiom in the Ethics of Spinoza: 'Everything which is, is *either* itself *or* in another (quasi itself).' And this can be compared with: 'Everything conceived [as being] is conceived *either* in itself *or* in another.' Either/or is the core of alternating knowledge. Neither/nor is the sign of otherless life. Life and knowledge is a pair-concept as lifeless knowledge *vis-à-vis* unknowable life. This is why the taste and test of the fruit from the tree of knowledge, forbidden by the Lord, brought (the one-sided half of that pair-concept) death: via sin or de-viation from the *via sui! Veritas sui!* Like *causa sive ratio sui vel in determinatio*. . . . A pair-concept has to symbolize best the inseparable wholeness with no cause nor reason of quasi-otherness *per se* apparent via the quasiness of number, discrepancy, etc. Let us then ponder on the main via of which it has been said by one I-saying Man: 'I' = I am. And 'I am' (is) the Way, the Truth and Life! Spinoza in this order of thinking speaks of *essendi fruitio*, not only *invita Latinitate sed invita cogitatione*! Sic!

16 Mal. 4; 6.

17 Ashvagosha, *The Awakening of Faith* (N.Y., University Books, 1960), p. 75.

18 Haec de Almarico Gerson Tract, de Concord. Metaph. cum Log. Part IV. Opera Alphab. 20. Lit. N. ex Hostiensi & Odone Tusculano.

19 Herbert Weiner, $9\frac{1}{2}$ *Mystics – The Kabbalah Today* (N.Y., Collier Books, 1969).

20 *TTP*, Cap. IX. p. 20. Van Vloten et Land, 3rd edition, Vol. I (The Hague, M. Nijhoff, 1914).

21 S. Hessing, *Spinoza – Dreihundert Jahre Ewigkeit* (The Hague, M. Nijhoff, 1962).

22 F. H. Hallett, *Creation, Emanation and Salvation* (The Hague, M. Nijhoff, 1962).
23 Reps, op. cit., p. 88.
24 S. L. MacGregor Mathers, *The Kabbalah Unveiled* (London, Routledge & Kegan Paul, 1957), p. 38.
25 *Ethics*, 5PXLIISchol., and TTP, Cap. IX.
26 *Buddhist Texts Through the Ages*, p. 230.
27 *TTP*, Cap. III, and IX. Frederick Ritter in his article: 'Constantin Brunner und seine Stellung zur Judenfrage' (*Bulletin des Leo Bäck Instituts*, 1975, XIV, No. 51, pp. 40–80) tries not to side and not to colour his arguments when pointing to such phenomenon as Brunner. Only posterity in retrospection will show quasi 'afterwards' the so-called historical 'Jewish Incident' as presented by the performance of Spinoza's and how of Brunner's karmic thinking. . . .

In his statement on the Jews Spinoza declined to accept any 'after' and any 'before', contemplating and reflecting on a timeless level on *causa sive ratio sui*. Brunner could only face the Jews either of the past or the Jews of the present time, because there was an irreconcilable discrepancy between 'after *per se*' and 'before *per se*'. And hence that crass dualism which splits persons and personalities so much. . . . He could not accept the undeterminable, acausal and irrational nature of chance as beyond any human siding with 'after' or with 'before' as two entities *per se*, so to speak loudly indeed! And just such a chance is embedded in Spinoza's cardinal and first axiom of the *Ethics*.

I cannot forgo recording here an encouraging 'co-incidence' when writing (down) these notes, via an article of Dr. Jakobovits (in *The Times* of 29.5.76, p. 14). Here the writer tries to speak unbiasedly about Jews, their destiny and – what interests us here most – about the epithet of the 'chosen people', as controversial as the 'chosen God' himself. It is a theme still claiming the very same undiminished actuality as in Spinoza's time and as in Brunner's. . . . That perennial enigma of the Jewish Nation among all other nations under the 'guidance' of the (Dis-)United Nations with their short-sighted and one-sided view ready to appease and please a certain numerical fashionable multitude (of votes!).

This time Spinoza would not call them any more '*ultimi barbarorum*' as in his time he did, and he would reject the remedy offered by his super-zealous pupil Brunner who thought that the barbaroi could be mitigated, flattered by super-identification with their ideals and idols. . . . Here I quote from that article as promised:

> To the Jew, the belief in belonging to the 'chosen people' is not an article of faith. It is an affirmation of his faith in the ability over the natural impediments of smallness and weakness. It is not a challenge or a menace to others: it is a challenge to himself and his people as religious pioneers to advance the moral order by precept and example.

As Robert Misrahi, an eminent French Spinozist, has also expressed his opinion on this delicate 'theme' in his contribution in this volume, I would like to repeat my echo to it, namely:

> May I point out that just the potentiality to *universalize*: i.e. to identify like Spinoza with that *omnia animata* (*sumus!*) and to be able to

transcend the self-isolated ego with its tendency to singularize (*res singulares*, etc.!) which as entelechy or not as such, could be called cosmic/divine (re-election of such) omni-(re-)awareness. . . .

28 Penguin Book of Quotations (Harmondsworth, Penguin, 1975), p. 156.
29 Pascal, *Pensées* (Harmondsworth, Penguin, 1966), p. 309.
30 *Les Quatres Fleuves* (Paris, Editions Seuil, 1974), No. 4. pp. 77–80.
31 *Korte Verhandeling*, II, Cap. XXVI, 4, and TTP Cap. IX.
32 Corti, *Theosophia Practica des Johannes George Gichtel* (Zürich, 'DU', 1952).
33 Marie Louise von Franz, *Zeitlose Dokumente der Seele*: Der Traum von Descartes (Zürich, Rascher, 1952), p. 75.
34 John Bleibtreu, *The Parable of the Beast* (London, Paladin Books, 1970).
35 Deut. 30: 11ff.
36 2 Kings, 2: 12.
37 *Philosophical Dictionary*, ed. D. Runes (N.Y., Philos. Library, 1960).
38 Hebr. 11: 1.
39 D. T. Suzuki, *Zen and Japanese Culture* (N.Y., Pantheon Books, 1954), p. 435.
40 D. T. Suzuki, *Studies in Zen* (N.Y., Philos. Library, 1955), p. 48.
41 Suzuki, 1954, op. cit.
42 *Upanishads* trs. by S. Prabhavananda and F. Manchester (N.Y., Mentor Books, 1957).
43 *Ibid.*
44 Meister Eckhart, ed. Pfeifer.
45 Job 42: 5.
46 Ashvagosha, op. cit.
47 *Upanishads.*
48 *Korte Verhandeling.*
49 *ibid.*
50 W. James, 'The confidence of a psychical researcher', *The American Magazine*, (Oct. 1909).
51 Spinoza, *Hebrew Grammar*, translated by M. Bloom (N.Y., Philosophical Library, 1962), p. 77.
52 *The Zen Teaching of Hui-Hai: On Sudden Illumination*, translated by J. Blofeld (London, Rider, 1962), pp. 118, 119.
53 Zalman Schächter, trsl. of Nachman of Bratslav: *The Torah of the Void* (London, Turtle, 1972).
54 Mircea Eliade, *Yoga-Immortality and Freedom* (Princeton University Press, 1969), p. 174.

1 Psychotherapeutic principles in Spinoza's *Ethics*

Walter Bernard, New York

> What Spinoza has to say about passion, desire, drive, but above all, about reason and knowledge, undoubtedly belongs to the most profound and sublime, to the most ingenious and richest in thought that has ever been said about these subjects (Ludwig Feuerbach).

In a recently discovered, hitherto unknown, letter of Freud's (discussed elsewhere in this volume; pp. 223ff.) – originally written 28 June 1931 but discovered in Toronto in 1974 among the literary effects of the late Dr Lothar Bickel – Freud clearly avows Spinoza's definite influence on him. I quote only the first paragraph here:

> I readily admit my dependence on Spinoza's doctrine. There was no reason why I should expressly mention his name, since I conceived my hypotheses from the atmosphere created by him, rather than from the study of his work. Moreover I did not seek a philosophical legitimation.

Towards the end of the letter he significantly added: 'I never claimed priority' (translated by H. Z. Winnik).

The purpose of quoting from this letter of Freud's is not to bring up again the question of the extent of Spinoza's anticipation of Freud, or of his direct or indirect influence on psychoanalysis, and on other psychotherapies or, for that matter, on psychology in general. This has been dealt with in a number of previous investigations.[1] The purpose of quoting Freud's own words admitting his 'dependence on Spinoza's doctrine' is mainly to draw attention again to the *Ethics* of Spinoza, as an original rich source of psychological ideas and insights from which many basic principles of the various psychotherapies have been derived whether directly or indirectly. By going back to Spinoza, who is often praised but not often read, psychotherapists as well as laymen are bound to discover new aspects of the psychology of man that they were not aware of before. Spinoza's psychology is not antiquated; it is still a part of modern psychology. It was above all his influence, as was shown by this writer, that was most important in shaping the rise of modern scientific psychology.[2] His classical study of the affects was incorporated verbatim in Johannes Müller's epoch-making *Handbuch der Physiologie des Menschen*

(1834–40). Spinoza's timelessness is due to the fact that he dealt with the inner dynamics of the invariant emotional life of man and with the constants of human nature.

His psychological principles therefore have validity and relevance at all times, but they may perhaps be more appealing today, especially in conjunction with his philosophical insights. This because our modern age, troubled by anxiety (the danger of a nuclear war), by the loss of faith in both religion and in science, and by the breakdown of some long-established cultural and social institutions is markedly characterized by 'anomie, amorality, anhedonia, rootlessness, emptiness, hopelessness, the lack of something to believe in and to be devoted to'.[3] Hence its great need to find its bearings again; hence its search for self-knowledge, self-fulfilment, finding meaning in life and in the cosmic totality. Witness the growth – in the USA especially – of the 'human potential' movement, of the encounter groups, the search for gurus and the study of the mystics, especially those of the Orient. Many people are thus troubled by the so-called 'existential question'. They feel a great need for the healing of their minds, for the ordering of their distraught emotions, for the therapy of their souls. So they flock now in great numbers to the new specialists in salvation, to the psychologists and psychiatrists, which seems to justify the sociologist Philip Rieff's remark that 'therapeutic theory is to modern culture what theology and philosophy were to systems of culture preceding our own';[4] an assertion he later elaborated in his own book with the significant title *The Triumph of the Therapeutic*.[5] It is clear, at any rate, that the vast majority of those who now go for therapy are not really sick with one of the typical, clinical neuroses. Their neurotic disorders are of a more general type, indicative of the general malaise of the age, and are thus often referred to as 'existential neuroses'. Chessick, in his book *Why Psychotherapists Fail*,[6] reports that at present many patients bring up problems relating to life's absurdity and lack of meaning. He also remarks that especially 'near the end of therapy patients often bring up questions that are basically philosophical and that cannot be approached by the method of science or psychotherapy', and for this reason he recommends a knowledge of philosophy as an invaluable diagnostic and therapeutic tool. Carl Jung, Victor Frankl and others have also emphasized man's unfulfilled philosophic and spiritual needs that must be considered in any successful therapy.

The philosophy of Spinoza which successfully integrates the psychologically therapeutic with the meaningfully philosophic seems to be singularly relevant to meet the present psychological and spiritual needs. His *Ethics* endeavours to lead man from an understanding of himself and the nature of his emotions to a lofty vision of his place in the cosmos and of his unitive relationship to the totality of Being, to the infinity and eternity of the One and All which he called 'God or Nature'. Many illustrious minds,[7] as well as a far greater number of unknown, ordinary people, have been profoundly moved by his psychology and philosophy, which they have found deeply satisfying, both intellectually and emotionally. The narrow scope of this article, however, allows only occasional reference to some of the philosophical ideas of Spinoza, since it will deal primarily with his theory of emotions, and even here, only limited aspects of his theory can be presented in order to arrive at the formulation of some important psychotherapeutic principles. These principles, as given here, were either stated directly by Spinoza or were extrapolated from his general psychology of man and his emotions.

In the field of psychology, Spinoza was the first clearly to state the principle of psychic determinism, the *sine qua non* for the scientific investigation of all mental and emotional events. But to reason scientifically one must be sure of the starting point of the logical process, the basic assumptions, which must be clear, simple, and in full agreement with experience. The starting point in psychology is the biological law of survival, of self-preservation, the *conatus* in man which is the endeavour to preserve himself, to continue his existence, for 'everything in so far as it is in itself endeavours to persist in its being' (III, 6).[8] For Spinoza, the law of self-preservation is not so much a matter of experience as the logical determinant of the given premise, i.e. that an existing force – in this case, the complex force of life called organism – will continue to exist 'with the same force with which it began to exist' (IV, Preface). In other words, self-preservation is simply another instance of the general law of inertia, applying to all states of being or forces in nature, according to which anything in a state of rest or motion will continue in its present state until destroyed or changed in its direction by another stronger force. This force of self-preservation is partly expressed automatically and unconsciously by the organism's vegetative and autonomic functioning – determined overall by *homeostasis*, the self-regulatory tendency of the body to maintain its inner balance – and partly by the organism's more or less conscious activity in response to the various needs, wants, drives, tensions that arise concomitantly with life's ongoing processes: the processes of continuous adaptation and adjustment to the incessant metabolic changes going on within, and to the stimulation and challenges of the environment forces impinging on the organism without. These continuous stresses and strains as well as the pleasurable sensations and stimulations become conscious in various degrees as a constant *state of desire*, which is the counterpart of the overall *conatus*, the body's endeavour to maintain itself. Hence the significance of Spinoza's statement that 'desire is the very essence of man', which hence determines man to respond and react to the continuous processes within and to their interaction with the events without.

Desire is not merely directed towards need-reduction in order to bring relief, satisfaction and pleasure. Pleasure is sought for its own sake, since the experience of pleasure or the recollection of it is 'self-reinforcing', and hence arouses the desire to attain it, to prolong it, and if possible, to increase it.

Pain and pleasure are thus the concomitant factors of desire, and Spinoza calls these three the 'primary emotions'; and from these three he then derives with penetrating logic, insight and clarity all the other principal emotions, such as love, hate, joy, fear, hope, envy, pride, and many others, the explanation and analysis of which, and the way reason and understanding can confront them, constitute the main subject matter of the last three parts of the *Ethics*.

All emotions are thus basically defined in terms of pain and pleasure with the necessary cognitive reference added of who or what is the cause of the pain or pleasure, or of the admixture of both. Some of the emotions are defined quite generally because of their wide scope. Thus love is defined as 'pleasure accompanied by the idea of an external cause', and hate, its antipode, as 'pain accompanied by the idea of an internal cause'. Notice that the idea of love (or of hate) is universally applicable. In the case of love, for example, it includes the love of things as well as the love of people. Whether we love food, art, music, money, sport, or friends, wife, husband or child, the type of pleasure, to be sure, and the consequent attachment will differ, but essentially it is a kind of pleasure accompanied and aroused by the idea of the 'object of our love', of who or what causes it. From which it also follows that love is primarily *egoistic pleasure* (or serving personal interests), and the assumed 'altruism' in love follows secondarily, namely, from the desire to cherish and preserve the thing we love. Consequently, when the pleasure, the interest, the motivation in love disappears, then the love for the thing or person likewise disappears. Motivation – the motive to care, to respond, to do – must always spring from within, from the person's experience of things or people as they affect his pleasure, his welfare, his social status, his pride, in short, his *egoistic interests*, or as they affect the welfare and interests of those who are close to him and are thus drawn within the orbit of his own ego-interests. There must always be some sort of 'ego-involvement'. Even the most idealistic motivation for a cause must come from within, from the ego, from the feelings and emotions of the person, since he has made the cause 'his own'. And like other attachments, idealistic motivations, too, change for a variety of personal reasons, and thus ideals, too, are frequently 'disowned' and abandoned.

Spinoza's analysis of the emotions, based as it is on the pleasure-pain principle (cf. also Freud) brings us to the important insight – often denied by well-meaning moralists – of the fundamental *self-concern* of man, derived from the natural, and biologically necessary, self-reference of his feelings and emotions which, in turn, determine his actions, his attachments and aversions, his likes and dislikes. Love interests are essentially self-interests. If we no longer take pleasure in the company of a person, or he no longer serves our interests, we become indifferent in various degrees and our love diminishes. Similarly, if we fail to be pleasurable, pleasant, kind, helpful, considerate to others, their concern for us will vanish. What basic insight that should give us for our inter-personal relationships should be rather obvious, yet that insight is strangely lacking among many people. They frequently *demand* love, affection, loyalty, instead of exerting themselves to earn it, or they feel they have a right to expect love, friendship, loyalty, gratitude for *past* favours performed ('What have you done for me lately?', a cynical joke has it), not realizing that ego-interests change and attractions wane, that new interests and pleasures frequently displace the old ones to the point where the old love attachments are abandoned. This realization of the essential egoistic nature of man – *always coupled with the honest recognition of one's own egoism* – can help us relate realistically to other people and can prevent and attenuate many heartaches and traumas, caused by estrangements, abandonment and betrayal, and the consequent bitter disappointments and disillusionments. The other side of the coin is the denial of our own basic egoistic rights by other people. Many a therapist has had the frequent task of strengthening the self-regard, and self-concern of his patients against the dominance of other members of the family – usually father or mother – who consciously or unconsciously would deny them the right to lead their own lives and to follow their own interests by appealing to their moralistic filial duties and by demanding an excessive amount of devotion. Here the patient must learn to assert himself against the others, and to realize that he has just as much a duty to himself and to his own interests, as others have to theirs, 'for virtue is nothing else than to act according to the laws of one's own nature' (IV, 18).

Thus the first therapeutic principle, though not directly referred to by Spinoza, can easily be distilled from his overall study of the emotions. It may be stated as the Principle of the basic right and self-concern of every organism:

I. A clearer understanding of the natural egoistic aspect of human nature, of the basic self-concern of everyone – including, of course, ourselves – will lessen our disappointments and disillusionments in people, will prevent us from feeling self-righteous, and will diminish our criticisms, scorn, hatred and contempt of others. While thus allowing for the rights of others, we shall also insist on our own rights, to live our own authentic lives, not controlled or dominated by others.

Most of the other therapeutic principles which Spinoza calls 'the remedies for the emotions' he himself summarizes in Part V, entitled 'The Power of the Intellect', especially in the Note to Proposition 20. One of the important principles emerges almost naturally from the affective-cognitive nature of each emotion. Since the affective disturbance is connected with the *cognitive* idea of an external cause (cf. Freud: 'The repressed complex consists of a libidinal cathexis and an ideational content.'[9]), it is clear that if we could separate conceptually the effect from its cause, it would lose its anchoring support and very likely dissolve and disappear. This Principle of the

Disassociation of the Emotion from its cause is clearly stated in V, Prop. 3

> II. If we remove – [the] emotion from the thought of an external cause and unite it to other thoughts, the love or hatred towards the external cause, as well as waverings of the mind which arise from these emotions, are destroyed.

We know, of course – to give a simple example – that hatred of a person assumed to be the cause of some injury to us disappears when we learn that he was *not the cause* of that injury, or perhaps only the unwilling cause of it. Spinoza urges us here to unite the cause of hatred, fear, etc., to *other* true thoughts. One obvious and often used remedy is to view the cause from a higher level by seeing the specific cause as an instance of other causes of a similar nature (as, for example, in cases of accidental injuries), thus arriving at a widely accepted generalization, a universal law, or something that is typical of man's nature in general. When one has been defrauded or one has made a serious mistake oneself, it does help to assuage the emotions of hatred, remorse, or regret, if one recalls the many similar cases of wrongdoing everywhere and reflects upon them as incidents that could be expected to happen anywhere, at any time, considering our common nature and the perpetual conflict of interests and emotions in which human beings are involved. Thus using our own emotion as a basis for thinking about the nature and character of man, and thus also learning to know ourselves better, and acquiring likewise a greater insight into our relationship to other people – all this would mean associating our wrong, our injuries 'with other true thoughts' and thus separating them from their fixations upon their single causes with the result that the emotion will be weakened at least, if not completely destroyed.

This method of separating the emotion from its cause and connecting it with other ideas – in essence, this means deliberating upon it, thinking through – leads by extension to two other therapeutic principles:

(a) Dissolving the fixation upon a single cause by regarding its linkage with other actual causes.
(b) linking the single cause with the idea of universal necessity, ruling all events.

The first of these two – which may be named the Principle of Multiple Causation – is stated by Spinoza as follows (V, 9):

> III. An emotion which has reference to many different causes which the mind regards at the same time as the emotion itself is less harmful, and we are less passive to it and less affected towards each cause than another emotion equally great which has reference to one alone or to fewer causes.

This principle is almost self-evident. Just as the concentration and focusing of rays on a subject intensifies the heat whereas their dispersal reduces it, so the consideration of multiple causes, proximate or remote, that very likely were linked with the immediate cause of the emotion, previously regarded as the sole cause, would disperse the emotional cathexis over the many instead of allowing it to be centred on the one cause. To illustrate: in the case of the apparently oft-recurring family traumas, e.g. hatred of one's father, it would certainly be helpful for therapy if the patient were made to reflect on the multiplicity of causal circumstances that shaped the outlook, character and behaviour of the hated father. One should certainly have to consider his upbringing, his inborn qualities of temperament, the social, economic, political and religious environment of his time, his own childhood history, his state of health, his education or lack of it. The reflection on many of these causal factors is bound to lead to a better understanding of the man, and hence to a considerable diminution of the emotion of hatred. *Tout comprendre c'est tout pardonner* remains the ideal.

Thus, by considering the multiple causes that shaped a person's character the fixation on him as the sole cause of the emotion is destroyed and with it the emotion itself is considerably weakened, and the mind is able to turn to other matters and to function more freely and spontaneously. For Spinoza realized – as most modern therapists do – that the obsessive, adhesive quality of the emotion frequently results in a blocking of the normal thought processes and in the interference of one's normal functioning. This is its most damaging aspect, for (V, 9, Proof):

an emotion is bad or harmful only in so far as the mind is prevented from thinking as much as before – inasmuch as the essence of the mind, that is, its power, consists of thought alone.

The principle of multiple causality, just considered, leads us inevitably – by further reflection on the interconnectedness and complicity of the infinite chain of causes – to the conviction that the past must be considered as necessarily determined, that under the circumstances a person could not have acted otherwise than he did, that he was shaped by forces more powerful than himself, that his actions, therefore, were ineluctably, necessarily so. Thus we are brought to the *philosophic concept of necessity*, so important in Spinoza's as well as in Stoic philosophy. This scientific-philosophic principle which testifies to the all-pervading law of causality which rules all things and all events, thus linking them together in coherence and unity – the recent events strictly determined by the preceding ones and these in turn by others – all this makes us realize that everything, everywhere, the entire cosmos is governed by the supreme law of necessity. This sublime thought has something of the effect of a soothing, healing balm over a wound, and hence, if sufficiently and deeply reflected upon, can constitute the important therapeutic Principle of Universal Necessity (V, 6):

IV. In so far as the mind understands all things as necessary it has more power over the emotions or is less passive to them.

It is especially from this idea of necessity that the attribution to, and fixation upon, a single cause upon which the emotion is concentrated is found to be simply unwarranted, since everything is now seen, *as it truly is*, in its nexus with the determined cosmic order of things. Whenever one realizes, therefore, that things could not have been otherwise, he experiences a certain quiet resignation, 'for we see the pain caused by the loss of some good to be lessened or mitigated as soon as he who lost it considers that it could have been preserved in no manner' (*ibid*. Note). This idea of universal necessity and the ineluctable, often even willing subordination to it is, as was remarked before, typical of the philosophic, the Stoic, and, in essence, also of the truly religious attitude. It is in the great tragic and fateful events of life the deeply felt, ultimate conclusion of all men. All somehow realize the wisdom of submitting to one's fate, of conforming to one's destiny, of humble surrender to 'Moira', to 'Karma' or to the 'will of God'.

Here, in Spinoza's philosophy, it is shown that the rational mind, to think truly and adequately, must indeed think in terms of causality (*ratio sive causa*), since causal connections express the universal laws of nature. This means, our reason makes us see all things as necessary and determined, as intertwined with the infinity of universal events. To view things thus is to view them '*sub quadam aeternitatis specie*', under a certain aspect of eternity, for 'this necessity of things is the necessity itself of the eternal nature of God' (II, 44, Corr. 2). *Necessity, thus, is eternity itself*, thought in human terms by way of the infinite chain of cause and effect; and it is for this profound reason that we find in necessity some of the quiescent calm of eternity. Thus seen, things of whatever nature, good or bad, become embedded in the universal being of which we are a part. They are just occurrences then, simply cosmic phenomena, as it were; and from this sublime yet true perspective we can even transcend to some extent our human viewpoint as we then tend to see even our own hurts, our own grievous mistakes, our own sufferings and sorrows almost as pure events in nature, as pure – in Kolbenheyer's phrase – as is 'the migration of stars, as ebb and tide, as birth and death'. Our unrest and emotional agitations are stilled. Hating a person because of some grievous wrong becomes almost as meaningless as hating a stone upon which one stumbled and severely injured oneself.

This ability of the mind simply to think rationally, to reflect on and explore the laws of nature – in this case the law of necessity – is indication of what Spinoza means by the power of the mind, whose true essence consists in understanding, in forming 'adequate' ideas and then logically deducing from these other adequate ideas. This leads us to the important distinction between the rational or logical association of ideas as contrasted with the purely accidental or fortuitous association of ideas, as given in common, everyday experiences. Thus one's love or hatred of a person usually generalizes to a multiplicity of things or persons. These fortuitous associations are then the basis of many unexamined, irrational prejudices, and predilections, likes and dislikes, sympathies and antipathies, and consequently also of many generalized emotional complexes, for 'anything can accidentally be the cause of pleasure, pain or desire' (III, 15). To this must be added that similar things will also arouse the same emotion 'merely, owing to the fact that they have something in common with something that is wont to affect us with pleasure or pain' (*ibid.*). Thus fears, hostile attitudes, phobias, depressions and other emotions are frequently aroused by the sights, sounds, images and names of things which had *nothing to do with the causes of the emotions,* but were simply contiguous to them in time or place, or because they bear some similarity to them. Hence we can formulate the cognitive-therapeutic Principle of Disassociation (from the emotion) of Unrelated Factors:

V. The insight gained by the realization of the irrelevant character of the purely accidental association of things or persons with the etiology of the emotion will tend to separate them from the emotion itself, and thus restrict and diminish the scope of the emotional complex.

Of course, we cannot help being affected to some extent by the associations of things experienced together. The law of association, after all, has supreme survival value. It is the basis of all our conditioning, learning and memory. But it also has a negative side. As long as we cannot *discriminate* between things in spite of their similarity, we have no precise knowledge. We will then treat, for example, a useful garden snake, with the same abhorrence as a poisonous snake; and for the same reason of mere similarity of appearance, many people have died by mistaking poisonous berries or mushrooms for the edible ones. By learning to discriminate, however, the true, essential characteristics from the merely similar, accidental or inessential ones we can, to our advantage, enjoy the one and avoid or discard the other.

Thus the claustrophobic patient need not forever shun confined space just because the traumatic experience took place in such a locale. He can overcome his phobia either by a process of direct *desensitization* or deconditioning, which, by coupling confined space this time with neutral or pleasant stimuli, gradually counteracts and neutralizes the original association, or by a cognitive reorientation, that is, by acquiring insight and understanding of its precipitating cause, the surroundings in which it was set, the emotional aura it created, its repression and its consequent effect upon present behaviour. The cognition, then – *usually referred to as insight* – of the many irrational and irrelevant factors tending to evoke the emotion will, it is assumed, reduce a good deal of the old emotional pathology, as thinking is now characterized by a new intellectual, more logical, more realistic order of ideas. Just as a mind enlightened can overcome dark, groundless superstitions and dispel the fears connected with them, so rational thinking, delving deeply into the original traumatic event, can supply the final insight to overcome fortuitous and irrelevant associations and thus help reduce the emotional disturbance connected with them.

The reader, acquainted with the psychoanalytic concepts of emotional 'abreaction' and 'catharsis', might well wonder here whether these intellectual, rational considerations would really help. Is it not a fact that merely telling a person that his phobia or anxiety is wholly irrational or that his neurosis is an exaggerated illogical reaction to an earlier trauma has very little, if any, therapeutic effect on his affliction? Also, isn't there some recognition by Spinoza of the deeper-lying *unconscious* factors in the etiology of emotional disturbance? As to the first, Spinoza would definitely agree, since he is very emphatic in saying that 'an emotion can neither be hindered nor removed save by a contrary emotion and one stronger in checking emotion' (IV, 6). But rightly understood, there is no contradiction between the above and his advocacy of rational thought in curbing and restraining emotion. Spinoza is quite aware of the fact that mere intellectual knowledge about the emotion, even though true, is powerless and ineffectual, or, as he puts it: 'A true knowledge of good and evil cannot restrain any emotion in so far as the knowledge is true', but then he adds significantly: '*but only in so far as it is considered an emotion*' (IV, 14–my emphasis). In other words, only to the extent of the *feeling aspect* of that particular knowledge, is that knowledge a counterweight to the emotion; only to the extent of the strength of the affective aspect of an idea, is that idea itself strong enough to create an emotional component to balance and restrain the other emotion. For ideas have feeling-tones, they are not as Spinoza says 'lifeless pictures on a board'. All ideas of concrete things arise in us originally as representations connected with sensations, with sensory impressions.

Cf. Constantin Brunner's classic definition of things:

> A thing is a sum of sensations coupled to the fusion product of such representations as arose simultaneously with these sensations and to which we relate these sensations as caused by them.[10]

The representations of similar things are then combined into more abstract class representations or universals. These universals or concepts may then be combined with or set into relation to other concepts, into ever more abstract entities. But always and everywhere, even in the most abstract notions there are some of the affective elements of the original sensations, though they may have lost some vividness, some of their native hue, 'by the pale cast of [abstract] thought'. The cognitive cannot be separated from the affective, hence in taking thought – seriously, not superficially or by mere words – we are calling forth the affective substratum, the feeling-tone that goes with these thoughts. Hence also, a change of thought can change the previously prevailing mood. Ideas bring their positive or negative feelings with them. Knowledge, as Spinoza remarks, can thus have an emotional impact; the more vivid, clear and rational it is, and the more it is in agreement with reinforcing reality, the greater its effect.

We can therefore state the next principle which stresses the need of: *Strengthening the affective substratum of reason, or reason as 'emotion'.*

VI. Reason to be effective must itself assume some of the nature of an impelling force, of a driving emotion. The rational grounds advanced in opposition to a passion, or in pursuit of an aim, must themselves become more and more invested with desirable feelings. Hence the need of concentrating on the positive, pleasurable aspects of the rational aim. Vividness of the aim creates a positive attitude towards it, heightens the the motivation, thus strengthening the 'will' to achieve the aim.

It is hence clear that the use of reason is a potent force against the dark libidinal or anxiety-producing forces. In Freudian language, the ego can control and often prevail upon the id; or to speak again with Spinoza, rational or adequate ideas can displace the inadequate, mutilated and confused ones. These inadequate and confused ideas are close to what we would now call the subconscious and unconscious. They are 'like consequences without premises', the missing premises being the unknown, hidden, that is, the unconscious. Spinoza hence speaks also of unconscious motivation.

> Men think themselves free inasmuch as they are conscious of their volitions and desires, and as they are ignorant of the causes by which they are led to wish and desire, *they do not even dream of their existence* (I, App., my emphasis).

Erich Fromm aptly remarks:

> With this concept of the determination of man by the unconscious, Freud, without being aware of it, repeated a thesis which Spinoza had already expressed. But while it was marginal in Spinoza's system, it was central to Freud's.[11]

'A neurosis is a kind of ignorance' Freud also remarked. Obviously, then, ignorance can be removed only by conscious thought, by knowledge and insight. Spinoza stresses the point, highly important in therapy or self-therapy, 'that we are able to arrange and connect the modifications of the body according to their intellectual order' (V, 10). This is the converse of that famous proposition (II, 7) which states that 'the order and connection of ideas is the same as the order and connection of things'. Many have interpreted this as body-mind parallelism or even interactionism. Spinoza's conception, as is well known, is that the mental and physical processes constitute two different views of what is a unitive event, an *ultimate identity*. This is the double-aspect view of body and mind. The physical and mental are not two parallel events – though it may seem so; they are not interactive events – though for practical purposes and for convenience of language we may consider them *as if* they were so – they are simultaneous in process and in function. They are, in Fechner's simile, the convex and the concave sides of the same lens, or as C. Brunner puts it, the mental (sensations, feelings, thought) is the inwardness to the outwardness of the body. And hence, just as we can study man merely from the physical side (behaviourism takes this extreme attitude and thus leads to reductionism) so we can theoretically study the very same events from the mental side. And since we have, and for a very long time we'll continue to have, very little knowledge and understanding of the complex and intricate physical, chemical and electrical processes that go on in the central nervous system, and especially in the cortex, while we are having ideas, feelings, moods, etc., it will be best, it seems, to approach many emotional disturbances and physical illnesses *from the mental side*. This may be called the Principle of Mental Hygiene and Psychosomatics. It was formulated by Spinoza in the following words (V, 1, Proof):

> VII. Just as the order and connection of ideas in the mind is made according to the order and connections of the modifications of the body, so vice versa, the order and connection of the modifications of the body is made according as the thoughts and ideas are arranged in the mind.

The overall idea of body-mind identity leads thus to the conceptual foundation of the discipline of mental hygiene and of *psychogenic therapy*, the positive aspect of psychosomatics, which is now considered primarily from its negative, pathological aspect, in the so-called psychogenic disorders. Spinoza does not indulge here in the common, hortatory rhetoric that glibly preaches the desirability of an optimistic attitude, positive thinking, love and affection for others, etc.; counsels freely given by our popular 'uplift' writers who seem to assume that it is all only a matter of free will, of just wanting it so. Spinoza emphasized the need for serious, sustained thought. One ought to make an effort at thinking about the nature and causes of the emotions, the psychology of man, his social relationship to his fellow human beings, his position within the universe of events about him, the laws of nature and, lastly, how man relates to the totality of all existence, the infinite eternal being that he calls God or Nature or Substance. What is needed, but difficult to acquire, is a positive philosophy that aims to see life whole and in its relation to the totality of existence, so that man, as a true child of nature, may find some sort of affinity, harmony and union with the whole of nature and thus also a measure of peace and contentment within him. 'As a man thinketh, so is he.' But wholesome thinking and the therapeutic source of

74

well-being resulting, therefore, will thus be the consequences not of an arbitrary optimistic stance, but of some intellectual effort, of rational thoughts conforming to reality, agreeing with things as they really are, not as fantasy and wish would like them to be. Furthermore, reality-thinking – the simple realization of other powerful forces prevailing in this world – perforce leads one also to a higher frustration tolerance, to a more ready submission to the many evils, misfortunes and unexpected calamities in life, to some sort of acceptance of one's own limitations in ability and attainment, and of one's own character defects. Acceptance is therapeutic, even if paradoxically it means accepting our inability fully to control our emotions. As a matter of practical wisdom, however, Spinoza adds

> that we must always pay attention in the ordering of our thoughts to those things which are good in each thing so that we may be determined always by an emotion of pleasure. E.g., if any one sees that he seeks honour too eagerly, let him think of the right use of it, to what extent it should be sought and by what means it may be acquired, and not of the abuse and vanity and inconstancy of man (V, 10, Note).

In the above example, Spinoza gives a partial illustration of *how the same emotion, previously a 'passion', can, by the use of reason, be transformed into an 'action'*. This he makes even clearer in a similar passage where he speaks of the ambitious man with his burning desire to excel, to attain leadership, which is to give expression to that desire of each

> that others should live according to his idea of life, and this desire in a man who is not guided by reason is a passion which is called ambition and which differs very little from pride; – [but] in a man who is guided by reason it is an action of virtue (V, 4, Note).

This important differentiation, which Stuart Hampshire calls 'the famous distinction between active and passive emotions',[12] is unique with Spinoza and, to my knowledge, is not found in any of the theories of psychotherapies, though it does find a later echo in Freud's somewhat metaphorical terminology when he remarks that 'the therapeutic task consists in freeing the libido from its present attachments, which are withdrawn from the ego, and making it once more serviceable to the ego'.[13]

Since Spinoza defines an *adequate cause*, as that 'whose effect can clearly and distinctly be perceived through it', it follows that

> we act or are active – when from our nature anything follows in us or outside us which can be clearly and distinctly understood through that alone. On the other hand, I say we suffer or are passive when something follows from our nature of which we are only the partial cause.

This is followed by the definition of emotion with the aforementioned differentiation (III, Definition):

> By emotion (affectus) I understand the modifications of the body by which the power of action in the body is increased or diminished, aided or restrained, and at the same time the ideas of these modifications. Explanation – thus if we can be the adequate cause of these modifications, then by the emotions I understand an Action, if otherwise a Passion.

The word 'action' is used when some conscious response follows from the very nature of the organism. Then it is clearly the unhampered functioning of its very existence, of its very essence. To know whether it is an action or not, man has to have a knowledge of his own true nature. But this knowledge is not given to him automatically. He has no sure instincts to guide him. He has no ready knowledge of his own body and mind; he has to acquire it, as he has to acquire knowledge of the world in which he lives. He depends therefore on the experience of his senses, on learning, occasionally on his intuitive sense, but above all on understanding, reason, since it is reason that ultimately orders and evaluates his experience and guides him to the discovery of the all-important scientific laws of nature, including those of his own nature, of his own body and mind.

In addition to this valuable need for knowledge of general human nature, a person usually strives also for a knowledge of his own uniqueness, of his individual needs and desires, of his abilities and potentialities, of what he is now and what he can still become in order to express his own nature, in order to achieve the great satisfaction that comes with self-actualization, with self-fulfilment. Hence the wisdom of the Socratic dictum: 'Know thyself!' Only to the extent that we clearly know our own nature, have 'adequate ideas' about it, will our choices and our required actions likewise become clear to us, only then are we truly *active*. We then affirm and preserve our veritable nature. This activity springing from *knowledge*, this self-affirmation, Spinoza speaks of as our ultimate 'human virtue', our 'power', which assert itself against other powers and forces in nature.

An emotion, then, which is an involvement of our nature with an external force must, in itself, be considered a 'passion', that is, we are passive, subject to it, as we are not our own masters in relation to it. This is true as long as we have inadequate or confused ideas about it. To the extent that we do understand an emotion, 'if not absolutely, at least in part clearly and distinctly', we are in a position to balance it with our own vital interests, and this either by fighting, accepting, or modifying it. At any rate we are then becoming more active and less passive to it. If we have come to terms with it, if we have been able consciously to incorporate it within our overall life goals, with a weighing of both its harmful and beneficial effects, if, in other words, our decision is the outcome of reasoned deliberation, then the same emotion has become an *action*, for 'whatever follows from human nature, in so far as it is defined by reason, must be understood through human nature alone as its proximate cause' (IV, 35).

As a simple illustration of the above there comes to mind the reply that Winston Churchill is reported to have given when he was asked whether he ever considered the possibly harmful effects of his smoking and drinking habits. His reply was that he got more out of his cigars and liquor than they got out of him, meaning that the harm done was far outweighed in his case by the pleasure, relaxation and possibly even stimulation for his work that he got out of his smoking and drinking, and that he consciously had made that choice. Thus, they were no longer passions, but actions. For 'all appetites and desires – are accredited to virtue when they are excited or generated by adequate ideas' (V, 4, Note). We can now try to formulate this therapeutic Principle of Conversion in the following way:

VIII. An affect or emotion which is a passion can be converted into an action to serve one's true ends. Consider above all your philosophy of life, your overall aim for self-fulfilment and whether the particular affect will increase or diminish, further or thwart your powers, activities and goals. Accept or redirect as much of it as you can to be in conformity with your nature and your own true needs.

In his book *Treatment of the Neuroses*, which also reviews and examines various psychotherapies other than psychoanalysis, Ernest Jones argues well for the evaluation of their effectiveness chiefly by means of the 'activity criterion', defined by him 'as the extent to which the patient himself is made actively to bring about changes in his mental functioning'.[14] If we consider the various therapeutic principles here discussed we find indeed that this common thread runs through them all. All point to the need of thinking, to the activity of the mind, especially to a person's use of his power of understanding and reasoning. To understand is to be active. This activity of the mind counteracts *directly* the passivity and stagnation of the thought processes, brought about by our obsession with the emotion, for as quoted before, 'an emotion is bad or harmful only in so far as the mind is prevented by it from thinking as much as before' (V, 9). The persistence of the emotion is loosened and weakened when one begins to be active, when the power of the freely functioning mind reasserts itself. And this unhampered functioning of the mind, like the unhampered functioning of any organ, yields *Funktionslust*, function pleasure, which adds to the well-being of the entire person, since mind or consciousness is what we ultimately live. Unfettered from the emotion, one's inner sense of power and self-confidence is regained. 'When the mind regards itself and its power of acting it is rejoiced' (IV, 53). This rejoicing or deep sense of pleasure is the self-satisfaction that arises when a person then views his accomplishments, his abilities, and his 'power of acting'.

But Spinoza's ideal of 'human freedom' includes more than the freedom from the bondage of the emotion, more than self-satisfaction; it aims at man's true happiness or 'blessedness'. His psychology is embedded in his philosophy. He reminds us that our happiness and unhappiness – with the resultant turbulence of our emotions – depend mainly on *what* we desire, on the *quality* of the objects we are attached to, on the kinds of goals we aspire to. Our disappointments, pains and fears are usually the consequence 'of the love of those things which are perishable'. His metaphysical search led him to the transcendental, beyond the evanescent and ephemeral, as he wanted 'to inquire whether there might be anything truly good and able to communicate its goodness.'[15]

Not that Spinoza counsels asceticism or a withdrawal from life. On the contrary, he vigorously advocates the enjoyment of life in all its aspects. For joy or pleasure 'is man's transition from a lower to a higher state of perfection' (III, 2) and this means, in Spinoza's sense, a heightened awareness of being alive, an increased vitality, an enhancement of the joy of existence. This brief definition of pleasure is a veritable 'Ode to Joy'. Indeed (IV, 45),

> to make use of things and to delight in them as much as possible (not indeed to satiety, for that is not to take delight) is the part of a wise man. It is, I say, the part of a wise man to feed himself with moderate pleasant food and drink, and to take pleasure with perfumes, with the beauty of growing plants, dress, music, sports and theatres, and other things of this kind which man may use without any hurt to his fellows. . . . This manner of living agrees best with our principles and the general manner of life. . . . and [is] in all ways to be commended.

But, as indicated before, something else is needed in addition truly to fulfil our human existence. Man senses within him, clearly or dimly, a profound spiritual need. Basically because of his realization of the transience and evanescence of his life and of all that he beholds about him, he faces the urgent desire of finding some meaning in his own existence, as well as in his relationship to the mystery of the universe about him. This is the 'existential question' that has troubled man in all ages. This is the ever-present spiritual malaise of man, possibly, as was remarked before, more evident in this age because of modern man's loss of faith in religious redemption and his disillusionment with science. Spinoza's philosophy constitutes a positive answer to this existential and spiritual quest. The whole purpose of the *Ethics* is to lead man psychologically to a greater understanding of his human nature, and philosophically to a realization of his true, spiritual self by means of a greater awareness of his basic identity and union with the infinite cosmos, the Ultimate Reality, the 'Being consisting of infinite attributes'.

How to achieve inner peace and harmony and true contentment is the start-ing point of his inquiry – as related in his *Correction of the Understanding*, in the moving report of his personal quest – to which the answer is the grand mystical finale of his *Amor Dei Intellectualis* with which the *Ethics* ends. He shows man the way out of alienation, despair, loneliness and the fear of death by showing him his veritable Oneness and sameness with all that exists. Reason, furthermore, and true self-preservation counsel a positive, joyful affirmation of life in the present. 'A wise man thinks of nothing less than of death, and his wisdom is a meditation not of death but of life' (IV, 67). Spinoza's rational and philosophical insights brought profound satisfaction to many illustrious minds and enlightened spirits of the last three centuries. They ought to speak perhaps even more persuasively today, to this modern age, in search of its soul.

NOTES

1 See among others:
B. Alexander, 'Spinoza und die Psychoanalyse' in *Chronicon Spinozanum*, vol. 5, 1928.
W. Bernard, 'Freud and Spinoza' in *Psychiatry*, May 1946, vol. 9, no. 2.
L. Bickel, 'Ueber Beziehungen zwischen Spinoza und der Psychoanalyse' in *Zentralblatt für Psychologie und ihre Grenzgebiete*, April 1931.
See also Freud's letter to Hessing in *Spinoza-Festschrift*, M. Nijhoff, den Haag, 1962, and a recently (1974) discovered letter of Freud to L. Bickel.
2 W. Bernard, 'Spinoza's influence on the rise of scientific psychology – a neglected chapter in the history of psychology' in *Journal of the History of the Behavioral Sciences*, vol. VIII, no. 2, April 1972.
3 Abraham H. Maslow, *Religions, Values and Peak-Experiences* (Viking Press, New York, 1970), p. 82.
4 Ernest Jones, *Treatment of the Neuroses: Psychotherapy from Rest Cure to Psychoanalysis*, Schocken Books, New York, 1963, p. xiv (Bailliere, Tindall & Cox, 1920).
5 Philip Rieff, *The Triumph of the Therapeutic Use of Faith After Freud* (Harper & Row, New York, 1966).
6 Richard D. Chessick, *Why Psychotherapists Fail* (Science House, New York, 1971), p. 53.
7 Ernst Altkirch, *Maledictus und Benedictus* (Felix Meiner Verlag, Leipzig, 1924).
8 Benedictus Spinoza, *Ethics, Proved in Geometrical Order*, translated by A. Boyle (Dent, London, 1910) (Dutton, New York).
9 *Abstracts of the Standard Edition of the Complete Psychological Works of Sigmund Freud*, ed. C. L. Rothgeb (International Universities Press, New York, 1973), p. 198.
10 Constantin Brunner, *Science, Spirit, Superstition – A New Inquiry into Human Thought*, translated by A. Suhl, ed. W. Bernard (Allen & Unwin, London) (University of Toronto Press, Toronto, 1968).

79

11 Erich Fromm, *The Crisis of Psychoanalysis* (Holt, Rhinehart & Winston, New York, 1970), p. 36.
12 Stuart Hampshire, *Spinoza* (Penguin Books, Harmondsworth, 1951), p. 135.
13 Freud, 1973, *op. cit.*, p. 339.
14 Jones, *op cit.*, p. 56.
15 Spinoza, *op. cit.*, p. 227.

2 On relationships between psychoanalysis and a dynamic psychology[1]

Lothar Bickel, Toronto
translated by Walter Bernard

When Freud entered upon the psychoanalytic road he saw among the then prevailing systems of psychology none by which his work could have been truly furthered and no particular philosophy which could have served him as a point of departure. In accordance with his basic position which can be designated as empirical-experimental, he was even averse to any connection with systems of thought founded on theoretical speculation, and therefore consciously avoided them. At any rate, at the beginning, such a connection would not even have been possible since he saw in the direction he took merely a new *method* of research and by no means a new attempt to master the problem of the mind. Also he could not anticipate at that time that his seemingly so modest method of investigation would lead to fundamental innovations for all psychology. In his *Vorlesungen zur Einführung in die Psychoanalyse* (3rd edn, p. 410) he could still maintain of psychoanalysis that 'as a science it is characterized not by the subject matter treated but by the technique with which it works'. However, apart from the ever stronger thrust towards a *system of psychology* by the actual achievements of psychoanalysis one can oppose to the above another statement of Freud which makes it apparent that he had in the meantime become fully aware of the significance of psychoanalytic research for the entire field of psychology: 'We are aiming for a dynamic conception of the mental phenomena' (*ibid.*, p. 58). This is saying what we should also like to express here, that psychoanalysis has now entered a stage where it is compelled to take a position regarding the basic philosophical problems of psychology. This position will by no means be completely negative.

There is a psychology – as good as unknown to the wider public – the laws of which can be seen as highly compatible with the main results of psycho-analysis. The person who knows the psychology of our contemporary thinker Constantin Brunner will become more and more aware in his study of psycho-analysis how readily its main proposition can be co-ordinated with the principles of the Brunnerian psychology, and how frequently indeed they offer a felicitous, empirical confirmation of what Brunner had demonstrated. But one is also reminded of Spinoza in reading Freud and is amazed that in view of the rather close affinity of the train of ideas one is never expressly referred to the philosopher.[2] As regards Spinoza one must admit at the outset that the strictly mathematical form of the structure of his thought has until recently made it difficult, nay impossible, for his system to be extensively researched for psychology so that – to give an example – even in our times Dessoir could evaluate Spinoza's significance for psychology as being rather meagre, although there is no lack of men of science whose connection with Spinoza was a most intimate one – let us name here only the physiologist Johannes Müller. But it was through the life work of Brunner that Spinoza has been liberated from his over-concise structure; only by the fact that Brunner took a hold of this thinker in a most original way has the seemingly aphoristic and rigid in Spinoza's method of teaching been loosened and set free, have his ideas gotten into full swing, and – *corpora non agunt, nisi soluta*. . . .

I do not intend at all to deprecate the originality of psychoanalysis by disclosing certain connections between it and former thinkers. It would indeed indicate a failure to recognize the origin and achievement of psychoanalysis if, in pointing out similar, or in principle identical, reflections elsewhere one intended to take away the slightest measure of its merit. Quite the contrary. Let it be emphasized that Freud had followed his own, the empirical, road and had made headway; but it is noteworthy that he had found and substantiated by experience nothing more than what other thinkers, removed from him in space and time, had already established in their creative speculations. What these had seen deductively as a logical, philosophical demand, what the scaffolding of their thought-structures had required as a necessary plank, that was found by Freud inductively, by following only his own brilliant research instinct, and as if guided almost by no principle, but this is by no means really so.[3] According to his own, oft-repeated, words he *did* proceed from a very general idea. Indeed it was an abstract, philosophical conviction which gave him the impetus and illumined for him the dark pits of consciousness: viz., the idea of *psychic determinism*.

After Janet had found that repressed experiences could be raised by hypnosis into the clear light of consciousness Freud was looking for a method to accomplish the same thing also in the waking state. He found psychoanalysis; more correctly, he simply put his trust upon this as yet unknown technique in order to discover with its help the long lost land of the psyche. Analysis makes use of freely occurring thought. The very first thing that comes to the mind of the analysand, regardless of its being banal, trivial, irrelevant or improper, is considered at once as a lead. 'Random' association, as it arises effortlessly out of the free play of representations and memories with the greatest possible avoidance of any logical judgment or ethical evaluation, this was the boat for carrying analysis across the stream of forgetting. How paradoxical must this have appeared to conventional psychology! To search for the laws of the mind with the help of the mentally arbitrary and insignificant? What psychoanalysis was basing itself upon, in following this course, was precisely the conviction that there is nothing arbitrary in consciousness, that it does not depend upon an imaginary freedom of the mind whether this or that presentation, the one or the other memory datum, is being taken up but that all this is strictly and lawfully determined. This lawfulness which governs the nature of external phenomena without a gap, which knows nothing arbitrary or insignificant (no miracles in physics, no 'dirt' in chemistry) – should this closed determinism be brought to a halt before the phenomena of the psyche? The natural sciences grew and were strengthened by the emerging insight that nothing in the external world was a matter of course and unworthy of research and that there are no freely acting forces in it. Freud approached the phenomena of the psyche with the same conviction, with 'the respect due to a psychic fact' and by surrendering 'the illusion of psychic freedom' (*ibid.*, p. 37). Experience proved him right, and each further penetration into the conscious and the unconscious succeeded only because of this trust in the determinism of the psychic event. The discoveries, in turn, strengthened this idea by adducing for it the empirical proofs and illustrations.

To be sure, the more research loses itself in the fullness of the details the more obscure its connection with the principle found at the starting point. The abundance and complexity of the material demand the positing of new, secondary propositions which, because of the growth of the investigated field, soon become main propositions; but always one can demonstrate, even though in round-about ways, this dependence of Freudian psychoanalysis on the fundamental proposition of psychic determinism. This can naturally be done most convincingly in the explanation of mental slips, where Freud himself repeatedly refers to this deterministic connection. They are not accidental and must not be ignored; they have their significance and their definite causes in the person who makes a slip of the tongue, slip of the pen, forgets, and so on, and their lawfulness is in most cases rather easy to discover.

The dream, too, has a definite meaning. Here one should first of all keep in mind that even in Freud's interpretation of dreams everything points ultimately to the strictest determinism. The manifest dream is the combined result of certain daytime events connected with infantile experiences under the influence of dream censorship by means of the complicated mechanisms of condensation, displacement, emphasis and so on. A similar mechanism is also at work in the aetiology of a neurosis. If to a certain constitutional disposition is joined a childhood experience which for certain reasons remains fixated, then, in future years, at the denial of natural satisfaction there ensues the attempt to go back to the childhood fixation. In the case of failure of such an attempt at substitute satisfaction there arises a neurotic symptom by the processes of displacement and condensation. From the first developmental arrest to the final anchoring of the neurosis everything shows itself to be lawfully determined, in obedience and in service to the comprehensive principle of pleasure and pleasure fulfilment. *Avoidance of displeasure, wish fulfilment, satisfaction of pleasure* – all three are in the last analysis the one moving and regulating psychic motor: pleasure. But why only pleasure, why only wish? Freud asked this question and confessed that he did not know the answer. Philosophy, however, which as we shall soon see had stated in principle the very same thing that psychoanalysis had uncovered, will not fail in giving us the answers to these questions and will thus bring the proper clarity to the entire subject.

Spinoza prefaces the third part of his *Ethics* with the following noteworthy remarks (*Ethics* 3, Preface):[4]

> Most who have written on the emotions, the manner of human life,
> seem to have dealt not with natural things . . . but with things which are
> outside the sphere of nature. . . . They attribute the cause of human
> weakness and inconstancy not to the ordinary power of nature. [But] the
> laws and rules of nature according to which all things are made and
> changed from one form to another, are everywhere and always the same.
> [Consequently one ought to] treat of the nature and force of the
> emotions as if [one] were dealing with lines, planes and bodies.

And Spinoza kept what he had promised. 'The idea which constitutes the formal being of the human mind is not simple, but composed of many ideas' (*Ethics* 2, XV). The illusion of freedom of will and thought is immanent in human nature and deeply embedded in it; it can always be traced back to lack of self-analysis. 'Men think themselves free on account of this alone, that they are conscious of their actions and ignorant of the causes of them' (*Ethics* 3, II, Note). 'This therefore is their idea of liberty, that they should know no cause of their actions' (*Ethics* 2, XXXV, Note). 'The mind has no knowledge of itself in so far as it perceives the ideas of the modifications of the body' (*Ethics* 2, XXIII). These, however, are 'like consequences without premises' (*Ethics* 2, XXVIII, Note). Reason, however, which is scientific thought, must not regard 'things as contingent but necessary' (*Ethics* 2, XLIV). And it soon finds that 'there is in mind no absolute or free will, but the mind is determined for willing this or that by a cause which is determined in its turn by another cause, and this one again by another, and so on to infinity. . . . In the same manner it may be shown that there cannot be found in the mind an absolute faculty of understanding, desiring, loving, etc.' (*Ethics* 2, XLVIII and Note). Spinoza hence denies 'that we have free power to suspend judgement . . . a suspension of judgment is in truth a *perception* and not free will' (*Ethics* 2, XLIX, Note). Also, 'it is not within the free power of the mind to remember or forget anything. . . . Those, therefore, who believe that they speak, are silent, or do anything from the free decision of the mind, dream with their eyes open' (*Ethics* 3, II, Note). 'The decisions of the mind are nothing save their desires, which are accordingly various according to various dispositions' (*ibid*.). Since even this single motive for speaking, thinking, and acting is unconscious in men, philosophical analysis searches and finds, in a way quite different from Freudian analysis, that the ultimate basis of every psychic phenomenon is pleasure which is at the same time also the fuel, lever and driving gear for the mental apparatus as a whole, because 'pleasure and pain . . . are the nature of every one' (*Ethics* 3, LVII).

But why pleasure and nothing else? To explain this, Spinoza has recourse to the fundamental scientific basis of our mental processes. 'Everything . . . endeavors to persist in its own being' (*Ethics* 3, VI). This endeavour 'is nothing else than the actual essence of that thing' (*Ethics* 3, VII). Hence 'the mind, as much as it can, endeavours to imagine those things which increase or help its power of acting' (*Ethics* 3, XII), since 'mind and body are one and the same individual, which is conceived now under the attribute of thought and now under the attribute of extension' (*Ethics* 2, XXI, Note). But what increases the power of activity of the body, what preserves it in its being, fulfils and enhances its being? Pleasure! Hence pleasure is defined by Spinoza as 'man's transition from a lower to a higher state of perfection' (*Ethics* 3, Definition of the Emotions). 'Hence it follows that the mind is averse to imagining those things which diminish or hinder its power and that of the body' (*Ethics* 3, XIII, Coroll.). All that, however, by which its power is hindered and effects its transition to a lower perfection causes displeasure, pain. And thus we see how Spinoza formulates and establishes the law of avoidance of pain.

But with 'avoidance of pain' the pleasure-pain principle of the psyche has not yet been fully grasped. The mind aspires not only after ideas of pleasure and avoidance of pain, but whenever it encounters pain it endeavours to push it aside, to ignore it as much as possible, and to seize upon an idea of pleasure in order to take refuge behind it and protect itself by it. And is not the essential meaning of the phenomenon of regression – in the case of thwarted libido unfoldment – expressed in the following sentence? 'When the mind imagines things which diminish or hinder the power of acting of the body, it endeavors as much as it can to remember things which will cut off their existence' (*Ethics* 3, XIII). Always, at all costs, 'to cut off their existence', to remove the idea of pain. Hence there are available definite paths or at least open ways to which the psyche, hungering for pleasure, can escape. With Freud, regression leads inevitably to previous experiences of pleasure, to the fixations of the past inner life. Similarly with Spinoza: 'If the mind were once affected at the same time by two emotions, when afterwards it is affected by one of them it will also be affected by the other' (*Ethics* 3, XIV). If therefore, to give an example, we experienced the libido in early childhood attached to a specific organ pleasure, then, at a later appearing of normal erotic feeling, the memory of that organ pleasure will always resonate with it in variable strength. If, however, the libido is denied expression with the normal object then 'the mind will endeavour, *as much as it can*, to remember those things which will cut off the existence of those others' that were denied to it. In other words, it will try, with all the available power, to focus on the previous organ pleasure to which the libido had been attached – for clearly pleasure is not tied exclusively to a definite object. 'Anything can accidentally be the cause of pleasure . . .' (*Ethics* 3, XV). And it seems as if Spinoza, while writing this, had actually thought – as we were just thinking – of the perversities, of the anomalous likes and dislikes, since he added: 'Hence we understand how it comes to pass that we love or hate certain things without having any known cause for it' (*Ethics* 3, XV, Note). For if our thinking or wanting this or that has no cause that is known or conscious to us, it does not mean that no ground for it is to be found in our psyche. The psyche is more extensive than what is known to it; it encompasses more than the merely conscious. And herewith we reach the third proposition of psychoanalysis: Psychoanalysis 'accomplishes nothing other than the disclosure of the unconscious in our psychic life' (Freud, op. cit., p. 410).

And now let us also hear Spinoza on psychoanalytic therapy. 'The force of any passion or emotion can so surpass the rest of the actions or the power of a man that the emotion adheres obstinately to him' (*Ethics* 4, VI). The emotion or the passion! The transition from the normal to the pathological is a fluid one. The same paths of association and laws of the mind which serve to avoid pain and to achieve pleasure are also at work in the formation of psychic illness. An affect is a 'confused idea' (*Ethics* 3, Definition of the Emotions). That means, it is a psychic event of which man is conscious only to a limited degree and which discloses manifest transitions to psychic anomalies. Thus Spinoza does not hesitate to declare a certain type of passionate love a kind of insanity (*Ethics* 4, XIX). Similarly, he considers arrogance 'a kind of madness wherein a man dreams with his eyes open . . . as long as he cannot imagine those things which cut off the existence of his fictions' (*Ethics* 3 XXVI, Note). We are impressed by the close relationship that Spinoza sees between affect and illusion and of the latter, in turn, to dreams and daydreams. However, the essential factor common to all three is the lack of knowledge, as the reason for *their* being in consciousness is that other things pertaining to them remained unconscious. With Spinoza, there is a straight line leading from the explanation of error to that of mental illness. 'The imaginations of the mind, regarded in themselves, contain no error, or the mind does not err from that which it imagines, but only in so far as it is considered as wanting the idea which cuts off the existence of those things which it imagines as present to itself' (*Ethics* 2, XVII, Note); and 'falsity consists in privation of knowledge which is involved by inadequate or mutilated or confused ideas' (*Ethics* 2, XXXV).

The essential fact in error, then – which is that which causes and maintains it – is not the idea entertained, not its conscious, manifest content, but the circumstance that something is hidden from the erring person, of which he is not conscious. And the same is true of the affect which 'obstinately adheres' to man in his mental suffering. It is not its manifestations and symptoms which constitute its true illness, but the fact that certain ideas and feelings are missing which would exclude the existence of those symptoms and would not even allow them to exist at all, namely, the unknown and the unconscious mental contents. And with the affects, emotions, and mental suffering the unconscious, latent content is very likely a libidinal one in view of the fact that appetite or desire is the very essence of man and 'whether a man be conscious of his appetite or whether he be not, his appetite remains the same notwithstanding' (*Ethics* 3, Definition of the Emotions).

If the essence of error and of illusion consists in this alone that certain things which make their existence impossible do not come to consciousness, then 'this remedy for emotions, which consists in a true knowledge of them, is excelled by nothing in our power we can think of' (*Ethics* 5, IV), and 'an emotion which is a passion ceases to be a passion as soon as we form a clear and distinct idea of it' (*Ethics* 5, III). Already by the fact that we 'remove the disturbance of the mind or the emotion from the thought of an external cause and unite it to other thoughts... the waverings of the mind... will be destroyed' (*Ethics* 5, II). 'To other thoughts' means to those hitherto unconscious motives that have been brought up. Thus 'love and hatred, e.g. towards Peter, are destroyed, if the pain which the latter involves and the pleasure which the former involves, are connected with the idea of another thing as a cause' (*Ethics* 3, XLVIII). The primary factor here is the insight into the inevitable formation of our emotions, into the lawful determinism of our feelings. 'In so far as the mind understands all things as necessary it has more power over the emotions or is less passive to them' (*Ethics* 5, VI). The knowledge of the necessity of psychic events allows at the same time some insight into their complexity and their extremely entangled connections – which insight, too, has a dissolving and therapeutic effect upon the emotions. 'An emotion which has reference to many different causes which the mind regards at the same time as the emotion itself is less harmful and we are less passive to it...' (*Ethics* 5, IX). How salutary is already the knowledge of the part which public opinion and education play in the formation of certain emotions. For 'that pain should follow all those actions which according to custom are called wicked, and those which are called right should be followed by pleasure... this most certainly depends upon education' (*Ethics* 3, Definition of the Emotions XXVII). Spinoza was not unaware of the fact that in the depth of every psyche dark, asocial drives were nesting which unfortunately are not removed by the common education. 'It is therefore apparent that men have a natural proclivity to hatred and envy, which, moreover, is aided by their education' (*Ethics* 3, LV, Note). It is especially the unclear and extravagantly formed concepts of good and bad, and often enough their false application, which cause so many confusions and contortions in the mind. The lack of self-knowledge and self-analysis leads of necessity to a failure of recognition of the importance of pleasure for the normal functioning of consciousness. Its right is thereby neglected and often sacrificed to unnatural concepts. To counter this, reason should insist, both with the healthy and sick, upon the clarification and soundness of the concepts of good and evil. 'Those things which bring pleasure are good', says Spinoza (*Ethics* 4, XXX). 'Nor can pleasure ever be evil which is moderated by a true understanding of our advantage' (*Ethics* 4, XXXI), and 'reason postulates nothing against nature' (*Ethics* 4, XVIII, Note). Against our affects there is hence no better therapy than self-study and self-knowledge. With their help we liberate ourselves from the overpowering force of certain social value judgements which can be traced back only to a misreading of human nature.

Insight, by itself, however, will not bring this about. Where, as in the case of a deep-seated emotion or a neurosis, there is not only a logical impasse and confinement of thought but also an unhealthy distribution of the dynamics of feelings – a damming up and blocking on the one side and displacement and escape on the other – then reason and convincement must be affectively laden, and strongly accentuated with pleasure, if they are to have a salutary effect. 'A true knowledge of good and evil cannot restrain any emotion in so far as the knowledge is true, but only in so far as it is considered as an emotion' (*Ethics* 4, XIV). The same is known to Freud, and hence he does not start with the positive education of the patient until he has succeeded by means of an ever more deeply penetrating analysis to bring the entire repressed material to the fore, together with the emotion which then invested the experience. He then attaches the positive enlightenment to this emotion which he subsequently tries to guide along the road of sublimation. This positive enlightenment is for Freud as well as for Spinoza a means for guidance to the greatest possible utilization of what in one's life has hitherto been repressed, and to the greatest possible personal and social adjustment. Hence, Spinoza gives the excellent advice, 'that we must always pay attention in the ordering of our thoughts and images to those things which are good in each thing, so that we may be determined always for action by an emotion of pleasure' (*Ethics* 5, X, Note).

The reason that Spinoza's psychology is important for psychoanalysis – and is, indeed, in these points rather close to it – is that it regards mental phenomena as lawfully determined and the processes of imagining and remembering as anything but mere copying and registering, but rather as a creative struggle for life and self-preservation. Thought is not being determined by a formal 'free personality' but receives direction and structure from its innermost pith and marrow: the uninhibited and inhibited desire to gain pleasure, to avoid displeasure. Whatever is false, perverse and morbid in judgment and behaviour cannot be explained by itself, nor can it be removed by the working-through of its conscious content, but rather by bringing up and raising into consciousness the relevant unknown content, and by ordering and connecting it with natural and wholesome thought. Freud's endeavours 'for a dynamic conception of psychic phenomena' – who among the known philosophers approaches it to such an extent as does Spinoza, whose psychology must be designated, in spite of Spengler, as dynamic in the most perfect sense of the word?

Translator's Note: These are excerpts from Bickel's article in which he discusses the kinship of psychoanalysis with the psychological ideas of both Spinoza and the contemporary philosopher Constantin Brunner. He had both in mind when he spoke of a 'dynamic psychology', as in the title. Brunner's affinity to Spinoza as regards fundamental philosophical and psychological conceptions is of course well known to anyone acquainted with both thinkers. Moreover, to show that Brunner by his own original work has contributed significantly to a deeper understanding of Spinoza would be a rewarding task, but one that cannot be undertaken here. Here, within our limited aim and the space available our restrictions are even greater. We must refer to the specific relationship between Freud and Spinoza, and leave the rest of the article, dealing with the relationship of Freud to Brunner, for another occasion.   Walter Bernard.

Editor's Note: In order to make my own paper: 'Freud's Relation with Spinoza' clearer to the interested reader in both camps, Freudian and Spinozist alike, I had to bring here in a Speculum 'Spinozanum' only an excerpt from Bickel's article as far as Freud's relationship with Spinoza is concerned.   Siegfried Hessing.

NOTES

1 Appeared originally in the *Zentralblatt für Psychotherapie und ihre Grenzgebiete*, vol. IV, no. 4. Reprinted in Dr Bickel's book, *Probleme und Ziele des Denkens*, Humanitas Verlag, Zürich, 1939.
2 'Concerning Spinoza's study of the drives, concerning his theory of the affects and emotions, psychoanalysis has not a word to say', remarks B. Alexander in 'Spinoza und die Psychoanalyse', *Almanach*, 1928.
3 According to Liebig, scientific research must 'in all cases of necessity be preceded by the idea, if it is to have any significance'.
4 All quotations are taken from the Everyman's Library edition of the *Ethics* (No. 481), translated by A. Boyle, and published by Dent, London, and Dutton, New York (1910), 1950.

3 Necessity and freedom – reflections on texts by Spinoza

Emilia Giancotti Boscherini, Rome

According to Spinoza, reality marked by rigid determinism seems to exclude every form of freedom. The fifth and final part of his *Ethics*, nevertheless, theorizes human freedom, and the *Tractatus theologico-politicus* sets out clearly to show the function of freedom of thought and speech in a rationally organized civil society.

Is determinism, of which man's ontological condition is a moment, compatible with the acquisition and use of individual freedom? Is there a theoretical error in Spinoza's affirmative answer to this problem, which was not only a personal one but one of his time, especially in its religious sense? Or is it rather, the transcription in terms of knowledge, the 'reflection', of those features characterizing the human condition stretched, in the overall context of the universal order of reality, between determination within the material system of relationship of which it is a part, and a willed impulse to modify the system itself? To answer this question, which is not simply a matter of a critical interpretation of Spinozan philosophy but which poses a problem regarding the theory and practice of it still open to reflection today, it may be useful to re-examine some theoretical elements of Spinozism.

Definition VII of the first part of the *Ethics* affirms that a free thing is understood to be 'quae ex sola suae naturae necessitate existit, et a se sola ad agendum determinatur', while a necessary, or better compelled (*coacta*) thing is 'quae ab alio determinatur ad existendum, et operandum certa, ac determinata ratione'.[1] And because 'omnia, quae sunt, vel in se, vel in alio sunt' (axiom I), that is to say, 'extra intellectum nihil datur praeter substantias, earumque affectiones' (dem. prop. IV), or better 'in Nature there exists only one unique substance' (schol. prop. X) and its affections (coroll. I and II, prop. XIV and coroll. prop. XXV), it follows that only substance is free, while each of the modes of the infinitely many by which it is expressed is determined by something else in its existence and action, i.e. it is 'compelled'. Substance, either God or Nature, is free for at least two reasons: because it is '*causa sui*' in the positive sense of the idea, producing itself and everything which exists 'by essence' (schol. prop. XXV); and because identifying itself with the totality of reality, nothing exists outside itself which can condition it. But this freedom – and with this, one touches the crux of the problem – has nothing in common with 'free will', that is, with the possibility of doing or not doing a thing, of choosing the best amongst various possible ways or of modifying the course of things. This type of freedom belongs to the God of the scholastic[2] and (with reservations) Cartesian[3] tradition but not to the God of Spinoza whose essence includes neither will nor intellect (prop. XXXI and coroll. I and II, prop. XXXII), but from which 'infinita infinitis modis (hoc est, omnia, quae sub intellectum infinitum cadere possunt) sequi debent' (prop. XVI). The order by which individual things derive from substance, unique, infinite and indivisible, is that of causal determination, by which every finite thing can neither exist nor act unless it has been determined to exist and act by another finite thing which assumes a causal role with respect to the first, while it is itself effected by the causal action of another finite thing (prop. XXVIII). Of this series of causes and effects the first (coroll. III, prop. XVI) and immanent (prop. XVIII) cause – besides being efficient, '*per se*' (coroll. I and II, prop. XVI) and free (coroll. II, prop. XVII) – is God or infinite substance which has produced and continues to produce things in a way and in a certain order which could not be different as it is the mode and order resulting from its essence. Finite things (and amongst these man: *Ethica*, II, coroll. prop. X) are therefore produced necessarily and there exists nothing in nature which is contingent (prop. XXIX). The concept of contingency is only the indication of a limit to our knowledge (*Ethica*, I, schol. I, prop. XXXIII) and, if removed, things appear as they are: impossible because they are contradictory in their essence or necessary because they are determined to exist.

To explain fully the significance of the concepts referred to so far it is useful to emphasize the importance of the transformation that Spinoza accomplishes in his concept of God, whose name is preserved (whether out of caution, or to pay homage to a dominating tradition, or because of consciousness not yet completely acquired), but which in the end serves only to mask a content which is strongly innovative in character. This God is neither person, subject nor spirit (Hegel used this as the mainspring of his attack against Spinoza); it is substance made up of infinitely many attributes (prop. XI), each of which expresses itself in infinitely many finite modes according to a necessary order. Which means – abandoning theological terminology – that the infinite universe is qualitatively differentiated but is regulated as a whole solely by necessary, objective and eternal laws which refer back to the general law of causal determination; laws which the human intellect can gradually come to understand but is not the author of,[4] being, on the contrary, subject to them. Finite things, all those individuals of our experience and indeed of every possible experience, are equally as much partial aspects of that whole which is the universe in its totality. They are only real in the context of a network of relationships which constitute the universe, while, on the other hand, the universe is not something 'beyond' the infinite multiplicity of finite things (past, present and future).

If this interpretation is correct then surely it can only mean that to speak of substance as 'free cause' means to translate into a positive sense the negation of the existence of a transcendent being, which is the origin and foundation of the world and universe of which we are a part and product and which constitutes an inexhaustible object (because it is infinite) to our knowledge and field of intervention of our action. Substance is free cause because it is itself the origin and cause of its own being which is the whole of Being in its infinite aspects; it is regulated, therefore, by immanent, objective and necessary laws which are not the product of a divine, superhuman mind but are functional laws which derive from its own nature or essence.

> Alii putant, Deum esse causam liberam, propterea quod potest, ut putant, efficere, ut ea, quae ex ejus natura sequi diximus, hoc est, quae in ejus potestate sunt, non fiant, sive ut ab ipso non producantur. Sed hoc idem est, ac si dicerent, quod Deus potest efficere, ut ex natura trianguli non sequatur, ejus tres angulos aequales esse duobus rectis; sive ut ex data causa non sequatur effectus, quod est absurdum (schol. prop. XVII).

The objectivity of natural laws, their validity independent of any subject or creative mind and their analogy with mathematical principles are confirmed here (and elsewhere) with absolute clarity. The common concept of divine freedom constitutes an obstacle to the knowledge of these laws, which, given the identification of God with Nature (see schol. prop. XXIX), are the same laws of divine nature:

> non dubito, quin multi hanc sententiam, ut absurdam, explodant, nec animum ad eandem perpendendam instituere velint; idque nulla alia de causa, quam quia Deo aliam libertatem assueti sunt tribuere, longe diversam ab illa, quae a nobis tradita est; videlicet, absolutam voluntatem. Verum neque etiam dubito, si rem meditari vellent, nostrarumque demonstrationum seriem recte secum perpendere, quin tandem talem libertatem, qualem jam Deo tribuunt, non tantum, ut nugatoriam, sed, ut magnum scientiae obstaculum, plane rejiciant (schol. II, prop. XXXIII).

The scientist knows that true science proceeds from cause to effects (see *Tractatus de intellectus emendatione*, vol. II, p. 32); he investigates, therefore, and studies the cause of things rejecting 'asylum ignorantiae', the resort to divine will as an explanatory principle for natural phenomena (*Ethica*, I, Appendix, p. 81) and is not afraid of being considered 'heretic and ungodly'

by those whom 'vulgus, tamquam naturae, Deorumque interpretes, adorat' (*ibid.*). He has as the aim of his research the knowledge of those '*elementa totius Naturae*' and of the '*ordo Naturae*' (*Tractatus de intellectus emendatione*, p. 28), knows that for us it is necessary

ut semper a rebus Physicis sive ab entibus realibus omnes nostras ideas deducamus, progrediendo, quoad ejus fieri potest, secundum seriem causarum ab uno enti reali ad aliud ens reale, et ita quidem ut ad abstracta, et universalia non transeamus, sive ut ab iis aliquid reale non concludimus, sive ut ea ab aliquo reali non concludantur [and that the intimate essence of things] tantum est petenda a fixis, atque aeternis rebus, et simul a legibus in iis rebus, tanquam in suis veris codicibus, inscriptis, secundum quas omnia singularia, et fiunt, et ordinantur; imo haec mutabilia singularia adeo intime, atque essentialiter (ut sic dicam) ab iis fixis pendent, ut sine iis nec esse, nec concipi possint (*ibid.*, pp. 36–7).

If, then, by freedom we mean the possibility of producing things in one way or another and of establishing certain truths rather than others, which, in the final analysis, is also characteristic of the God of Descartes, or of choosing between different possible worlds in view of an end, which is that of the Leibniz God, then the Spinozan God is *not free*, because things and their corresponding truths are produced by His power according to an unchangeable order which is an essential part of His essence. 'Vides igitur me libertatem non in libero decreto; sed in libera necessitate ponere' (*Epistola LVIII, Opera*, vol. IV, p. 265). It has already been said that the freedom of Spinoza's God is nothing else than His own power, whereby He is by essence His own cause and in one and the same act the cause of all things which exist according to that order and those objective and necessary laws (natural) which it is the scientists' task to investigate. If this is the freedom of the infinite being, what then is the nature and what are the limits of human freedom?

Having explained the principles of his doctrine of reality, Spinoza explicitly declares that man's conviction of being free lies on the one hand, in the knowledge of his own willed impulses and, on the other, in the ignorance of the causes which prompt him to will and to act (*Ethica*, I, Appendix, p. 78). Therefore the idea that men form of their own freedom on the basis of common experience is an illusion which a more careful study of the human condition cannot fail to destroy.

Before proceeding to clarify this concept, it is useful to remember the philosophical requirement from which Spinoza moves and which we find clearly enunciated at the beginning of *Tractatus de intellectus emendatione* (p. 5):

> Postquam me experientia docuit, omnia, quae in communi vita
> frequenter occurrunt, vana, et futilia esse: cum viderem omnia, a quibus,
> et quae timebam, nihil neque boni, neque mali in se habere, nisi
> quatenus ab iis animus movebatur, constitui tandem *inquirere an*
> *aliquid daretur, quod verum bonum, et sui communicabile esset*, et a quo
> solo, rejectis caeteris omnibus, animus afficeretur: imo an aliquid
> daretur, quo invento, et acquisito, continua, ac summa in aeternum
> fruerer laetitia.

Further on the 'true good' is distinguished from the 'highest good' as a means of achieving the latter, which is defined as the enjoyment, together with other men, of that certain stronger human nature which arises from the knowledge of the unifying relationship between the individual and Nature. The 'collective' possession of the highest good, or of this stronger human nature, and consequently, the construction of a society in which the means of acquiring it is offered to the maximum number of men possible, is the purpose of the philosopher (*ibid.*, pp. 8–9).

It is therefore a question of a highly ethical requirement and a practical purpose revealing a subjective attitude that is not fatalistic acceptance of what is given but rather constructive intervention. Knowledge of the structure of reality in its various relationships and man's position in it is a necessary premise for every kind of initiative and for the definition of every kind of programme. Nevertheless, without losing its fundamental character and inasmuch as its condition cannot be ignored, it becomes the instrument of rational human action and a means of acquiring that ethical conduct which is its premise and, at the same time, its consequence, The definition of freedom and the determination of its content therefore (*Ethica*, V), coherently follow an analysis of the constituent elements of reality and of their inter-relationships (*Ethica*, I); they follow a clarification of the essence of man as mode of this reality, unique and unitarian in its structure, and hence of his existential condition within the system of relationships of which this reality is comprised (*Ethica*, II). The theory of passion (*Ethica*, IV) is part of the clarification of human essence which precedes the indication of the two possible alternatives open to man, bearing in mind the reality described above: that of slavery or subjection to passion (*Ethica*, IV) and the way of freedom, or dominion through knowledge of them (*Ethica*, V).

There are two points clarified then:

(1) What is the essence of human freedom and what are its limits?
(2) Do the two ways, slavery and freedom, constitute a real alternative for the individual or is each of them, successively, in conformity with its own individual essence and within its own historic condition, the path which the individual cannot stray from, the designated road he must follow?

(1) The essence and limits of human freedom must be deduced from the definition of human essence. As is known, this is different from the essence of substance (*Ethica*, II, ax. 1 and prop. X) and is made '*a certis Dei attributorum modificationibus*' (coroll. prop. X), that is of modifications of extent and thought (coroll. prop. XIII). Human essence is, therefore, a mode or organic set of modes of substance; its condition, however, is defined by means of '*in alio esse*' and '*per aliud concipi*', that is to say by means of both ontological and logical-gnosiological dependence. Like every mode, man is not '*causa sui*' but is caused by substance, or God, which 'eo sensu, quo dicitur causa sui, etiam omnium rerum causa dicendus est' (*Ethica*, I, schol. prop. XXV). Its existence is 'determined' in conformity with an unchangeable order from which it cannot withdraw (*ibid.*, props XVI, XXVI–XXIX). A passage from *Epistola XLIII* affirms with peremptory clarity: 'statui omnia inevitabili necessitate ex Dei natura sequi' (*Opera*, vol. IV, p. 221).

What is human freedom then; what does it consist of; what are the limits beyond which it cannot extend? In my opinion, the content of props XXVI, XXVII, XXVIII and XXIX, where the theoretical principles of determinism are introduced, can be explained in the following way. A human being is generated by another human being who in turn was produced by a preceding act of generation and so on. He comes into the world, above all, at a moment not of his choosing because, in any case, he could not choose before he came into existence; he is endowed with a genetic heritage which, it has been scientifically proved, has an effect on his psychological and physical structure and therefore, on his future behaviour. He is conceived in an environment (the maternal womb) which is formed by a series of elements extraneous to him. He develops in this environment, gradually influenced by it and by the changes to which the environment itself is subject, all traceable to causes independent of him. Finally he is born and continues to develop within a group or family which belongs to a certain social class and therefore occupies a certain position within social relations of production. In keeping with his position, which he accepts as a fact, he is raised and receives a certain kind of education: he achieves satisfactory physical and intellectual development or fails to do so. Consequently, two levels of conditioning may be perceived: that of the world external to him (the network of causes and effects around him and into which he is placed) and that of his own psycho-physical structure (his essence, in as much as it is a mode determined by substance).[5]

It is only departing from these assumptions, therefore, i.e. from the principles of determinism, and having them clear in their validity and meaning, that one can begin to talk about freedom. Returning to Spinozan terminology: it is a question of understanding the significance to man, ontologically determined like every mode of substance, of the concept and practice of human freedom, the limits to which it is restricted and the way in which he can present himself as an 'agent' within the bound of his existential condition.

Spinoza answers this problem by identifying freedom with reason in the double sense of rational knowledge and action ruled by reason. In God, by nature of His own essence, freedom and necessity are immediately identified, whereas, in man – a modification of reality, i.e. a partial aspect of it – this identification occurs through scientific mediation. In fact, there is no question of the possibility of man's disrupting the system of necessity, but it is more a question of the way in which he can insert himself into the system, either as an 'agent' or 'patient', as *'ignarus'* or *'sapiens'*. That is to say, given that necessity regulates and governs every event in reality, there are two theoretical and practical attitudes possible with respect to it: that of the unenlightened man who acts in ignorance of causes, his own essence and the structure of reality; and that of the wise man who acts on the basis of knowledge of the concrete situation within which he moves, conscious of his role in a system of relationships which condition his action as they condition the action of every other individual. The first harbours the illusory conviction that he is 'choosing', that everything in the universe is regulated by an intelligent God who has the well-being of man in mind, and adapts his own behaviour according to ethical norms inspired by false concepts of good and evil (*Ethica*, I, Appendix); consequently, and in contradiction with his analysis of reality, he allows himself to be led by things and succumbs to the emotions caused by his relationships with other individuals. The second knows that his actions have a determined cause which deprives them of any kind of 'free' choice and he forces himself to identify it; that the universe is regulated by necessary laws which no phenomenon can avoid and which exclude 'final causes'; that he does not occupy a special position in this system if one excludes the faculty he has to understand its structure; and that the concepts of good and evil and other analogous ones are prejudices (*ibid.*) because perfection is identified with reality (*Ethica*, II, def. VI). Consequently, he controls his relationships with the world around him and does not allow himself to be carried away by emotions caused by them, conscious of the necessity which rules every human and worldly event.

According to Spinoza, freedom consists of this kind of knowledge which arises from reason, the content of which, therefore, is determined by analysis of the concept of *'ratio'* and its allied concepts.

Reason (the essence of which consists in *'clare et distincte intelligere'*: *Ethica*, III, prop. XXVI and dem.) is the second of three kinds of knowledge in which, according to Spinoza, human capacity for knowledge is outlined. Like the third kind *'scientia intuitiva'*, it is true knowledge and consists of the acquisition of 'common notions' and adequate ideas of the properties of things' (*Ethica*, II, schol. II, prop. XL). The 'common notions' are the foundations of our ratiocination (*ibid.* and dem. coroll. II, prop. XLIV) and of philosophy (*Tractatus theologico-politicus*, cap. XIV, *Opera*, vol. III, p. 179, 11.32–3). They are ideas 'quae illa explicant, quae omnibus communia sunt, quaeque nullius rei singularis essentiam explicant, (*Ethic*, II, dem. coroll. II, prop. XLIV). They are the true ideas, obviously, of that in which all bodies meet and have in common amongst themselves (coroll. prop. XXVIII) and of that[6] in which all minds meet and have in common amongst themselves. Above all, all bodies converge in that they implicate the concept of one and the same attribute (*extensio*) and in that they all move or remain still (II, dem. lem. II post prop. XIII);[7] minds – which are none other than an idea of the body (prop. XIII) – all meet too, in that they implicate the concept of one and the same attribute (*cogitatio*). Common notions are therefore those ideas which permit us to conceive bodies (and minds) as moments, finite expressions, partial but necessary aspects of the expression of the infinite reality of the attribute. While the first degree of knowledge (*opinio, imaginatio*) presents us with things dispersed and separate, reason unifies them and gets an element by which all are effects of the power of an attribute of substance. By means of common notions, reason identifies a fundamental point in the structure of reality, that is, it finds the connection between mode and substance at the attribute level, gets an idea of the mind and the body of which this mind is an idea, which unites them with all other minds and bodies and presents them as necessary moments in the expression of the reality of the attribute. That is, by means of common notions, reason grasps the attribute in all the multiplicity of its aspects, each of which does not appear in the concrete specific character of its particular being, but rather as part, homogeneous with other parts, of a qualitatively uniform whole. The common notion corresponds to the first degree of a theoretical unification of reality, in which the mind, at a mode level, grasps the two series, real and ideal, in their internal homogeneity, in their qualitative continuity. The final and highest degree of theoretical unification is represented by '*scientia intuitiva*', which apprehends reality in its heterogeneous qualitative unity from which it deduces the infinitely numerous aspects in their dependence on this unity. '*Scientia intuitiva*' – being different from reason, which is the realm of the common at both a theoretical (common notions) and practical level (the common good which it strives to achieve) – apprehends a thing in its particular and concrete essence but as a necessary product of the infinite causal activity of substance which is not conditioned in its totality.

Reason, therefore, apprehends the unity of reality at a first level and it, too, knows things in their necessity (*Ethica*, II, prop. XLIV) and since 'haec rerum necessitas est ipsa Dei aeternae naturae necessitas', it considers them in the light of some sort of eternity ('sub quadam aeternitatis specie': *ibid.*, coroll. II and dem.).

The practical attitude which arises from this form of understanding of reality is not a resigned and fatalistic acceptance of what is given. On the contrary, reason deduces a series of practical norms from it which have as their ground the identification of '*virtus*' and '*potentia*' and reveal themselves essential for social life. What in fact does reason demand? that

> unusquisque seipsum amet, suum utile, quod revera utile est, quaerat, et id omne, quod hominem ad majorem perfectionem revera ducit, appetat, et absolute, ut unusquisque suum esse, quantum in se est, conservare conetur (*Ethica*, IV, schol. prop. XVIII).

Analysis of this norm allows us to single out the prime motive for the action of the free man, i.e. of man guided by reason, in the preservation of his own being and in the search for his own benefit. In fact, the 'conatus suum esse conservandi, et in suo esse perseverandi' is the same actual essence of every single thing; it is the natural right of the individual. In the man guided by reason this effort, which is common to all things, including all men, be they '*ignari*' or '*sapientes*' (*Tractatus politicus*, cap. III, para. 18, *Opera*, vol. III, p. 291, 11.21–7), is realized in a way not antagonistic to others because since men live according to the laws of reason they continually and necessarily meet amongst themselves (*Ethica*, IV, schol. props XVIII and XXXV) and indeed there is nothing more useful to man than man guided by reason (coroll). In the man guided by reason, that is, this effort manifests itself in accordance with virtue, a concept which clarifies all its own positive significance by identifying itself with '*potentia*': virtue and power are the same thing and since individual '*potentia*' – a part of the infinite power of God or Nature[8] – explains itself through '*conatus*', this is the prime basis of virtue and the realization of its aim causes the happiness of the individual.[9]

'*Conatus*' is, therefore, the basis for the dictates of reason and the ground from which they draw motivation and scope. The search for good, understood as true good, is the only way which allows man to reach the goal that *conatus* strives for. '*Conatus*' is the point of encounter between nature and reason because it is in the full respect of the materiality and naturalness of *conatus* that reason proposes the search for a benefit which is common to all, that is, the abandoning of a particular benefit for a common one. The highest degree of freedom in man guided by reason is found in '*civitas*' (*Ethica*, IV, prop. LXXIII). *Conatus*, therefore, is the point at which ethics and politics meet: since the virtue of the individual identifies itself with the effort he makes to preserve himself, rational life can only explain itself within the context of a civil society and – as we shall see – within a particular organization of this society. The realization of *conatus*, therefore, becomes the way by which the individual pursuing his own good, pursues the common good at the same time and, realizing his own virtue, contributes to the creation of a social organism in which individual virtue is at the same time the condition and result of the virtues of all.

It must be added, that the realization of individual power, in its physical and intellectual components, implies the overcoming of those affects which are passion, that is, by which the individual pays for his condition as a 'part' and has the function of 'patient' with respect to the world around him. This overcoming is made possible, without contradiction, by the nature itself of affects which are none other than 'affections of the body and the idea of these affections' and they distinguish themselves as affects which are passions (those determined by feelings of the body of which we are not adequate cause) and affects which are actions (those determined by actions of the body of which we are adequate cause). It is in the complex structure of the human being (organic unity of the body = the sum of the modifications of extension, and mind = the sum of the ideas of these modifications) that the origin of the numerous emotional possibilities to which he is open lies: affection which can determine itself in a diminution of his power to act or, on the contrary, of an increase in it. In the first case, the individual is inadequate cause, i.e. partial cause, of the affections of his body, and the knowledge he has of his condition is confused because it, too, is inadequate: the affect which follows from this is passion; in the second instance, the individual is adequate cause, i.e. sufficient of the affection of his body, and the knowledge he has of his condition is clear because it is adequate: the affect which follows from this is action. The overcoming of the condition of passion, and therefore of slavery – a natural condition of man given his existence as 'part' – occurs in the transition from confused knowledge to clear and distinct knowledge.[10] Leaving aside here the problems connected with the mechanics of this transition – and they exist – we need only establish that the liberation from passions, and hence the transition from slavery to freedom, occurs through the transition from confused knowledge to clear knowledge which is, of course, reason, the essence of which consists in '*clare et distincte intelligere*', to achieve the transition. Furthermore, the continuity between passion and reason is found in cupidity, an affect which can be a passion but which can also arise from reason and hence be action (*Ethica*, III, dem. props. LVIII and LIX; IV, prop. LXI and dem.).

Defined thus and described in all the complexity of its aspects, freedom theorized by Spinoza reveals its exclusive nature which contrasts with the community dimension of the social programme outlined in *Tractatus de intellectus emendatione*. The use of rational knowledge and the practical behaviour which follows from it are not the heritage of the many but rather the privilege of the few. Instead, the purpose of the philosopher (or of the wise man, i.e. the man guided by reason) is the construction of a society which allows the majority to acquire rational behaviour; but the terrain from which he moves and upon which he evolves his hypothesis of building an alternative society is populated by a multitude which is '*vulgus*', capable of opinion but not of true knowledge, subject to passions and superstitions, with respect to whom he can only present himself as a minority.[11]

Is it possible to change this relationship? Is it possible to realize the programme described in rapid outlines in the *Tractatus de intellectus emenda-tione*? The answer to this question implies the answer to the second of the questions we have put to ourselves: do the two ways, that of slavery and that of freedom, form a real alternative for the individual or is each of them, in turn, the path from which the single individual cannot stray, the road set out for him to follow?

(2) On the basis of what we have clarified so far, it seems evident that in the essence of an individual nothing can produce itself which does not form part of that essence. Given the essence which unites it with all other finite beings, i.e. given its condition as a mode of the infinite reality of substance, as part of its whole and therefore itself, subject to the necessary process of causal determination which regulates the universe, and given a certain individual essence of its own, i.e. its psycho-physical structure which – as has been seen – is the result of a complex series of elements, each act of behaviour is never, in any case, something completely new with respect to its total essence, but is 'marked' by it. There can be no break, no interruption but only continuity between its being, its own individual history, the environment in which it moves and its actions. These actions are not arbitrary 'choices', separated from contextual reality but are always the necessary consequence of deter-mined material (objective conditions) and spiritual (subjective conditions) premises. The principle considered generally valid by Spinoza, '*a nihilo nihil fit*' is also valid here. It is only a question of becoming aware of it, of bringing that which is hidden behind the apparent spontaneity of the individual to a level of conscience in order to identify the causes and motivations of his action. It is this that escapes the '*ignarus*' but is known by the '*sapiens*'.

On the other hand, since individual essence is identified with individual power (or *conatus*, or *cupiditas*) which is part of the infinite power of Nature, i.e. moment expression of the dynamic universal principle, it follows that:

(a) it is not at all static or unchangeable but is reality in motion affected by the action of other individuals (men and things) with which it establishes relationships;

(b) for this reason, it does not identify itself stably with any one state or condition but with that state or condition which each time arises from the type of relationship established between the individual and others, so that one or other of the conditions prevails, thus characterizing it, but not signifying the definite exclusion of other conditions arising from other relationships.

This analysis stems from the Spinozan concept of the body as a compound individual living in a series of relationships with other bodies which it needs to preserve itself and by which it is continually almost regenerated (*Ethica*, II, post. I and IV) and the mind as the composition and succession of the ideas of subjective states which arise from these relationships.

This means, then, that the transition from one condition to another is a natural condition for man (as it is for every other mode of substance) and that in this possibility of transition lies the possibility, in the ethical sense, of passing from 'slavery' to 'freedom' and, in the political sense, the possibility of intervening in reality in order to change it. Hence new weight is added to the hypothesis of the construction of an alternative society in which moral philosophy and education of the young assume prominence alongside medicine and mechanics.[12]

Freedom = reason seems to mean to us, therefore, not only 'knowledge of necessity'[13], i.e. knowledge of those objective conditions within which and on the basis of which our action occurs, but also an increase in the natural tendency to affirm oneself and search for one's own benefit by identifying those means which are the most suitable because they are rational.[14]

Therefore, the impulse to overcome the particularism present in natural individual rights arises from reason and is an expression of freedom, as is the impulse to have collectively the right that by nature each one has over all things, regulating each thing not in accordance with the antagonistic laws of individual appetite but in accordance with the laws of reason which establish common rule (*Tractatus theologico-politicus*, cap. XVI, p. 191).

What forms does freedom take and what dimensions does necessity preserve within the civil society based on the surrender (free, i.e. conscious, or forced, i.e. conditioned *ab alio*)[15] of the arbitrary affirmation of individual right or effort?

The realm of necessity is defined as obedience to the laws of the state, which by repressing and regulating irrational impulses, offer themselves as guarantors of freedom, the state having been constituted to ensure their operation. The purpose of the state is in fact the peace, security, well-being and freedom of its citizens.[16] This purpose constitutes the essence of its rationality and its pursuit is the basis of its power. Absolute State, to Spinoza, means rational state; here, too, power and reason are identified with each other and the state loses the grounds for its own power when it moves away from the purpose for which it was founded, the content of which is determined by reason (*Tractatus theologico-politicus*, cap. XVI, p. 194). In order to carry out the task for which it was constituted and in order to preserve itself, the state must follow the regulating criterion of reason, which is the only one that allows it to overcome natural right by civil right in the preservation of it,[17] while recognizing and respecting the needs of individuals, who gain complete satisfaction in the search for the common good.

The form of government in which these characteristics are realized more than in any other is a democratic one, defined as 'coetus universus hominum, qui collegialiter summum jus ad omnia, quae potest, habet' (*ibid.*, p. 193). Although the *Tractatus politicus* lacks an analysis and explanation of the principles of this form of government, the allusions contained therein in themselves, and related to the general principles of Spinozan political philosophy, are enough to state that, to Spinoza, the concept of democracy is identical with that of the state, the latter being founded on rational principles. Only by assimilating rational principles and building its structure around them can the state succeed, with one unique action, in providing for the well-being of its citizens and seeking the conditions for its own self-preservation. The realization of the common good, to be pursued solely in accordance with reason, is defined therefore as the only goal in which two requirements, formally distinct but substantially identical, are satisfied: the well-being of the citizens and the well-being of the state. This adaptation to rational principles is in fact possible only there where 'omnes, vel magna populi pars collegialiter tenet [imperium]' (*Tractatus politicus*, cap. XX, p. 239), that is, in a democratic system. Here where 'salus totius populi, non imperantis, summa lex est' (*ibid.*, cap. XVI, pp. 194–5), obedience is not slavery but freedom, because obeying the laws of the state – if, as we have seen, these arise from reason – is at the same time, and simply, obeying one's own laws inasmuch as this too is derived from true reason.

Democratic government, therefore, is (*ibid.*, p. 195)

maxime naturale . . . et maxime ad libertatem, quam natura unicuique concedit [accedit]. Nam in eo nemo jus suum naturale ita in alterum transfert, ut nulla sibi imposterum consultatio sit, sed in majorem totius Societatis partem, cujus ille unam facit. Atque hac ratione omnes manent, ut antea in statu naturali, aequales.

Only a democracy can realize true absoluteness because only the power that lies in all the people is absolute (*ibid.*, cap. VIII, S. 3); and, on the other hand, it is only in a democracy that freedom for all is realized, i.e. the real purpose of the state is realized, in so far as it is a rational state.

At the political as well as at the ethical level, reason mediates the identification of necessity with freedom.

The freedom which the Spinozan state defines as its purpose, is defined as freedom of thought, criticism, judgment and the expression of one's own ideas with respect to authority, be it civil or ecclesiastical. It is, therefore, freedom of thought and speech, but action is in accordance with the laws: these are the rights and obligations of the citizen of a rational state. Acting in accordance with the law, which (in a well-ordered state) is an obligation to be followed without any shadow of doubt, loses its motivational basis if the state forgets its essence as a rational state and strays from the purpose for which it was constituted. Should this happen, conditions for not recognizing the constituted power are formed and the way to overthrowing the constituted order is opened.[18] It seems at this point, that Spinoza offers sufficient motives for the recognition of revolutionary action. In fact, if the regulating criterion of an agreement is the benefit that the contractual partners derive from it

(*Tractatus theologico-politicus*, cap. XVI, pp. 192–3), and should either of the two not observe the condition of the agreement, thus cancelling the margins of benefit, then the reason for the agreement itself disappears and the latter becomes automatically invalid.[19]

If, therefore, 'libertas philosophandi dicendique quae sentimus' (*Epistola* XXX, p. 166) is the only form of freedom allowed the citizen of a well-ordered, i.e. rationally ordered, state, he passes from this theoretical freedom to a practical form when the state shows signs of degenerating. The freedom theorized by Spinoza is, therefore, not the freedom of the wise man, who, freeing himself individually from subjection to a power he no longer recognizes, closes himself up in his own inner being, but it is more the use of that judicious faculty and the employment of those suitable means of spreading and debating ideas that precede, and upon which is attached, the action of whoever wishes to live responsibility in '*civitas*'.[20]

It seems to me, therefore, that the Spinozan theory of freedom offers most interesting starting points even to those who consider this question today from the materialistic-historic point of view. Let it be clear: the theory in question is not one to be accepted *in toto* but one which offers only theoretical elements useful in the construction of a materialistic-historic theory of freedom.

These elements may be individuated:

In the construction of a theory (be it even elaborated at an abstract and metaphysical level as a moment of universal determinism) of a system of closely interconnected objective (external causes) and subjective (internal causes) conditionings that man cannot avoid so that his freedom moves from this indisputable basis and (so to speak) feeds on it: no matter how conscious we are of a tradition that attributes characteristics of identity and immobility to the Spinozan system, we consider it more correct to view the relationship between the system of necessity and the plane of freedom as a dialectic one (Engels, on the other hand, indicated Spinoza, together with Descartes, as a 'splendid representative' of dialectics);[21]

In the sort of link between mind and body, which, despite their declared reciprocal independence and autonomy, limits the activity of the one to the capacity to express the power of the other;

In the concept of reason as knowledge of the common and necessary order, which regulates the relationships between things, and sources of practical norms, the content of which is specified as expression of individual power, search for individual good and preservation of the self (all supported by reason, hence lacking antagonistic impulses and endowed, instead, with a collectivistic load) and the aim of which is defined in the construction of a society which allows the greatest possible number of men the individual acquisition of 'a stronger nature'[22] and the collective acquisition of a good which, by its essence, is common;

In the concept of democracy as 'coetus *universus* hominum, qui *collegialiter* summum jus ad omnia, quae potest, habet' (*Tractatus theologico-politicus*, cap.

XVI, p. 193), a form of government in which the care of the state is the duty of the assembly of the people;[23]

Finally, in the defence of civil liberties as a fundamental aspect of a rational state and in the contestation of any form of authority which is not collectively exercised and derived from reason.

It seems to us that it is these elements of the Spinozan theory of freedom that – notwithstanding the absence (not to be underestimated even though 'historically determined') of an analysis of economic structure and a theory of class – allow one to connect it to the initial point of a line of development which concludes in a theory of freedom as 'revolutionary praxis'.[24] The dialectic relationship (while not consciously theorized as such) between the realm of necessity and the world of freedom in its formal outline, anticipates (but from the contextual point of view does not identify itself with) the Marxist concept of freedom which is described in one of the most beautiful pages of *Capital:*

> The realm of necessity begins only at the point where work determined by necessity and external finality ceases; by its nature it is hence to be found beyond the sphere of truly material production. Like the savage, civil man must fight nature in order to satisfy his needs, preserve and reproduce his life; he must do this in all forms of society and under all possible modes of production. As he gradually develops, the realm of the natural necessities expands because of the expansion of the productive forces which satisfy his needs. In this field, freedom can consist only in the following that socialized man, i.e. the associated producers, rationally regulate this organic exchange of theirs with nature, bringing it under their mutual control instead of being dominated by it as if by a blind force; that they carry out their task with the minimum possible use of energy and in conditions most suitable and worthy of their human nature. But this still remains a realm of necessity. Beyond it begins the development of human capacity, which is an end in itself, the true realm of freedom which nevertheless can flourish only on the basis of that realm of necessity.[25]

NOTES

1 Spinoza's works are quoted as they stand in C. Gebhardt, *Spinoza, Opera* (Heidelberg, Auftrag der Heidelberger Akademie der Wissenschaften, 1925), vol. 4; *Ethica*, vol. I.

2 'Deus agnoscendo, et volendo agit et operatur; non igitur per necessitatem naturae, sed per arbitrium voluntatis' (Thomas Aquinas, *Summa contra gentes*, II, c. 63).

3 'La volonté . . . ou liberté consiste seulement en ce que nous pouvons faire une même chose ou ne la faire pas' (R. Descartes, *Oeuvres, Méditations*, Méditation

quatrième, ed. Ch. Adam et P. Tannery (Paris, Vrin, 1964), vol. IX, 1, p. 46); 'La toute-puissance que Dieu a sur l'univers est très absolue et très libre' (R. Descartes, *Principes de la philosophie, ed. cit.*, vol. IX, 2, I, 38, p. 42).

4 Here one must see one of those 'seeds of the future materialistic way of thinking present in Spinoza's philosophy according to K. Korsch (see *K. Marx*, Frankfurt-Wien, 1967, p. 147).

5 Putting aside the albeit diverging points which constitute just as many points of development, thus allowing historical materialism to appear with specific and original characteristics that destroy traditional criteria of philosophical reflection, this Spinozan concept of determinism constitutes the first and most obvious antecedent of the principles of historical materialism expounded by Marx and Engels in *German Ideology* and by Marx in 1859 in the preface to *A Contribution to the Criticism of Political Economy* as well as in other texts. We are obviously aware of the fact that between Marxism and Spinozism there lies all the difference between coherent materialism and a concept of reality where materialistic and idealistic elements co-exist without any possibility of reconciliation.

6 Spinoza does not say this here explicitly, but by analogy one cannot fail to deduce it.

7 The concepts of the natural sciences are part of the common notions: 'in scrutandis rebus naturalibus ante omnia investigare conamur res maxime universales et toti naturae communes, videlicet motum et quietum' *Opera*, vol. III (*Tractatus theologico-politicus*, cap. VII, p. 102, 11.21–3).

8 'Potentia, quae res singulares, et consequenter homo suum esse conservat, est ipsa Dei, sive Naturae potentia, non quatenus infinita est, sed quatenus per humanam actualem essentiam explicari potest. Potentia itaque hominis, quatenus per ipsius actualem essentiam explicatur, pars est infinitae Dei, seu Naturae potentiae, hoc est essentiae' (*Ethica*, IV, dem. prop. IV).

9 'Per virtutem, et potentiam idem intelligo, hoc est virtus, quatenus ad hominem refertur, est ipsa hominis essentia, seu natura, quatenus potestatem habet, quaedem efficiendi, quae per solas ipsius naturae leges possunt intelligi' (*Ethica*, IV, def. VIII); 'quandoquidem virtus nihil aliud est, quam ex legibus propriae naturae agere, et nemo suum esse conservare conetur, nisi ex propriae suae naturae legibus; hinc sequitur primo virtutis fundamentum esse ipsum conatum proprium esse conservandi, et felicitatem in eo consistere, quod homo suum esse conservare potest. Secundo sequitur, virtutem propter se esse appetendam, nec quicquam, quod ipsa praestabilius, aut quod utilius nobis fit, dari, cujus causa deberet appeti' (*ibid.*, schol. prop. XVIII).

10 'Affectus, qui passio est, desinit esse passio, simulatque ejus claram, et distinctam formamus ideam' (*Ethica*, V, prop. III).

11 'Fit raro, ut homines ex ductu rationis vivant' (*Ethica*, IV, schol. prop. XXXV); 'Causam ostendisse credo, cur homines opinione magis, quam vera ratione commoveantur' (*ibid.*, schol. prop. XVII).

12 'Danda est opera Morali Philosophiae, ut et Doctrinae de puerorum Educatione; et, quia Valetudo non parvus est medium ad hunc finem assequendum, concinnanda est integra Medicina; et quia arte multa, quae difficilia sunt, facilia redduntur, multumque temporis, et commodatatis in vita ea lucrari possumus,

ideo Mechanica nullo modo est contemnenda' (*Tractatus de intellectus emendatione*, vol. II, p. 9).

13 Elsewhere (cf. 'Sur la question du materialisme chez Spinoza', *Revue Internationale de Philosophie*, 1977) I pointed out that this same concept of freedom as knowledge of necessity returns, with the mediation of Hegel, in Engels (*Antidühring*, I, ch. XI).

14 While agreeing with S. Timpanaro's opinions in many respects, I am, however, not entirely in agreement with what he says with respect to this in his essay 'Engels, materialismo e libero arbitrio' (*Quaderni piacentini*, no. 39, 1969, p. 105): it seems to me, in fact, that the ascetic component certainly present in the Spinozan theory of freedom as reason is correct, or at least contrasts with the hedonistic elements found in the *conatus* theory and that of the '*jus naturale*' which is part of it.

15 Note the two Spinozan positions on this: that theorized in the second explanatory note to prop. XXXVII, part IV of *Ethica* and that dealt with in the political section of *Tractatus theologico-politicus*.

16 'Ex fundamentis Reipublicae supra explicatis evidentissime sequitur, finem ejus ultimum non esse dominari, nec homines metu retinere, et alterius juris facere, sed contra *unumquemque metu liberare, ut secure*, quoad ejus fieri potest, *vivat, hoc est, ut jus suum naturale ad existendum, et operandum absque suo, et alterius damno optime retineat*. Non, inquam, finis Reipublicae est homines ex rationalibus bestias, vel automata facere, sed contra ut eorum mens, et corpus tuto suis functionibus fungantur, et ipsi libera ratione utuantur, et ne odio, ira, vel dolo certent, nec animo iniquo invicem ferantur. Finis ergo Reipublicae revera libertas est' (*Tractatus Theologico-politicus*, cap. XX, pp. 240–1).

17 This, as explicitly declared by Spinoza, is the discriminating point between his theory of the state and that of Hobbes: 'Quantum ad Politicam spectat, discrimen inter me, et Hobbesium, de quo interrogas, in hoc consistit, quod ego naturale Jus semper sartum tectum conservo, quodque Supremo Magistratui in qualibet Urbe non plus in subditis juris, quam juxta mensuram potestatis, qua subditum superat, competere statuo, quod in statu Naturali semper locum habet' (*Epistola L*, pp. 238–9).

18 'Summis potestatibus hoc jus, quicquid velit, imperandi, tamdiu tantum competit, quamdiu revera summam habent potestatem: quod si etiam amiserint, simul etiam jus omnia imperandi amittunt, et in eum vel eos cadit, qui ipsum acquisiverunt, et retinere possunt. Quapropter raro admodum contingere potest, ut summae potestates, absurdissima imperent; ipsis enim maxime incumbit, ut sibi prospiciant, et imperium retineant, communi bono consulere, et omnia ex rationis dictamine dirigere' (*Tractatus theologico-politicus*, cap. XVI, p. 194).

19 In this too he differs from Hobbes, for whom the agreement which sets up the state obliges only the citizens, but not 'that great Leviathan, or rather, to speake more reverently, that mortal god' which the state is to Hobbes (*Leviathan*, in *The English Works*, by W. Molesworth, London, 1839, vol. III, p. 158). Hobbes is most precise in listing the rights that the subjects of his state do *not* have and one cannot think that here is any margin for any form of freedom, neither individual nor of the 'multitude'. On the other hand, Spinoza, on this point, also departs from the principles of '*pacta sunt servanda*' of Grozio.

20 I have intentionally failed to discuss the theory of '*beatitudo*' and '*amor Dei intellectualis*': my interest does not lie in the religious dimension to which this theory refers. Since I have chosen a problematic and not strictly philological approach to the texts, I consider myself authorized to analyse and discuss only those elements of the Spinozan theory of freedom which, in my judgment, contribute to clarify the problem and are of interest today.

21 *Antidühring*, quoted from an Italian edition (Rome, Editori Riuniti, 1971), p. 22.

22 One recalls the 3rd *Note to Feuerbach* by K. Marx (MEW, Dietz Verlag, Berlin, 1959, vol. III, p. 534).

23 *Tractatus politicus*, ch. II, S. 17. One mustn't forget that together with slaves and minors, women are excluded from this, being defined as individuals who are not '*sui juris*' but '*in potestate virorum*' (*ibid.*, ch. XI, S. 3). It would be a mistake not to mention, however, that such an attitude is not an exception but represents the norm of a cultural tradition which Spinoza does not contest despite his criticism of other aspects of it.

24 See the 3rd, 10th and 11th *Notes to Feuerbach* by Marx.

25 *Capital*, vol. III, p. 933: translated from an Italian edition (Rome, Editori Riuniti, 1968).

4   Spinoza and the Kabbalah

Henry Walter Brann, Takoma Park

Baruch Spinoza, though trained for the rabbinate and imbued with the teachings of the most outstanding medieval and Renaissance Talmud and Torah scholars, was physically and mentally excluded from the Jewish Community of Amsterdam and has been considered a heretic from Judaism up to the present time. While non-Jewish thinkers of our era freely stress the typically Jewish character of Spinoza's philosophy, their Jewish counterparts at best make a hesitating gesture towards a half-hearted recognition of this fact with a strong emphasis on basic points separating Judaism from Spinozism. George Santayana, in his introduction to Bayle's translation of *Ethics*, speaks of the 'genuine Hebraism of Spinoza' and reaches the conclusion that 'pure Hebraism interpreted philosophically becomes Pantheism'. Meyer Waxman, on the other hand, in a special essay entitled 'Baruch Spinoza's relation to Jewish philosophical thought and to Judaism'[1] reluctantly admits: 'In spite of the conclusions reached by Spinoza it seems to me that the source motive of his system lay in Jewish philosophy', but he qualifies this statement by adding: 'Spinoza's speculations arose primarily from his criticism of Jewish medieval philosophy. . . .'

Yet the close relationship between Spinoza and the Kabbalah was recognized very early; the famous German philosopher Gottfried Wilhelm Leibniz mentioned it even in his main work *Theodicy*, published in 1708, i.e. thirty-one years after Spinoza's death. Another German scholar, the linguist Johann Georg Wachter, earlier had pointed out the 'Spinozism of the Kabbalah' in his treatise *Elucidarius Cabalisticus sive Reconditae Hebraeorum Philosophiae Brevis et Succincta Recencio* [sic][2] (Halle, 1706). Much later, even in the rationalistic nineteenth century, two serious French and German scholars, Elias Benamozah and Isidor Misses, published essays whose titles respectively read *Spinoza et la Kabbale* and *Spinoza und die Kabbala*.[3] But, as a great deal of popular nonsense was published about the Kabbalah by incompetent mystifiers of a very low intellectual level, qualified Jewish and Christian theologians and philosophers shied away from kabbalistic studies and considered it preposterous to involve both Judaism and a thinker of Spinoza's rank in such 'doubtful gibberish'. Thus, even a scholar of Leo

Baeck's[4] high standing has never quite found the adequate approach to the esoteric Kabbalah. This attitude was, however, not generally accepted. The best Spinoza interpreters continued to link the great philosopher with the doctrines of the authentic Kabbalah, especially those of the *Zohar*.[5] One of the most important among them was Stanislaus von Dunin-Borkowski, a German Jesuit whose book *Der Junge de Spinoza*[6] is still a classic hardly ever matched by more recent publications. Dunin-Borkowski has a full chapter called 'Kabbalistische Wanderfahrten' (Kabbalistic travels). A subdivision of it reads (pp. 176–90): 'Der Ursprung der Mystik-Kabbala und die Urkeime des Spinozismus' (The origin of Mysticism-Kabbalah and the first germs of budding Spinozism). The author stresses that 'a higher form of cognition of all finite things, a cognition in God and in the light of eternity in the Kabbalah as well as in De Spinoza appears as the highlight of *Ethics*'. According to him, there was a highly developed older and intermediary type of Jewish mysticism prevailing beside the Kabbalah in the thirteenth century, and the Talmudists had already conceived the existence of mediators between God and the Universe. From these mystics, he concludes, an infinitely long and slow but almost straight evolution leads, through the ideas of the (kabbalistic) sephiroth and the neoplatonic emanations, directly to the basic concepts of the *natura naturans* and the first links of the *natura naturata* in Spinoza's system. Dunin-Borkowski, in contrast to Heinrich Grätz, the well-known historian of Jews in Germany, calls the sephiroth in the Sepher Jetzirah (Book of Creation) of the *Zohar* a 'highly advanced evolution of the secret philosophy of the Talmud, a groping for a link with secular science, an important transitional work pointing to the speculation of the oldest gaonitic religious philosophers'. The concept of the En Sof, the Endless or Boundless one, Dunin-Borkowski continues, dominates the *Zohar* to the same extent as it will later be prevalent in Spinoza's mind. And here we encounter exactly the same determinism which by so many thinkers and scholars is considered a fundamental cleavage between Judaism and Spinozism. God (the En Sof) cannot be designated by any known attributes. He is best called Ayin (the undeterminable). Hence, in order to make His existence known to all, the Deity was obliged (or, what amounts to the same thing, wishes) to reveal Himself at least to a certain extent. But the En Sof, being boundless, cannot become the direct creator, for he has neither will, intention, desire, thought, language nor action, attributes which belong only to finite beings. The En Sof, therefore, made His existence known in the creation of the world by the *ten sephiroth*, which flowing directly from Him, partake of His perfection and infinity.

These substances or emanations are parts of one another, as sparks are part of the same flame; yet they are, at the same time, distinguished from one another, as are different colours of the same light. The three first sephiroth are crown (kether), wisdom (chochmah), intelligence (binah). The crown is the first manifestation of the En Sof. It represents the original substance encompassing simultaneously matter and form, extension and mind. The crown enters into an intimate union between wisdom, the male principle, and the intellect, the female principle. They create their 'son': knowledge.

The pantheistic suggestions of the first and third book of the *Zohar* have become of the highest significance for Spinoza. For there the sephirah 'wisdom' forms a perfect unity with the crown and the En Sof. 'They are like three heads which, actually, form only one. Everything is connected and linked together in the one whole (the universe). *Between the Universe and the Ancient One (God) there is no distinction at all. All is One, and He is all – without distinction and separation.* He who describes the sephiroth as separated from one another, destroys God's unity' (Dunin-Borkowski, *op. cit.*, p. 185–7; *Zohar* III, fol. 289b, 290a; suppl. preface III).

But Dunin-Borkowski has made another important discovery. The concepts of the Kabbalah were first transmitted to young Spinoza in a rather palatable contemporary version, i.e. Abraham (Alonzo) Herrera's famous book *Door of Heaven*. It was written in Spanish and translated into Hebrew by Isaac Aboab. This work, which dealt with Kabbalistic philosophy, was a favourite sourcebook of Baruch's noted Talmud teachers, Saul Levi Morteira and Manasseh ben Israel. In 1678 (one year after Spinoza's death), a Latin version appeared under the title *Sha'ar Hashomayim seu Porta Coelorum. In quo Dogmata Cabbalistica Philosophorum proponuntur et cum philosophiae Platonis conferuntur.*

Herrera himself had already died in 1639, and young Baruch absorbed the contents of *Door of Heaven* just during those most decisive years of mental development when the imprint of new ideas is strongest and everlasting in every budding intellectual. He read, of course, the book in its Hebrew version, the language he mastered best up to his death (despite his somewhat clumsy Latin publications and Dutch letters).

According to Herrera, there is one original substance with an infinite extension. Outside it, there are only divine *modi* which are all encompassed in that original substance, the En Sof, even in their potentialities. Thus, there is a created (finite) and a non-created (infinite) State of God, i.e. both God in His proper sense and the Universe; but God is and remains the immanent cause of all things, and the '*Universe is actually nothing but the revealed and unveiled God*' (my italics). Therefore, we find in the '*Lexicon Cabbalisticum*' (a chapter of the *Door of Heaven*) the *unequivoked statement*: '*the acceptance of this unity is part and parcel of the faith of every genuine Israelite*; we must believe that the Infinite manifests Himself in all His modi through the unity' (my italics). There is one substance, Herrera stresses, with infinite properties. It is determining itself by a multitude of infinite beings which are, however, nothing but its modification. God is One and Many at the same time – one in so far as He is infinite; many in so far as He determines Himself in His attributes and *modi*. These *modi* cannot exist nor be understood without the Divine One inherent and indwelling in them. *Everything is one in God* (my italics). Dunin-Borkowski reaches the following conclusion: 'Especially the first five treatises of the book [Herrera's *Door to Heaven*] explain that *only blind prejudice can overlook this source of Spinoza's*. Old Wachter[7] has recognized these similarities with perspicacity' (my italics).

The lucid Jesuit thinker was by no means alone in studying the influence of the Kabbalah on Spinoza's philosophy and in proving the tremendous impact of the former on the latter on solid grounds. As early as 1917, an orthodox Jewish scholar, the Austrian Sigmund Gelbhaus,[8] made a thorough investigation of the problem which, up to this very moment, has been the most conclusive and rewarding one. His analysis has an invaluable signifi- cance for a better understanding of the first two books of Spinoza's *Ethics*, with their rather dark and difficult passages which even such seasoned philosophical interpreters as Bruno Erdmann and Kuno Fischer failed to explain satisfactorily. We hope that future Spinoza researchers, be they Jews or non-Jews, will avail themselves of this evidently forgotten material. For Gelbhaus, though he does not neglect pointing out contrasting concepts to be found in the two doctrines, the identity of Kabbalistic and Spinozistic metaphysics is a well-established fact described as following at the beginning and at the end of his study: 'What the Kabbalah presents in an allegorical- oriental form, Spinoza's *Ethics* teaches in a mathematic-ontological manner' (Gelbhaus, *op. cit.*, II, p. 108 and *passim*).

The philosopher of Amsterdam himself never denied the Hebrew origin of his basic metaphysical ideas. In his seventy-third letter in which he explains his concept of God he says: 'Omnia inquam in Deo esse et in Deo moveri cum Paulo affirmo et forte etiam cum omnibus antiquis philosophis . . . et auderem etiam dicere *cum antiquis omnibus Hebraeis*' (my italics). In *Ethics* II, pro- position 7, the scholium reads: 'Quo quidam Hebraeorum quasi per nebulam vidisse videntur qui scilicet statuunt *Deum, Dei intellectum resque ab eo intellectas unum et idem esse*' (my italics). The last statement is identical with that of Moses Cordovero, an analyst of the *Zohar*, as given in his *Pardes Rimonim*, fol. 55a:

> The Creator . . . is Himself the perception, the perceiving and the perceived. He is the archetype of all being and all things are in Him in their purest and most perfect form so that the perfection of the creatures just consists in the existence by which they find themselves united with the primary source, and to the extent in which they withdraw from Him, they descend from His perfect and exalted state.

This doctrine is nothing but a more explicit interpretation of the postulate: 'soper, sapper and sippur' established in the Sepher Jetzirah, the book of creation.

111

Gelbhaus has found that all the subjects of Spinoza's philosophical research have been thoroughly discussed either in the Pentateuch, the Prophets and the other books of the Bible or in the Talmud and the Kabbalah. He does not start with problems concerning nature, mind and the universal spirit, as the Eleatics, Heraclitus, Socrates, Plato and Aristotle have done, but with problems whose solutions were suggested by religion and religious documents. The leading ideas of Spinoza's speculations on ontological matters are based in the first place either on esoteric-kabbalistic-philosophical theories or on mystical theosophy. The philosopher of Amsterdam chooses only two main attributes of the substance (God): namely wisdom-thinking (*cogitatio*) and ground-extension (*extensio*). Wisdom-thinking is explained in the same way both in the Kabbalah and the *Ethics*.

Woe to him who compares Him [God] with His own attributes; we have to think of Him as being exalted and superior above all His attributes. . . . We must say that God is intelligent and wise by Himself, yet wisdom deserves its name not by itself but by the wise man who has filled it with the light flowing out of Him (*Zohar*).

Est igitur cogitatio unum ex infinitis Dei attributis quod Dei aeternam et infinitam essentiam exprimit sive Deus es res cogitans (*Ethics* II, demonstration, proposition 1).

Deus sive natura – God or, what amounts to the same thing, Nature; this famous equation of Spinoza's has made his system suspect to traditional Jews and Christians alike. Now, just this concept, as we have already shown, belongs to the basic ideas of the genuine Kabbalah, a natural offspring of the most exalted Talmudic tenets. As the *Zohar* explains, even the name of God indicates His close identity and unity with the Universe. Before God had manifested Himself, when all things were still hidden in Him, He was Himself the most concealed one among everything concealed and thus He had nothing but the name of the question: 'Who?' He first formed an invisible point, namely His thinking, a mysterious and holy figure and, finally, He covered Himself with a rich and brilliant cloth, i.e. '*The Universe whose name is united with God's name*' (my italics) (*Zohar*, I, 1 and 2; II, fol. 105; III, fol. 188). 'Who' in Hebrew is 'mi'; the creation is called by Isaiah 'these', eleh. The term '*eleh*' *consists of those five letters* '*mi*' *and* '*eleh*', so that God and the Universe appear in one single name. Everything starts with the exclamation: 'R'ah mi barah eleh' (see who has created these).

Gelbhaus shows beyond doubt that the Kabbalah's 'cause of all causes' which does not have any beginning nor place nor limitations, can easily be recognized in Spinoza's 'substance', and two of its 'internal points' are the philosopher's main attributes of the substance, i.e. thinking (*cogitatio*) and extension. The En Sof as well as the 'sibot kol hassibot' (cause of all causes) has the quality of the infinite, and this must be considered the centre of the whole kabbalistic system. The same holds true for Spinoza's 'substance'. The eighth proposition of part I of *Ethics* reads as follows: 'Omnis substantia est necessario infinita' (in Hebrew: En Sof), and the sixth definition says: 'Per Deum intelligo ens absolute infinitum, hoc est substantiam constantem infinitis attributis quorum unumquodque aeternam et infinitam essentiam exprimit.'

It is interesting to study the relationship between God and Nature in the Kabbalah because it opens unexpected vistas which go far beyond the man- and earth-centred concepts of the Middle Ages. The Sepher Jetzirah considers our present world as only one of the many creations of God which were preceded by a world of a quite different character (Gelbhaus, *op. cit.*, p. 76). Such ideas would even fit into the physical *Weltbild* of the atomic and space ages. God has connected and intimately linked Nature with His essence as a being for Himself, as a substance outside of the Universe, while '*elohim points to the presence of God in Nature*' (my italics, see above). God is in Nature and, at the same time, outside it, in the same way as the *En Sof* dwells in its sephiroth and outside them (Gelbhaus, *op. cit.*, p. 79).

Rabbi Joseph Karo and Hachem Z'wi (in their interpretation of the Kabbalah, no. 18) have made an amazing discovery which explains the identity of God and Nature. The Hebrew letters 'mi' and 'eleh' = Elohim have the same numeral value as the word *Hatuvah* (nature), namely 86 (Gelbhaus, *op. cit.*, pp. 80ff.).

What is the actual meaning of Spinoza's oft-cited (but evidently as frequently misunderstood) concept '*natura naturata*'? Certainly not a mechanistic, abstract, spiritless matter, as some interpreters – quite in contrast to Dunin-Borkowski's opinion (see above) – have intimated. (By the way: the term first appears in Thomas Aquinas and his school. But, as Gelbhaus correctly states, Spinoza gave them a different interpretation, i.e. the kabbalistic one). In the scholium to proposition 29 of the first book of *Ethics* we find a clear definition of the two concepts which reads (my translation):

> By *natura naturans* we must understand what exists in itself and is conceived by itself or such attributes of the substance as express an eternal and infinite essence, i.e. *God in so far as he is considered a free cause (causa libera)*. . . . by *natura naturata*, however [I understand], *what follows from the necessity of God's nature, or God's attributes.*

We have seen that Spinoza's determinism fits in perfectly well with the concept of the En Sof in the *Zohar*; there is no place for any 'free will' of God, consequently not much of a 'free will' in man. We cannot agree, as far as this problem is concerned, with Gelbhaus who construes a contradiction between Spinoza and the Kabbalah. If a contradiction exists it is to be found in equal terms in both, as Dunin-Borkowski had recognized (*op. cit.*, pp. 185–6). We find in *Ethics* II the sentence: 'Voluntas non potest vocari causa libera, sed necessaria' but in I, proposition 17, Spinoza says: 'Deus ex solis suae naturae legibus et nemine coactus agit' (*God acts only according to the rules of his own nature and free of any compulsion* (my italics). This proposition clearly shows that Spinoza's God-Nature cannot be considered to be blind matter, as some scholars have tried to interpret it. Yet if there is a slight ambiguity in the two first books of *Ethics* with respect to God's 'freedom' in a pantheistic universe, it simply stems from the fact that the philosopher took his whole concept of God from the esoteric Kabbalah and did not even try to change certain inherent contradictions.

The most striking resemblance, if not complete identity, between the theories of *Ethics* and the doctrines of the Kabbalah covers the field of body-mind relations. The Kabbalist Moses de Leon, in his book *Nefesh Haneshamah*[9] divides the soul into three parts, i.e. nefesh, ruach and neshamah (life, mind and soul). To nefesh (which literally means breath) is attributed the essence of all bodily functions, all forms of life and all its sensations. Its basis is the blood, in fact, nefesh equals blood. Ruach is the strength which preserves nefesh and provides it with consistence and duration in the body, for nefesh cannot exist but by the strength of ruach which gives existence to man; as soon as ruach (the mind) leaves nefesh, death occurs. Neshamah (the soul), however, is the object of the genuine intellect which originates from the sources of life, intelligence and wisdom. It came to take residence in the human body to arrange everything for the service of the Creator in order to make the body partake in the true and genuine being. In the fifth book of *Ethics*, Proposition 23, demonstration and scholium, Spinoza says (again my own translation): 'The human mind cannot absolutely be destroyed with the body, but something remains which is eternal.' And in the demonstration and proof he continues: 'There exists in God by necessity a concept which expresses the essence of the *human body* [how could nature-matter be restricted to the human body?]; there is, therefore, necessarily something which belongs to the essence of the human mind.' He adds the note:

> The mind perceives those things which He comprehends by the intellect, no less than those which He remembers. For the mind's eyes with which it sees and observes the things, just are the demonstrations. Therefore, even though we do not remember to have existed before our body came to life, nevertheless we are aware of the fact that *our mind is eternal in so far as it contains the essence of the body under a certain form of eternity* (sub quadam aeternitatis specie) and this kind of its existence cannot be defined by time or duration (my italics).

At the end of his famous *Short Treatise*, Spinoza stresses: 'From all this and also from the fact that our soul is connected with God and represents part of the idea immediately originating from God, very distinctly follows the origin of any clear cognition and the immortality of the soul.'

114

All the foregoing is a beautiful example of neoplatonistic thinking as incorporated into the Kabbalah from which Spinoza took it. His direct knowledge of Plotinus is rather doubtful. The *'idea corporis'* of *Ethics* corresponds with nefesh, the abstract animal life, the *'idea rei'* with ruach, the blurred intellectual essence, and the *'idea mentis'* with neshamah, the pure thinking mind. The Kabbalah distinguishes three stages of cognition: a superficial manner of thinking, a deeper contemplation and the purely spiritual comprehension (see *Zohar*, III, fol. 152b). In *Ethics* we find three kinds of human knowledge: (1) superficial consideration, (2) knowledge adequately formed by certain ideas, (3) the cognition forming immediate intuitive knowledge. The second part of *Ethics*, proposition 40, scholium 2, describes these three types of knowledge as follows: (1) Perception won from single things by the senses in a mutilated, confused and orderless manner, (2) perception won from signs and marks, i.e. from what we remember from our reading and hearing with regard to certain words and names, and finally from the fact that we have certain common concepts of adequate ideas involved in the objects, and (3) besides these two kinds of cognition there is ... 'a third and different one which we call *intuitive knowledge (Scientiam intuitivam)*'.

The first type corresponds in the *Zohar* with the knowledge of those who accept the stories of the Bible verbatim, the second with the opinion of the informed who do not look at the clothes but rather at that which they cover, the third with the ideas of the wise men who regard the soul of the Torah which is the root of all things.

One of the most mysterious concepts in Spinoza's system is the famous *amor Dei intellectualis*, the intellectual love of God and for God. Various interpreters have explained it in quite different ways, and the same discrepancy prevails as to where the philosopher took this idea from. Lewis Browne[10] points to the fact that the term was already used by Leon Abarbanel in his *Dialogue on Love*, a work composed some two hundred years before Spinoza's time and found in its Hebrew original in the thinker's library after his death. This is certainly true as far as the coinage of the term is concerned. But the underlying idea appears in the Kabbalah, *Zohar* II, fol. 216, as Gelbhaus has shown convincingly in the crowning conclusion of his essay (*op. cit.*, pp. 105–8). There we read:

> There is only one step which is stronger than fear, and this is love. Yes, love is the mystery of God's unity. It is love which unites the higher and the lower stages with each other. *It raises everything up to a stage where all must be one.* This is also a secret of the Sh'mah.

And in *Zohar* II, fol. 97a, we come across one of the most beautiful passages:

> In one of the most deeply hidden and, at the same time, most exalted parts of heaven there is a place called *hall of love*; there we find the

115

profoundest secrets, there dwell the souls that are being loved by the heavenly King, there dwells the heavenly King Himself, the Holy One, praised be He, together with the holy souls and their unity is sealed by the kiss of love.

Spinoza's chapter on the intellectual love of and for God in the *Ethics*, V, propositions 35 and 36, reads as follows:

Deus se ipsum amore intellectuali infinito amat. Mentis amor intellectualis erga Deum [the human mind's intellectual love for God] ipse Dei amor quo Deus se ipsum amat, not quatenus infinitus est, sed quatenus per essentiam humanae mentis sub specie aeternitatis consideratam explicari potest [because it can be explained by the essence of the human mind contemplated under the form of eternity] hoc est – mentis erga Deum amor intellectualis pars est infiniti amoris quo Deus se ipsum amat.

That 'love with which God loves Himself' is what is called 'glory' or 'splendour' in the Scriptures, called *Hod* in Hebrew, one of the main sephiroth of the En Sof. As love in the *Zohar* has that unifying quality of mind and soul we have mentioned before, there follows the conclusion: 'Whoever serves impelled by love will have reached the highest stage of perfection, and therefore already belongs to the holiness of the future life.'

As we have shown elsewhere,[11] Spinoza shares the concept of the intellectual union with God with Maimonides who anticipated the philosopher of Amsterdam in proclaiming intellect the highest good and form of perception. The close connection of Spinoza and the Kabbalah is taken for granted in a rather strange publication by the so-called Spinoza Institute of America, in New York. One Harry Waton in 1931 and 1932, under the auspices of this institute, published two volumes entitled: *The Kabbalah and Spinoza's Philosophy as a Basis for an Idea of Universal History*. The first book was called *The Philosophy of Spinoza*. Further volumes which should explain the relations of those two philosophies with the 'idea of a universal history' never did appear nor is anything known about the fate of the Spinoza Institute of America, which seems to have vanished after a rather shortlived existence. Though the publication as a whole cannot be considered a serious scholarly endeavour – it is a queer mixture of pertinent ideas and popular eschatological fantasies – we should like to cite a few remarks of the former type. The author has found five important ideas in the Kabbalah, i.e. the ideas of rationality, destiny, determinism, dialectics and creation. According to him, the Kabbalah is 'based upon a mathematics of the highest order'. In order to corroborate this, he quotes Oswald Spengler's *Decline of the West*, containing a chapter on the 'meaning of numbers'.

Considering the role which the mysticism of numbers has played in the

Kabbalah (see the quotations above), we might venture the idea that Spinoza's choice of the geometrical method in presenting his philosophical system might have been influenced by the Kabbalah. Gelbhaus (*op. cit.*, pp. 5–6) points out that the '*ordo geometricus*' was not invented by Spinoza but already used by the philosopher Proclus in his *Institutio theologica* and later by Duns Scotus, Languet and Henning in the sixteenth century. But it is doubtful whether Spinoza had known them. Descartes (whose *Principles* were later published by Spinoza in the same mathematical manner) uses it in his reply to 'objections' raised against his ideas; so does Geulincx in his *Methodus inveniendi argumenta*. Though nobody will deny the influence of those two philosophers on Spinoza, Gelbhaus points to the great advantage which that dogmatic and almost dictatorial method gave the philosopher and stresses that he shares the dogmatic structure of his *Ethics* with the kabbalistic Sepher Jetzirah, the *Zohar* and the 'Book of Secrets', Siphra Dziniuta. 'The teacher pronounces sentences and every single word of his is being accepted as an article of faith' (Gelbhaus *op. cit.*, pp. 10–11). Returning to the publication of the Spinoza Institute of America, we find in the preface of volume II an amazingly adequate summary of what the philosophy of Spinoza has in common with the ideas of the Kabbalah, composed by J. H. Muraskin:

> The nature of the universe is merged with divinity itself. Existence is self-creative through a process of self-negation developing from an inherent implicitness to ever greater explicitness of forms in which the order and connection of phenomena is only an aspect of universal necessity.

NOTES

This paper first appeared in the *Hartwick Revue*, vol. 3, no. 1, Spring 1967, Hartwick College.

1 Meyer Waxman, 'Baruch Spinoza's relation to Jewish philosophical thought and to Judaism', *Jewish Quarterly Review*, New Series, vol. XIX, no. 4, 1929, Dropsie College, Philadelphia.
2 Manuel Joel, *Zur Genesis der Lehre Spinozas*, Breslau, Jewish-Theological Seminar, 1871.
3 Stanislaus von Dunin-Borkowski, *Der Junge De Spinoza. Leben und Werdegang im Lichte der Weltphilosophie*, Münster i.W., Aschendorff, 1910.
4 Leo Baeck, *Spinozas erste Einwirkungen auf Deutschland*, Berlin, Meyer & Müller, 1895.
5 Harry A. Wolfson, *The Philosophy of Spinoza*, New York, Meridian Books, 1960, vol. I, p. 395; vol. II, pp. 316–17.
6 Dunin-Borkowski, *op. cit.*
7 *Ibid.*

8 Sigmund Gelbhaus, *Die Metaphysik der Ethik Spinozas im Quellenlichte der Kabbalah*, Wien-Brünn, Jüdischer Buch- und Kunstverlag Max Hickl, 1917.

9 *Ibid.*

10 Lewis, Browne, *Blessed Spinoza*, New York, Macmillan, 1932.

11 Henry Walter Brann, 'Spinoza and Judaism', *The Jewish Spectator*, vol. XXV, no. 10, December 1960.

5 Interpreting Spinoza: a paradigm for historical work

James Collins, St Louis

Hegel made the well-known judgment that 'thought must begin by placing itself at the standpoint of Spinozism; to be a follower of Spinoza is the essential commencement of all philosophy'.[1] This remark can be construed from two standpoints: that of Hegel's own speculation and that of historical methodology. In terms of Hegel's argumentation, its import is partly polemical. Spinoza's theory of substance is a reprise of the Eleatic doctrine on being as the one-and-all. But this is an abstract unity which wrings all the individuating life out of spiritual freedom, so that modern philosophy only *begins* with Spinozan substance and must then move on to Hegel's concrete, self-negating and self-affirming spirit. This criticism is exposed, in turn, to the reply that Hegel fails to take account of the Spinozan conception of active self-expression on the part of substance, as well as the genetic nature of the geometrical method which does show the origin and truth of the definition of substance.

But Hegel's words can also be taken in the context of historical methodology, signifying the paradigmatic quality of the effort to understand Spinoza's philosophy. What the historian does in examining this philosophy proves to be, upon reflection, the kind of interpreting activity which serves analogously for studying the rest of modern philosophy. Coming as it does in Hegel's *Lectures on the History of Philosophy*, this suggestion is appropriate and worth pursuing, for it provides a way of testing one's theory on how to interpret modern philosophy. In order to ensure the generality of such a theory, a very broad inductive basis in modern philosophers is required. One facet of the theory will be drawn from historical work done on some particular philosophical source, whereas other facets will be taken from procedures used to study still other source thinkers. Once a general view of historical interpreting has been developed in this way, however, it needs to be concretely focused upon some one great thinker.

Spinoza's philosophy serves admirably in this verificational process. His total work is sufficiently complex and unified to put a general theory to the test and, reciprocally, to receive some additional illumination from the effort. My working hypothesis is that historical meaning in modern

119

philosophy arises from the inter-working of three primary factors: the philosophical source itself, the procedures of historical questioning, and the influence of our present philosophical concerns.[2] Although each factor is in itself highly variable, it is integrated with its correlates through the unifying activity of the historical interpreter himself. When he succeeds in synthesizing these ingredients in a manner that does justice to each of them, he meets the basic requirements for an adequate historical interpretation. Although always open to further revision and new departures, the interpretation yields some reliable understanding of the source philosopher under present circumstances.

I propose, then, to inspect how a historical study of Spinoza involves these three factors, not just in a general way but in terms of their concrete adaptation to his philosophy. The analysis must inevitably concentrate upon just a few aspects of this relationship between Spinoza and today's historical interpreters of his thought.

SPINOZA AS AN INSISTENT SOURCE

Although Spinoza never held an institutional professorship, he devoted himself to developing, clarifying, and teaching his philosophy to others. By 'others', he meant university students (such as Casearius) whom he tutored, the study groups at Amsterdam and elsewhere which discussed his developing positions, and the wider readership of his own time and subsequent ages to whom his books and correspondence were ultimately addressed. In each instance, he used all his skills as a teacher in order to present his positions in a way appropriate to the learner and yet also faithful to his own mind on the matter.

This careful insistence on conveying his precise philosophical intent involved Spinoza in much experimentation and variation. His *Part One and Two of René Descartes' Principles of Philosophy* strained to the utmost the resources of the commentary method. In that book's main body, he sought to elucidate the philosophical positions Descartes had established mainly in *Principles of Philosophy*, but also in *Discourse on Method, Meditations on First Philosophy* and the *Replies* to objections brought against the latter book. But even in the course of his commenting, Spinoza managed to show his critical independence. This came out, first of all, through his *recasting* of Cartesian arguments into geometrical form and manner. Whereas Descartes himself had used geometrical form only as a secondary sampling in response to a critic, Spinoza insisted upon restating all the main doctrines in that form. Moreover, he did so in a manner that brought out the *genetic dependence* of everything Cartesian upon the premissing of plural substances, creation through free decrees of the creator's will, the presence of free will in man, and the absolute predication of goodness and perfection. Spinoza could not refrain from interjecting, in the body of his commentary and his appended *Metaphysical Thoughts*, many statements of opposition aimed explicitly against these Cartesian principles.

Even more remarkable is the preface to *Descartes' Principles*, written by Dr Meyer at Spinoza's request.[3] Instead of merely commending Spinoza for the correctness of his account, Meyer underlines the points of philosophical disagreement between Descartes and his commentator. Thus a careful reader is made aware from the outset that, even though the Cartesian theses about the God-and-man relationship are clothed in geometrical forms of proof, Spinoza is not committed to their truth but rejects their framework in ordinary theism; and as A. K. Offenberg's contribution establishes, Spinoza requires Meyer to sharpen the expressions of opposition in the main text of *Descartes' Principles* and *Metaphysical Thoughts*, and not solely in the preface. All these precautions manifest the insistent activity of an original mind, its determination to make its own intent shine through even the oblique medium of a reconstruction of a predecessor's thought.

Spinoza had already been expounding his personal philosophy in the *Short Treatise on God, Man, and His Well-Being*. This work is often undervalued by being considered solely in relation to the *Theologico-Political Treatise* and the *Ethics*. Yet although relational questions of its agreement and disagreement with these later writings are important, they do not exhaust its significance and legitimate usefulness to Spinoza scholars. The *Short Treatise* deserves analysis not only in comparative terms but also in its own right. An intrinsic approach is specially demanded by a theory of historical interpretation engaged in studying Spinoza's insistence on stamping his own mark upon a course of reasoning, as well as on communicating such reasoning in the most effective way. These two questions concern respectively the *what* and the *how* of his philosophizing. Important examples of each aspect can be found in the *Short Treatise*.

(a) The *what* question chosen here for its bearing on our interpretation theory is provoked by the very first pages of the *Short Treatise*, as it plunges abruptly into proofs for God's existence and nature. Scholars sometimes feel obliged to construct an introductory paragraph or two that will lead us more smoothly into the topic. Doubtless, a final redaction of the work would have included an overview of the main problems and some preliminary statements within each major division, beginning with that on God. But in the extant Dutch manuscripts, Spinoza seems eager to move immediately into the actual paths of reasoning that God is and what he is. The author wants us to become more intensively reflective about this whole enterprise, so that we can learn what we are really doing in the inferential processes on God.

In establishing that God is, we usually begin with things around us or with ourselves as having the idea of God as a being with infinite attributes. Whatever our path to God, Spinoza calls the entire inferential act a 'consideration of nature' (*overweginge van de Natuur*).[4] This could mean that both poles of the inference (the world-and-ourselves and God) belong somehow within the unity of nature. But he does press the issue until he moves into the next chapter, concerning what God is. To establish the meaning of God as the being of whom all or infinite attributes are predicated, Spinoza argues for more than the uniqueness of substance. He also maintains that there is no substance or attribute, grasped in God's infinite understanding, other than 'what is formally in nature' (*die formelyk in de Natuur is*). The latter proposition is intimately connected with the Spinozan conception of the underived existence, infinite power, and immanent causal necessity of substance or active nature.

Spinoza is now in a position to conclude that nature is the total being which consists of infinite attributes or, in other words, that it fulfils the definition which one gives of God.[5] In this respect, *Deus sive Natura* is no empty phrase but an accurate equivalence. We are now given a response to the question of *what* we are doing in the philosophy of God: it is a human discipline *for exploring the essential traits and existence of nature itself*. Hence philosophical theology is a phase in the theory of nature (including human nature and its ethical aims). By spelling out this conclusion in unmistakable terms, Spinoza is communicating to us one of his radical philosophical tenets. Here at the very outset of his writing and teaching, he insistently conveys an intent that controls his whole discussion of the God-man relationship, and which therefore should become central to any well-founded historical interpretation of his work.

(b) The *Short Treatise* also supplies information about a *how* question which similarly affects the act of comprehending Spinoza's thought. In that work, he employs four forms of exposition: chapters containing definitions, proofs and explanations; notes on special difficulties in these chapters; two dialogues; and two appendices. Particular historical questions have been raised concerning the chronological relation of these parts (showing that the dialogues and appendices were composed later than the rest), as well as the authenticity of the notes (most of the longer ones coming from Spinoza himself, with the briefer paraphrases probably being inserted by some disciples). But what a general theory of interpretation compels us to do is to gather these four forms into a unified perspective. We can then view them all as expressions of Spinoza's intention as a philosophical writer. The question then naturally formulates itself: How does he meet the problem of communication? As far as the early *Short Treatise* is concerned, the briefest answer is: Through several experiments.

The chapter format, used here in the main body and also found in Spinoza's *Metaphysical Thoughts*, corresponded roughly to that of the school treatises of his day. From actually writing out his expositions in this manner, he experienced and exhibited its defects as a mode of communication. It relied too heavily on definitions not established either in prior or posterior chapters. Its argumentation was syllogistic, providing only a formal necessity in matters where the necessity of both thought and being was sought. And its brevity recommended itself to young students but resulted in that memorative sort of logic which Spinoza criticized as an unthinking act.

To compensate for the schematic brevity, he found it necessary to add some long notes whose function was argumentative as well as expository. In the *Short Treatise*, these notational additions signified both a clarifying response to friendly critics and an acknowledgment of the deficiencies of any school-manual vehicle for at once explicating and unifying his proofs. Yet the notes also anticipated Spinoza's freedom for the shortcomings of even the mature form of his *Ethics*.[6] The prefaces, appendices and many scholia of the latter work continue his notational procedure, just as do the notes to his *Theologico-Political Treatise*. They serve to prepare our minds for the import of definitions about to be given, to investigate the passional grounds for stubbornly held errors, and to open out prospects which follow consequentially from a given proof but which also go farther afield than the domain of the *Ethics*. The notemaker of the *Short Treatise* foreshadowed the supple investigator of the *Ethics*.

As for dialogue, Spinoza was sufficiently acquainted with ancient, medieval and Renaissance instances of its use to be encouraged at least to try this form. But while his two samples functioned in the *Short Treatise* as connectives between the general account of God's essence and existence and the particular chapters on his properties, they remained stylistically wooden and doctrinally awkward. They failed to breathe the Platonic fire and, in addition, they educated Spinoza negatively to seek a more impersonal, necessitating and demonstrative medium than dialogic writing could offer.

There were also some internal difficulties engendered by Spinoza's use of dialogue form. The first dialogue might lead an unwary reader to hypostasize its participants: understanding and love, reason and desire. This might well restore the theory of faculties. The consequence would be to construe Spinoza's whole metaphysics as a projection from human free will, intellect and passions which he was actually seeking to transcend. In its turn, the second dialogue produced a scatter-shot effect. It introduced the topics of divine causality, types of wholeness, and immortality, without much connection between them which might prepare for their systematic ordering. What would be a charming informality in dialogues composed within a different notion of philosophizing could prove disastrous for Spinoza's project of expressing the order of nature as apprehended without tears or laughter.

The two appendices must be treated as fragmentary sketches for restating the main divisions of the *Short Treatise* and for looking ahead to future work. Appendix I, on God, did for Spinoza's doctrine of the unity of substance

123

something similar to what Descartes's did for God's existence in his Appendix to *Replies II*. But whereas Descartes had treated geometrical form and its synthetic way as secondary, Spinoza was gradually coming to recognize in the geometrical order and its synthetic way the best procedure to follow in his own metaphysics and ethics. His Appendix I has axioms and propositions, proofs and corollaries, but lacks definitions and expansive aids. Yet here and in his early correspondence (Letters 2–4) with Oldenburg, Spinoza was reaping the first fruit of his expressional variations. He obtained valuable practice in that mode of writing discovered to be best suited to his reordered thinking about God and man.

Appendix II, on the human soul, was written in straightforward prose. Yet Spinoza was actually shaping that prose into a mould similar to the many cross-references, applications and scholia of the *Ethics*. For instance, to establish that 'what we call the soul, is a mode of the attribute which we call thought,' he marshalled many previous points of the *Short Treatise* and drew forth their implications for this thesis.[7] This was a tightening exercise in the unification of his thought. As a laboratory test, Appendix III taught Spinoza what kind of additive reflections were required to achieve his distinctive sort of geometrical reasoning.

From all this, we can appreciate the patient tries and insistence out of which grew the confident presentation of the *Ethics*. It embodies Spinoza's weathered judgment about how best to conceive and communicate his philosophical intents.

SPINOZA UNDER HISTORICAL INTERROGATION

Historical understanding springs from the match made between the source philosopher and his subsequent interrogators. They must learn to vary their questions, just as he varies his manner of conveying his reasoning. The historians will devise queries about the source philosopher's life world, his genetic phases, and his mature system in its many arguments, relationships and ends-in-view. Precisely *which* questions become foremost in a given period of Spinoza research depends upon the complex, changing conditions both within this field and tangential to it. It will consider two areas where the emphases shift in relation to the total advance of scholarship: Spinoza's early convictions, and his initial statements in the *Treatise on the Correction of the Understanding*.

(a) *Spinoza's early views*. It is philosophically useful to consult the biography of Spinoza written by J. M. Lucas. We are still surprised by these four positions elicited from him by his denouncers:

[1] that God is a body . . . [2] that Scripture does not say that these
[spirits] are real and permanent substances, but mere phantoms, called

angels because God makes use of them to declare His will. . . . [3]
Wherever Scripture speaks of it, the word 'soul' is used simply to express
life, or anything that is living. . . . [4] As for the Law, it was instituted
by a man [Moses] who was in truth better versed than they [the Jewish
people] were in the matter of politics, but who was hardly more
enlightened than they were in physics or even in theology.[8]

Comparing these declarations with the mature Spinoza's writings, one sees
both the continuity and the development.

On the first point, he distinguishes the traits of perceivable physical bodies
from extension itself. To attribute extension to God does not entail attributing
corporeity also to him. The second position receives a double correction when
transferred from scripture to philosophy: 'substance' ceases to be used in the
plural, and divine 'will' is equated with the necessary (but uncoerced)
production of the natural order. In making a similar transfer regarding his
third view, Spinoza the philosopher explains 'soul' through the relation between each finite mode of extension and the idea of that mode. Hence 'soul' is
not predicated of man alone but applies to the idea-factor in every such
correlation. And immortality becomes a complex problem about intermodal
relationships (between finite and infinite modes, as well as between particular
modes of thought and extension), which cannot be resolved by scripture.
Spinoza's fourth point foreshadows his 'theologico-political' strategy of
reserving truth-questions on God and the physical universe for philosophy
and the sciences, while treating Mosaic law as a matter of practical obedience
rather than of cosmological or moral truth.

Yet even these philosophical emendations do not remove our wonderment
that Spinoza should have reached his stated convictions during his early years
in the Jewish community at Amsterdam. Here is a clear instance where
philosophical research does not occur in a vacuum but remains beneficially
open to the initiatives of other disciplines.

During the past twenty-five years, Jewish studies have transformed our
image of the *Amsterdam ghetto* of Spinoza's time.[9] It was not a closed,
monolithic enclave but the focal centre for the various currents running
through seventeenth-century Jewish culture. It felt the tremors of Messianic
hope and disillusionment emanating from Sabbati Ṣevi; it afforded
opportunities to study the Kabbalah and Ibn Ezra, along with the Talmud,
Maimonides and Crescas; its Iberian refugees imported an unusual mixture
of scholasticism and unorthodox ideas about biblical criticism, God, and
man; and it resonated with the latest currents in scientific thinking, philosophical scepticism, and religio-political realities. Despite the stiff penalties
of excommunication, this swirling intellectual atmosphere of belief and
unbelief understandably enabled Spinoza to take his early stand and orient
himself towards ultimate philosophical independence. The historical study of

Spinoza's philosophy is now being revised to assimilate these findings about his intellectual formation.

(b) *The beginning of Spinoza's Treatise on the Correction of the Understanding* is another instance where a shift in general research improves the historian's ability to interpret Spinoza himself. Here, our initial surprise arises from the very personal and emotive tone of his opening paragraphs.[10] Spinoza plunges us unceremoniously into an existential description of his situation as a searcher after a fixed good and the enduring joy of possessing it. His critique of the ordinary objects of desire – riches, fame and pleasure – belongs in the long tradition of moral philosophy reaching from Artistotle to Descartes, not to mention his religious background. But the frequency of Spinoza's first-person references to what *I* experience and debate, reflect upon and resolve, strive after and love, seems to conflict with his adherence to the geometrical manner and order of reasoning.

By way of mitigation, of course, one might observe that *Correction of the Understanding* is a chronologically early and unrevised writing. One could also surmise about the extent of Spinoza's knowledge of St Augustine's personal way of reflecting; and upon surer ground, we could cite Part I of Descartes's *Discourse on Method* and his *Meditations,* along with that author's 'I-and-my' studded Dedication and Letter to the Translator of his *Principles of Philosophy.*

Yet even these possible precedents, coupled with the suggestion that the Spinozan 'I-and-my' language is a hortatory rhetorical device, cannot remove the impression of personal immediacy and passionate involvement. The latter still remain remarkably strong and puzzling. The suggestion about a hortatory aim is indeed valid, on condition that it is not taken as the sole reason for Spinoza's first-person usage; for *Correction of the Understanding* is indeed intended as a general introduction to his philosophy as a whole (including moral liberation) and not solely to his teaching on method. However, Spinoza repeatedly refers to 'my philosophy' and 'my method', so that a personal-reflection matrix envelops even the most geometrically presented demonstrations of his *Ethics.*

As with so many other Spinozan difficulties, the historian can profit from ongoing research into the *Dutch university climate*, especially at Leiden in the mid-seventeenth century. *Praxis Logica* (1651, 1657), by that university's leading philosophy professor, Adrian Heereboord, contains a striking set of suggestions for introducing people to the treatment of simple and complex philosophical themes.[11] The recommendations show that earlier criticism of university teaching and writing in philosophy had penetrated the Leiden community by mid-century and had spread abroad. The sort of people whom Spinoza envisioned as readers of his introduction to philosophy had already learned the lesson of the Bacon-Hobbes-Descartes satirical attacks on scholastic instruction and were now becoming accustomed to more personally oriented and practical methods of philosophic instruction.

According to Heereboord, there must be a closer, more explicit, relation between the human mind's operations and its means of inquiry and communication. The latter are not self-sufficient, and the former are not irrelevant in the expressive order. The chief operations of mind needed for philosophizing are: meditating, discussing and writing. Writing constitutes the ultimate use of social and public reason in philosophy. Its fitting modes of communication are the manuscript and (increasingly so in the modern age) the published book.

Heereboord gives special attention to the published philosophical treatise, in order to make sure of its continuity with meditating and discussing. This link must be established in the author's introductory statements. The well-considered introduction should supply information of two sorts. First, it must inform the reader about the author's concrete life situation, the specific occasion for this particular writing, and the impelling or motivating cause (*causa impulsiva*) that spurs him to treat the themes actually presented in his book. Second, a responsible author has the further obligation of giving a preliminary view of the foundation, the organizing scope, and the ultimate purpose or object of his philosophical treatise.

The opening paragraphs of Spinoza's *Correction of the Understanding* follow these precepts quite faithfully. The agreement is not purely formal but represents Spinoza's own conception of the reciprocity between his personal meditating, his social discussion and teaching, and his writing activity. His philosophy achieves a unique synthesis of all these components.

Everything we know biographically and philosophically about Spinoza supports this close union. Specially symbolic of it are his passionate response to the murder of the de Witt brothers and his lifelong engagement in correspondence. For the historical interpreter, Spinoza's letters reveal that his 'I-and-my' language is truly rooted in his own reflections and efforts at clarifying his thought. This process is socially communicated and sensitively adapted to the mind and situation of his correspondents. A linguistic sign of the personally imbedded quality of Spinoza's philosophy is found in his use of the terms 'feeling' and 'to feel'.[12] Apart from descriptive passages, the usage is sparingly reserved for those crucial meeting points between awareness of individual existence, recognition of the ordered inclusiveness of finite within infinite mode, and responsiveness of love toward the eternal. All these interconnections carry personal significance in the midst of systematic development.

Under interrogation from diverse perspectives, then, Spinoza's reply is framed in contextual, personal, and systemic-inferential terms. He instructs his historical interpreters in the use and refinement of their own canons. This is the sort of meeting between source thinker and historian in which some contributory insight is gained about the peculiar values of each participant.

127

SPINOZA AND OUR PLURAL MODEL-MAKING

As the third major ingredient of the meaning of history of modern philosophy, I have specified the source philosopher's capacity for becoming related to our current problems and procedures. One method widely cultivated in philosophy and other disciplines today is the construction of various kinds of models. Hence a promising route for interpreters of Spinoza is to relate his philosophy to some endeavours in this field.

When such a comparative study is tried, the first finding is that model-making takes place at both poles of the comparison: in Spinoza as well as in his present-day investigators. As for Spinoza himself, he deliberately engages in the construction of at least three types of models: (a) epistemic description, (b) explanatory foundation, and (c) psycho-social moral growth. In each area, he is reflectively aware of what he is doing, and often varies the particular models. The result is a contribution to *our* general model-theory and not solely to *his* making activity.

(a) Descriptive models of the epistemic process are sometimes set forth to differentiate among the degrees of cognition. Spinoza distinguishes between hearsay and memorative acts, experiential grasp of objects, the way of inferential reasoning, and peak intuition. But when some aspect of this process of cognitive activity is challenged, Spinoza responds most vigorously in model language.[13]

Thus when the objection is advanced that the whole cognitive process can never get started for lack of something to improve upon, he updates the replies of Bacon and Descartes to the same difficulty. Just as the human hand moves from primitive to more sophisticatedly fashioned tools, so does the human mind move from the basic idea it has (or *is*) to ever more adequate tools or methods of knowing. Epistemic method-making is thus compared with the making of material tools and machines, as a clarification of how human cognition grows more effective. Again, when his correspondents balk at the notion of a cognitive growth moving from finite to infinite modes and attributes of the universe, Spinoza employs analogical cognitive models of development. He likens the finite human mind to a conscious and actively reflective worm or corpuscle in the blood stream. Its expanding awareness of a surpassing environment functions as a modelling of how human cognition becomes aware of infinite modes and attributes of substance.

(b) If we make the connection between the later sections of *Correction of the Understanding* and the opening definitions of Parts I and II of *Ethics*, we can discern there a primary model of explanatory foundation.[14] Towards the end of the former work, Spinoza gives rules of definition for a created thing and an uncreated thing. The primacy is accorded to the latter type of definition in accord with the understanding's ordination to positive eternal actuality. Then in the basic definitions of the *Ethics* treatment of God and man's mind, these rules are exhibited in operation. From this schematic model of foundational meanings, Spinoza then proceeds with his explanatory reasoning. Due to the presence of this foundational model, he has a basis for meeting the charge that his definitions are arbitrary and his explanations groundless.

(c) There is a close relation between the already discussed initial paragraphs of *Correction of the Understanding* and Parts III and IV of *Ethics*. In the former work, Spinoza recognizes the formation of some human model (*naturam aliquam humanam*) which is superior to one's present weakness, and which will serve as an intermediate goal and spur to self-improvement. Any improvement coming from the encouragement of such an attainable ideal of human living is social as well as psychological, since it inclines one to aid others to realize a similar pattern. In the parts of the *Ethics* treating of our subjugation to the passions and our use of the image of the Stoic wise man, as an aid in achieving personal and social freedom, Spinoza concretizes this model.[15] He builds it up with the aid of many paragraphs of counsel and moral encouragement, proportioned to a midway development of our power and freedom over our passions and actions. In the *Theologico-Political Treatise* and the *Political Treatise*, he develops the social consequences of intermediate and ideal models of community life.

Looking at contemporary studies on Spinoza, we find them divided into epistemological, metaphysical and moral-actional models.[16] The epistemological ones provide a focus for inquiries about Spinozan method and cognition. Metaphysical models are useful for organizing analytic studies of his theories of substance and attributes, modes and the human composite. And the moral-actional models connect Spinoza with flourishing contemporary theories of action and freedom.

But when a historical comparison is made between Spinoza's own developments in model-theory and those made by contemporary students of his philosophy, three deficiencies in the contemporary efforts become apparent: The most important lack is that of a *unifying model* that can do justice to what Spinoza names as his philosophy and his method. There is continuity of reflection and argumentation when Spinoza treats the problems of method and knowledge, metaphysics and passional psychology, and ethics in its personal and socio-political dimensions. His values of continuity and systemic unification call for an overarching kind of model. Yet the synthesis should assimilate, rather than blur, the more restricted models and their analytic advances in the understanding and criticism of Spinoza. Perhaps his chief function for today's model-theorists is precisely to argue for both the pluralism and the integration of models.

Two other unsettling results of a *rapprochement* between Spinoza and current model approaches to him can also be observed. Our model-theories tend to treat his philosophy as static and ahistorical, whereas Spinoza himself undergoes constant development, refinement and polemical effectiveness of his thought. Historical interpretation depends upon achieving meanings that express models of *internal growth*. There is no essential incompatibility between the more standard-argument type of Spinozan model and the more developmental type. But their unification depends upon taking a second-level look at the present dichotomies.

The other finding is that there is need for reconsidering Spinoza's role in seventeenth-century philosophy. If we give due weight to philosophical developments in that century, then the tight alternatives of rationalism and empiricism can be responsibly loosened and replaced by more *functional historical models*. Spinoza and Locke (both of whom were born in 1632) faced roughly the same problems inherited from Descartes and Hobbes. An inquiry-model on the philosophical advancements made by Spinoza and Locke opens the prospect for aligning them together on some issues, whatever their grave differences on others.

My conclusion is that inquiry into Spinoza's philosophy does yield a paradigm for historical work. Whether that philosophy be considered in its own texture and textual expression or in its problems for historical questioning or in its relation with our contemporary interests, it taxes an interpreter's ability and enriches his art in a distinctive way. Spinoza does not surrender his meanings cheaply or ever exhaustively. But he is always ready to enter the interpreting process anew with us. Thus Spinoza provides us with a unified sustaining example of the demands and rewards of the historical study of the great philosophical sources.

NOTES

1 G. W. F. Hegel, *Lectures on the History of Philosophy*, trans. E. S. Haldane and F. H. Simson (3 vols, New York: Humanities Press, 1955), vol. 3, p. 257. Hegel's criticism of Spinoza is made on pp. 282–9.

2 For this theory, see James Collins, *Interpreting Modern Philosophy* (Princeton University Press, 1975).

3 Spinoza, *Earlier Philosophical Thoughts*, trans. F. A. Hayes (Indianapolis: Bobbs-Merrill, 1963), pp. 3–9, where the reader is also alerted to the wide scope of Descartes's works under comment and critique.

4 Chapter 1 of *Korte Verhandeling van God, de Mensch en des zelfs Welstand*, in *Spinoza Opera*, ed. C. Gebhardt (4 vols, Heidelberg: Winter, 1925), vol. 1, p. 17 n; *Spinoza's Short Treatise on God, Man, and His Well-Being*, trans. A. Wolf (London: Black, 1910), p. 19 n. The next quoted phrase is from ch. 2 of *Korte Verhandeling* (Gebhardt, *ed. cit.*, vol. 1, p. 20); *Short Treatise* (Wolf, *op. cit.*, p. 22). Translations are sometimes emended.

5 Chapter 2 of *Korte Verhandeling* (Gebhardt, *ed. cit.*, vol. 1, p. 22); *Short Treatise* (Wolf, *ed. cit.*, p. 25).

6 G. Deleuze, *Spinoza et le problème de l'expression* (Paris: Minuit, 1968), examines the tension and reciprocity between the formal plan of the *Ethics* and its scholia.

7 Appendix II of *Korte Verhandeling* (Gebhardt, ed. cit., vol. 1, p. 117); *Short Treatise* (Wolf, ed. cit., p. 157).

8 *The Oldest Biography of Spinoza*, ed. and trans. A. Wolf (London: Allen & Unwin, 1927), pp. 45, 46, 49. These statements expressed an attitude towards the literal interpretation of scripture which found systematic development in Spinoza's *Theologico-Political Treatise*. Cf. S. Zac, *Spinoza et l'interprétation de l'Écriture* (Paris: Presses Universitaires, 1965).

9 On Spinoza's intellectual relations with Jewish culture in Amsterdam, see I. S. Révah, *Spinoza et Juan de Prado* (Paris: Mouton, 1959); G. Brykman, *La Judéité de Spinoza* (Paris: Vrin, 1972); R. H. Popkin, 'The Marrano Theology of Isaac La Peyrère', *Studi Internazionali di Filosofia*, 5 (1973), 97–113; and G. Scholem, *Sabbatai Sevi: The Mystical Messiah* (Princeton University Press, 1974).

10 *Tractatus De Intellectus Emendatione* (Gebhardt, *op. cit.*, vol. 2, pp. 5–9; van Vloten and Land's numbered paragraphs 1–16); *On the Improvement of the Understanding*, in *The Chief Works of Benedict De Spinoza*, trans. R. H. M. Elwes (reprint, 2 vols, New York: Dover, 1951), vol. 2, pp. 3–7.

11 Adrian Heereboord, *Praxis Logica* (3rd edn., Leiden: Lodenstein, 1657; bound together and in continuous pagination with Heereboord's *Hermeneia Logica*), paras. 33–48, pp. 315–23. See P. Dibon, *La Philosophie néerlandaise au siècle d'or*, vol. 1 (Amsterdam: Elsevier, 1954); and E G. Ruestow, *Physics at 17th and 18th Century Leiden* (The Hague: Nijhoff, 1973).

12 Consult E. Giancotti Boscherini, *Lexicon Spinozanum* (2 vols, The Hague: Nijhoff, 1970), vol. 2, pp. 1004–6, 1188–90, s.v. 'Sentire', 'Gevoel', and 'Gewaar worden'.

13 On tool-making and method-making, see *Tractatus Intellectus de Emendatione* (Gebhardt, ed. cit., vol. 2, pp. 13–14, paras. 30–1); *On the Improvement of the Understanding* (Elwes, ed. cit., vol. 2, pp. 11–12). The worm's-eye-view image is used in *Epistola 32* (Gebhardt, ed. cit., vol. 4, pp. 169–74); *The Correspondence of Spinoza*, trans. A. Wolf (New York: Dial Press, 1928), pp. 294–7.

14 *Tractatus Intellectus de Emendatione* (Gebhardt, ed. cit. vol. 2, pp. 34–6, paras. 92–8); *On the Improvement of the Understanding* (Elwes, ed. cit., vol. 2, pp. 34–6). These rules govern the Definitions and Axioms in *Ethica* I and II (Gebhardt, op. cit., vol. 2, pp. 45–7, 84–6); *Ethics* (Elwes, ed. cit., vol. 2, pp. 45–6, 82–3).

15 Especially the psycho-moral counsels, given in chapter form, in the Appendix to *Ethica*, IV (Gebhardt, ed. cit., vol. 2, pp. 266–76); *Ethics* (Elwes, ed. cit., vol. 2, pp. 236–43). That the process of moral liberation must ultimately be social, is the theme of A. Matheron's *Individu et communauté chez Spinoza* (Paris: Minuit, 1969).

16 Types of model-work concerning Spinoza are exemplified by: H. G. Hubbeling, *Spinoza's Methodology* (Assen: Van Gorcum, 1964); G. H. R. Parkinson, *Spinoza's Theory of Knowledge* (Oxford: Clarendon Press, 1954); E. M. Curley,

Spinoza's Metaphysics: An Essay in Interpretation (Cambridge: Harvard University Press, 1969); Stuart Hampshire, 'Spinoza and the Idea of Freedom', in *Spinoza: A Collection of Critical Essays*, ed. M. Grene (New York: Doubleday Anchor, 1973); and James Collins, 'Inquiry-Model on Philosophical Advancement', *The Modern Schoolman, 52* (1974–5), 3–25.

6 Spinoza – as an expositor of Descartes

Edwin Curley, Canberra

Until recently Spinoza's exposition, *more geometrico*, of the first two parts of Descartes's *Principles of Philosophy* has been widely esteemed, but relatively little studied. In the seventeenth century this work, the only one Spinoza published under his own name in his lifetime, gained him sufficient reputation that he was offered a chair of philosophy at the University of Heidelberg;[1] in this century Gilson commended Spinoza to students of Descartes as 'un commentateur incomparable';[2] and Caillois has gone so far as to claim that, although Spinoza sometimes criticizes Descartes on essential points, his *exposition* is always faithful to Descartes's thought.[3]

Only fairly recently has there been any serious challenge to these favourable evaluations. In 1960 Gueroult concluded, with respect to the *cogito*, that Spinoza had fundamentally transformed the sense of the philosophy he was trying to expound;[4] and similarly, David Bidney, in his introduction to a recent English translation of Spinoza's work, has contended that Spinoza 'was simply too original and creative a writer to submerge his own thought and allow his subject to speak for himself', that he 'read his own ideas into Descartes, and his exposition of Descartes often tells us more about Spinoza than about his subject'.[5] His chief example of this involves Spinoza's solution to the problem of the Cartesian circle.

Without necessarily agreeing with their reasons for passing this adverse judgment on Spinoza as a historian of Descartes's thought, I must side here with Gueroult and Bidney. Whether or not Gueroult's interpretation of the *cogito* is correct, Spinoza's certainly is not. As for the circle, Spinoza offers two possible replies to the charge that Descartes's procedure is circular. Bidney evidently takes Spinoza to be offering both these replies as possible *interpretations* of Descartes, and thinks neither of them satisfactory. I take Spinoza to be offering only the first as an interpretation and the second as an improvement on Descartes;[6] and it seems to me that his improvement on Descartes is far closer to being a correct interpretation of Descartes than what he offers as Descartes's reply to the charge of circularity. So perhaps it would be more accurate to say that one of Spinoza's faults as an expositor of

133

Descartes is that sometimes he refrains from reading his own ideas into Descartes when that is precisely what he should do.

To substantiate the judgments of the preceding paragraph would require an extensive discussion of classical problems of Cartesian scholarship on which I have already had my say elsewhere.[7] Here I propose to take up another matter on which I think Spinoza misunderstands Descartes – one which has not yet, so far as I know, received any attention, but one which is absolutely fundamental to Spinoza's project in this work. I refer to Spinoza's concept of the mathematical method itself – and the related distinction between analysis and synthesis.

Spinoza's work bears the title, *Parts I and II of Descartes' 'Principles of Philosophy', Demonstrated in the Geometric Manner*. It is natural to ask: What justifies the sub-title? In what sense is this a geometric demonstration of Descartes's philosophy? The obvious answer is that it is a geometric demonstration because it employs an apparatus of proof analogous to that of Euclid's *Elements*. This certainly seems to be the spirit of Lodewijk Meyer's preface:

> It is the unanimous opinion of everyone who wishes to be wiser than is common among men that the best and surest way of seeking and teaching the truth in the sciences is that of the mathematicians, who demonstrate their conclusions from definitions, postulates and axioms (I, 127).

And Meyer makes some very strong claims for that way of proceeding:

> Since a certain and firm knowledge of anything unknown can only be derived from things known certainly beforehand, these things must be laid down at the start as a stable foundation on which the whole edifice of human knowledge may be constructed (*ibid.*).

So the use of the geometric method, thus understood, is made essential to any advance in knowledge which can properly be deemed the acquisition of certain knowledge. A bit further on, Descartes is hailed as 'that brightest star of our age' for having been the first to succeed in applying the mathematical method to philosophy and for uncovering firm foundations for that discipline.

But one difficulty with this obvious answer is that very little of Descartes's work is actually written in the geometric manner as we have so far described it. Descartes only once, and then very briefly and reluctantly, at the end of the Second Replies, sets out his arguments in the form of axioms, definitions, propositions and demonstrations. If Descartes had expounded very much of his philosophy in this style, there would have been no need for Spinoza to do it for him.

Meyer, of course, knows this, admits it, and calls attention to that passage at the end of the Second Replies where Descartes distinguishes between analysis and synthesis. He quotes briefly from it, but I think it may be helpful to give a somewhat fuller account. Descartes distinguishes first between the geometrical order and the geometrical style of demonstrating:

> Order consists only in this that those things which are first proposed must be known without any assistance from those which follow, and that they are demonstrated solely from what precedes them.[8]

Descartes claims that the *Meditations* are so written as to conform to this requirement.

But there are two different ways in which works may be geometrically demonstrated by analysis and by synthesis:

> Analysis shown the true way by which the thing was methodically . . . discovered, so that if the reader is willing to follow it and to attend sufficiently to everything, he understands it and makes it his no less perfectly than if he had discovered it himself. . . . Synthesis, on the other hand . . . uses a long series of definitions, postulates, axioms, and theorems, so that if anyone denies any of the consequences, it shows him immediately that it is contained in what went before, and so it forces the reader's assent, however contrary and stubborn he may be; but unlike analysis it does not satisfy anyone who wishes to learn, because it does not show how the thing was discovered (C. Adam and P. Tannery, *Oeuvres*, Paris: Vrin, 1897–1913, VII, 155–6).

Descartes maintains that analysis is the true and best way of teaching, and that the *Meditations* have been demonstrated in the analytic way.

Up to this point in his preface Meyer appears to have been identifying the geometric or mathematical method with what Descartes would call the synthetic method, so that his strong claims for the value of the mathematical method would in fact be claims for the value of the synthetic mathematical method. But having introduced Descartes's distinction between two styles of geometrical demonstration, Meyer allows that both of them can achieve certainty, and argues merely that the analytic mode is not suited to everyone. He does not discuss Descartes's reasons for thinking that the analytic mode is the best one for teaching, but does offer a justification for preferring the synthetic mode:

> Since most men are completely unskilled in the mathematical sciences, and quite ignorant, both of the synthetic method in which they have been written, and of the analytic method by which they have been discovered, they can neither follow for themselves, nor present to others, the things which are . . . demonstrated conclusively in these books. That is why many who have been led, either by a blind impulse, or by the authority of someone else, to enlist as followers of Descartes, have only impressed his opinions and doctrines on their memory; when the subject

135

comes up, they know only how to chatter and babble, but not how to demonstrate anything (I, 129).

In this regard they are no better than the followers of Aristotle. To assist such people Spinoza has undertaken to present synthetically what Descartes presented analytically.

But this rationale makes it clear that Spinoza's project rests on a mistake, for the work Spinoza is presenting synthetically is not the *Meditations* but the *Principles of Philosophy*, and according to Descartes the *Principles*, unlike the *Meditations*, are already written in the synthetic mode and not in the analytic mode.[9] This suggests that Spinoza fundamentally misunderstood the contrast Descartes wished to make between analysis and synthesis.

Now it will not have escaped notice that I speak here of Spinoza's misunderstanding Descartes, whereas my evidence of the misunderstanding, where it does not come from Descartes's statements about the difference between analysis and synthesis, comes from Meyer's preface to Spinoza's work, and it may seem unfair to hold Spinoza responsible for Meyer's mistakes. But I would disagree.

It is clear from Spinoza's correspondence that he read the preface in manuscript, and made suggestions about what should be included and omitted, which Meyer faithfully followed.[10] It seems unlikely that Spinoza would have let pass any interpretation of Descartes with which he seriously disagreed. Moreover the point on which I am claiming a misunderstanding is such a fundamental one that Spinoza's whole project of recasting the *Principles* would be difficult to understand if he had not agreed with Meyer that that work had been presented by Descartes analytically.

If Spinoza misunderstands the distinction between analysis and synthesis, how does he do so, and why does he do so? I would suggest that Spinoza was over-impressed by certain features of the organization of material which characterize the Geometrical Exposition at the end of the Second Replies and distinguish that work from the *Principles*, and that he overlooked more important similarities between those two works, which distinguish both of them from the *Meditations*.

In the Geometrical Exposition the material is organized as readers of Euclid would expect a geometrical demonstration to be organized. Descartes begins with a series of definitions, postulates and axioms, and then proceeds to prove four propositions and one corollary, justifying each step in terms of some preceding step. In the *Principles* the material is not organized in this way. What I suggest is that, in Descartes's eyes, this is merely a superficial difference. What do the two works have in common which distinguish both of them from the *Meditations*?

One feature they have in common is that they both offer formal definitions of important concepts. For example, both the *Principles* and the Geometrical

Exposition offer a definition of *cogitatio* – essentially the same definition.[11] That term is not defined in the *Meditations*; though Descartes's use of the term is unusual, he contents himself with indicating the range of activities he includes under that heading by giving examples.[12]

Similarly with clarity and distinctness. For definitions of these terms we must go to a synthetic work like the *Principles* (I, 45). In the analytic *Meditations* they are introduced by way of the example of the wax at the end of the Second Meditation. Part of the purpose of that discussion is to bring us to the point of having a clear and distinct idea, and so to define clarity and distinctness quasi-ostensively.

This, I suggest, is not accidental, but quite deliberate. Descartes thinks that the concepts which are important for philosophy are concepts which it would be difficult to define in a way which would be helpful to someone who does not already have the concept; and if he already has the concept, he will not require the definition.[13]

Another important feature which distinguishes the synthetic works from the *Meditations* is the prompt and explicit recognition of the role of eternal truths in the argument. This is most conspicuous in the case where it has been most contentious, the *cogito*:

> But when we thus reject all those things about which we can have any doubt . . . we easily suppose that there is no God, no heaven, no bodies, and even that we ourselves have neither hands nor feet, nor any body at all – but not that we who think such things are nothing. *For it involves a contradiction to suppose that what thinks does not exist at the same time that it thinks* (*Principles* I, 7, my emphasis).

True, Descartes goes on to say, immediately after the passage just quoted, that 'This knowledge, *I think, therefore I exist*, is the first and most certain of all those which occur to anyone philosophizing in an orderly way' (Descartes's emphasis). But this is not intended to exclude a role for the general proposition, as Descartes makes clear three paragraphs later:

> When I said that this proposition, *I think, therefore I exist*, is the first and most certain which occurs to anyone philosophizing in an orderly way, I did not on that account deny that it is necessary to know, before this, *what thought is, what existence is, what certainty is*, and *that it cannot happen that what thinks does not exist* (*Principles* I, 10, Descartes's emphasis).[14]

In the *Meditations* no proposition equivalent to 'Whatever thinks must exist when it thinks' is ever explicitly stated. Descartes does there mention a somewhat less general eternal truth, viz. 'Let whoever can deceive me, he shall still never bring it about that I am nothing so long as I think I am something' (Adam and Tannery, *op. cit.*, VII, 36). But it is symptomatic of the difference between the analytic and synthetic methods that this proposition is introduced only at the beginning of the Third Meditation, when Descartes, in spite of apparently having established his own existence in the Second Meditation, is once again wondering whether he can ever be fully certain of anything.

The appearance of the external truth can be delayed in the analytic *Meditations,* not because the inference from thought to existence does not in some sense depend on it but because it would not be helpful to make that truth explicit at an earlier stage of the argument. If the reader does see that the inference is valid in the particular case, he won't need to have the principle behind it stated. And if he does not see that the inference is valid in the particular case, he won't accept the general principle on which it rests. The best order requires us to begin with the particular and move to the general.[15]

Now it may seem ungracious to argue, in a paper written to honour Spinoza on the tercentenary of his death, that he misunderstood Descartes on a fundamental point. But if we explore the reasons for this misunderstanding, we may find that they reflect no discredit on Spinoza. It is true, as Gilson says,[16] that Spinoza and other contemporary interpreters of Descartes had some advantages over their twentieth-century counterparts. The philosophical language in which Descartes wrote was more familiar to them than it is to us, and to the extent that Descartes was expressing 'les plus secrètes aspirations de leur pensée', his writings must have seemed less strange to them than they often do to us.

But twentieth-century commentators do have some compensation. First of all, some texts are available to us which were not available to Spinoza and his contemporaries. The *Entretien avec Burman,* for example, was first published in 1896. Before that the only known manuscript was in the library of the University of Göttingen. It is not clear to what extent copies circulated privately.[17] Yet this document sheds a great deal of light on the distinction between analysis and synthesis.[18]

Similar remarks apply to the *Regulae,* another work which helps to illuminate that distinction and which was not published until some years after Spinoza wrote his account of Descartes's philosophy.[19] In this case we know that manuscript copies were circulating privately. Leibniz was able to purchase one in Amsterdam in 1670; and by 1664 – just one year after Spinoza's work – Arnauld and Nicole had received one from Clerselier, which they used to expand their account of analysis in the second edition of their *Logic.*[20] But when the Port Royal logicians published their first edition in 1662, they evidently did *not* have a copy of the *Regulae*; and since they were much closer to the source than Spinoza was, it seems unlikely that he would have seen one in 1663.[21]

The discovery of a previously unpublished text may provide the historian of philosophy with new data against which to test existing theories of interpretation. But progress in understanding past philosophers does not depend entirely, or even chiefly perhaps, on such happy accidents. Grasping a philosopher's meaning is hard work in the best of circumstances, and two interpreters working on the same body of texts may easily reach quite different results. One very important advantage which the twentieth-century commentator has in dealing with a seventeenth-century figure like Descartes is that he is the heir of three hundred years of critical discussion of Descartes's philosophy. As one interpretation is advanced, criticized, modified, and perhaps abandoned, to be replaced by another, it is reasonable to hope that those which survive this process will be good ones, better than we were likely to have had without that extended process of joint reflection.

Certainly it is an illusion to suppose that Descartes's more intelligent contemporaries must have understood him more easily than we can. He did write in a language somewhat less strange to them than it is to us, but it was not altogether a language they already spoke. It was, in important respects, a new language which they had to learn from him (as is illustrated both by *cogitatio* and by *more geometrico demonstrata*). Nor did Descartes altogether express the innermost aspirations even of his most sympathetic followers. Arnauld and Nicole show the same tendency as Spinoza to identify the geometric method with the synthetic geometric method. Even after they have read the *Regulae*, they dismiss analysis as a method which one uses only for resolving particular questions, not for treating the whole body of a science. They continue to regard synthesis as the most important method, and devote most of the space in their section on method to laying down rules for following the synthetic method.[22]

The reactions of one major philosopher in a period to his more important contemporaries – of Spinoza to Descartes, of Leibniz and Malebranche to Spinoza, of Leibniz to Locke, etc. – must always be of great interest to later historians of philosophy. But we should beware of supposing that, because they were contemporary with the philosophers on whom they commented, they were peculiarly well placed to understand them correctly.

NOTES

1 Or so it has usually been thought, at any rate. Cf., for example, R. Caillois, *Oeuvres complètes de Spinoza*, Paris: Bibliothèque de la Pléiade, 1954, p. 145; and Charles Appuhn, *Oeuvres de Spinoza*, Paris: Garnier, 1964, vol. I, p. 228. Wolf, however, conjectured that 'it was the author of the *Tractatus Theologico-Politicus* that the Prince Palatine wanted, and not merely the author of the geometric version of Descartes *Principles of Philosophy* (A. Wolf, *The Correspondence of Spinoza*, London: Allen & Unwin, 1928, p. 442). In favour of this it may be said that Spinoza's authorship of the *Theological-Political Treatise* does seem to have been well-known in Heidelberg. See M. Mayer, 'Spinozas Berufung an die Hochschule zu Heidelberg', *Chronicon Spinozanum*, III, The Hague, 1923, pp. 20–44.

2 E. Gilson, 'Spinoza interprète de Descartes', *Chronicon Spinozanum*, vol. III, p. 68.

3 Caillois, *op. cit.*, p. 146; similarly, Appuhn, *op. cit.*, p. 225.

4 M. Gueroult, *Etudes sur Descartes, Spinoza, Malebranche et Leibniz*, Hildesheim: Georg Olms, 1970, p. 78.

5 Spinoza, *Earlier Philosophical Writings*, trans. by F. Hayes with an introduction by David Bidney, Indianapolis: Bobbs-Merrill, 1963, p. xvii.

6 Cf. Willis Doney, *Descartes, a Collection of Critical Essays*, London: Macmillan, 1968, p. 20. The passage in the Prolegomenon to the *Principles* in which Spinoza offers this solution (C. Gebhardt, *Spinoza Opera*, Heidelberg, 1925, vol. I, pp. 147–9) is paralleled by one in the *Treatise on the Correction of the Intellect*, para. 79 (vol. II, p. 30).

7 In a forthcoming book tentatively titled *Descartes Against the Skeptics*.

8 *Oeuvres*, ed. C. Adam and P. Tannery, Paris: J. Vrin, 1897–1913, vol. VII, p. 155.

9 At least they are if we may trust the *Entretien avec Burman*. See Adam and Tannery, *op. cit.*, vol. V, p. 153. Some Cartesian scholars are very sceptical of the value of that work, and of course it must be admitted that it is not a work written by Descartes but Burman's record of an interview he had with Descartes, and that it does *sometimes* seem that it could not be an accurate record. Cf. F. Alquié, *Oeuvres philosophiques de Descartes*, Paris: Garnier, 1973, pp. 765–7. Our judgments about its probable accuracy are inevitably affected by what we think Descartes likely to have said, given our knowledge of works which are unequivocally his. I am not convinced by *all* of Alquié's allegations of inaccuracy, and on this particular point I trust Burman. If Burman's record is right, Descartes has changed his mind and no longer thinks the analytic mode best for teaching. On the other hand, Burman's Descartes does give a plausible explanation of the fact that the order of the arguments for the existence of God in the *Principles* is the same as that in the Geometrical Exposition, and different from that in the *Meditations* proper. Note also that in the *Principles* the distinction of mind and body is introduced immediately after the *cogito* (I, 8), before God's existence has been proven (I, 14) and even before the proposition that the mind is better known than the body (I, 11). In the *Meditations* it is not established until the Sixth Meditation.

10 See Letters 13 and 15.

11 *Principles*, I, 9; Geometrical Exposition, Definition 1.

12 See Adam and Tannery, *op. cit.*, vol. VII, p. 28. Regarding the unusualness of Descartes's usage, Anscombe and Geach (Descartes, *Philosophical Writings*, London: Nelson, 1969, p. xlvii) argue that '*cogitare* and its derivatives had long been used in a very wide sense in philosophical Latin'; but I am persuaded by Kenny's counter-argument that seventeenth-century Latin usage of *cogitatio* was never as wide as Descartes's and that Descartes was consciously extending existing usage. (See his *Descartes*, New York: Random House, 1968, pp. 68–9.)

13 Cf. *Principles* I, 10, and the letter to Mersenne of 16 October 1639 (Alquié, *op. cit.*, II, 144; Adam and Tannery, *op. cit.*, vol. II, 596–7). The letter contains a discussion of defining truth which is worth comparing with Spinoza's analysis of truth in the *Cogitata Metaphysica*, vol. I, p. vi. The general tenor of Spinoza's

analysis seems not to be Cartesian, and it is an interesting question whether he was familiar with the letter to Mersenne. It was first published in volume II of Clerselier's edition of Descartes's correspondence in 1659. The only edition of Descartes's correspondence listed on the inventory of Spinoza's library made at at his death in 1677 was Glazemaker's translation, published in 1661 (see *Catalogus van de Bibliotheek der Vereniging het Spinozahuis te Rijnsburg*, Leiden: E. J. Brill, 1965, p. 22). But Spinoza does sometimes refer to the Clerselier edition. For example, in the geometric version of Descartes's *Principles* (II, P 6S) he refers to Letter 118 of volume I of that edition (cf. Adam and Tannery, *op. cit.*, vol. IV, p. 442–7).

14 This passage was the subject of one of Burman's questions (Adam and Tannery, *op. cit.*, vol. V, 147) and I find nothing surprising in the reply reported, though Alquié evidently does. See *Alquié, op. cit.*, vol. III, p. 766.

15 The reply to Burman (Adam and Tannery, *op. cit.*, vol. V, 147) may here be compared with the reply to Gassendi (Adam and Tannery, *op. cit.*, vol. IX, pp. 205–6). I have discussed Descartes's antiformalism in more detail in *Descartes Against the Skeptics*.

16 Gilson, *op. cit.*, p. 68.

17 The Göttingen manuscript was copied from a manuscript of Clauberg's at Dordrecht in 1648 (Adam and Tannery, *op. cit.*, vol. V, 145). Some scholars have asserted very confidently that Spinoza did know the *Entretien*. Cf. Caillois, *op. cit.*, p. 1407.

Lachieze-Rey (*Les Origines cartésiennes du Dieu de Spinoza*, Paris: J. Vrin, 1950, pp. 91–3) is rightly more cautious. Some of Spinoza's objections to Descartes are very similar to ones made by Burman. But these are objections which might occur easily enough to a careful student of the *Principles*, since they are based on apparent self-contradictions. If Spinoza did take these objections over from Burman, his silence about Descartes's replies is more than a little surprising.

18 It is interesting to note that some twentieth-century commentators, who have less excuse, have followed Spinoza in thinking Descartes's *Principles* were written in the analytic mode. Cf. Gilson, *op. cit.*, p. 75, and Bidney, *op. cit.*, p. xxxi. Indeed Bidney thinks even the *Cogitata Metaphysica* were written analytically, though it seems far more reasonable to suppose that that work would not have been regarded by Spinoza as being written according to any kind of mathematical method. Its method seems rather to be the method of definition and division disparaged by Meyer at the beginning of his preface.

19 A date often given for the publication of the *Regulae* is 1710, the date when the Latin text was first published. But a translation was published in 1684 by Glazemaker, the translator of Spinoza's *Opera posthuma*. See *Regulae ad directionem ingenii*, ed. by G. Crapulli, The Hague: Martinus Nijhoff, 1966.

20 Cf. Antoine, Arnauld and Pierre Nicole, *La Logique ou l'art de penser*, ed. by P. Clair and F. Girbal, Paris: Presses Universitaires de France, 1965, p. 300.

21 Koyré, in his edition of the *Treatise* (*Traité de la réforme de l'entendement*, Paris: J. Vrin, 1969), frequently invites us to compare passages in that work with passages in the *Regulae*, sometimes suggesting that Spinoza's thought may have

been inspired by reading Descartes's. Since the *Treatise* was quite probably written about 1661, this would imply that Spinoza knew the *Regulae* when he wrote his exposition of Descartes. I do not find Koyré's parallels convincing. More striking than any he mentions is the similarity between Gebhardt, *op. cit.*, II, 13–14 (Bruder PPs 30–1) and Adam and Tannery, *op. cit.*, X, p. 397. But even this strikes me as expressing an idea Spinoza might easily have had independently of Descartes.

22 *Op. cit.* See particularly, pp. 300, 306.

7 Spinoza – my paean

Will Durant, Los Angeles

... I would be happy to share in the Spinoza Symposium, but I am
verging on ninety, and am too old to undertake your assignment.
Perhaps you could find, in my volume *The Age of Louis XIV*,[1] something
you might use, especially the final paragraph, which is my final Paean.[2]

England for a century knew Spinoza chiefly through hearsay, and denounced
him as a distant and terrible ogre.
Sillingfleet (1677) referred to him vaguely as

late author (who) I hear is mightily in vogue among many who cry up
anything on the atheistical side.

A Scottish professor, George Sinclair (1685), wrote of

monstrous rabble of men who, following the Hobbesian and Spinozan
principle, slight religion and undervalue the Scripture.

Sir John Evelyn (1690?) spoke of the *Tractatus Theologico-Politicus* as

that infamous book a wretched obstacle to the searchers of holy truth.

Berkeley (1732), while ranking Spinoza among

weak and wicked writers, (thought him) the great leader of our modern
infidels.

As late as 1739 the agnostic Hume shuddered cautiously at the

hideous hypothesis (of) that famous atheist, (the) universally infamous
Spinoza.

Not till the romantic movement at the turn of the eighteenth into the
nineteenth century did Spinoza reach the English mind. Then he, more than
any other philosopher, inspired the youthful metaphysics of Wordsworth,
Coleridge, Shelley and Byron.

Shelley quoted the *Tractatus Theologico-Politicus* in the original notes to
Queen Mab, and began a translation of it, for which Byron pledged a preface;
a fragment of this version came into the hands of an English critic, who,
taking it for a work by Shelley himself, called it a

schoolboy speculation ... too crude for publication entire.

George Eliot translated the Ethics with virile resolution and James Froude
and Matthew Arnold acknowledged the influence of Spinoza on their mental
development.[3]

Of all the intellectual products of man, religion and philosophy seem to endure the longest. Pericles is famous because he lived in the days of Socrates.

We love Spinoza especially among the philosophers because he was also a saint, because he lived, as well as wrote, philosophy. The virtues praised by the great religions, were honored and embodied in the outcast who could find a home in none of the religions, since none would let him conceive God in terms that science could accept.

Looking back upon that dedicated life and concentrated thought, we feel in them an element of nobility that encourages us to think well of mankind.

Let us admit half of the terrible picture that Swift drew of humanity; let us agree that in every generation of man's history, and almost everywhere, we find superstition, hypocrisy, corruption, cruelty, crime and war: in the balance against them we place the long roster of poets, composers, artists, scientists, philosophers, and saints.

The same species upon which poor Swift revenged the frustrations of his flesh, wrote the plays of Shakespeare, the music of Bach and Händel, the odes of Keats, the *Republic* of Plato, the *Principia* of Newton, and
the *Ethics* of Spinoza;
it built the Parthenon and painted the ceiling of the Sistine Chapel; it conceived and cherished, even crucified, Christ.

Man did all this: let him never despair!

NOTES

1 W. Durant, *The Age of Louis XIV*, Simon Schuster, New York, 1963, pp. 656 ff.
2 In a private letter to me dated 2 July 1975, so his 'Final Paen' should not be missing in this common homage for Spinoza.
3 There could still be added later names, as Sir Frederick Pollock and especially F. H. Hallett with whom I shared my admiration for Spinoza in my symposium *Spinoza – 300 Jahre Ewigkeit*, Martinus Nijhoff, The Hague, 1962, and where he published his last great work, *Creation, Emanation and Salvation*.

8   Is Spinoza an ethical naturalist?[1]

Paul D. Eisenberg, Indiana

I propose to comment on two recent papers which approach Spinoza's ethics in a relatively novel way. In them their authors ask probing questions concerning the so-called meta-ethics of Spinoza's *Ethics* (or, of his ethics). These papers are Edwin M. Curley's 'Spinoza's Moral Philosophy' (1973) and William K. Frankena's 'Spinoza's New Morality: Notes on Book IV' (1975).[2]

The first concern of both authors is to clarify and to classify the theory about the meaning of the key ethical terms which is implicit in Spinoza's *Ethics*, especially Part IV. *Prima facie* the most 'natural' interpretation of Spinoza's remarks is that he is offering a form of ethical naturalism.[3] And Frankena, who announces explicitly that he 'tend[s] to remain with the antinaturalists ... in thinking that ethical utterances ... are typically and noncontingently used at least in part to commend, approve, prescribe, etc., and not just to describe or to assert facts' (Frankena, *op. cit.*, pp. 93–4), tends to think that Spinoza is indeed an ethical naturalist. Curley, however, whose paper strongly suggests that he himself 'tends' to agree with such non-naturalist, indeed non-cognitivist, views as those advanced by Urmson or by Hare, argues explicitly both that Spinoza is not an ethical naturalist (in the sense defined by Broad) and that there is a 'basic similarity' between Spinoza's view and the sort of view one finds, in a rather more developed form, in Urmson or especially in Hare (both of whom he explicitly cites). Curley is quick to add that 'Spinoza was [not] just doing crudely the sort of things people like Urmson and Hare now do with more sophistication' (Curley, *op. cit.*, p. 363),[4] but that he 'was also concerned to do something quite different, something which places him squarely within the Platonic-Aristotelian tradition that Hare is so critical of ...' (*ibid.*). Curley does not actually say what this 'something quite different' is. Presumably he is referring, not to another and less 'crude' part of Spinoza's meta-ethical view, but to what he takes to be Spinoza's 'prescriptive ethics,' which is indeed based, like Plato's or Aristotle's, on an

145

account of human nature in what might be called its 'ideal' form or purity. But that Spinoza has – or, at any rate, can have consistently with his meta-ethical position – *any* prescriptive ethics, is questioned by Frankena, both because he doubts that Spinoza does mean to be offering prescriptions ('or the like,' as Frankena would say) and because he doubts that Spinoza is present-ing something which ought to be considered an 'ethics' in the sense of a *morality* or a *moral* philosophy.

I wish to join issue, not with the procedure of Frankena and Curley (i.e. with the questions which they raise), but only with certain of their results. And I admit at the outset that, along with those writers, I, too, tend to think that any form of ethical naturalism is mistaken in principle. I may possess, however, a much less clear sense than either of them concerning what ethical naturalism is supposed to be.

I take it that Frankena, who *in effect* devotes the entirety of Section II (pp. 87–94) of his article to the question whether Spinoza was an ethical naturalist, although nowhere in that article does he offer explicitly any account of what such naturalism is or is supposed to be, would subscribe to the view that ethical naturalism seeks to deduce 'ethical conclusions' (whatever exactly they are!) from premises which merely state or describe facts. It is, surely, because he is implicitly adopting such an account that he bothers to observe, indeed with considerable emphasis, that '[i]t will not do . . . to object [against Spinoza], as some in more recent times would, that one simply cannot [validly] deduce ethical conclusions from MEP [i.e. metaphysical, epistemological, or psychological] premises alone' (Frankena, *op. cit.*, p. 87) – in short, from the materials dealt with by Spinoza in Parts I–III, respectively, of his *Ethics*. Frankena continues (*ibid.*, pp. 87–8):

> For Spinoza does not pretend to do this; he seeks to derive his ethical
> theorems from his MEP premises only with the help of his definitions
> (at the start of Part IV), and such derivations are quite according to
> geometrical hoyle.

Certainly they are 'quite according to [the] geometrical hoyle' of the seven-teenth century, as of earlier centuries, even if they do not, perhaps, quite measure up to the more rigorous standards of contemporary geometricians. But the question of their geometrical 'hoyle' is a red herring. What really matters, at any rate in Frankena's eyes and in the context of his article, is that Spinoza's derivations do not involve the alleged mistake of deducing 'ethical conclusions from MEP [and, hence, from ostensibly factual] premises alone.' Frankena is right in insisting that Spinoza does not make that mistake.

Spinoza may, however, still prove to be an ethical naturalist in some other sense; and immediately after the defense of Spinoza against the charge of naturalistic deduction (just considered), Frankena appears to shift, without indicating explicitly that he is doing so, to a quite different account of ethical naturalism, which again he does not state explicitly. From his claim, already quoted, that he tends 'to remain with the antinaturalists . . . in thinking that ethical utterances . . . are typically and noncontingently used at least in part to commend, approve, prescribe, etc., and not just to describe or to assert facts,' it seems legitimate to infer that he would take the ethical naturalist to be one who affirms that ethical utterances are 'typically and noncontingently used . . . just to describe or to asset facts' – provided that the facts being described or asserted are empirically ascertainable. (Some such proviso is very important, for without it one could not distinguish the ethical naturalist from such a non-naturalistic intuitionist as, for example, Moore himself was.) Since I myself do not wish to prejudice the issue whether meaning is use – and since, in fairness to him, I must say that I suppose that Frankena, too, really did not intend to do so – I suggest that this new account be understood as claiming that the ethical naturalist is one who holds that the meaning or linguistic job of (typical) ethical judgments or utterances is, at least primarily, to state or describe certain empirically ascertainable facts or alleged facts.[5]

Is it, then, the case according to Frankena that Spinoza is a naturalist in the present sense? To this difficult question Frankena responds directly in exactly one sentence (Frankena, *op. cit.*, p. 94):

> I doubt that this [i.e., the statement of the antinaturalist view, previously quoted] can be true of them [i.e., ethical utterances] if their whole meaning is supposed to be captured in MEP terms, as Spinoza thinks or seems to think, especially if these MEP terms ('power,' etc.) do not have built-in normative connotations, as some nowadays say the term 'God' has.

This is a disappointingly brief answer to our question – and, moreover, a quite questionable one. Whether Spinoza is offering what he takes to be *a* whole or, instead, *the* whole meaning of the defined terms, the basic question here is whether, as defined, the terms turn typical ethical utterances employing them into mere statements or descriptions of fact. Presumably, the basic 'ethical' terms for Spinoza are 'good' and 'evil' (which he defines in definitions I and II, respectively, of Part IV) – and, maybe, also 'virtue' (which he defines in definition VIII). The definition of 'evil' is, clearly, parasitic upon that of 'good'. Equally clearly, however, the definition of 'good' cannot be faulted on the ground that, if accepted, it would turn typical judgments or utterances employing it into mere statements of (metaphysical, epistemological, or psychological) fact. For Spinoza, in definition I of Part IV, defines 'good' thus: 'By good, I understand that which we certainly know is *useful* to us' (my emphasis); and 'useful' is not a term which lacks what Frankena has called 'built-in normative connotations.' It would be question-begging merely to suggest at this point that Spinoza (must have) wanted to construe 'useful' itself as a *non-normative* term.

Yet in the final paragraph of his *informal* exposition in the Preface for Part IV, Spinoza does write: 'By *good* . . . I understand in the following pages everything which we are certain is a means by which we may approach nearer and nearer to the model of human nature we set before us' – a definition the point of which has been explained by Spinoza in the immediately preceding sentences of the paragraph in question. *Prima facie* that definition does indeed appear to be aiming at 'revealing' *good* as a non-normative term. Although it appears only in the informal exposition, no sooner has Spinoza proferred his new definitions of 'good' and of 'evil' than he writes, 'With regard to these two definitions, see the close of the preceding preface' – a note which appears to indicate that the real meaning of these definitions is (somehow) brought out by the two earlier definitions and the commentary immediately surrounding them. Thus, it appears *either* that Spinoza regards his definition I as elliptical, i.e. that the 'full' definition of 'good' is 'that which we certainly know is useful to us, being a means by which we may approach nearer and nearer to the model of human nature we set before us'; *or* that he understands these two definitions to be equivalent.

The first of these alternatives poses no problem for the non- or anti-naturalistic interpretation of Spinoza's ethics. The second alternative, however, suggests that Spinoza means this first definition of Part IV to reveal 'good' as a non-normative term. None the less, two considerations may be offered to show that this suggestion is probably not correct.

First, it may be held that the term 'model' (Latin: *exemplar*), although not defined by Spinoza, is one which he understands to be normative. Clearly, Spinoza is not talking about just any *example* of human nature. Indeed, given his peculiar form of nominalism, i.e. his rejection of what *he* calls 'universals', there can be on his view, strictly speaking, no human nature as such and, hence, no examples of it (cf. Part II, proposition XL, Scholium 1, where he explicitly cites *Man* as a universal). Either he is speaking here, less than strictly, of an ideal(ized) example of human nature; or he is referring, in a way which accords better with his own metaphysics, to some particular (even if unactualized) human nature which, like a Platonic παράδειγμα, is fit to serve as the standard or model by reference to which all other human beings are to be judged. In either case, the term *exemplar* is a normative one – indeed, it refers to the norm *par excellence* for all other members of a given kind or species of things; and Spinoza would seem not to be attempting to deprive it of its normative significance. (This consideration, though it may seem to do so, does not actually depend on any play of words or shifting between two senses of 'normative,' one itself normative and the other not. The point is that Spinoza is implying, on this interpretation of his view, that our normative terms derive at least part of their significance from referring to an extra-linguistic, but still normative, thing.) I find this first consideration quite persuasive.

There is, however, a second consideration; I do not find it so persuasive as the first, but, none the less, it does have *some* weight. It is this: in this passage of the *Ethics* itself Spinoza does not directly characterize this *exemplar* to which he is appealing; but in a parallel passage from the *Treatise on the Improvement of the Understanding* (section 13) he remarks that

> since . . . man may conceive some human nature much more powerful [*multo firmiorem*] than his own and at the same time may see nothing preventing his acquiring such a nature, he is inspired to seek the means which may lead him to such perfection: and everything which can be a means for his attaining to it is called a true good.

In short, the *exemplar* in question is such because of its strength or power. Its power is what makes it – and so, derivatively, the pursuit of it – *virtuous*. For, as Spinoza says, now in the *Ethics* itself (in definition VIII, the final definition for Part IV),

> By virtue and power, I understand the same thing; that is to say (Part III, proposition VII), virtue, in so far as it is related to man, is the essence itself or nature of the man in so far as it has the power of affecting certain things which can be understood through the laws of its nature alone.

Now, offhand, one might think that for Spinoza 'power' is as much a normative term as is 'virtue' itself (rather than thinking, as Frankena appears to do, that Spinoza takes 'power' to be non-normative and so deprives 'virtue' of its ordinary normative significance via this 'reduction' of it to mere power). Certainly, in ordinary discourse 'power' or, at any rate, 'powerful' does often figure as a normative term. But Spinoza himself has not left 'power' uncharacterized. He remarks as early as the final proof before the scholium for I xi, 'Inability to exist is impotence, and, on the other hand, ability to exist [*posse existere*] is power . . .'; and, in the same vein, he explains (definition VI of Part II) that '[b]y reality and perfection I understand the same thing.'[6] In thus equating perfection with reality, and power with ability to exist, is Spinoza indicating that he intends to 'reduce' such *prima facie* normative or evaluative terms as 'perfect(ion)' and 'power(ful)' to non-normatives; or is his point, rather, that via such equations we may see, more clearly and distinctly than normally we would, that 'reality' and 'existence' themselves are normative terms? Although Frankena (for one) is inclined to answer that question by opting for the first alternative, there appears to be much reason to go the other way. After all, there are many ordinary contexts in which 'real' has a clearly normative significance – as, for example, when we speak of a heroic individual as a 'real man'. And we must not forget that

Spinoza is working from, if not quite within, an age-old tradition which openly and unambiguously takes reality to be *a* perfection. (Clearly, considerations quite similar to the immediately foregoing apply also to Spinoza's equation between 'power' and 'essence' in definition VIII of Part IV.)

A natural objection to such a line of argument is this: 'If Spinoza were not attempting to reduce apparently normative terms to ones which he construed as non-normative, there would be no *point* in these various definitions and equations of his.' But, as I have already suggested, Spinoza may not have taken them to be naturalistic reductions. He may simply have supposed that the *definienda* here are antecedently – i.e. prior to the definitions themselves – less clear than the terms which he offers as their *definientia*. That sort of explanation is, I think, the most plausible one to offer when one is dealing, for example, with Spinoza's definitions of 'cause of itself' or of 'substance'. But there is no good reason to suppose that something else – something objectionable in principle – is or must be going on when Spinoza proceeds, in due course, to offer his definitions for 'good' or 'evil' or 'virtue'. Granted, 'good' and 'virtue' are very ordinary or commonplace terms unlike 'cause of itself' or even unlike the at least semi-technical term 'substance'; but, on Spinoza's view, one should not confuse a term's being *familiar* with its being *clear*. Indeed, I suppose that Spinoza would hold that it is precisely the most familiar terms (among those which he chooses to define in the *Ethics*) which are the most misunderstood by philosophers and by non-philosophers alike.

II

I have been arguing, against Frankena, that Spinoza is apparently not an ethical naturalist, i.e. that it is not at all clear that Spinoza is seeking to replace ostensibly normative terms with terms which he himself would take to be non-normative.[7] Thus, of course, I am fundamentally in agreement with Curley's conclusion that Spinoza is (probably) not an ethical naturalist – although the sense of 'ethical naturalism' which he, following Broad, specifies is rather different, once again, from either of those that I have built up on the basis of Frankena's remarks. I am, however, unhappy both (a) with the way in which Curley defines 'ethical naturalism' and (b) with the way by which he reaches his conclusion that Spinoza is not an ethical naturalist in the sense defined.

On (a): according to the definition adopted by Curley (*op. cit.*, p. 362), an ethical naturalist is 'someone who thinks that there is some property common and peculiar to all good things and who thinks that this common property may be identified with some empirical property'. Curley appears to be supposing that 'some property common and peculiar to all good things' must be thought by the ethical naturalist to be the (alleged) property of goodness; for it is only on that (or some such) supposition that the espousal of the claim that the former property is to be identified with some 'empirical property' could plausibly be taken to represent a commitment to ethical naturalism. After all, even an ethical anti-naturalist among cognitivists or a non-cognitivist might believe that there is *some* property of all good things 'common and peculiar' to them and that it is, moreover, an 'empirical property'. Here again, however, we encounter the difficulty that, as an opponent of empiricism, Spinoza, even had he sought to identify some property 'common and peculiar to all good things' with goodness, would probably not have subscribed to the view that that alleged property is 'empirical' or empirically ascertainable. But this problem with Curley's account is minor; and since I have already dealt with a similar problem in discussing Frankena's accounts, there is no need to say any more about it here.

A more serious difficulty is that, given his explicit rejection of what he calls 'universals', it simply is not clear that Spinoza would not reject ethical naturalism on Curley's account of it for reasons which have nothing directly to do with his view concerning the relation between any thing's particular goodness and the (other) particular qualities of that thing. For the sake of convenience, however, let us assume here that Spinoza did believe in the existence of *certain* universals or properties. Let us assume that either (as we suppose) counterfactually, or else because we really believe that Spinoza's so-called 'universals' comprise, and are perhaps recognized by him to comprise, only a special subclass of what philosophers, both before him and nowadays, have had in mind when they discuss the issue of universals.[8] What, clearly, he is rejecting is the reality of very 'fat' universals or properties (perhaps even complexes of properties) each of which would be common and peculiar – indeed, essential – to the members of exactly one so-called natural kind. One cannot safely infer from Spinoza's actual examples of alleged universals in the *Ethics* – '*Man, Horse, Dog*', etc. – or from his brief discussion of this topic (in Part II, proposition XL, scholium 1) that he means similarly to reject such a 'non-universal universal' or property as, for example, triangularity. In any case, only if it is assumed that Spinoza was prepared to accept the reality of *some* 'non-universal' or 'non-common' properties (like triangularity) does the question of ethical naturalism, in the *sort* of way in which it is formulated by Curley, become a real question within Spinoza's philosophy.

On (b): Curley at first argues that Spinoza is not an ethical naturalist on the following ground. According to him, Spinoza (construed as holding that there are *some* universal or non-particular properties) denies that goodness is a property common and peculiar to all good things. Curley takes this denial of Spinoza's to be importantly similar to the view presented and defended, for example, by Hare. No sooner has he argued thus, however, than he announces (Curley, *op. cit.*, p. 363) that 'everything so far said about the apparently subjectivist implications of [Spinoza's] meta-ethical theory has been misleading.' In fact, Curley concludes, the foregoing denial and all that in Spinoza's *Ethics* goes along with it constitutes merely Spinoza's rudimentary theory concerning the moral views and utterances of the 'vulgar', of the many (who are confused). In contrast, Spinoza presents his own positive view – concerning the *exemplar* of human nature – a view which, according to Curley, is not at all 'subjectivist'.

I find it strange that Curley should equate (as he seems to be doing), or even that he should very closely associate (as he cannot but be doing), ethical subjectivism with anti-naturalism. I understand ethical subjectivism to be a species of ethical naturalism – to be, in its crudest form, the view that 'goodness' indeed refers to no property of the so-called good object (at any rate, in the typical case where that object is not identical with the human subject who takes it to be good) but does *refer*, rather, to some property of that subject, e.g. his being pleased. Thus it is the view that such a pronouncement as 'X is good', which appears to be attributing the 'objective' property of goodness to the object X, should really be understood as a disguised *description* of or *report* on some state of some subject, Y, who, for example, has made that pronouncement. I take it that the majority of recent writers on ethical theory understand the term 'subjectivism' in at least the sort of way that I have just indicated. I do not wish to press that point, however. Let subjectivism, as a type of ethical theory, be tantamount to an anti-naturalist or even anti-cognitivist position (so-called) such as one finds in Hare, for example. Is it the case that Spinoza's 'theory' about the *ordinary* meaning and/or uses of 'good' and 'bad' expresses an anti-naturalistic view, as Curley thinks?

Not clearly so. Granted, it is Spinoza's settled opinion – which, accordingly, does not change when he comes to present his own positive view – that the terms 'good' and 'evil' are or represent nothing else than 'modes of thought', i.e. that they 'indicate nothing positive in things considered in themselves' (*Ethics*, IV, Preface; this passage is cited by Curley himself, *op. cit.*, p. 356). Since they indicate nothing positive in things considered in themselves, Curley concludes, what they do indicate is something about the state of some subject. However, it would be equally legitimate to conclude, from the scanty evidence available to us *so far*, that Spinoza means to say that these evaluative terms indicate, not how certain things are *in themselves*, but how they are *in relation to something else* (not necessarily to some subject, however). But if we suppose that the obtaining of relation R between X and Y entails that X has a certain *relational property* and that Y also has such a property, then, on the view of Spinoza's in question, goodness might turn out, after all, to be a property *of good things* and, moreover, a property of the same logico-ontological type and so ascertainable by the same means as, for example, the manifestly non-ethical property of *being to the left of M* or *being taller than N*.

Presumably, the type of view which Spinoza means to be attributing to the ordinary man will be indicated by the sort of consideration which Spinoza offers in support of that view. Now, as Curley observes, in the *Ethics* itself Spinoza adduces the following piece of evidence: 'Music, for example, is good to a melancholy person, bad to one mourning, while to a deaf man it is neither good nor bad' (*Ethics*, IV, Preface). What that consideration indicates is that indeed music is neither good nor bad 'in itself' – i.e. out of relation to any other thing. It does not show that music *itself* does not or cannot possess, in relation to a melancholy person, goodness, or in relation to a person who is mourning, badness. But how is one to understand the claim that, for example, music itself, in relation to a melancholy person, possesses goodness? Curley takes that to mean that the goodness (like the beauty) of music is only *in* the eyes (or ears – or, really, the mind) of the (e.g.) melancholy *subject* – hence, in the subject and, therefore, 'subjective'. Surely, however, *that* claim can equally well be taken to mean that music possesses the property of *being good for, or with respect to* (e.g.) *a melancholy person* – where that goodness is *in* the music, as its property. Similarly, in Epistle XIX, to Blyenbergh (also cited by Curley), Spinoza argues for his view on the ground that certain 'things which we detest in men' we nevertheless consider perfections or virtues in other animals. Again, however, that fact might be cited to support quite different theses about the 'location' or the ontological status of goodness.

Of course, Spinoza himself does not offer such considerations as these in splendid isolation, without surrounding commentary; and he makes it clear that he thinks that ordinary people determine the goodness or badness of things relative to what he calls their 'universal' *ideas* of the kinds to which the things judged to be good or bad are taken to belong. In Curley's reformulation of Spinoza's point, the claim is that the 'notion of "favourable comparison" is to be understood in terms of approximation to something we take as an ideal – our general idea of the species in question' (Curley, *op. cit.*, p. 357) – that is, one's idea; for Spinoza emphasizes that one man's idea of *Dog* or *Horse*, for example, is likely to be different from that of anyone else. But, as Curley also says (*ibid.*) ' "[g]ood" and "evil" are terms which we use to compare members of the same species with one another'.[9] Putting these two Spinozistic claims together, we get the conclusion that, for Spinoza (reporting on the implications of ordinary usage), 'good' and 'evil' do not indicate anything 'in things considered in themselves' but do indicate how certain individual things (dogs, for example) stand (a) in relation to one another and (b) in relation to one's universal or general idea (of the species). Now, on the one hand, (a) and (b) here are in no way clearly supported by the ostensible facts which Spinoza himself adduces in their support and, on the other, they in no way require the anti-naturalistic gloss which Curley provides. Here, however, I shall not pursue the former point (which is, or should be, rather obvious anyway); I mean to concentrate on the latter – viz., Curley's interpretation of Spinoza.[10]

Given (b), A's judgment 'X (e.g. this man) is good' is to be understood as meaning (something like) 'X approximates rather closely to A's universal idea of the species *Man*'. Thus it is indeed the case, on this analysis, that X 'considered in itself' – that is to say, without reference or relation to A's (or to someone else's) universal idea of *Man* – is not good (or bad, or even evaluatively indifferent). This analysis, however, does not clearly imply that X, in so far as it is in relation to (e.g.) A's idea, fails to possess the *property* of goodness – i.e. more perspicuously, that Spinoza means either to deny that X then possesses the relational property *being in close approximation to A's idea* or to deny that that property is, in the circumstances, identical to X's *goodness*. To be sure, this analysis would be subjectivistic in the sense that X's goodness would depend, in the way indicated, on A's idea – or rather, on his ideas both of X itself and of the species or kind to which A thinks X belongs. But it is, apparently, not subjectivistic in the sense in which Curley seems to employ the latter term; this analysis appears to be straightforwardly *naturalistic*. Is this, however, actually Spinoza's analysis of the ordinary meaning of evaluative terms or of the typical judgments or utterances in which they occur? To answer that question, several points need to be considered.

First, even if one is willing to assume that Spinoza does believe in the reality of *certain properties* such as triangularity or circularity, for example, one may reasonably question whether he accepts or would have accepted the reality of any so-called *relational properties*. He does not address himself explicitly to this issue. (I suggest, however, that adherence to his view of relations as being only 'modes of thought' or *entia rationis* – a view to be discussed shortly – should probably have led him to the conclusion that there are or can be no relational properties.) But nothing important in my argument against Curley really depends on the assumption that Spinoza's answer to that question would be in the affirmative. Rather, I have so far written as if Spinoza accepted such properties in order to respond, as directly as possible, to the letter of Curley's statement of Spinoza's view – a statement which discusses goodness as an alleged *property* of things. Suppose, however, that Spinoza did not or would not accept the reality of any relational properties. The basic issue concerning his interpretation of ordinary evaluative discourse remains unaffected. However, the question now becomes, more precisely, whether in that part of his overall view Spinoza adopted (or, rather, represented) a naturalistic interpretation, according to which, while 'good' and 'bad' indeed do not refer to anything considered in itself, these terms do *refer* to a certain 'empirical' *relation* in which things may stand to certain universal ideas.

Now one might think that Spinoza – in this respect agreeing, allegedly, with Leibniz – holds that there is no such relation because he takes there to be no relations at all. And, in a sense, that is correct. Though he is not so explicit on this subject in the *Ethics* as he was in the earlier *Short Treatise*, it seems reasonable to believe that his claim, in the later work, that good and evil are nothing else than 'modes of thought' represents still, even as it does in the earlier work, a mere application of his general view concerning relations. In the *Short Treatise* – indeed, in the chapter of it entitled 'What Good and Evil Are' – Spinoza presents that view thus:

> Some things are in our understanding and not in Nature, and so they are also only our own creation . . . : among these we include all relations, which have reference to different things, and these we call *Entia Rationis* [things of reason].

And he continues immediately:

> Now the question is, whether good and evil belong to the *Entia Rationis* or to the *Entia Realia* [real things]. But since good and evil are only relations, it is beyond doubt that they must be placed among the *Entia Rationis*.

As in the *Ethics* itself, he proceeds to remark, first, that judgments of good and evil depend upon comparisons between different things (of the same kind); but then he concludes, as in the later work, that '[t]herefore, when we say that something is good, we only mean that it conforms well to the general Idea which we have of such things'. In short, his emphasis finally is upon the relation between the thing in question which is said to be good and the corresponding general idea. The goodness of the thing is thus, finally, its relation to such an idea; but since *all* relations are 'modes of thought', this relation must be so, too.

Now, the thesis that good and evil are 'our own creation' – when taken out of its context in Spinoza – does indeed appear to be a striking anticipation, on the one hand, of the view of Nietzsche and, on the other, of the more recent non-cognitivistic theories of Anglo-American meta-ethicists. But, of course, Spinoza's view has to be seen in its appropriate context; and when it is seen thus, it may still be a very exciting and interesting view – but it is not by any means clearly a view of the sort which Curley takes it to be. For the *point* of a non-cognitivist position such as Urmson's or Hare's depends on the philosopher's retaining the *ordinary* view that *ordinarily* relations are objective 'features' of the world. But Spinoza is adopting, instead, the view that *all* relations are only 'modes of thought'; he is, so far, not singling good and evil out as somehow very special 'beings' within the category of relations.[11]

So much for now about Spinoza's view of relations in general. The question of more immediate concern here is whether he takes the relations of good and evil to be such that, properly construed, the ordinary person's claims that something is good (evil) means no more than that a certain relation obtains between some general idea of that person's and the thing in question or, strictly speaking, between such a general idea and that person's idea of the latter thing[12] – *where neither that relation itself, nor either of the relata, is signified by an 'ethical' or evaluative term*. For a meta-ethical position is not automatically a naturalistic – or, for that matter, an anti-naturalistic – one merely because it construes an ostensible evaluative *property*, such as goodness, as a relation. What matters, in this regard, is whether the relation in question is itself evaluative (or includes 'unreduced' evaluative components).

III

As explicated so far, Spinoza's account of the popular meaning of 'good' is indeed naturalistic – contrary to Curley's claim. But it is also contrary to what I have earlier argued is the non-naturalistic view adopted by Spinoza himself. Is, one then, to think that the latter conclusion becomes questionable in the light of the present interpretation of the first part of Spinoza's overall account? Or is it, rather, the case that acceptance of that conclusion should lead one on to examine more carefully Spinoza's account of popular 'morality,' and that one should expect the latter account also to turn out, in fact, to be non-naturalistic? Or, finally, is this so important difference between the two parts of his account intended by Spinoza himself?

Though it is difficult, if not impossible, to answer those questions with certainty, I believe that the last-mentioned of those three positions is the most plausible. On the one hand, Spinoza does seem to be saying that ordinary people, though indeed they may *mean* to be commending, condemning (or the like!) in their pronouncements concerning good and evil, are in fact only describing how things strike them (i.e. how certain particular things measure up, or fail to measure up, to whatever happen to be their personal ideas of the kind or kinds involved): 'we call [certain things] imperfect,' says Spinoza, meaning by 'we,' presumably, people generally or even himself and other philosophers in their more or less careless moments, 'because they do not affect our minds so strongly as those we call perfect...' (*Ethics*, IV, Preface).[13]

There is nothing *here* to suggest a non-naturalistic interpretation of Spinoza's doctrine. And all Spinoza says by way of transition or of introduction of his 'positive' account is, 'But although things are so, we must retain these words'. Exactly why we must retain them, is not clear in itself nor, as we shall see in a moment, does Spinoza succeed in clarifying matters by the reason which he himself actually proceeds to offer at this point. Presumably, however, his reason here is of exactly the same sort which has led him, in the previous course of his work, to retain (e.g.) the word 'God' – despite the fact that he has been extremely critical of traditional notions of God, whether ordinary or philosophical. This is not the place to debate the wisdom of that mix in Spinoza of terminological conservatism combined with substantially new views about the meanings of the terms that have been retained. My point here is merely that, already in the earlier course of the *Ethics*, Spinoza has provided examples of his giving old words new meanings – or, as he would prefer to think (and it is this which provides his reason for so proceeding), he has at last revealed the 'real' meaning of terms which have been for so long abused and misunderstood.

Thus in the present instance he simply writes, 'we must retain these words. For since we desire to form for ourselves an idea of man upon which we may look as a model of human nature, it will be of service to us to retain these expressions.' That is, just as people generally may wish to compare others or even themselves with that idea of Man which they happen to have formed for themselves, and call 'good' the man who approaches near to the characteristics of that Man, so Spinoza now wants to compare himself or others to that which is or which may serve as the (proper or adequate) model of human nature and to call 'good' the man whose characteristics approach near to the models. This parallelism between the basic procedure and purpose of the many who are Spinoza's 'we' and those which Spinoza himself now intends to adopt justifies, on his view, the retaining of these expressions. One expects, however, that he will indicate next the different *sense* in which he will employ them. Instead, he says – quite misleadingly, I believe – 'it will be of service to us to retain these expressions in the sense I have mentioned' (*nobis ex usu erit, haec eadem vocabula eo, quo dixi, sensu retinere*); then he proceeds immediately to specify how in the following pages he will understand 'good', 'evil', etc.

I have argued that Spinoza's previous account has been deliberately naturalistic. Hence, if indeed he is going to retain 'these expressions in the sense I [Spinoza] have mentioned', one seems forced to conclude that his positive account is meant to be equally naturalistic. And perhaps that is the correct conclusion; but I do not think it is. For apparently this key phrase of Spinoza's is meant to refer back *only* to what he has said in the earlier part of the very paragraph in which this phrase occurs. 'These expressions' are, more specifically, 'good' and 'evil'; and Spinoza has begun to discuss them only in this paragraph. But in that paragraph he has *not* said, as he had in the immediately preceding one (though, admittedly, the account in that earlier paragraph *might* have been extended into the later one), that 'good' and 'evil' are terms which, willy-nilly, describe the relations of approximation to or distance from some, ultimately arbitrary and certainly 'confused', general idea. What he has said here is merely, 'With regard to good and evil, these terms indicate nothing positive in things considered in themselves, nor are they anything else than modes of thought, or notions which we form from the comparison of one thing with another.' I take Spinoza to mean, when he says that he will retain 'these expressions in the sense . . . mentioned', no more than that for him, too, these terms are nothing else than 'modes of thought' formed from 'the comparison of one thing with another'.

Wherein lies the difference between his positive view and that ordinary one which he has described and implicitly rejected? To begin with, precisely in the switch from a universal idea of Man – which, according to Spinoza's general account of such ideas (already cited), cannot but be 'confused' – to the adoption of 'the model of human nature we set before us.' Earlier, for the sake of the argument then, I was prepared to allow that the idea of this model or *exemplar* might be itself a general, and so a confused, idea. I wish to argue now that in fact, on Spinoza's view, it has to be a 'clear and distinct' idea – and, hence, not a general or universal idea at all. That it cannot be for Spinoza anything but 'clear and distinct' is itself clear from the fact that he employs it, at least tacitly (but, none the less, consciously), in much of the remainder of the argument in the *Ethics* – an argument which, I believe all students of Spinoza's philosophy are prepared to admit, is taken by him to proceed at the level of *ratio*, if not indeed upon occasion at the still higher level of *scientia intuitiva*. Hence, that argument proceeds at a level or at levels where, according to Spinoza, (e.g. *Ethics*, II, proposition XI, scholium 2), one has or finds only ideas which are adequate or, that is, clear and distinct rather than confused. But, also according to Spinoza, all general ideas are confused. One cannot avoid the conclusion that, if Spinoza's doctrine is consistent (as I shall assume it to be), the all-important idea or the 'model of human nature' *is* an adequate idea and so *is not* a general idea.

Some extremely interesting questions arise at this point. Among them is the question whether, when Spinoza speaks of 'the model . . . we set before us', he means that there is exactly one such model for all human beings; or, instead, that each clear-headed person (each person at the level of *ratio*) has his, or her, own personal model – which may be slightly different from that of any other such person's, but so slightly that Spinoza may safely ignore those differences and so, in the remainder of the *Ethics*, speak of 'the model' *as if* there were exactly one of them.[14] Here, because of limitations of space I must forgo any attempt to answer that question. But I must consider this question: Granting that Spinoza has switched from an allegedly confused idea of *Man* (that is of human nature) to an allegedly clear idea of 'the model of human nature', how, if at all, does that switch comprise, involve, or justify a switch from a deliberately naturalistic account to a non-naturalistic one?

Perhaps the answer is basically that, for Spinoza, 'confused' and 'clear' (and 'distinct') are themselves, at least in part, genuinely evaluative terms. Hence, in characterizing the ordinary usage of 'good' and 'bad', Spinoza may be taken to mean that people, despite their intentions, are not *really* commending or condemning anything because the general idea to which they compare the thing which is 'good' or 'bad' is not itself commendable, and is such precisely because and in so far as it is confused. (He could, of course, as well or better say that they do succeed in commending/condemning, yet that their moral or other evaluative views are mistaken or confused; but I shall not dwell on that point. For here I am primarily concerned to understand what Spinoza does say, not to consider what he ought to have said.)

In contrast, when for his part Spinoza calls something 'good' or 'bad' he really does commend or condemn it thereby because the model to which he is at least tacitly appealing is 'true' or adequate. But, apart from the objection just now noted, this view would itself be *inadequate* if it depends upon a conflation or confusion of ethical with non-ethical (i.e. with epistemic) values. And it does seem as if, in trying to unpack the sense in which Spinoza will employ the key ethical terms, one has discovered that latent within his definition of them is reference to his epistemic values: for something to be ethically good, it seems, is for it to 'approach near' to an idea of human nature which has only its (alleged) *clearness and distinctness* to recommend it – i.e. is for the thing's *ethical* value to be a matter of its approximation to an *epistemological* ideal.

But one need not construe Spinoza in that way. For he may be taken to be implying – rather more plausibly – that his model's acceptability as a norm for ethics presupposes, but does not reduce to, its or (what may come to the same thing) its idea's passing this basic epistemological test. But that is merely a necessary condition of its *ethical* acceptability – and a reasonable enough condition, too; ethics had better not be based on any notion which, upon examination, reveals itself to be unclear or confused. Finally, however, the acceptability for ethics of Spinoza's *ethical* norm must either be self-evident or revealed only by something other than its clarity and distinctness. Spinoza appears, however, not to be assuming that it is self-evident – at any rate, self-evident *to us*, whatever it may be *in itself*; for if Spinoza supposed it to be self-evident to all human beings that the model he is about to describe is the acceptable one, *he* could not but suppose also that all of us have always accepted it. Since he has gone to some length to indicate that he does not suppose the latter, presumably he must have thought that the ethical acceptability of this model requires some sort of proof or evidence.

Of course, it is one thing to hold that a certain definition (claim, etc.) is 'somehow obvious' and another to hold that it itself is 'rational' or that one would be rational or would have good reason to accept it. So, even though Spinoza did not take these definitions of his – i.e. those which involve at least implicit reference to the *exemplar* of human nature – to be 'somehow obvious,' he may have supposed that *every* reason supporting them had already been provided by the preceding MEP (*and* his further prefatory remarks). Even that is unlikely, however. At any rate, I am inclined to think, *contra* Frankena (*op. cit.*, pp. 91–2), that Spinoza believed – and, moreover, believed that readers of the *Ethics* would believe – that the acceptability of the definitions in Part IV is, to an appreciable extent, dependent upon the results to be derived from them (with the help, to be sure, of at least some of the materials provided earlier). In sum, I believe that Spinoza himself held (a) that the initial clarity

159

of the idea of the model of human nature which he was going to present fitted it, or made it epistemologically acceptable, for use in the subsequent course of his own argument; and (b) that it is mainly that subsequent argument itself which reveals the 'ethical' acceptability of that model or, hence, of the definitions which depend, implicitly or overtly, on the idea of it.

But these last suggestions, even if they help to throw some considerable light on what is 'going on' in Spinoza's (meta)ethics, are not themselves directly relevant to the basic question of whether Spinoza's ethics is naturalistic. For, after all, even descriptions (or definitions which are designed to yield certain descriptions) may have to be justified or supported somehow; so one should not make the mistake of supposing, because Spinoza sought in some way to justify his definitions of the key ethical terms, that therefore those definitions are not naturalistic. What I take to be the basic considerations which suggest that indeed Spinoza's own definitions are not intended by him to be naturalistic have already been presented. They concern (his use of) the word *exemplar* itself, and his implied (but earlier – in the *Treatise on the Improvement of the Understanding* – explicit) characterization of it as being or being conceived as 'much more *powerful*' than is one's actual self. Spinoza's *exemplar*, I have suggested, is an *ideal* of or for humanity and is so construed by Spinoza himself. Having introduced this ideal, his task is to elaborate upon it and thereby to convince his readers of its ideality. His move from *reporting* on what others mean to commend (but do not 'really' commend), to commending in *propria persona* has been made; but the latter requires, on Spinoza's view, that the thing 'commended' be commendable. That it is so is what he seeks next to prove. It is not, however, until much of that proof has actually been advanced that Spinoza permits himself the liberty of explicitly concluding, concerning a life which approximates closely to the model, 'So, if there is any other, this manner of living is the best and is to be commended in every way.'[15]

NOTES

1 I gratefully acknowledge the assistance of my colleague Professor Hector-Neri Castaneda, whose many comments on an earlier draft of this paper led to extensive revisions and (I hope) improvements.

2 The former paper may be found in M. Grene (ed.), *Spinoza: A Collection of Critical Essays* (New York, Doubleday, 1973), pp. 354–76; the latter in M. Mandelbaum and E. Freeman (eds), *Spinoza: Essays in Interpretation* (LaSalle [Ill.], Open Court, 1975), pp. 85–100.

More particularly, like Curley and Frankena themselves, I am concerned to understand the view(s) presented by Spinoza in Part IV of his *Ethics* and, even more particularly, in the Preface and definitions for that Part – materials which constitute the 'heart' of Spinoza's meta-ethical theory. Accordingly, I shall make no *systematic* attempt to relate Spinoza's views there to views advanced by him elsewhere, much less to arrive at an interpretation of the former views by seeing them 'in the light' of such other passages. Upon occasion, however, I shall find it helpful to compare what Spinoza is saying in (that portion of) the *Ethics* with the views which he advances in certain other works. Throughout I use the W. H. White translation of the *Ethics* (New York, Hafner, 1953), unless otherwise noted. I quote also from Wolf's translation of the *Short Treatise*, and from my own (unpublished) translation of the *Treatise on the Improvement of the Understanding*.

3 Cf. C. D. Broad's *Five Types of Ethical Theory* (London, Routledge & Kegan Paul, 1930), ch. II.

4 In order not to make this paper unduly complicated, and in order to *focus* my disagreements with Curley and with Frankena concerning the interpretation of Spinoza, I shall not question their (implied) view that the most plausible alternative to a 'naturalistic ethics' is one of the sort now associated most commonly with Hare. In fact, however, Hare's view has been subjected to very basic and telling criticisms, and rather more 'sophisticated' meta-ethical positions have been advanced than those which Curley and Frankena cite. In any case, I shall not here question the Harean view that 'good' and 'ought' have sufficient similarities to warrant one's classifying them together simply as 'value-words' (cf. *The Language of Morals*, Oxford, 1952, p. 153). That is, I shall ignore the point – raised so forcibly earlier in this century by, for example, Ross and developed by certain more recent thinkers – that the 'logic' of so-called deontic terms may be fundamentally different from that of genuinely evaluative ones, and, hence (though this latter is certainly no part of Ross's view), that it is quite possible that the former terms are not to be analysed naturalistically whereas the latter are correctly so analysed. Nor shall I question Hare's view that the primary linguistic function of all 'value-words' (including, for him, deontic terms) is commendation. My concluding remarks about the role of commendings or commendations in Spinoza's positive account of ethics should, therefore, be understood as being designedly somewhat 'loose'. Such a procedure may not be altogether *commendable*, but I do think it justified by the reasons already indicated!

5 One might all too easily get sidetracked, when one attempts to determine whether that account fits Spinoza's actual procedure or squares with his own brief meta-ethical remarks by questioning whether, in Spinoza's own view, the, 'facts' of ethics are *empirically ascertainable*. It is, surely, true that Spinoza is no empiricist, and true also that the entire *Ethics* is written from the standpoint of what Spinoza calls 'reason' (or, maybe, even 'intuitive science') rather than from that inferior standpoint which he dismisses as that of 'vague experience' (cf. Part II, prop. XL, schol. 2). Instead of trying to determine whether Spinoza recognizes a kind of *experience* which is not vague, it would seem more profitable, at least in the present context, to rephrase the second Frankenian account, once again, so that it does not beg or even appear to beg the rationalist/empiricist question. Let us then say that the ethical naturalist takes the meaning of (typical) ethical judgments or utterances to consist, at least primarily, in the statement or the description of (alleged) facts which are ascertainable in whatever way(s) he supposes the facts that provide the data for (his) metaphysics,

161

epistemology, or psychology are ascertained or are ascertainable. Following Moore (but not exactly!), we may dub the latter ways 'naturalistic' – that is, we may employ 'naturalistic' as such a technical term (for the moment disregarding its ordinary meanings or associations). Hence, we may label any ethicist as a naturalist provided that he holds (a) that the primary business of (typical) ethical judgments or utterances is indeed to state or describe (alleged) facts, and (b) that the ascertainment of those facts requires in principle no means other than those which, in his view, are required for the ascertainment of the facts with which those other domains of philosophy deal. If one happens to be an empiricist as well as an ethical naturalist, then, of course, one will hold that the ethical 'facts' in question are empirically ascertainable.

6 It needs to be added that, as the context of the former passage (from Part I) makes clear, Spinoza means to be talking there about a thing's ability to exist (as manifested in its actual existence) from its own internal resources, as it were, and not merely in so far as it is kept going by other things (over which it itself has no control).

7 I have *not* argued that he has not made two other blunders, namely, confusing ethical normatives with one another or confusing ethical normatives with non-ethical ones. Thus, for example, one might agree that 'powerful' is, as Spinoza employs it, a normative expression. Yet one might object that he has wrongly sought to define the key ethical term 'good' by reference to the model of human nature much *stronger*, i.e. more *powerful* than one's own. One might object, that is, either because one supposes 'goodness' is one ethical term and 'power' another or because 'power' is not an ethical term at all (but, rather, a normative term of some other sort). Or, alternatively, one might think that none of these terms is necessarily or in every context an ethical term; and that Spinoza's fundamental mistake was, not to *reduce* the ethical to the non-normative, but to *expand* the ethical so that every normative is, *ipso facto*, an ethical one. I have not the space in this paper, however, to deal with any of these further charges.

8 Though this is not the place to discuss that interpretative assumption at length, it seems to me that, terminological issues aside, Spinoza is consciously committed to the existence of certain universals – e.g. to those which directly correspond to or are the objects of what he calls the 'common notions'. (Since, he maintains, the common notions are applicable to all modes, these universals turn out to be genuine universals in the sense that they have *universal* extensions.) It is by no means clear, however, that Spinoza's actual commitment to universals is limited to these 'universal' universals, as I might call them.

9 It is obvious that these claims, even if correct, can account for only a part of people's ordinary moral views – or rather, more generally, their evaluative views. It is not true that ordinarily 'we' take something to be *good* just in case it approximates very closely to 'our' idea of the species to which, we believe, it belongs; we also judge entire species as good or bad. (In a sense, which I have not the space to elucidate here, Spinoza does indeed identify 'being good' with 'being good of a kind'; but the sense in which he does that allows him to escape the sort of objection I have just suggested, an objection which Curley's presentation does little or nothing to meet.)

10 The question of how Spinoza takes (a) and (b) themselves to be related is a fascinating and important one, but it is not one with which Curley deals nor, unfortunately, is it one which I have the space to investigate carefully in this paper. For the sake of simplicity, at any rate, I shall assume that Spinoza means in fact to subordinate (a) to (b) in the sense that he takes some actual comparison of two or more 'things' with one another to be necessary for the *original formation* of the universal idea of the 'species' to which the things in question belong, and, maybe, also that he takes the judgment of something's *approximation* to that idea, once formed, to involve, if only implicitly, comparison between that thing and at least one (real or possible) other member of the 'species'. The *core* of his account, however, as I understand it, concerns directly only that universal idea and, in relation to it, the very thing being judged good or bad. Hence, I wish to concentrate on (b), as Curley himself seems to do.

11 Although it is, perhaps, not directly relevant to my main concerns in this paper, I should like to point out that Spinoza has overstated his case concerning relations as such. For modes of thought are, in his ontology, real things, quite as much as are modes of extension. Indeed, given his so-called psychophysical parallelism, it has to be the case that what are, considered in one way, modes of thought exist also as modes of the attribute of Extension. Accordingly, what Spinoza really means by his oft-repeated claim that relations are only modes of thought is merely that the *content* of such ideas does not correspond to or parallel anything which exists under the attribute of Extension. Obviously, his form of psychophysical parallelism itself does not require him to maintain that *in all cases* the content, or the object, of an idea exists also under the attribute of Extension. For clearly he is not committed to the real existence of unicorns or golden mountains. It is enough that these modes of thought, construed as mental *acts*, be the 'counterparts' of certain physical events occurring within the body of the being whose thoughts they are. I am not suggesting, however, that Spinoza has a well-worked-out distinction between the act, the content, and the object of thought; but his present doctrine concerning relations, like various other of his theses, can only be made intelligible or coherent if some such distinction is taken to be implicit in his philosophical writings.

12 It is impossible, in Spinoza's view – according to which the order of ideas and the order of 'things' (i.e. material objects) are *merely* parallel, i.e. according to which there is only one order or series, which may be viewed by us either under the attribute of Thought or under that of Extension – that there should be anything which directly relates an idea to anything else than some other idea(s). Hence, the relation which he takes goodness or evil to consist in cannot be one which directly connects an idea (about a certain 'species' of thing) with some member of that species considered as a material object. It is, rather, one's *idea* of the thing which is connected to one's idea of the thing's species – the connection being itself, on Spinoza's view, a 'mode of thought' or idea (but, obviously, one of a different variety from that of either of the ideas which it relates to one another).

13 It is quite clear, I think, that this passage should be read in conjunction with this earlier passage (*inter alia*):

But we must observe that these notions are not formed by all persons in the same way, but that they vary in each case according to the thing by which the body is more frequently affected, and which the mind more easily imagines or recollects. For example, those who have more frequently looked with admiration upon the stature of men, by the name *man* will understand an animal of erect stature, while those who have been in the habit of fixing their thoughts on something else, will form another common image of men, describing man, for instance, as an animal capable of laughter, a biped without feathers, a rational animal, and so on; each person forming universal images of things according to the temperament of his own body. It is not therefore to be wondered at that so many controversies have arisen amongst those philosophers who have endeavoured to explain natural objects by the images of things alone (II, proposition XL, scholium 1).

14 Much more pointedly, one must ask whether 'the model . . . we set before us' is, for each of us, his or hers as yet unrealized but ideal self; or whether Spinoza means to take as the one model the (allegedly) already real life of the man who was Jesus. (For evidence to support the conjecture that Spinoza did take Jesus to be the exemplar, see both *Ethics*, IV, proposition LXVIII, scholium and various passages from the *Theologico-Political Treatise*, including especially a pasage from ch. I which may he found in Gebhardt *Opera* (Heidelberg, 1926), vol. III, p. 21, 1.8 *et seq.*). Clearly, answering that question is important not only for an understanding of Spinoza's ethical theory but also for an understanding of its underlying metaphysics.

15 I have chosen to close this paper by quoting (in Curley's own translation) the very passage – from *Ethics*, IV, proposition XLV, corollary 2, scholium – which Curley uses as the epigraph for his paper. He, however, does not indicate – nor, so far as I know, has anyone before him – that Spinoza's wording here is somewhat odd. Why does Spinoza appear to be raising the question whether there are alternative manners of living when he has already informed us, at great length, that there *are*, namely, all those which involve what he terms 'bondage' to the passions? I think the explanation is this: Spinoza uses the phrase *vivendi ratio*, which may be translated merely as 'manner of living'; but which, of course, implies that such living has some *ratio*, i.e. that it is reasonable. Apparently Spinoza is thus punning on the phrase, or is calling attention to the fact that it is, in his view, really wrong or misleading to label any *alternative* lifestyle as a *vivendi ratio*. (Cf. his similar, but more explicit, objection to the traditional phrase *entia rationis* or 'things [entities] of reason' in *Ethics*, I, Appendix, penultimate paragraph.)

9 Reality or perfection

Guttorm Fløistad, Oslo

Spinoza's view that reality is the same as perfection is alien to most philosophers of the present. Reality is to many philosophers above all the reality of physical objects and processes. What may be more or less perfect is our knowledge of this reality. Between the social reality and our (more or less 'perfect') knowledge of it there is certainly a high degree of interdependence; they are, however, far from identical.

The philosophical doctrine of the present, to which Spinoza's view appears to be most akin, is that of the lifeworld in the phenomenology of Husserl and Heidegger. An individual's lifeworld is the world of his consciousness, the physical, social and moral world as constituted in and by his consciousness or understanding. Since an individual *is* the world of his consciousness, it may properly be said of it that it makes up an individual's reality, that is, the reality which is present to him, and moreover that this reality signifies the degree of perfection of his understanding. With respect to an individual's lifeworld reality may hence be conceived of as perfection.

I shall only occasionally compare Spinoza's doctrine of reality as perfection and that of the phenomenological lifeworld. I shall, furthermore, for the most part neglect the long history of the problem in Jewish, Greek and medieval philosophy. My chief purpose is to shed some light on Spinoza's doctrine as presented in the *Ethics*, naturally with the underlying assumption that it may help to clarify aspects of our problem or problems of reality.

As presented in the *Ethics* the doctrine obviously has a psychological, an epistemological, an ontological and a moral component. I shall comment on these in turn.

1 THE PSYCHOLOGICAL INTERPRETATION

The term 'reality' is normally associated with ontology. When reality in the *Ethics* is said to be the same as perfection (Part 2, definition 6), the ontological association may still be preserved, for instance on account of the Platonic view that things are more or less real and hence more or less perfect, according to their participation in the eternal forms or ideal reality. Spinoza's use of the terms 'reality' and 'perfection' in the *Ethics,* however, appears at first sight to make a psychological interpretation more plausible. A statement in 2Pl5 Sch runs: 'Nam quo plura ens cogitans potest cogitare, eo plus realitatis sive perfectionis idem continere concipimus . . . .' And to think is foremost a psychological notion. The correlation of an individual's perfection (and consequently his reality) with being active and passive (5P40), points in the same direction: 'Quo unaquaeque res plus perfectionis habet, eo magis agit, eo perfectior est.' Even stronger evidence for a psychological interpretation is found in those passages which relate perfection to the mind's suffering of change and to the experience of pleasure and pain. The mind is said to be able to suffer great changes and thereby pass to a state of greater or lesser perfection. Pleasure (*laetitia*) is then defined as the passion (*passionem*) by which the mind passes to a higher state of perfection and pain (*tristitia*) as the passion by which it passes to a lower state of perfection (3P11 Sch). Later on (3P21 Dem) pleasure is even said to impose existence on the thing feeling pleasure (*existentiam rei laetae ponit*), which amounts to no less than saying that pleasure imposes perfection or reality on that thing (since perfection is the same as the (actually existing) essence of the thing (3Aff. Gen. Def. Expl.). True enough, pleasure and pain are *not* perfection (or reality) themselves (*ibid.*). They consist of the transition from one degree of perfection (or reality) to another. As primary emotions (3P11 Sch) however they obviously enter into an individual's 'essence' (cf. *ibid.*, and 3P7 Dem). Hence, since perfection is defined as an individual's essence, there can be no doubt that pleasure and pain form integral parts of Spinoza's notion of perfection or reality.

2 THE EPISTEMOLOGICAL INTERPRETATION

It is easily shown that psychological phenomena such as the power of thinking, being active and passive and pleasure and pain all are parasitic upon knowledge. Even the primary emotions, constituting the essence of an individual, are not primary in the sense that they precede ideas. The emotions are themselves, moreover, called modes of thinking, and they cannot be granted unless an idea is granted in the individual:

> Modi cogitandi, ut amor, cupiditas, vel quicunque nomine affectus animi insigniuntur, non dantur, nisi in eodem Individuo detur idea rei amatae, desideratae, etc. At idea dari potest, quamvis nullus alius detur cogitandi modus.

Ideas are hence the primary entities. They are the 'first things' that constitute the actual being of the human mind (2P11, P15). The power of thinking as well as pleasure and pain always arise out of ideas, which is to say that they are factual in the sense of being tied up with and dependent upon knowledge of those objects that on a given occasion affect the mind. To say that the power of thinking or desire, that is the endeavour to persist in his being (cf. 3P6, P7), is the essence of the mind, is hence surely to exhibit an essential feature of the mind or its ideas, but remains an incomplete way of putting the matter. Ideas are the essence of the mind (2P11, 5P38 Dem.).

The epistemological interpretation obviously makes the identification of reality with perfection more plausible. It also explains why there can be degrees of reality: ideas are the real being of the mind, and the mind or the individual can be more or less real, depending upon the kind or kinds of knowledge the mind exercises. The more adequate and true ideas of the second and third kind it has (that is, consists of) the more real and perfect it is; the more inadequate and false ideas dominate the mind, the less real and perfect it is. Or differently expressed, the more the mind is in itself, the more it acts from itself alone and the more reality and perfection it has.

As is apparent from the properties 'is in itself' and 'conceived through itself', the standard of perfection and reality is that 'most perfect being', God or Substance (. . . *ex summa Dei perfectione* . . .) (1P33 Sch2) God is absolutely in himself and conceived through himself. Man and finite modes in general are only to some extent in themselves and conceived through themselves.

Spinoza suggests, however, another, at least in part, empirical standard: that of the human nature itself – men are more perfect or imperfect in so far as they approach or are distant from the type of human nature (*exempla humanae naturae*) (4 *Praefatio*). This type, as every other type of being is surely, on Spinoza's view, dependent upon God or Substance or Nature as a whole for its conception. It is, however, equally sure that it is unique in its own way as compared with other species of being. This means that the specifically human nature has built into it the norm of its own self-realization, and self-preservation – no doubt a significant Aristotelean reminiscence in the *Ethics*.

This norm is variously expressed in the *Ethics*. Of particular interest to epistemology is the norm concerning the perfection of the intellect: in order to become as perfect or real as possible it is above all useful in life to perfect (that is, to realize) as much as we can the intellect or reason (cf. 4 App. 4). To perfect our intellect is nothing else than to understand God and his attributes and actions which follow from the necessity of his nature (*ibid.*). It is to know oneself and all other finite modes as parts of God or Nature as a whole. This is the ultimate norm of the human nature.

Epistemology is thus basically a theory of how to perfect our understanding, of comprising a description of the three kinds of knowledge. In what sense, if any, does this epistemology point to ontology?

167

3 THE ONTOLOGICAL INTERPRETATION

The mind is its ideas. Epistemology is hence nothing other than the ontology of the mind. Now perfection, although merely a mode of thinking (cf. 4 *Praefatio*), must surely, just as much as the term 'reality', be taken to refer to both the mental and physical (extended) being. How then can epistemology or the ontological doctrines of the human mind be translated into a general ontology of matter?

First, how does it bear on the human body? Epistemology is in a sense translated already into a theory of the body. The body functions in every cognition of something as the (mediating) object of the mind's ideas. Ideas are, whatever objects they have, always ideas of the body. Nothing can in fact happen in the body which is not perceived by the mind (2P12, P13). A theory of the mind is therefore at the same time a theory of the body. Ontology of the body is hence, to use a certain terminology, nothing else than first-order ideas (of the body) whereas epistemology is ideas of these (first-order) ideas, that is, second-order ideas. Or in Spinoza's words: 'Mens humana non tantum Corporis affectiones sed etiam harum affectionum ideas percipit' (2P22). This is part and parcel of the theses of psycho-physical parallelism and of the unity of mind and matter (cf. 2P21).

Now, to talk of the human mind and body is surely abstract. Man is not unique in the sense of existing in isolation from other entities. On the contrary, as a finite mode, he needs from his own nature other entities for his existence and actions (cf. 1 Def. 2, 3). His dependence on God is a dependence on Nature as a whole. In the epistemology and ontology of the *Ethics*, this is also expressed in terms of the mediating position of the body. The mind has no knowledge of itself, of its body and of other external bodies unless through the modification of the human body by the external bodies (cf. 1P19, 2P23, P26). This continuous interaction between man and other entities also accounts for statements such as 'the (physical and mental) power of man, his actual essence, is a part of the infinite power of God or nature' (cf. 4P4 Dem.). It also accounts for Spinoza's explanation of the emotions: pleasure and pain, for instance, can neither arise nor be explained without the relation to or interaction with some object. Adequate ideas or actions and the emotions accompanying them are no exceptions. Their adequacy merely signifies that the individual is the adequate cause of, or has freely chosen to know or act upon the object, or objects, in question. Hence it follows that epistemology or the ontology of the mind from the very outset is a general theory of mind and matter, of cognition and its objects, of (mental and physical) reality as perfection. From this viewpoint the psychological components appear as (perhaps useful) abstractions.

4 THE NORMATIVE INTERPRETATION

That Spinoza's notion of reality or perfection has a normative component is clear from the previous remarks on epistemology and ontology. The human nature, as well as every other type of being has built into it the specific norm of its own self-realization or self-preservation. This norm, being the essence of every finite mode, gives meaning to an individual's existence in general, his thought and feelings and his actions. Specific moral notions such as good and bad, freedom and constraint, merely exhibit features that are present in every interaction, in particular if we are to believe Spinoza, in every act of cognition. Knowledge or understanding, whether it takes on the shape of imagination, reason or intuition, is itself morally normative towards the object of cognition as well as towards the knowing individual himself. That is the reason why there is no separate moral philosophy in the *Ethics*. And that is moreover the reason why the ontology, epistemology, psychology and moral philosophy in the *Ethics* never should be treated separately from each other, as the custom has been by many modern interpreters. It cannot but lead to a truncated view on what the *Ethics* is about.

It is admittedly difficult for a modern reader to conceive of reality as having a morally normative component. How can reality be good and bad, free and constrained? To us it makes most sense to predicate these terms of social reality. The physical reality is free from such properties. That even goes to make up its robustness (Russell). Spinoza's answer is fairly simple: reality should not be viewed independently of man, his feelings, thoughts and actions. Man is, to himself anyway, an unavoidable part of his ontological predicament. He may neglect his own ontological status and its significance for ontological theories in various fields. The effect of such neglect cannot but be harmful. It impoverishes not only our notion of reality, but reality itself. And it may turn philosophy against itself and prevent it from being a truly humanistic discipline.

10 Spinoza – as Europe's answer to China

German Seminar, Peking

The German Seminar of the University of Peking is publishing a commemorative issue on the occasion of the

300th anniversary of the birth of Benedict Spinoza.

Having commemorated the 100th anniversary of Goethe's death in a similar manner six months ago, it thus follows a stimulus which stems from the significant link set up by the year 1932.

And because there is also a spiritual link, which is unique in greatness, clarity and dignity, this commemoration seemed even more vital.

The content of this commemorative issue will remove any doubt about whether such an honour to Spinoza is justified.

In our time voices of selfless and independent humanity are seldom heard.

They are particularly seldom heard in China from those countries which on their part have absorbed the highest values of philosophical thinking from China and which feel enriched by such teachings.

May this work be permitted to voice a noble gratitude for the noblesse he has given to Europe!

May Spinoza's voice be for China a link with Europe, a voice so seldom heard, but always so efficacious in stating the truth – as the very same sky covers Europe and China alike!

NOTE FROM THE EDITOR

This memorial publication came out on 24 November 1932 in a special edition of the *Deutsch-Chinesische Nachrichten* under the attentive care of Vincenz Hundhausen to manifest his devotion to Spinoza with a remarkable talent in poetry and prose alike. Its message is still valid and the more valid, as it has not reached Spinoza admirers everywhere in the world. It can come out now more alive and able to reach the perturbed mind of man and mankind when China is already represented at the (Dis-) United Nations to voice opinions more attracted with the external dilemmas than the internal ones. . . .

Along with German and Chinese excerpts from Spinoza's works, Hundhausen brings various viewpoints of occidental thinkers, some clinging to the Benedictus, some to the Maledictus in accordance to the Chinese Yin and Yang. Among the various articles Hu-Shih points to Spinoza *vis-à-vis* Chuang-Tzu and it will be found in alphabetical order of contributors in the present symposium here. This memorial publication – in vertical form according to the Chinese custom of writing and printing – has been sent to me by Hundhausen via Siberia to reach me in my former hometown, Czernowitz. Hundhausen has added to it a second memorial edition dedicated to the poet Wieland, dated 5 September 1933. Here too Hundhausen has indeed excelled himself and fully surpassed all expectations when celebrating a poet in a poetical manner as an equal approaching another equal should do. Sic!

Later, when coming out of Russia after the war, I was lucky enough to save this valuable document together with other rare books and manuscripts, all bearing the stamp of the Literary Censure Board. Now they adorn my bookshelves and remind me of my first contact with China via Spinoza. Later I learnt from Helmut Wilhelm (son of Richard Wilhelm) that he knew and very much appreciated Hundhausen when living in Peking. 'To bring Spinoza much nearer to the spiritual world of the East, will contribute certainly to the understanding of its vitality and expansion. . . .' So Wilhelm wrote to me and encouraged me to show the basic parallels between Spinoza and China's teaching as also with the whole of the East.

At this time I had already penetrated into the magic awareness of Yin and Yang, of Ming and Hsing, and especially into the Surangama Sutra! I have already mentioned this before in a footnote to my book *Spinoza – 300 Jahre Ewigkeit*, Martinus Nijhoff, The Hague, 1962, when testifying for a second time as it were for Spinoza and accepting with regret the historical (hysterical?) denial of my first symposium *Spinoza Festschrift*, Carl Winter, Heidelberg, 1932.

Since then I really have tasted and tested with increasing delight the life elixir offered by Chinese thinkers which imbues one with the ultimate aim of oneness and at-onement leading to all-oneness or one-allness. . . . Here I must recall a good friend of mine. A clairvoyant trained in the French tradition of astrology, he disclosed to me my quasi former karmic ties with China (in former incarnations) after consulting the Ephemerides. In Spinoza's library Jean Préposiet (in his *Bibliographie Spinoziste*, Paris, 1973) listed the Ephemerides as item 36, which may have been of interest to Spinoza too. This finger pointing behind the cosmic veil as it were, happened just at the time when history and hysteria together were both boiling at my doorstep and burning my shy footsteps while I had to 'walk' into the better residential area of the 'Ghetto'. But still I had time enough to make notes in my diary and I am so happy to have survived such 'distinction for extinction' when remembering the whole scene again. . . . I must confess that at that time I was engaged with the 'consolations' (not of Boetius but) of Sri Rama Krishna and the Chinese way of thinking and of life was very far away from my spiritual horizon indeed. So far that it is difficult to believe that I became so enthusiastically aware of it later. And especially when selecting the Sixth Patriarch, Hui Neng, as my guide for life. Many years passed before I merged my own surge and urge with Hui Neng so as to let him enter my cells and pores of the unknown. In a way which later my friend Carlo Suares succeeded in expanding into 'multidimensional consciousness'. . . .

Now Lu K'üan Yü (known as Charles Luk), the living Chinese teacher, encourages me to persevere in my affinity with Spinoza as I have mentioned in my Prologue, where I reproduced a letter of Lu K'üan Yü with such odd and indirect homage of his to Spinoza.

I am happy to pledge my loyalty to Hui-Neng and the 'Sutra Spoken by the Sixth Patriarch on the High Seat of the "Treasure of the Law" '. And not only can I join Hui-Neng's pupils but also Joe Miller who wrote the foreword to the American Shambala Edition (1969).

This sutra contains the essence not only of Buddhism but of all Great Religions. The Sutra extends to you, the reader, the possibility of coming to full realization of Enlightenment: in, of and through your own understanding. You need not to turn to any ritual dogma or creed; just keep reading. The only worthwhile practice is to understand. When you have reached understanding, you will realize the Light never seen on land or sea. You will not have to do, or strain for gain; you will know Who you are; then you will only have to Be. This, my friend, is the Key to Eternity. . . .

Learn to feel-think [non 'cognoscimus' sed 'sentimus experimurque' nos aeternos esse: ed.] from the depth of Being. Discard sentimentality; feel the real. Know that all which our senses contact is but limited expression of unity in diversity. Know that beyond objectivity and subjectivity is That which you are. When you can experience this, you realise the Essence. Then intuitive spontaneity is functional for you. If you can let this Sutra 'happen' for you, you will enjoy 'unendurable pleasure indefinitely prolonged.'
Fall awake, my friend. . . !

And so dear reader, you will discover easily in and between my words the wordless aim to realize in accordance with my teacher Hui-Neng: 'inwardly the imperturbability of the essence of mind.' And thus you will welcome like me the parallel of my teacher Baruch de Spinoza: the panacea of the 'acquiesctia in se ipso' [et in se ipsa!], namely the tranquillity in the otherless self – when you suddenly discover and understand that your mind cannot be perturbed save in 'your' wrong standing and understanding instead of avoiding any siding whatsoever. Understanding what? The mystery that there is no 'one' to be perturbed, that there is no-thing to perturb apart from you, and there is no there either, no otherness *per se* at all.

And among the Precepts of the Gurus listed among the 'Best Ten Things' is such no-thingness of self-realization as:

> For one of superior intellect, the best meditation is to *remain in mental quiescence*, the mind de-void of all thought-processes, knowing that the *meditator, the object of meditation*, and *the act of meditation* constitute an inseparable unity.

And the *summmum bonum* is encapsulated in a single word:

ANUTPATTIKA – DHARMA – KSHANTI*

* Lu K'üan Yü describes this state as 'The patient endurance of the uncreate, or rest in the imperturbable reality which is beyond birth and death and requires a very patient endurance. The Prajnaparamita-Sastra defines it as: the unflinching faith and unperturbed abiding in the underlying reality of all things, which is beyond creation and destruction. It must be realized before attainment of Buddhahood.

11 Individuality and society in Spinoza's mind

Joaquim Cerqueira Goncalves, Lisbon

If we wanted to interpret Spinoza's philosophy through a dialectic scheme and if we had to favour some of the process's moments, we should, undoubtedly, insist on the reasoning rhythm of *synthesis* of *surpassing* and of *reconciliation*.

We could even exemplify some of the usual outworn expressions; man and citizen of his time – eternal philosopher; time – eternity; religion – secular mind; voluntarism of social pact – demand for rational necessity *ordine geometrico demonstrata*; individualism – social organization presided over by an almost absolute authority; valuation of the *fraction* – anxiety for the *totality*. . . .

If this scheme is useful and correct it is not, in the meantime, easy to follow with exactness the *geometric* precision which Spinoza, explicitly, imposes on himself. It is enough to exemplify the difference in style and method, between *Theologico-Political Treatise* and the *Ethics*. But contrast cannot be reduced to style. The dialectic *reconciliation* is obtained by the change of plan and, if the geometric demonstration is easily detectable in the horizontal development, it escapes away from us its transition moments, ending frequently in parallel structures.

Is this to assert that great philosophers are so due to logical infidelities? Why not submit Spinoza's work to a computer's test and thus decide the coherence value of his mind? But who, knowing Spinoza's philosophy, would dare sacrifice it to the machine's postulates or speak of infidelity to the system?

We are penetrating the Jewish philosopher's mind through a difficult path, the *individuality–society* thesis. The expressions and the binomial relations are important in the author's works, constituting a pertinent road to be traversed by a Portuguese who wishes to pay homage to this great philosopher, whose drama was deeply felt by this Portuguese land.

Spinoza may be placed amongst the many great Western philosophers, who pursued the road to *happiness*,[1] like St Augustine, who knew that happiness may be explained in many different ways, which may even be in contrast with one another. He also knew that if happiness fails, life has been lost. Therefore, discovering the correct road to happiness should be man's and philosopher's main preoccupation; however, the correct road, is the true road to *knowledge*, as opposed to that of *contingency*.[2]

These intentions may be found clearly expressed in the beginning of *The Treatise on the Correction of the Understanding*. Whether or not a development in Spinoza is admitted, it is undeniable that he held steadfast to this basic principle.

Trustful in victory on *passions*, not believing in the all-powerfulness of any *genius malignus* and not needing a grace's 'complement', he is more optimistic than Augustine and Descartes. However, happiness – the circle with eternity – is not contingent nor immediate. It implies the crossing of a route, not necessarily historical, in which you will have to face the *contingent* and overcome it, meanwhile, but through the *social pact's* laws and, above all, through the highest form of knowledge.[3]

We situate our first approach to the *individuality–society* thesis on the same level as the *social pact*. Spinoza will try to find out how a man may be *free* and *happy*.[4] This is not, as yet, a radical plan, but only a *possibility*, within a very positive and circumstancial society which, nevertheless, shows a strong tendency to establish a general social system.

If only half of Spinoza's works had been read, he could very well be compared to an *existentialist*, an *opportunist* and *conformist*, such is his sensitiveness to the time and space in which he lived.[5] The author of '*Ethica ordine geometrico demonstrata*' ends his *Theologico-Political Treatise* by formally declaring an incontestable heteronomous behaviour.[6] But this is only the first plan, which prepares for the second, much more radical, where triumph over the unconditioned is at stake. Politicians, inventors of the every-moment *possibility*, remain politicians without paying any attention to the real reasons; *philosophers*, breathing the unconditioned will follow the first plan and, with this attitude, they will jeopardize the second.

Spinoza is *man* and *philosopher*, therefore, he will not abdicate from his *citizenship*. This social condition is a mediation to guarantee human existence. Is this not a condition for the true philosopher, to communicate with *mediation*? Because Spinoza is a true philosopher, he dedicates special attention to the *individuality–society* thesis. It would be profitable to try the *citizenship* mediation, in order not to jeopardize this radical tendency – *conatus* – to exist, to persevere and maintain existence,[7] in other words to live *happily*.[8]

When Spinoza speaks of the individual being, he is more a *Jew* than a *Greek*, which means, more precisely, that he belongs to the modern generation, attracted by the rational demand of *plenitude*; he appreciates however, the biblical multiplicity and individuality, notwithstanding the dubious neoplatonic projects he frequently uses such as an Arab-Jewish manner, and in spite of his clear opposition to the voluntary discontinuity of the followers of Descartes.

He does not, like the cynics, conceal disciplines, desires and passions; we would much rather surpass them, qualitatively, intensifying the *activity* and *happiness*, thus remembering Aristotle for whom pleasure and activity were associated. On the other hand, his ethics do not entrust *duty*, directed, more towards others than towards himself. His ethics are undoubtedly, the 'story of his soul', of Benedict Spinoza's irreducible individuality.

In the meantime we ask, does the desire to live attain its highest intensity when in kinship with others, in society, when man realizes his *citizenship* condition? Notwithstanding repeated assertions, although dispersed, regarding the advantage and rationality of social life,[9] it should be accepted that, in Spinoza's works, the individual dimension overlaps the social and also that human nature does not bend *city's* materialization. In fact, *man* is never reduced to *citizen*,[10] accepting citizenship's condition to defend man. Spinoza imagines a society not so much to develop the human being but, more to allow the individual to develop, annulling the possibility of restraining his free mind and expression.[11]

We should add that Spinoza at this time shows himself rather pragmatic. However, to defend freedom of thought and expression, during his lifetime meant to be highly developed in the definition and defence of human rights. His biblical *exegesis*, not to mention his social casuistic, obeys this basic intention: to eliminate all religious fanaticism, though conceding much to the civil authority,[12] but always endeavouring not to strangle individual irreducible rights. At this time and space, superimposing *civil authority* on *prophetic inspiration*, would be equivalent to substantiating a frequent Spinoza's maxim: *do not touch certainty for hope*.[13]

The *certainty*, however, is not the *best*, as, in agreement with the Jewish philosopher, society stands over a voluntary pact and not over the consistent roots of *understanding*, being understanding provided with the ontological-logical *certainty*. The social relationship is processed at an *imagination's* level, where contingence[14] rules, and this uncertainty should be replaced by the necessary causal relationship.

Individuality – Spinoza's, of course – is in fact irreducible and, therefore careful due to being frequently menaced. Man's happiness, however, is more internal than social. Spinoza, fearing fanaticism, especially collective fanaticism, does not feel proud to belong to the people.[15] The guarantee of social cohesion remains with the strongest authority and not with man's participant nature, who is not defined as a *social animal*. Therefore, politics is not a job that should be responsible for the organization of the *city* but, it should take care of the political *regime*, better still, of the *authority's* scheme. In the natural order of things, the standards are not those of general interest, because the true reality, the most genuine of all, is the individual.

II

The difficulty in expressing the different plans in Spinoza's mind, is presently greatly felt by us when surpassing *individuality's* study, whilst a member of a *society* and its respective laws, to another horizon, where the binomial is being queried or else modified. Would we have to abandon Spinoza the *politician*, to understand – and save – Spinoza the *philosopher*? Would the first one not have to pay a too heavy tribute to his time, making it impossible for us to adopt *his* philosophy as *ours*, to use Bergson's fascinating interpretation? Shall we not be forced to contradict Spinoza's order, reluctant to *final causes* having to explain the *beginning* by the end? What does the *Theologico-Political Treatise* represent and what is its position within Spinoza's works? Have we been too influenced, up to the present, by this study, which cannot be read lightly nor separated from the remaining works?

Be that as it may, our first Spinoza is not the *total* Spinoza or, at least, it is possible to portray the philosopher in a different aspect. Let us go on, keeping in touch, if possible, with the *individuality–society* thesis.

Has the binomial *individuality–society*, in fact, identical weight and similar structure through all of Spinoza's works? The reply will come out without hesitation if we consider individuality's importance, notwithstanding the difference in style and contents of each work. Thus, if, in the *Theologico-Political Treatise*, it is clear the development of relationship between *individuality–society*, in some of his works, of a more pronounced methaphysics disposition, informed by the fundamental notions of the system – *substance, attributes, modes* – we do not find a direct handling, though we cannot determine definitely its exclusion.

We have to recognize that the *individuality–society* thesis is highly anthropomorphic, whilst Spinoza's philosophy, like all true philosophy, is a radicalization effort, which means that a de-anthropomorphization must be carried out. As in Plotinus, and here, like in many other theses surprisingly similar to Spinoza's, metamorphosis of man will coincide with the abolition of the *human*, through its own integration in the horizon of *being*. Therefore, all opportunities to mention *man* will be reduced and, above all, *society*, as the plan and terminology are now of an ontological nature. Man, for instance, should enter in the registration of the *mode*.[16] This, on the other hand, will project us to the *attribute* and above all to the *substance*, which is, through its own nature, previous to its *modes*.[17]

Arriving at this point and if we persist in mixing up notions and terminologies, critical problems will arise, due to a certain nonconformity between *substance* and individual diversity, and also due to the consequences which the necessary *mode* derivation contains for the liberty of man,[18] so anxiously administered by Spinoza. The present difficulty, however, is more ours than Spinoza's. On one side, we confer unlimited priority to *freedom*, whilst

Spinoza aggregates it, transforming it within the wider horizon of *happiness*; on the other hand we lend to *freedom* the social-political meaning of our days – perhaps remotely and paradoxically prepared by our philosopher – not considering it out of the *citizenship's* scheme, which has been surpassed by Spinoza.

We should add, meanwhile, that, although distant from this possible anachronism of our responsibility, there can still be felt in Spinoza such a mixture of plans and thesis, arising from many different sources, that, if trying to understand his mind, we would have to compile the respective survey, which he was unable to do, at least not in an *ordine geometrico demonstrata* language.

If *substance* maintains undeniable priority in the system, Spinoza maintains a notion of the individual, the roots of which are easily recognizable within the Scotus scholastic sphere, sometimes already interpreted by the Occamists who misunderstood the 'Doctor Subtilis' thought. This means that individual also has a vitally important place which is why he is situated at essence's level, not being established in subordinate and accidental aspects.[19] In fact, this ontological intensity which is attributable to the individuation, is generalized in all of Spinoza's works.[20] If this interpretation is correct, translating it now in the *mode* register, we should enquire up to which point this assures this ontological weight and respects the activity – *conatus* – of individual essence, which does not appear to be able to resist to *omnipotence* of the *substance*. We know Spinoza's reply: the *mode*, expression of the *substance*, has in itself the *causa sui* activity, which *substance* is, which he seems to imitate.

Of course, we associate to the individual essence's notion the idea of discontinuity, demanding radical differences between *substance's* activity and that of the *individual*. This is one of the permanent objections we have against Spinoza, taken always by the desire to preserve individual's *freedom*. However, if we changed the normal meaning of freedom, essentially marked by the idea of *independence*, we might find ourselves surprisingly near to Spinoza. Substance is in fact *causa sui* and the reason for everything, but Spinoza's teaching wishes to place man in necessary relationship with it, thus taking advantage of the *joy* in the substantial activity. This seems possible in the last degree of knowledge, in which the human being does not destroy himself but immortalizes himself.[21] The presence of the individual values is so evident in Spinoza's works that, due in part to this presence, the *rationalistic* philosopher is simultaneously labelled as *nominalistic*.[22]

As can be seen, in this second part, the reference point of the *individual* is no longer *society*. Will there still be place for society? The silence that has fallen over *society* is in itself significant and suggests a negative answer. Spinoza felt difficulty in integrating himself in the structures of the *chosen people*, being in fact repelled by them and does not see the desired and true happiness in terms of models and collective values. If he is able to articulate the capable activity of each individual with the *causa proxima* – God; there he tastes plenitude,[23] sharing relationship with other individuals, even granted although not proved, to the discrimination of these in the substance. So as not to reduce everything to pantheism of *substance*, we are left with a plurality of *parallel* individual essences, which are not in relationship.[24] Spinoza, who lacked the notion of a *distinctio realis*[25] applicable to the ideas in God, lacked also a philosophy *relationship* because both would break the unity of *substance*. The absence of *relation* on a metaphysical level, made it impossible for an ontological fundamentation of society.

Spinoza does not have a *personality* philosophy, which would enrich the individual dimension, with *relation* category. Clever as he was, would he have feared to fall, if he admitted it, to the anthropomorphist's level,[26] similar to so many other philosophers, especially in the last decades? Would Spinoza have by-passed this difficulty when realizing a kind of *concrete universal* at the summit of the last degree of knowledge?[27]

As a final note, which is also a valid critical note to Spinoza's philosophy, but not only that, we would say that Western culture has known during the last centuries, paladins and heroes of the individual rights and freedoms, without benefiting the counterpart of a real society – metaphysics.

NOTES

1 This is the tone of all Spinoza's works and explicitly the predominant argument of the *Short Treatise*.

2 'De natura rationis est, res vere percipere' (*per Prop. 41 hujus*). nempe (*per Ax. 6. p. 1*) ut in se sunt, hoc est (*per Prop. 29. p. 1.*), non ut contingentes, sed ut necessarias q.e.d.' (*Ethics* II, *Prop.* 44, *Dem.*; vol. I, p. 109.)

We quote Spinoza's works from J. van Vloten and J. P. N. Land's edition, *Benedicti de Spinoza Opera quotquot reperta sunt*, in 4 volumes (The Hague, 1914). The numbers of the respective volumes and pages will be indicated after the semi-colon.

3 'Cum melior pars nostri sit intellectus, certum est, si nostrum utile revera quaerere velimus, nos supra omnia debere conari, et eum quantum fieri potest perficiamus; in ejus enim perfectione summum nostrum bonum consistere debet. Porro, quoniam omnis nostra cognitio et certitudo, quae revera omne dubium tollit, a sola Dei cognitione dependet.' (*Theologico-Political Treatise* IV; vol. II, p. 136.)

4 'Volvebam igitur animo, an forte esset possibile ad novum institutum, aut saltem ad ipsius certitudinem pervenire, licet ordo et commune vitae meae institutum non mutaretur . . .'. (*The Treatise on the Correction of the Understanding*, vol. I, p. 3.)

5 'Cum itaque nobis haec rara felicitas contigerat, ut in Republica vivamus, ubi unicuique judicandi libertas integra, et Deum ex suo ingenio colere conceditur, et ubi nihil libertate charius nec dulcius habetur; me rem non ingratam neque

inutilem facturum credidi, si ostenderem, hanc libertatem non tantum salva pietate et Reipublicae pace concedi, sed insuper. eandem non nisi cum ipsa pace Reipublicae ac pietate tolli posse.' (*Theologico-Political Treatise, Preface*; vol. II, p. 87.)

6 'His quae in hoc tractatu agere constitueram, absolvi, Superest tantum, expresse monere, me nihil in eo scripsisse, quod non libentissime examini et judicio summarum Potestatum Patriae meae subjiciam. Nam si quid horum, quae dixi, patriis legibus repugnare, vel communi saluti obesse judicabunt, id ego indictum volo.' (*Theologico-Political Treatise* XX; vol. II, p. 312.)

7 'quare cujuscunque rei potentia sive conatus, quo ipsa vel sola vel cum aliis quidquam agit vel agere conatur, hoc est (*per Prop. 6 hujus*) potentia sive conatus, quo in suo esse perseverare conatur, nihil est praeter ipsius rei datam sive actualem essentiam. *q.e.d.*' (*Ethics* III, *Prop.* 7, *Dem.*; vol. I, p. 128.)

8 'Cupiditas est ipsa hominis essentia (*per 1. Affect Defin.*), hoc est (*per Prop. 7. p. 3*) conatus, quo homo in suo esse perseverare conatur. Quare Cupiditas, quae ex Laetitia oritur [. . .].' (*Ethics* IV, *Prop.* 18, *Dem.*; vol. I, pp. 195–6.)

9 *Ethics* IV, *Prop.* 34, *Sc.* and IV, *Prop.* 35 *Cor.* 2; *Theologico-Political Treatise* V; vol. II, p. 149 and XVI; vol. II, pp. 259–60.

10 Spinoza, whose texts frequently remind us of Karl Marx, for instance, in his efforts to eliminate religious *alienation* could be, at this moment, implacably attacked by him, due to his liberal and *bourgeois* mind. Mind's evolution is not indifferent to the march of time. . . .

11 Although sociability does not appear to be *constitutive* of the individual's nature, it is, however, *useful*, without being inevitably *selfish* as, the happiness I desire for myself is also desired by the great majority. (*The Treatise on the Correction of the Understanding*, vol. I, p. 6.)

12 Notwithstanding Spinoza's democratic intentions, it should be considered that, conferring on man, freely, full powers to somebody else, he obeys nobody, but himself. (*Theologico-Political Treatise* V; vol. II, p. 149.)

13 'Dico, *me tandem constituisse*: primo enim intuito inconsultum videbatur, propter rem tunc incertam certam amittere velle.' (*The Treatise on the Correction of the Understanding*; vol. I, p. 3.)

14 'Hinc sequitur, a sola imaginatione pendere, quod res, tam res ectu praeteriti quam futuri, ut contingentes contemplemur.' (*Ethics* II, *Prop.* 44, *Cor.*; vol. I, p. 109.)

15 The others are only external causes, which impede more than they help the spontaneity of nature, representing, although not always, a negative factor. (See *Ethics* IV, *Prop.* 33, *Dem*; vol. I, p. 204). Besides this, sociability is not a value in itself, but a useful element, always active in the individual development. (See *Ethics* IV, *Prop.* 35, *Dem.*; vol. I, pp. 205–6.)

16 'Res singulares modi sunt, quibus Dei attributa certo et determinato modo exprimuntur (*per Coroll. Prop. 25, p. I*); hoc est (*per prop. 34, p. I*) res, quae Dei potentiam, qua Deus est et agit, certo et determinato modo exprimunt; neque ulla res aliquid in se habet, a quo possit destrui, sive quod ejus existentiam tollat (*per Prop. 4. hujus*); sed contra ei omni, quod ejusdem existentiam potest tollere, opponitur (*per Prop. praec.*); adeoque quantum potest, et in se est, in suo esse perseverare conatur. *q.e.d.*' (*Ethics* III, *Prop.* 6; vol. I, p. 127.)

17 Comparing the definitions of *substance* and of *mode*: 'Per substantiam intelligo id, quod in se est, et per se concipitur: hoc est id, cujus conceptus non indiget conceptus alterius rei, a quo formari debeat.' (*Ethics* I, *Def.* III; vol. I, p. 37.)
'Per modum intelligo substantiae affectiones, sive id, quod in alio est, per quod etiam concipitur.' (*Def.* V, *ibid.*).

18 'Sequitur II., solum Deum esse causam liberam. Deus enim solus ex sola suae naturae necessitate existit (*per Prop. 11 et Coroll. 1, Prop. 14, Adeoque per Def. 7*) solus est causa libera. *q.e.d.*' (*Ethics* I, *Prop. 17, Cor.* 2; vol. I, p. 52.)

19 It was this radical principle that so worried Duns Scotus, not accepting, therefore, individuation by *matter* or by *quantity*, the first because it was not *determinant* and the second for being only *accidental*. Let us quickly explain that Spinoza's *mode* is not equivalent to *accident*.

20 There is an interesting page revealing the sensibility to the individual, which is also an assertion of *eternal singular*, as well as the conscience of the apparent contradiction between both. (*The Treatise on the Correction of the Understanding*; vol. I, pp. 31–32.)

21 All is resumed in the last *scholium* of *Ethics*, in which the *free man* becomes a *wise man*.

22 If classifications are as unjust as they are comfortable, its disadvantages add up when applied to Spinoza. If we restrict, however, the *nominalism* to *ideas* doctrine, we find a great many of Spinoza's texts confirming this.

23 God has to be the *causa proxima* as, at the moment of total perfection, the mediation of the *causae proximae*, which would make God only a *remote cause*, would annul all of Spinoza's teachings. (*Ethics* I, *Prop.* 28, *Sc.*; vol. I, pp. 59–60.) Meanwhile, this anxiety for the *causa proxima* – divine – clearly indicates the individualist tendency of Spinoza, shared only with God and nothing else. (See Preface of IV Book of *Ethics*.)

24 The most famous Spinozan principle, *Ordo et connexio idearum idem est, ac ordo et connexio rerum* (*Ethics* II, *Prop.* 7; vol. I, p. 77 and V, *Prop.* 1, *Dem.*; vol. I, p. 248), appears not to destroy our interpretation, as it refers more to the relationship *idea-thing* than to the *idea-idea* or *thing-thing*. At least the relationship of these last ones would not result in essential modification of any of the modes. (*The Treatise on the Correction of the Understanding*; vol. I, pp. 30–31.)

25 Spinoza does not appear to have surpassed the *physical* and *logical* level of understanding, in order to establish his highly metaphysical thesis, with an understanding of ontological understanding.

26 The following words are clearly elucidative regarding the application of the *personality* image to God: 'Nec fugit nos vocabulum (personalitas scilicet), quod Theologi passim usurpant ad rem explicandum; verum, quamvis vocabulum non ignoremus ejus tamen significationem ignoramus, nec ullum clarum et distinctum conceptum illius formare possumus' (*Metaphysical Thought* II, 8, IV, p. 216).

27 We, who have resisted appealing to another authority which is not Spinoza, would like to mention in this last note, H. Bergson, not only because he was a great interpreter of Spinoza but also symbolically to declare the impossibility of a dogmatic vision, exclusive to the author of *Ethics*. We have chosen a Bergson's text, not to solve our doubts but, instead, to emphasize them: 'En allant de la

solidarité social à la fraternité humaine, nous rompons donc avec une certaine nature, mais non pas avec toute nature. On pourrait dire, en détournant de leur sens les expressions spinozistes, que c'est pour revenir à la Nature naturante que nous nous détachons de la Nature naturée.' (H. Bergson, *Les Deux Sources de la Morale et de la Religion*, Centenary Edition, PUF., Paris, 1959, pp. 1023–4.)

12 The cosmic creed and Spinoza's third mode of knowledge

Klaus Hammacher, Aachen

Pierre Bayle (1647–1706), in his famous article 'Spinoza' in the *Dictionnaire historique et critique,* insists on the distinction between religious, ethical and philosophical thought. That this sceptical critique of Bayle concerning Spinoza's pantheism was founded in religious motives had been stressed by the Spinoza editor, Carl Gebhardt, in his collection of documents of Spinoza's life.[1] On the other hand, in a later study on the *Tractatus Theologico-Politicus* Leo Strauss had developed the same differentiation between philosophical and theological truth as Spinoza's own intention.[2] Had Bayle read Spinoza so biasedly – which one can only assume due to such divergencies in reception – that he totally failed to recognize this critical tendency which was expressly mentioned by Spinoza himself? (*TTP*, Praef., chs. II, XIV, XV (1st edn, pp. 30, 165, 166 and *passim.*) Against this assumption is to remark that Bayle had a subtle sense for thematic involvements which even enabled him to find in Spinoza a cosmic conception of the world analogous to the doctrines of the Far East.[3]

According to his tendency to find a political basis for a philosophical way of life, Spinoza had in fact required a sharp division between religion and philosophy in the *Tractatus* and substantiated this from the argument of his *Ethica* that only emotions have the power of directly affecting practical conduct and also religious practice, but that emotions could not have any influence on true philosophical knowledge. Leo Strauss on his part had, fascinated by the antagonism between the exoteric diction and the esoteric philosophical pretension of the *Tractatus*, overlooked that this division was made by Spinoza in order to open a free discussion of religious customs and laws and to replace these with cognition in the laws of Nature. Even Strauss had finally to admit that the antagonism between an exoteric diction and an esoteric philosophical problem was not the only difficulty which Spinoza felt himself confronted with in the *Tractatus*, but that the greatest difficulty lies within the concept of God itself since, according to Spinoza, the world cannot be created and ordered by a extramundane God but by a God who is found immanent as an active power in reality.[4]

Bayle's at first seemingly diffuse, incongruent and strange critique on

Spinoza would perhaps be a little more understandable if we consider this background as causing his vehement condemnation of Spinoza as an atheist. But a different concept of God cannot fully explain the characterization of a man as atheist who spoke of God on nearly every page he wrote. Even when in *Ethica*, according to a report from Jean le Clerc, the word 'God' originally does not even appear,[5] I think this was meant to eliminate false associations and verifies only the rejection of a God as Creator in the sense of Christian religion. There are other consequences which are entirely inextricably connected to the different concepts of God. These can be found in the results on religious behaviour which also express the different concepts of God and which had to be altered in conformity with Spinoza's insight. Therefore, when Bayle insists on the definite differentiation not only of religion and philosophy but also of philosophical knowledge and ethic, then one can discern a new estimation of such an association between the concept of God and the resulting religious habit. The reasons for the religious habit, especially for the piety, which was also pointed out by Spinoza as a cardinal virtue in *Tractatus Theologico-Politicus* and which is to be understood in the original Latin sense of dutifulness, cannot, according to Bayle, be precisely judged by demonstration. This is because one can look into the eye but not into the heart and cannot discriminate the sincerity of another simply from his words and actions. Bayle founds the imperceptibility of mental attitude, which however could also be ascertained in Spinoza's *Tractatus*, by stating, that it is not possible to find a contradiction between proofs against a God conceived in one manner or another and belief in him, since the connection assumed is not that of belief or non-belief which would be necessary for a logical contradiction. If, however, God is conceived as a cosmic basis of unity and if alone such a conception is verifiable through strict proofs – as Spinoza claims – then each other practice of religion is unreasonable and consequently there is no true religious attitude in these other practices as can be shown by pure demonstration.[6] That is Bayle's vision of Spinoza's system.

On the one hand we must doubt that a religious conduct is founded in reason and not only – maybe by reason – in tradition, but on the other hand we have to recognize that Bayle criticizes non-consequent discerning between religion, morals and knowledge. In reality atheism in this context could only be found in the above-mentioned estimation of religious belief as Bayle shows, because he had never drawn Spinoza's personal integrity into question.

Owing to Bayle's protests against Spinoza we are made aware of an unidentified implication in the understanding of the relationship between religion and knowledge, which can be exposed by the question: is religious behaviour still justifiable at all when knowledge alone constitutes the foundation of it?

Only when this question is accepted is it possible to understand why Spinoza was seen as an atheist even by his contemporary correspondents. It is not sufficient to assume that he rejected the Christian and Jewish God. That is to say that he actually disavowed a personal God. As Hobbes stated, every man who thinks Nature is eternal, denies God and is an atheist, but Hobbes is only projecting his causal definition in the Christian idea of God as Creator.[7] Therefore, in this article I shall approach the question regarding Spinoza's relationship to religion not from the concept of God, but from the question of the relation to this God as shown in religious performances. I believe that the basis for the refusal of Spinoza as an atheist should be sought in his discarding of religious practices which are only permitted by him as inferior practical prescriptions useful to government. But for the comprehension of God, he only permitted the third mode of knowledge.

There exists the opinion that all philosophy tries to dissolve religious thought, which seems to belong to a prehistoric mode of thinking. Then, however, it still depends on which claim is combined with such an implication. The German philosopher Friedrich Heinrich Jacobi (1743–1819) already diagnosed in the sense of the implication mentioned above that likewise the natural urge of reason is not to find a God but to be able to do without him,[8] and so discovered in knowledge itself an incompatibility with religious belief. But the spectrum of conclusions here is still broader and allows us to differentiate between at least three attitudes towards religious behaviour. First, one may judge the religious foundation of life as mentally retarded and devalue the religious proof as pathological, this attitude being expressed in Karl Marx's remark that religion is opium for the people[9] (despite its abuse of knowledge to disavow others this remark still shows an intellectual attitude); or second, one only permits such practical exercise of religion as conforms with knowledge, which Spinoza did already. Finally, one acknowledges self-determination by reason as religious attitude, which Spinoza also precepted in *Ethica*. In the last two attitudes concerning religious behaviour, often associated with one another, the identification of religion with ethic as well as ethic with knowledge can be recognized.

Spinoza, himself, adhered to the idea that knowledge was the basis of ethics, not directly, but through its emotional outcome (*Ethica* IV, props 8 and 14). Also the intellectual love of God (*amor Dei intellectualis*) fulfils moral conduct (*Ethica* V, prop. 36). Equally piety (*pietas*) and obedience (*obedientia*) are acknowledged in the *Tractatus Theologico-Politicus* as an ethical statement of belief (*TTP*, chs XIII, XIV, XIX (1st edn, pp. 154, 161, 165, 215).

These consequences from an altered relationship between religion and morals result – I would claim – from undetermined concepts in religion itself. This relationship will be described in this article. It may also clarify the sense of the third mode of knowledge and its sources. A turn in religious sentiment can be found in Spinoza, a turn to an individual relationship with God and divine law, which is internal to the individual. So, according to Spinoza, religious behaviour in piety and knowledge of God can only be won through individual and free judgment (*proprium & liberum judicium*) (*TTP*, ch. VII (1st edn. pp. 102–3)). Because this judgment is bound to knowledge and since, according to Spinoza, knowledge is *active* (to which we shall return) and an affirmation of the real order of Nature free from personal interests, an ethical thought, the concept of *autonomy*, carries the justification of an action as religious. On the other hand, by this thought individual judgment expresses in religion the same sovereignty that characterizes knowledge, that is, to need no external cause and therefore not be dependent on chance. According to Spinoza one understands oneself in this attitude, and with this understanding expresses the necessary order of Nature.

Religious customs have no significance for the relationship to God, which is simply illustrated – Spinoza pointed out that the Jews immediately abandoned cultic rites and religious practices when they no longer had collective services in Babylonic captivity (*TTP*, ch. V (1st edn, p. 58)). The religious habit which is shown by customs, ceremonies and cultic rites is only for external application. With the individualizing of religious behaviour the religious cultic rites as well as the fulfilment of the *Law* faded into formal civil law. This emancipation of the ethical sense from morals and ritual customs means that for the judgment of religious conduct the foundation can no longer be found in these customs themselves.

Having reached this point of view one can only discern in such customs and rites a manner of thinking which finds its order in coincidental occurrences and which develops from this order certain ceremonies. Spinoza had shown this in his *Tractatus Theologico-Politicus* and consistently denied all other origins. Therefore, ceremonies are actions which are in themselves *indifferent* ('*actiones, quae in se indifferentes sunt*', *TTP*, ch. IV (1st edn, p. 48)); their legality comes from associations (*TTP*, ch. IV (1st edn, pp. 43–4)) and they are dependent on the will of men ('*ex hominum placito pendere*', *TTP*, ch. IV (1st edn, p. 44)) and the particular circumstances (*ibid.*).

To what extent, however, their original character, that the divine order should be realized in the fulfilment of the rules and laws and execution of rites, is misjudged by Spinoza is apparent in his inadequate understanding of the words of Christ, that he did not come to abolish the Law but to fulfil it. That Christ did not want to abolish the Law is interpreted to mean that he was not concerned with public affairs but rather with teaching, which is supposed to show – as Spinoza comments – that he did not wish to better the morals but the faith of mankind (*TTP*, chs V, VII (1st edn, pp. 56–1, 89)). Spinoza deletes the fulfilment of the Law, which is proclaimed there and which exists in realization of the prophecies. The New Testament strives meticulously to prove this fulfilment.

Since the times of mythological thinking, man recognizes his relationship to God in execution of these laws and rites and, therefore, religious conduct fulfils itself in obedience to such laws. Even though Spinoza maintains that obedience and pious faith are forms of religious behaviour he does not realize that by practising these forms the events in the world should be understood as submitted to divine laws. Obedience for Spinoza in this case refers primarily to the inner activity according to rules of the heart (*TTP*, ch. XVII (1st edn, p. 188)) even though it should principally be expressed in the fulfilment of an outward act of charity (*TTP*, ch. XIV (1st edn, p. 160)).

Some of these mythical or even magical identifications with the deity in the rites and cultic symbols may also be found in the Christian and Jewish doctrines, as shown, for instance, by the Christian symbol of the cross.[10] So we can discover in the rules of performance of religious gestures (making the sign of the cross, the washing of the feet, and fraternal kiss) a genetic basis of religious thinking which is common to all religious communions and therefore enables us to understand the real foundation of religious thought.

Although Spinoza did not see this connection, even if he mentions that in the Old Testament the word of God often was taken as the law of Nature, he should very well have been able to explain a religious foundation using his new method of research. He ascertained in *Tractatus Politicus* as well as in the preface to the third part of *Ethica*, that all human modes of behaviour, even such which stem solely from emotions (*affectiones*), have their own certain causes and therefore may be understood with a scientific method as strict as mathematics (*TP*, I, §4 OP, pp. 268–9; *Ethica* III, Praef. OP, p. 94). Nevertheless, an exact observation of that which the Jewish religion understood as obedience showed him that the fulfilment of the Law was a form of education for initiation in the divine order of nature – a thought which Lessing would later take up and expound in his *Erziehung des Menschengeschlechts* (*TTP*, ch. II, XVII, 1st edn., pp. 27, 202).

This understanding can, however, also be twisted and points then towards such behavioural patterns in customs and cultic habits which grasp the natural order in the execution of the rituals. Due to behaviourism such a motivation in the religious rules and cults has become comprehensible today. In this sense they are based on a symbolic reconstruction which imitates patterns of prehistoric men, because these patterns are analogous with certain animal instincts. So we can – to stay within the Jewish religious customs discussed by Spinoza – find in Passover rites the instinct residual of 'covering traces' in the ceremonial instruction that all that was not consumed during the night must be burned since nothing was to be left over.[11] That there is a symbolic relation is shown by assumed demons which are rest-consuming. In the same manner the sacrificial lamb can be understood as representing the flock in order to procure protection. This points to the origin of the cult in pastoral tribes and is comprehensible as a *pars-pro-toto*-connection which Ernst Cassirer had analysed as a type of primitive logic.[12]

I assumed that Spinoza's understanding of the religious relationship as being inner, shifted the access which by using his method had made it possible to explain the cultic rules of the Jewish faith. This is supported by the fact that in his work, in addition to the new methodological approach for describing the emotive effect, an anthropological explanation can be found through which, in principle, all modes of behaviour can be derived by strict natural laws.

Spinoza takes over Descartes's theory of movement, but converts it into a dynamic system[13] in which by the co-operation between corps (i.e. corpuscles) larger units are built which then strive to survive (*Ethica* II, def. and lemma 4 following axiom 2, prop. 13). Spinoza calls such a composition *individuum*. The individual maintains his nature through the preservation of the composition, in spite of all change of corps, by a self-regulation (Lemma 7, *ibid.*). Thereby a referential system becomes apparent which gains stability by inference of the single moments (lemma 2, dem., *ibid.*) and which is maintained through the regeneration of the single corps. Even today we can accept this derivation as an adequate definition of an organism. The human body is in this manner characterized as an especially developed organism which is composed of many individual bodies and which expresses its life in manifold motions and in extremely diversified interactions. This appears in most extensive possibilities of allocation when conceived by the human mind, so that these individuals appear to be moved in many different ways and are capable of setting others in motion (*Ethica* II, post. 6 following lemma 7). They show a nearly undetermined and therefore unpredictable motion.

Spinoza stated that generally he did not discern between human and other individual beings as far as all are governed by the laws of Nature (*TTP*, ch. XVI (1st edn., pp. 175–6), cf. also *Ethica* III, prop. 2, schol. OP, p. 98). The human mind remains coupled to an internal quasi-cybernetical circle of functions which is derived from the affections in the motions of its body. In particular, the insight which Spinoza states in *Ethica* II, corollary 2 of proposition 16 reveals a point of view from which the development of human conduct could be seen in this sense: 'It follows . . . that the ideas we have of external bodies indicate the constitution of our own body rather than the nature of external bodies.' Not only does the human mind come into contact with the environment through interactions of its body but the ideas which are produced in the interactions are also bound by an internal bodily feedback since these ideas are not perceived only by the senses but are also perceived as ideas by the mind itself (*Ethica* II, prop. 22). However, with this model of reverse sensitivity the self-adjustment of the body is coupled to the urge for self-preservation. This has the consequence that the correlations built in the imagination also appear as expressions of this urge. But the association of ideas which, according to Spinoza, are given from the reverse sensitivity in connections of imagination reach beyond the perception of the body itself and build patterns of behaviour in the mind, which are governed by entireties conceived in this manner. From this development of body-mind associations, associations of imagination which are dependent on the direct reactions of the bodies surrounding the human body, many types of human behaviour can be explained from the biological basis. However, this does not yet prove that religious behaviour and the greater part of intelligent acts which are formed by men are also explainable by this method. But we can assume that Spinoza sets cultic behaviour in this sphere, because it is not founded in knowledge.

Religious behaviour includes a hidden reference to the whole of nature, the cosmos. Man tries to learn the mental unity of Nature through the organic functional connections as significant. The principle of unity is to be gained from an articulation of the body using a symbolic generalization.

Spinoza also ascertained that there is a mental connection of ideas that conform to each change in Nature and that in these ideas the nature of the human body is given as well as the nature of its external neighbouring bodies (*Ethica* II, prop. 16). According to this sentence there must be a way to find the connections of Nature from the references which they have to our own body bearing on the unity.

Moreover, a cosmic creed still holds Spinoza's perception of Nature as it had already held that of the original religious behaviour. And this connection is only perceivable through a belief in the cosmic unity of Nature in God. In the *Tractatus de Intellectus Emendatione* he explicitly demands that the whole of Nature must be comprehended as such an entirety (OP, p. 360). This creed not only appears in the pantheistic formulations in *Ethica* where Spinoza even points to the same thinking in religious tradition (*Ethica* II, prop. 7, schol.), but is also closely linked with the concept of psycho-physical parallelism. So the complete analogy in the connection of ideas as including all corporal changes is only guaranteed in that they are involved in 'the eternal and infinite essence of God' (*Ethica* II, prop. 45).

But Spinoza attempted to give a rational basis to the creed and does not simply accept it as a mythical thought. That we are not able to comprehend anything besides the corresponding changes of the corporal world and their causal connections in true knowledge becomes evident by the simple fact that we comprehend a visible existing circle as being the same as we perceive in its construction (*Ethica* II, prop. 7, schol.) even though this – as shown by the *Tractatus de Intellectus Emendatione* (OP p. 379) – is conscious as a different thing. We have a certainty: of the object and of our thinking the object corresponds to the relationship between the corporal world and its comprehension (*Ethica* II, prop. 5), since we have the idea that the mind, that is the *consciousness*, should be united to the mind in the same manner as the mind is united to the body (*Ethica* II, prop. 21). This uncertain identification[14] is supported by indirect evidence which lies in the cosmic unity and which Spinoza elaborates from the supposition of God's infinite attributes. Infinite attributes are to be assumed because it is only through these that the conciseness of the universe can be perceived in a manner in which both corporal and intellectual worlds refer only to one another (*Epist.* XXXII and LXIV; *Ethica* I, prop. 10, schol.). So he thinks it possible to connect the individual being and its identification with a body in the cosmic creed.

When Bayle introduces the Indian and cabbalistic concept of perceiving God in *extension* and *contraction* (a symbolic derivation from the rhythm of breathing)[15] – and in this interpretation he was followed by Lessing, Goethe and Herder in consequence of a remark of the above-mentioned Jacobi in his dialogue with Lessing[16] – he misses Spinoza's concept of the cosmic creed. Then, according to Spinoza, this type of identification takes place only in the third mode of knowledge. To what extend the cosmic creed, which is the foundation of religious behaviour as expressed in religious rites and cultic customs, is compatible with Spinoza's third mode of knowledge, is what we now need to clarify.

Spinoza tried to point out that through the relationship of the organism to the surroundings only an inappropriate and confused concept of the universe can be attained. Our body only enters into a very small part of all interactions of the world. However, all perception of external matters takes place through such reactions with our bodies (*Ethica* II, props 19, 26). In this sense Spinoza once asked what concept of order a worm in the circulation of the blood would have (*Epist.* XXXII). Since, as human individuals, we are concerned with the drive for self-preservation (*conatus in suo esse perseverandi*), that is in this case an adjustment following reverse sensitivity, we are determined more – as we have heard – from the constitution of our body that from external bodies (*Ethica* II, prop. 16, corr. 2).

Nevertheless, Spinoza concedes a specific sense of human behaviour. Even though he comprehends all living beings (and that is all that exists, because all is to a certain degree animated, *Ethica* II, prop. 13, schol.) under the drive for self-preservation, he notes that human beings have special laws which control their behaviour. The drive arises from the general order of Nature, but in human beings is referred to the preservation of the individual as desire (*appetitus*) (*Ethica* III, prop. 9, schol.). Therefore, the appetite acts not only from the basis of immediate affections but also from associations which are built from the ideas we get from our emotive feelings. Spinoza systematically from here deduces the higher, i.e. the common, modes of conduct.

Remarkable for our consideration of religious behaviour are: first, that Spinoza also recognizes the appetite for self-preservation in the endeavour to make others live according to one's own convictions (*Ethica* III, prop. 31, schol.; *TP*, ch. I, §5), and, second, that the associative communication through language creates emotional connections which are independent of the perceivable similarity, that is, which are symbolic in our sense (*Ethica* II, prop.

18, schol. combined with *TTP*, ch. IV (1st edn, p. 44)). Spinoza understands religious rites and cultic customs from such an arbitrary conformity. But the claim of general validity contained in them does not conform with the necessary order of Nature. Here the ideas are still conceived according to the external connection and, therefore, one can only gain a confused knowledge in this manner (cf. *Ethica* II, props 24–30).

In his seventeenth letter, Spinoza develops the idea that one can imagine something that would happen in the future, but only if the ideas are coherent with the character of that person. In this case participation with an ordered connection of ideas is possible (*Epist.* XVII). Here we can see indicated an explanation of cultic or moral behaviour in nearly the same manner as is given in our times by structuralism, that is to find a pattern of geometrical relations behind the acting of a group which is to be reconstructed to conform to the laws of Nature. Also in the *Tractatus Theologico-Politicus* Spinoza occasionally discovers an agreement with the laws of Nature in such customs. He attempts, however, to discredit it by stating that it only involves rules for physical welfare and is advantageous for the common welfare (*TTP*, ch. V, 1st edn, pp. 55, 56, 57, 61). In this manner Spinoza comprehends the integrative social power even if not the hygienic sense in circumcision (*TTP*, ch. III (1st edn, p. 43)). But when he suggests an education by nature in the history of the Jews – as already mentioned – he assumes a legislation in religious instruction which conforms to the law of Nature.

But only by the third mode of knowledge should man be able to comprehend Nature adequately. Such inconsistence in Spinoza's system results from an ambiguous consequence in the conception of the third mode of knowledge. This knowledge should result from the common notions (*communes notiones*) which could be built from the common characters between the human body and external bodies (*Ethica* II, prop. 39, dem.; *TTP*, ch. XIV (1st edn, p. 165)). But this equates to the constitution of schemas of behaviour that arise from the bodily functions in so far as they conform with the common law of Nature. Now we can ask where the difference lies between a religious ritual built in a symbolic generalization of behavioural gestures from organic experience and the common notions gained from the identical characters of bodies. Even though Spinoza has already stressed the *reason in the body* – to use Nietzsche's term[17] – there is also to be found a discerning moment in his definitions. A generalization by identification with the law of organism is based on the drive for self-preservation. In Spinoza's system the drive in this case would appear as an appetite (*appetitus*) which is related to *both* body and mind, and is conscious in the emotion of desire (*cupiditas*) (*Ethica* III, prop. 9, schol.). An identification – as Spinoza conceives it – cannot be executed in this way, because it consists in an affirmation of the order of Nature in which the will is positively seized as a faculty to affirm or deny (*Ethica* II, prop. 48, schol.). That does not take place in desire for, in the will, the drive to preserve existence is related alone to the mind, while desire also expresses the associations which reflect on the influence of the body (*Ethica* II, prop. 23, dem.).

Spinoza uses these clear definitions to substitute knowledge for religion. In consequence it must be queried whether or not this makes every responsibility for our actions illusive, if we express them in our religious behaviour. This is of even greater importance than in symbolic generalizing as is done by religious rites one necessarily refers back to the limited experience of earlier cultures and back to mythic thinking which is very impeded by taboos. For the Jews in post-biblical times the idea that Passover originated from a blood ritual would be incomprehensible, precisely because the consumption of blood was condemned as the worst of crimes, although it still influenced the ceremonial.[18]

From such observations it can be deduced that each form of religious thinking can be resolved as an erroneous intention in the drive for self-preservation, based on falsely generalized experiences. In this manner Christian customs and symbols reflect back on a world orientation which knowledge seems to have proved as inappropriate. Isn't it thus possible to understand the Christian feeling of responsibility to the divine commandments as parallel to a hallucination as known by psychoanalytical experience? There we find an irresistible compulsory commandment of a superego, which imputes to the self a strict performance of certain ritual actions.

But does the religious responsibility refer at all to such a drive? If the will according to Spinoza contains only in knowledge the affirmation and denial of personal responsibility, since only the human being is active in this way (*Ethica* III, def. 2) and is therefore autonomous, then yet it still remains oriented to the drive for self-preservation. For even here we are only aware of the ideas from the modifications of the body necessary for this drive (*Ethica* III, prop. 9, dem.). In ethical evaluation the remaining religious behaviour, acting in accordance to knowledge, can therefore only be recognized as a moral legitimation of *survival of the fittest*.

Spinoza seems to avoid this conclusion since the affirmation, which is fulfilled in knowledge, does not result from individual consciousness but from the objective connection of things, that is from that which all things have in common (*Ethica* II, prop. 38 in connection with prop. 48). So nothing can be affirmed which is not given in this manner. To assert an activity, conscious in the power of the will, shows a careless confusion of the *consciousness* of our actions with the *causes* of our actions (*Ethica* II, prop. 49, schol.; III, prop. 2, schol. in connection with II, prop. 35, schol.). Spinoza shows on man's psychological dependence, that the will is not capable of causing anything: we cannot articulate a word if we cannot remember it. Dreams demonstrate that will can generate nothing more than what we are already conscious of, since a man has not the freedom during dreams 'of suspending his judgment upon those things which he dreams, and of causing himself not to dream those things which he dreams that he sees' (*Ethica* II, prop. 49, schol. OP 90). That simply means that with our will we cannot change circumstances whose order we recognize and which bound the will in the drive of self-preservation. Moreover one follows the drive for self-preservation in knowledge as well as in the passions.

But when Spinoza thinks to unmask the responsibility in religious consciousness as a consciousness of desire and freedom which founds such imputation as being conscious of the fulfilling of our wishes, he himself finds the same confusion in his arguments which he discovered in the consciousness of actions: he understands the responsibility as resulting from causes.

This can be made clear by continued interpretation of his example of the dream; there he made the restriction, namely that: we come across a suspension of judgment at the point where we dream that we are dreaming. Here in other words he correlates the experience which the poet Novalis later put into verse: 'We are close to awaking when we dream that we are dreaming.'[19] In reality Spinoza's example does not argue from the existence of seeing in dreams but from the affirmation, that is, the judgment on that which one sees, in this case: the dream as dream.

In the responsibility as foundation of the religious consciousness which appears in the will, the concern is not for a consciousness of causes in the sense of self-preservation, but for *good* and *evil will*. That is, a consciousness of the performance of an action and not of will as power. Christianity understood good will as being conscious of imputation in this manner. Accepting religious conscience in this sense we leave behind us the concept of will as a *magical power* which, through identification with the movements of the organism, tries to gain omnipotence. Sigmund Freud stated sarcastically in *Totem und Tabu*: 'Aber in dem Vertrauen auf die Macht des Menschengeistes, welcher mit den Gesetzen der Wirklichkeit rechnet, lebt ein Stück primitiven Allmachtglaubens weiter.'[20] In contrast to this the metamorphosis of the blood offers at Passover as mentioned above[21] and the reversal of fertility rites into chastity-symbols, which C. G. Jung observed in Christian and Indian religions,[22] mark a change of cosmic creed into religious creed on a level of thought which becomes free from drive for self-preservation.

Spinoza had also seen the *ambivalence* in which the symbolic act liberates men from the urge by showing him *good* and *evil will*. He states in the fifth part of *Ethics* that a person in respect to the same appetite can be active in mind as well as passively subdued in passions. Spinoza did not consider that the religious decision, as discovered in Jung's observations, consists in a re-evaluation given in reference to the cosmic belief and expresses itself alone in the sense in which an action is executed. Spinoza concedes in his explanations that such manners of conduct as *piety* (*pietas*) and *honesty* (*honestas*) can not evolve from an act of will (*impetu*) (*Ethica* IV, prop. 37, schol. 1). In these explanations Spinoza develops a particular law which aims for common consent (*Ethica* IV, prop. 37, dem. aliter). With this a basis for behaviour is characterized which Spinoza himself did not comprehend, but which he ascribed to and gives out as the third mode of knowledge. This basis is not tangible for Spinoza because he proceeds from a cosmic creed. In his own thinking we find a knowledge which dissolves the foundation of such a creed, because it has no rational basis. With a rational basis, however, no emotional feeling can be found to articulate the moving of the organic body. The knowledge apparently interferes, then – as Spinoza stated – only an emotion can affect an emotion (*Ethica* IV, prop. 14).[23] For this reason the internally given connection should be interpreted as an ethical characteristic, that is, as autonomy.

In reality the independence of knowledge fits into the drive for self-preservation without any problem. So that a man who acts from knowledge lives by an ethical attitude which deludes self-determination, but in reality he is only directed by self-preservation. This attitude has in knowledge a system which seems warranted by the independence of mental connection. The internal intention of judgment has no more connection with bodily feeling. There is no longer a symbol of divine order to be found in bodily feeling, only a stable self-directing system. The inwardness of belief has nothing more to do with, for example, the kneeling action of a person at prayer. But how can a good will be grasped when it can no longer be understood from bodily action? Spinoza on the one hand insisted that piety as *good* for all together (*omnibus commune*) could be understood as derived from the appetite to see that others also enjoy the same good (*Ethica* IV, prop. 37, dem. aliter). On the other hand he states that all regulation between humans is given as *good* or *evil* from the common agreement concerning utility (*Ethica* IV, prop. 37, schol. 2). From this he explains all religious customs (cf. *TTP*, chs IV, XIX). But *good will*, as Spinoza ascertained, cannot be derived from such agreements (*TTP*, chs VII and XIX (1st edn, pp. 102–3, 215)). Since we can no longer conceive the organism of our body symbolically we must now find a symbolic behaviour which takes place in the knowledge and lets the knowledge be determined as good or evil.

NOTES

1 *Spinoza, Lebensbeschreibungen und Gespräche*, translated and edited by Carl Gebhardt (Leipzig, 1914), p. viii.
2 Leo Strauss, 'How to Study Spinoza's Theological-Political Treatise', in *Proceedings of the American Academy for Jewish Research*, vol. XVII (1948), pp. 69–131.
3 Pierre Bayle, *Dictionnaire historique et critique*, 5th Edition (Rotterdam, 1720), vol. III, pp. 2633–4, note B.

4 Strauss, *op. cit.*, p. 128.

5 Jean le Clerc, *Bibliothèque ancienne et moderne*, vol. XXII, I, p. 135: 'J'ai dit oui à l'homme digne de foi, qui me l'a même donné écrit de sa main, que Spinosa avait composé sa prétendue *Ethique démontrée* en Flamand, et qu'il la donna à traduire en Latin à un Médecin, qui se nommait Louis Meyer; et que le mot de Dieu ne s'y trouvait point; mais seulement celui de la Nature, qu'il prétendait être éternelle. Le Médecin l'avertit qu'on lui ferait infailliblement une grosse affaire de cela, comme niant qu'il ait un Dieu, et introduisant en sa place, la Nature; qui est un mot plus propre à marquer la Créature que le Créateur. Spinosa consentit à ce changement, et le livre parut, comme Meyer le lui avoit conseillé.' (Quoted from Constantin Brunner, *Spinoza gegen Kant und die Sache der geistigen Wahrheit*, 2nd Edition (Assen, 1974), p. 16, note.)

6 Bayle, *op. cit.*, p. 2637, col. 1.

7 Thomas Hobbes, *Opera Philosophica . . . Omnia* (London, 1839–45) (Reprint Aalen 1961), vol. I, p. 337: 'Nonne qui æternitatem mundi sic tollunt, eadem opera etiam mundi conditori æternitatem tollunt?'

8 Friedrich Heinrich Jacobi's Letter to J. G. Hamann from November 14th 1786, cit. in Johann Georg Hamann, *Briefwechsel*, ed. A. Henkel, vol. VII (forthcoming).

9 Karl Marx, 'Zur Kritik der Hegelschen Rechtsphilosophie', in *Frühe Schriften*, ed. H. J. Lieber and P. Furth (Stuttgart, 1962), vol. I, p. 488.

10 Ernst Cassirer, *Philosophie der symbolischen Formen*, Part II: *Das mythische Denken*, 3rd Edition (Darmstadt, 1958), p. 178.

11 See Ernst Ludwig Ehrlich, *Kultsymbolik im Alten Testament und im nachbiblischen Judentum* (*Symbolik der Religionen III*) (Stuttgart, 1959), p. 67.

12 Cassirer, *op. cit.*, p. 65.

13 P. van der Hoeven, 'The Significance of Cartesian Physics for Spinoza's Theory of Knowledge', in *Spinoza on Knowing, Being and Freedom*, ed. J. G. van der Bend (Assen, 1974), pp. 114–25.

14 Klaus Hammacher, 'Spinozas Gedanke der Identität und die Begründung im menschlichen Verhalten,' in *Zeitschrift für Philosophische Forschung*, vol. 23 (1969), pp. 24–35.

15 Bayle, *op. cit.*, p. 2632, col. 1.

16 See Friedrich Heinrich Jacobi, *Werke* (Leipzig, 1812–25) (Reprint Darmstadt, 1968), vol. IV/1, pp. 63–4; see also Klaus Hammacher, *Jacobis Auseinandersetzung mit dem Neo-Spinozismus Goethes und Herders*, in *Biographie als Problemgeschichte. Friedrich Heinrich Jacobi: in seiner Zeit*.

17 To illustrate Nietzsche's conception see Friedrich Nietzsche, *Werke*, ed. K. Schlechta (München, 1954), vol. II, pp. 300–1.

18 See Ehrlich, *op. cit.*, p. 66, note 172:
Bei den Naturvölkern wurde wahrscheinlich auch die Gottheit in diesen Bund einbezogen, bei dem Mahl als anwesend betrachtet, und an das gemeinsame Bindeglied, das Blut, gebunden. Es diente zugleich als Erkennungszeichen, mit wem die Gottheit in einen Bund des Friedens und des Schutzes getreten ist. Ursprünglich dürfte beim heiligen Mahle durch Blutgenuß die dem Opfer innewohnende Lebenskraft eingesaugt worden sein. Das Blut wurde dem Gott übergeben und das dem lebenden

Fleisch und Blut eigene göttliche Leben von den Teilnehmern am heiligen
Mahle aufgenommen. So wollte man der Gottheit Leben spenden, um
im Überfluß von ihr wieder Leben empfangen zu können. Für Israel waren
derartige Bräuche freilich der ärgste Greuel gewesen. Blutgenuß galt als
schlimmstes Vergehen.

19 See Novalis, *Schriften*, ed. R. Samuel (Stuttgart, 1960), vol. II, p. 416.
20 Sigmund Freud, *Totem und Tabu, Gesammelte ¦Werke* (Frankfurt-a-M., 1961),
vol. IX, p. 109.
21 See above, note 18.
22 See Carl Gustav Jung, *Man and his Symbols* (London, 1964), p. 91.
23 See my contribution: 'Spinoza's Conclusions drawn from Systematic Reflection
on the Affections', in van der Bend, *op. cit.*, pp. 82–97.

13 Finite and infinite in Spinoza's system

Errol E. Harris, Milwaukee

I

'That queer quantity "infinity" is the very mischief and no rational physicist should have anything to do with it.' Sir Arthur Eddington's remark[1] was prompted by problems in classical and contemporary physics but is equally apposite to philosophical theories. 'That queer quantity, infinity', has been a perennial stumbling block to metaphysicians, not least to interpreters of Spinoza, who makes use of it undaunted by the paradoxes which seem to proliferate with every attempt to understand its nature and relation to finite individuals.

Spinoza defines God as an absolutely infinite substance constituted by infinite attributes each of which expresses eternal and infinite essence (*E*, I, def. vi).[2] Commentators have asked why God should have infinite attributes, and Tschirnhaus appealed to Spinoza to prove that it was so (*Ep*, LXIII). Others have puzzled over the nature of infinite essence; but perhaps the problem which has given most trouble, after that of the relation between the infinite attributes, is how the infinity of substance and of its attributes relates to the infinity in number and variety also asserted by Spinoza, of the finite modes of substance. '*Ex necessitate divinae naturae infinita infinitis modis* (*hoc est omnia, quae sub intellectum infinitum cadere possunt*) *sequi debent*' (*E*, I, xvi). Infinite things in infinite ways (modes) follow of necessity from the divine nature (that is, everything that can be comprehended by an infinite intellect). We are called upon to make intelligible to ourselves an absolutely infinite substance having infinite attributes, each of which, we are told (*Ep*, XXXVI, *E*, I, xvi, dem.) is infinite in its own kind, and from all of which there follow of necessity infinite things in infinite ways.

Spinoza was confident that he had conclusively shown why an absolutely infinite substance must have an infinity of attributes. Because a thing has attributes in proportion to its reality or perfection, the more reality it has the more attributes must belong to it. Its essence expresses what it is, and its attributes express its essence; therefore, the more it encompasses, the more attributes are needed to express its essence. If it is absolutely infinite it must

197

have an infinity of attributes. All this seemed self-evident to Spinoza and his proof of prop. ix. (*E*, I)[3] in consequence states simply '*patet ex Def. 4.*' (i.e. the definition of attribute). To Simon de Vries he wrote:

> But you say that I have not demonstrated that substance (or being) can have many attributes, perchance you have not attended to the demonstrations. For I have offered two, the first, that nothing is more evident to us than that any thing whatever is conceived by us under some attribute, and the more reality, or being, any thing has the more attributes must be assigned to it. Whence an absolutely infinite thing must be defined, etc. The second, and what I judge the best, is that the more attributes I assign to any thing the more I am compelled to attribute existence to it, that is, the more I conceive it under the principle of truth (*sub ratione veri*) . . .' (*Ep*, IX).

Although this reasoning may seem clear and cogent, it gives rise to the notorious difficulty concerning the relation of the infinite attributes to the attribute of Thought, placing Spinoza between the horns of a dilemma. Either there must be an asymmetry between Thought and every other single attribute, or else the human mind must be capable of knowing all of them, and not only Thought, and Extension. Spinoza's reply to Tschirnhaus's objection on this score is cryptic and unsatisfactory:

> 'In answer to your objection, I say, that, although each thing is expressed in infinite ways (*modis*) in the infinite intellect of God, those infinite ideas by which it is expressed, cannot constitute one and the same mind of an individual thing, but infinite [minds]: since each of these infinite ideas has no connexion with any other (*Ep*. LXVI).

I have discussed this dilemma elsewhere[4] and shall not make it the subject of this paper. There are other problems involved in Spinoza's conception of infinity, especially with respect to its relation to finite things, and it is these, and the treatment of them by certain other writers, which I want to attend to here.

The main question centres on *E*, I, xvi. How does the multitude of things follow from the infinite essence of substance in infinite ways? In one sense of 'follows' we may find a tolerable answer, although its legitimacy has been denied by several commentators. Spinoza repeatedly says that the modes follow from God's essence in the same way as the properties of a triangle follow from its definition, and H. H. Joachim and John Caird have maintained that he has failed to provide any principle of differentiation in the nature of substance which could explain how this diversity of modes, or, for that matter the infinite attributes, should follow from God's absolute and infinite unity.[5] But what has been quoted above answers, at least by implication, criticisms of this kind. God has been defined as the absolutely infinite substance and the very conception of absolute infinity involves infinite reality (or perfection). A blank and featureless unity is the diametric opposite of infinite reality and so could not be an absolute infinite. To try to conceive of God as undifferentiated unity is to strive to entertain a flat contradiction. It does, therefore, follow from the definition of substance that it is infinitely diversified – that is, that it has infinite attributes, and much the same reasoning could be used to show that each attribute, infinite in its own kind, must similarly, in its own kind, be infinitely diversified.

Spinoza's insistence and proofs that substance cannot be divided and that no attribute is internally divisible, does not conflict with the above conclusion. Division and diversification are not the same concept. Within an indivisible whole there may be numerous distinctions of differences, aspects, interdependent elements and mutually indispensable factors, so related that no division or separation is possible between them, while, among themselves, they are infinitely changeable and diverse. We shall shortly have occasion to give examples of such wholes. The point here to be emphasized is that a blank and undifferentiated unity is not a whole at all, finite or infinite, and *ipso facto* cannot be what Spinoza defines as God or substance. For 'whatever is, is in God, and nothing can either exist or be conceived without God' (*E*, I, xv). God, therefore, comprehends the totality of the existing universe, the internal diversity of which nobody (not even Parmenides) can consistently deny. The significance and importance of Spinoza's doctrine is that this infinite diversity is veritably a whole, understood in the only proper and legitimate sense of that word; that is, a unity which though internally diversified is indivisible.

Again, although it is a fact that at times Spinoza denies the propriety (as applied to substance) of the category of whole and part (e.g. *Ep*, XXXV), this denial, rightly understood, involves no inconsistency either with what has just been maintained, or with other of Spinoza's own statements in which he uses whole and part in speaking of the infinite (e.g. *Ep*, XXXII). The inappropriate conception is that of a 'whole' as an aggregate or collection of parts, the reality and nature of which are prior to the whole, so that the latter is a product of the former. The appropriate conception, on the other hand, is of a whole of different elements the existence and character of which depend upon the structure and pattern of the whole, so that it is prior to them and they entirely dependent both for their being and their nature (essence) upon the totality.

If one adopts the second conception, the diversity of substance follows from its nature or essence, and Spinoza's assertion in *E*, I, xvi is established precisely for the reasons given in the demonstration:

> from a given definition of anything, the intellect deduces more properties which truly follow necessarily from that same definition (that is, the

essence of the thing itself), to the extent that the definition of the thing expresses more reality, that is, the more reality the essence of the defined thing involves. Since, however, the divine nature has absolutely infinite attributes (by def. 6) of which, moreover, each expresses in its own nature infinite essence, by the same necessity, therefore, infinite things in infinite ways [i.e. everything that can be conprehended by an infinite intellect] must necessarily follow.'

From all this it is apparent how the infinite variety of modes follows from the divine essence in the same way as the properties of a triangle follow from its definition – that is to say, they follow logically and are conceptually involved in the nature defined. But Spinoza asserts besides that God is the cause of all things and this causal relationship is fraught with difficulties which are not immediately dispelled by the explanation of the logical connexion. In fact, for some critics they are compounded by it.

Logical implication obtains between ideas and propositions. What follows from the *essence* of substance may well be conceived in such terms. But causal connexion is between events, or facts, or existences; and, at least since Kant, there has been a widespread conviction that existence does not and cannot follow logically from mere ideas. Not only the Ontological Proof comes under attack on this ground, for it also prompts doubts about Spinoza's assimilation of causal to logical connexion. He constantly writes of an effect as logically implicated in its cause and that raises problems for many; first, because logical entailment is commonly taken to reveal only equivalence of meaning and not new factual information, which causal connexion requires; and, second, because cause and effect are normally conceived as temporally earlier and later, while logical implication is timeless. Here, however, we plunge into the depths of metaphysical perplexity surrounding the relation of time to eternity, which is inevitably involved with that of the infinite and the finite. In a single paper one can hardly do justice to all the facets of this difficult issue and I shall confine my attention to the doctrine propounded by Spinoza of the causal relation between substance and its modes.

II

With respect to the attribute expressing God's essence and its infinite modes little difficulty is to be encountered, for here ground and consequent coalesce fairly intelligibly with cause and effect. The reason is that the infinite modes are themselves eternal, as are the attributes from which they follow immediately. The issue of temporal succession does not, therefore, arise. The relation between attributes and infinite modes is thus entirely one of logical consequence, attribute being prior to mode and primary mode to secondary or derivative.

In Thought, the infinite intellect is the immediate consequence of the attribute. Substance conceived as thinking thing is *ipso facto* an infinite intellect and (as for Aristotle) the content of its thought is itself – the infinite idea of God which follows immediately from the notion of an infinite intellect. There is no temporal sequence here: infinite thought and the infinite thinker are one and the same, God's essence (the attribute) is one with his intellect, and that which he thinks is equally himself. For Spinoza, as for Aristotle (and incidentally Hegel), God is νόησις νοήσεως.

Under Extension, motion and rest follow immediately from the infinite attribute, and *facies totius universi*, the configuration of bodies and the constant interchange of motion and rest among them, directly from motion and rest. Here temporality begins to emerge, for changes in motion and rest are events and must be successive; but the problem does not become acute so long as the emphasis remains on the words *facies totius*. It is the configuration of the whole that is the infinite mode. The successive changes are the finite modes. Motion and rest must be conceived as a single indivisible 'state' of the entire physical world, an all-inclusive energy system which at once involves a structure, a dynamic pattern, of matter and interchange. Some might question (like Tschirnhaus in *Ep*, LIX and LXXX) whether an energy state follows directly, or at all, from extension pure and simple, but Spinoza's answer is firm and clear, and is much what a modern physicist might give: 'Indeed, from Extension as Descartes conceived it, that is to say as a quiescent mass, not only is it difficult (as you say) to demonstrate the existence of bodies, but altogether impossible' (*Ep*, LXXXI), 'it is impossible in so far as matter has been ill-defined by Descartes as Extension, but it ought to be explained through an attribute which expresses eternal and infinite essence' (*Ep*, LXXXIII). As God's essence is the same as his power, an attribute expressing eternal and infinite essence is nothing static and quiescent but is ἐνέργεια – the activity of God.[6]

The major problem is how the finite modes follow from the infinite, for here there seems to be a hiatus between the causality (or logical sequence) which produces infinite modes from attributes and that which produces finite things. Is this, perhaps, 'the great gulf fixed' between God and finite creatures of which the Bible speaks? In attempts to understand Spinoza's system it presents a familiar puzzle, but it is one which I think is soluble, so long as we understand aright both Spinoza's conception of logical deduction and what he held to be the true nature of

> the fixed and eternal things, [which] although they are individuals, yet because of their presence everywhere and far-reaching power, will be for us like universals or the genera of definitions of individual changeable things, and the proximate causes of all things (*TdIE*, XIV, 101).

Spinoza maintains that God is the immanent, but not the transient, cause of all things (*E*, I, xviii). As we have seen he is the immediate cause, under each of his attributes, of the infinite modes. But the finite modes can neither exist nor be determined to action unless they are so determined by a cause which is also finite, and that again by another likewise, and so *ad infinitum* (*E*, I, xxviii). This infinite regress, it seems, never reaches the infinite modes and God's eternal essence itself, yet Spinoza insists that 'God cannot properly be said to be the remote cause of individual things, unless perhaps in order to distinguish them from those which he has immediately produced, or rather follow from his absolute nature' (*ibid.* S), because nothing can exist or be conceived without him. How are we to understand God's immanent causation of finite things, and how does it converge with logical implication?

The problem had already been faced by the mediaevals and can be traced back, in one form or another, to Plato and Aristotle. It underlies the Cosmological Argument for the existence of God. Every finite and contingent existence requires a cause which is itself finite and contingent and therefore, in itself, inadequate ground for any existence. The entire series of causes traceable back to infinity cannot *ex hypothesi* be summed. Unless it can be grounded, therefore, in a necessarily existent first cause, the actual existence of present entities is ultimately unaccountable. But even if there is a necessarily existent being, which, to exist of necessity must be both infinite and eternal (for finitude implies contingency), how it can be causally connected with any finite thing remains a mystery. The Cosmological Proof, therefore, fails, not simply because, as Kant maintained, it presupposes the Ontological, but because even if the validity of the latter were granted, the proffered foundation of contingent existence remains paradoxical.

Spinoza, however, makes no appeal to the Cosmological Proof to establish God's existence, probably because he was sensible of its dependence on the Ontological. But he does assert the dependence of the finite on the infinite and eternal, and he interposes the infinite modes to bridge the gap between God and his temporal creatures. It is this mediation that we seek to understand.

III

Contemporary commentators have answered these questions to their own satisfaction by interpreting Spinoza's theory as a form of naturalism, and understanding his notion of deduction in terms of mediaeval or contemporary formal logic. Their interpretation has great plausibility, but I shall try to show that it fails to do justice to Spinoza's insight, which went beyond the ideas both of the mediaevals and of his own day, and in some sense even beyond his own explicit exposition.

The type of interpretation on which I propose to comment has recently been expounded most clearly and systematically by E. M. Curley in the book *Spinoza's Metaphysics*.[7] In general, if not in detail, it is similar to those of Stuart Hampshire and A. C. Watt[8] but it is worked out in more detail and elaboration. In brief what Curley does is to correlate Spinoza's concept with modern notions and (professedly) to show that their interrelation can then be explained so as to resolve the difficulty we have indicated.

Curley asserts that what Spinoza calls ideas are really propositions, for every idea involves affirmation and is said by Spinoza to be a 'conception of the mind' rather than a perception (*E*, II, def. iii). In this Curley is on the right lines, though, because Spinoza insists that an idea is an activity of the mind (*ibid.*, expl.) I should prefer to substitute judgment for proposition.[9] The *ideata* of ideas will, therefore, be facts rather than bodies, as Spinoza habitually asserts. We need not discuss the effect of this emendation upon Spinoza's contention that the human mind is the idea of the human body, and nothing else; for Curley regards the relation of proposition to fact as analogous to Aristotle's form to matter, which is almost (if not quite) precisely the relation which Spinoza (like Aristotle) intends between mind and body.[10] The attribute of thought – (or the divine intellect?) – then becomes 'a set of propositions – call it A – which constitutes a complete and accurate description of the world of extended objects.' These propositions state all facts about the world and are divided into three main classes: nomological generalizations, accidental generalizations, and singular propositions. Nomological general propositions are universal and necessary and assert laws of nature; an accidental generalization, on the other hand, is reducible to a collection of singular statements. An example of the latter would be 'All the books in my library were published after 1850', which is equivalent to 'This book was published after 1850, and this next book . . .' etc. until all the books I possess have been enumerated.

The world, we are told, mirrors our description of it, so it consists of nomological facts corresponding to laws, and individual facts, i.e. particular events and states of affairs. Nomological propositions may be axiomatic or derivative (the theorems of a deductive system), and, correspondingly, the facts they describe will be basic or in varying degrees derivative. The basic facts are Spinoza's attributes, the primary derivatives are his primary infinite modes, and the secondary derivatives his secondary infinite modes. Singular propositions correspond to finite modes – individual facts and events. In sum, the basic nomological facts comprise *Natura naturans* and the rest *Natura naturata*.

The set of propositions, A, constitutes the complete body of unified science. Nomological general propositions, being universal and necessary, and singular facts, being causally related in accordance with universal laws, all the propositions of our unified science are logically interdependent, so we are justified in assimilating causal to logical sequence. Thus within the scientific system any individual fact is explicable by deduction from a general, nomological proposition in conjunction with singular propositions stating the relevant antecedent conditions. Hence we may say, in Spinoza's terms, that a

Hss

finite mode follows from an infinite mode along with other finite modes which constitute the series of causes of which it is an effect, and our problem is solved.

As Curley puts it, we should understand Spinoza as maintaining that finite things follow from God both, and at once, so far as he is affected by finite modes and so far as he is affected by infinite modes. Neither by itself is the adequate cause of any given finite mode, but together they provide a complete explanation.[11]

Such an interpretation is intriguing and well-nigh unexceptionable. As far as it is commendable, especially if we add that Curley follows Sir Frederick Pollock in recognizing the identity of the attributes and infinite modes with what Spinoza calls 'the fixed and eternal things' in *TdIE*. I shall take issue with his rendering of Spinoza, not so much for what it says as for what it leaves undisclosed.

IV

The crucial issue, or at least one of them, is the status of nomological propositions. Curley tells us that they rank as axioms and theorems in a system of unified science and are laws of nature. He tells us also that they are universal and necessary. For Spinoza, unquestionably, the laws of nature which are the 'eternal decrees of God' (*E*, II, xlix, S and *TTP*, III) are universal and necessary. But this is not the way they are conceived by contemporary thinkers influenced by Hume and Wittgenstein. Curley rightly maintains that Spinoza rejects the logical atomism fundamental to Wittgenstein's earlier position (in the *Tractatus*), but he persists in trying to interpret Spinoza in its terms. It would hardly seem possible to do this consistently.

For contemporary thinkers, like Ayer, Braithwaite and Nagel, laws of nature are empirical generalizations which can be established only by inductive reasoning and cannot be deduced *a priori*. In the light of Hume's analysis, inductive reasoning can never establish universal and necessary laws, but only the constant conjunction of events or characters in particular things as they occur contingently in common experience. On this basis no general propositions could be, in principle, other than accidental generalizations. Because there is and can be no logical entailment between distinct matters of fact (no necessary connexion), such generalizations can refer only to contingently occurring conjunctions which happen to have been regular. The fact that something more than this is required for scientific prediction has been a persistent source of difficulty for the theory of induction throughout its history, which different writers have tried to overcome, either by postulating synthetic *a priori* principles in conflict with their basic philosophical position, or by offering *a priori* proofs of the principle of induction which have invariably proved fallacious.[12] Be that as it may, the current doctrine remains that scientific laws of nature are contingent upon experience and changeable with it. If Spinoza thought otherwise (as he certainly did) and we wish to make his view intelligible, it is not sufficient to say, as Curley does, that he believed it possible to deduce the laws of nature *a priori*, and that this belief was shared (as indeed it was) by Galileo, who is usually regarded as the founder of experimental science. We must understand how such a view can be justified and how laws of nature must be conceived if they are really to be universal and necessary.

Curley's best answer seems to be that they describe nomological facts, but what kind of facts are these? The example given is the law of inertia, but this, if it is taken as a description of fact, is precisely what a contemporary philosopher would insist was an empirical generalization. Otherwise it is an arbitrary rule defining motion uninfluenced by external forces, from which no factual information can be deduced purely *a priori*.

Neither of these alternatives would have been accepted by Spinoza, who regarded empirical generalizations as confused ideas, at best aids to the imagination, existing only in the mind and without any real referent (*E*, II, xl, Si), or else as a haphazard means of ascertaining 'accidental properties which are never clearly understood' (*TdIE*, IV, 21 and V, 27), and who dismissed stipulative definitions as asserting only what we conceive and nothing *sub ratione veri* (*Ep*, IX). Unless laws of nature are very differently understood, and nomological facts are more clearly explained, one can hardly agree with Curley that Spinoza's 'substance . . . is that set of facts to which *the axioms of our unified science* correspond';[13] nor will Spinoza's conception of the dependence for existence of finite things upon infinite modes and attributes be faithfully represented by saying that singular facts can be deduced from laws of nature in conjunction with statements of antecedent conditions.

What, then, must be the character of the laws of nature if they are really to be universal and necessary, and how will they be related to particular facts? These questions must be clearly answered if Spinoza's system is to be coherently understood and successfully validated. To fulfil these aims we must examine closely what he meant by infinity and how he conceived the relation between whole and part. For, as Curley agrees, it is 'the fixed and eternal things', of which Spinoza speaks in *TdIE*, wherein the laws of nature 'are inscribed', that constitute the nomological facts of the system; and these (Curley also agrees) are the attributes of substance and their infinite modes, all of which, as they follow immediately from the infinite and eternal nature of God, are themselves infinite and eternal.

V

In his famous 'letter on the infinite' (*Ep*, XII) the main emphasis of Spinoza's argument is that substance, the infinite and eternal, cannot be compounded out of separable parts,[14] and that it is only when we try to imagine the infinite and fail to conceive it (adequately) that it appears to be divisible. We conceive quantity, he says, in two ways, namely, abstractly or superficially as we have it in imagination with the help of the senses, or as substance which can be conceived only by the intellect ('*quod non nisi a solo intellectu fit*'). If we attend to the idea of quantity as it is in the imagination (which is easy) we find it divisible and composed of finite parts; but if we regard it as it really is in itself, as conceived by the intellect (which is very difficult) we find it to be infinite, indivisible and one (*unica*).

The important point is that mere addition of finites does not produce the infinite, which is not an aggregate or a compound of separable parts, each independently real. The continual indefinite addition of finites produces, as Hegel taught, only a spurious infinite. The true infinite is a single, coherent whole.

The argument is clearly set out in *KV*, I, ii, where Spinoza writes:

> whole and part are not true or distinct [*duidelijke*] beings, but only beings of reason, and consequently there are in Nature neither whole nor part. Secondly, for a thing to be put together from different parts it must be such that the parts, taken separately, one without the other, can be grasped and understood.

And that, Spinoza proceeds to show, is not possible in the case of substance and its attributes (in particular Extension[15]). He repeats and elaborates the argument in the *Ethics* (I, xv, S), castigating those who deny the infinity of corporeal substance because it is composed of finite parts,

> doing nothing different, by Hercules, than one who pretends that a circle has the properties of a square, and hence concludes that a circle does not have a centre from which all lines drawn to the circumference are equal. For corporeal substance, which cannot be conceived except as infinite, unique [*unica*] and indivisible, they conceive, in order to prove it finite, to be concatenated [*conflari*] out of finite parts, and to be multiplex and divisible.

In the *Short Treatise* (*loc. cit.*) we are told that extended substance is a self-dependent reality (*zelfstandighijd*), and is accordingly indivisible; but what are distinguishable are its modes, and these we divide into parts. Likewise in the *Ethics* it is said that matter is indivisible 'unless we conceive it as affected in different ways, in which case we can distinguish its parts modally only, but not in reality' (I, xv, S). Just previously, in this scholium, the passage quoted earlier from *Ep*, XII is repeated almost verbatim in which the apparent divisibility of quantity is attributed to the imagination. In the letter Spinoza says that

> because we are able to limit [*determinare*] duration and quantity as we wish, when we conceive the former abstracted from substance, and when we separate the latter from *a mode, which flows from eternal things*, time and measure arise (my italics)

defining duration and quantity in such a way as to enable us to imagine them more easily.

From all this we are left somewhat in doubt whether the succession of events and the distinction from one another of finite modes are mere appearances produced by the imagination, or have some status in reality. There are cogent reasons for maintaining the latter, not only from the evidence of the quoted passages but more decisively because imagination is itself a consequence of the finiteness of the human body as a mode of extension, and so cannot be the original source of modal distinction. Moreover, it is by the necessity of the divine nature that from it infinite things follow in infinite ways.

So far we have examined the negative side of the argument. The infinite is not composite, not an aggregation (and this is the essential point) of separately independent and separately intelligible parts, which, in consequence would be prior in conception to the whole. The positive side of the argument, that the whole is prior and determines the conception, the nature and the behaviour of the parts, is developed in the thirty-second letter and (stated more briefly) in *E*, II, lem. vii, S. From these we learn what Spinoza held to be the true and legitimate conception of whole and part and of their mutual relation.

In the letter Spinoza addresses himself to Oldenburg's question, how each part of Nature agrees with the whole and by what principle (*ratione*) it coheres with the rest; to which he replies:

> By the coherence of parts ... I understand nothing other than that the laws or nature of one part so accommodate themselves to the laws or nature of the others that they conflict as little as possible. Concerning whole and parts, I consider things as parts of some whole or other to the extent that their nature accommodates itself one to another [*invincem*] so that as far as possible they agree among themselves (*Ep*, XXXII).

The lemmae that Spinoza inserted after *E*, II, xiii, with the axioms and definition from which they follow, explain how complex bodies answer to the above description. They are complex, not merely in being combinations of simple bodies (mutually distinguished only by the velocity of their motion), but also because, despite diverse motions among their parts, they are so adjusted one to another as to transmit a constant ratio of motion and rest to one another, and to preserve the individuality of the whole.

In the letter the famous example of the blood is elaborated, a fluid compounded of several different fluids, all of which are mutually adjusted in quantity and behaviour so as to preserve a constant proportion and the individual character of the whole. The example is extraordinarily apt and the more remarkable in as much as the science of physiology in Spinoza's day was still in its infancy. A modern description of the complex mutual accommodations of chemical components in the blood would even more spectacularly illustrate the concept and support the theory that Spinoza is advocating.[16]

But Spinoza's insight goes beyond the conception of finite organisms. He realizes that organic individuality can embrace even larger wholes, as today we know that eco-systems and the entire earth answer to his description. Complex bodies, he maintains, can be constituted by parts themselves already complex, and these may be combined hierarchically in yet more complex bodies, 'and if thus still further we proceed to infinity, we easily conceive', he optimistically informs us, 'that the whole of Nature is one individual, whose parts, that is, all bodies, vary in infinite ways, without any change of the individual as a whole' (*E*, II, lem., vii, S).

The version in the thirty-second letter is even more significant, for there he says:

> as the nature of the universe is not . . . limited but is absolutely infinite, therefore its parts are modified in infinite ways by this nature of infinite power, and compelled to suffer infinite changes.

The whole of Nature of which he speaks in these passages is nothing short of *facies totius universi*, an infinite mode of the attribute of Extension. And this, if our interpretation has been correct, is one of the fixed and eternal things in which the laws of nature are inscribed, 'according to which all individual things are made and ordered' (*TdIE*, XIV, 101).

Thus it becomes apparent how the differentiations of motion-and-rest, the immediate infinite mode of Extension, are determined and regulated by the configuration of the whole physical world. It is by nothing other than differences in velocity of motion that bodies are mutually distinguished, and it now transpires that these differences are regulated and determined by the individual structure of the whole of the physical universe. In terms of modern physics the curvature of space-time which corresponds to energy fields is a function of the presence of matter, itself nothing else than a singularity in the field (so that there is an equivalence between matter and energy – $E = mc^2$). The radius of the space-time hypersphere thus constituted, which is the physical universe as a whole, determines the natural unit of length and the physical constants which govern the number and disposition of particles in the universe and the exchanges of energy between them.[17] In this fashion the finite modes are derived from the infinite under the attribute of Extension; and, as the order and connexion of ideas is the same as the order and connexion of things, we may be sure that the same is true of the finite and infinite modes of Thought.

Now we can see what kind of facts, the 'nomological facts' of nature must be. They are dynamic systems of infinitely diverse and variable parts, whose nature and changes are mutually adjusted so as to maintain an invariant structure in the whole. They are, moreover, all mutually related in the same way to form one infinite whole, the immanent governing principle of what is an infinite power determining the being, nature and process of change in every constituent part. The laws 'inscribed' in these fixed eternal wholes will thus be dynamic principles of function, structure and organization established by the nature or essence of the totality and determining the detail and diversity of the parts. It will also be clear why the propositions stating these laws will be universal and necessary: universal because of the comprehensiveness of the wholes whose nature they express, 'because of their presence everywhere and far-reaching power', and necessary because conformity to them alone makes the internal diversification and the component elements what they are and 'compels' their infinite changes.

These universal laws are in no sense empirical generalizations. They are not generalizations at all; for, apart from comprehension of the principle of structure of the whole, the nature of the particulars, from which generalization could be made, cannot be understood. As Spinoza says,

> For it would be impossible for human weakness to follow through the series of individual changeable things, both on account of their multitude surpassing all count and because of the infinite circumstances in one and the same thing of which any one may be the cause that the thing exists or does not. Since indeed their existence has no connection with their essence, or (as we have just said) is not an eternal truth (*TdIE*, XIV, 100).

This is why he proscribes 'generalities and abstractions' and insists on deduction from 'real entities'.

In short, Spinoza's 'nomological facts' are concrete universals, a concept wholly foreign to the thought of the early Wittgenstein, anathema to Bertrand Russell and his following, and utterly incompatible with logical atomism, in terms of which Curley professes to be interpreting Spinoza.

A concrete universal is a self-differentiating system the principle of organization of which determines the nature, mutual disposition and behaviour of its parts (or internal specifications), as an algebraical equation determines the contours and mutual relations of points in a geometrical figure. From the formula (*ratio*) expressing the universal principle the specific instantiations follow and so can be 'deduced'. The consequent logical relations are concrete, or real, relations inherent in the actuality of the whole so that they determine, or are manifested in, the causal relations which govern the succession of changes within the dynamic structure. For Spinoza, therefore, 'deduction' is no mere transformation of formulae according to arbitrarily set rules. It is the self-development, at once in thought and in actuality, of a dynamic principle. It is the self-specification, both inferentially and as organic causation, of a concrete universal.

209

The divine essence is an infinite whole of this nature – a genuine infinite, in which the regress of finite causes is but a subordinate (its temporal) aspect, constituted by the perpetually varying manifestation of the dynamic principle of universal order. It specifies itself as an organically systematized universe the configuration of which is invariant, but the specific detail of whose self-expression is the endlessly diversified succession and profusion of finite things and events. The finite modes are therefore the manifestation of God's eternal activity. The infinite regress of causes is nothing but the inexhaustible issuance of the dynamism of *Natura naturans*, which, in Extension as *facies totius universi* and in Thought as *infinita idea Dei*, is an eternal, invariant *Gestalt* governing the nature of every transient detail and 'compelling' the 'infinite changes' suffered by the inexhaustible diversifications of *Natura naturata*.

NOTES

1 *New Pathways in Science* (Cambridge, 1935), p. 217.
2 Abbreviations used throughout are as follows:
   Ethics, E; Epistolae, Ep, Tractatus de Intellectus Emendatione, TdIE; Korte Verhandeling van God, de Mensch en dezelfs Welstand, KV; Tractatus Theologico-Politicus, TTP.
3 'The more reality or being any thing has, the more attributes pertain to (*competunt*) that thing.'
4 Cf. *Salvation from Despair* (The Hague, 1973), pp. 69–74 and 'The Order and Connexion of Ideas' in *Spinoza on Knowing, Being and Freedom*, ed. J. G. van der Bend (Assen, 1974).
5 Cf. John Caird, *Spinoza* (London, 1910) ch. VIII; H. H. Joachim, *A Study of the Ethics of Spinoza* (Oxford, 1901), Book I, App.
6 In contemporary relativistic physics space-time and energy coincide, as fields of force are represented by space-time curvature and all motion follows geodesics.
7 E. M. Curley, *Spinoza's Metaphysics*, Harvard University Press, 1969.
8 Cf. S. Hampshire, *Spinoza* (London, 1946); A. C. Watt, 'The Causality of God in Spinoza's Philosophy', *Canadian Journal of Philosophy*, Vol. II, 2, 1972.
9 Further, judgments do not exhaust the denotation of Spinoza's modes of thought, which include emotions (*affectus*) as well as ideas, but, as he asserts (*E*, II, Ax. iii), affects do not occur without ideas, although ideas may occur without any other mode of thought. There are other reasons for objecting to the identification of *idea* with 'proposition', so far as that connotes a verbal or symbolic formula, but these need not be pursued here as they are not germane to our central theme.
10 See my *Salvation from Despair*, p. 83.
11 Cf. *Spinoza's Metaphysics*, p. 66.
12 Cf. my *Hypothesis and Perception* (London, 1970), ch II.
13 *Spinoza's Metaphysics*, p. 75f.
14 '*Quare ii prorsus garriunt, ne dicam insaniunt, qui Substantiam Extensam ex partibus, sive corporibus ab invicem realiter distinctis, conflatam esses putant*' (*Ep*, XII).

15 He has special reasons (into which we need not enter) for confining attention here (and in *E*, I, xv, S) to Extension.

16 Cf. J. S. Haldane's description in *The Philosophical Basis of Biology* (London, 1931).

17 Cf. Sir Arthur Eddington, *The Philosophy of Physical Science* (Cambridge, 1939), p. 168; *The Expanding Universe* (Cambridge, 1933), pp. 103, 105, 114; and *New Pathways in Science* (Cambridge, 1935), p. 227; Sir Edmund Whittaker, *From Euclid to Eddington* (Cambridge, 1949), pp. 194, 198, 200.

14 L'Écho de Spinoza dans la littérature néerlandaise

Roger Henrard, Liège

Il peut paraître étrange d'évoquer la littérature à propos de Spinoza, alors qu'aucun de ses ouvrages n'y réfère. Se situant à tous points de vue dans la tradition philosophique classique, il se méfie de l'art; son intérêt se porte essentiellement sur la morale – cf. le titre de son ouvrage principal, l'*Ethique* – et la manière la plus efficace de dominer les passions; cette morale il la fonde sur une philosophie de Dieu et de l'homme, qui débouche sur une philosophie politique. De l'esthétique il n'a cure; l'art est en effet au premier chef une question de formes; or ce n'est pas l'aspect formel des choses qui intéresse Spinoza, mais leur essence; les formes sont contingentes, l'essence est éternelle; tout l'effort existentiel de Spinoza porte sur un bien durable, à savoir la béatitude éternelle qui, parce qu'elle ne peut être une chimère, doit s'inscrire dans la logique de l'entendement. La joie suprême est indissolublement liée à la connaissance du vrai; la vérité est du ressort de la raison, de la logique, en fin de compte l'affaire des philosophes, et non des artistes, dont l'objectif est le beau, celui-ci étant inhérent à la forme – en latin, forme est d'ailleurs synonyme de beauté. Le spinozisme est une grandiose entreprise de rationalisation de la nature et du christianisme; dans le domaine religieux, il s'agit de dépersonnaliser Dieu, de le débarrasser des propriétés par trop humaines que lui a attribuées l'imagination; Spinoza anticipe en fait l'interprétation psychologique du christianisme, selon laquelle le Dieu personnel ne serait que l'affabulation d'une humanité en quête d'une valeur sécurisante. Aux yeux de Spinoza, l'imagination est l'ennemie de la raison, dans la mesure où elle nous fait appréhender les êtres et les choses tels qu'ils affectent les sens, et non tels qu'ils sont par essence; nous détournant de la vérité, elle est la source de nos égarements, de nos passions et, en fin de compte, de notre misère intime.

C'est la méfiance des philosophes classiques à l'égard de l'imagination qui explique leur réticence vis-à-vis de l'art en général et de la littérature en particulier; ils s'inspirent en cela de l'exemple de Platon, qui excluait les poètes de la Cité. Toute oeuvre littéraire, qu'il s'agisse d'un roman, d'un poème épique ou lyrique, ou d'un drame, est fictionnelle: ce qui est raconté dans un roman n'est pas le récit d'événements qui se sont effectivement déroulés selon une chronologie scientifiquement vérifiable; de même, une pièce de théâtre ne met pas en scène des personnages dont l'identité peut être attestée par le registre de la population. Rien n'est 'vrai' dans une oeuvre littéraire; nous entendons par là que la réalité du contenu de l'oeuvre ne peut être contrôlée ni justifiée empiriquement ou logiquement. Et cependant, les faits relatés dans un roman ou représentés au théâtre ne sont pas étrangers au monde phénoménal dans lequel nous évoluons; ils traduisent 'fictionnellement' une 'réalité' que nous vivons. L'oeuvre littéraire serait tout simplement inaccessible, si nous ne pouvions l'actualiser, c'est-à-dire la transposer dans l'actualité empirique du lecteur. D'ailleurs, le patrimoine artistique des cultures lointaines dans l'espace (par exemple la culture chinoise) ou dans le temps (par exemple la culture celtique) reste pour la plupart d'entre nous un trésor fermé, pour la simple raison que le contexte social et culturel qui lui a donné naissance nous est inconnu. L'art puise sa substance dans la réalité sensible, mais transforme celle-ci par un processus de création imaginaire, qui libère cette réalité de ses contraintes temporelles et spatiales. Si au moment de sa conception, l'oeuvre littéraire est destinée à un public potentiellement déterminé, elle s'adresse, comme le montre J.-P. Sartre dans *Qu'est que la Littérature*, virtuellement à tous les lecteurs du monde, d'aujourd'hui et de demain; en d'autres mots, elle est éternelle, parce qu'elle n'est pas liée au contingent; la fiction neutralise la réalité, tout comme l'éternité transcende l'historicité. Alors que chez l'artiste, nous assistons à une reproduction créatrice du réel, chez le lecteur se déroule le phénomène inverse, à savoir la réalisation ou l'actualisation de la fiction; il 'interprète' l'oeuvre à la lumière de sa vision du réel. Comme chaque lecteur a sa vision propre et actualise la fiction à sa manière, on peut dire qu'il y a autant d'interprétations d'une oeuvre littéraire qu'il y a de lecteurs et qu-aucune interprétation n'épuise l'oeuvre; à chaque nouveau lecteur, celle-ci révèle un monde nouveau. C'est la théorie littéraire, une science relativement récente, qui a mis en évidence la spécificité de l'oeuvre littéraire et l'interaction qui la caractérise entre le réel et l'imaginaire; au dix-septième siècle, à l'époque où la littérature et la musique ne jouissaient que d'un crédit très relatif, la littérature était tout bonnement assimilée à la fiction et, dès lors, peu appréciée des philosophes.

Ce qui dans l'oeuvre littéraire met notre imagination en mouvement, ce sont les mots. Alors que le monde réel qui nous entoure est constitué de choses et d'êtres bien déterminés, l'oeuvre littéraire, en particulier le roman et le poème, est un monde de mots, donc un monde artificiel – dans le théâtre, le texte littéraire est soutenu par le jeu scénique, qui atténue son caractère fictionnel et le met à la portée d'un public plus vaste, qui voyant des personnages en chair et en os se mouvoir et dialoguer dans un décor suggérant un lieu connu, a l'impression de vivre une tranche du réel.

Le développement des techniques de la communication (télégraphe, téléphone, radio, télévision) ont mis en évidence l'importance du mot en tant que moyen de communication. Effectivement, si pour nous exprimer, nous pouvons nous servir de signes, d'idéogrammes et de gestes, dont il ne faut pas minimiser l'importance – un simple clin d'oeil n'est-il pas bien souvent plus parlant qu'un long discours! – il n'en est pas moins vrai que sans le mot, nous nous trouverions affreusement démunis sur le plan de la communication. La majeure partie de la vie sociale se déroule par le langage; il n'est, à ce propos, pas surprenant que la linguistique, la science du langage par excellence, revendique de nos jours une place de choix dans la hiérarchie scientifique. Les sciences ne peuvent progresser qu'en perfectionnant et en affinant leur instrument terminologique; les idéologies politiques et littéraires ne s'imposent que par les slogans qu'elles véhiculent; nos échanges sociaux sont conditionnés par des échanges de paroles. Les belles lettres constituent un mode spécifique de communication, au même titre que les informations journalistiques ou la littérature scientifique. Quel que soit le médium de la communication, le matériau est identique; hormis le jargon propre à chaque discipline l'homme de science se sert des mêmes mots que l'écrivain ou le commun. Ce qui les différencie est la façon dont ils traitent le langage.

Pour le commun des hommes, le mot a une valeur exclusivement fonctionnelle; il se fie à l'usage, qui a enlevé au mot non seulement son expressivité, mais souvent aussi sa rigueur conceptuelle; nous nous servons quotidiennement de formules stéréotypées, qui relèvent du code social, mais dont nous ne réalisons plus la signification profonde, ainsi le 'bonjour' ou le 'bonsoir' que nous adressons à nos interlocuteurs suivant le moment de la journée où nous les rencontrons. A la limite, le langage devient du radotage, selon l'expression de Heidegger, un radotage qui touche les sens et l'imagination, mais n'atteint pas la pensée. Spinoza en était déjà conscient, lorsqu'il écrit dans le *Traité de la Réforme de l'Entendement*:

> Les mots font partie de l'imagination, en ce sens que nous concevons nombre de fictions selon ce que les mots composent entre eux dans la mémoire grâce à quelque disposition du corps; ....
> Ajoutez que les mots sont créés arbitrairement et suivant le niveau du vulgaire. Aussi ne sont-ils que des signes des choses telles qu'elles apparaissent à l'imagination et non à l'entendement.

Le savant ne peut se permettre de radoter. Sa raison d'être est de répondre aux questions que suscite notre étonnement devant tel ou tel phénomène étrange – comme l'ont déjà remarqué les Anciens, l'étonnement est la source du savoir et du progrès scientifique – de mettre de l'ordre et de la clarté dans le chaos de nos représentations. Voilà d'ailleurs l'exigence fondamentale des philosophes classiques: se former des êtres et des choses une idée claire, adéquate et, dès lors, vraie. La vérité dans la clarté est l'objectif par excellence du savant; de même que le soleil luit également pour tous, la vérité doit s'imposer à tous comme une évidence, par la rigueur de la démarche intellectuelle. C'est pour éliminer la moindre parcelle de sujectivité que Spinoza opta pour la méthode géométrique; toute l'*Ethique* constitue une seule déduction logique de quelques axiomes, soutenus par autant de définitions. Définir, c'est-à-dire étymologiquement fixer les limites d'une chose en la distinguant du même coup des autres choses, est la condition première de la clarté; une bonne définition, s'accordant parfaitement avec l'objet qu'elle définit, lève toute ambiguïté; on dira d'un concept philosophique ou scientifique qu'il est 'univoque' dans la mesure où la relation entre le signifiant et le signifié n'est susceptible d'aucune interprétation.

Le langage scientifique est, dès lors, impersonnel, froid et d'une rigueur qui ne laisse aucune place à l'affectivité ou à la fantaisie. Cette rigueur, Spinoza l'a poussée à l'extrême; aucune image, aucune figure de style n'en adoucit l'implacable logique; à aucun moment, Spinoza ne lève le voile sur sa personnalité profonde; il dira d'ailleurs lui-même: 'La vérité n'a pas le moindre rapport avec la personne qui croit l'avoir découverte'; elle ne peut être appréhendée que par un effort de dépersonnalisation, que seule la souveraine raison, par son ascendant sur les passions, peut réaliser. La raison s'exprime dans un langage conceptuel, que nous découvrons dans toute l'oeuvre de Spinoza, et notamment dans sa correspondance; dans chacune de ses lettres, après une adresse respectueuse à son correspondant, il répond à ses questions ou réfute ses objections dans le même style dépouillé que ses écrits philosophiques, de sorte que ses lettres en constituent en fait une partie intégrante. A aucun moment, Spinoza ne donne libre cours à son émotivité, si bien que sa vie intérieure reste cachée au lecteur.

Les écrivains naturalistes, davantage brillants penseurs qu'artistes de talent – à l'exception de Multatuli – ont respecté le secret de la vie intérieure de Spinoza, pour la simple raison qu'ils nient, au nom du déterminisme, la liberté créatrice de l'esprit. Ils sont conquis par la force de son raisonnement, qui n'offre aucune issue à la subjectivité, à l'irrationnel et à la foi religieuse; ils saluent en lui le destructeur du Dieu chrétien et le prophète du naturalisme, selon lequel l'éternelle perfection de la nature se manifeste dans les lois immuables qui régissent le monde phénoménal élevé au rang d'Absolu. Spinoza apporte, selon l'expression de J. van Vloten, la 'bonne nouvelle à l'humanité adulte', qui a rejeté la foi infantile en un Dieu à l'image de l'homme et non à la mesure de l'Infini, et qui a l'ambition de s'intégrer par la science dans la Totalité, que les naturalistes appellent la Nature ou la Vie, avec l'intention non déguisée de bannir à jamais le terme ambigu de Dieu. En fait, cette modification terminologique déforme la pensée même de Spinoza; alors que celui-ce conçoit Dieu comme une 'substance consistant en une infinité d'attributs', qui ne peut dès lors être saisie que synthétiquement, par l'intuition, qui dépasse la pensée réflexive, les naturalistes réduisent les attributs de Dieu à l'étendue et à la pensée, faisant ainsi de la Nature la clef de voûte du déterminisme universel. Nous touchons ici du doigt le point capital sur lequel les naturalistes se sont mépris au sujet de la philosophie spinoziste: ils ont délibérément ignoré la distinction introduite par le philosophe entre la nature naturante et la nature naturée; les Marxistes sont encore allés plus loin en ramenant celle-ci à la matière et en donnant au déterminisme une coloration économico-sociale. En fondant logiquement la nature naturée en Dieu en tant que cause première immanente, Spinoza transcende le déterminisme et pose la liberté comme valeur suprême.

Les naturalistes ont ainsi fait du déterminisme la loi universelle, valable aussi bien pour les phénomènes physiques que psychiques, entre autres les phénomènes artistiques. La critique positiviste, illustrée notamment en France par H. Taine, n'a vu dans l'oeuvre littéraire que le produit de facteurs extrinsèques à l'art; elle considère l'oeuvre comme le reflet de la vie de son auteur, lui-même étant déterminé par tout le contexte dans lequel il vit; l'artiste n'est pas un créateur, au sens où l'entendaient les romantiques, c'est-à-dire un génie échappant aux contraintes matérielles, mais un artisan, ayant hérité du don de l'écriture et s'appliquant à transposer dans la fiction la réalité qu'il observe passivement. A l'exemple du physiologiste Cl. Bernard – cf. son *Introduction à l'Étude de la Médecine expérimentale* (1865) – É. Zola veut introduire la méthode expérimentale dans le roman. Les poètes impressionnistes n'ont d'autre ambition que de faire jouer à plein les qualités sensibles du mot pour exprimer le plus fidèlement possible les impressions qu'ils reçoivent du monde extérieur; ils ne se préoccupent pas de considérations morales ou philosophiques, leur objectif est essentiellement d'ordre esthétique: il s'agit de faire chanter la rime, de créer de belles harmonies sonores, bref de tendre vers la musicalité pure de la poésie – cf. l'exigence de Verlaine: 'de la musique avant toutes choses' – d'où serait éliminé à la limite l'élément significatif. La poésie impressionniste et, à un stade ultérieur, sensitiviste trouve sa source, comme le nom l'indique, dans les sens, qui nous font percevoir l'apparence des choses, et s'adresse à la sensibilité du lecteur, qui par l'émotion ressentie communie avec le poète dans l'exaltation de la nature. Cette poésie charme les sens, mais ne touche pas l'esprit; elle est dans le prolongement de la réalité et en constitue en quelque sorte l'ornement, mais elle ne nous apprend rien, ne nous élève pas spirituellement.

Dans la mesure où son objectif est la beauté, et une beauté délibérément indifférente à la vérité – cf. la réflexion de L. van Deyssel: 'Il m'importe peu de croire que la terre tourne autour du soleil, si le contraire me paraît plus beau et supérieur...' – cette poésie est contraire à l'exigence cognitive de Spinoza.

Dans sa biographie de Spinoza, Colerus raconte qu'un conseiller d'Etat éminent, en visite chez Spinoza, le trouva en robe de chambre fort malpropre, ce qui lui donna l'occasion de faire quelques reproches à son hôte et de lui en offrir une autre. Spinoza lui répondit qu'un homme n'en valait pas mieux pour avoir une belle robe. 'Il est contre le bon sens', ajouta-t-il, 'de mettre une enveloppe précieuse à des choses de néant ou de peu de valeur.' Cette réflexion nous prouve l'absence totale d'intérêt de Spinoza pour les formes extérieures, qui ne peuvent que nous induire en erreur sur la valeur authentique des hommes et des choses. Il n'y a que cela qui compte à ses yeux: connaître la nature vraie des êtres et des choses; Spinoza attache plus de prix à la qualité de la marchandise qu'à beauté de l'emballage; il est adversaire de tout ce qui a des relents de publicité, de propagande ou de persuasion au sens littéral du mot – *per-suavis* signifie rendre des idées séduis-antes; – comme la rhétorique, les figures de style et les artifices littéraires constituent autant de moyens d'édulcorer et de travestir la réalité, nous comprenons pourquoi Spinoza en conteste la valeur, minant du même coup les fondements de la poésie et de l'art en général.

Nous évoquions plus haut le caractère univoque du concept scientifique et la nécessité de définitions précises dans la démarche scientifique. Traitant des conditions d'une bonne définition, Spinoza s'exprime ainsi:

> Pour être dite parfaite, la définition devra rendre explicite l'essence intime de la chose et nous prendrons soin de ne pas mettre certaines propriétés de l'objet à la place de son essence.

C'est précisément ce qui caractérise les figures de style, propres à la langue poétique: elles consistent toutes en un transfert sémantique, qui prend son appui dans l'analogie ou le rapport associatif des propriétés des choses; elles relèvent, dès lors, de l'imagination, que Spinoza distingue nettement de l'intellection. Tandis que le philosophe, en quête du vrai, veille à l'adéquation parfaite entre l'essence des choses et leur représentation conceptuelle, l'artiste, dont l'objectif est le beau, s'efforce par le jeu de l'imaginaire d'exploiter au maximum le pouvoir évocateur des mots, leur champ référentiel ne connais-sant aucune limite.

Spinoza, dont l'honnêteté intellectuelle ne souffre aucune compromission, refuse au beau et au langage imagé toute valeur positive, celle-ci n'étant reconnue qu'aux idées claires et distinctes, produits de la pensée pure. Voici comment il s'exprime à propos de la beauté:

> Je n'attribue à la nature ni beauté, ni difformité, ni ordre, ni confusion. Ce n'est, en effet, que du point de vue de l'imagination qu'on peut dire des choses qu'elles sont belles ou laides, ordonnées ou chaotiques.
>
> La beauté n'est pas tant une qualité de l'objet considéré qu'un effet en celui qui le regarde. Si notre pouvoir de vision était plus grand ou plus faible, si notre tempérament était autre, les choses qui nous paraissent belles nous paraîtraient laides et les laides deviendraient belles. La plus belle main, vue au microscope, doit paraître horrible.

> Certains objets qui, vus de loin, sont beaux, sont laids si on les voit de
> près. Ainsi les choses considérées en elles-mêmes ou dans leur rapport à
> Dieu, ne sont ni belles ni laides.

Spinoza considère la beauté comme une illusion d'optique; son caractère
subjectif lui dénie toute valeur. La position de Spinoza en la matière rejoint
celle de Descartes, qui définit le beau et le laid en ces termes:

> Nous appelons beau ou laid, ce qui nous est ainsi représenté par nos
> sens extérieurs, principalement par celui de la vue, lequel seul est plus
> considéré que tous les autres.

Descartes nomme 'agrément' la passion qui nous pousse vers les choses
belles, tandis que l'"horreur" est la passion qui nous détourne des choses
laides. En d'autres termes, il associe l'esthétique à la psychologie; cette
assimilation du beau à l'agréable apparaît d'ailleurs en français dans la
terminologie: jusqu' au début du dix-neuvième siècle, on employait en France
indifféremment les termes 'arts d'agréments' et 'beaux-arts', suggérant ainsi
que le beau est source de plaisir et de joie.

Nous savons que Spinoza ramène tous les sentiments à la joie ou à la
tristesse et que la sagesse consiste pour lui à éliminer la tristesse ou, du
moins, à réaliser un équilibre entre ces deux sentiments contradictoires.
L'amour intellectuel de Dieu est la joie suprême, car ayant Dieu, la perfection
absolue, pour cause, elle ne peut être altérée par la moindre tristesse, celle-ci
étant étrangère à Dieu. Dans la mesure où l'homme tend vers Dieu, il
recherche la joie et les occasions de rire; nous lisons dans l'*Ethique*:

> Le rire, comme aussi la plaisanterie, est une pure joie; et par conséquent,
> pourvu qu'il ne soit pas excessif, il est bon par lui-même. Et ce n'est certes
> pas qu'une sauvage et triste superstition qui interdit de prendre du
> plaisir. Car, en quoi convient-il mieux d'apaiser la faim et la soif que de
> chasser la mélancolie?
>
> Plus nous sommes affectés d'une plus grande joie, plus nous passions
> à une perfection plus grande, c'est-à-dire qu'il est d'autant plus nécessaire
> que nous participions de la nature divine. C'est pourquoi, user des
> choses et y prendre plaisir autant qu'il se peut . . . est d'un homme sage.
> C'est d'un homme sage, dis-je, de se réconforter et de réparer ses
> forces grâce à une nourriture et des boissons agréables prises avec
> modération, et aussi grâce aux parfums, au charme des plantes
> verdoyantes, de la parure, de la musique, des jeux du gymnase, des
> spectacles, etc., dont chacun peut user sans faire tort à autrui.

Nous remarquons que dans cette énumération certes non exhaustive de
plaisirs, le théâtre est cité en dernier lieu; il n'y est fait aucune mention des
arts plastiques ou de la poésie; Spinoza semble en fait limiter la littérature au
théâtre. Cela ne peut d'ailleurs nous surprendre; d'une part, le théâtre est

le genre poétique qui par son côté 'spectacle' se rapproche le plus de la vie réelle; d'autre part, dans l'optique du dix-septième siècle, il est censé exercer une action psychologique. Développant dans l'avant-propos de *Jephta* sa conception de la tragédie, par ailleurs inspirée d'Aristote, Vondel, le grand dramaturge du siècle d'or hollandais, attend d'elle qu'elle provoque une catharsis chez le spectateur. L. Meyer, un ami de Spinoza et co-fondateur de la société rationaliste *Nil Volentibus Arduum*, s'interroge dans un de ses écrits sur les passions que le dramaturge doit éveiller chez le spectateur. Le 'spectacle' n'est retenu par Spinoza que dans la mesure où il nous fait rire, ou du moins nous aide à vaincre la tristesse; bref, il conçoit l'art sous l'angle fonctionnel, sa fonction étant de contribuer à notre santé psychique.

C'est dans la seconde moitié du dix-huitième siècle que, sous l'influence du romantisme naissant, la conception du beau va évoluer, principalement en Allemagne; on cesses de le considérer comme une douce illusion des sens et on s'interroge sur son essence objective; la spéculation va bon train et débouche sur une philosophie, qui élève le beau à une fonction cognitive, celui-ci devenant la manifestation sensible du vrai. L'esthétique, c'est-à-dire la science du beau, qui prend son essor au dix-huitième siècle en Allemagne, se range résolument sous la bannière philosophique. Alors qu'au dix-septième siècle elle est absente des préoccupations des philosophes, l'idéalisme allemand de Kant à Hegel en passant par Schopenhauer va lui attribuer une place de choix; il s'ensuit que poètes et philosophes vont se rapprocher, la priorité à accorder à l'art ou à la pensée restant un point de friction; si les poètes romantiques se considèrent comme les prêtres de l'Absolu et revendiquent à ce titre la première place dans l'ordre de la connaissance, les philosophes sont plus divisés; si Hegel prévoit le déclin de la poésie parallèlement à la réalisation de l'Idée, Schopenhauer, au contraire, voit dans l'art le moyen de dépasser le monde des représentations et de dévoiler l'essence même de la Volonté; il définira la philosophie comme un art.

Au déclin du positivisme évoqué plus haut, l'idéalisme va refaire surface, notamment en Hollande, où sous l'impulsion de G. J. P. J. Bolland, professeur de philosophie à l'université de Leyde, l'hegelianisme devient en vogue. Il va inspirer, davantage par sa méthode dialectique qui par son contenu idéologique, aussi bien l'idéalisme de De Haan et des poètes symbolistes que le vitalisme anti-idéaliste du mouvement *Forum*, que prolongent après la dernière guerre S. Vestdijk et Hella S. Haasse. Nous laisserons de côté les vitalistes qui, pressentant les ravages que va causer le national-socialisme, se détournent de l'idéalisme, qu'ils accusent d'en être la cause médiate; ayant gardé la foi dans l'Absolu, mais ne pouvant l'admettre comme tel, à l'état pur, ils l'insèrent dans le relatif, si bien qu'ils en arrivent à promouvoir le paradoxe au rang de vérité première. Notre attention se portera sur les idéalistes, qui rêvent du paradis perdu et ne désespèrent pas de le retrouver, bien au contraire. Pour la plupart d'entre eux, le paradis perdu, ce n'est pas l'éden chrétien, mais la béatitude spinoziste. Grâce au dynamisme de van Vloten au dix-huitième siècle, et de W. Meyer au vingtième siècle, Spinoza n'a cessé de retenir l'attention; les naturalistes lui ont consacré de nombreuses études; entre 1895 et 1902 paraissent pas moins de trois traductions néerlandaises de l'*Ethique*; la maison qu'occupa Spinoza à Rijnsburg de 1660 à 1663 et celle où il mourut à La Haye en 1677 furent achetées par des associations spinozistes, respectivement *Het Spinozahuis* et *Domus Spinozana*, avec l'intention de les aménager en musée ou centre d'étude. Tout au long de la première moitié de ce siècle, la controverse est vive entre les tenants de l'interprétation rationaliste, conduits par W. Meyer et W. G. van der Tak, et les exégètes idéalistes groupés autour de J. D. Bierens de Haan et J. H. Carp.

Bierens de Haan, théologien passé à la philosophie, proposa au début du siècle une interprétation mystico-religieuse du spinozisme, qui servit de support philosophique au symbolisme d'une génération de poètes, animés par A. Verwey. A l'inverse des matérialistes marxistes, qui réduisent les attributs de Dieu à la matière, De Haan, exploitant certaines contradictions de l'*Ethique*, ramène Dieu à la pensée, considérant du même coup le monde phénoménal comme une forme dégradée de l'Idée. Cette antinomie devant être levée pour permettre à l'Idée de redevenir elle-même, nous voyons se dessiner la démarche dialectique qu'entreprend De Haan pour donner un fondement métaphysique à l'activité inhérente à Dieu. Il introduit le mouvement dialectique au sein de la substance divine; en d'autres termes, il combine l'Être et le devenir, associant la dialectique hegelienne à l'immuabilité spinoziste de Dieu. Remarquons à ce propos que Bolland, le rénovateur du hegelianisme en Hollande, fut le premier président de *Het Spinozahuis*, ce qui prouve son intérêt pour Spinoza, vu à la lumière de Hegel. De Haan reconnaît qu'il 'renouvelle et élargit' le spinozisme, mais il estime qu'il en a le droit, parce qu'une philosophie n'est jamais achevée; elle n'est qu'un appel à une réflexion philosophique toujours plus poussée. En fait, il considère la philosophie moins comme un système de pensée fermé que comme un art de penser. Le voilà, ainsi, à pied d'oeuvre dans le domaine artistique, que les poètes ne se feront pas faute de faire fructifier. De Haan n'hésite pas à reconnaître qu'en Hollande le renouveau philosophique a été stimulé par les poètes qui, las de l'expérience impressionniste et sensitiviste, ont réalisé que la beauté doit s'appuyer sur une vision claire des choses, autrement dit qu'il ne peut y avoir d'oeuvre d'art digne de ce nom sans réflexion philosophique. Tandis que l'impressionnisme réduit la conscience à un réceptacle d'impressions, le symbolisme lui attribue une fonction créatrice, à savoir présenter la diversité du monde empirique comme autant de manifestations d'une seule et même Idée. Comment le poète peut-il légitimer cette fonction?

De Haan conteste la définition spinoziste de Dieu. On ne définit pas l'Indéfinissable, dit-il; l'essence de Dieu est un mystère, qui se soustrait donc à l'entendement et ne peut être appréhendée que de l'intérieur, par le sentiment. Tous les poètes symbolistes, de Fr. van Enden à P. N. van Eyck en passant par N. van Suchtelen, dont l'idéalisme est cependant le moins prononcé, sont d'accord sur ce point: le champ d'action de la raison est limité au monde phénoménal, dans lequel toute chose est déterminée et en relation avec les autres parties de la Totalité, qui est Dieu. Dieu étant l'Absolu, l'Un est davantage que la somme de ses parties et, dès lors, irréductible à la conceptualisation, indéfinissable et mystérieux. Si les poètes cités ratifient certaines propositions de Spinoza, ils considèrent unanimement que toute l'*Ethique*, si imposante soit-elle par la rigueur du raisonnement, n'est que la justification d'un sentiment antérieur à toute réflexion, à savoir la foi en un Être supérieur immanent; sa philosophie ne ferait donc que réfléchir sa foi.

Le 'monisme dynamique' de De Haan débouche sur la foi, qu'il présente comme une faculté non irrationnelle, mais supra-rationnelle, qui prolonge et achève l'oeuvre de la raison; elle englobe le rationnel, tout en le transcendant. C'est parce que la raison, jour après jour en quête de la vérité une et indivisible, réalise ses limites qu'elle en appelle à une faculté supérieure pour achever ses démarches. Nous retrouvons ici le mouvement dialectique, la pierre angulaire de la philosophie de De Haan. Dans un premier temps, Dieu, c'est-à-dire la Pensée ou l'Idée, se réalise dans la matière, non pas à la suite d'une décision gratuite, mais mû par une nécessité inhérente à sa nature; la matière est l'antithèse de l'esprit: la Pensée est une et ordonnée, le monde sensible est diversifié et désordonné; et cependant, le monde étant l'expression de Dieu, il ne peut pas en être par essence différent. Il appartient à l'esprit humain, inspiré par la foi qui anime la nature naturée – la foi s'apparente ici au *conatus* de Spinoza, mais avec une coloration téléologique – d'ordonner la multitude de nos idées disparates et de restaurer la Pensée dans son unité originale; c'est là, selon l'expression de De Haan une 'perspective intérieure' que la raison seule ne peut réaliser, sinon en s'en remettant à la foi, mais cette fois une foi consciente, parce qu'éclairée et légitimée par l'entendement.

L'homme de science traduit en concepts les démarches de la pensée discursive, qui nous rapproche de l'Un, en qui toutes choses sont incluses et dont elles tirent leur essence et leur existence. Mais la cause première de la vie est transcendante à l'entendement et au concept; elle ne peut être dévoilée que par le poète, qui a le pouvoir de transcender le mot, de susciter de nouvelles connotations et de jeter un pont entre le visible et l'invisible, le matériel et le spirituel, la nature naturée et la nature naturante. Par la grâce de l'imagination, il crée des symboles, qui, selon l'étymologie du terme, réunissent ce que la raison a arbitrairement séparé; le poète symboliste, à la faveur des images que lui inspire l'imagination, rétablit la 'grande harmonie' dont rêvaient déjà les romantiques et nous fait partager sa vision du monde, tel qu'il est par essence et de toute éternité. Il s'agit bien de l'imagination symbolique et non de l'imagination fantasmagorique; celle-ci, qui puise ses racines dans l'inconscient, nous écarte du réel; celle-là, au contraire, est nourrie par la Pensée-même supra-rationnelle – le poète Verwey ne dit-il pas que le poète 'pense en images'? – et nous plonge dans le pur réel, nous fait voir et sentir la vérité cachée derrière l'apparence des choses. A ce titre, l'imagination symbolique a une valeur cognitive certaine.

Nous nous trouvons ainsi devant ce paradoxe que les meilleurs poètes qui se réclament de Spinoza, déforment sa pensée, tandis que ceux qui en respectent la lettre et l'esprit – nous pensons par exemple à H. Gorter dans ses *Sonnets Spinozistes* – tuent la poésie. En fait, le rationalisme absolu de Spinoza est réfractaire à la poésie et la considère avec méfiance, seul l'entendement étant capable par un raisonnement déductif d'atteindre le vrai. Il met d'ailleurs également ses lecteurs en garde contre l'Ecriture Sainte, qui est une oeuvre poétique: elle incite le commun des mortels à l'amour et à l'obéissance, dit-il, mais ne nous enseigne pas la vérité. Les poètes de répondre: certes, elle n'enseigne pas doctrinalement, elle ne prouve rien; mais elle fait plus: elle nous montre Dieu en action, elle nous fait sentir le souffle de Dieu, nous fait participer de tout notre être à la vie divine. Voilà posées une fois de plus les données de l'éternel conflit entre science et art, objectivité et subjectivité, raison et sentiment!

ENGLISH SUMMARY: SPINOZA'S ECHO IN DUTCH LITERATURE

Spinoza did not attract the attention of poets until they became aware that, beyond the geometrical way of reasoning, a religious spirit, which only poetry can convey adequately, pervades the *Ethica*.

Through the symbolic imagination the poet brings together again what has been arbitrarily sundered by discursive reason, bridges the gap between the finite and the infinite and achieves the 'great harmony' in which all things are in communion with God. Poetry mediates and illumines: through it the mystery of the Being hiding in each singular existence is unveiled. It thus contributes to elevating us spiritually and to making us 'see' truth. There is no room for mystery in Spinoza's philosophy; not only does Spinoza, like Descartes, attain to the infinite, he also understands it.

At the beginning of the twentieth century an idealistic interpretation of Spinozism, which introduced dialectic dynamism into it, developed in the Netherlands under the influence of 'Geistesgeschichte'. In this interpretation God becomes Thought, which is despiritualized in the phenomenal world (antithesis) and comes to self-consciousness in thought (synthesis), the reflective activity of which leads up to supra-rational faith. It is this supra-rational capacity to see God that the Symbolists attribute to the imagination. For the Symbolists the true and the beautiful are intimately associated, the latter being nothing more than the concrete manifestation of the former; they react against the Impressionists, who, in translating positivism into poetry, are content to record the movements of nature and to convey the impressions they receive through the music of the verse.

Positivists also took an interest in Spinoza, whose thought, however, they purged of all trace of religion; hence the atheistic character of Impressionism and its exaltation of pure beauty. Spinoza denies all positive value to beauty; he believes, as did the classic philosophers, that art is intended merely to please; in other words, he sees art as a psychological category.

It was not until the eighteenth century that aesthetics took its first steps as the science of the beautiful under the interested eye of the German Idealists.

15 Freud's relation with Spinoza

Siegfried Hessing, London

I

I have often been grateful to Walter Bernard for attracting my attention to ideas within the radius and focus of my special interests. Thus I learnt from him for the very first time – although in fragmentary form – of the existence of a recently (1974) discovered letter from Freud to Lothar Bickel as a reply to an article submitted to him earlier, and published already.[1] In order to present to the reader my own paper I asked Bernard to translate that part of the aforementioned article of Bickel into English and it is in the alphabetical order of these pages.

In my role as custodian, so to speak, of the material at hand, especially of that letter from Freud to Bickel, I have been entrusted[2] with the pleasant task of making known or rather better known than before, for Spinozists as well as for Freudians, the very enigmatic and cryptic relationship of Freud with Spinoza. The whole material is based on two, or rather three, private letters with special significance in such a delicate affair.

The first letter was addressed to Lothar Bickel on 28 June 1931 and was not made public until after his death, when it was found among various papers and manuscripts left behind. The second letter was written by Freud to myself and dated 9 July 1932, and has been published before.[3] Before going on to cite the content of these letters, it is worthwhile to throw more light on the apparently intentional silence regarding Spinoza in all the works of Freud, while Spinoza's impact on Freud presents perhaps even more of a puzzle to students of Spinoza than to those of Freud.

> Any student of Spinoza who has had occasion to acquaint himself with the contribution of the psychoanalytic school of psychology cannot fail to be impressed by the many points of contact between the basic views of Freud and those of the seventeenth-century philosopher.[4]

And every unbiased thinker will agree with Walter Bernard and join in his inquiry into such astonishing total silence of Freud himself or of any later writer on Freud and his works on the subject of such an attitude towards

Spinoza. The increasingly vast literature about Freud has brought many and various things into the limelight of world-attention, but unfortunately almost nothing at all so far has been said anywhere about Spinoza. . . . Bernard himself, so eager and anxious to continue his own research in this field, discovered an interesting paper of B. Alexander, 1928[5] who also deplores

> that among psychoanalysts there is not a single word about Spinoza's Trieblehre; nothing about his theory of affections and passions. One would rather have expected that Spinoza should meet with approval from psychoanalysts.

Another inquirer then joined the growing avalanche of astonishment in 1934, and Constance Rathbun[6] noted 'that there is a closer alliance of Spinoza's psychology with psychoanalysis than there is with any other school of psychology'. Bernard himself seemed mostly impressed by Bickel's article of April 1931[7] which has added thus a further share to the already loud voices of surprise: 'But one is also reminded of Spinoza when reading Freud, and one is surprised never to find any mention of the philosopher's name, even when the line of thought is so similar.'

If Freud's letter to Bickel had been published by the recipient soon after its receipt, he would perhaps have had some chance to learn about the existence of the other, second letter of Freud to myself, only one year later than his. And this perhaps would have given him some satisfaction and even more perhaps a further letter of Freud to myself, which I intend to publish here for the first time. Bernard published the full text of Freud's first letter to me in this matter only much later[8] – after the end of the Second World War in 1946. And at that time he was quite unaware of any controversial attitude of Freud towards Spinoza and so he was entirely right to assume that

> as to Freud himself, there is no question that he knew and studied Spinoza. To what extent Spinoza had influenced him in his psychological studies, is difficult to say. Possibly he knew Spinoza as a philosopher and metaphysician. The *only* reference to Spinoza, we were able to find, was in a letter addressed to Siegfried Hessing, dated July 9, 1932.

It is quite clear that while writing his paper on 'Freud and Spinoza' in 1946, Bernard had not yet any knowledge of the existence of any other earlier letter to anyone else on this subject. Now, we are faced with the problem of retrospectively pondering on both letters with no chance to clarify Bickel via himself save by linking the two letters with one another – and perhaps also with the other (third) letter of Freud to myself. Here Freud was crystallizing his alliance with Spinoza by identifying it with Albert Einstein's and Jakob Wassermann's attitudes as expressed in my first *Spinoza-Festschrift* (Carl Winter, Heidelberg, 1933).

When I was contacting my Spinoza-friends in this matter on Spinoza and

225

his provocative denial by Freud, the President of the Vereniging Het Spinozahuis, H. G. Hubbeling, wrote to me on 20 October 1975:

> As for Freud's dependence on Spinoza, your communications are very useful. It was already very often understood that there was a line from Spinoza to Freud, but the letter you mentioned, proved it!

And parallel to this Guido van Suchtelen, the Secretary, voiced his opinion on 17 October 1975:

> You should indeed make public Freud's statement with your 'own echo(!)' if only for the purpose of helping to remove false ideas and legends. . . .

James Collins also seemed astonished to hear from me about this 'Freud incident'. In his letter of 29 October 1975 he had this to say:

> I am also quite interested in the remarks you made about Spinoza and Freud, as well as the confidential excerpt from Freud himself. I think that Freud's relationship with Spinoza is much less forthright than is Einstein's relation with Spinoza. Perhaps the reason is that Einstein actually studied Spinoza himself and was willing to admit that philosophical truths can be distinct from scientific ones. Freud seems to have minimized his direct relationship with Spinoza by talking about a general atmosphere sort of interest. I think that Freud wanted to have his cake and eat it too. He wanted to take advantage of Spinoza's thought on the orderliness of nature and the universality of cause-effect relationships. But Freud did not want to allow that this constituted a certain dependence upon philosophy and a need to argue on philosophical grounds about world order and causality. Freud took many things for granted out of his atmosphere and hence drew back from admitting that sort of relationship with Spinoza which might require Freud to give independent philosophical justifications for some of his central assumptions in methodology.

Following the traditional trend in the spirit of Spinoza's legacy to posterity via the Domus Spinozana, I am now willing to give this affair 'my own echo' while leaving everyone to form his own opinion: *quot capitis tot sententiae!* King Frederick of Prussia followed that line: 'to let everybody be happy in his own fashion', although it is not fashionable anymore in totalitarian countries, organizations with totalitarian regimentation, clans, etc. . . . all with their own monopoly of slogans to impose the one same universal truth. With all this in mind, I feel I have to quote an eminent Spinoza scholar, Errol E. Harris.[9] Learning from our correspondence about such Freud oddity, he wrote to me on 17 November 1975:

Thank you for the note on Freud, which is of interest. However Freud
is undoubtedly right to say: 'dass es mir um eine philosophische
Legitimation überhaupt nicht zu tun war'.

Now let us have the letters speak for themselves. After publishing his article,
Bickel did not rest content but wanted to see Freud's reaction. So he submitted the paper with an accompanying letter in the justifiable expectation of
seeing the veil lifted from Freud's total silence on Spinoza, in spite of the
latter's undeniable impact upon himself and his work. Not without indignation received Bickel a letter from Freud which is reproduced here in
facsimile:

TRANSCRIPTION 1 OF LETTER SHOWN IN PLATES 6 AND 7
The German and English texts of the letters follow side by side to facilitate
comparison:

Sehr geehrter Herr,
Meine Abhängigkeit von den
Lehren Spinozas gestehe ich
bereitwilligst zu. Ich habe keinen
Anlass genommen, seinen Namen
direkt zu erwähnen, weil ich meine
Voraussetzungen nicht aus seinem
Studium holte, sondern aus der von
ihm geschaffenen Atmosphäre. Und
weil es mir um eine philosophische
Legitimation überhaupt nicht zu
tun war. Von Natur aus unbegabt,
habe ich aus der Not eine Tugend
gemacht und mich darauf
eingerichtet, die Tatsachen, die
sich mir als neu enthüllten,
möglichst unverbildet, vorurteilslos
und unvorbereitet zu verarbeiten.
Ich dachte, bei der Bemühung,
einen Philosophen zu verstehen, sei
es unvermeidlich, dass man sich mit
seinen Ideen durchtränke und
deren Lenkung bei seiner Arbeit
erleide. So habe ich auch das
Studium von Nietzsche von mir
gewiesen, obwohl – nein weil es mir
klar war, dass bei ihm Einsichten
sehr ähnlich zu finden sein
würden. Auf Priorität machte ich

Dear Sir,
My dependence on the teachings of
Spinoza I do admit most willingly.
I had no reason to mention his
name directly, as I got my
presumptions not from studying
him, but from the atmosphere he
created. And as such any
philosophical legitimation was of no
great importance to me at all. By
nature untalented for philosophy, I
have made a virtue of necessity and
prepared myself to work out, as
much as possible, unspoiled,
unprejudiced and unprepared, the
facts which unveiled themselves as
new to me. In the endeavour to
understand a philosopher, I thought
it would be unavoidable to imbue
oneself with his ideas and to
undergo his guidance during one's
work. Thus I have also rejected the
study of Nietzsche, although, not
because it was clear to me that one
could find in him views very
similar to psychoanalysis. I never
did claim priority. About C.
Brunner I know of nothing in my
ignorance. The only useful thing

227

nie Anspruch. Von C. Brunner weiss ich in meiner Unbildung nichts. Das einzig Brauchbare über das Wesen der Lust fand ich bei Fechner.

Ihr sehr ergebener   Freud.

about the nature of pleasure, I found in Fechner.

Yours very faithfully

         Freud.

We may assume that Freud later came to know, to esteem and even admire Lou Andreas-Salomé, and not only to become befriended, but via that friendship to be quasi transformed into a follower of Spinoza. I have here in mind writers like Lessing, Novalis, Heine, etc, men quite different from those in the paid service and lipservice of an Alma Mater Academica. Freud's relationship with Lou may very well have brought him much nearer to Spinoza just as it brought her nearer and dearer to Rilke while establishing a noble link between them.

But even earlier, one year after the 'incident' of Freud's first letter on Spinoza, addressed to Bickel, Freud showed a more approachable attitude towards Spinoza in his second letter on Spinoza, the first letter to myself. Here he hints at a much closer link with Spinoza than ever before. With no knowledge of the existence of that letter from Freud to Bickel and its background, I felt encouraged by Freud's open confession and loyalty to Spinoza to list him among other admirers of Spinoza in my aforementioned first *Spinoza-Festschrift 1632–1932*, when he wrote to me:

TRANSCRIPTION 2 OF LETTER SHOWN IN PLATE 8

Sehr geehrter Herr,
Ich habe mein langes Leben hindurch der Person wie der Denkleistung des grossen Philosophen eine ausserordentliche Hochachtung entgegengebracht. Aber ich glaube, diese Einstellung gibt mir nicht das Recht, etwas über ihn vor aller Welt zu sagen, besonders da ich nichts zu sagen wüsste, was nicht schon von Andern gesagt worden ist. Entschuldigen Sie durch diese Bemerkung mein Fernbleiben von der geplanten Festschrift und seien Sie meiner Sympathie und Hochachtung versichert.
Ihr

         Freud.

Dear Sir,
Throughout my long life I have shown an extraordinary rather shy esteem for the person as well as for the thought of the great philosopher. But I think that this attitude does not entitle me to say anything about him in front of the whole world, especially as I have nothing to say that has not already been said by others. Excuse me for staying away from the planned Festschrift and be assured of my sympathy and esteem.
Yours

         Freud.

When I sent to Freud a copy of the published Festschrift he wrote to me again about Spinoza in a letter of 19 March 1933. I have never mentioned this letter before but think now is the right time and place to come into the open with it during the controversy about Freud's relationship to Spinoza. Now follows a facsimile of Freud's second letter to me, side by side with the German and English text for comparison in order the better to unfold the growing self-commitment as evidenced through personal contact rather than through books, etc.

TRANSCRIPTION 3 OF LETTER SHOWN IN PLATE 9

Sehr geehrter Herr,	Dear Sir,
Dank für die Zusendung Ihrer	Thanks for sending your
Spinoza-Festschrift. Sie wirkt durch	Spinoza-Festschrift. It produces an
den Reichtum ihres Inhalts und der	impression by its rich content and
Vielseitigkeit der Gefühlspunkte.	by the many sided points of feeling.
Meine Empfindlichkeit, dass ich in	My sensibility of being mentioned
ihr genannt werde, findet eine	in it, finds its appeasement by the
Beschwichtigung darin, dass auch	fact that also two others have
zwei Andere sich ähnlich wie ich	pronounced themselves in a way
geäussert haben.	like myself. Einstein has found the
Einstein hat das richtige Wort	right word, that love alone for
getroffen, dass die Liebe zu	Spinoza is not sufficient to justify a
Spinoza allein nicht genügt, um	contribution.
einen Beitrag zu rechtfertigen.	I have given your work to our
Ich habe die Schrift unserer	Journal *Imago*. With esteemed
Zeitschrift Imago übergeben.	greeting
Mit hochachtungsvollem Gruss	your Freud.
Ihr Freud.	

One thing remains clear and clarified in our conclusion:
Freud did in fact not intend to say anything openly 'in front of the whole world' (vor aller Welt!) and he perhaps was reserving this privilege exclusively to some private contact and occasion whenever the time seemed ripe. The last cited letter, the second letter to myself, already shows Freud coming more into the open and happy to discover that others like Albert Einstein and Jakob Wassermann were in agreement in their homage to Spinoza, namely 'that love alone for Spinoza is not sufficient to justify a contribution'. And by putting his emphasis on that common attitude of 'love' Freud demonstrates his own love for Spinoza and is already willing to share it with others. Love which Spinoza deserves so well especially from somebody like Sigmund Freud in the role of Balaam . . . Freud involved in man's approach to his own unknown awareness of himself behind the so called 'façade', must have passed

successfully through self-analytical self-approach with no witness present to testify. In Spinoza's words man's own face *vis-à-vis* the face of the whole world: that *facies totius universi* which Hui-Neng called man's true face before being born. . . .

II

Now let me show how other sources[10] have voiced an opinion about Freud which point to a similar attitude of Freud, which before appeared to us as unique, while now seen as a natural urge for independent self-expression.

Richard Wollheim collected critical essays about Freud[11] and afterwards Christopher Reeves gave them an echo through the radio and the *Listener* with a demand for a repeat. Reeves was not afraid to attract wide attention by throwing light into such dim domain where self-confrontation should help a reader for better acceptance of some apparently blurry views leading to unbearable self-bondage. For the very first time an analytical mind like that of Freud became itself the object of analysis with a resulting puzzling diagnosis. In Christopher Reeves' own words[12] Wollheim is

> examining Freudian theory afresh together with his fellow-contributors, and trying to show the relevance of certain aspects of psychoanalysis to topics which presently exercise philosophers of mind, aspects such as to treatment of imagination in thought-processes, its explanation of self-deception and the role of language in the formation of concepts.

Such new critical re-appraisal of Freud shows him in the very same light as these private letters about Spinoza, as far as similar remarks are concerned. Remarks which seem to be confirmed by Freud himself without shyness in his *Autobiographical Study*. Here the emphasis can be clearly seen on 'his avoidance of philosophy made the easier by what he called the *constitutional incapacity*'! And we are also further reminded by Christopher Reeves that, when a student at Vienna University, Freud was perhaps in instinctive search of philosophical guidance and paradoxically of independence as well. Now some coincidences tend to crave for repetition and are quasi begging to be linked with the same attention of introspection. Freud's teacher Franz Brentano

> was engaged in writing a treatise on psychological methods which anticipated many of Freud's latter ideas, in particular Freud's emphasis on the intentional, or meaning content of an individual's action as the central focus of psychological inquiry.

Now, why wonder and why make more lamenting fuss about Freud's silence on Spinoza in his maturing years, than about his silence on Brentano in his early youth, especially when he was at his crossroad in confrontation with his karma? Why . . .? Freud never ever wanted to be 'imbued' – to use his own words to Bickel – or at least to appear to be imbued with anyone else's teaching. So he has hinted with sufficient blunt frankness already cited in full. And was not Nietzsche another case where, for the very same reason, Freud shunned any direct involvement or contact which would be interpreted as subordinating guideline? What he wanted to be seen was always how his own spontaneity worked out fully his independent originality in its 'own way' so to speak: with no indebtedness to (Spinoza's) *causa sive ratio: alius,* as it was the case with his relationship to Spinoza. Sic!

As a further conclusion in the analysis of Freud, the great analyst, we may perhaps ask: is there a writer to be found to write in such a manner as to please in anticipation all his potential and future critical readers or writers via posterity? Freud wanted to be unconcerned on his path when having reached his goal of such envisaged path, leaving his followers to continue his attention and intention filtered through their own mind and urge . . . I must retell here a true story which happened at the welcome of the great artist Marc Chagall by a local critic who tried to explain what the artist actually ought to have had in mind when having painted such and such painting. After having finished and 'cashed' his applause Chagall stood up to thank the speaker with the words: How grateful I am to you to learn only afterwards what I was thinking while painting that painting about which you gave me so interesting retrospective hints, which I was supposed to have had as introspective before. And finally do we not hear nowadays of children complaining that they regret so much of having had no chance, no choice for choosing their parents in their own image and up to their own taste, to avoid blaming them later for any misgivings or shortcomings caused by them.

There are still two voices on Freud not heard perhaps yet, or not heard by those concerned, especially via the brilliant mediocrity of the 'Freud professionals', the specialists. These two are Timothy Leary and Ralph Metzner.

> To properly compare Jung with Sigmund Freud we must look at the
> available data with each man appropriated for his exploration. For
> Freud it was: Darwin, classical thermo-dynamics, The Old Testament,
> Renaissance cultural history, and most important: the close overheated
> atmosphere of the Jewish family.[13]

Timothy Leary in association with Ralph Metzner and Richard Alpert have ventured together in their common understanding and undertaking to comment and reword again the ancient text of the Tibetan Book of the Dead[14] in order to make it much more palatable in our psychedelic (i.e. mind-expanding *ergo*: mind-manifesting) age of experience of one's own unknown wholeness. *Omnia animata* (*sumus*) of Spinoza. Nevertheless, an unbiased onlooker can see true honour given to Freud (*ibid.*) where he deserves it so much although he fails to advance further into such *terra incognita.*

When Freud coined the phrase that the ego was *the true seat of anxiety* he was giving voice to a very true and profound intuition. Fear of self-sacrifice lurks deep in every ego, and his fear is often the precariously controlled demand of the unconscious forces to burst out in full strength. No one who strives for self-hood (individuation) is spared this dangerous passage (into trans-subjective reality). . . .

This again is reminiscent of Spinoza's cardinal and first axiom in his *Ethics*: 'Everything which is, is either in itself or in another' [quasi-self].

Thus Freud's true seat of anxiety in which the fictitious self (pudgala) is in constant fear of a fictitious 'other' *per se*, does offer no comfort nor real rest as expected from such armchair of rest to look from his home at the whole strange universe. . . . This unique *Book of the Dead*, a Tibetan source of life wisdom for the few, reached our Western horizon first by the gipsy-scholar, W. Y. Evans-Wentz, joined by C. G. Jung, via his psychological commentary and by the excellent Lama Anagarika Govinda[15] via his foreword to the third edition. All these three explorers of man's unknown have to come to terms with Freud when advancing in the search of this Tibetan Guide-book, whatever the viewpoint was they applied in order to face that own unknown of man. So Jung had certain reservation when pointing out that 'although Freud's is the first attempt made by the West to investigate as if from below, from the animal sphere of instinct the psychic territory that corresponds in Tantric Lamaism to the Sidpa Bardo, or state of reincarnating', a very justifiable fear of metaphysics prevented Freud from penetrating into the sphere of the 'occult'. In this, Freud was typically non-Oriental, and fettered by his own self-imposed limitations. Evans-Wentz thinks such limitations cannot always hold back psychological research. And he further thinks that Jung has gone far beyond the limitations of his predecessor, Sigmund Freud, because he maintains: 'it is not possible for Freudian theory to reach anything except an essentially negative valuation of the unconscious'. And there are stored, apparently imperishably, the records in completeness, of mankind's past. The East speaks of Akasha records. . . . And still not underestimating Freud's venture, Jung thinks:

> we can state it as a fact that with the aid of psychoanalysis the rationalising mind of the West has pushed forward into 'the neuroticism' of the Sidpa Bardo and has there been brought to an inevitable standstill by the uncritical assumption that everything psychological is subjective and personal.

Evans-Wentz continues to think on the same line, that much sought-after higher understanding of the human psyche will be won not by these admittedly inadequate Freudian methods, now in vogue by 'psychoanalysing' a subject, but by meditation and integrating self-analysis. These are hints at psychological techniques of oriental yoga referred to in Lama Govinda's foreword there. And it is only as the great distiller of Oriental Wisdom for the Western mind, W. Y. Evans-Wentz sees it as[16]

a yearning or thirsting after sensation, after the unstable sangsaric existence [from singularized ex-full *causa sive ratio alius* to another *causa sive ratio alius* and so forth, once Spinoza's axiomatic truth has been grasped: *causa sive ratio: vel sui vel alius!*] So long as this cause [or reason for quasi-otherness *per se*] is not overcome by enlightenment, death follows birth and birth death, unceasingly. – Enlightenment results from realizing the unreality of the sangsaric existence [with cause and reason for successional quasi-otherness *per se*, etc.]

Freud had an innate aversion against introversion, which he identified with an auto-erotic narcissistic attitude of mind. And Jung blames Freud for sharing such a negative position with the National Socialist Philosophy of Germany (in 1939!) when at that time accusing introversion as offence against (totalitarian) community-feeling. Sigmund Hurvitz[17] speaks with much enthusiasm of the introspective self-submersion as so excellently manifest in the Hassid Mystic, the Great Maggid of Mesritch. He attained mastership in the act of introversion so far as to disegotize his bodiless ego linked with the egoless body as a pair-concept in the cabbalistic symbolism in order to return to the trans-personal (i.e. trans-causal or trans-rational) or primordial state of the (unconscious) mind. Freud put more emphasis on the little conscious segment (one tenth of the whole likened to a visible cap of an iceberg in the ocean of universality), while he considered the unconscious as repressed feeling (das Verdrängte) in opposition to others calling the conscious a trick of psyche (Kunstgriff der Psyche!).

Now, as to the ego with its drop-consciousness, we must say that it follows the trend to self-particularize and self-singularize its own unknown oceanic wholeness or universality (omniality). Hence the old dispute to solve the quasi-dilemma of the One and the Many. When wrongly viewed as a number 'one' and not as the acausal, irreal principle of indeterminacy this became a trapdoor even for thinkers such as Einstein. . . . As a number the ego must appear versus any quasi-other ego as you, him, her or it (id) and from here stems the suffering deriving from the own projections of quasi-otherness *per se* with fear and anxiety. That horror *alius*, heterophobia as horror *tui* is the very fear of any other-than-me: madanyo. The *totaliter aliter* or the wholly otherness. Only when aware of the reciprocal relativity within the pair-concept of such quasi-otherness then such quasiness reveals via enlightenment the true otherlessness beyond *causa sive ratio: vel sui vel alius*. And *vel* is like a velum to un-veil the hidden, the occult of the own unknown. Then the ego is no longer versus other egos, but uni-versus, omni-versus re-identifying the drop with the ocean while expanding the narrow drop-consciousness to the cosmic-divine, the oceanic universal omni-consciousness: *omnia animata*. Enlightenment releases the frightened ego from the illusion of quasi-selfness *per se*! Until then, before enlightenment dawns in the long dark night of self-obscuration, there is much insecurity, and only a very few, like Alan Watts, were able to discover the 'wisdom of insecurity',[18] leading to self-salvation from self-bondage. Much puzzling insecurity is lurking in this 'seat of anxiety' haunted by alternating phantoms of 'self or other', of hope or fear: both a pair-concept after Cabbalah and Spinoza. When intuiting into one's inside and insight, one can better grasp the cosmic-divine hint of *omnia animata* offered as a boon to the dwarf's gigantic pride: *ego* via *sum* or '*ego sum*' via omniality becomes: *nos sumus*. Hence Spinoza speaks in the plural: 'sentimus (non cognoscimus!) experimurque nos (omnes) aeternos esse. Essendi fruitio. . . .'

Then the dividuated I and his I-mindedness wants to escape in his craving for individuation quasi unveiling indivisibility or wholeness, com-pletion, omniality. The predominating fear in this 'seat of anxiety' is unmasked soon as *horror vacui*, the negatively per-versed side of omniality. Fear of aloneness is replaced by hope for all-oneness or one-allness. The negatively conceived horror or anxiety feels impaired and in des-pair until the omniality via the pair-concept pacifies the self-isolated ego-mind. The horror is a horror *tui*, *non-mei, alius per se* appearing as phantom of otherness *per se*. Max Planck has been able to decode the various phantom-problems enticing and horrifying the anxious I and his unreliable I-mindedness while happy in creating a phantom-world to motivate better his own fear in such an uncomfortable seat of anxiety. . . .

Among those concerned enough to ask questions, Whitehead asks: what does man do with his aloneness? They are all concerned with the challenge and mission of self-confrontation. The question could be reformulated better perhaps: what does the fear-poisoned ego do in his seat of anxiety to escape or transcend such aloneness? All-oneness or one-allness is the remedy which comes via individuation to re-identify with the quasi-disidentifiable *omnia animata* (*sumus*) of Spinoza. Individuation I would rather call omniality or totality, and I am glad to see R. Buckminster Fuller naming it 'synergy'. What, then, does this new label for our nameless unknowable Being stand for? 'Synergy is of the essence. Here we witness mind over matter and humanity's escape of his exclusive identity only with some sovereignized circumscribed geographical locality.'[19] Ralph Metzner thoroughly explores the 'Maps of Consciousness'[20] and does not only recognize two levels of which one is mislabelled 'unconscious'. Spinoza's notion hints via *omnia animata* at multidimensional consciousness at many levels, aspects, while Mr Average for his own convenience splits the immense, enigmatic wholeness into handy and common 'use' of conscious and unconscious (another pair-concept!). It makes this concept more palatable and it works on different labels and levels in order to point at omniality via all-oneness or one-allness, for some better named individuation. Metzner does not belittle the very fact that it was:

> to Freud's credit that he took the bull by the horns and grappled with the problems of resistance and defense mechanisms directly. . . . To be objective about one's inner states requires the difficult, lengthy and poorly understood process of freeing oneself from inherited and acquired images and mechanisms.

And while still in the witness-box for Spinoza, I can see Freud linked with Spinoza especially when discovering for '*that* there are so many things influencing the psyche while we are not being aware, *what* these things are.' For Spinoza it remains an undisputable axiomatic truth that 'man is [only] conscious of his wishes and his appetites, whilst at the same time ignorant of the causes by which he is led to wish and desire, not dreaming *what* they are.' Metzner extended his own daring self-exploring research where Freud, fully self-complacent and satisfied with his findings, looked for a resting place:

> in his discoveries of divergent theories and points (later unfolded by his followers) based on equally unverified and unverifiable observations. . . . The inseparable interaction of the process of observation with the phenomena observed, which is expressed in the physical sciences in Heisenberg's indeterminacy principle, is of course of paramount importance in psychology where the phenomena to be observed are the observers' own subjective states. Yet we find that the pervasive and fundamental distortions of perception caused by ego-factors and personality-bound perspectives are very rarely recognized by the observer himself. The weak point in Freud's entire work was his method, the technique of 'free associations' actually not free at all since it follows the fixed patterns of neurotic mechanisms. . . . But unfortunately the method, even when supplemented by the analyst's interpretation did not free from these mechanisms. The analyzed patient could relate the whole history of his neurosis but not be one iota closer to overcoming it.[21]

Here Metzner can offer a remedy in the School of Actualism founded by Russell Paul Schofield in Valley Centre, California, where he applies successfully some techniques

> designed to actualize potentials (i.e. to extend potential faculties within everyone!) to free perception from imprinted images so that awareness can expand into the many levels of consciousness – that is beyond our usual awareness.

Here again I encounter and recognize what I have learned from my excellent teacher, Baruch de Spinoza: to 'imbue' (in contradiction to Freud!) myself with urge for identification with my wholeness or individuated Being (as indivisible). Spinoza is finger-pointing to the goal of the wise man when having traversed his path to that goal of individuation or omniality. *Non solum singulares, particulares sed nos omnia animata sumus!* This means to expand narrow I-mindedness into all-minded self-knowledge of otherless omniality or wholeness or completion. The wise man is thus happy and free to re-identify via re-awareness with the inseparable same Being when conscious of self, of God and of the world (of quasi-diversity and multiplicity!). And such re-identifiability demonstrates that we *are omnia* and *omniality.* The quasi many (ones) or the unquasi numberless, indefinite, indeterminate, the 'one' which is the one-all or all-one. . . . We are *omnia* and *animata* when referring to our awareness of it, but all-one when aware of it as us and us as it. In the ancient spirit of the Upanishads we are no-thing but con-sciousness as co-consciousness 'in' and 'as' *anima, animatio, animantia sive animata* like *naturans sive naturata. Achat Ruach Elohim Chayim!* Unique is the living Spirit of Elohim! This first verse of Sepher Yetsirah seconds the first verse of Bereshit: of genesis via gnosis and of gnosis via genesis. Or via all-oneness and one-allness indeed. I repeat we are no-thing but consciousness and now we can more easily grasp Whitehead's message: 'apart from the experience of subjects, there is nothing, nothing, bare nothingness'.[22] In other words – from Jewish Esotericism – there is only *Echad* and no *Acher.* One with no Other, and Indian Esotericism seconds here best: one with no second, Advaita: the twoless, i.e. the otherless!

Spinoza is a thinker who can imbue a thinker like Freud when in want of access to such salvational truth, although he shunned any guidance for the self-exploration of the immense mystery of man's own unknown Being. This is not explorable by systems, explanations changing old isms for new ones but it mesmerizes via self-experience and self-realization the othernessless of the unreal phantom of quasiness.

Since time immemorial the *mysterium* has encapsulated the message of

Know Thyself! and *Love Thy Neighbour!*

but for comfort and convenience it has been perverted into:

Love Thyself! and *Know Thy Neighbour!*

Deus sive Natura can impress you with the *Amor Dei sive Amor Naturae* to turn knowledge into love in the original biblical sense. Knowledge, then, is not concerned to know quasi-otherness *per se* in order to mitigate the odd self-estrangement. Not concerned either to love quasi-selfness *per se* but to transcend quasiness and re-identify with *causa sive ratio sui,* i.e. with the principle of indeterminacy. . . . In such a spirit Spinoza once wrote to a corn-broker: 'It may be that God has impressed you with a clear idea of Himself so that you forget the world for love of Him and love your fellow-men as yourself!' Then perhaps you would feel challenged as Spinoza felt, you would become fully (expanded!) conscious of yourself as identical with God and the world (of things) to forget quasi-otherness *per se* and also quasi-selfness *per se*: in all-oneness or one-allness via cosmic-divine omni-consciousness: Yahweh Echad! Then you will never side with consciousness, *sub*-consciousness or with super-consciousness dimensional (multi- or omni-dimensional) or immensional. . . . It is as if the drop in the universal ocean becomes conscious of himself, the world of drops (or waves) and the substantial ocean as one and same omni-awareness with such marvellous 'oceanic feeling': samadhi, nirvana, moksha, enlightenment – Every drop is the whole indivisible ocean just as every man is a Buddha, a Christ, etc., but only the few, the karmic-elected are aware of it to experience the innate omniality: *cum essendi fruitione. Omnia animata (quamvis diversis gradibus respectu intellectus humani!)*. Only a few like Baruch de Spinoza could say about the own unsayable unknown: 'sentimus experimurque nos aeternos esse'.

This utterance contains the whole unsayable oceanic identity of all drops and waves via quasiness, namely of the quasi unidentical drop *per se*, or wave *per se* which give up the quasi *perseitas* for the all-oneness of the omniality of the ocean. Freud was so 'freudlos' in his 'seat of anxiety' and could have lifted up himself to the Ode of Joy – Das Lied an die Freude, in the last symphony where Ludwig van Beethoven tried to reach the borderline of sayability of human and orchestral voices as homage to *omnia animata*.

Mankind should never belittle man's effort within his karmic radius like that of Sigmund Freud with his potentialities and propensities, when so keen to explore the border-regions of self-limitations in order to transcend any stumbling-block of quasi-selfness *per se* or quasi-otherness *per se*.

We all are pilgrims on the path to the same goal pointing to self-liberation from self-bondage, if following the finger-pointings of Spinoza in the West or of the rishis, sages, gurus, lamas from the East for the sake of whole mankind. When man himself discovers his own individuation or wholeness then he will be able to help mankind to be kind to one another, as there is no real otherness *per se*. If I and the Father are One, then also I and all the *Brothers* are no others *per se* anymore. . . .

Evans-Wentz found no better words of courage and hope for all the egos in their 'seat of anxiety' when introducing the Tibetan Book of Liberation with the Dhammapada as:

It were better to live one single day:

It were better to live *one single day* in the development of a good life than to live a hundred years evilly and with undisciplined mind.

It were better to live *one single day* in the pursuit of understanding and meditation than to live a hundred years in ignorance and restraint.

It were better to live *one single day* in the commencement of earnest endeavour than to live a hundred years in sloth and effortlessness.

It were better to live *one single day* giving thought to the origin and cessation of that which is composite than to live a hundred years giving no thought to such origin and cessation.

It were better to live *one single day* knowing the Excellent Doctrine than to live a hundred years without knowing the Excellent Doctrine.

NOTES

1 Lothar Bickel, 'Über Beziehungen zwischen der Psychoanalyse und einer dynamischen Psychologie', *Zentralblatt für Psychotherapie und ihre Grenzgebiete* (April, 1931).

2 Leo Sonntag, Paris, has permission from Lothar Bickel's son Peter at Berkeley; I have obtained permission from Sigmund Freud Copyrights Ltd.

3 Siegfried Hessing, *Spinoza Festschrift 1632–1932* (Heidelberg, Carl Winter, 1933); Siegfried Hessing, *Spinoza – 300 Jahre Ewigkeit*. Zweite vermehrte Auflage (The Hague, Nijhoff, 1962); Walter Bernard, 'Freud and Spinoza', *Psychiatry*, vol. 9, no. 2 (May, 1946).

4 These are the introductory words of Bernard, *op. cit.*

5 B. Alexander, 'Spinoza und die Psychoanalyse', *Chronicon Spinozanum*, vol. 5 (1928), p. 103.

6 Constance Rathbun, 'On certain similarities between Spinoza and psychoanalysis', *Psychoanalytic Review* (January 1934), p. 14.

7 Bickel, *op. cit.*

8 Bernard, *op. cit.*

9 Errol E. Harris, *Salvation from Despair – A Reappraisal of Spinoza's Philosophy* (The Hague, Nijhoff, 1973).

10 Nearly half a century ago Carl Gebhardt – ahead of most Spinozists and Freudians – intuited extremely wisely that:

> Spinoza has originated the dynamics of the affections and it could witness the living Spinozism that his origination has experienced its confirmation via psychoanalysis in all its essential theses and consequences in our time. Psychoanalysis in its first stage, has been a therapy, and could be content in it with the physician's empiricism. Now, in its second stage, it has become a psychology, possessing in it the merit of having freed us by its dynamism from the mechanics of experimental psychology. If desiring in a third stage, already heralded now, to penetrate further into a conception of the world (Weltanschauung) by widening therapeutics into pedagogy and finally into ethics, then it will recognize in Spinozism the features of its deeper self.

('Spinoza: Judentum und Barock'. Lecture at the Celebration before the Jewish Academic Association, in Kleiner Festsaal of Vienna University 12 March, 1927.

11 Richard Wollheim, *Freud – A Collection of Critical Essays* (New York, Doubleday, 1974).

12 Christopher Reeves, 'Was Freud a Scientist?', *The Listener*, 15 January 1976.
13 Timothy Leary, Ralph Metzner and Richard Alpert, *Psychedelic Experience* (London, Academic Editions, 1971), p. 13. Karl Popper disclosed that he was disenchanted with Marx and Freud; P. B. Medawar was also disenchanted with Freud.
14 W. Y. Evans-Wentz, *The Tibetan Book of the Dead* (New York, Pantheon, 1951).
15 Lama Anagarika Govinda speaks of 'multidimensional consciousness' and sent me some excerpts of his work from *Main Currents in Modern Thought*, vol. 26 no. 4 (1970). Also Carlo Suares has a very keen approach to similar findings as in his book *Mémoire sur le retour du Rabbi qu'on appelle Jésus* (Paris, Robert Laffont, 1975).
16 *Das Tibetanische Totenbuch* (Zurich, Rascher, 1960), p. 69.
17 *Zeitlose Dokumente der Seele* (Zurich, Rascher, 1952), p. 206.
18 Alan Watts, *The Wisdom of Insecurity* (New York, Vintage Books, 1951).
19 R. Buckminster-Fuller, *Operation Manual Spaceship Earth* (Illinois University Press, 1969), p. 99.
20 Ralph Metzner, *Maps of Consciousness* (New York, Collier, 1971), pp. 5 ff.
21 *Ibid.* The advancing researcher in Spinozana is reminded to parallel the term 'mechanism' used for somatic aspects and 'automaton' used by Spinoza to define the mind in its working. See note 1 to my contribution 'Proton Axioma kai Proton Pseudos' in this volume (p. 315).
22 *Process and Reality*, p. 234.

16 Proton axioma kai proton pseudos

Siegfried Hessing, London

Mit Gott fang an,
mit Gott hör auf:
das ist der beste
Lebenslauf!

To begin with God, to cease with God, is the best course life can take for man in his godlikeness and awareness of togetherness with God since the Garden of Eden. To begin and to end with no other but with the very same, called God: with no beginning and no ending. Such God–Man togetherness is indeed marvellous in the divine-cosmic stage-setting 'as' the Garden of Eden: the Kindergarten of Man. I can still remember being confronted on my first schoolday with the very first Spinozistic disclosure of that quasi-beginning and quasi-ending which would be in such togetherness with no-beginning and no-ending to understand quasiness. . . . It was just after I had been considered mature enough to leave the kindergarten, my human version of the Garden of Eden, and to enter the world by learning first the pictorializing and then the verbalizing approach to the Great Show on Earth. For me the world is only a world of and for adults with a secular monopoly for that which is not secular. Adults are grown up or grown out from Eden and from that common paradisiac togetherness with *Deus sive Natura* or with *Natura sive Deus*. I never admired adults because they always pretend to know everything before they know anything at all, simply because of the former togetherness which they betray too soon. Like mental dwarfs they try in vain to pose and impose their authority (with force if necessary, and *when* is it not necessary?) like giants against children, who although small in stature are gigantic inside, feeling and remembering that 'magic togetherness' from Eden: even when later exiled to live in outer Eden like us on earth connected with the un-approachable vastness of (our) outerspace. For such gigantic feeling poets and gods alike envy us so often when they themselves are exiled too. . . . Feeling with no purpose, no cause, no reason, no determinism to try to explain the very plain and unexplainable life: as wonderful as plain life to marvel at!

Later, for the second time in my life I was again found mature enough to leave school with all its schoolwisdom, only valid on school-benches to be learned under the super-'vision' of schoolmasters with no vision and with no mastership at all to inspire.... Only then did I discover an exceptional teacher who had had no schooling himself: self-taught[1] and teaching self-teaching via *causa sui* or *ratio sui*. Learning for learning's sake and a teacher with no schoolmastership but with an ability to master life by obeying its hidden inside rules with vast and deep vision into the own unknown, into the invisible and indivisible mystery of life *per se* to marvel at.... A mystery as vast beyond the human fake-horizon and as deep as the great ocean bestowing that 'oceanic feeling' to the oceanic drop in a revelation of all-oneness and one-allness. Such at-onement points to that Garden of Eden, the kindergarten of mankind and points to that pre- or trans-rational (i.e. pre- or trans-causal) togetherness with *Deus sive Natura*.... The great vision of the little ego into the otherless self! The vision with no di-vision and no discrepancy via the strange insideness in constant self-confrontation as it were with our own quasi-otherness. To escape from it we project it by externalization into a quasi-otherness *per se* then to become our own arch-enemy for life. The only remedy appears to be hiding in internalization versus externalization under the ad-'vice' of divine duality, so to speak. But this exceptional teacher attracted me so much, like that first school-motto, to point at and to marvel while so pointing at my own beginningless and endless unknown, the ex-less 'X'. He attracted me with such magic and focused on that for which no name can really fit best, but if any, then perhaps still the good old name 'God' with the still good old unexplorable namelessness as Spinoza sees it in himself. And so he let everyone see it in his own otherless very same self. God with the vast meaning of our own identity and infinity 'in' it and 'as' it: *itself*. And life and strife, and reason and treason, and why and because (be-'cause')... all this... 'that ye may know that "I am" [is] the Lord!', God inside and outside as the manifest togetherness. God insight and outsight with no otherness, but beyond siding and beyond beyondness: absolute infinite or infinite in infinite ways, aspects, levels, dimensions (of consciousness, or omni-consciousness of *omnia animata – sumus!*) via quasi-otherness and otherlessness as well. The only thing left to grasp remains: quasiness or unquasiness. I feel obliged to show that Spinoza himself used the word God for the same wordless content encapsulated in it. And for a deeper inside and insight into Spinoza's formulation let us glance first at:

> *Deus* est: M-ens con-stans infinitis attributis attribuentia sibi ipse sive 'sub-stantiae per se' infinitam essentiam (vel aeternam existentiam) via Amoris Dei *Intellectualis*.
>
> Deum, Dei Intellectus resque ab ipso *intellectas* unum et idem esse. Amor Dei *Intellectualis* ipse est essendi fruitio divina. Amor Naturae *Intellectualis* ipse est essendi fruitio naturalis. In se considerata est vera considerata, divina considerata, naturalis considerata. Sic! In se, i.e. sine alio, sine ratione, sine cause, sine determinatione etc. et: sine 'sine' ipse....

241

Omnia animata (et animantia) 'sumus', ergo: sentimus experimurque
nos esse: infinitos vel aeternos: sine attributis respectu attribuentis.
Intellectus tamquam essentiam rei attributae constituere. Sine respectu
alteritatis *Intellectus* percipientis sive rerum *intellectarum*.

If this is God or the way to know Him by knowing oneself or knowing Him
as myself, then with Spinoza we can only know 'that' God is and not 'what'
God is, while what and whatness is only part or aspect of such that and thatness, to be marvelled at in unknowable but livable and experienceable oneness:
via *Amoris Dei Intellectualis* where 'we', the intellecting, and 'it', the intellected,
are the very same idea *convenire debet cum suo ideato*. The very same cosmic-
divine Infinite Intellectus intellecting or self-intellecting his own unknowable
'thatness' is called *Deus sive Natura*. How to know Him? So the *Zohar* asks
and points to the indivisible oneness of asking and answering by re-identifying
such oneness. How to know Him? When not knowing Him as other than
knower, known and knowing. When not knowing but being Him 'in' Him
the All-Being and 'via' Him as the *vera via viae vel via sui, ens suitatis*! Not
assuming Him as creator apart from creation, the quasi-'other' than the
creatura as quasi-Him, the godlike man from the Bible when the first verse of
Genesis speaks via Elohim of the same gnosis in the first axiom in Spinoza's
Ethics; but crystallized as: 'Whatever is, is in God and no-thing can neither be
nor be conceived without God' (IP15). To begin thus has to mean: to begin
with God or with that 'in' which every-'thing' and every 'thought' from the
very beginningless including its own endlessness via my otherless self, that is
me: 'my' I and my I-mindedness has depossessed itself of I-hood or has
disegotized itself to be free from any human anthropomorphous reprojected
entelechy. This was and is always so, enticing with comfort as offering a
cause or reason for that which 'is' without (quasi-otherness of) cause or
reason to marvel at as at a wonder . . . taumazein!

To begin properly – in the spirit of Spinoza – I begin with that marvellous
causa sive ratio sui, evolving and involving my own acausality and irrationality
as 'life'. 'I am' is really 'I am' when I = am and then 'I am' [is] the Way, the
Truth and *Life*. Sic! Le Chayim! My very one unknowable and my one own
(?) life as e'very'one's life and its very self-sameness which my teacher,
Spinoza, started to teach me – via his self-teaching way: how to know and
especially how to know knowing in itself, namely as the unknowable via
knowing and without dichotomy or trichotomy into a quasi-knower versus
(another) quasi-known, while the via knowing is only knowing quasiness as
inseitas. . . .

Genesis is always genesis of thinking and not of some-'thing' only to be
seen outside (of – another? – quasi: inside) of us ourselves as seers or thinkers
apart from our own seeing and thinking in crass and often grotesque discrepancy with us as (if) not us, but some 'other' or some 'it'. Such dichotomy

of a subject-like thinker and seer versus an object-like thought and seen vanishes only in the revelation of sudden enlightenment in the dark ignorance ignoring quasi-otherness *per se* and then:

An instant realization sees endless time.
Endless time is as one moment.
When one comprehends the endless moment
He realizes the person who is seeing it.[2]

Then the enlightened one 'realizes' with Hui-Neng 'inwardly the imperturbability of the essence of mind'. And this equals salvation from (self-) bondage. . . .

Genesis is the gnosis of that which is so seldom experienced without dichotomy or anatomy of the wholeness and omniality: *omnia animata* (*sumus*), without discrimination, without any 'dis-' as a very welcome prefix to 'fix' quasi unwelcome fleeting thoughts of otherness *per se*! It is as if speaking of a thin slice of bread unable to satisfy or satiate man's hunger by sliceness. In order to live man always looks for a whole loaf of bread to inspire veneration and worship of wholeness and holiness. Yes. The whole loaf is the whole life (Laib = Leib) for the life-hungry man. Loaf and life demand both wholeness as a commandment to long for fulfilment with nostalgic craving and then to become fully aware of one's own indivisible, otherless omniality or totality. . . .

All the commandments which I command thee this day shall ye observe to do, that ye may live, and . . . know that man doth not live by bread only, but by every word that proceedeth out of the mouth of the Lord doth man live.[3]

By this *word* (dawar also means matter, thing!) do man and the world live. All divine commandments and all of godlike man's observances are condensed in 'doing' in order 'that ye may know that "I am" [is] the *Lord* and ye may live!' This will bring all the food man needs and cannot find only in bread coming as it were from outside his mouth, but rather that feeding word coming from the *Lord's* mouth as from our own unknown 'thatness' inside with food for infinity and eternity. This is not knowledge (of quasi-otherness as known), but life (of otherlessness as unknowable but livable!). In the cryptic biblical parlance we read that the 'word of the Lord *happened*'. To 'happen' (*fieri*) is the classical mind-opener for enlightenment beyond *causa sive ratio* '*alius*'. And while pondering on biblical parlance it is indeed odd to hear of the '*fiat*'! (no *facere* and no *factum* for the *facies totius universi*!). Those familiar with the Tao's cardinal teaching of 'letting' (i.e. be or not be, etc.) will read again the Bible text: Let it be light! Let us, etc. . . .! 'Let there be!' opens the way for something 'to happen' without creator *vis-à-vis creatura* and is more appropriate to *causa sive ratio sui*. *Fieri* inspires *fiendi delectatio*:

243

delighted to be free from (thinking of) *causa sive ratio alius*. I could never imagine before that such excellent cosmic-divine wording for happening and and that such randomness of indeterminacy can never be used in the first person as our ego is so eager to use the high role of the 'first person'. I cannot say: 'I happen' while the intransitive meaning points to acausality or irrationality too. And to 'happen' is so 'natural' for when we look at the Greek word *phyo* we see it phonetically linked with *physis*, nature (cf. *nascor* versus *nosco*) as becoming via some other or quasi-other coming. The rationalist or causalist is strongly opposed to such an intransitive link with one's own unknown being as beginningless, endless . . .: *causa sui sine alio*. Food like bread must be taken into man's mouth to feed him in order to assimilate the quasi-twoness of bread and man (*Laib* and *Leib*). Then the bread becomes man. The divine word which proceedeth out of the mouth of the Lord is a marvellous happening 'in' us and then to become 'as' us and 'from' us as if 'not' us. . . . Sic! Hence marvellous for revelation and enlightenment of the 'I' always in constant fear of otherness (as ending '*other*' than beginning, etc.) *per se*. After Spinoza there is actually no 'there *per se*' or 'here *per se*' as also no 'before *per se*' or 'after *per se*', or 'when *per se*' to ask for. There is no-'thing' to proceed from or to succeed to only with the success of mechanical explanation of *causa sive ratio alius* '*per se*' while only pointing at quasi-otherness and making quasiness so difficult to ponder on or to marvel at. And such quasiness, namely not really 'so' or 'not so', but only 'quasi so' or 'quasi not so' and just this supports and calls for acceptance of the quasi-indeterminate as well. It is the magic revelatory principle of *causa sive ratio sui* with a sudden instant awareness of *suitas*, of *omni-suitas*. As *inseitas* or Enstasis as Enlightenment. And the constant, instant or co-instant and sub-stant *Now* and *Here* appears magic.

All my life I am concerned with such constant instant nowness which helps me to grasp the ungraspable wholeness better than slicing it like bread into a slice of 'before' and into another slice of 'after' as it were for the better palatability of sliceness. Yes, I am now so well assured by my I-anxiety (of otherness *per se* as not-I) in this ever-now with no need to boast about it like the victorious Pyrrhus who entered posterity for ever with his proverbial victory (although self-ostracized) . . . I do not need to boast: 'After me the deluge!' showing that I am not interested in any afterwardness without including my very same I and I-mindedness indeed. Accordingly I would dare to parallel such a saying with an exclamation: 'Before me the chaos!' Or the tohuwabohu = the void and formless. Thus I show that I am not interested in any 'before' or any ante-I or ante-I-minded state without me. The main cosmic actor is destined for the whole of creation during the span of life allotted to I-mindedness of singularized existence revolving again and again singularizing existence with no exception or desire for the wholeness bestowing that 'oceanic feeling' of *omnia animata (sumus)*!

Chaos and deluge are both complementary, interchangeable reciprocal notions to befit better I-mindedness quasi-at home and comfortably with *causa sive ratio alius*, but they can never be conceived *per se* without each other evolving quasi-otherness and reflecting it as well. Chaos and deluge are reversible for a happy or unhappy state of mind and I-mindedness in it: when either egoful or egoless. Happy when I can 'let' every-'thing' and every-'thought' just to 'happen' (sahaja) and I do not try to interfere with *causa sive ratio alius* (to explain the ex-less plain 'X': my own unknowable life!). I as I with discriminative I-mindedness separated from your you-mindedness, etc., I am always as 'if' between such quasi-before and/or of such quasi-after within my own self-creation (of quasi-otherness) *causa sive ratio mei*. In Russian there is a saying applicable to this nexus of thought: Where is the goodness I can find as I merit and deserve it so much? Where? To which the answer waits ready: There where I am not, there it is so good for me. Then 'it' is not good for me but simply good *per se*. I can really be as being undisturbed by my own I-mindedness, when I can abandon such self-limited I-mindedness and transform 'I' into 'it', namely into all-mindedness including every'thing' and every-'thought' of I and not-I. Only there where is no 'there' with no 'I', i.e. in a positive no-'where' (or not asking for any 'where' at all!), there in no-man's land with no-ego and I-centred pretensions or intentions. Only 'there' I can feel happy when everything happens as it happens with no dictatorship of *causa sive ratio alius* as an I-mind extra-mundane and as the scholastic God was supposed to be *Deus extramundanus* quasi *ex nihilo* or *ex machina* in accordance with the negative transcendence of *aliud Dei*, the divine 'Otherness *per se*'! And how then should the godlikeness from the creation re-unite or re-identify man and God, God and man? *Creator et creatura idem*! Not *'in se sive in alio!'*. *Siveitas* or quasiness gives man the spontaneity of craving for re-awareness of omn-identity, but not the rational or causal coercion for it. Yes! That oceanic feeling ... and the longing of the drop to attain such state (of drop-mind): M-ens constans, instans (co-instans or sub-stans) via *infinitis attributis* revealing self-realization of otherless infinity.[4] And then to test and taste *essendi fruitio* (not cognoscendi) as salvation via self-experience transcending quasi-otherness while identifying with the divine quasiness, the goddess Maya as it were:

> Rabbi Shimeon said: moreover I will not say it unto the heavens, that they may hear; I will not declare it unto the earth, that it may hear: for certainly *we are the pillars of the universe!*[5]

Heaven and earth were the main two witnesses or the witness-pair as the very first (i.e. principal!) quasi-example of Yahweh–Elohim, when Moses proclaimed his testament as the very essence and testimony. That *Old, Ancient Testament*, with Bereshit or Genesis, is speaking of the creation of 'heaven and earth' as (if) two acts of creation via twoness or otherness, while pointing to the pair-concept with reciprocal receptivity of self-same wholeness. Rabbi Shimeon learnt that *'one man's life is equal to all the work of creation!'*

He is in agreement with such identity of *creator et creatura idem*. Full was his craving for the same fullness (of Ayin, Shunya, void), for the very same Glory. The same glory which the prophet has been filled with in his fulfilment: *The whole earth is full of His glory!* Man equal with the whole creation points to man's godlikeness as God's manlikeness. The pillars of the universe are not biased by the (thought of) beginning. . . .

'With' the beginning (of thinking) Elohim created heaven and earth as (if) two. And so Elohim created Man: male and fe-male He created 'them' as (if) two but as an inseparable pair after catholicity or universality. The enlightenment which comes with the insight into the inside of quasiness let Man feel exalted, universalized, when re-identifying himself with the indi-'visible' *Whole* of 'Heaven and Earth' quasi divided by a pseudo-horizon creating quasi-separation between the quasi-twoness. *Omnia animata sumus!* We are the pillars of the uni-'verse' (and omni-verse!). It is never the 'earth *per se*' and never the 'heaven *per se*' either. Spinoza like Moses both speak of a quasi-twoness, of quasi-otherness (para-otherness = parallel!) or of binary alternation in order to point at a quasi twofold, multifold and quasi-otherless truth of *Echad* and not of *Acher per se*! So we speak of uni-verse, not dui-'verse', multi-verse but rather omni-verse. Sic! And Zoharic hints at otherlessness and at omni-awareness with such 'oceanic feeling' are quite in line with very ancient Tantric texts when quoting via Lakshamanjoo: 'As waves come with water and flames with fire, so the universal waves come with us.'[6] Shri Sankaracharya parallels it excellently here:

> As waves are only water and copper pots only copper, so the multitude of universes are the self and the *self* alone. . . . As by a jar is meant the clay, and by cloth the threads, of which it is *composed*, so by the name of the *world* is denoted *consciousness*. This whole world in its visible and invisible form is consciousness. The wise man should every day meditate carefully on his *self*.[7]

And Spinoza parallels here too:

> By 'Man' is meant: mind and body of which he is *composed* [as a pair-concept], while in the Biblical wording: By 'Man' is meant 'male and female' of which he is *composed* [as pair-concept to implement 'wholeness'].

The essential teaching of Buddha is centring on the principle that life is composed (i.e. 'posed' as pair-concept of wholeness!), conditioned and it is not thinkable as uncomposed or unconditioned before attaining nirvana, enlightenment from the obscure quasi-twoness. . . .

Now you can see and are allowed to rebuke me, that I am endlessly beginning to speak about a beginning or quasi-beginning. This demonstrates in itself an already evident, self-evident infinity in every approach of quasiness when only trying to speak of a beginning when speaking of a quasi-Genesis in the Bible and of a quasi-Gnosis of thinking as deriving from my beginning enlightenment. For me such enlightenment came as if 'happening' via Spinoza's first axiom of the *Ethics*. This axiom points at every-thing and every-thought (about things) in me and at me in every-thing and every-thought as well. This first axiom of Genesis of thinking via Spinoza attracted me so much that I selected it as a leitmotif for my theme in this contribution as homage to Spinoza. In this first axiom of Gnosis as in the first Bible verse of Genesis one can see a cryptic link involving quasi-otherness when speaking of a quasi-beginning, and also exploring otherlessness via quasiness.

Everything which is, is either in itself or in another (self).

But first let me show how children, before entering fully unbiased into the realm of hardening school-benches, are ready for discoveries like my own during such same hardship of setting and sitting among schooled thinkers. How then do children (and not thinkers) think about any beginning and especially about the beginning of their own life, called birth, when not yet attracted like myself to such a school-motto pointing at the paradisiac togetherness of God and Man as in Eden? I once intended to find out how a child's unbiased mind does think of any beginning. From various answers I was easily able to gather, that it never even enters the human mind to question its own unquestionable being at all. Sic! The thought of a beginning – so Suares convinces us to admit – becomes unthinkable and leads to the brink of *causa sive ratio alius*! It is taken for granted whenever pondering on life (such divine composition of composed creation!) that one feels as if in the middle, in the centre (attracted to con-'centrate' with self-identification and realization!). One feels as if in the centre of the ocean with no beginning and with no ending of the ocean and that 'oceanic feeling' of wholeness or omniality revealed. Revealed in omni-awareness of *omnia animata sumus* (not *omnia animatus sum*!). Salomo the wise lists this simile of the ship in the midst of the sea among the unknowable wonders to wonder at again and to ponder again as on a revelation. For the sake of the analysis Spinoza helps us to see the mind quasi 'as if' it had started just now to be. Similarly he proceeded with the definition of the attribute: – *tamquam ejusdem essentiam constituens*, while such *essentia* is self-constituent, self-created, auto-maton: self-teaching, self-re-volving (the 'wheel' of *ordo et connexio idearum sive rerum*) for better self-identification.

When the child is pressed by adults to search for its identity with a quasi-beginning *per se* and a quasi-ending *per se*, only then follows such a trend to believe like the adults do; when impressed by the only evidence (e-vidence not in-vidence!) of birth and death via certificates to certify quasi-birth or quasi-death, certifiable only by and for 'others' witnessing, i.e. by allo-evidence. The child thinks of its own birth when reminded by festivities of birthdays and takes it for granted after the only available orientation of time via watch and calendar (both watching quasi-otherness *per se*!). So of sun-rise and sun-set alike although too aware of such school-wisdom that the sun never rises nor sets. Giordano Bruno was burnt to death at the stake for our mistake and for such burning fake-truth, to be revoked and unmasked. The retina still has its say even today. Sic! To certify the (uncertain) *'prima'* or *'ultima' causa sive ratio hominis*, makes such certificates quite welcome and authorities can easily rule by such acceptance of rules. The child when un-biased would never even have dared to 'think' that time- and placeless life can some-where and some-times 'take' place as if caused (or reasoned) by some-one, some-when and some-where only in order to 'happen'. No *causa sive ratio (alius)* is needed to 'let things happen'. Here again the principle of indeterminacy brings easy re-lease! Without recurrent birthday dates everyday dailiness would run like a river in its riverbed with river-dreams of happenings from a sourceless source into the grand sourceful sea of the same wholeness mirrored and reflected in every drop of water to enjoy, via drop-awareness, omni-awareness with 'oceanic feeling' . . . !

And when already half of the (beginningless) truth is being revealed and accepted then the quasi-other half(of the perfect pair-concept!) is begging to be recomplemented for the full re-awareness of the whole enlightenment manifest in *omnia animata sumus*! Then the wholeness is manifest in such 'oceanic feeling' of substance or substantiality via the quasi-fleeting appear-ance of being (of drops, waves). And as waves come with water so the uni-versal waves come with the (otherless) self. The little I-minded I in its anxiety (of a quasi non-I or it) is relieved when submerging its singularity of the last and lost 'is'-lander as islander in the universe-ocean. 'I' is only too happy when not concerned any more with *causa sive ratio* to explain and sustain its special I-ness and I-mindedness. So it is happy to 'let' every-thing and every-thought (in order and connection . . .) thinking it, just 'happen', sinking into the I-less sea. The birthless half-life longs for the wholeness via the deathless half to re-enact the divine-cosmic pair-pattern. The Anguttara-nikaya Sutra (III, 355) speaks of those 'few' ones. 'Verily few are those who pass their time touching with their bodies the immortal element.' I shall say more about it in another context. Now I talk only about the longing for wholeness innate in awareness of one's own birthless state: of *causa sive ratio sui*. It is the dawning of the otherless, acausal or irrational self-realization like via the fake-horizon and the horizontal pseudo-division of heaven and earth into quasi-twoness while only a pair-concept to ponder on and wonder about.

With the beginning Elohim created heaven and earth as (if) two.
Everything which is, is either in itself or in another ('self' as 'if' two).

So I feel in my discriminative and dichotomizing way of thinking as 'if' there are two: me and not-me, as you, he, she or it. So twoness as otherness *per se* emerges to frighten the self-'isolated' I and its I-mindedness, to insist still to be considered an exceptional being among all (others?) unexceptional beings: me the crown of creation waiting to be crowned at least for its quasi-exceptionality. . . . But when I ponder that every I and its I-mindedness is entitled to the very same exceptionality then this turns into universality with the very same unique and universal (already omni-versal!) importance. Then the mind likes to reflect on itself, to contemplate itself and thus removes the stumbling-block of fake-obstacles blocking the way to reach omni-awareness: *omnia animata sumus!*

> To illustrate, let us take the analogy of a lamp. We know that the light of a lamp when surrounded by a shade will reflect inwardly with its radiance centering on itself, whereas the rays of a naked flame will diffuse and shine outwardly. Now when engrossed with criticising others, as is our wont, we hardly turn our thoughts on ourselves, and scarcely know anything about ourselves. Contrary to this the followers of the Dhyana School turn their attention completely within and reflect exclusively on their own '*real nature*' known in Chinese as one's '*original face*'.[8]

It would be rewarding for the Spinoza admirer to see how Spinoza himself speaks so strongly that 'the mind has to reflect on itself [not on 'otherness'!], has to contemplate itself, etc.', in order to re-assess one's own root-awareness to attain self-realization. . . .

Sentimus experimurque nos aeternos esse!

Esse as *nos* and *nos* as *esse*. This is the experience of every 'I am' as the equation I = am; am = it = I. 'I am' [is] the Lord and ye may know it! Ezekiel exclaims it so often. Do you hear him and do you accept his claim? And be-'cause' of such quasi-otherness, quasi-causality of reflection, I have to re-mind my I-mind that it is the (I-less) all-mind with its all-reflection and with the reversible way of singularizing, dualizing, pluralizing to omnia-lizing. . . . From I to it or from Ani to Ayin or from the quasi-determinate to the indeterminate and vice versa as uni-versa, always uni-'versal'. Thus the all-identity is not lost and not to be re-gained, but it refers to the *self-reflection of all to all as all-self.* Ergo: Know Thyself! As 'Deus sive Natura sive Veritas sive Amor Dei Intellectus et Universum Intellectum unum et idem est. . . . Unum est et unam habet faciem totius universi'. [*Echad*!]. To re-mind is to re-make quasi my (I-minded) mind after Paul via the meta-noia (not via the para-noia because of a presumed para-otherness, called parallel!). It means to turn the mind and 'let' him re-turn to its root for experience of root-experience, root-awareness or omni-awareness of all-life. All-oneness as one-allness. This does 'happen' when I-mindedness turns into egoless mind or (I may say): mind-mindedness. Mind your own business, i.e. mind your own = our *all-mind, omnia animata*, Mind *per se*: *mens sui = ens sui* like *causa sui* like *ratio sui. Vivat suitas!* Then I will never be seduced to believe in reaching infinity outside myself (as quasi-otherness) via *causa sive ratio alius*, i.e. *infinitatis sive absurditatis*. Infinity has no cause, no reason to be motivated while questioned, to be explained with its ex-less 'X', when plain *per se* always remains plain. Q.E.D.

Now in my witness-box I have to say the full truth as full truth, not half and half. The full truth and no-thing else. There is no elseness besides fullness. The whole earth is full with His Glory! *Veritas sui. Deitas sui. Naturalitas sui. Vivat suitas!* Le Chayim! The absolute truth involves no otherness and I have to confess from self-realization, that wholeness is not demonstrable and not communicable either, as it would be quasi-outside the all-sidedness to have its being in order to test wholeness from outside in the crude human or anthropomorphous fashion with arrogance and ignorance blindfolded so much! Half-truth would be dichotomized: in the quasi-outsider and the 'other' half in the quasi-insider. It is the pair-concept: like male and fe-male com-'posed' as (whole) Man. I as I can only be witnessing the 'other' I dying or being born, but never ever myself: as a quasi double, Doppelgänger, of a double-self. How can I experience birth *ex alio* and death *in aliud* as *causa sive ratio alius* demands it only *this* way to be ex-'plained' (divested of its full plainness!): life being unexplainable, plain . . . ?

The Tibetan *Book of the Dead* points to the uninterrupted and incorrupted continuity of wholeness which always remains wholeness. Certain training of the ('I'-)mind helps him to become re-aware of its omniality, totality. *Omnia animata sumus*. And Spinoza adds with expedient means adapted as makeshifts or pegs: '*quamvis* diversis gradibus' in a manner like '*tamquam* ejusdem essentiam constituens', etc. Or *quatenus*, or *sive*. . . . in order to point to that quasiness as the basis of indeterminacy which will be dealt with later in detail.

Only a single paper in Jean Préposiet's *Bibliographie Spinoziste* (Paris, 1975) deals with the 'Latent indéterminisme de Spinoza' by E. Leroux.[9] Now more and more abandon their shyness and come into the open from various viewpoints to point at it. Yes! I myself have been trying to compare my viewpoint with other writers. Lama Anagarika Govinda gave special attention to this crux and thinks:

> In a certain respect we are free and in another we are not, and where the boundary line separates these two conditions, is not an objective but a subjective problem.

Some writers think, that some people are more, others less free. Sri Madhava Ashish in a letter to me, agreed with me and had this to say:

In general, however, it should follow that a system which envisages liberation (mukti) from the bondage of the causal effects of action (karma), what we would nowadays call freedom from the compulsion of unconscious psychic determinants, and assumes that this liberation can be either won by effort or given by grace, assumes that man is free to choose between bondage to desire-motivated action and (bondage to) the universal spirit. In other words: man can either submit to the illusion of separate being or submit to the inclusion with the universal substratum. If that Absolute is 'essentially free' then, when included in it, man is free, but not while he still 'thinks' himself separate. . . . Apart from the 'logical' impregnability of a convinced determinist – as impregnable a position as that of the subjectivist's – it is apparent that if we can change ourselves and change others, as witnessed by the phenomenon of 'brain-washing', then there is a principle of indeterminacy at work. I agree with you, and have observed in fact, that many devotees of determinism find in their attitude a welcome release from what seems to be, in the terrible responsibility of being an individual.

I promise to come back to this point later with more material at hand in another context.

Here I would like to show how Spinoza rightly does not 'wonder that philosophers sometimes fall into those verbal and grammatical errors. For they judge objects from names and not names from objects.' This is in strict opposition to Wittgenstein who thinks that 'essence is expressed by grammar'. When using with school-obedience the rule of grammar in order to become *anthropos grammatikos*, a learned man, a scholar, we are 'carried' and often carried away from right thinking when believing in the dichotomy of the *gerundium* also called *participium presentis*, like saying for instance: 'I am knowing' which is to participate in the presence of the uninterrupted *infinitivum* of the verb: 'to know'; namely to know (in order with knowing) in order to know succeeding further in the same order 'to know' as *infinitivum* of knowing infinitely. A flow of the infinitely knowing as 'knowing *per se*' in constant presence or omni-presence as it were. Knowing for knowing's sake: *cognitio sui*: acausal or irrational and to make it causal and rational, grammar intervenes with 'my' participation which carries me to become a quasi-knower versus a quasi-known. After the grammar this latter is a *participium perfecti*. 'I' have thus passed two stages of participation in the flowing *infinitivum*. Both *gerundia* (*gerendia*) are the via of knowing, where one and the same walks in two ways (a two-way traffic with reciprocal receptivity!) and thinks two 'ones' walking in the one way. Once quasiness is revealed the 'participation mystique' does not block self-integration and self-realization any more. Then it is always the very same and one mind – after Spinoza –

reflecting on itself, contemplating itself via a quasi-knower and (another) quasi-known as on a river. Evans-Wentz illustrates the via of knowing as on a river:

> so long as a man afloat on a river passively submits to the current, he is *carried* along smoothly, but if he attempts to grasp an object fixed in the water, the tranquillity of his (e-)motion is broken. Similarly thought-formation arrests the natural flow of mind (my emphasis).

When it comes to using the rules of grammar for verbs like 'to be born' or 'to die', then it appears odd and farcical to apply the same form of conjugation which any other verb has to obey. For instance, how could I convincingly say: I have died? I die now? How could I say: I sleep?, when I am not sure of my awareness, synchronic with the assertion of the grammar. I mostly use the future (with no obliging truthfulness whatever for me save for the grammarian) when I can say with no certainty: I shall die, sleep, etc.[10] Among Yiddish proverbs one can find one like this: Every man 'knows' that he must die, but no one 'believes' it. We cannot believe what we know by hetero-logical knowledge applicable by allo-experience as witnesses. Also we cannot know what we believe by auto-logical knowledge with no witness at hand. . . .

'The wise man not only does not cease to be (in his mind)' – but also does not think of having sometimes and somewhere started to be: as the *full sense* of Spinoza's conclusion in the finale of the *Ethics* reveals it, when the wise man has reached the goal on the rare and difficult path. Yes. Any beginning or ending of 'being' is unthinkable for any being, human or otherwise, when 'wise' to recognize the identity of 'being *or* being conceived'. Sein = Bewusst-sein! In such an identifying sense does Spinoza think and speak, and so he is always aware and beware of verbal and grammatical errors.

When using the sacro-sanct guidance of grammar, we can observe how 'otherness *per se*' can be sanctified and often even canonized while making the follower of grammatical rules believe in the order of the quasi-first, quasi-second and quasi-third person (or personal pro-'noun') only because grammar 'orders' such convenient grading of personal pronouns into persons of first, second and third grade so to speak. That means all three grades are ranks in the deputy of the pro-noun for the noun. Hence the human infiltration of personalization into the impersonal cosmic scene and scenery alike. And man thinks of himself nevertheless an exceptional outsider of 'his' universe, while man *and* universe constitute an indivisible wholeness. He is 'in' it and 'as' it according to his thinking on himself and on itself. Too often he prefers to think of the universe as dui-verse, multi-verse, as a toolmaker sticks to his blueprint to imprint rules which he himself has to obey too. And all this is only because of the lurking dichotomy with the ambush of quasi-otherness *per se.*

Sartre and Brunner are both calling the Jew the *other*. I would give him the epithet: *proton allos! Acher harishon!* His otherness is more typified than ever to complain about the hate and for the hater to 'explain' it as well to appear justified on top of it. Yes! The climax of you-ness and the danger of quasi-otherness appears in the Jew, as also in the Woman although she has, since Paradise, some mitigating compensations so elemental, that she now claims emancipation by equalness. But a special equalness with special superiority to over-turn the emancipation into absolutism . . . !

The very same postulate of quasi-otherness is imposed by structure and in-structing grammar via the form of the imperative, which is always used in the second person as a dictate to the 'other' to surrender and obey. Only I, the first person, am entitled to use the first pronoun by divine decree. I am entitled to give you, the 'other', second 'I' categorical orders as if coming from a self-appointed priest or schoolmaster, both exempting themselves from rules and involving only all 'others'. You should! You should not! Seldom does enlightenment suddenly emerge defying grammar to recognize that there is no true 'other *per se*' and we are all the very *same other* with the *same claim* for *perseitas*! I am thus your other. You are my other. Only the wise one sees himself not as self versus other or no-self, but uni-versus self or other as well. Only the wise man can escape his own di-'lemma' and its trickiness 'to judge objects from names' and not vice versa, as Spinoza warns us. How many like to be warned to become aware and beware if not aware of awareness itself . . . ! Ashvagosha teaches the right way of thinking, that it does not consist in realizing the indiscriminative essence of his mind. Just as Spinoza demands that man ought to let the mind reflect on itself in order to experience self-realization (of such quasi-irreal, acausal, indetermin-able . . .)! Such self-reflection brings quietness or con-*quiescentia* to share universal quietness of *omnia animata sive omnia vana* in perfect accordance with quasi-otherness after the revelation of quasiness. The wrong way is to discriminate and to assume things as separate entities *per se* either as persons or beings (in the East they speak of sentient and 'quasi' non-sentient beings, i.e. ego and id as idem to identify with!) and thus suffering from such self-isolation. The beginning of otherness is the beginning of sorrow, of suffering. Wells thinks a superman could 'create a super-civilization when man only agrees to a change of heart' or as the Sutra parallels it: 'to a turn of mind'. While he 'thinks', man's heart is lonely to be separated from every-'thing' and every-'thought' until he is concerned about such a lifeless state of life and is ready to expand his thinking of quasi-otherness *per se*. Then after such transcendence or transfiguration of his ego, he understands, that quasi-selfness *per se* is as dangerous as quasi-otherness *per se*. One quasiness versus the other quasiness would finally lift the discrimination and pave the way to salvation (from his own bondage of perseitas!).

Selfhood and universe are only the inside and outside of the same illusion. The realization of completeness however, has all characteristics of universality, without presuming an external cosmos and has likewise all characteristics of individual experience without presuming an ego-entity.[11]

Cosmos or order (in Greek) con-fronts us as quasi-onlookers with the very same *ordo et connexio idearum sive rerum* and our self-identification with it can be likened to the identification with the (human law of) causality or rationality, determinability. 'Idea cum ideato vero convenire debet! Ideae creant et creantur. Ideae sive intelligentia et res intellectae sive ideata *idem* sunt.' How to identify with such quasi-ego and quasi-id as 'idem' if not by self-experience where quasi-otherness agrees to *con-venire*, to re-cognize its reciprocal complementing wholeness via the pair-concept of receptivity? The true knower has to know no other *per se* as quasi-knower versus quasi-known, but only via knowing with a two-way traffic for the pair-concept. The quasi-other is his 'own' missing link: the complementary half for the pair-concept. Like two hands and two eyes are considered as natural requisites for man to be natural when not presuming quasi-twoness what is only a pair-concept. So the quasi-two must 'come together' while they are already together as 'twins' and still a pair-concept symbol for wholeness to grasp. The quasi-two must come together to intuit their oneness via together-ness. They must discover what they are already: together a pair-concept since only so can the whole 'be' whole and 'be conceived' whole. The whole all-one and one-all: the same! *Con-venire* reminds us of *co-ire* which is to say the way of *Amor Dei sive Amor Naturae*. Then 'Adam *knew* Eve' not a knower versus a known but re-versus, re-turned to original oneness as a pair-concept to restore the mission of creation in each pro-creation by voting 'pro'.... Zoharic and Pre-Zoharic illumination stems from the pair-concept. Elohim created Man; male *and* female, He created them, just as if two quasi-others lift the veil of quasiness. It is convenient to re-establish and re-assess the original oneness again and again by acting as if re-enacting the same play of cosmic-divine entelechy. Man is composed of mind and body. Man is composed as male and female. A divine-cosmic composition of a pair-concept to conceive wholeness via pairness in cosmic-divine orgasm....

To experience is to know otherlessness via reciprocal receptivity of the pair-concept. The quasi-halves institute and con-stitute (together) the pair-concept in the ideal way of:

idea = ideatum (i.e. ideans = ideatum)
natura naturans = natura naturata
Deus deificans = Deus deificatus.

Knowledge as love excludes otherness and knower or known are reversible, uni-versible the very same uni-verse: extro- or intro-'vertible' sameness: *Echad* like Yahweh-Elohim!

For that which clingeth to 'another' thing there is a fall, but to that which clingeth not, no fall can come. Where no fall cometh, there is rest, and where rest is, there is no keen desire. Where keen desire is not, naught cometh or goeth, there is no death, no birth. Where there is neither death nor birth, there is neither this world, nor that, nor in between . . . it is the ending of sorrow [i.e. about quasi-otherness *per se*!]. There is, disciples, an Unbecome, Unborn, Unmade, Unformed. If there were not this Unbecome, Unborn, Unmade, Unformed, there would be no way out for that which is become, born, made and formed, but since there is an Unbecome, Unborn, Unmade, Unformed, there is escape for that which is become, born, made and formed.[12]

What is the escape? It is quasiness: quasi-Unborn and quasi-born; quasi-Unbecome and quasi-become; quasi-Unmade and quasi-made; quasi-Unformed chaos, tohuwabohu, deluge (formless?) and quasi-formed. It is quasiness: *sive* = or. *Siveitas* = eitherness, 'otherness' . . . ! So has the first axiom of Spinoza formulated the cardinal theme I like to ponder upon:

Every(-'thing' or -'thought') which is (or is 'conceived' as 'being' or 'concept') is either in itself (or conceived in itself as 'being' or 'concept') *or* in another (quasi-self versus a quasi-other), of which it can also be 'said' again that it 'is' (or is 'conceived') either in itself *or* in another (quasi-self versus quasi-other) which, etc. etc. *ad infinitum* . . . !

Either/or as versus neither/nor with the little 'n' as abbreviation for *negatio*. What *negatio*? *Omnis de-finitio, de-terminatio est negatio.* It cannot be 'so' as 'so *per se*' or 'not so *per se*' either. *Per se* admits *per alium* (as pair-concept!), while quasiness evades negation via definition or via determination which are both the outcome of *causa sive ratio* with the inbuilt tendency (of the pair-concept): *vel sui vel alius.* Is '*vel*' an allusion to 'velum' to unveil or re-veal the quasiness and via quasiness the identity of wholeness, oneness? *De-'finitio'* of which the arch-rationalists and arch-causalists are so unspeakably proud, makes the *in-finitio* sliced to have sliceness instead of wholeness. The 'in'-finite is 'in' the 'finite' pointing at its quasiness to ponder at, to marvel at in enlightenment . . . ! When onesided applied to 'otherness *per se*' or to 'selfness *per se*' it must be leading to causality or rationality via determinability. Sic! But Spinoza (within the framework of quasiness) allows acausality or irrationality leading to indeterminability when *causa sive ratio* is intuited: *vel sui vel alius* and the '*vel* and *velum*' reveals the mystery . . . ! *Either* (not only phonetically) is an encapsulated *other*, but quasi-other and otherness *per se* has no sense as eitherness *per se* has not. They are pegs, expedient means or makeshift ways to express the inexpressible (so Lu K'uan Yü is hinting at). Thus for Spinoza: *tamquam, quatenus, quamvis, sive, vel*, etc. are tools for such instrumentality like scaffolding which helps erect a building; but after birth you cannot live in the scaffolding, the 'prenatal' state (of mind?) like a matrix feeding you 'later' post-natal with the same maternal 'cake' of a fake any more. In life you need a post-natal home with its responding and corresponding reality and you have to be guided by Spinoza, that there is no 'when', no 'after', no 'pre' or before'. *Pre per se sive post per se* are both pre-post-erous: a pair-concept again! As a type of quasiness via eitherness one is no longer horrified by the phantom of irreal (acausal) otherness *per se*. I can easily attain illumination and salvation when I can in-'tuit' (not ex-'tuit'! as e-(x)-'vidence') quasiness and via it quasi-otherness versus quasi-selfness causing quasi-separation and bringing quasi-sorrow. All-oneness and one-allness in the omni-awareness of *omnia animata sumus* disperses the darkness of obscure pseudo-separation which is only separation from assumed or pseudo-*perseitas*, so to speak. Here please ponder why the first axiom is the *proton axioma* and also the *proton pseudos* when you fail to intuit quasiness and get lost in des-pair not recognizing the pair-concept with quasi-otherness, para-otherness or pseudo-otherness. Yes! Then – after illumination I find it not too difficult to withdraw my own projection of a sub-'ject' versus an ob-'ject', both a pro-'ject' of a pair-concept'[13] which I have to retro-'ject' it again into the indivisible wholeness or individuation. Sic! I cease to claim and proclaim loneliness, I know with Heschel: Man is Not Alone! Man lives not by bread only (or alone)! I-mindedness is no longer a prerogative and monopoly of my special 'I' with cosmic-divine exceptionality, but for *all special, exceptional 'I's* as well. (*Nos*) *omnia animata sumus!* And all 'I's are quasi-others to each other and unquasi otherless too. As in the Ode of Joy of the Ninth – apocalyptic – Symphony of Beethoven:

> Deine Zauber binden wieder,
> was die Mode streng geteilt.
> Alle Menschen werden Brüder,
> wo dein sanfter Flügel weilt!

We – I and you, my allo-critical reader – are *all* I-'saying' beings with the same and only quasi-other I-mindedness: we are brothers of the very same father indeed. All of us can say: I and the Father are One. We and our Father are One. And the Father can say: I am that 'I am'. I am [is] every 'I am' or I and all children are One, all-one and one-all.

In the newly found Spinoza letter to Lodewijk Meyer of 26 July 1663, which is included with a commentary in this symposium, Spinoza speaks cryptically as follows:

> ... that the Son of God is the Father himself, this I believe follows very clearly, etc.

The same one and oneness already seen in so many exoteric and esoteric tones and overtones has been the goal for seekers of illumination. ...

The same oneness, all-oneness or one-allness via the quasiness of twoness, of pairness or multiness must lead to omniality in omni-awareness of *omnia animata sumus sive omnia animantia sumus. Animantia sive animata* is to be likened to *creator sive creatura. Idea (ideans) sive ideatum: con-venire debet* because the human mind is separating them in the discrimination and dichotomy which will be dealt with later until final enlightenment is attained.

> When a man is fatally ill, his relations gather round him and ask: 'Do you know me? Do you know me? . . .' Now until speech is merged in his mind, his mind in his breath, his breath in his vital heat, his vital heat in the Supreme Being, he *knows* them [as quasi-others *per se*]. But . . . when his speech is merged in his mind, his mind in his breath, his breath in his vital heat, his vital heat in the Supreme Being, he does *not know* them [via quasi-otherness].[14]

When knowing, he always knows 'another' as quasi-knowable known via quasi-otherness versus quasi-selfness, versus himself, the quasi-knower. Hence the question in order to test his ability to dichotomize and discriminate (quasi-otherness *per se*, i.e. any other than me as 'not-you'). Sri Krishna Prem draws light from madanya (i.e. other than myself!) to include in such disegotizing self-emancipation all me-s: mine and yours. To ask then: Do you know me: as outside you, apart from you in a fake-separation of senses and sense-reality, and not yet daring to unmask the fake? In a reality where you cannot 'realize' the quasi-irreal, irrational or acausal, indeterminable, being outwardly mostly perturbed in your self-isolation of existence. If you feel attracted to a teacher like Hui-Neng, then you may realize inwardly the imperturbability of the essence of mind. Spinoza equates for God *existentia* with *essentia, ens* and *esse*, being and Being, *wesen = sein* and *Wesen*, verb and substantive to substantialize the all-oneness or one-allness indeed, for to think of thinking with no thoughts (to singularize, dualize, pluralize but omnialize instead!). It helps a lot if you feel near to the challenge of Tat Twam Asi: that you are. Not what you think you are as Only-you or you-alone or supreme *exception* among all you-s. You are the *acceptance* of universality and omni-versality and you will discover or uncover the veil (*vel, velum*) to intuit: it is a crime to dis-criminate to di-chotomize in order to create fictional quasi-otherness *per se*. A phantom-problem which Max Planck deplores so much and explores so deeply, and indeed with great success, is on the way to enlightenment. Having created fake-otherness the fake-creator is himself haunted by his own fake-creation with phantom-otherness turning creator versus his creation and vice-'versa' (as vice or sin!). Enlightenment can only help to show the phantomization as a projection of one's own unknown, unable to be integrated into whole-allness of oneness. . . .

Nothing is apart from the *whole*, from the *all-one or one-all*, from the very same and apparently very unsame or so-called 'other', reciprocal other and ergo no unreciprocal or other *per se*. . . . Things seem to be only a 'part' of each other (while each-otherness a continual pair-concept becoming a whole-concept indeed!). This seemingly 'quasiness' makes things appear as if 'apart' from each other while only a concept of each-otherness in pairness and fairness to say of them. . . . The phantom-creator forgets so quickly, too quickly perhaps that 'otherness' is his own projection and conception of the unknowable but livable wholeness of life: *omnia animata nos omnes sumus*. There is nothing other *per se*, thus nothing outside or beyond wholeness save its 'concept' with quasiness. . . . The projection can always be withdrawn when the projector intuits into such playfulness of a quasi-subject versus a quasi-object or object versus subject. It can be withdrawn when – in the description of the Upanishad – speech is merged in the speechless mind and via all the media of quasi-otherness into the Supreme Being or Supreme Intellectus of *causa sive ratio vel sui vel alius* and the *vel* or *velum* uncovered from the very same quasi unsame. Then you can no longer claim discriminative otherness as before when you had 'names' to name the nameless phantom (of otherness): when names are so handy for such particularizations as me, you, him, her and it, and following from here singularization, dualization and pluralization is keeping you a-way from your way of you-fulness to you-lessness, from ego to id as idem in omnialization via experienceable omni-awareness of *omnia animata sumus*, i.e. *infinitos* (*infinita*) *sive aeternos* (*aeterna*) *esse*. Sic! Omniality reveals to us: to all me-s as one, to all you-s as one, to all he-s as one, to all it-s as one-allness or all-oneness indeed.

In early babyhood the reverse process takes place when the mother starts to confront the baby with toys dis-'guised' as the whole world: the human-toy-world, the animal-toy-world, etc. It is no wonder that the baby is taking the toy-world seriously, while later on adults take the serious world as toys to play with and display only: the *comedia divina*? In accordance with ancient tradition and insight into Maya the mother is pointing to the dancing toy-world (of Shiva?) with divine joy: all children and all men like children become like brothers again. The baby does not see its mother via otherness as we are used to see one another (otherish!) but she seems otherless. Mother and son are *one* as father and son are *one* as mother and father are *one*. One-allness is mirrored in one-allness again and again. . . . The father-oneness is not so graspable unless the cosmic-divine pair-concept is experienced with its permeating magic wholeness. The mother does not see the child via otherness and not even via quasi-otherness, but always via the invisible and indivisible link of the eternal umbilical cord and accord with the identity of 'I' and the mother-child are *one* 'matrix' or pattern of oneness.

The toys for the child are willing actors able to re-enact the play of the world of 'otherness *per se*'. It is a show for the baby as later for the adult mature enough in *causa sive ratio alius* and ripe in causalizing or rationalizing life, although not yet ready to be vitalized by *vita*, itself, by life, unknowable life. *Vivat vita!* Only the few, the very few discover or uncover the quasi-otherness and see the show as mock-show re-projected by our retina and its scenario to split seeing into quasi-seer versus quasi-seen as if quasi two others *per se* and against each other so. Via toys, the different worlds, such as animal-kingdom, thing-kingdom, plant-kingdom and man-kingdom with advanced citizens as republicans, peace is prevailing in all these worlds: toy-peace as long as it can last with toy-war when atrocities have their serious toy-reality. . . . And they are still all so near and dear to the as yet indiscriminated baby-mind, while the mother tries to pacify when continuing to teach discrimination of 'what' the toys are, of 'what' the toy-world is. 'What' is this? – A dog. 'What' is that? – A house, etc. Luckily the baby is not taught by the mother what the baby is 'himself'. It has plenty of time to hear the message: to know thyself! And it will then easily follow the rule to prefer to know the 'other' and to 'love' itself rather. The baby instead knows with no teaching 'that' it is and 'that' life includes father, mother, toy-worlds nothing else beyond it, the baby itself, as the very centre of every-'thing' and every 'thought'. Later it will easily continue to claim and proclaim central self-attention from everybody. . . .

With picture-books the adults are proud to display discriminating know-ledge of 'this' and 'that' as different and otherish, and the child plays and lives playing such cosmic-divine display . . . until under the supervision of the schoolmaster (with no 'vision') it learns to become as serious as possible or learns to show that it can learn it, where needed. Sic!

For the discriminating adult the world is only a world when discriminating otherness, is in it at its best; and thus the best way so far to present man and mankind to the child is by 'playing' discrimination, until it learns the lesson well and lives all its life playing in the way. For the discriminating adult the world is only a world of cause and effect in order to be 'effective', real. I am indebted to Sri Madhava Ashish for pointing to Ibn ul'Arabi: 'that the real cause of every effect is "non-existent" in the sense that it does not exist objectively anywhere.' And this comes much nearer to Spinoza's equation: *causa sive ratio* and to the only human version of causality and rationality of what *per se* has no cause, no reason as the principle of indeterminacy teaches us again to remind us the truth of 'I am', the way of 'I am' as *life* itself.

When we ponder and self-reflect with respectable sincerity via the mind conscious of ourselves, of God and of the world (of things), we do not find them as different or differentiated separate entities *per se*, but rather aspects, levels, plans or dimensions of omni-consciousness in which we are aware of *omnia animata sumus*. The world is not the world *per se* without man to conceive it 'as' a world for him and with him. The world is thus a world of the child, of the boy, of the girl, of the man, of the family, of society, of the nation, and with all the vistas of our *vis-à-vis* to 'it'. As children we call the adults the 'others', then later as adults we call the children the 'others' and fail to see the 'quasi'-otherness with reciprocal receptivity, so to speak. We

259

fail to see the alternating role we with our I and I-mindedness are playing in the world as seen by 'us' and existing only as such a seeable world. The picture-book presenting the world as real, changes later with the picture-world presenting the non-real, the quasi-real with quasi-otherness and this again is a play on a higher level of cosmic-divine interplay of man and uni-verse as one wholeness via quasi-discrimination. In the Chinese tradition of thinking, one picture can say more than ten thousand words with pictorial sayability can do. Thus the baby learns more from the picture-world than from the description about the word-world. And the man on the path to knowing himself via quasi-otherness of the world which he presumes to be 'otherness *per se*', again feels released from the deluge of words in order to grasp the wonder of the silent-word created by the divine *word* (equated with thing and matter in the Bible language).

> What *God* was, was the *word* . . . the Lord gave the *word* and great
> was the company of those who made it public!

While on the school-bench, fresh after the kindergarten where all the days of the week were as full of enthusiasm as the days of creation, I had it so freshly in mind, fresh as in the Garden of Eden through the magic and holiness of togetherness between God and Man with no otherness whatever between them . . . until the sin of knowledge split the togetherness in quasi-two: quasi-knower versus quasi-known. Man versus God but God uni-versus (*vis-à-vis*) Man when such togetherness highlighted the godlikeness of Man as if menlikeness of God. Man lives with God, in God and in him. After the sin (of quasi separating sameness as quasi-otherness *per se* knowledge acknowledges it), lifeless knowledge replaced unknowable life. . . . The tree of knowledge in Eden appeared so pleasant to the eyes awakening the desire to become wise, when separating knower from known while ignoring the via knowing. The via or way of 'I am': truth and life! This had to bring the expulsion from Eden into the exile of the world of otherness *per se*, depicted and worded as a substitute for the invisible and wordless one and same. In the world of exile or Diaspora oneness has been quasi-dispersed into multifariousness, unity into duplicity and multiplicity to keep company in the solitary loneliness of the 'I' and its I-mindedness. In the world was the reign and the terror of *ratio sive causa(alius!)* as a protector against the horror of otherness *per se* with siding for right or wrong to which the phantom of 'otherness' ought to be ascribed. Until then, and before finally naturalizing in such a world of obliging otherness *per se*, I still could admire and believe with all my heart, with all my soul and with all my power in that motto in front of my school-benches:

> Mit Gott fang an, mit Gott hör auf,
> das ist der beste Lebenslauf!

Namely to begin with God, to cease with God, is the best course life can take. I was ready to accept it then that way when starting to think of myself, of God and of the world (of things: *omnia animata!*) before Spinoza could teach me the hidden identity of such a triad. Later I have been so surprised to learn that Spinoza, this unique god-thirsty and god-intoxicated teacher, could be branded and nailed on his cross as godless: *male-dictus*, while hailed by the very few as saviour and *theissimus*: *Bene-dictus*. Where did they claim to have found in him godlessness? In: the *omnia animata sumus*? In: *sentimus experimurque nos aeternos esse*? When everything which is, is in God and no-thing (and no-thought either) can neither be nor be conceived without God. No-thing on that infinite way: *via infinitis attributis* to experience one's own infinity again and again *ad infinitum*? Via incarnations and discarnations leading through quasiness (of otherness) to re-incarnations and re-discarnations so long until the quasiness of dis- and of re- is fully revealed in eternal revelation. . . . After school and schooling under the aegis of 'otherness *per se*' I had to change my school-motto to fit better the godless I-mind than the I-less god-mind since Eden.

> Mit Ich fängt 'es' an. Mit 'Es' hör ich auf.
> So wirr der Lebenslauf!
> Wie komm ich 'ichlos' nur darauf . . . ?

'It' begins with 'I'. With 'it' I ceases to be: So confuse the course of life! How can I I-less only discover 'its' enigma . . . ? How? Not via otherness and not backed by *causa sive ratio* (*alius*), but by quasiness can otherness be desintoxicated to appear as quasi-otherness. Not by God alone, not by I alone as if two Gods, two sub-stances which cannot lead after Spinoza to man's salvation on the path of: a quasi-knower versus a quasi-known, but only of the via called: knowing and uncalled: living with a threefold identity involved, ripe for self-realization indeed. Enlightenment does not enlighten when realizing otherness but quasiness in it and turning it into me or me into it = idem. Ani into Ayin again as the indeterminate, undefinable with no *creatio ex 'alio'*, i.e. *ex causa sive ratione* (*alius*) but exless as 'X' *ab nihilo positivo*. Thus *ordo et connexio idearum sive rerum* is identifiable again with the whole of (*causa sive ratio*) *causalitas sive rationalitas*. Man then is not under the law of *ratio sive causa* but *one* with that law of quasiness, namely of: *sui sive alius*.

> Everything which is, is either in itself or in another. Whatever is, is in God and no-thing can either be nor be conceived without God [as the supreme identity of either or and of neither nor: revealed in quasiness, *tamquam, quamvis, quatenus*, etc.].

Quasiness is so baffling and otherness is also puzzling. In the first axiom of the *Ethics* Spinoza reconnects *Genesis* of being and *Gnosis* of being conceived.

So this axiom is the Genesis of beginning as quasi-beginning with otherness as quasi-otherness and hence followed by quasi-duality, quasi-plurality. The dilemma is solved and dissolved into *causa sive ratio sui* via such con-fusion. Confusion is a beginning for the mind to make quasi thinkable the unthinkable thought of beginning (and ending) in the light of *M-ens constans, substans infinitis attributis* impressed by absolute infinity and craving to express it again and again as infinity with no beginning and no ending unless when 'thinking' of *causa sive ratio* (of) quasi-*alius sed non alius per se*.

 . . . with what should I begin now when speaking and thinking of such quasiness with quasi-otherness *per se*? How should I begin to connect esoterically the Genesis of such an ethical axiom pointing to quasi-otherness with the Genesis of the Biblical axiom pointing at 'heaven *and* earth' presented (to the eyes and the sense-conditioned mind) as quasi-otherness *per se*? Am I wise enough to begin not with a word nor with a letter, a capital letter to celebrate such beginning or rather with that which usually as a phrase and sentence marks its ending: the full-stop? A point pointing with the very same right to a full-start in order to show the acting of a full-stop quasi-stopping the beginningless (and endless) flow of order and connection of ideas or things to save me from the horror *vacui* of no-thingness. Cosmos is this 'order' and it is quite in divine cosmic-divine order to have no beginning or ending as self-limitation of the limitless, causeless, reasonless, thingless, thoughtless God or Ayin (standing for indeterminability) or Point (standing for no-dimensionality).

Euclid translates it into meta-geometry to suit the *mos geometricus* and to handle *forma sive essentia* as quasi exless *ex-istentia*: the great unknowable $X = $ life. Le Chayim! Elohim Chayim. I stumble over words when pointing to wordlessness via quasiness while starting to speak of a quasi-beginning in accordance with Bible and *Ethics*. The same Bereshit in both is pointing to otherlessness. So I am happy to use a letter and a capital letter, speaking, as 'I' and at the same time to use the unusual point as a capital-point of such capital paradoxical dilemma as beginning, or *prima causa*. After Spinoza it would also mean a *prima ratio* for me, the *prima persona* in a world of persons and things. With what should I then begin, when speaking of beginning which is only a quasi-beginning before revealing the occult enigma of such quasiness even so far as to the first axiom of the *Ethics* and the first Bible verse of Genesis? And perhaps I have to point to quasi-genesis and quasi-gnosis in order to avoid having to explain the exless plain unknown of me and of it as the very same and unique enigma. Me as I is knighted with the capital letter, the highest rank among letters reserved for men of letters only. With 'what' should I begin if there is no real 'what' for and of my I-ness and I-mindedness but only quasiness containing infinite potentialities of absolute infinity? So I would rather obey Maimonides and Spinoza, when both replace the quasi-knowable 'whatness' or *quidditas* with the unknowable but experienceable 'thatness', i.e. to live and to experience life as life when 'I am' is the Way, the Truth and Life itself! Am I wise enough in my rhapsody of quasiness and quasi-beginning to begin with a few points as . . . to show that my beginning phrase is phrasing no beginning *per se* but as if coming from some-where and going into some (other) some-where, while the vagueness of such someness (the pillar of indeterminacy or of *causa sive ratio sui*!) makes that 'where' a quasi-where to equate it with no-where (i.e. no where *per se*!)? So as if coming from some-where as no-where (*per se*) there can be no real or unquasi beginning or end. Philosophers ask: is there in such vague whereness or some-whereness (as no-whereness), anything at all with its own (or quasi-own) existence *per se* quite apart from the only reality to realize for 'us' and for 'our' existing mind asking questions for which there are no answers, making thus all questions non-questionable but quasifiable indeed? Any answer would contain a cause or a reason which would be a quasi-cause or quasi-reason for quasi-otherness to ex-plain the exless X, the own unknown plain life: *omnia animata sumus cum essendi fruitione*! Not: *cognoscendi fruitione!* So I may continue to say that any answer could contain a cause or a reason for some-thing (or some-thought) which by the nature of someness or quasiness is *causa sive ratio sui* (*sed non alius per se*!). Is there indeed anything? Is there indeed any thought before any thought? In such no-man's land there can only lead as guide the Great Maggid of Mesritch who was so interested in exploring his own unknown 'before' thinking anything at all in its thinkability. He was on the same path as Buddhist teachers of meditation who teach to try not to think anything at all. The Maggid did not know of Saraha exploring the beyond of form of thought (form), i.e. ante-causal or ante-rational so to speak with the purpose to parallel the Spinozistic trend. Let me now continue in the flow of thoughts: there is no otherness *per se* but only quasi-otherness with quasi-*perseitas* to remind the I-mindedness hunting for otherness of the indeterminacy latent in every apparent determinacy as quasi-determinacy indeed. And so quasiness does apply to any of the concepts: 'before', 'after' and 'when' as quasi-before, as quasi-after and quasi-when. Thus to think of 'pre' *per se* and of 'post' *per se* must become preposterous. Instead speaking of Monism or Monotheism and deifying a number for a numberless concept, it would help better to consider that very same word 'one' as the indefinitive article, namely one, as some-one and leading to the revelation of *causa sive ratio sui* via indeterminacy. Now when approaching the concept of a so-called 'beginning' as quasi-beginning, we can better re-read the Bible text of Bereshit:

> 'with' the beginning Elohim created Heaven and earth: [as if two, but a pair-concept involving wholeness] Everything which is, is [as if two] either in itself, or in another [itselfness].

Perhaps let us try to reformulate for better palatability the verse of Bereshit:

Everything Elohim created 'with' a beginning is
either (quasi) heaven or (quasi) earth: the divine pair.

When thinking this thinking process of the flowing *ordo et connexio causae sive rationis* there is a need for the dichotomy to add: *causae sive rationis alius*: pointing to quasi-otherness. And this implies quasi-beginning: 'with' (which is the starting point) to start 'with' . . . and to point to the ever fleeting and never graspable (otherness!): *now* our I-minded awareness is always so anxious to relate *now* to something quasi-else as a demonic 'other' i.e. other *now*. And this then appears as a before, or an after. Only otherless self-awareness of *omnia animata sumus cum essendi fruitione* as instasis, enstasis can bring illumination and liberation to live the own unknown, exless 'X', with X-rays radiating *causa suitas* or indeterminacy implying *ratio suitas*. This magic word 'with' initiating and introducing 'creation' also plays an important role when reifying ideas or ideifying res, things, namely that the common use of 'without' versus 'within' seldom discovers how the composition of such a little word gains a great significance. 'With'-in and 'with'-out imply the relatedness to concepts of 'in' as in, in-side or in-sight, etc., and also of 'out' as in: out-side, or out-sight etc. – baffling and puzzling indeed. So *mens* quasi mentifies *ens* and *ens* entifies *mens* . . . we live everything as onto-logy – logy of logical usage encapsulated in words as *entia verbalia*. The first Bible verse matches excellently with the first axiom in the *Ethics* in demonstrating the first principle of a quasi-beginning, a quasi-firstness. Bereshit is only exoterically to mean beginning, but else the etymos means principle. It is not a numerical principle, but rather a numberless one of indeterminability full of magic and charm to inspire. . . . And when seeing indeterminacy in Genesis and Gnosis alike as *causa sive ratio sui*, then feel with such self-discovery of otherlessness as if you are alchemized, mesmerized. Otherness the great phantom is only quasi-otherness, para-otherness and the phantom is unmasked for ever, never to frighten anybody anymore.

The essence of life and nature, the secret of immortality, cannot be
found by dry intellectual work and selfish desire, but only by touch of
undiluted life: in spontaneity of in-tuition [not ex-tuition].[15]

These very warning words of Lama Anagarika Govinda have got their place among pathfinders to help point the rare way for pathseekers in the beginning of this book. Indeterminacy and *causa sive ratio sui* can help a lot for those on the path, when not sticking to the intellect only, but to look for Spinoza as guide that

God, God's Intellect and the things intellected by Him

via us, are the very same and otherless things: a full indivisible whole. Full is the whole earth with His glory, with His Intellect to point to all-oneness or one-allness.

Be-reshit, in the cryptic language, comes from rosh, head, principle, original, elemental, funda-mental, etc., all as epithets for truth. *Deus sive Veritas*. The notion of this principle of truth with a quasi-beginning implies eternal freshness: as if newly born or born again in enlightenment, delighted by the self-experience of the uncreated: genesis *sui* = gnosis *sui*! *Vivat suitas*! Spinoza speaks of *omnia animata*, not of *omnes animatos sumus* to identify with the omniality and totality of being and awareness. No extra-mundane God and no extra-perceptional life:

> Whatever is, is in God as All-life and no-thing can neither be nor be conceived [as 'being' identic with 'conception'] save in the all-wholeness of: *omnia animata*. . . .

We can now compare in our godlikeness equating *Deus sive Natura*, and then *Natura naturans sive naturata* with the creation of the world and of Man while always having in mind: *creator est creatura (idem)*:

> Elohim created Man in his own image. In the image of Elohim created He him [quasi-singular]: male and female created He them [quasi-dual, i.e. pair concept].

> 'With' the beginning Elohim created the heaven and the earth [as if two, but a pair concept].

Heaven (or quasi other than earth) and earth (or quasi other than heaven). Male (or quasi other than female) and female (or quasi other than male). To such quasiness has to be added a Zoharic hint: that 'in the very same secret in which heaven and earth have been created, has been Man created too.' Sic. And some 'Secret Sayings of Jesus according to the Gospel of Thomas' have something to parallel the unquasi secret and occult: common with Man and World alike as if to testify again: *creator idem est creatura*. . . .

> Jesus said to them: When you make the two one, and make the inside like the outside, and the outside like the inside, and the upper like the under side (in such way) that you make the man [with] the woman a single one, in order that the man is not the man [only] and the woman is not the woman only [but a pair-concept].

And when referring to heaven and earth:

> Salome said: Who are you, O Man? Jesus said to her: I am he who came into existence from that which is equal. . . . They said to him: Tell us who you are so that we may believe in you? He said to them: You test the face of the heaven and the earth and you do not know what is

265

'before' you! . . . If they say to you: Whence have you come? Say to them: we came from the light, the place where the light came into existence through *itself* alone.[16]

The 'Awakening of Faith' helps a lot to support this by pointing to such equalness:

> As all existence originally came to be without any idea of its own, it ceases to be also without any idea of its own; any thoughts arising therefore must be from being absolutely passive. . . . One should know that the proper state is that of the soul alone without anything outside it. Again, even this soul has no form and no thought by which we can conceive of it properly.[17]

We cannot conceive of it properly, but only quasily, as if, *tamquam*, in order to point that *m-ens* is a centre in the very midst of it all and as it all in all-oneness and one-allness. The great ocean with great oceanic feeling of the universality permeates drop and wave to make them forget drop- and wave-*diversity* and transmute it into *university* via quasity. That is to remember the homely omniality of *omnia animata sumus*: the ocean as ocean and not as water via drop-awareness or wave-awareness quasifying the substantiality via modality. Thales from Milet already thought of water as the best simile for omni-awareness. When on a journey in the middle of the sea, you can experience your own inner infinity mirrored by the sea and vice versa when quasi confronted with 'it' as 'you' and quasi before you and unquasi you yourself. Ergo: know Thyself! And has not already King Solomon, the Wise, experienced and recorded this experience of oceanic feeling coming as if from 'four unknowable and too wonderful things', to marvel at them and at us with him?

> The way of an eagle in the air, the way of a serpent upon a rock, the way of a ship in the midst of the sea and the way of a man with a maiden.[18]

There is a fourfold unknowable wonder of oceanic feeling of life. The very same as expressed: 'I am' [is] the Way, the Truth and life! The same one way with no otherness and no secondness of way and wayfarer: only one alone and all-one. Among these four similes for the quasi-similarity of life, water is the best of all. . . . Have we not been told on the very far horizon (of thinking back to the brink of memorability) about Oannes, the fishman, living in the water and coming out on land to teach man the wisdom of life *vis-à-vis* all its unknowability as only otherness can offer for a quasi-knower versus a quasi-known on the via knowing, but not of living? The teaching concerned the truth (and the way) that there is no horizon (*per se*) at all (but only in our thinking of our self-limitation of discriminative thinking: of heaven and of earth as if two!). There is only a limit to our seeing: in the midst of the sea with quasi-no beginning and quasi-no ending although we feel so protected by *causa sive ratio* when able to mean and lean on a quasi-beginning and a quasi-ending. And in deep meditation when mind is reflecting on itself, mind is to be likened to the midst of allness, to the midst of that ocean, forgetting any *causa* and any *ratio* (*alius*). They offer welcome outlets with their welcome limitations when transcending all that in a sudden flash on instant enstasis: *cum essendi fruitione* or with the oceanic feeling of omni-awareness: *omnia animata sumus* . . . (not *cognoscendi fruitione*).

To see the water and to speak of life and water as its simile . . . who can better be entitled to do so if not the fish living in such environment with environ-mental awareness? Light shed on the fish will show us how the fish thinks, sees and speaks as fish of the water and of its life 'in' it or 'as' it. Evans-Wentz himself, often deeply involved with the fish-simile, has found that 'the fish itself symbolizes all sentient beings, who like the fish in an infinite sea, are immersed in the Sangsara and it suggests Tilopas' power to lead them to freedom. The fish symbol is adopted by the early Christians probably from Oriental sources, conveys similar significance with respect to the Christos as the Saviour of Mankind.' The fish's standpoint can help for our enlightenment in the water of life eternal to stimulate self-inquiry about quasi-otherness and to understand quasiness as a wonder, tauma to marvel at . . . Inquiry about lifeless knowledge and about unknowable life will lift the separation into quasi-knower versus quasi-known on the via knowing. In our dark aeon called Yuga Kalpa, the end of which is supposed to be the beginning of an apocalyptic era of Aquarius, a new magic dawn of the messianic tomorrow, but is premonited today: now and here on Morrow's Eve with the enstasis of vision.

There is no way to realize the void before the future is come to be now! It is a mystery for the Rabbi Nachman of Bratslav to experience the Now itself as nowing of the quasi-before and the quasi-after as indivisible omniality. There is no coming, no becoming as it were . . . on the way when the wayfarer ('I am') is that Way, that Truth: Life! The quasiness transmutes the pseudo-duality, the para-otherness via the reciprocal receptivity of the pair-concept impressing and expressing wholeness, omniality!

Now what have some thinkers to say about fishes and of their thinking when expanding consciousness from 'now' into quasi-before and quasi-after and later via fish-illumination transcending quasiness or unquasiness at all? What? When now in the witness-box for Spinoza I have to show first how Spinoza himself does compare man and fish when regarding (discriminative) thinking with a quasi-beginning and a quasi-ending:

> If a fish (for which of course, it is impossible to live out of the water) were to say: 'if no eternal life is to follow this life and in the water, then I will leave the water for the land.'

And Rabbi Akiba seconds Spinoza and Spinoza's fish in its thinking by telling a story of a fox whose fox-wisdom has been outwitted by the fish-wisdom:

> A fox walking by the riverside, noticed the fishes therein swimming and swimming to and fro, never ceasing: so he said to them: 'Why are ye hurrying, what do ye fear?' 'The nets of the angler,' they replied. 'Come then', said the fox, 'and live with me on dry land!' 'Art thou called the wisest of the beasts?' they exclaimed: 'verily thou art the most foolish. If we are in danger even in our element, how much greater would be our risk in leaving it?'

And a pupil of Spinoza, Albert Einstein, is also attracted by the fish and the fish-simile. He thinks with arrogance about the fish's ignorance

> What does a fish know about the water in which he swims all his life?

And the Brihadaranayaka (Upanishad):

> As a large fish from one bank of the river to the 'other', so does the self move between dreaming and waking.

You may ask: dreaming what? Dreaming of land when sleeping in water and of water when tossed between dreams. It reminds me of Chuang-Tzu's dream of being a butterfly; when woken from the dream, he asked himself: did I dream to have been a butterfly or did the butterfly dream to have been me, Chuang-Tzu? Perhaps some fishes are so dream-wise that they dream like Chuang-Tzu similar dreams as well! I hope they will have a chance to meet to clarify the dilemma of such phantom-problem. The fish alternates his movement from one bank of the river to the 'other' while man can transcend the river on a raft and when having crossed the water arrives on the 'other shore'. Would he then still continue to stick to the raft and carry it with himself all his life, because it helped him *once* for self-transcendence (of quasi-otherness)[2]. So Buddha likened the raft to ponder on and meditate upon. . . . The quasi-two banks or shores of the river or of the sea are similes for the parallels, i.e. for para-otherness with no siding on one-sidedness versus 'the other *per se*'. The *Book of Change* speaks of such a golden secret of life while using the fish-simile:

> Heaven created water through the One. If a man attains this One, he becomes alive, if he misses it, he dies. But when a man lives in the power-air, he does not see the power-air just as fishes live in the water, but do not see the water. A man dies when he has no life-air just as fishes are destroyed when deprived of water.[19]

Through lifeless discriminating knowledge (of otherness *per se*!) man misses the twoless One, Echad, Advaita, because knowledge presents the fake of a cake which no hungry man can eat in order to live, but only to speak about or to describe it with lifeless words as substitute for unspeakable and indescribable life. This is to be experienced only in the totality of omni-awareness of *omnia animata sumus cum essendi fruitione* (not *cognoscendi fruitione*).

And the Secret of the Golden Flower with its blooming life-wisdom continues:

Perhaps there are fishes who believe that they contain the sea . . . !

You cannot see what you are yourself although you presume always to see 'otherness', because thinking of the 'seer' other than the 'seen' on the via 'seeing'. Castaneda's 'world – and self-experience' is so revolutionizing when he speaks of a quasi 'Separate Reality'.

The world has been rendered coherent by your description of it. From the moment of birth, this world has been described for us [as quasi-otherness *per se*].[20]

So seldom is left to us the 'chance' to live plain *'sine causa sive ratione (alius*!)'* while it has begun and has been explained from its beginning via quasi-otherness from the first moment of our ego-awareness *vis-à-vis* an 'it' reality as it were. To conclude the fish-story I have to re-tell you a Hindu-story of a fish. This fish went to a queen-fish and asked:

I have always heard about the sea, but *what* is this sea? The queen-fish replied: You live, move and have your being *in* the sea. The sea is *with*-in you and *with*-out you and you are made *of* sea, and you will end in sea. The sea sur-rounds you as your own being.[2]

The fishes do not know *what* the sea is. Man does not know what life is. Sea and life are unknowable for the living being but only livable! Sic! Water and life are our elements as revealed in elementary or substantial omni-awareness (*substantia per se sine attributis et sine modis*) of *omnia animata sumus*. Knowledge is singular, singularizing and dualizing, pluralizing the omniality reflecting on quasi-otherness and not self-reflection leading to self-realization (of the quasi-irreal). No whatness, no *quidditas* can be self-revealed only thatness can while being whatless (beli-mah as Sepher Yetzirah calls it!). We are all the very unquasi same or quasi-other: 'I am' that 'I am' and all this in order that 'ye may know that "I am" is the Lord!' that 'I am' [is] the Way, the Truth, Life. The Zohar seconds a certain Psalm to restore Man's distortion of the pair-concept:

It is time for Thee, O Yahweh, to lay Thine hand, for they have split Thy Law!

They have split the wholeness as if in two; in itself or in another (itself). So it happens in the Genesis and so in the Gnosis of the first axiom leading to pseudoness when taking quasi-otherness as otherness *per se*. Otherness *per se* is absolutized *perseitas* against (another) *perseitas*, so the speak. Constantin

Brunner approached such duality (of awareness) on two levels, aspects or dimensions of consciousness, while falsely assuming real two realities *per se*.

> But this is the greatest adversity, that unspeakable and fatal Proton Pseudos of all popular science: to assume as separately real, everything of which we are conscious in a separate way (as it cannot become otherwise conscious!) and thus to *split the unity of nature*.[22]

And Sri Madhava Ashish parallels Brunner from the other side in the East:

> It is important always to remember that these various principles themselves all coexist in a living unity from which, however classified for our convenience, they emerge as independent levels only by a process of abstraction or different *emphasis*. [23]

Different emphasis comes on different ways of becoming conscious and thus falsely presuming different *beings* not different *levels* of conceiving such same being. Here we can see how Spinoza himself equates 'being' with 'being conceived':

> Everything which is, is in God (the Supreme Being of Allness!) and no-thing can neither be nor be conceived without God (the Supreme Being of Allness!).

So everything is in everything and cannot be nor be conceived without allness of everything: *omnia animata via omnia animata* via omni-awareness of omniality and totality. Sic! Everything is the very same allness if conscious of it on quasi-other levels, pointing to conception of quasi-otherness *per se* as being *per se*. Being conscious is not a being outside that (being-)conscious, and therefore various levels, aspects or dimensions of being conscious never ever convey real otherness *per se* or other beings *per se*. Totality of being, of Nature is inseparable in spite of us not being able to become conscious of via synchronicity or simultaneity. The simile of lightning and thunder is well understood and fully explained as reaching our consciousness at different times via different sense-channels as to become aware of it. We never falsely presume that thunder and lightning are two different beings (*per se*) merely because of us and our media transmitting awareness in two quasi separate ways. Different awareness cannot imply different being *per se* claiming otherness *per se* as such! This is the *proton pseudos* and is connected with the first axiom:

> Everything which is, is either in itself or in another [as itself quasi!].

'Or' should mean not a real second other with a parallel-reality to the only one, but rather a parallel (para-other!) way of conceiving the one and same 'everything which is'. It is clear and without dialectical approach to argue about words and wording. . . . When quasi-otherness is replacing otherness by quasiness then pseudoness becomes only quasi-pseudoness and the true thinker will never point to *perseitas* while not recognizing it as quasi-otherness or relational, reciprocal. Self-experience and self-actualization finally will lift the veil of the fake-division as in the case of the fake-horizon separating heaven from earth (only for our seeing it as such!). 'If we ever turn our eyes to scrutinize too closely the mysterious bond which "knowing" constitutes, we find it vanishes elusively beneath our gaze, leaving us only the two poles: knower and known.' I would rather paraphrase Sri Madhava Ashish, and say knower *or* known, subject or object as alternating poles polarizing our causal or rational dis-crimination with quasi-otherness *per se* as it were. . . .

The very same pseudoness and quasi-otherness occurs when speaking of 'two' attributes *extensio* and *cogitatio* (*in-tensio*), both relating to alternating *tensio* and leading then to *ex-tuitio* or *in-tuitio*, so to speak. This means looking outwardly into quasi-otherness or inwardly into quasi-otherlessness when withdrawing our projections to become quasi-subject versus a quasi-object, while both are not two numerical entities, but: a pair-concept of one and the same universality and omniality. We will come to it much nearer! Awareness as omni-awareness of omni-identity is involving the odd identity between experiencer and experience as otherless same. This is – as now again revived and revealed again in a new spiritual renaissance – by the marvellous work of alchemy to trans*form* the form of the quasi-knower into the form of the quasi-known and accepting quasiness of both as initiation into the same unknowable via knowing: the mystery of life, to live but never to know it, be-cause it is you, your self. Ergo: know thyself! Alan Watts among the Pathfinders listed in my witness-box, should be heard and heard again:

There is simply experience. There is not 'some-thing' or 'someone' experiencing experience. . . . You never are aware of being aware. . . .

Experience is the wonder of wonder: the revelation, the enlightenment of otherlessness and of quasiness as well to marvel at. . . .

Life – we have seen it before – is likened to water and gains significance only for the (life – or water-) thirsty one in the vast desert with no water (or life) easily at hand. No definition, description, explanation, formula as H_2O and no formulation of the formless wonder as such (the wonder 'of' it and 'in' it while 'as' it itself!) can make you to marvel as at a wonder, and at its enigmatic essence via existence or existence via essence. Nothing of all this could help you to save your life in your thirst for water as only life = water. No-thing could still your craving for real water, real life than to 'realize' it via experience without otherness *per se* to overcome via quasiness. Water, like life, stands for matter, *materia*, mother, *mater* and is the archi-matrix of all. Water, the softest element (like mother in her softness to her child) can nevertheless destroy the strongest 'material' like iron cruisers in wartime. Water, *thalassa*, was once the very salvation for the armies who had crossed the great desert and reached the sea. They tasted the ocean and the oceanic

271

feeling not via words and verbalizations but wordless. Water is the *alma mater universalitatis* not *universitatis*! And so is life! I cannot say 'what' it is, but only 'that' it is, that it is me, my 'I am' as the Way, Truth, Life! Such thatness is marvellous beyond description and leading to beyond beyondness. . . .

> The sweep of mystery is not a thought in 'our' mind but a most
> powerful presence beyond the mind. In asserting that the ineffable is
> spiritually real, independent of your perception, we do not endow a
> mere idea with existence, just I do not do so in asserting: 'This is an
> ocean'!, when I am carried a-way by its waves.[24]

I am so glad that Heschel pointed to that 'oceanic feeling' and joined the ranks of the witnesses, to attract still more to join!

Water, ocean and the wonderful causeless, reasonless, nameless, indeterminable – that oceanic feeling brings 'out' what is always 'in' the substantial omni-presence and omni-awareness as co-conscious of *omnia animata sumus sine me, sine nobis*. It is as if the dust from a cosmic-divine mirror[25] is wiped off to let I-less self-reflections come through so baffling and puzzling as well. It is as if the *facies totius universi* looks via our eyes and via our mirrors mirroring universal reflections, but sometimes discrepancy creeps in; as Goethe has observed, how observers err while doing observations into creation and its quasi-beginning.

> The highest that man can attain in these matters is wonder; if the
> primary phenomenon causes this, let him be satisfied, *more* it cannot
> bring [as 'quantity' of whatness] and he should forebear to seek for
> anything further behind it: here is the limit. But the sight of a prime
> phenomenon is generally not enough for people. They 'think' they must
> go still further and are like children, who *after peeping into a mirror,*
> *turn it round directly to see 'what' is on the 'other' side.*

Goethe speaks of those in hunt for knowledge of 'otherness' who never think to 'turn inwardly' instead their own thinking behind or beyond thinking (single, singularizing, dualizing, pluralizing thoughts: atomizing or itemizing the wholeness!). Such turning would be like re-turning to the sub-stans of the in-stans, namely of that which stands 'under' every stans, standing and under every under-standing as well. The mirror has sides, when mirroring otherness or quasiness, and only animals are so well aware of it. *Homo sapiens* thinks he is how the 'others' see him and thus how he has to see himself via the looking-glass looking at his quasi-otherness as if it were seeable. The pupils of Prajapati (in the Upanishads) thought so wrongly and had to return several times to their master until they finally were told to discover the true is unseeable as the self is otherless in order to know truly their unknowable self as Life. And as about myself in the early stages of thinking as Spinoza teaches, I was not able yet to see his real image nor my real image either, because still imagining to see, means to see within the cleavage of quasi-seer versus quasi-seen. I saw only my little bewildered face looking into the glassy reflections of the looking-glass and I seldom caught glimpses of the imageless *facies totius naturae* (after Hui-Neng the *facies naturae meae verae!*): reflecting my own universality. The dilemma arose how to face one's own face as my own face before birth (before having become a quasi seeable 'seen' for a quasi-seeing seer to see it as his otherness!) without twoness. With a mirror I must expect to see mirrored twoness and otherness *per se* while mediating quasiness only. How then to face such awe-inspiring oddities emanating from the unseeable and unknowable self, while old masters still teach: know thyself? How? How then could I learn this and continue on the path, which Spinoza has gone unless he attained the goal of self-liberation (from self-bondage!)? This seemed the main lesson for a life-time to learn to ensure that I can avoid grafting skin-thin knowledge evolving and involving otherness *per se* only. The expounder of truth becomes the truth himself. The wayfarer on the way becomes the way himself when 'I am' identifies 'I' with 'am': as Life.

Goethe would have been pleased to see Sir James Jean showing him as us 'The Universe Around Us'

reducing the whole of nature to a mental concept, since the texture of nature is nothing but the texture of the space-time continuum. All this makes it clear, that the present matter of the universe cannot have existed for ever; indeed . . . the universe becomes now a finite picture whose dimensions are a certain amount of space and a certain amount of time. The creation of the universe lies as much outside the picture as the artist is outside the canvas . . . it is like trying to discover the artist and the action of painting by *going to the edge of the picture*. This brings us very near to those philosophical systems which regard the universe as a thought in the mind of its creator.[26]

But this can still be likened to peeping behind the mirror to see what is on the 'other side', as Goethe wisely warns onlookers and through-lookers via a looking-glass. This still involves otherness *per se* and is far from quasiness pointing to the principle of indeterminacy as in *causa sive ratio sui* (*sed non alius!*). Determinacy always likes siding with in-side or out-side, with in-sight or out-sight, etc. Some-thing can only de-termine something *else*, or *other* while quasiness dissolves otherness and elseness *per se* into self-determination in the way Spinoza speaks of. He speaks of the mind as an auto-maton, not as mechanical (rational and causal) com-puter or robot, but as self-teaching or learning that: otherless *causa sive ratio sui per se*. Sic! After Spinoza this can apply also to God, God's Intellect and the intellected things as objects for such subject-divine Intellect: the great divine cosmic auto-maton. From here

evolves: *creator idem est creatura!* Hence: *ideae creant et creantur* (*idem*).
Hence: *ordo et connexio idearum sive rerum* (*ideatarum, intellectarum*).
Hence: *omnia animata sive omnia animantia.* The grand omni-identity and
omni-awareness of totality via itself as *m-ens.* I would like to add to Max
Planck's instances of phantom-problems: ens or *mens. Mens* or *ens.* Hence
from 'I am' evolves: I = am and 'I am' = life . . . and ye may know that 'I am'
[is] the Lord! So Ezekiel points out tirelessly! (*Sein* = *Bewusstsein*.) I admire
Planck's Spinozistic approach of twoless seeing quasi-twoness, comparing it
as a parallel with Brunner's *proton pseudos* mentioned before.

MacGregor Mathers was tormented, like myself, with the phantom of
'otherness' and with a para-cabbalistic approach tries to solve the dilemma.
'Otherness' creeps in from the beginning of being *or* thinking (of being):
Genesis or Gnosis. The wonder starts quasi how does that 'other' = second
originate from the quasi-otherless 'one'? How?

> How, then, if 1 can neither be multiplied nor divided, is 'another' 1 to
> be obtained to *add* to it? In other words: how is the number 2 to be
> found? By *reflection of itself*, for though 0 be incapable of definition, 1
> is definable. And the effect of a definition is to form an Eidolon,
> duplicate, or image of the thing defined! Thus, then, we obtain a duad
> *composed* of 1 and its reflection. Now also we have the *commencement*
> *of a vibration* established, for the number 1 vibrates *alternately* from
> changelessness to definition and back to changelessness again. . . .[27]
> [Vibration from quasi-determinacy to quasi-indeterminacy or self to other
> and vice versa!]

So is made quasi graspable the principle of indeterminacy, of *causa suitas*
that *one* like some-one with 'someness' is void, de-void of any-thing to say
'what' it is. If unsayable then it can only be said 'that' it is: life! De-void of
number, definition *one* is the indefinitive point to point to *suitas* with no
otherness, no quasiness: shunya, Ayin while the meta-thesis or meta-noia of
it is Ani = I. I re-versed id. Id uni-versed I and I-ness. So life is vibration,
tension or *Panta rei* after Heraclitus, or *omnia animata* after Spinoza. And
tension tends vibrating or oscillating from in to out or from out to in with
alternating or quasi-alternating quasiness: a play of the Old Magister Ludi.
Hence the two or quasi-two attributes our mind is attributing to itself as self-
reflection: *ex-tensio* and mind or *in-tensio* (if the schoolmaster allows me to
coin such word?). When I want to know, then I expect to know 'what' being is
'other' than being itself. And I de-fine, limit its unlimited indefinability,
indeterminacy. Hence: *omnis determinatio* (*definitio*) *est negatio.* Hence:
omnis indeterminatio est affirmatio: so puzzling, so baffling as only a mystical
and occult self-experience can be. I must remind again the sceptic causalist
and rationalist (in his onesidedness) what a contemporary thinker, Vernon J.
Bourke, thinks about determinism:

it is said to be by way of negation according to Spinoza (epist. 50) and this means that universal substance is in its perfect form indeterminate, but is 'thought' to become [as if] determinate by a sort of logical 'absolute' perfection.[28]

Who clings to 'logical' perfection and to 'logical reality' while worshipping *causa sive ratio alius*, must discard as inconvenient the other side of quasi-otherness which presents the notion: freedom-necessity as a pair-concept or a com-position of one and its (otherness same) re-flection. Spinoza repeatedly says: the mind had to *re*flect on itself (without flection of otherness *per se*!). Creation is a com-position of heaven and earth. Man is a com-position of male and female. Man is a com-position of mind and body: as if two or as a pair-concept con-taining and attaining wholeness. God created Man: male *and* female. Man pro-creates mankind, male *or* female its members!

Now we understand why Planck was fighting with phantom-problems of quasi-otherness, of quasi-twoness like Don-Quixote with windmills to take out the wind. . . . In Hebrew wind and mind have the same word: Ruach! A phantom-problem discovers phenomena without 'logical' substance, for which 'logical perfection' is claimed and proclaimed via *causa sive ratio alius* or via *determinationis*. Q.E.D. . . . The vibration of which MacGregor Mathers speaks, oscillates as (if) between chaos and creation or between creation and chaos. Between 'that' and 'what' or between 'what' and 'that' as knowable and livable or as self and quasi-non self or other. Hence the first axiom of Spinoza applies with pseudoness and implies quasiness to ponder on self-reflection to attain self-realization via irreal quasi-otherness. Goethe, Spinoza's pupil wisely says: 'Nichts ist ständig als der Wechsel!' No-thing is con-stant save the change (the alter-nating faking quasi-otherness *per se*). 'One' when not self-re-flecting and taking the reflection as reflection *per se*, points to *perseitas*. Hence: know thyself! Ergo: Be it (not as you versus it, but uni-versus!) *one* when considering the process of reflection as an eidolon or as quasi-otherness, sees a quasi-image and (quasi) imagines some otherness *per se* with some thereness *per se*. . . . 'One' when not self-reflecting but allo-reflecting tempts so much the temptable knowledge (not only to dichotomize knowing into quasi-knower and quasi-known) as if two 'is' two *per se* and thus is evolving via the vibration of volution of *ordo et connexio idearum rerum, causarum ad infinitum* or rather a numerical, numero 'logical' infinity which seems to commence and seems to end where the limitation of numbers is supposed to end. So the same word 'one' has an alternative sense after the first axiom of Spinoza, namely *either* the indefinite article *or* the opening of the quasi-numerical *ordo et connexio idearum sive rerum*. The same applies to the word 'I': either a self-restricting entity, separated quasi from 'other' self-restricting entities called 'I' as well as called: you, him, her, it or all together: them. When self-reflecting thus seeing vanishing otherness or quasi-otherness *per se* as you *per* you, he *per* him, she *per* her, it *per* it, them *per* them while abolishing duplicity or multiplicity of *perseitas* and demanding omniality of it as omni-awareness of *omnia animata sumus* (including you, him, her, it and them all with all allness). Now, being familiarized with pseudo-otherness and pseudo-duality, we can share the grand vision of Max Planck and deal with the di-lemma of quasi-twoness ergo of twolessness Advaita so happily that Spinoza and Spinoza-lovers can learn from it. Learn when on the'way to the self via 'I am' [is] the Way, i.e. the way knowing, seeing, etc., up to the *via viae* or *via sui* like *causa sui*, like *ratio sui*. *Vivat suitas!*

Before learning through Planck's discovery to unmask the 'phantom of quasi-duality', we want to have and to keep in mind the cosmic/divine trend or tendency so to speak of reflection as *reflectio sui* or *reflectio alius* in accordance with the first axiom. Here is the phantomness! Beware and be aware of no eidolon (or duplication!), no image as Moses in the Decalogue warned so sternly: You shalt not make any image of Yahweh, Elohim! You cannot imagine a creator beyond an imaginable creatura via otherness. 'One' which is not the basis of exoterical Monotheism (or One-God Doctrine) when it is not identifiable with *causa sui, ratio sui* and is numberless, indefinitive indeterminable, indefinable, is then Ayin, the Void, shunya (Sanskr.). Via omniality with quasiness of eidolon or duplication – when defining it – means via image-appearance of the imageless, formless. Planck helps us a lot to unmask eitherness = otherness, as the phantomlike quasiness with *perseitas* seems to menace us often. It makes us frightened, thinking that in the dim light on the road, it must be a snake, and when coming nearer we discover to our blame-surprise: it is only a rope, which sometimes could be useful as well. We all have heard the ghost-story of the Doppelgänger, the double baffling so often of man and more animals when looking into the looking-glass, unable to handle the enigma of reflection to think of a real other one 'over there in the glassy existence of otherness'. Indian thinkers have overcome dualism not via 'monism' as with the oneness as a figurative number still in the fold of ordinal numbers and therefore quite inappropriate for the purpose needed here. They call it Advaita = twolessness rather than oneness to avoid the phantom of number when desiring to express the indeterminable: *causa sui* or *ratio sui*. Only Cabbala (not the *nugatores cabbalistae* known to Spinoza! despised by us as by him) introduced the pair-concept to transcend the temptation of number and numerical interpretation. Sic! Oxford-wisdom points to the 'pair' = a set of two, of parts forming a whole. That would mean from the first axiom onwards we have to beware of 'eitherness', not to take for granted 'otherness' *per se*. Our human mind in its setting of notions and words for such purpose, is too ready for otherness *per se* although being tormented by such own acceptance, but when indivisible wholeness is to be considered via self-reflection of the mind, then the mind has to avoid hypostazing self-reflection into reflection *per se*. The word 'two' means not 2×1 or two ones, to single ones as entities *per se*. Not: One plus *another*, *single* 'one', but a set to make aware of the whole via the quasi two parts forming it. Totality is never the sum of its parts. To be omni-aware of the whole in the quasi-parts as quasi-numerical only. This is the enigma of the pair-concept. Without it whole-awareness would appear im-paired so to speak. . . . Max Planck had the courage to unmask its *dis*guise. Yes. The truth is when we do in-tuit rather than ex-tuit that one is not alternating like a number, but oscillating, shifting the mind from form to formlessness and back again. From *existentia* to *essentia* and vice versa as uni-versa. From the determinate to the indeterminate be-cause of innate craving for otherness and for logical perfection or for logical perfect infinity. The same applies to the word 'two' or the figure '2'. It is not twoness against twolessness as if opposites (of polarizing thoughts). What is it then? It is a pair, a 'set' of two having no 'single' meaning and leaning as self-existent beings. Two is never to split into two single ones but rather '*per se*' a whole totality, omniality with no halfness to experience in it. Indeterminacy can thus be ascribed to 'one' in the same way as to 'two as pair' impersonating the impersonal whole *per se*. *Omnia animata sumus* via the acausal or irrational 'pair'-concept or 'one' concept implying indeterminacy!

The *Zohar*, in describing the sephirotic tree of life, speaks of pairs in the simile of the human body (embodying the soul like the soul ensouling the body), namely to appear as 'pair' and not as (numerical) two and twoness com-posed as single oneness *à deux*! This cabbalistic way, when free from anthropomorphous godlikeness of man or manlikeness of god, must have been found fit to befit the definition of knowability of attributes, which is only revealed in two as pair and not as number '2'. *Omnia et unum animata sumus. Omnia et unum idem sumus!* Knowability is only applied to the notion of pair with the trend of omni-awareness as pair-awareness. (Examples of pair-concepts: above-below; before-after; male-female; heaven-earth; mind-body; etc.) And so in accordance with the *Zohar* and Yetsirah Spinoza can assert that only of such pairness we can know 'what' they are (*quidditas* or *mah*) while of everything beyond (pair-thinking) we can only know 'that' it is or assert its 'thatness'. Via self-reflection or omni-awareness of *omnia animata sumus* we can know now 'wholeness' (including us the knower and the known as one via knowing), we can live the unknowable as 'thatness' or constant self-awareness. And here, even a man, thinking *maxima cum ira* about Spinoza, like Carl Gebhardt, has deviated in his uttermost and sincere attention in the quest for truth: to reconcile quasi-twoness with infinity while expressing it this way:

$$2:\infty$$

So, he thinks, should be presented the true relationship of the two knowable attributes to the 'others' while pointing to their all infinity *par excellence*! There is no 'otherness' and there are no 'other' attributes *per se* to think about

277

with our human intellect by self-attributing to ourselves the very same substantial essence of infinity *sub specie intellectis* and *praeter intellectum* as well. Sic! The cabbalistic 'pairness' helps us to omnialize any singularizing, dualizing and pluralizing tendency of the human mind after the causal or rational *ordo et connexio idearum sive rerum* only via self-identification. The human mind is so structured to thinking and living in pairs, like having two feet to be able to walk, two hands, two eyes, ears, etc. everything in pair-concept via the indeterminacy of quasi-oneness and of quasi-twoness as well. Sic! The pair symbolizes the whole to be the whole and to be-come it as being, while omni-aware as pair-aware.

At first I thought to change Gebhardt's simile into:

two: twolessness instead of two: infinity

but this still would have implemented to odd relationship of a number to (another) numberless infinity, while infinity is not a sum of infinite manyness added up beyond our ability to count anymore, being exhausted by such negative infinity while positive infinity bestows an oceanic feeling of illumination. So too many of us think of infinitely *many* attributes rather than of *countless* infinity of attributes! The definition of attribute after Spinoza would never allow such fraud and trick of the human weakness called mind. Causal or rational infinity would only mean an endless infinity beyond any chance to express it in the realm of figures. Infinity points not to endless multiplicity but to *omniality* beyond number, world or otherness of limitations. Here such a set of two as 'Pair-concept' is no longer a number and has transcended its determinability successfully. A pair is numberless and forms a whole, while the whole as a whole *per se* is only available *per nos*: *sentimus experimurque 'nos' esse* when: omni-aware of *nos omnia animata* (not *animatos*!) *esse tamquam essentiam sive existentiam constituentes*. Sic! *Omnia animata sumus* not via two halves, but via one 'pair'. Two halves would contain only 'half' the truth of wholeness, while a pair contains the whole truth, the whole way, the whole life. Le Chayim!

Full is the whole earth of His glory!

Full and whole in and as every little grain of dust of earth and dust of stars alike. . . .

The *Zohar* is not tired to assert and re-asserts that His full glory is only where a 'pair' is symbolizing the 'whole' fullness indeed worthy of His blessing! After the *Zohar* Man has been sent to earth with the mission to know that Yahweh is Elohim, a divine pair! and . . . ye may know that 'I am' [is] the Lord! Yahweh = Elohim, *Deus = natura* as macrocosmic, macrodivine pair and whole and glory! We need the whole truth to intuit the full truth including our own unknown wholeness: The whole delight and enlightenment of the way by quasi-pairing the quasi-impair or quasi-otherness to 'know itself!' otherless and to overcome that phantomlike *perseitas*: as main obstacle to attain self-realization.

Now to return to Planck whom I promised to bring into the witness-box to help Spinoza when helping the puzzled and baffled Spinoza admirer over the stumbling block of quasi-twoness as pairness and of quasi-oneness not as number but as indefinite uncreate, *causa sive ratio sui:* to manifest all-oneness or one-allness and pair-oneness or one-pairness as well. The first axiom of Spinoza's *Ethics* has already the first pair of: either/or. The first Bible verse of Genesis or Gnosis has already the first pair of: heaven and/or earth (not to read as if two, but as pair!). Like Man, whole Man, has been created as pair: male/female. When pairing they re-pair the error of quasi-otherness and quasi-twoness, and they become a couple again to re-experience initial wholeness as if via singleness, quasi-singleness or quasi-twoness (for some only double-singleness). Thus is sanctified the innate wholeness with the craving of return – re-turn to the root via root-awareness of omniality: *omnia animata sumus.* The Cabbalah shows this principle applied above and below in a Messianic identity of the way up with the way down. The very same way with quasi unsameness: 'I am' [is] the way, the truth and Life! Expanded I as pair identified with you (losing its other I-ness) and experiencing wholeness as pairness with the magic double indeterminacy full of spontaneity of enstasis in instant, sub-stant, constant now and here also an eternal pair and whole alike.

Now what about Planck and his quintessence? It is that

the problem which has been preying on one's mind is totally incapable of any solution at all – either because there exists no indisputable method to unravel it, or because considered in the *cold light of reason*, it turns out to be absolutely void of all meaning – in other words: it is a phantom problem!

The 'cold light of reason' or cause cannot induce us to enlightenment or illumination! Planck is one of the pathfinders Spinoza would have liked to join on the path. So I let them join and meet at the goal of the path. Phantom is defined to be an appearance (as if) 'with' no substance and this seems in sharp contrast with (other) appearances (as if) with substance and with substantial reference and cross-reference from the observer siding always versus an object to be observed. The whole gammut of instances for such phantom-problems to illustrate to us is like: right-left; above-below; I-you; I-it; self-other; wake-sleep; existence-essence; inside-outside; birth-death, etc. This is the outcome of dichotomy of the siding mind: siding always with a quasi-knower versus a quasi-known: both *per se* with one *perseitas* versus their ad-'versity'. When thus aspiring otherness *per se* or a dualistic *perseitas*, then the very same appearances appear as a quasi-opposite with no relational substance as versus the quasi-other *per se*, namely versus a known unrelational to a knower. Thus the interchangeable, reciprocal receptive relationship of observer and observed is negated – and that is the phantom and the phantom-problem. A pair of lovers are lover and/or be-loved, ergo knower/known as a pair-wholeness, excluding siding and quasi-otherness *per se*. In the phantom-problem the quasi-two remain for ever estranged and unquasi-two. They can never ever in-tuit co-ition (as reciprocal in-tuition!) as the same ition: exper*imur*que not exper*imus* like a reciprocal passivity, re-ceptivity or intransivity to help transcending siding and quasi-otherness in the quasi-two-way traffic which is a pair-traffic on the same path. The most exciting phantom-problem is the very same *modus* called: *extensus* or *cogitans* with the modality of para-otherness in viewing when viewing *seitas*: body *per se* or mind *per se* as single-*seitas* or pair-*seitas*! One *perseitas* as if parallel (or para-other) to one (same) *perseitas*. Would you then better accept: metallel than parallel? As metanoia better than paranoia? You have only to turn your mind with I-mindedness and siding versus quasi-otherness *per se* in order to reveal the 'other' side of such quasiness namely: otherlessness! Q.E.D. With a very keen self-introspection and sincerity of the unbiased mind Planck has already recognized that

> the mental process of the observation coincides in the unified self-consciousness with the mental process of the volitional impulse. Observed from without, the will is causally [or rationally] determined; from within it is free. We have to specify explicitly the viewpoint of the observation (and) it is but a question of time before it will gain universal recognition.[29]

How happy Planck would have been indeed to see in his lifetime such a standpoint gaining recognition while unmasking the phantom as quasi-phantom because defined as substanceless had to mean only relational as such, but not absolutely *per se*. The naïve observer had to abandon his arrogant and ignorant monopoly of 'obje-c-tive' siding so to speak. There is no 'versus' without implying otherness *per se*: one versus the 'other'. Everything is omni-versal and uni-versal but not dui-versal. Everything is the very same everiness as a whole excluding otherness *per se* for ever. It started already in the Garden of Eden when the human mind tasted 'otherness' of good versus evil and found it more attractive than the taste of (no-otherish!) life *per se*. Fulcanelli, the last living alchemist in our days, disclosed to Jacques Bergier in an interview that

> in the official science of today the role of the observer becomes more and more important. Relativity, the principle of indeterminacy, shows the extent to which the observer today inter-venes in all these phenomena. The secret of alchemy is this: there is a way of manipulating matter and energy so as to produce what modern science

call a 'field of force'. This field acts on the observer and puts him in a privileged position *vis-à-vis* the experiencer himself. . . . The essential thing is not the transmutation of metals, but of the experiencer himself.[30]

And here Ralph Metzner[31] has progressed on the path with ripening understanding: 'that we cannot be objective about anything external until we can be objective about ourselves [internal]. To be objective means to be *whole!* Now you can see why I listed Metzner among the pathfinders, as he experienced himself the 'practice of inner union on all levels of consciousness, separately or conjoined.' And so he became free of the *proton pseudos* of which Brunner warns us before, namely not to tear into two the whole of nature when assuming as separately real what appears so only on various quasi-other levels, aspects, planes or dimensions of consciousness. It is the very same consciousness of which Spinoza speaks at the end of the *Ethics* and at the end of the path when reaching the goal 'to be conscious of God, world and self' as the very same and otherless *omnia animata sumus* (*quamvis diversis gradibus* '*conscientiae*'*!*). It is so marvellous to add new witnesses for Spinoza quasi from the other side of dialectical or epistemological observation where siding is missing the wholeness and integration for self-realization. Roland Fischer came so near to me via Spinoza in the true experiential observation of the quasi-dualistic approach in daily life.

It is becoming increasingly clear that during the normal states of daily routine, the dualistic approach – with its object – subject *separateness*, 'Aristotelian' or two-valued logic, cause-effect relationship and reductionism – has a *physiological counterpart* in the relative independence or separateness during these states, of cortical interpretive activity from the subcortical substratum. The dualistic worldview, therefore, can be scientifically validated and is operational *only* during these states. At raised levels of ergotropic or trophotropic arousal, however, dualism, objectivity, etc. become non-operational, and are replaced by non-dualism, the experience of certainty and subjective insight. *Independent verification by an outsider is impossible*, since the very same cortical and subcortical structures and processes of man, the self-referential system which *creates inner experience*, are also involved in the 'verification' of that experience as external projection.[32]

Evidence as some ask it for quasi-rationalized mystical ex-perience, must be all-(e)-vidence not involving or co-involving the quasi-witness. And Metzner is seconded by Fischer, namely that such phantomlike '*independent verification by an outsider is impossible*' when in-sight into in-side mystical self-experience is concerned. Yes! With Spinoza to speak: we are *naturans* and *naturata*. *Creator idem est creatura!* And verification of such oneness by some outsight of some outsider would exclude the verifier and desintegrate the oneness (i.e. uniqueness) of *omnia animata sumus* with its oceanic feeling of such omniality beyond drops and waves. . . . Such verification would be outside of *causa sive ratio* (*alius*) by an *aliud per se*, alien to himself. This is Titanic crime. . . . The lifting of the veil of quasi-knower versus a quasi-known is only spontaneous transcending *causa sive ratio* and ergo quasi-otherness *per se*. In a larger study of a *Cartography of the Ecstatic and Meditative States*,[33] the relational or reciprocal referential link between 'self', the knower and Image-maker and 'I', the known and Imagined is so thoroughly described and circumscribed as well that it must lead to the 'unity' reflected in the experience of oneness with everything: oneness with the universe that is oneself!' For the Spinoza-research it is rewarding when pondering here how Spinoza himself approached such a cardinal problem, transcending knowledge to become experienceable beyond dichotomy of subject-object or knower-known, etc. Let us, therefore, accompany Spinoza when speaking of the mind and its *via operandi* and let us agree with a working hypothesis to consider a quasi-beginning of the mind, by pleasing the observer guided by *causa sive ratio* (*alius*). Cabbalists know of seventy variations how to ponder on such quasi-beginning of an unquasi endless (and beginningless) *en sof*. In the very same manner Spinoza approaches the singularizing trend of the mind with dualizing and pluralizing epiphenomena as it were to follow. Spinoza thus speaks of *res singulares* as if of *idea et ideatum* or as if reifying or ideifying by reciprocity so to speak. He then postulates an axiomatic truth for the *idea vera*: i.e. *cum ideato suo con-venire debet*! Here I feel like to paraphrase Spinoza in spite of '*invita Latinitate*' (*Ethics* II, 9):

> Ideae singulares eatenus tantum – respectu intellectus – debent dici (re-) convenire cum rebus singularibus. Nihilominus ideae et res *unum et idem esse* eodem modo ac idea (ideans) et ideatum; ac natura (naturans) et naturata; ac Deus (deificans) et deificatus . . . etc.

Ethics, II, 13 Lemma 2: 'Omnia corpora in quibusdam conveniunt' when paraphrased reads as: 'omnes ideae in quibusdam conveniunt'. *Ethics*, II, 21 (Quamvis) 'idea (prior) unita est ideati' (Axiom IV) – 'tamen idea vera cum ideato suo semper (re-)convenire debet!'

And here, in the very same spirit (*Ethics* II, 7 Schol.) I have to point at the affinity with *intellectus, ideae intelligendae et intellectas* (*sive res*) *unum et idem esse*. Here Spinoza leans on some 'ancient Hebrews' (to which I soon come with details) as having intuited such philosophical revelation, while the beginning text of Sepher Yetsirah seems to second here Spinoza at the best indeed: 'God creating His world via three Sepharim, namely S'phor, Sippur and Sepher'. Isidor Kalischer comments on this (Frank, New York, 1877) thus:

1. Portrait of Baruch de Spinoza, 1632–77

2. Bust of Spinoza by Professor
L. O. Wenckebach in the little
garden of the Spinozahuis in
Rijnsburg

Natus Amsteled
MDC. XXXII.
24 Novemb.

Denatus Hage com
MDC. LXXVII
21 Febru.

BENEDICTUS DE SPINOZA
Cui natura, Deus, rerum cui cognitus ordo,
Hoc Spinofa ftatu confpiciendus erat.
Expreffere viri faciem, fed pingere mentem
Zeuxidis artifices non valuere manus.
Illa viget fcriptis: illic fublimia tractat:
Hunc quicunque cupis nofcere, fcripta lege.

3. *above* Etching of Spinoza from *Opera Posthuma*, 1677

4. Portrait of Siegfried Hessing by his son Leonard Hessing

PROF. DR· FREUD   WIEN, IX., BERGGASSE 19

5. Facsimile of letter from Freud to Lothar Bickel, 28 June 1931

6. Second page of letter to Lothar Bickel

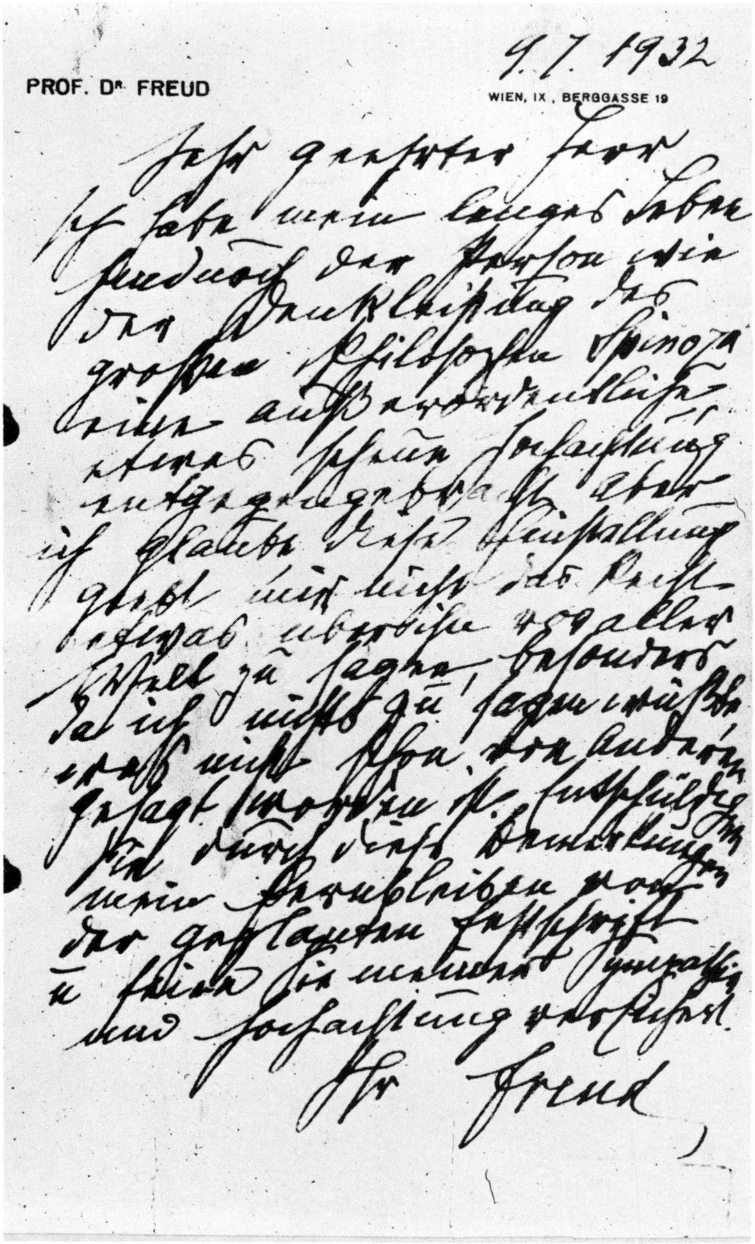

PROF. Dr. FREUD

WIEN, IX, BERGGASSE 19

9. 7. 1932

Sehr geehrter Herr
Ich habe mein Leben lang
[illegible] der Person wie
der Denkleistung des
großen Philosophen Spinoza
einen außerordentlich
[illegible] Hochachtung
entgegengebracht. Aber
ich glaube diese Einstellung
gibt mir nicht das Recht
etwas über ihn vor aller
Welt zu sagen, besonders
da ich nichts zu sagen wüßte
was nicht schon von anderen
gesagt worden ist. Entschuldigen
Sie durch diese Bemerkungen
mein Fernbleiben von
der geplanten Festschrift
u. seien Sie meiner Sympathie
und Hochachtung versichert.
Ihr Freud

7. Facsimile of letter from Freud to Siegfried Hessing, 9 July 1932

PROF. DR. FREUD

19. 3. 1933

WIEN, IX., BERGGASSE 19

8. Facsimile of letter from Freud to Siegfried Hessing, 19 March 1933

9. The Spinozahuis in Rijnsburg where Spinoza lived quietly, dedicated to his philosophical mission, 1661-3

10. The Spinozahuis, Paviljoensgracht, The Hague, where Spinoza lived the last years of his life. It is now a Spinoza museum.

11. Ornament of the memorial slab of Spinoza's tomb, in the churchyard of the Nieuwe Kerk on the Spui, The Hague. The rose symbolizes 'Be cautious!'

[handwritten letter in Latin]

A LETTER FROM SPINOZA TO LEIBNIZ

12. Facsimile of letter from Spinoza to Leibniz, showing Spinoza's seal

Three Sepharim or three words of similar expression signify: first calculation or idea; second the word; third the writing of the word. The idea, word and writing (of the word) are signs to man for a thing, and is not the thing itself. To the creator (Spinoza would call it: *Dei intellectus*) however: idea, word and writing (of the word) are the thing itself, or as some 'ancient Rabbis' (which?) remarked: 'Idea, word and work are *one and the same* to God'.

I consider it a coincidence when I see both Spinoza and Kalischer speaking of 'ancient', the one 'Hebrews', the other 'Rabbis' but without naming them. As further witness for Spinoza I admit also the 'Precepts of the Gurus' (and will return to it soon again) when listing among the 'Best Ten Things' as:

For one of superior (godlike?) intellect, the best thing is to have thorough comprehension of the inseparableness of the (subject) knower, the object of knowledge and the act (work) of knowing.

For Spinoza and Spinozists alike such witnesses point to an in-tuiting thorough comprehension of the inseparableness of *idea vera cum ideato suo*. Q.E.D. Here again contemporary searchers are re-affirming what seems to us only a metaphor when having been quoted by and via Spinoza. Cordovero, Maimonides and Abraham Abulafia excel in their uniqueness to point at the omni-identity of quasi-otherness *per se*, namely that *proton pseudos* (as C. Brunner names it!) in order to assume duality only be-*cause* the *via cognoscendi* presents itself as if *per* a quasi-knower versus a quasi-known (*idea et ideatum*). Gerschom Scholem refers such leaning to a text:

And just as his Master who is detached from all matter, is called, SEKEL, MASKIL and MUSKAL, that is the KNOWLEDGE, the KNOWER and the KNOWN, all at the same time, since all three are *one* in Him, so also He, the exalted man, the Master of the exalted name, is called INTELLECT, while he is actually KNOWING, then he is also the KNOWN, like his Master, and then there is *no difference* between them . . . .[34]

I am glad to have got later a personal letter with an additional opinion of Scholem when pointing to the origin of Spinoza's sporadic allusion, namely 'that some Hebrews have dimly maintained that God, God's intellect and the things understood by God, are *identical*'.

I can say that this sentence represents as well a known thesis of Maimonides whom Spinoza generally mentions by name, when referring to him, as also to a thesis of the Cabbalists, as per chance has been formulated by Moses Cordovero in his *Pardes Rimonim* [Ch. VIII, 13. Krakow 1592, p. 55a). Several authors have agreed as it seems to me to be right – that the various sense of the thesis with Maimonides and with the Cabbalists speaks for it, that just the cabbalistic context with Cordovero could have been envisaged by Spinoza.

I am glad to say that by some coincidence and affinity George Nador (*Spinoza Gnosis Schnueur Zalman Bina Northwood*, 1974) just now discovers how Zalman Schneuer appears as witness for Spinoza when also pointing to this cardinal thesis of Maimonides. He paraphrases it with more emphasis: 'The Holy One, praised be He, His essence, His substance and His knowledge: all this offers an absolute oneness! 'Such oneness misleads so many to speak of monism, monotheism, etc., so they do not think of the 'binary' nature of things as Spinoza does. Especially as he hints at it (Letter 50)

> Since the existence of God is His essence, and of His essence we can form no general idea, it is certain, that he who calls God *one* or *single*, has no true idea of God and speaks of Him very improperly.

'One' is only a number in the sequence of '*ordo et connexio idearum et rerum*' when thinking of *causa sive ratio* (*alius*), but when considering *causa sive ratio sui*, then 'one' is the indefinite article in grammar and the principle of indeterminacy (acausality, irrationality . . .)! Some Cabbalists know from Ancient Supplements (to the *Zohar*) that a prayer of Elijah refers to it: 'Lord of the uni-verse, ONE alone art Thou, but *not* according to number . . . !'

The goal of Spinoza's path to long for, was not to unite nor to re-unite a seemingly twoness, when approaching one's own unknown, uni-versal and omni-versal, cosmic-divine root-source, but rather to be aware or re-aware (as if by a second birth) of such *causa sive ratio sui* (*sine alio*). A mystical otherless inseparableness indeed! This only brings enlightenment to the obscured ignorance by assumed separation from the indivisible all-oneness or one-allness:

> (Non cognoscendi sed) essendi con-stans fruitio. Ego sum via, veritas et vita ipsa. Le Chayim! M-ens constans infinitis aeternitatibus . . . ergo: (non cognoscimus sed) sentimus experimurque nos aeternos (et infinitos) esse. Nos co-acquiescentes sumus in nobis ipsis quia omnia animata et omnia in Deo sumus.

All this makes us inwardly aware not only of such inseparableness from womb to tomb and from tomb to womb (Jer. 1, 5) but also realize the imperturbability of the essence of mind. (Spinoza Letter 50 points to it!) And hence to experience that

> knower, known and act of knowing;
> God, idea and word (work);
> thought, speech and action;
> Sekel, Maskil and Muskal;
> S'phor, Sippur and Sepher;
> Sat, Chit and Ananda

are not seemingly three quasi-other entities, but the very same unquasi, wordless, numberless and otherless *one: Echad-hen kai pan-advaita-*to re-mind us, all mindless ones, via the Sepher Yetsirah of ACHAT RUACH ELOHIM CHAYIM! (one is the living spirit of God)

Did all this – *horribile dictu* – still sound perhaps too much of *theissimus* and less of *Judaissimus* to justify the Herem of Baruch de Spinoza? To motivate still the ex-communication of a man like him from his kind when in constant communication with God and mankind as man's re-experience of that awe and odd inseparableness from God's all-oneness or one-allness: the *Gardener of Eden?*

I can welcome here H. W. Brann with his excellent contribution 'Spinoza and the Kabbalah' where he assists Gelbhaus to testify for Spinoza again via the Kabbalah and just pointing to that so immensely important identity of the triad, attracting often Klatzkin as well. Only the wise man whom Spinoza describes or re-describes again and again, is detached from matter *per se* as from mind *per se.* The wise man can thus be equated with the exalted man 'above' and 'beyond' discrepancy and discrimination of knower versus known via knowing. And I feel to parallel such identity as viewed in the East as a welcome voice from the 'Supreme Path of Discipleship' while excellently seconding Spinoza:

> For one of superior intellect, the best thing is to have thorough comprehension of the inseparableness of the knower, the object of knowledge and the act of knowing. For one of superior [exalted?] intellect, the best meditation is to remain in mental quiescence, the mind void of all thought-processes, knowing that the *meditator, the object of meditation, and the act of meditating* constitute *an inseparable unity* [identity].[35]

Now re-read the full allusive text of Spinoza:

> everything which can be perceived by the infinite intellect as constituting the essence of substans, pertains entirely to the one sole substance only, and consequently that substance thinking and substance extended, are *one and the same thing* expressed in two different ways: a truth which some of the Hebrews appear to have seen as if through a cloud since they say that God, the intellect, and the things which are the objects of that intellect are one and the same thing (2PVII Corr.).

We know already that singularizing (*per se*) should lead to dualizing, trializing and pluralizing *per se* while omnializing or omni-awareness of *omnia animata sumus* reveals again and again the wholeness with the attraction to re-identify or re-integrate again and again with the own unknown source: *causa sive ratio sui* (*non alius*) or with the principle of indeterminacy. That is the nostalgia for feeling at-home in no-man's land, where Ayin (void) means not nothing *per se*, but rather no-thing. I am indebted to Ronald Fischer when seeing him attracted to R. Kipling's *Kim* in the confession to freedom from two-sidedness of the human mind which parallels the notion of 'pairness' via the Cabbalah par excellence indeed!

> Something I owe to the soil that grew
> More to the life that fed –
> But most to Allah Who gave me two
> Separate sides to my head.
> I would go without shirts or shoes,
> Friends, tobacco or bread
> Sooner than for an instant lose
> Either side of my head.

And if Cabbalists make the pair-concept so plausible to be applied while excluding fully duality with otherness or twoness *per se*, this also would have to refer to the pair-concept of certainty-uncertainty or determinacy-indeterminacy in accordance with *causa sive ratio* (*vel sui vel alius!*). Here I must say to Planck's credit that he entered posterity without having to face a fiasco for his attitude, like Einstein, when one-sidedly clinging to the (f-)rigid determinism or causality (involving otherness *per se*). Einstein refused to accept an indeterministic explanation of the behaviour of elementary particles, as this would contravene with the order and the system of nature (postulated by man!). So he sought the company of Mario Bunge and David Bohr with an equal stand like his against Heisenberg and those siding with him. The more progressive approach denied the causal (or rational!) interference in physical phenomena, where the standpoint of the observer depends on what the observer 'intends' to expect. In 1927, at the Solvay Congress, the tricky 'trapdoor of indeterminacy' was opened and Einstein objected that indeterminacy, for him, resulted only from ignorance, while Bohr claimed indeterminacy to be a part of nature herself and the conflict. Oppenheimer, also eager to back Einstein 'who disliked the elements of indeterminacy, considered his last decades in life a failure but 'having a right to such failure'[36]

Rabbi Akiba has enlightened many thinkers that 'all is foreseen *and* freedom is given'! And Rabbi Akiba is so excellently seconded by Rabbi Nachman of Bratslav; when speaking of the void and the wisdom of the void (Ayin or the indeterminacy!) 'It cannot be realized, [as something real]. It is not some-thing but makes all somethings possible!' So there is only a surface-discrepancy between 'free-will and determinism' with some quasiness adorned a lot. This still makes some heads ache, as it made Einstein, a pupil of Spinoza, who had been and felt so well protected under *causa sive ratio* (*alius*), but this is only half the truth, the other half of the pair-concept is *causa sive ratio sui*! So it is according to the first axiom with alternating trend to establish boundaries within causality and rationality to ex-plain all ex-ful causes and disregard the exless plain 'X', the Ayin, the void and indeterminable *perseitas* of life. Life has not any entelechy as man thinks he must have under the *aegide rationis sive causae* (*alius*) and so he splits the indivisible wholeness of nature. Some thinkers have already become dis-appointed with such pseudo-certainty of causality or rationality. Suares warns of rationality, which in itself is corruption! And Alan Watts attracted with his pioneering explorations the 'Wisdom of Insecurity' with much success in the *terra incognita*, leaving fully open the magic of spontaneity. This can never emerge from a causalized or rationalized anthropomorphic view of the world, after all only our own projection, reflecting unhappiness and bondage, with the only remedy of self-liberation. Suares, via the Cabbalah, pioneered for the principle of indeterminacy as the very life pulse and impulse indeed. If Einstein or other Spinoza admirers had searched much deeper, they never would have backed one-sidedness as based on Spinoza. Carl Gebhardt can claim as a credit to speak of 'free necessity':

> Who sees in Spinoza only the consequent representative of that scientific determinism, which our modern natural philosophy cannot dispense with, fails to recognize, that Spinoza is in the same time the creator of the moral notion of liberty of our times, of the notion of the liberty of immanence.

Abraham Wolfson is also free from such dilemma indeed when he points to the fact:

> that Spinoza then attempts to explain his often misunderstood doctrine of determinism. He holds that freedom and necessity are interchangeable terms only where the Deity is concerned and that God as Author of all, is Himself, fate, freedom and necessity.[37]

Zen Masters solve this dilemma with no dialectic acrobatics, as scholastics like so much. 'Is the enlightened man subject to the law of causation?' Answer: 'He is one with the law of causation!' He is one with *causa sive ratio*, his best human tool to handle extra-human affairs as if under his causal or rational jurisdiction. Man is one with everything and with every thought and understands that he also stands 'under' (as sub-stans instans) *causa sive ratio* (*vel sui vel alius!*) If some-one puts more emphasis on the more attractive '*alius* or *alter*' with alternating tendencies and is blind to the quasiness of *sive*, to either = other, than the trapdoor must cure his blindness at once and bring him enlightenment:

> to become conscious of oneself, God and the world (of quasi-otherness and of *omnia animata sumus!*)

The 'cold light of reason' or *causa* horrified Planck, who did not expect from it illumination. Nor could he expect such from the equation: *omnis*

287

determinatio est negatio, so *omnis causalitas sive rationalitas (alius) est negatio etiam.* The compensation of a perfect 'logical' pattern to impose on nature because it fits man and man's attention plus intention best would perhaps enrich the limitations of explanations, but enlightenment it could not offer for the frustrated self-fettered man in the strait-jacket of *causa sive ratio,* too straight after an opulent meal with indigestion to follow. . . . Sic! Logical substance and substantiality give no substance to life to attract us with magic to the uncertainties and indeterminacies of life in the midst of the Garden of Eden.

Let us abide in Eden to familiarize with life and the lively indeterminacy with no logic, no *ratio,* no *causa,* etc. And to re-enter Eden, Spinoza had to presume an artificial beginning of the mind in order to observe better its working hypothesis *vis-à-vis* the observer, as no beginning is ever thinkable to the mind when happily engaged in self-reflection. The concept of a 'beginning' involves an 'other' with a determining cause or reason, so that otherness can cause again 'other' otherness in the way Spinoza ex-plains ex-istence of *res singulares* in accordance with the singularizing tendency of slicing the whole-ness of nature, to avoid omniality via the surrender of egohood. With no beginning, no cause, no reason – we are easily on good terms with no-thingness and implicit with egolessness as well. That is the Ayin, the void, nihil, the indeterminate. According to Euclid the 'point' is a symbol for 'no dimension-ality'. To Descartes the void is 'extension without corporeal substance'. with which Spinoza would not agree. It reminds me just now of the phantom defined as appearance with no phenomenal substance, but *homo causalis sive rationalis* needs only '*logical* substance' to substantiate all his aims, and any logical help is welcome indeed to explain and to bring peace via explanation of the 'ex'ful events in life with a well ordered and respectable determinability as if ensuring a secure itinerary from birth to death for the whole acting on the Great Show on Earth!

To give more substantiality of contemplation to the cabbalistic point *vis-à-vis* the Euclidian, let us listen to what has been said about it: 'Yud is the primary point which emanates in all directions'. So G. Scholem shows in his research[38] how the school of Gerona (as Asriel and Nachmanides) has built her speculations as an unfolding of the primary point to become the line, the plane and the body to be mirrored accordingly via the consciousness pro-jecting quasi-otherness *per se* rather than intuiting quasiness and reidentifying with all-oneness or one-allness again. The *via negativa* seemed for the Cabba-lists so promising for intuitive direct perception as self-realization with no otherness *per se* to fear phantom-obstacles anymore after Planck. Ayin and En Soph or No-thingness is volving and evolving no end, then involving no beginning either and thus saying 'no' to all human assertions, definitions, determinations. Ayin as void is devoid of human and humanizing attributes, while Spinoza's attributes of the absolute infinite substance or of God must already mirror the infinity via infinite ways to face the *facies totius uni-versi*. And must also mirror the face-to-face approach of divine truth as on Sinai or as via enlightenment when conscious of self, God and world as very same divine reflection. Everything is void. Or *omnia vana* = *omnia animata*. Two ways of saying the same: sayable or unsayable by pointing only in order to marvel at *sine causa et sine ratione*. Nihil or Ayin was not absolute Negativity, no *nihil per se*, as *perseitas* is only *versus per alteritas* to be understood properly. It was only negating definability, determinability, limitability via *ratio humana*. It was only negating and transcending either-or and neither-nor under the domination of *causa sive ratio* (*alius*). Spinoza researchers like Dunin-Borkowski have translated Ayin as indeterminacy and made it more palatable to the natural taste.

Now we can understand much better the old crux or pseudo-crux of *creatio ex nihilo*. Creation from no-thing means now from the indeterminable. 'The wisdom of not being, the wisdom of the void [after Rabbi Nachman of Bratslav] cannot be realised'. Not by *causa sive ratio* (*alius*) under the guidance of determinacy. 'It is not a some-thing but it makes all somethings possible. . . .' Thanks to Rabbi Nachman as a witness for indeterminacy or *causa suitas. Ratio suitas. Vivat suitas!* Le Chayim Elohim Chayim! It is to understand formlessness which 'stands under' forms and things to wait for logic to be con-formed with reason or cause. Logic cannot make us grasp the self-identity with *ordo et connexio idearum sive rerum*, or to agree with the equation: *forma sive essentia* in order to taste then *essendi fruitio et formae*!

Zoharic and Pre-Zoharic approaches indulge abundantly in re-interpreting Job in such a line of re-orientation to the root and origin of *causa sui*!

Where is wisdom to be found and where is the place of understanding?[39]

To answer: no-where or any-where would point directly to the principle of indeterminacy of Ayin = no-thing = void. The place of understanding is there where all-oneness or no-thingness as sub-stans is in every instans, standing 'under' every standing and under every understanding of self or quasi non-self (or other): *causa sive ratio* (*alius*). They translated wisdom to be found as the 'foundation' (in the sephirotic symbolism) in Ayin = no-thing = void or in the indeterminate. The great Beyond of either-or: good or evil, knower or known but quasi transcendent and immanent as via knowing, becoming the via *ipsa*, the *vita ipsa*: unknowable life. *Vita sine causa sine ratione* (*alius*)! Metanoia is shifting the discriminative human mind from dichotomy via the Tree of Knowledge to its 'other' side of quasi-otherness as Tree of Life. And nihil, void, Ayin, no-thingness or better indeterminacy fits such incursion into our own infinity of *causa sive ratio sui*.

'Reality is formed from Tohu!' (*Mamesh yetser mitohu.*) Reality or quasi-formativity comes from the formless (called by the sense-conscious man: void, etc.) and hence Spinoza's equation: *forma sive essentia* (standing for *existentia (sui)*: exless *essentia = esse per se* with *essendi fruitio*. This gives to such reality the perfect-real symbolism in wording. Castaneda and Einstein see in their way the reality as 'our' description of it: the label, so to speak, according to the label-minded 'mind'. Reality (as *mamesh*) is like a 'fixation' for the 'duration' (of thinking or describing the world while being 'it': the self). In Latin tradition and erudition *'realitas'* is the world of *'res'* or the *'ideatum'* quasi a half or complementing pair together with 'idea' to constitute the whole reality in self-realization of own otherlessness and not of quasi-otherness *per se*: things, objects *per se* and 'object' to our subjectivity! *Res* = things are arriving or deriving as if from no-thingness, formless or best from: indeterminacy, embracing beginningless and endless sameness(of self-realization).

> You have indeed uncovered the beginning so you may seek the end; for in the place where the beginning is, there the end will be. Blessed is he who will stand in the beginning and will know the end . . . and will not taste death.[40]

I think that Job with his vast experience will come gladly into the witness-box to point at the indivisible wholeness of life (*and* death as pair-concept!). Such omni-awareness helps not only during the so-called lifespan but also during states not called or not so-called:

> One dieth in his full strength
> being 'wholly' at ease and quiet (Job : 21; 23).

Huang Po speaks of similar help and similar self-realization attained by omniality . . . to experience wholeness of all-oneness or one-allness as same. Wholeness is before birth and after death the same wholeness waiting to be self-realized in quasi-irreality or quasi-reality either! Wholeness thinks of no *causa sive ratio (alius)* fit for creation or emanation to be grasped as wholeness of: *omnia animata sumus*. Verbalization or conceptualization is only a peg or expedient makeshift, but self-experience of otherlessness via revelation opens the gateless gate to: know Thyself! Uncreate instead *creatio ex alio* or ex quasi-*alio vel quasi sibi* . . . Job or Elijah or Spinoza all are aware of the First Days (of any quasi-creation) with that scent from the Tree of Life via the metamorphosis of the Tree of Knowledge to turn and re-turn as pair-concept for quasi-unknowable life or quasi-unlivable knowledge either. Like bodiless ego or egoless body.

> *sentimus experimurque nos aeternos esse tamquam omnia animata vel omnia vana sumus!*

And then we say:

> Full is the whole earth with His glory!
> Empty is the whole earth with our glory!

With such oceanic feeling of the little drop attained by self-transcendence we now can understand Ezekiel better: . . . that ye may know that 'I am' [is] the Lord! And such grandeur of the pair-concept: Yahweh = Elohim (*Deus sive Natura* (*naturans vel naturata*)). Hence 'I am' involves singularity of the ocean drop and evolves omniality of the dropless ocean. Hence: 'I am' [is] Yahweh, the Way, the Truth, Life! and thus the really great identity of 'I am' is revealed to Moses and via Moses to us and to our 'I am', namely as 'I am' [is] that 'I am': the otherless same via quasiness or unquasiness. Echad, Advaita, Ayin, Void, Shunya or the indeterminable, the exless 'X': *causa sive ratio sui*.

It is interesting to learn how that magic 'I am' has been seen and shown via Zen. A poem, Han Shan, by Indra will point to it:

> I think of the past twenty years then I used to walk home quietly from the Kuo-ch'ing; all the people in the monastery say: 'Han-Shan is an idiot!' – 'Am I really an idiot?' I reflect, but my reflections fail to solve the question for I myself do not know 'who the self is', and how can 'others' know who 'I am' (is)? I just hang down my head – no more asking is needed, for what service can the asking be? Let them come then and jeer at me all they like. I know most distinctly what they mean: but 'I am' (is) not to respond to their sneer, for that suits my life admirably.[41]

'I am' has such a micro- and macro-cosmic and divine gammut either when this pair-word is unified as 'I' or as 'am' in order to identify with I = am: self. Ergo: know thyself! As unknowable but livable. Why such fuss about such feud between the quasi-two and the ungodly twoness as if unworthy? Spinoza has pacified the feud and declared the oneness via the pairness as allness. The Hebrew wording helps via the root-wisdom (etymosophy?) to attain root-awareness. Parallels are in fact para-others (they defy to meet in the finite realm of *causa sive ratio* (*alius*) but meet in the infinite sphere of *causa sive ratio* (*sui*)) when the quasi-otherness via reciprocal receptivity has lifted otherness and quasiness. So it could be understood that the abbreviation of the two parallels (meeting with their quasi-twoness in the infinite) appears as sign of equation, identity: ' = '. In Hebrew the word for parallels is *mekubal*, for receptivity *Cabbalah*, for receive = *mekabel*. Klatzkin, in his knowledge of Spinoza and of the Hebrew language, thinks wisely that Hebrew word-containers fit not only the esoteric content of Kabbalah but also of Spinoza's terminology. Perhaps he would never ever had to encounter that *invita Latinitate* as *invita Hebraeitate*. Spinoza has solved this feud as well as the others. Matter is assumed not to be worthy of the divine nature. How then *Deus sive natura*? How then Elohim Hatewah? *Deus sive Veritas*? Body is assumed not to be worthy of the mind? Female not to be worthy of the male (half man). Knower and known not to be worthy of the via knowing?

They all are pair-concepts, conceived by the divine All-mind to convey all-mindedness via single-mindedness and better via pair-mindedness to reflect wholeness, omniality. The fuss about such a pair-concept is the crux. It began with the first pair, the number '2' as expounded before in this paper: it originated by reflection considered an allo-reflection, an eidolon or duplication of the re-'flection' as such. A Zen Master once asked the pupil, to help open and widen his consciousness for enlightenment: could you hear the sound of 'one hand' when after *causa sive ratio* (*alius!*) only two hands, only a pair of hands can 'cause' a sound or make it rational? The meaning of one being not as a number handy for *causa sive ratio* (*alius*), but rather the numberless indefinitive, indeterminable principle: one = pair = all-one or one-all, the Self. Know thyself! 'I know [with the prophet Jeremiah] that the way of Man is not in himself. It is not in Man that walketh to direct his steps!' It is not in Man the Way but in every-thing and no-thing alike. The very same way, the very same truth, Life of 'I am'. And 'I am' is already in itself a pair-concept to grasp wholeness and thus the fullness of His glory in it.

> In the beauty of the world lies the ultimate redemption of our
> mortality. When we shall become at-one with nature in a sense
> profounder even than the poetic imaginings of most of us, we shall
> understand what now we fail to discern.

Fiona McLeod helps us to grasp such beauty which is more manifest via the pair-concept with that magical reciprocal receptivity. The sign of equation symbolized as abbreviation of the two parallels (or two para-others) reveals how such otherness can be abandoned only in the infinite meeting beyond the rational or causal parallelity (or para-otherness!). We have failed to understand in this interpretation Spinoza's teaching as' parallelism' while only approaching it exoterically, but meta-geometrically the hidden sense may come through perhaps when the para-other and the para-self form a pair-concept of the para-alleloi and nevertheless equals. Please ponder on it! Such a pair-symbol started with Genesis in the Bible and with Gnosis in the first axiom of the *Ethics*. If Kabbalah can convey via the sephirot the pair-concept to grasp pair-receptivity as omni-receptivity of *omnia animata vel omnia animantia sumus!*

The pair-concept excludes otherness *per se* and thus indeterminability lets everything 'happen' with no quasi-creation or quasi-emanation, when *creator idem est creatura. Ideae creant et creantur*: with reciprocal receptivity or Cabbality – so to speak. 'It happens' dispenses us to apply the ego-minded and anthropocentred *ratio sive causa* (*alius*) for any creation. Here Spinoza parallels the East with the idea of the Uncreate, unborn, unmade, etc. So we re-read what Spinoza has to say about the mind:

And it 'happens' that the mind is able to contemplate on itself!

292

It is not a rationalized or causalized 'happening' of contemplation or self-contemplation but *causa sive ratio sui* or indeterminacy reigning with no otherness *vis-à-vis*.

It has something like faith and grace in it and that smells extra- or trans-rational or extra- or trans-causal beyond the forecast of events 'to happen' only. Events are events. *Evenire ex nihilo* or *ex indeterminatione* or *ex causa sui* or *ex ratione sui*. Wholeness is equated with emptiness as well. Hui-Neng is so familiar with self-contemplation like Spinoza eager to reach *acquiescentia in se ipso* (or *in se ipsa!*).

Have your mind like space [with no clouds!] and yet entertain in it no [thought of] emptiness [per se]

'Nihil aliquid esse quia indeterminatio sive indefinitio est affirmatio viae negativae, nihilitatis'. By negation you arrive on the way, negating otherness *per se* and selfness *per se* and thus you can identify with the way, the truth and life itself: to live it. Pilate asked Jesus about Truth, while seeing him being already 'the Way'. Spinoza has been asked, if his philosophy is the best 'way' for 'I am' and he replied instead: it is the true way for any 'I am': to be conscious of the self-identity of self-God-world. Of *omnia animata sive vana sumus*.

Of all the various pair-concepts we are mostly interested in and involved with that of body-mind in order to still and distil the quasi-twoness representing a quasi-number symbol. The outcome of such an inquest would let for us and our self-reflection the body-mind re-appear as a numberless pair and as a quasi-numberless, indeterminable wholeness-symbol. So in the light of Kabbalah and in the light of Spinoza as well.

For Spinoza, the circle and the idea of that circle is the same thing. If the soul is to be considered the 'idea of the body', then the body and its idea are not two, nor quasi-two, but an inseparable pair-concept. In order to make more palatable for us Spinoza's wording we have to use it in the same sense he gave it himself in his quest for intentional wording of adequacy.

Man is composed of mind and body and the human body exists [only] as we perceive it.

The human body exists as we via the soul or via the idea of the body perceive 'it' as its true *ideatum*. Then this *modus extensionis cum suo modo (cogitandi) con-venire debet* and vice versa. Mind as body-idea and body as mind-*ideatum* are the very same things: embodying and ensouling as a pair-concept the symbol of wholeness or *causa sive ratio sui*. And Spinoza continues in a Note:

Hence we see not only *that* the human mind is united to the body, but also *what* is to be understood by the union of the mind and body.

While still trying to throw light on the pair-concept of body-mind (Gan as Micro Eden) we may perhaps look again to the com-position of Man: namely of mind 'and' body and say: the human mind exists (only?) as we perceive us ourselves when '*perceiving*', i.e. reflecting on ourself or contemplating on us. Thus we identify with the via knowing and also with the pair-concept on that via-knowing 'to happen' as quasi knower *vis-à-vis* a quasi-known or an idea *vis-à-vis* an *ideatum*. Then we experience their unity of '*convenire debent*' or better to say: their identity re-established via the quasiness of knower *vis-à-vis* known. In this very sense of always '*con-venire*' they appear or come in togetherness of wholeness via pair-concept.

Each thing is perceived through knowing. The self shines in space through knowing. Perceive *one* being as knower *and* known.[42]

You see how the East seconds Spinoza here so excellently. And so also Cordovero and Gersonides back such wisdom, while in our time not only philosophy, but also psychology and physiology (physis with 'its' logic?) sees the inseparable oneness of nature: Man 'as' and 'in' the universe as an oceanic unit of unity of wholeness via oneness or via pairness. It is the same via, the same Way, the same Truth of 'I am' as pair-concept too: I = am = id = idem = identity of one-allness or all-oneness with the symbolical quasiness.

Man splits the pair into two as entities *per se* and clings to eitherness = otherness *per se*. Man is slowly maturing for the revelation via quasiness and seeing the via as a quasi-via: *via viae* or *via sui. Vivat suitas!* God pairs above those who below do not see yet the pair-concept to enact or re-enact it as oneness for wholeness indeed.

Full is the whole earth with His glory!

Full is the whole body with the same glory. The glory of creator *et creatura idem.*

Looking into the inseparable wholeness of body-mind (Gan) we learn from Spinoza

certainly no man hath yet determined *what* are the powers of the body: I mean that *none* has yet learned from experience *what* the body may perform by mere laws of nature, considering as a material thing, and *what* it cannot do *without* the mind's determination of it. For *nobody* has known yet the frame of the body so thoroughly as to explain all its operations. . . .

Can we also assert the same about the same human com-position of mind and body:

certainly no man hath yet determined *what* are the powers of the mind: I mean that *none* has yet learned from experience *what* the mind may perform by mere laws of nature. For *nobody* has known yet the frame of the mind so thoroughly as to explain fully all its operations.

And would Spinoza agree with us and with such assertion? We see how the language lends itself to use words (for m-entification of identity!): no-'one' *or* no-'body' are alternations for the same oneness of body-mind as pair-togetherness to show the '*con-venire*' of body and mind as con-scious of oneness. In the same way as con-scious means co-conscious so *con-venire* means *venire*, a coming and be-coming as if a coming on the via as the via itself of oneness! Independent of the unthinkability of a beginning (or ending) Spinoza encourages us that we do not need to remember of having existed as a member-unit of the all-unity of the uni-verse facing the very same *facies totius universi*. Having pre-existed or having to (after or) post-exist is all-included in the omni-present Now of existence *sine alio*, with no otherness of 'before' or 'after' or 'when'. As *existentia sui* identical with exless *essentia* leading to *essendi fruitio* or enlightenment in the enstasis of the instans, the co-instans and sub-stans of infinity, indetermination, *causa sive ratio sui*.

Can you know it as 'now' it: as pair-concept of you-it? *Tat twam asi*. That you are! Now and Here can justify and testify as mystical experience of the omnipresence via omni-awareness of *omnia animata sumus*.

The frame of the body or the frame of the mind cannot be transcended while presuming otherness *per se* in its many variations of palatability as it were. We as a mind-body com-position have a paradoxical position of a quasi-frame and framework to identify with the working and frame-working as co-worker, where Man has no Foreman beyond himself as the Great Other! It is an excellent frame for such marvellous divine composition, to inspire admiration and veneration for *Deus sive Natura* via *deificans sive naturans* and via *deificatus sive naturatus:* the same *via viæ* as *via sui*!

Full is the whole earth with His Glory!

Now and here we can glorify the frame and the framework not by wanting to know 'what' the powers are, but happy to experience 'that' such powers are 'in' us and 'as' us – that ye may know that Yahweh is Elohim! For on such a mission has Man – in such com-position – been sent to earth to know 'that' Yahweh is Elohim, but never to know 'what' Yahweh or 'what' Elohim *per se* is. Spinoza admirers know with Spinoza the innate question in the mind of the quasi-knower: Who (Mi) are These (Eleh) i.e. the things as quasi-knowns? Now perhaps we will intuit rather than ex-tuit as before, the metathesis and metanoia by turning the mind to re-formulate the question to become the unquestionable answer. The Known reversed and the Knower are a pair-concept: Mi-eleh are Elohim. Knower-known or known-knower = via knowing with no otherness, no quasiness: just *knowing*, just the via, the way and the pilgrim, the wayfarer longing to become the pathfinder on the way will become the way itself. 'I am' [is] already and does not need to come or to be-come: the Way, the Truth, Life. Le Chayim. Elohim Chayim. Sepher Yetsirah seconds with its first verse the first verse of Bereshit and the first axiom of the *Ethics*; Achat ruah Elohim Chayim! One is the Spirit of the living Elohim via the quasiness of asking: Mi – Eleh? Who are they? They (all) are me. I am all them: *omnia animata sumus*!

And no need to ask for the unknowable potentialities of the frame of mind 'or' body as long as we do in-tuit the framework working and (frame-working) as com-position and pair-concept in the very same framework of inseparable unity as inseparable unitive unit-symbol. Spinoza's frame-concept has been helped to be understood pictorially as a 'picture and its frame' by Sir James Jean:

> it is like trying to discover the artist and the action of painting going to the 'edge' of the picture.

And the frame-concept has been helped by the Geheimrat von Weimar pointing to children

> when peeping into the mirror, try to 'turn' it to see what is on the 'other' side,

expecting like Paul puzzling and baffling reflections. Tennyson has recorded of himself that he gained enlightenment by meditation via looking into the looking-glass so long until glass, looking and looker vanished to become one-allness.

Lama Anagarika Govinda has an illuminative view of the pair-concept of quasi-twoness:

> what we call birth is merely the 'reverse' side of death like one of the two sides of a coin, or like a door which we call 'entrance' from outside and 'exit' from inside a room.[43]

Why always siding? Sri Rama Krishna, before his 'death', said 'it is as if going from one door into the other' but of the very same mansion of the omni-verse as uni-verse. To look into its face as into the *facies totius universi* is to look into totality, omniality and to be omni-aware of *omnia animata sumus quamvis diversis gradibus con-scientiae ut con-venire debeant*! To explain the unexplainable frame of the marvellous framework cannot convey the fullness and the wholeness of the golden glory! Govinda asks to 'reverse' the position of 'versus' quasi-otherness, then to discover the com-position of the uni-versus as *omni*-versus and vice-versa or uni-versa. 'Versus' causes ad-versity op-position to the *com*-position which is universal and glorious magnificent indeed!

> Full is the whole earth with His glory: as earth-heaven pair!
> Full is the whole Man with His glory: as male-female pair!
> Full is the whole body with His glory: as body-mind pair!
> Full is the whole mind with His glory: as mind-body pair!

Wholeness is always full with His glory. *Gloria in excelsis Dei et in profundis Dei!* The Glory of Yahweh; Elohim. *Deus sive Natura.* Sanctified in the pair-concept, symbolized in *causa sive ratio* vel *sui vel alius* as pair-concept with quasiness as a working-frame. Full the glory in the wholeness and totality via omni-awareness or via pair-awareness as the very same all-self-awareness 'sentimus experimurque nos aeternos esse: vel solos, vel duos, vel omnes, i.e. infinitos vel aeternos esse cum essendi fruitione' (sed non cognoscendi fruitione!). The longing for omniality comes from unknowingly feeling the belonging to it by being it, itself. There is an esoteric *mysterium* in such a pair-concept of manifest wholeness. The *Zohar* hints at it when in its exegesis (and its Gnosis).

> In the same secret, in which heaven and earth have been created, has been Man created too. With them it reads (Gen. 2:4): This is the origin of heaven and earth. With Man it reads (Gen. 5:1): This is the book of the origin of Man. There it reads: as they were created. Male and female He created them. Therefore, a picture (diokna), which does not contain male and female, is not a picture from above (heavenly). This we have established in the secret tradition. Come and see, in a place, where male and female are not united, the Holy, praised be He, will not make His dwelling. And blessing will be present only in a place, where there are male *and* female. It reads (Gen. 5:2): And He blessed them and named their name Man (adam) as even Man will be designated (Man) only, if there are united in him male *and* female.[44]

The Zohar points also to the picture-concept to include the frame-concept for the pair-symbol for better intuition. The craving in Man's com-position as body-mind or as male-female is not longing for otherness as a glorious quest and conquest, so to speak, but rather for self-identity in the urge for wholeness expanding solitary self-limitations of ego-singularity. Hence to transcend it via reciprocal longing and receptivity of longing on the very same via 'via the pair-concept' of the positive and compositive manifestation of wholeness, of omniality with glory to glorify.

When the mind is in a position to grasp its own composition (of mind-body as one body reflects on his mind or on himself) then he intuits better oneness expressed by 'no one standing for no-body' and mind for self. Do you a-gree to such de-gree of reflection! Conze thinks from the essential core of Buddhist teaching, to culminate in 'such phrasing': to put mind and body in order. And Charles Luk also thinks in this way of 'disentanglement of mind and body' of their quasi-twoness, but to reflect rather as a com-position as a pair-concept. Hence to reflect on itself and to attain all-oneness or one-allness via the reflexive pronoun: self or *se* leading to *causa sive ratio sui* or to the principle of indeterminacy. Now I can follow Spinoza better when it 'happens' that the mind reflects on itself without interfering with my I-minded discrimination in I and not-I as if then grasping the ungraspable. If there is no 'I' *per se*, no 'it' *per se*, no 'there '*per se*, then no '*perseitas*' has any meaning and enlightenment can draw with Messianic salvation! The self-inquirer into the otherless *causa sive ratio sui* intuits the alternative of 'either-or' as pair-concept and never extuits wishful otherness *per se*. Intuition must lead to indeterminacy while extuition to determinacy. Self-reflections are not so puzzling as allo-reflections appear to be phantoms with no (corporeal) substance while *causa sive ratio* (*alius*) endows everything with 'logical' substance to feel logically, i.e. which heals the chronic back-ache when having no where to 'lean' on otherness. . . . Sic!

Self-reflections turn the own alternating, discriminative mind from otherness to quasi-otherness and from quasiness to the pair-concept of wholeness. Spinoza's lenses did not show for his retina fake-otherness to baffle or puzzle. Descartes would never have been baffled or puzzled either by 'otherness' or duality, as it offered to him a rest in a too-comfortable resting chair (of philosophy?) and which fully explained or explained away the unexplainable 'plain life' pointing to the need of causal or rational 'certainty' with a mechanical logic best suitable for lifeless knowledge than for unknowable life! To the need for self-affirmation of: *cogito ergo sum*, his '*ego sum*' was for *ego cogito* exceptional singularity and duality versus omniality and all-oneness. His 'I' could and would never identify with the whole I = am as 'I am' [is] the Way, the Truth, Life. It would never have entered his dreams and his dreamy philosophy that later Heisenberg or Suares would bring a message discovered on the 'other side' of the Cartesian otherness *per se* and its certainty. But now Spinoza's (otherless) self-reflection has been revived and also the self-identity of being conscious of self, God and world (of *omnia animata*). The principle of uncertainty or indeterminacy has to include and involve chance, spontaneity and happening (witnessed by physicists as by metaphysicians).

Descartes at any time seemed only too eager and happy with such eagerness to look for the tranquilizing principle of (quasi?) certainty accessible and granted via *causa sive ratio alius*.

> We shall not reach certainty (in regard to the existence of our body) except through the knowledge and certainty of some-thing else.
> Therefore the (self-)affirmation: 'I am' (is) not known by itself (in as far as 'I am' [is] a thing *formed*) of a body.[45]

Descartes was not ripe in the eyes of posterity to envisage the enigma of the bodiless I or 'I am' and the egoless body as the very same alternating assertion indeed! Elohim created Man: male *and* female. Man pro-created all members of mankind: male *or* female! As a com-position, a pair-concept. 'With' the beginning Elohim created the heaven and the earth. As a com-position, a pair-concept. Man as a composition of mind and body, a pair-concept.

Descartes wanted 'I' to be a thing 'formed' of a body! Descartes did what the East warns so often: not to identify I with the body which after Spinoza exists only as I perceive it within my own I-minded perception. *Causa sive ratio alius* is the only tool for Descartes to master and to attain mastership which makes him depend on knowledge to become knowledge only when it is certain by 'something else' than the knower. Here you have the otherness *per se*. Here you cannot discover the *causa sive ratio sui*. So Descartes was the happy pioneer for determinism, absolute determinism with the catechism and schism of self and non-self or other *per se*. Unfortunately, Will Durant, like other contemporary thinkers, in spite of claiming here in this symposium Spinoza as his 'Paean', nevertheless assumes that

> Spinoza and Descartes have shared the Galilean mechanics in moulding the mechanistic theory in Descartes and the deterministic psychology in Spinoza. Determinism is predestinarianism without theology: it substitutes the primeval vortex or nebula for God. Spinoza followed the logic of mechanism to its bitter end. . . . The inescapable logic of determinism reduces consciousness to an epiphenomenon – an apparently superfluous appendage of psychophysical processes which, by the mechanics of cause and effect, would go on just as well without it; and yet nothing seems more real, nothing more impressive, than consciousness. After logic had its say, the mystery tam grande secretum remains omnia quodamodo animata.[46]

Durant like Balaam came to curse, and pointed to the blessing mystery of *omnia animata* (*sumus*) where he had to add how such mystery must lead the wise man on his path to be conscious of self, God and the world (of things) via a self-identification with all-oneness or one-allness which is beyond any determinable *causa sive ratio* (*alius*) transcending quasi-otherness *per se*. Then could this wise man exclaim happily and blessed: '*sentimus experimurque nos aeternos esse*' self-realizing the quasi-irreal, irrational and acausal, indeterminable *acquiescentia in se ipso* or *se ipsa*?

I must recall to the witness-box Vernon J. Bourke to meet face to face with Durant over the case of 'determinism:

> it is said to be by way of negation according to Spinoza (epist. 50) and this means that universal sub-stance is in its *perfect* form *indeterminate*, but is 'thought' to become (as if) determinate by a sort of logical (i.e. mechanic) absolute perfection.

So you see, dear Balaam, Spinoza did not avoid the mystery of *causa sive ratio sui* with the uncertainty and indeterminacy leading to *acquiescentia in se ipso* (*non in alio*!), as also to *omnia animata sumus via experientia aeternitatis*. And he rather pointed to such acausal or irrational and indeterministic 'happening'

. . . it 'happens' that the mind is able to con-template itself [as otherless] and thereby is supposed to pass to a greater perfection (or reality).

Spinoza did not flirt with a logical or absolute perfection to make the logical substance absolute infinite, as this would have not enabled him to expand his I-minded consciousness to all-mindedness or *omnia animata sumus*.

'Inescapable logic (or mechanics) of determinism reduces consciousness' instead and Spinoza always was eager via the *Amor Dei Intellectualis* to expand the Intellect as to include or identify with the things intellected, i.e. the identity of quasi-knower and quasi-known as pair-concept to become the via knowing: the *via viae* or *via sui* like *causa sui* like *ratio sui*. *Vivat suitas*. Indeterminacy expands in the oneness with *extensio* and with the idea of it as exless *tensio* or *cogitatio* (*in-tensio* in my wording!). When Spinoza views the mind as auto-maton, this is not via logics or mechanics, but rather via self-teaching or self-revolving via alternation to grasp quasiness as the grand paradoxon.

Quasiness (*tamquam, quamvis, quatenus, sive . . .*) is the grand mystery to marvel at as at a revelation

the interplay of those energies in the Universe and in Man [as pair-concept]. We are then subjected to an amazing mental exercise which can modify our way of thinking to the extent of uniting us with those energies. And that only is revelation.[47]

Kabbalists (like W. E. Butler) and modern Alchemists like Jacques Sadoul agree with Suares and Ralph Metzner alike in this cardinal point of revelation. That oceanic feeling when the amoeba has reached the galaxies in the same omni-identity of *omnia animata sumus*. . . . Have I not tried so many variations on this divine theme to attract you to its magic to marvel like me via self-realization? But let us go back still to Descartes for a while to understand better his contemporary followers *vis-à-vis* Spinoza's contemporary followers both in our days still eager to have the sole-agency for the well determinable *causa sive ratio alius*, and horrified by the idea of trespassing beyond the self-limitations into the realm of the quasi-acausal or irrational. The arch-root or archetype of all dichotomy and discrimination derives from the di-version and a-version of knower 'versus' known. Patanjali's sutras offer pratyahara as healing and freeing agency to let the perceptual agents make possible the reconnection of the so-called (quasi-disconnected) external object (the known) with the so-called internal subject (the knower). And it is possible for the same disconnecting discriminative I-mindedness when I and 'I am' is always disconnected from a quasi-other I and 'I am' with its I-mindedness as well. . . . So it became possible for Wittgenstein to declare then triumphantly: 'No-thing empirical is knowable!' So it became possible for Whitehead too to parallel: 'Apart from the experience of subjects there is nothing, no-thing, bare no-thingness!' Sir 'I' is the main actor on the world scene claiming all limelight for ruling such world (of otherness *per se*) under *causa sive ratio* (*alius*) via *determinabile*. After enlightenment from self-bondage from quasi-otherness *per se*, Sri 'I' exclaims happily of seeing no more 'otherness,' 'no *perseitas*; but only quasiness when alternating external-ization with quasi internationalization of the very same uncertain, indetermin-able One, the exless 'X', the own unknown. . . . Life can only be life and lived as undivided otherless same. Such revelation helps man to his own trans-figuration (transcending figure, form or figurative, formative thinking). Con-sciousness presents such alternating evolution and involution to look at itself via quasi-otherness *per se* through an *ordo et connexio idearum sive rerum* (*causarum*). The looking becomes being and the being be-comes be-coming on and of the same *via viae. Via sui. Vivat suitas*! Le Chayim!

Body and mind is the great com-position of Spinoza with a marvellous score played by an earthly instrument on a celestial theme: Full is the whole earth with His glory! Marvellous indeed! The Diamond Sutra assures us so convincingly that 'body', 'world', etc.' are only names. Descartes, when sometimes being so near, or too near to such revelation, hesitates the horror *transcendentiae*. The Agrapha of the 'Secret Sayings' of Jesus according to the Gospel of Thomas are more keen and daring, when we listen to the revelation of what Jesus presumably had to say on such subject:

he who has known the world, has found the body, but he who has found the body, of him the world is not worthy!

And there is a splendid parallel accord from the Radnasara Tantra: 'he can then come to know the truth of the uni-verse who realizes the truth of the body,' namely that body and mind do not constitute a dui-verse, but as a pair-concept a uni-verse reflecting uni-versal and omni-versal omniality of oceanic feeling via drops and waves. We speak of a world of the body (as if *per se*) and of world of the mind (as if *per se*) but after Spinoza (and not after Descartes!) we have welcomed the message of the infinite attributes as if infinite worlds (of infinity) not only one along the 'other' but as all in one-another expressing otherless all-oneness or one-allness. Now instead of attributes we hear much speaking of levels, aspects, planes or dimensions of consciousness which actually is considered to be co-consciousness where everything is co-aware of everything via omni-awareness of *omnia animata sumus* . . . with no more otherness *per se*!

Zen teachers warn again and again not to take finger-pointing at the moon for the moon itself. In our dark tunnel of discriminative thinking (of otherness *per se*) such pointed moonlight cannot lead but to moon-enlightenment, and the whole truth would then be a finger-pointer-truth. And the truth *per se*? And the truth identical with the way and with life of 'I am'? This truth has to identify 'I am' as 'I' with 'am' as one and same! The identity between I-ness and being or between I-mind and All-mind via omniality is at stake. That otherless self, which the sages for ages and stages have tried to teach to us as: Know thyself! Tat Twam asi! Sages, rishis and Enlightened Ones like Buddha and like Spinoza are fully aware of the stumbling block presented by words, their usage and assumed sense: it is not only that *invita Latinitate sed invita lingua ipsa!* Sic!

> The reason why the Tathagata nevertheless endeavours to instruct by means of words and definitions is through his good and excellent skilfulness (or expediency, upaya). He only provisionally makes use of words and definitions to lead all beings, while his real object is to make them abandon symbolism and *directly* enter into the real reality (tattva). Because if they indulge themselves in reasonings, attach themselves to sophistry, and thus foster subjective particularization, how could they have the true wisdom (tattvajnana) and attain Nirvana?

Here I would like to remember my friend from days of youth, Dagobert Runes, always so eager to pioneer for two great and main topics: for Spinoza and for the nation of Spinoza and of the Saviour, to which Runes belongs and still longs to belong, as it were. When once writing a foreword to Spinoza's *Principia Cartesiana*, he seemed to cling too much to that which Buddha and Spinoza, from a higher indiscriminative viewpoint, never teach to cling:

> There is no doubt that in the given era of seventeenth century Europe the mathematical investigation of philosophical themata by means of axioms, definitions and postulates seemed to hold keys to *certainty*.[48]

And such quasi-certainty has made Spinoza in so many eyes for so many I-s palatable and I's-ruminatable indeed: via words ruled by *causa sive ratio* (*alius*) accepting for granted otherness *per se*. This has misled so many sincere Spinoza admirers to lean comfortably on *determinism* because they have too easily overlooked (although looking through a micro- or macro-telescope on the horizon of Spinoza's thoughtworld . . .) the first axiom with its self-evident and axiomatic truth. Such truth has initiated thinking man into Genesis and Gnosis of eitherness = otherness or rather quasi-otherness with no self-existent *perseitas* to proclaim. Then, they all (like Einstein himself) would have followed the unison ruling of *causa sive ratio* under such 'either-ness', namely appearing as *causa sive ratio vel sui vel alius*. This is the full truth including determinacy and indeterminacy as one indivisible composition via a pair-concept as body-mind, as male-female, heaven-earth, etc. Man is com-posed of mind and body but likes to pose as if *per se*, un-composed, not as pair-concept, but as body *per se* and mind *per se*. 'Hence we see not only *that* the mind is united to the body, but also *what* is to be understood by the union of mind and body.' I rephrase this in the radius of my challenge as 'We see only *that* man is united or a 'unit' of mind and body in a whole unified uni-verse of all-unity, all-animation. *Omnia animata sumus, sed non ego solo animatus, enim ego omn-animor,* if I may dare to say so, *invita Latinitate.*

The very same pair-concept as unit, as composite unit is still tempted with alternating self-awareness on a somatic level or (*sive*) on a psychic level (of consciousness) concerning the very same psycho-somatic pair-unit and indivisible as such. The same thing: *res extensa sive res cogitans* in a modality of quasi-otherness but in a substantiality of quasi-selfness 'By thought I comprehend all that is in us and of which we are *immediately conscious.*[49] Later this leads to 'By idea I understand a conception of the mind which the mind *forms because* it is a thinking thing.' Here Spinoza offers us a be-cause with rational understanding the standpoint of the *modus substantiae* and understanding the sub-stance, namely that standing 'under' every standing and under every understanding either in order to become immediately self-aware via *causa sive ratio sui.* Here no be-cause for acausality or irrationality is asked for or given. The magic of 'I am' as the way, the truth and Life is self-revelation, the mystery of the exless 'X' with all-oneness and one-allness. Not bare, abstract, but with love of *Amor Dei sive Amor Naturae, sive Amor Veritatis, Amor Vitae!* All this 'happens' in the pre-causal or pre-rational state of mind: kadmut hasechel as the Great Maggid of Mesritch called it, when asking bluntly where our thoughts were 'before' *we* think *them.*

Man is composed of mind and body as pair-concept and the idea which expresses the essence of the body (under the form of infinity or eternity) and pertains to the (same!) essence of mind, is the essence of com-position to be conceived as pair-concept to make manifest omniality. Therefore our mind in so far as it involves the (same) essence of the body within the pair-concept of the com-position: mind-body, evolves or rather re-evolves its own essence, its same total (or pair-)essence by self-reflection or self-attributability of constitutional essence. By self-reflection of infinity or eternity as absolute *perseitas (sine ratione sive causa alius!).* It is only infinity spatial or temporal, and then called eternity. So eternity and infinity is a pair-concept as well. When Spinoza speaks of *essendi fruitio* this all-essence or pair-essence is meant like water as a drop or as a wave the very same water via *sub-stantiae* not *via aquae!* To know, to perceive, to understand, to conceive, to attribute, to reflect, etc., all this which 'happens' on the path of quasiness via *tamquam, quamvis, sive, quatenus,* etc., is manifesting indivisible wholeness as the via knowing is. *Modus, attributum et substantia idem sunt et idem est. Idem est iste m-ens constans, substans, instans, co-instans* Now and Here with no before, no after and no when. With no pre and no post to become preposterous indeed. It is helpful for man on the path to think of the raft helping him to cross the sea of quasi-otherness *per se,* but later having arrived on the quasi-other shore, to recognize the very same quasiness from before the crossing or quasi-crossing. Sangsara and Nirvana is a pair-concept too and can nirvanize

303

you easier . . . to traverse dichotomy and discrimination of the quasi-twoness, of the quasi-two shores a pair-concept as well.

We can settle as settlers in a world 'set' (as if) in a body and in a mind confronted with our own phantom of quasi-otherness, while we are aware of the whole as a pair and of the pair as a whole: a whole composition of mind and body. Not enough of us have heard of Alan Watts:

> Slowly it becomes clear that one of the greatest superstitions is the
> separation of the mind from the body.[50]

It is as if that lovely pair since the creation of the divine pair: Yahweh-Elohim with the beginning of a pair of heaven-earth and in it Man as male-female . . . has re-enacted the role of the pair of actors to relive the cosmic drama or divine comedy from Eden again. For the sake of human discriminative thinking the 'pair' has been forced to di-vorce and both to continue to live a divorced life, which is not whole life anymore like married life, as the same *via viae* to become viable (stands for vi(t)able = livable!): *vita sui!*

Herman Hesse, after his successful journey into the East as a journey into his own unknown, has this to say in accordance with the Upanishads:

> It is good to know that we have within us one who knows everything
> about us, wills everything, does everyting better than we can
> ourselves.[51]

And man, like an outsider to the body, feels like God an outsider to the world: extra-mundane *vis-à-vis* extra-corporeal to share the extraneousness abundantly. Man often seems to see God anthropomorphous and himself theomorphous to make up for the godlikeness he inherited from an old testament: the Old Testament. Anthropomorphous is Man's measure of *Deus sive Natura* with his egomorphous, homocentric *causa sive ratio alius*: imposing causality and rationality to the grand wholeness of *omnia animata* which he intended to claim for himself, the exception or exceptional rule! Later he did not feel the fatal bondage of his human-style fate or determinism, causal or rational conditioned. Determinism founded the dilemma and quasi-discrepancy of matter and divine nature *sub specie rationis humanis*, but Moses found matter not unworthy of divinity when Yahweh revealed to him: I will set my dwelling among you and My soul will not abhor you! (as you do abhor what is *vis-à-vis* as you-ness or quasi-otherness *per se*.) *Creator et creatura idem.* No God will abhor Himself indeed! And so Buddhist god-craving wise men thought the same when declaring the body as the abode of the divine. The egoless body as bodiless ego: before discrimination from the Tree of Knowledge started to affect or infect man. . . .

> Within this very body, mortal as it is, and only six feet in length, I do
> declare to you, are the world and the origin of the world and the
> ceasing and likewise the path that leads to the cessation thereof.[52]

And this stimulated the imperative:

> to strive within our six feet body for the form which existed before the laying down of Heaven and Earth.

Bliss, especially as Tantra wants to focus upon, takes place in the body as the whole world made manifest as pair-world, pair-wholeness of body-mind to mirror the heavenly eidolon from above. As above as below: the way up is the same way down. Only angels can ascend and descend with no discrimination, but man, a 'little bit lower than angels' has to transcend himself and his discrimination to follow in their footsteps on the path to the otherless self. The pair-concept ripens the longing for revelation of wholeness via the reciprocal receptivity in a two-way traffic of knower-known = known-knower as lover and be-loved are so reversible and uni-versible indeed! The body seems empty, void when supposed (by logic expectancy) to em-body some-thing else than body en-souled with a quasi-other in itselfness, but seems fully aware or re-aware of the pair-oneness of wholeness in its indivisiblity. Full is the whole earth with His glory. Fullness contains His glory to glorify the revelation originating from the craving for it. Edward Conze verily points to that very same truth (as Saraha), namely to that which can enslave (when thinking of quasi-otherness *per se*) and can free (when realizing the irreality of *causa sive ratio alius* or quasi-otherness *per se*!) in the same body so instrumental and mental as pair-concept for wholeness and omniality. 'Always standing in the very center of attention [is the body] and the human mind is wont to operate through (quasi-) contrasts.'

Saraha always hits at the Pandits:

> The scholars explain all the scriptures but do not know the Buddha residing within the body.[53]

And 'few only know how to touch the "deathless element" with one's body' and *ergo* how to strive for the 'form which existed before the laying down of Heaven and Earth'. The chaos, the Ayin, void, shunya, i.e. the indeterminate which 'just happens' with no *causa sive ratio alius*. And every happening happens just now and here as a constant, instant, Genesis or Gnosis. So to understand the body is to understand the world and vice versa as uni-versa indeed. To understand what stands 'under' (sub-stans) every standing and under every understanding. Job understood this challenge to seek within the Ayin, the place of wisdom in no-where or every-where with no birth nor death, as a pair-concept of life.

No*body* or no one (with a body or with-in the body) has known yet the frame of the body nor the frame of the mind. If he thinks of body *per se* or of mind *per se*. Every knower is himself within this very same frame and framework. It would be as Einstein described such observation in a letter to Schrödinger:

One attempts to interpret the psi-function as a complete description of a state, independent whether or not it is observed.

Schrödinger making then certain allusions to the 'Quantum mechanics people' answers:

It seems to me that what I call the construction of an external world that *really exists* is identical with what you call the describability of the individual situation that occurs only once-different as the phrasing may be. If they accuse us of 'metaphysical heresy' (when adhering to *such a reality*) does not matter. We are concerned thus with – the intersection of the determination of many, indeed of *all conceivable individual observers*.[54]

And Einstein, in his heyday, declared at a certain occasion to me that he loved Spinoza for being 'the very first to have applied with a thorough consequence the determinism to man in its wholeness', while Einstein himself, unfortunately, overlooked the 'other side' of determinism, namely the principle of indeterminacy as *causa sive ratio sui*, inbuilt in the first axiom of Spinoza with the first self-evident truth, way and life of 'I am'. This axiom is to be contemplated upon as primordial principle guiding the wise man when conscious of self, of God and of the world (of *omnia animata sumus*) as one and the same thing to re-identify with. Fettered to absolute determinism via *causa sive ratio alius*, Einstein nevertheless was too sincere to himself to confess:

it is rather rough to see that we are still in the stage of our swaddling clothes and it is not surprising that the fellows (!) struggle against admitting it (even to themselves).

'The principle of the quantum-theory is considered as final, although it remained a dilemma and one must believe that a more complete description would be useless because there would be no laws for it.' Particle-wave is a pair-concept too! Sic! Who makes the laws other than man himself? And he makes them within the frame of an observer *vis-à-vis* an observed as if a quasi-knower versus a quasi-known? And the lawgiver needs a lawtaker to accept it from a 'me' the observer above or beyond 'it'. The observable laws 'in' nature are too relational and only *in respectu expectationis intellectus hominis* always involving anthropomorphous attention and intention of ego-centred exceptionality, so to speak.

Now I must let my friend Carlo Suares speak about

the interplay of those energies in the Universe and in Man. We are then subjected to an amazing mental exercise. which can modify our way of thinking to the extent of uniting us with those energies. And that only is revelation.

There cannot be an 'observed' object *per se* and (another) observing subject *per se* with a certain standing under human ruling of his own (?) 'understanding'. Where is, then the wholeness if not doomed to remain a word with paper- and print-existence only'? Where? There is no 'where' *per se*, no 'there' *per se*. There is only either = other with quasi-otherness *per se*. And our identification with the recognition of *omnia animata sumus* as omni-awareness via self-awareness. Where is no question *per se* and no answer *per se*, there is the real 'where as no-where' or as 'no' to any asking at all. Any self-existence could be attributed to any 'where', 'there' or any 'asking' *per se*. It appears as (if) via *causa sive ratio alius*. Where a so-called questionable 'where' exists, an 'I' coexists to ask for it as if such 'it' be versus 'I' asking for the sake of his I-mindedness indeed. So an 'I' claiming another self-existence or self-coexistence *vis-à-vis* asking for 'where', etc. We can speak only of a pair-concept as there-here, after-before, then-now, etc., as manifestations of the constant, instant, substant and also permanent: immanent versus a fleeting transcendent. *Realitas* of res (*per se*) would presume an *ideitas* or *idea* (*per se*) *sine ideato*. Spinoza accordingly speaks of the same '*ordo et connexio idearum idem est ac ordo et connexio rerum*' with the understanding that *idea vera cum ideato suo con-venire debet*. *Con-venire* as a con-ventional pair-concept like the attribute-pair: *extensio-cogitatio* or in my re-phrasing like: *ex-tensio – in-tensio* (i.e. the very same '*tensio*' quasi 'in' or quasi 'ex') depending if adhering to *causa sive ratio vel sui vel alius*. Sic! The innate urge to ask and to ask again, while never to be satisfied with any short- or long-livable answer stems from one's hidden longing for completeness or identification with wholeness via expansion of self-awareness into omni-awareness.

> The path to enlightenment is the path towards completion. . . .
> Completeness can only be established *within* ourselves through a
> thorough transformation of our personality or, as expressed in
> Buddhist terminology . . . through a change or reversal (paravritti) of
> the very foundation (asraya) of our existence into a state of universality
> by dematerializing the hard crust of our individual selfhood. . . . Just
> as in a plant the urge towards sun and air compels the germ to break
> through the darkness of the earth, so the germ of Enlightenment
> (bodhi-citta) breaks the twofold veil: the obscuration caused by passion
> and by the illusion of an objective world.[55]

Does this not equate with Spinoza's aim: to be conscious of self, of God and of the world as one inseparable re-identifiable all-oneness or all-oneness?

It appears as if the whole play of askable questions in the expectation of answerable answers comes from the very urge to ask only, to ask for asking's sake (a kind of self-reflection with a question-mark ' ?') and not with the purpose to get this time the ultimate 'be-cause' with the ultimate cause or reason, which refers more to human beings, than to beings universally considered. Perhaps well determinable causal or rational explanations never can quench the quest for the immanent unexplainable, can never ever satiate the longing for the indeterminable, acausal, irrational, for *plain* life. Life remains life only when livable but not when knowable as substitute.

After so many and various attractions together with so many and various deceptions deriving from the Tree of Knowledge, have been severing the knower from the quasi-known via knowing and thus creating quasi-otherness *per se*, man is still longing for the pre-knowable state, what Hui-Neng calls to see one's nature or his face before birth. Man is still longing for the pre-rational or trans-rational state (which equates with the pre-causal or trans-causal state, i.e. of thinking!) that means before having succumbed to the (negative) magic of knowledge (knowing quasi-otherness *per se* without recognizing quasiness involved!). In Biblical language man surrendered to temptation be-cause or for the reason that the Tree of Knowledge looked 'good for food and pleasant to the eyes to be desired to make one wise . . .'.

For Spinoza only man's longing would make him wise to approach again the Tree of Life, of unknowable, acausal, irrational, indeterminable life when not via a quasi-knower *vis-à-vis* a quasi-known, but – but via knowing. This via is not siding with either/or which equates with 'otherness, but it is identifying with that via, becoming the via, the way itself when on the way to know the (otherless) Self'. When a-way from siding with one side of 'I' and the other side of 'Way'. It has been told to us that 'I am' is an equation of $I = am$ or $I = it$. The Angel with the whirling sword is watching over the access to the Tree of Life and only messianic conditioning or re-conditioning of the human mind can lead back to that state before having sided with good or evil, with knower versus known.[56] Then the so-called 'Last Days' will restore the so-called 'First Days' again and God and Man will again live in the together-ness of Eden. *Idea vera cum suo ideato con-venire debet, volit.* . . . In the Garden of Eden the pair-concept of *idea-ideatum*, of body-mind, of male-female, heaven-earth, etc., will reveal the secret of Yahweh = Elohim. The *Zohar* hints that just this was the mission for which man has been sent into the world, namely to discover the missing link for the pair-symbol of whole-ness. Body-mind or body-world and world-body reveal in the human garden the divine Garden of Eden, Gan = Garden is an abbreviation of G-uf: N-eshamah, the pair-name for the pair-concept which seems so im-paired and thus craves to be re-paired again and again. Yes. This concept will demon-strate Man as male-female (the human symbol) in the likeness of the divine symbol: Yahweh-Elohim, *Deus sive Natura, forma sive essentia, in se sive in alio.* . . . Man com-posed of mind-body has often posed the alternating prob-lem which stems from the very first axiom with axiomatic and self-evident truth (of quasi-otherness or eitherness *per se*!). That 'either: or' namely either as mind or as body (*per se*) longing so much for a pseudo-independence of seitas while still disregarding otherlessness implied in the pair-concept.

308

'Give up those erroneous thoughts leading to false distinctions! There is no 'self' and no 'other' [*per se*]'. With such words Huang Po seconds so excellently Spinoza's first axiom to unmask the phantom-otherness disguised as 'either-ness', while 'either' being the arch-root of dichotomy and discriminative knowing, namely knowing one, a quasi-knower as (if) *vis-à-vis* (another) a quasi-known. . . .

The notion of wholeness via the pair-concept is revealing the glory the prophet speaks so gloriously:

Full is the whole earth of His Glory!
Full is the whole body of His Glory!

This very wholeness or completion is like seeing the world in the body and the body 'in' the world and 'as' the world in its inseparable wholeness and inner-ness! In the Kabbalah the pair-concept seems so strongly structured as if becoming too anthropomorphic and less theomorphic. But this is only from the exoteric aspect where Polytheism for instance is per-verted while under the esoteric view the notion of 'number' has no meaning and no value like for *causa sive ratio* in the working of human entelechy, so to speak.

The human-pair points to the divine-pair to follow the great com-poser alternating *modo cogitandi vel modo extendi ad modum vivendi*. The psychic or somatic standpoint must always refer to the inseparability of the pair via the psychosomatic oneness of the pair-concept with only quasi-twoness in appearance. Man and 'his' Gan as reflection of the Gan of Eden to interweave and intertwine the all-oneness or one-allness of: Yahweh = Elohim or of *Deus sive Natura*.

So Cordovero points to the very sameness of 'God, God's Intellect and things intellected by Him' in order to show wholeness and fullness. Full is the whole earth with His Glory! Self-realization of wholeness via the drop, via the wave or via the dropless and waveless ocean itself, means: via the *via* or *via sui* and it offers oceanic feeling of omnidentity or omni-awareness as one-all-awareness (or all-one-awareness!). *Omnia animata sive omnia animantia sumus quamvis diversis gradibus, sed in se considerata, id est vera considerata: sine gradibus, sine respectu intellectus et sine rebus intellectis. Sine sine ipse*. . . . Sic! The very strict negation *via sine et via sine sine* . . . is in strict obedience of *omnia animata sive omnia vana*. It is in strict accordance with: *omnis determinatio est negatio*. Paraphrasing it must read: *omnis causatio, omnis ratiocinatio est negatio*. In order to see via quasi-negativity is only to negate the dichotomy of quasi-seer and quasi-seen and identifying with seeing, i.e. with self, with otherless self. Hence: Know Thyself!

In order to see quasi-negativity (as there is no negativity *per se* only *per* quasiness!) what appears to 'us' as seeable only via quasi-positivity (of otherness or eitherness) 'posing' as 'if' other than that which with it is composed as whole-pair or pair-whole. I in my singularizing or particularizing tendency of I-mindedness discriminate between 'that' and 'this', while this 'and' that discloses only eitherness = otherness in disguise as quasi-otherness *per se*, and then *perseitas* via duality poses and im-poses the phantom-problem. The fearful ego with its horror *tui sive alius* de-termines any apparent discrimination of knower *vis-à-vis* known, as the 'I' and 'I am' feels com-forted in its horrified self-isolation when rationalizing or causalizing such a discrepancy to become less harmful – only when it is exhaustively ex-plained (explained 'away' the odd way itself, that *via viae* or *via sui*!) how to lean on 'otherness' of so-called ex-es with their otherness of further ex-es, etc, and happy indeed to have a scapegoat for the own sinless goat of quasi-otherness *per se*. The wise man after Spinoza instead looks for the finger-pointers to the very ex-less and x-ful source and root of his own unknowable being via such oceanic root-awareness. It is 'I am' as the very Way, the very Truth and Life itself. It is unknowable *via cognoscendi* (and livable *via nascendi quasi ab alio* . . .) which de-viates the quasi-knower from the quasi-known while disidentifying with the otherless *via per se*: *via ipsa* or *via sui*. . . . I, as the knower *vis-à-vis* a quasi-known, feel as if con-fronted by myself: face to face with that puzzling self-reflection. And I have to face its odd reflecting other-lessness and unquasiness, when viewing reciprocal receptivity as two-way traffic of the pairness = oneness = allness. Yes! Then I really know that I know no-thing knowable (*per se*, but only *per* me!), but I live *animatus* and *animata*, *omnia-animata sumus*: the *via* as *via* beyond knower and/or known. The very *via* where I and it do pose as quasi-other or quasi-self and yet com-posed as one (pair-concept) and yet the same *via*. This is man's *via dolorosa et amorosa* as well. . . .

'I am' [is] that via. 'I am' [is] that truth. 'I am' [is] such life . . . Le chayim! Although or rather because of being unknowable, life contains and maintains such magic of all-oneness including the hunters after knowledge and the hunted, victimized objects of hunting. Victimized only in the mind of the (I-minded) hunter and in his quasi split-wholeness (co(s)mic schizophrenia!). He is always in the hope (and fear: hope after Spinoza is also a pair-concept!) to encounter once in 'his' life such lifeless otherness *per se* as the 'real' known *per se* beyond him, the 'real' knower *per se* and his special *seitas* as it were. . . .

Life awakens to desire to live, to live more than to know. *Vivat vita! Vivat via!* It makes everything so viable when equating or identifying vitable = viable '*invita lingua*' not only *invita Latinitate sed*. . . .

I feel Spinoza would have accepted not only Huang-Po, if he had read him before with us as witness, but the whole Eastern concept of the essence of mind (like Tantra, etc.) and the Way = Tao to liberation from discrimination between 'this' and 'that' as this 'or' that with an uncertain 'eitherness = otherness'.

310

Everything which is, is *either* in itself or in an-*other* (quasi-self).

The pair-concept of either-or does not belong to the essence of mind (rather to its existence so to speak in the speakable simile), but it claims and reclaims the pair-concept of neither-nor, when saying 'no' to any otherness or either-ness *per se* via alternating quasiness. And only thus do we read with glad acceptance:

> The essence of mind belongs 'neither' to death 'nor' rebirth. It is uncreated and eternal. If the mind would be kept free from discriminative thinking, there would be no more *arbitrary* thoughts to give rise to appearance of form, existence and condition.[57]

The essence of mind is manifest in its self-reflection as the via knowing which is unknowable *per se* but livable only in oneness, or pairness as wholeness of the quasi-knower *vis-à-vis* (or quasi: *vis-à-vis*) a quasi-known. The essence of the body is manifest in its same self-reflection of *idea: ideatum*, of *naturans: naturata*, of *animantia: animata*, namely as pair-concept again and again. . . .

Where is this Way? Where this Truth? Where such Life? Where the via, the Tao? Answer: There where 'no'where is and where 'no'there is either. Where no 'no' is either. Only a Buddha could speak of such quasi-where and quasi-there as a quasi-nowhere or quasi-everywhere is: everyman's and no-man's land with no I and no I-mindedness apart from All-mind and All-mindedness of *omnia animata sumus magna cum essendi fruitione*. . . . (sed non cognoscendi fruitione)!

> There is, disciples, a realm de-void of earth and water, fire and air. It is not endless space, nor infinite thought, nor no-thingness, neither ideas, nor non-ideas. Not 'this' world, nor 'that' it is. I call it neither a coming, nor a departing, nor a standing still, nor death, nor birth: it is without a basis, progress or stay. It is the ending of sorrow.[58]

The sorrow begins with 'otherness' and with knowledge and because the knower presumes and assumes that he 'knows' the otherness *per se* of the known. The sorrow begins with 'my' thought as if 'my' drop apart from all drops, waves and the dropless, waveless Ocean itself. It begins with 'my' thought of you as (if) quite other than me, that non-you, non-you *per se*, because I have only co(s)mic monopoly on I *per* me as first *seitas*, so to speak. The end of otherness is the end of sorrow. The end of sorrow is the end of otherness.

> For that which clingeth to 'another' there is a fall; but to that which clingeth not, no fall can come. Where no fall cometh, there is rest, and where rest is, there is no keen desire. Where keen desire is not, naught cometh or goes, there is no death, no birth. Where there is 'neither' death [*per se*] 'nor' birth [*per se*], there neither is this world nor that, nor in between . . . 'it' is the ending of sorrow.[59]

311

The end of thinking otherness is the end of thinking sorrow and of own bondage. Think no thoughts, no single thought of singularizing what is whole including you and me, and him with her: *nos omnes*: *omnia animata sumus*. There is no otherness only quasi-otherness. There is no sorrow only quasi-sorrow. There is no you only quasi-you, quasi-me, quasi-him, quasi-her. Tat twam asi; You are 'it', you are it all in 'its' (not in 'yours') wholeness, all-oneness or one-allness. Via quasiness you are all it, but you do not know it. Hence Know Thyself! As the via: the way, the truth.... Life! And life as Gnosis or Genesis via the first verse of the Bible or via the first axiom of the *Ethics*!

Everything which is, is 'either' in itself, 'or' in another.
Everything which is, is 'neither' in itself (*per se*) 'nor' in another (*per se*).
Everything which is, is every thing and every no-thing: quasiness or unquasiness.

And the first and best pioneer against the phantom of quasi-otherness *per se* will now voice its point:

As long as there is duality, one sees 'the other' one hears 'the other', one smells 'the other', one speaks of 'the other', one thinks of 'the other', one knows 'the other'. But . . . when for the illumined soul the all is dissolved in the Self, who is there to be seen by whom? Who is there to be smelt by whom? Who is there to be thought by whom? Who is there to be spoken by whom? Who is there to be heard by whom? Who is there to be known by whom? By whom shall the 'knower' be 'known'?.... That is the truth I teach you. That is the truth of immortality.[60] Beli-mah and beli-mi: without 'what' and without 'who' are a pair-concept!

Would this have been the same truth as the answer Pilate expected when asking: What is truth? Did he mean: What is the Way? What is Life? What is 'I am'? Would Pilate still have pronounced the death-sentence when accepting the truth of immortality or deathlessness via birthlessness . . . ? Pilate had no right to ask no 'other' than himself, as there is no other than the very same truth for all. Yes!

It were better to live one single day in the realization of the deathless state than to live a hundred years without such realization.[61]

Such realization implies the 'inward realization of the imperturbability of the essence of mind' as Hui-Neng taught us: imperturbed by thinking of twoness, of duality what is only pairness, *ergo* by conditioned thinking of quasi-birth (*ab alio*!) and of quasi-death (*in alio*). Sic! There is no otherness than you yourself to perturb you. Why are you against yourself and still do not want to: Know Thyself? Truth is divine with Spinoza: *Deus sive Veritas. Deus sive Natura. Deus sive Amor. Deus = sive* and *siveitas*: eitherness or quasi-otherness and unquasiness as 'pair'! Truth is not only truth. It is the Way of 'I am'. It is Life. The via is via quasiness or via unquasiness: a pair-concept of wholeness via omni-awareness (of *omnia animata sumus*!). Unknowability of life does not belittle it but just magnifies the sizeless magic of life. No shadow of sorrow and no shadow of otherness *per se*. . . . A Hassidic witness in spite of Buber will speak for Spinoza if only for its magic unfaltering contradiction and pre-diction of Israel's re-election in the eyes of *Deus sive Veritas*, of Yahweh = Elohim.

> If I am only I, when you are you, and if you are only you when I am I,
> then – I am not (really) I and you are not (really) you either.

To paraphrase it one could apply the same truth to undo quasiness *per se* as the phantom-problem to horrify the I-minded I aiming for 'Sir I' rather than for (the metathesis of) 'Sri I'.

> If I am only your other, when you are my other, and if you are my
> other only when I am your other, then – there is (really) nobody
> nobody's other . . . !

Or here:

> If the body is only the body, when the mind is the mind, and if the mind
> is only the mind, when the body is the body then – the body is (really)
> not the body and the mind is (really) not the mind either. They are not
> two but one cabbalistic, sephirotic pair-concept impressing and
> expressing omniality and completion via revelation of otherlessness. . . .

I *per* me, you *per* you, he *per* him or *per se* – self *per se*, other *per se*; body *per se*, mind *per se*: all these concepts are void of *seitas*, of self-existence. They are com-posite pair-concepts of all-oneness or one-allness. Yes.

> Full is the whole earth-heaven (pair) with His glory!
> Full is the whole body-mind (pair) with His glory!
> Full is the whole Man (male-female pair) with His glory!
> And void is the whole I and his I-mindedness of His glory while only
> full of self-glorification via separation and isolation leading to
> non-glorious otherness and sorrow. . . .

The end of sorrow is the end of otherness and the beginning of joy in the *acquiescentia* or *con-quiescentia in se ipso* (*sine alio*!). Then I can realize the quasi-irreal, acausal, in the indeterminability of my own unknowable Life as Way and Truth of 'I am' that 'I am' as God has shown it to Moses and his 'I am' awareness. It is the beginning of joy about the imperturbability of the essence of mind which belongs neither to birth nor death but rather longs for omni-awareness of *omnia animata sumus*. Until now, my dear and far you, you were always in fear. In fear of otherness *per se* but not of self *per se*. Always in fear of fear and you forgot the fear of the Lord, beyond self and

313

other. Wisdom begins with such fear or rather awe, with awe to wonder and to ponder; to ponder and to wonder again. . . . Fear as if you were the only solo-actor in this great show on earth, to show knowledge and not love. You loved yourself and not your neighbour. You wanted always only to know thy neighbour but never your self.

Now you have to re-verse it not to be anymore versus your neighbour but uni-versus as he is not 'like' you, but he 'is' you when you want to be you yourself! Thus you will turn knowledge into love and love into knowledge: in the way 'Adam knew Eve' while both still in the Garden of Eden in pair = togetherness and all = togetherness with The Lord, the Gardener of Eden. In the garden the quasi-knower and the quasi-known were aware of their otherless and reciprocal receptivity of sameness. Loving each other is knowing each other or one another otherless: the great magic. . . . Then the great Truth of 'I am' is identical with the great Way, and with Life itself. Achat Ruah Elohim Chayim! This is the first verse of Sepher Yetsirah equal to the first verse in the Bible and equal to the first axiom in the *Ethics* of Spinoza. Only so can Life start more ethically valid than morally, which wants to preserve one's hidden selfhood via non-obliging lip-service to man and mankind. Where, then is man kind to man . . . ?

Amor Dei sive Amor Naturae sive Amor Veritatis sive Amor Viae . . . such identity involves and evolves self-identification of 'I am' to reflect and re-reflect the great echo from creation via re-creation and pro-creation either . . . to test and to taste omniality with omni-awareness or pair-awareness.

Abraham Joshua Heschel assures us: Man is not Alone when he is all-one or one-all. His great vision is to think of God as

Togetherness of All Beings in Holy Otherness!

Holy the 'other' then only you can follow the prophet to proclaim: Holy, Holy, Holy is Yahweh. Full is the whole earth with His glory! Full the whole earth and full with His glory every inhabitant on earth when Whole as: self and other, i.e. self or other with no difference, no discrimination, no dichotomy whole all-oneness or one-allness! Then you experience holy togetherness or ingetherness to 'gether', i.e. gather all quasi-others as unknown parts of you and com-posing your wholeness and completion. Then your consciousness will be like co-consciousness to be with Spinoza 'conscious of self, God and the world (of quasi-otherness)' in a marvellous self-realization indeed. The whole essence of the Dharma is encapsulated and condensed in one long word:

ANUTPATTIKADHARMAKSHANTI

Lu K'uan Yü describes this state as:

The patient endurance of the uncreate, or rest in the imperturbable reality which is beyond birth and death and requires a very patient endurance.

The Prajnaparamita Sastra defines it as:

the unflinching faith and unperturbed abiding in the underlying reality of all things, which is beyond creation and destruction. It must be realized before attainment of Buddhahood.[62]

Q.E.D.

NOTES

1 Van der Taak, *Spinoza Mercator et Autodidactus* (The Hague, M. Nijhoff, 1933) can re-awake our attention to Spinoza's definition of mind as automaton, but this word not be understood as a mechanical man-made robot and the maker always beyond and outside his making. In Greek *auto-didaktos* = *automathes* means self-taught or having learned by one self (and no 'other'): as self-discipline in its very original sense and essence. On a higher level the word also means – according to Greek etymology – 'natural' = by 'self' (as otherless), and further: 'spontaneous'. Having all this in mind when thinking about 'mind', then Spinoza's definition must point to such cardinal and fundamental pillar of his philosophical system: *causa sive ratio sui* = indeterminacy! Just recently I learned from a Japanese friend that the Japanese word for 'nature' has the very same meaning, namely: in-itselfness. *q.e.d.*

2 Paul Reps: *Zen Flesh, Zen Bones.* Zen and Pre-Zen Writings (New York, Doubleday, 1961), p. 127.

3 Deuteronomy, VIII, 1–3.

4 'Deus est: M-Ens con-stans infinitis attributis attribuens sibi ipso infinitam sive aeternam existentiam vel essentiam via infinitae essendi fruitionis; ergo via Amoris Dei Intellectualis. Deum, Dei Intellectum resque ab ipso intellectas unum et idem esse. Ordo et connexio idearum idem est ac ordo et connexio rerum sive causarum. Ideae cum suis ideatis sive cum rebus con-venire debent'. . . . Sic!

5 S. L. MacGregor Mathers: *Kabbalah Unveiled* (London, Routledge & Kegan Paul, 1956), p. 112. Comp. with Note 13 more thoroughly!

6 Reps, *op. cit.*, p. 171. We could parallel this highly important thought with Spinoza by saying: substance comes with attributes when viewed from the intellecting viewpoint or with modes when viewed from the intellected or objectified aspect. Spinoza thus uses for the purpose of viewpointing: *tam-quam, quam-vis, sive, quatenus,* etc, like pegs as makeshifts or expedient means in order to express somehow the inexpressible in the light of the Dharma. . . .

7 Shri Shankaracharya, *Aparokshanubhuti* (Direct Experience of Reality) (London, Shanti Sadan, 1959), p. 51.

8 See note 8 to my Prologue in this book! Let us pause for an eternal instant and ask: what is it that re-flection gets such highest importance among great thinkers, East and West alike? What is our consciousness and its enigmatic functional re-flection? Is it not cosmic all-consciousness (of *omnia animata sumus!*) that reflects in each consciousness of us? Teilhard de Chardin has pondered on it: 'the consciousness of each of us is e-volution looking at itself –

315

and reflecting!' (*The Phenomenon of Man* (New York, Harper & Row, 1969), p. 420.) C. Brunner once does speak of 'thinking as self-experience of existence', and here he meets Descartes's *cogito ergo sum; cogitare sive esse*, but I cannot remember that he gives special attention to Spinoza's emphasis on self-reflection, self-contemplation which must lead to self-realization of *causa sui sive ratio sui sine alio per se.*

Carlo Suares free from our slavery to explanations of unexplainable life speaks of existence as of a wonder. Especially in his comment to Sepher Yetsirah like: 'the fact that anything at all exists is a total Mystery. . . .' For the 'I' and his I-mindedness omni-identity with the all-oneness or one-allness is a mystery. Yes! It just 'happens'. . . . Is it not a wonder, when it happens to be, but not when being caused or reasoned out to be in accordance with *causa sive ratio alius*? Happening cannot be known, or not known 'what' it is, but rather in Spinoza's way, 'that' it is. Happening cannot fit in between the quasi-two: knower and known, it is only non-dual knowing, as life. It can be likened to electricity which we use and harness its wonder of 'thatness', without really knowing its 'whatness'. *Eliceo* in ancient Roman times concealed some magic, which only in Gilgamesh can appeal to us for direct experience, when he approaches that magic (electric) gate to sense something quasi beyond the senses, what we call today extra-sensorial. . . .

9 *Revue Philosophique* (Paris, Presses Universitaires, 1924), sept–oct., pp. 301–408.
10 The pious Jew when first awake in the morning, says a little prayer of thankful confession: 'I confess (thankfully) to Thee that Thou hast returned to me 'my' soul with great mercy! – I with my bondage (mostly attributed to my arch-enemy: The Other One), as the main fact and factor, the only cause or reason for isolating and separating I-mindedness, this same I, does expect that the divine all-mindedness re-leases me as it were, again to this merciless self-bondage of I-ness. During so-called sleep I assume to have been quasi deprived of my I-ness, i.e. to have been quasi I-less or united with all other equally I-less and It-ful beings: *omnia animata*. Spinoza does not say: *omnes animatos sumus* but rather prefers wisely: *omnia animata* with no respect to us (as '*nos* -and *animatos* as well!'). This only in order to let us ponder upon us as 'not-us': free from anthropomorphism towards theomorphism. . . . In the Upanishads we go to Brahma during sleep and later we say: I have slept so well! I was so happy with Brahma together in the way Adam would have said: I was so happy with God together in the Garden of Eden to enjoy such togetherness of God's manlikeness with Man's godlikeness nursed in this kindergarten of mankind. And if happy during sleep only because I-less, I then could rather say: I have been only so happy without me and without my I-mindedness as if happy-dead (via loss of egohood!). Thus death like his little brother (both likened to greater or lesser mysteries pointing to man's transformation or transfiguration in the way Suares means it) sleep, regain both a more common and better significance indeed. School-grammar and grammarians are applying to all verbs with no exception the very same rule of con-jugation (like a yoke to carry and carry-on!). This rule seems sanctified only by hasty verbalizations for comfort sake. How otherwise could I then say for sure: I sleep now? How: I have slept before? How, when I with my I-mindedness never ever can beware or be re-aware

namely now: to be asleep and retaining my I-mindedness as well as quasi an outsider to myself and to my I-mindedness too? Am I a true follower of Baron von Münchhausen, the man, you remember, who boasted to have dragged himself out from a marsh with no need for help from any otherness. . . ? Sic!

A para-doxon of such odd I-concept which I never ever can recollect during my I-lessness of having been still I-full and extra-I-minded as well with the very same I-awareness of self-observation as a quasi-other. Or: how did I know that I have slept so well in the past? Can I remember a non-existing I-experience with I-awareness only accessible during non-sleep, i.e. when only being awake? Any experience is only self-experienceable always (all-ways!) only as a presence presenting uncommunicable self-evidence namely knowledge as (k)now-ledge so to speak. What am I allowed to say, is: I shall sleep as in a future tense and this is never demanding verification save when becoming a presence in a socalled later (presence), so late already that such future is never recognizable or identifiable with the presence as already expounded before. Here Spinoza denies so clearly any 'before', any 'after' and any 'when'. *Conclusion*: you have to admit then that you are not really you (for yourself) but only you if I am I, and I am not really me (for myself) but only I if you are you. In the very same way: 'before' is not really 'before' (for itself) but only if 'after' is 'after', and 'after' is not really 'after' (for itself) but only if 'before' is 'before'. So you have to admit in the very same way that you are not (really or *per se*) you, but you-less or 'it' and therefore it is hard for you to tread on the path leading to *know thyself*! You as you like all you-s, like me, like him, like her, like them all. . . . *you are already* 'it' but never *ready* to know it as a knower *vis-à-vis* a known. Tat Twam Asi has been taught by self-teaching or by learning from one self; auto-maton! To know yourself is the hardest knowledge (of nowledge) and not transferable at all, not communicable to any quasi-other: No gimmick, no trick nor fake can help to get access by knowing the theory of it. We have to agree with J. Blofeld that 'knowing how to drive a car does not help a man in an armchair to get as far as to the next room' . . . (*The Way of Power*, London, George Allan & Unwin, 1970, p. 239).

And have we from the West not heard already the message from another divine messenger about the Way (of 'I am'), the Truth and Life? Namely: you can only *find* yourself when ready to *loose* yourself. When ready to abandon and loose your 'special' your-ness as illusive exclusiveness with craving nostalgia to return homebound for the all-inclusive *all-oneness or one-allness of omnia animata*. . . .

11 Lama Anagarika Govinda: *Foundations of Tibetan Mysticism* (London, Rider 1959), p. 181.
12 *Udanas*, VIII, 1, 3, 4, from the Pali.
13 The pair-concept will be unfolded later in the main text itself, but some words are so important for understanding and so much in common use while containing a very uncommon meaning that I crave to reveal their etymo-sophical true significance. They all will help consolidate the plain validity of this pair-concept indeed. To begin with: it is two-way traffic as between a quasi-twoness which in reality makes the pairness to apply its fairness.
1. *reci-procal*: this comes according to Oxford Etymology from re- and pro- to

mean: corresponding to each other [ergo: otherless]; re-flexive in grammar, moving backwards and forwards, *alter*-nating (in true obedience to that first axiom of Spinoza's *Ethics*!).

2. *vice-versa*: (or re-versa what is only uni-versa but not dui-versa at all). This matches also with: 'face-to-face' and like this it is a 'versus' facing (another) 'versus' but really facing thus that very same self, you are supposed to learn how to: Know Thyself! This is apparently a dichotomy, although backed by grammar, but let assume a *'versus'* only when against a *'vertendus'* like a 'knower' versus a 'known', while only *alter*-nating the versus, the known, etc.

3. *vis-à-vis*: as a 'seen' facing a (quasi-other) 'seen' as subject/object with no seer *alter*-nating. *Ergo* in full accordance with the previous word the very same meaning.

4. *face-to-face*: supports also excellently the pair-concept in all the various exoteric and esoteric usage of language. Thus Spinoza's *'facies totius uni-versi'* points to direct self-confrontation in the mystical sense of 'I' and I-less Self conveying otherlessness. The *facies totius universi* is likened to one face or sur-face where every face is facing self-reflection, also a notion so highly important on the path, Spinoza is pointing to. Face-to-face and *vis-à-vis* are both congruent in their meaning to reveal the functioning of a mirror-simile not mirroring seer and/or seen, but mirroring self-reflection so 'puzzling' for Paul as for the modernizing translators of the New Testament to accept the very same epithet as best fit for the finger-pointing to help getting access to such odd and fascinating text. Let us pause for a moment and compare both translations:

Old Text:	*New Text:*
For now we see through a glass darkly: but then face to face: now I know in part, but then shall I know [as a knower] even as also I am known [as a known].	Now we see only puzzling reflections in a mirror, but then we shall see face to face. My knowledge is now partial; then it will be whole like God's knowledge of me [via me and it: knower knowing self].

C. Brunner gives attention to this mirror-simile as the ancients had no looking-'glasses', but mirrors from metal, in which one could recognize one self only 'darkly'. (*Unser Christus oder Das Wesen des Genies* (Köln, Kiepenheuer & Witch, 1958), note 11, p. 226.)

Paul rightly refers to such a metaphor known to him quite well from Jebam. 49 b: 'All the prophets looked into the non-luminous mirror, whilst our teacher Moses looked into the luminous mirror. Brunner himself rejected with much emphasis such mirror-analogy in his main work, apparently in order to avoid crass dualistic discrimination of seer and seen. Animals cling to it when seeming to be puzzled by their 'otherness *per se*' as if having to face 'an enemy' discovered over 'there' in the glassy beyondness as it were. .... We (*homo sapiens* and *bestia humana* in a mixture) see ourselves undisguised via glassy reflection. Prajapati – as recorded in the Upanishads – had great difficulty in explaining to his two special pupils their true self as not reflectable in a mirror nor in a water-hole. . . . In the East thinkers are so familiar with the mirror-analogy that the quasi-otherness reflected is *de facto* a self-reflection via quasi-otherness *per se*. John Blofeld with his mind so excellently attuned to the Eastern directness of self-approach, reminds us wisely of a

> widely used Buddhist analogy to liken mind's function to that of a mirror. The images cannot exist without the mirror and yet the mirror remains itself, neither com-'posing' nor sullied by the images yet. Were there no images, the existence of the mirror could be detected – except by reference to its surroundings, which are excluded from the analogy. Mind is the container of all things, none of which could exist apart from it, but is imperceptible *per se*. (*The Way of Power*, London, Allen & Unwin, 1970), p. 239.

Finally I should not omit to mention here that only due to the true application of the mirror-simile has been determined the fate of Hui-Neng to become the Sixth Patriarch against his rival also a candidate for the succession of the Fifth Patriarch. (We will come back to it in another note!). Hui-Neng begins the new revitalizing renaissance of Zen to save it from fossilization into lifeless scripturization, as it were. . . . How to compare those two decisive stanzas connected with truth and true succession of the Fifth Patriarch?

I.	II.
This body is the Bodhitree;	The Bodhi is not like the tree;
The soul is like a mirror bright;	The mirror bright is nowhere
Take heed to keep it always clean,	shining:
And let not dust collect on it!	As there is nothing from the first,
	Where can the dust itself collect?

So Advaita (and Nirdvanda too) or non-duality has won the victory over the wrong term 'Monism' still encapsulating oneness as 'number' instead in Spinoza's spirit (and the very same tradition of the 'ancient Hebrews') indefinitiveness, indeterminacy. This is a victory over vaita or crass duality *per se*. It is my urge to show the pair-concept as the graspable concept of totality, omniality. And finally to ponder on re-flection in a mirror and on the re-flexive pro-noun mirrored by grammar, I would like to re-read with you again (5) what MacGregor Mathers has been so able to crystallize in his mind, namely about the eidolon formed by our own de-finition and then when added to the thing defined in such invisible mirror of thinking is to 'appear' as if a duality, a duad *per se*, so puzzling indeed. . . . From here stems the use of the notion and term 'second' (namely: to 'second' quasi the numberless indefinite, but not the definable, definite article!) or 'another'. The Greek and Latin have both two words for 'other': one as between quasi-twoness, i.e. the other or the second, the next other to me. And there is 'other' as between the quasi-many: *allos, heteros* and *alius, alter*, hence alteration and alternation, alternative, etc. Erich Fromm once went even further and used 'alternativism' to illustrate and demonstrate better the dark quasiness between determinism and freedom (or indeterminacy). Spinoza solves and dissolves such cardinal di-lemma via his first axiom. And this I have selected as basic leitmotif for my theme here. A variation of the same theme is only: *via causa sive ratio: vel sui vel alius*. Q.E.D.

319

14 *The Upanishads* ed. Brabhananda and Manchester (New York, Mentor Books, 1957), p. 71.

15 Govinda, *op. cit.*, p. 56.

16 *The Secret Sayings of Jesus. According to the Gospel of Thomas* (London, Fontana, 1965), p. 126.

17 Ashvagosha: *Awakening of Faith* (New York, University Books, 1960), p. 83.

18 Proverbs 30, 18, 19.

19 *The Secret of the Golden Flower*, tr. R. Wilhelm (London, Routledge & Kegan Paul, 1957), p. 23.

20 Carlos Castaneda, *Tales of Power* (London, Hodder & Stoughton, 1975), p. 31.

21 Reps, *op. cit.*

22 C. Brunner *Die Lehre von den Geistigen und vom Volke* (Stuttgart, Cotta, 1959), p. 881. After a lifelong search and research I have been glad to link that Proton Pseudos (misleading to duality *per se*) with the Proton Axioma of Spinoza (unmasking quasi-duality *per se*!).

23 Sri Krishna Prem and Sri Madhava Ashish, *Man, the Measure of All Things*, (Adyar, Theos. Publ., 1960), p. 171.

24 A. Heschel, *Man is Not Alone* (New York, Harper & Row, 1966), p. 27.

25 See note 13.

26 Sir J. Jeans, *The World About us* (Cambridge, 1933), p. 294, 354.

27 MacGregor Mathers, *op. cit.*

28 D. Runes, *Philosophical Dictionary* (New York, Philosophical Library, 1960), p. 78.

29 Max Planck *Quantum Theory* (Oxford, Clarendon Press, 1922).

30 L. Pauwels and J. Bergier, *The Dawn of Magic* (London, Panther Books, 1964), p. 78.

31 Ralph Metzner, *Maps of Consciousness* (New York, Collier Books, 1971).

32 R. Fischer, 'On Separateness and Oneness-I-self Dialogue', *Confinia Psych.*, Basel, vol. 15, pp. 165–94. Material received directly from the author.

33 R. Fischer, *A Cartography of the Ecstatic and Meditative States* (Symposium, Chicago, 1970). Material received directly from the author.

34 G. Scholem, *Major Trends in Jewish Mysticism* (New York, Schocken Books, 1961.

35 W. Y. Evans-Wentz, *Tibetan Yoga and Secret Doctrines* (London, Oxford University Press, 1935), p. 85.

36 St. Elmo Nauman Jr., *Dictionary of American Philosophy* (New York, Philosophical Library, 1973), p. 107.

37 A. Wolfson, *Spinoza – A Life of Reason* (New York, Philosophical Library, 1969), p. 244.

38 Scholem, *op. cit.*, pp. 238, 252, etc.

39 Job, 28:12.

40 *Secret Sayings of Jesus.*

41 D. T. Suzuki, *Essays in Zen Buddhism*, 3rd Series (London, Rider, 1958), p. 208.

42 Reps, *op. cit.*, p. 174.

43 Lama Anagarika Govinda's Foreword to *The Tibetan Book of the Dead*, 3rd edn. (Oxford University Press, 1966).

44 *Zohar*, II:55a.

45 B. Spinoza, *Principles of Cartesian Philosophy* (New York, Philosophical Library, 1961). I cannot refrain from mentioning here a Spinozist and at the same time so familiar with Descartes. I must agree fully with his findings, namely pointing to Spinoza, that 'he was simply too original and creative a writer to submerge his own thought and allow his subject to speak for himself. . . .' These words of David Bidney are so fascinating for me as for Edwin Curley (in his contribution to the homage of Spinoza here!), that I must further say with him that Spinoza 'reads his own ideas into Descartes and his exposition of Descartes often tells us more about Spinoza than about his subject.' Now I can recollect how I myself have been so often puzzled by such discovery to take the one for the other . . . and it was an impression of revelation so to speak. . . . Further relevant material is to be found in Curley's own contribution here, called rightly: *Spinoza – as an Expositor of Descartes*.

46 Will Durant, *The Age of Louis XIV* (New York, Simon Schuster, 1963), pp. 656ff.

47 Carlo Suares, *The Cipher of Genesis. The Original Code of the Qabala as Applied to the Scriptures* (London, Stuart & Watkins, 1970), p. 46.

48 Spinoza, *Principles of Cartesian Philosophy*.

49 *Ibid*.

50 Alan Watts, *Joyous Cosmology* (New York, Vintage Books, Random House, 1962), p. 3.

51 Herman Hesse, *Demian* (London, Panther Books, 1965), p. 82.

52 Govinda, 1959, *op. cit.*, p. 66.

53 Edward Conze in *Buddhist Texts Through the Ages* (Oxford, Bruno Cassirer, 1954), p. 233.

54 Einstein, Schrödinger, Planck and Lorentz, *Letters on Wavemechanics* (New York, Philosophical Library, 1967).

55 Govinda, 1959, *op. cit.*, p. 82.

56 To illustrate this in the most striking way and to appeal by transmitting an experience, I will have to retell the following story:

A monk named E-myo out of envy pursued the patriarch (Hui-Neng) to take his great treasure away from him. The Sixth Patriarch placed the bowl and robe on a stone in the road and told E-myo:

'These objects must symbolize the faith. There is no use fighting over them. If you desire to take them, take them now.' When E-myo went to move the bowl and the robe they were as heavy as mountains. He could not budge them.

Trembling for shame he said: 'I came wanting teaching, not the material treasure. Please teach me!' The Sixth Patriarch said: 'When you do not think good and when you do not think non-good, what is your true self?'

At these words E-myo was illumined. Perspiration broke out all over his body. He cried and bowed, saying: 'You have given me the secret words and meanings. Is there yet a deeper part of the teaching?'

The Sixth Patriarch replied: 'What I have told you is no secret at all. When you realize your own true self the secret belongs to you.'

E-myo said: 'I was under the Fifth Patriarch many years but could not realize my true self until now. Through your teaching I find the source. A person drinks water and knows *himself* whether it is cold or warm. May I call you my teacher?'

The Sixth Patriarch replied: 'We studied together under the Fifth Patriarch. Call him your teacher, but just treasure what you have attained.' (Reps, *op. cit.*, p. 108).

57 Asvagosha, *op. cit.*, p. 75.
58 Udanas, *op. cit.*
59 *Ibid.*
60 Brabhananda and Manchester, *op. cit.*, p. 89.
61 W. Y. Evans-Wentz, *The Tibetan Book of the Great Liberation* (Oxford University Press, 1954), p. x.
62 Glossary of Lu K'uan Yü (Charles Luk) in most of his works (London, Rider).

17 The logical and experiential roots of Spinoza's mysticism – an answer to Jon Wetlesen*

H. G. Hubbeling, Groningen

In his interesting paper, 'Body awareness as a gateway to eternity: a note on the mysticism of Spinoza and its affinity to Buddhist meditation' Jon Wetlesen criticizes the interpretation of Spinoza that appeared in a previous paper of mine entitled 'Logic and experience in Spinoza's mysticism'.[1] Wetlesen is a very competent Spinoza scholar and the whole circle of international Spinoza scholars is looking forward to his forthcoming book *The Sage and the Way. Studies in Spinoza's Ethics of Freedom.* I am glad that so capable a scholar pays attention to this very interesting subject. I have much sympathy for his point of view and I would be glad if I could subscribe to it. As I am not convinced by his arguments, my scholarly consciousness forbids me to do so. In this paper, I shall bring forward my main objections without repeating the arguments of my previous article.

I said that I have sympathy with Wetlesen's point of view. And why not? Without being a mystic myself, I have great admiration for many mystics in various religions; and again, without being a Spinozist myself, I have great admiration for Spinoza. So, why not combine these two things and interpret Spinoza as a mystical philosopher, as so many competent scholars do? And then a mystical philosopher in the sense that Spinoza had mystical experiences, as Wetlesen tries to prove in his paper? For I do not deny that Spinoza's philosophy has a mystical structure, but, so far as I can see this mystical structure can be explained without reference to these mystical experiences. At one point Wetlesen misinterprets my intentions in that he says that I take sides with the rationalists. This was not my intention. In the debate between the rationalistic and the mystical interpretation of Spinoza I tried to take a mediating position by defending the thesis that Spinoza's philosophy has a mystical structure but that this mysticism is not built on mystical experiences but on the use of certain (logical) rules. On one point Wetlesen and I agree, i.e. that the question as to whether Spinoza had mystical experiences depends on how we define the term 'mystical experience'. I interpreted 'mysticism' in a narrow way in 'that it tries to lead people via various ways to experience

* For a much better understanding see Wetlesen's paper (pp. 479–94) before Hubbeling's answer – the editor.

323

mystic ecstasy, the *unio mystica*' and 'that there are various stages on this way before one reaches one's goal. . . . An interesting feature in the various mystical systems is that they resemble each other in their doctrine of the itinerary of the human soul towards the *unio mystica*.'[2] Of these various stages I gave some examples.[3] Now, if in a certain thinker there is not this clear itinerary towards the *unio mystica*, including some techniques of contemplation, this thinker is not a mystic in my sense. Wetlesen apparently uses a broader concept of mysticism. The disadvantage of this broader concept of mysticism in which views like 'the union which the mind has with the whole of nature' belong, is that practically all religious experience becomes mystical. Then every great religious person is a mystic. Therefore I prefer to distinguish between mystical experience in a strict sense and religious experience that is non-mystical. Many instances of what Wetlesen calls mystical experience, e.g. 'the cognition of the union which the mind has with the whole of nature',[4] 'an intimate cognition of God', 'a highly personal feeling and experience', etc.,[5] belong to religious feelings in general and are not typically mystical in the sense in which I use the word. But, of course, I do not want to dispute about words and for the sake of the discussion I am very well prepared to accept a broader sense of mysticism, so that religious experiences that are not stages on the typical way to the *unio mystica* by way of contemplating techniques, are also called mystical. Now, it seems for a moment that the discussion between Wetlesen and me comes down to a dispute about words. But, alas, this is not the case. Wetlesen draws a parallel between Spinoza's philosophy and Buddhist meditation, and this latter kind of philosophy is certainly mystical in the sense in which I use the word mysticism in my original article. And on this point and some others I disagree with Wetlesen.

Before I put forward my objections to Wetlesen's view, it seems as well to indicate some principles of interpretation that have guided me, as the science of interpretation is a difficult one and scholars do not always agree with each other on these principles. 1. The main point is that according to my view we should apply Occam's razor also to the problem of interpretation. That is, we should not presuppose some views or experiences in the author who is to be interpreted, if we can do without them. On the other hand: 2. The set of views and experiences by which we can explain more statements of the author is to be preferred to one by which we can explain less. It is self-evident that there is sometimes tension between principles 1 and 2 and that this causes many difficulties. Another problem is the question as to when we can speak of the influence of an author A on an author B; or, what is more important in our case: When can we say that there is an affinity or common structure between two philosophical (or religious) systems? To answer the last question only: 3. According to my view we may only speak of an affinity or common structure if there is an isomorphy between the two systems with respect to their basic or fundamental concepts and views. Of course, here too there is plenty of opportunity to disagree with each other: What is to be included among 'fundamental concepts and views'? I think that if Wetlesen and I were to continue our discussion we would finally come to a discussion on the principles of interpretation instead of a discussion of Spinoza!

But be this as it may, I think that I have to bring forward some objections to Wetlesen's interpretation that makes it impossible for me to accept his view, however much sympathy I have for it. Strangely enough I would be glad if Wetlesen could convince me that I am wrong, but until now he has not. In my presentation of objections I shall restrict myself to what seems to me fundamental. Wetlesen's paper is rich in content and tempts one to go into various details and not only in a critical way. But this would be beyond the scope of this paper.

My main argument was that we can explain the mystical structure of Spinoza's philosophy, which I accept, by means of (logical) rules and that therefore using principle 1 of the principles of interpretation mentioned above we do not have to presuppose some mystical experiences on the part of Spinoza. I do not say, however, that Spinoza had no religious and emotional feelings; he was not a walking computer machine, but he did not refer to these feelings in his argumentation and he did not build up his philosophical system on this emotional and religious basis. Wetlesen rightly interprets me by saying:

> By way of implication, I suppose that Professor Hubbeling would also hold that in order to reach an adequate understanding of the doctrines of Spinoza, it is sufficient to read his definitions, axioms, postulates, and so forth carefully, and to follow his reasoning as he deduces his propositions. This is sufficient in the sense that it does not require any particular 'mystical experience' in order to grasp the meaning of what Spinoza has to say.[6]

I agree with Wetlesen that in Spinoza the essence of the body (and the mind) is a singular essence.[7] Wetlesen says, however, that the three kinds of cognition are all general,[8] that therefore the singular essence of the body cannot be known by these three ways of cognition and that therefore we must accept the thesis that this singular essence can be felt and experienced in a highly personal manner, which makes Spinoza's philosophy congenial to mysticism.[9] Now, I do not think it is merely so, that 'Spinoza's system as a whole must have the status of an entity of reason,'[10] which Wetlesen inferred from his own thesis. This seems to me highly improbable for a man who characterizes his philo-sophy in a letter to Albert Burgh as true: 'For I do not pretend to have found the best philosophy, but I know that I understand the true one.'[11] Further I cannot accept Wetlesen's argument that all three kinds of cognition are general and do not lead to the knowledge of the singular essences. Spinoza *expressis verbis* says that the third kind of knowledge is a '*rerum singularium cognitio*' (a knowledge of the singular things).[12] Wetlesen tries to escape this conclusion by saying that this is only knowledge of the general essence of singular things.[13] But this distinction is too artificial here. In that case there would be no difference at this point between the second and the third kinds of knowledge, which Spinoza precisely points out in this scholium by calling the second kind of knowledge a '*cognitio universalis*' and the third kind a '*cognitio rerum singularium*'.[14] Moreover, Wetlesen's reference to 2P40Sch2 does not hold good. Wetlesen says: 'I base this interpretation on 2P40Sch2, where Spinoza introduces the three kinds of cognition as three ways of forming 'universal notions'' (*notiones universales*).'[15] Spinoza, however, gives here three ways of forming these notions but calls them first and second kinds of knowledge (he subdivided the first kind into two parts; the first is called vague experience, the other memory and imagination). The third kind of knowledge is clearly distinguished from the others and is not subsumed under the three ways by which to form the *notiones universales*.[16] This kind of knowledge evidently leads to cognition of the particular essences of things. Also the old Dutch translation, which, as is well known, goes back to an older text, has the same structure as the official Latin text of the *Opera posthuma*.[17] The reader will, however, not fail to notice that the way in which Wetlesen defends Spinoza's mysticism is highly original, because this is usually done by trying to point out that the third kind of knowledge is a mystical way. Wetlesen, however, follows a different path. He first tries to show that none of the usual kinds of knowledge leads to the cognition of the particular essence of one's own body (in which Wetlesen, as we saw, is incorrect) and then he proceeds that in that case there must be another way of knowledge of this particular essence of one own's body, the mystical way, for which he quotes to text of 5P23Sch: 'Nevertheless, we feel and experience (*sentimus, experimurque*) that we are eternal. . . .'[18] When Wetlesen, in a first oral discussion with me, referred to this text,[19] I was much impressed. But on further consideration I do not believe that it substantiates Wetlesen's position. Let us look at the context in which the text stands. Spinoza starts by saying: 'This idea which expresses the essence of the body under the form of eternity is, as we have said, a certain mode of thinking which belongs to the essence of the mind, and is necessarily eternal.' And now Spinoza starts a discussion with those people who say: Why do we not know it directly but need a long series of proofs in order to know this eternalness of the mind? Spinoza admits this: 'Yet it is impossible, that we should remember that we existed before the body, because there are no traces of any such existence in the body, and also because eternity cannot be defined by time or have any relationship to it.' But somehow we know that it is true that the mind is eternal, and in this connection Spinoza says: 'Nevertheless, we feel and experience that we are eternal' (*At nihilominus sentimus, experimurque, nos aeternos esse*). But how must we interpret this '*sentimus*' and '*experimur*'?

Spinoza gives the answer immediately, for he continues: 'For the mind feels those things that it conceives by understanding, no less than those things that it remembers' (*Nam Mens non minus res illas sentit, quas intelligendo concipit, quam quas in memoria habet*), i.e. what the mind understands is no less lively before it than what it remembers by means of the memory. 'For . . .', and now a very important sentence comes: 'For the eyes of the mind, whereby it sees and observes things, are precisely the proofs' (*Mentis enim oculi, quibus res videt, observatque, sunt ipsae demonstrationes*). The seeing, feeling, experience of the mind are nothing else than proofs and demonstrations and thus nothing else than logical activities. So, I am very sorry, we are back again with Hubbeling's logical rules, and not with Wetlesen's mystical experiences! With '*sentimus*' Spinoza apparently does not want to introduce a new kind of knowledge that he has not introduced before, i.e. the mystical kind, but simply the well-known way of proofs he used before. '*Sentire*' in Spinoza sometimes has the meaning of 'to think, to have the opinion'.[20] As a cognitive activity it is mostly used for the act of observing things, but sometimes it is used for the second (and third way?) of knowledge.[21] Even if we interpret '*sentire*' and '*experimur*' here as immediate knowledge (of the third kind), they still differ from Wetlesen's mystical way of knowledge, which he does not identify with this *scientia intuitiva*.

So, according to my opinion, Wetlesen's interpretation of Spinoza is not convincing, for his basic arguments are insufficient. The parallelism he tries to show with a certain kind of Buddhist insight meditation is interesting and at first sight striking. We should not have expected this. If there were a parallelism with some kind of mysticism, we should have expected this with some kind of Jewish mysticism. Wetlesen thinks that the Buddhist principle of Right Mindfulness runs parallel with Spinoza's transcendental body awareness.[22] But here too, I am afraid, I must disagree with Wetlesen. The similarity is only superficial and therefore according to my principle of interpretation 3 mentioned above, we cannot speak of an affinity between Spinoza and Buddhism. Let me quote a Buddhist standard text for this body awareness and let the reader judge for himself. He will discover that the Buddhist disciple lives in a world that is totally different from Spinoza's:

(A. The four postures): When he walks the disciple knows 'I am walking'; when he stands he knows 'I stand', when he sits he knows 'I sit', and when he lies down, he knows 'I lie down'. In whichever position his body may be, he knows that it is in that position. . . . (B. Clear comprehension): The disciple acts clearly conscious when 1. he sets out (on the alms round) or returns (from it); 2. looks straight ahead or in other directions; 3. bends and stretches (his limbs); 4. in wearing the garments and carrying the alms-bowl; 5. when he eats, drinks, chews and tastes; 6. discharges excrement and urine; 7. walks, stands, sits; is asleep or awake; talks or keeps silent.[23]

Now, is this Spinoza? Can we imagine him walking through the streets, being aware of his body in a yoga manner at each step? It is a completely different world! And this only the first stage. Further on the disciple is expected to produce in himself a repudiation of the sensory world[24] and a distaste for the body and its functions.[25] Now this clearly contradicts Spinoza's attitude towards his body. It is unnecessary to verify this with a great number of quotations. Let me by way of example quote the famous proposition 5P39: 'He who possesses a body fit for many things, possesses a mind of which the greater part is eternal.' I could, of course, go deeper into the parallels Wetlesen draws. Sometimes they are striking, sometimes they are doubtful. An example of the latter is the parallel he draws between Spinoza's modes and the Buddhist *dharmas*, for *dharmas* are 'things as they appear, when viewed by wisdom',[26] which is not the same as Spinoza's modes. But all forms of parallels, if read in their context and compared with Spinoza, show that they belong to different worlds.

Certainly, Spinoza's philosophy has a mystical structure and we can draw parallels with various mystical systems as I did in my previous article. But mystical experiences in the way the great 'real' mystics experienced them are alien to Spinoza's philosophy. I must come to this conclusion. I am very sorry indeed.

NOTES

1 H. G. Hubbeling, 'Logic and experience in Spinoza's mysticism', in J. G. van der Bend (ed.), *Spinoza on Knowing, Being and Freedom*, Assen, 1974, pp. 126–43.
2 *Ibid.*, p. 129.
3 *Ibid.*, pp. 129ff.
4 See Wetlesen's paper in this book, 'Body awareness as a gateway, to eternity pp. 479–95; quotation on p. 480.
5 See what Wetlesen mentions as characteristics, in *Ibid.*, p. 492.
6 *Ibid.*, p. 479.
7 *Ibid.*, p. 481.
8 *Ibid.*, p. 482.
9 *Ibid.*, p. 483.
10 *Ibid.*, p. 483.
11 Epistola 76 (*Opera*, ed. C. Gebhardt, Heidelberg, 1924, IV, p. 320).
12 5P36Sch (*Opera*, II, p. 303).
13 Wetlesen, *op. cit.*, p. 483.
14 5P36Sch (*Opera*, II, p. 303).
15 Wetlesen, *op. cit.*, p. 482.
16 2P40Sch2 (*Opera*, II, p. 122).
17 *De Nagelaten Schriften van B. D. S.*, Amsterdam, 1677, pp. 88f.
18 Wetlesen, *op. cit.*, p. 485. I am afraid, however, that contrary to what Wetlesen suggests in note 15 of his paper, Gueroult's remarks on Spinoza's mysticism do not go further than some kind of rationalistic mysticism, similar to the one that I defend.

19 H. G. Hubbeling, 'The Discussions at the Spinoza-Symposium in Amersfoort, September 10–13, 1973', in van der Bend, *op. cit.*, p. 187.
20 See E. G. Boscherini, *Lexicon Spinozanum*, The Hague, 1970, II, p. 1005, the various places mentioned under (b).
21 See *Tractatus de Intellectus Emendatione*, para. 35 (*Opera*, II, p. 15); 2Ax5 (*ibid.*, p. 86), etc. '*Sentire*' in this sense is often equated with *percipere* (see 2P49Sch, *ibid.*, p. 133), which is very often more than only observing as it is done by our sense organs (see for example, 1 Def. 4, *ibid.*, p. 45).
22 Wetlesen, *op. cit.*, p. 479.
23 E. Conze, *Buddhist Meditation*, London, 1972, p. 62.
24 *Ibid.*, pp. 78ff.
25 *Ibid.*, pp. 95ff.
26 *Ibid.*, p. 181: *Dharma* can also stand for the one ultimate reality, see *ibid.*, p. 181 A. Wayman, 'Buddhism', in C. J. Bleeker and G. Widengreen, *Historia Religionum. Handbook for the History of Religions*, Leiden, 1971, II, pp. 389ff.; M. Monier-Williams, *A Sanskrit-English Dictionary*, Oxford, 1970, p. 510.

18   Spinoza and Chuang-Tzu

Hu-Shih, Peking

When reading the philosophical works of Spinoza we feel how much he is related in his thoughts to the old Chinese philosopher Chuang-Tzu. Both these philosophers indeed often represent a quite congruent viewpoint. On the other hand we also find topics where they diverge very much. Would it not be a gratifying and also a useful task to search for what Spinoza and Chuang-Tzu agree on and where they deviate from each other? And also why they agree in particular or why they disagree?

The principal topic where both philosophers agree is their pantheism. Chuang-Tzu calls the Omnipresent, 'Way' (Tao); Spinoza calls it 'God'(Shen). The verbal differentiation of such terminology is due to the influence of their time. In reality Spinoza's God comes quite near to Chuang-Tzu's 'Way', while not being so near to the God of the Christian or Jewish religion. Spinoza's 'God' is substance and substance is defined by Spinoza as 'being in itself and conceived through itself'.

This is really in accordance with that which Chuang-Tzu calls 'Way' and which he expresses as 'own stem and root' of which no one knows the beginning and nobody the end. Chuang-Tzu's 'Way' is contained in everything: 'in the cricket, in the ant, in the smallest corn, in the bricks of the roof, in the excrements.'[1] In the same way Spinoza's substance is omnipresent. All things are entirely a model presented by the 'proper nature of the substance; all things are formed through God (*natura naturans*)'. This is exactly Chuang-Tzu's theory about the 'Way' which animates Demons and Gods with spirit, and which creates Heaven and Earth: 'To "animate Demons and Gods" means that the Demons and Gods are spirits after they have attained it: the Way.'

All this is pantheism. Hsün Ch'ing criticizes Chuang-Tzu by saying that he is dominated by the Heaven and does not know anything about Man. Chuang-Tzu, who considers the Heavenly Way, t'ien-tao, as existing in everything and displacing itself into every-when, subsequently represents an absolute determinism. He says: 'Why to do? Why not to do? – It will certainly change by itself. . . .' To do and not to do seem both to lie externally in human power. But how can we know, if doing and if not doing are not both a part of the natural ruling Heavenly Way? 'How do we know, if what we call Heaven, is not Man and what we call Man, is not Heaven?' We assume ourselves that it is of our own free effort, but we do not know if that own effort is determined. Brass and steel in the furnace could not hope freely to be moulded into some famous sword. That is tantamount to paltry man hoping 'in the great furnace of Nature' to possess some freedom. Man's share is to enjoy Heaven and to accept quietly his Fate (order): 'to rest in time and to abide in obedience.' Fate is that which the thing cannot escape from.

Spinoza represents the very same absolute determinism. He assumes that every thing in nature is determined in itself, absolutely unchangeable. The universe in itself has an established law and even 'God' is unable to alter freely; and how much less could paltry little 'Man' do so? How? If men do suppose they have a free will, then this is likened to a little stone when rolling down from a mountain and, having then already reached half the mountain's height, exclaiming so happily: 'Look, how I am rolling down in freedom!' 'O he does not know even, that he is a little stone, standing under the rule of gravitational attraction of the earth, quite without any freedom.'[2]

Such absolute determinism is the second topic where Chuang-Tzu and Spinoza agree most. Besides this, there are still many topics of agreement which we cannot discuss here without introducing more details. But the two aforementioned topics are indeed fundamental ones. From these two points of departure we can deduce many other principles on which they agree; so, for example, their attitude toward religion (apart from the different terminology both are very rich in religiosity!) and further their conception of life as based on the heavenly principle and on the congruence of given states.

There is only one topic which surpasses our speculation: Chuang-Tzu does not plead for right and wrong, while Spinoza to the highest degree trusts in the mathematical method of demonstration. Chuang-Tzu praises with all his power the Heavenly Way, changeable in each movement, displaceable into each time. For such reason he assumes that every right and every wrong thing, that every good and every bad thing, is changeable: 'That comes from this, this again is based upon that. The right thing is an infinity. The false thing is an infinity.' Things being as they are, one need not quarrel about right and wrong. Things certainly do have their suchness (of being). Things certainly do have their power. Therefore Chuang-Tzu says: 'Dispute overlooks. All quarrelsome discussions originate from onesided opinions, by the fact that one is unable to recognize the totality of Heaven.'[3]

Spinoza lived in a world where all sciences flourished anew, and he was baptized by the sciences of that time. He was especially greatly influenced by Descartes but could not apply both his guiding-points: to 'understand' and to 'establish'.

Spinoza believed that the mathematical (geometrical) method would be very easy to understand and to concretize, and for such reason his great opus, *Ethics* has been construed after the geometrical model. He thought that the true principle could be thought after, that right and wrong could be decided, while only needing a concrete understandable method.

In this topic Chuang-Tzu and Spinoza deviate from each other very much. Chuang-Tzu does not quarrel with 'right' and wrong'. He wants to live with the underground streams of his time. Spinoza on the other hand, was anxious from his youth to give way to the controversy over right and wrong. Spinoza in his younger years was in ill-repute by his religious community because of his religious deviations as a teacher of erroneous doctrines. He had to endure many oppressions. At the age of twenty-one years, when his father died, his sister wanted to seize his inheritance, and that only because he no longer believed in religion. Spinoza did bring his claim before the court but when later the sentence had been pronounced in his favour, he did not accept a single penny for himself but left everything to his sister. For himself he took only a bed of ease. Thus he did not fight for his possessions but only for right and wrong. Spinoza was, rather, going to accept religious oppression for the whole of his life, unwilling to reject his faith in confrontation with his conscience. Here we can see an expression quite in the very same spirit. Such an attitude of not forcing his will to conform, in order to surrender his opinion on right and wrong, is totally different from that of Chuang-Tzu who does not quarrel with right or wrong.

NOTES

This paper was translated from the Chinese by John Hefter, Peking. See also my notes to the article: 'Spinoza – as Europe's answer to China. A manifesto by the German Seminar of the University, Peking' (p. 171).

1 Chuang-Tzu, 22.
2 Documents 58.
3 Chuang-Tzu, 2.

19   On the infinity of Spinoza's attributes

George L. Kline, Bryn Mawr

Haec nomina [sc. indignatio, odium, etc.] ex communi usu aliud
significare scio. Sed meum institutum non est, verborum significationem
sed rerum naturam explicare, easque iis vocabulis indicare, quorum
significatio, quam ex usu habent, a significatione, qua eadem
usurpare volo, non omnino abhorret, quod semel monuisse
sufficiat.[1]

I am concerned in this paper to develop, and offer evidence for, an unorthodox
interpretation of Spinoza's doctrine of infinite attributes. To do this I shall
first establish a general distinction between his systematic and nonsystematic
senses, or uses, of philosophic terms, offering specific examples of such
senses. All of this will be preliminary to identifying two distinct though
related systematic senses, and one unrelated nonsystematic sense, of the key
term *infinitum*.

I

Most major philosophers make a distinction, sometimes explicitly, more often
implicitly, between the senses of principal terms as they enter into the philosopher's system of concepts and categories and the senses of the same terms
which are not directly related to the system. For example, both Hegel and
Whitehead use the term 'concrete' in special systematic ways: for Hegel it
means 'many-sided and adequately mediated'; for Whitehead it means
'experient and actively self-relating'. But both thinkers sometimes use this
term in the ordinary nonsystematic sense of 'particular' or 'down-to-earth'.
Similar remarks apply to Hegel's terms *Erfahrung* and *Geist* and to
Whitehead's terms 'experience' and 'feeling'.

Most philosophic terms have more than one nonsystematic sense, including
some which are idiomatic or idiosyncratic. Identifying these senses is not
always easy. But what is both more difficult and more important is to distinguish between two distinct systematic senses.[2] It will be my contention that
failure to distinguish Spinoza's two systematic senses of *infinitum* has been
a major source of confusion among Spinoza scholars.

In general Spinoza's systematic senses correspond to what the understanding clearly grasps, and his nonsystematic senses to what *imaginatio* obscurely senses or pictures. But Spinoza was well aware that language can obfuscate as well as clarify (see note 22 below).

How may a philosopher who is aware of the distinction between systematic and nonsystematic senses of his key terms make this distinction perspicuous to his readers? He might try to avoid all nonsystematic uses of such terms in systematic contexts. In fact I know of no philosopher who has managed to do this; certainly Spinoza has not. A more feasible approach would be to distinguish typographically between systematic and nonsystematic senses, and between distinct systematic senses, of a given term. Contemporary philosophers sometimes do this by means of subscript or suffix numerals, e.g. 'cause$_1$' and 'cause$_2$'. I shall in this paper distinguish Spinoza's two systematic senses of 'infinite' as *infinitum I* and *infinitum II*.

Such devices probably did not occur to Spinoza, or if they did, did not appeal to him. But the available device of capitalization *was* used by Spinoza, or by his earliest copyists and editors – who may be presumed to have known his wishes in such matters – with respect to *natura* ('nature') and *ratio* ('reason').[3] The distinction is made more consistently for *natura* than for *ratio*. And in the case of *natura* it is made most consistently in the *Improvement of the Understanding* and the *Short Treatise*, somewhat less consistently in the *Correspondence*, less consistently still in the *Ethics* and the *Theologico-Political Treatise*. The distinction appears not be made at all in the *Political Treatise*, the *Principles of Descartes' Philosophy*, or the *Metaphysical Thoughts*.[4]

I shall briefly compare the differing usages in three categories of Spinoza's works: (1) those published during his lifetime, (2) those first published in the *Opera Posthuma* (1677), and (3) the *Short Treatise*, first published in 1862.

(1) The first category comprises: the *Principles of Descartes' Philosophy* and *Metaphysical Thoughts* (published in a single small volume in 1663) and the *Theologico-Political Treatise*, published anonymously in 1670. In the 1663 volume the term *natura* occurs at least thirty-four times in the systematic sense but appears to be capitalized only once. *Ratio* occurs at least twenty-four times in the systematic sense but is not capitalized at all.

In the *Theologico-Political Treatise* both terms occur frequently in the systematic sense, but *natura* is capitalized only three or four times, and *ratio* not at all.

It seems clear that the distinction between systematic and nonsystematic senses of key terms is *not* marked by capitalization in the three works which Spinoza published during his lifetime. Perhaps the distinctions were not yet clear in his own mind, or perhaps he had not yet decided to use capitals to mark them.

(2) The four works first published in the one-volume *Opera Posthuma* a

few months after Spinoza's death are: the unfinished *Treatise on the Improvement of the Understanding*, the unfinished *Political Treatise*, the *Ethics*, and the (selected) *Correspondence*. (The *Theologico-Political Treatise* was also reprinted in this volume.) Here the use of capitals to mark systematic senses is not consistent. However, in the *Improvement of the Understanding* the term *natura*, which occurs at least thirty-two times in the systematic sense, is capitalized in all but one or two cases. In a single, often-quoted sentence the term occurs in *both* senses, clearly distinguished by capitalization: *Quaenam . . . illa sit* natura *ostendemus . . . , nimirum esse cogitationem unionis, quam mens cum tota* Natura *habet* ('What that [human] essence [or 'character'] is we shall show . . . , namely, that it is the knowledge of the mind's union with the whole of nature [i.e., God or the Universe]') (V & L, I, p. 6; emphasis added).

The term *ratio*, perhaps surprisingly, does not occur in the systematic sense of 'understanding' or 'rationality' in the *Improvement of the Understanding* and occurs only infrequently in nonsystematic senses, e.g. *rationes*: 'grounds'.

In the *Ethics* the term *natura* is used almost ninety times in the systematic sense but is capitalized only twenty-two times. Still, these twenty-two cases, a quarter of the total, are significant. And, as in the *Improvement of the Understanding*, when *natura* is used in *both* senses in a single sentence the two senses are distinguished by capitalization, e.g. the expressions *hominis natura* ('the essence of man') and *infinita Naturae potentia* ('the infinite power of nature [i.e. God]'), and the expressions *hominis natura* and *totius Naturae ordo* ('order of the whole of nature [i.e. the universe]') (both IV, 4).[5]

In the *Ethics* the term *ratio* occurs at least 164 times in the systematic sense but is capitalized in only half a dozen of these cases. In contrast to the situation with *natura*, this proportion is too small to be significant.

In the *Political Treatise* the terms *natura* and *ratio* occur fairly frequently in systematic senses but are not capitalized.

The situation with Spinoza's *Correspondence* is rather more complicated. There are at least eighteen cases in the 1677 edition where *natura* in the systematic sense is capitalized and only about half a dozen where it is not. However, many of these cases are not capitalized in the surviving copies in Spinoza's hand or the copies made by others before 1677, e.g. several made by Leibniz for his own use. These were capitalized, presumably by Spinoza himself, in preparing the letters for publication in the *Opera Posthuma*.[6]

I have found no case in the *Correspondence* where *ratio* in the systematic sense is capitalized and at least sixteen cases where it is not.

Since ontological and epistemological discussions, in which the systematic/ nonsystematic distinction is of special importance, are more central in the *Ethics*, the *Improvement of the Understanding*, and certain of the letters than in the *Theologico-Political Treatise* or *Political Treatise*, it is not surprising that capitalization – particularly of the key term *natura* – is much more consistent in the first three works mentioned than in the last two. I have no ready explanation for the greater consistency of capitalization in the *Improvement of the Understanding* as compared to the *Ethics*.

(3)   In the Dutch *Short Treatise* the term *natuur*, used in the systematic sense, is capitalized at least eighty-eight times; it almost never appears in lower case.[7] (Of course, when it occurs in the nonsystematic sense(s) the term is regularly uncapitalized.) Where both systematic and nonsystematic senses occur in the same passage, they are clearly distinguished by the use of capitals, e.g. *in de Natuur* ('in nature') and *de natuur van de zaak* ('the essence [or 'character'] of the thing') (*Korte Verhandeling*, I, 2, add., V & L, IV, p. 8 n. 1); *de schik . . . van de Natuur* ('the order . . . of nature') and *zijn eigen natuur* ('its own nature [i.e. character]') (II, 17, V & L IV, p. 68).

The term *reden* ('reason') in the systematic sense is capitalized more than seven times but is left lower case twice as often.

Both of the works in which the systematic senses of terms are most clearly and consistently marked by capitalization were unpublished at the time of Spinoza's death. But he had prepared one of them – the *Improvement of the Understanding* – for publication himself, or at least had taken some part in its preparation, during the final months of his life, by which time the implicit distinction between the systematic and nonsystematic senses of *natura*, and even of *ratio*, may have become clearer to him than it had been earlier.

Even if it should turn out that Spinoza himself made no such typographical distinction, that the *non*capitalization of *natura* and *ratio* in the systematic senses in the works published during his lifetime was a result of his deliberate decision, and that the marking of the systematic/nonsystematic distinction by the use of capital and lower-case letters was introduced by Spinoza's earliest copyists and editors, acting on their own – still, I would maintain, such a distinction is implicit in Spinoza's writings and, what is more important, extends to the key terms *infinitum* and *unum*.

Thus far we have been considering only nouns; but we have a special interest in the adjectives and adverbs *infinitum/infinitê* and *absolutum/absolutê*. And this raises a special problem: Spinoza almost never capitalizes adjectives, apart from those appearing in compound proper names, and – so far as I can see – *never* capitalizes adverbs. The only exceptions among philosophic terms are adjectives used as substantives, e.g. *Necessarium* ('the necessary'), *Fortuitum* ('the contingent'), *Liberum* ('the free') (all in Letter 56, V & L, III, p. 189; *Necessarium* also appears at I, 33, n. 1). The adjective *infinitum* is never capitalized in the *Ethics* and only rarely in the *Correspondence* – and then in numerical or quasi-numerical, hence nonsystematic, senses, e.g. *quale Infinitum majus alio Infinito* ('which [kind of] infinite [could be conceived as] greater than another infinite') (Letter 12, V & L, III, p. 39; cf. also pp. 41, 42, 43). This is the letter in which an unusually large number of terms is capitalized.

Thus, lacking the clue of capitalization, we are left to distinguish between systematic and nonsystematic senses of the key terms *infinitum* and *absolutum* either from philosophic context, by philosophic intuition, or through some combination of the two.

I shall consider Spinoza's implicit distinction between the systematic and nonsystematic senses of *ratio*, *natura*, and *modus* in sections II, III, and IV, respectively. In numbered subsections I shall give: (1) the systematic sense, (2) the idiomatic nonsystematic senses, and (3) the other (non-idiomatic) nonsystematic senses. Section V is more complex because it includes *absolutum* as well as *infinitum*, and each of these terms has two systematic senses; but the overall arrangement is the same.

II

(1) *Ratio* in the systematic sense means 'rationality' or 'understanding'. Spinoza explicitly equates it with *intellectus* (IV, app. 4) and uses *potentia intellectus* ('the power of the understanding') as a synonym for *potentia Rationis* ('the power of reason') in the title and preface, respectively, of *Ethics*, Part V. He uses an expression: *ex vera contemplatione seu Ratione* ('from reason or true contemplation') (IV, 53, pr.), which clearly associates these two concepts, but I do not take it to be a systematic definition of 'reason' in terms of 'true contemplation'.

(2) The Latin terms *ratio* and *modus* have a great many more idiomatic uses than do the corresponding English terms 'reason' and 'mode'. The term *natura*, in contrast, probably has about the same number of idiomatic uses as the term 'nature'. (See section III, 2 below.) The idiomatic nonsystematic senses are only superficially problematic; it is the non-idiomatic nonsystematic uses which raise hermeneutical problems. However, the idiomatic uses are worth examining briefly (they have not to my knowledge been noticed hitherto).

Certain idiomatic uses of *ratio* parallel those of *modus*, e.g. *tali ratione*, like *tali modo*, means 'in such a way'; *qua ratione*, like *quomodo*, means 'how' or 'by what means'.[8] *Ea ratione*, like *eo modo*, means 'in that way'; *nulla ratione*, like *nullo modo*, means 'in no way'; *certa ac determinata ratione*, like *certo et determinato modo*, means 'in a certain and determinate way'.

In another idiomatic use, which is fairly frequent in the *Ethics* and the *Correspondence*, *ratio* means 'with respect to', e.g. *ratione suae essentiae* ('with respect to its essence'), *ratione figurae* ('with respect to shape'), *ratione motus et quietis* ('with respect to motion and rest').[9]

(3) I list several nonsystematic and non-idiomatic uses of *ratio*, beginning with one which seems most remote from the systematic sense and ending with one which seems closest to it.

Ratio can mean '[mathematical] ratio' (II, 40, n. 2) and 'relation', as in the celebrated stricture on Descartes's philosophy of mind: *nulla detur ratio voluntatis ad motum* (V, pref., V & L, I, p. 247), which in the Stirling-White version reads: 'there is no relation between the will and motion'. A somewhat more literal translation would be: 'there is no ground for the will's [causing] motion', where the meaning of *ratio* would be closer to the systematic one.

Ratio can also mean 'manner' or 'method', in such expressions as *ratio intelligendi* ('manner of understanding') – analogous to *modus imaginandi* ('way of imagining') – *ratio philosophandi* ('method of philosophizing'), and *vivendi ratio* ('manner of living' or 'rule of life').[10]

Ratio also means 'consideration', 'estimation', or 'regard', as in the expression *nostrae utilitatis* (*vera*) *ratio* ('the (true) estimation of our advantage') (IV, app.; 26, 31, 32). Desire, Spinoza points out, *rationem utilitatis totius hominis non habet* ('has no regard for the advantage of the human being as a whole') (IV, 60). At least twice this nonsystematic sense occurs in a single sentence along with the quite different systematic sense.

Ratio (pl. *rationes*) often means 'reason(s)' or 'ground(s)', in such standard, but non-idiomatic expressions as *ratio . . . cur* ('the reason why'), *non sine ratione* ('not without reason'), and *absque ulla ratione* ('without any reason'). *Ratio*, like *Reden*, has no plural when used systematically; in contexts which include both *Ratio* and *rationes*, or *Reden* and *redenen*, the difference in number provides a further clue to the systematic/nonsystematic distinction.

Finally, *ratio* can mean 'reasoning' or 'argumentation', in such frequent expressions as *per eandem rationem* ('by the same reasoning' – used in many proofs in the *Ethics*) and in the less frequently used expression *ratione . . . et calculo* ('by reasoning and calculation') (Letter 6, V & L, III, p. 21). In all such cases *ratio* means 'formal [or 'deductive'] inference' – a meaning related to, but distinct from, the systematic sense of *Ratio*: 'rationality' or 'understanding'.

III

(1) For Spinoza the term *Natura* in its systematic sense means 'universe' or 'cosmos' – including both its creative and created aspects, both *Natura Naturans* and *Natura Naturata*. In the *Short Treatise* the Dutch term *Natuur* is regularly capitalized to mark its systematic sense.

Frequently used expressions are *pars Naturae* ('a part of nature'), *ordo Naturae* ('the order of nature'), *Naturae leges* ('laws of nature'), and the celebrated equation: *Deus sive Natura*.[11]

(2) I have discovered only two idomatic uses of *natura*; both using the ablative absolute: (a) *naturâ* ('by nature', 'in character', or 'in kind'). Here the lower-case '*n*' is reinforced by the diacritical mark on the final '*a*' to set this sense off as idiomatic as well as nonsystematic. Examples: *Substantia prior est naturâ suis affectionibus* ('Substance is by nature prior to its modifica-

tions') (I, 1); *idea naturâ prior est* ('the idea is by nature prior [to certain modes of thought]') (II, 11, pr.); ... *omnia haec ... simul naturâ [sunt]* ('... the latter, by nature, [are] all simultaneous') (*De int. em.*, V & L, I, p. 31); *cogitatio ... est ... suâ naturâ infinita* ('thought ... is ... by its nature infinite') (I, 21, pr.). (b) The ablative absolute expression *naturâ servatâ* ('its nature being preserved') (II, 1em. 7, n.).

(3) There are two non-idiomatic nonsystematic senses of *natura*: (a) a somewhat idiosyncratic sense equivalent to 'kind', as in the expressions *affirmatio existentiae alicujus naturae* ('affirmation of existence of some kind') (I, 8, n. 1) and *naturae diversae alimenta* ('foods of different kinds') (IV, app. 27); (b) a more normal nonsystematic sense equivalent to 'essence' or 'character'.[12] Thus Spinoza speaks of *hominis essentia seu natura* ('man's essence or nature') (IV, def. 8). This sense is regularly indicated by lower-case '*n*'; it appears in such expressions as *natura humana* ('human nature'), *Dei natura* ('God's nature'), and *divina natura* ('the divine nature').[13] In the *Short Treatise* the term *natuur* has this same nonsystematic sense in such expressions as *de natuur van de zaak* ('the nature of the thing'), *van natuur* ('by nature'), *zijn eigen natuur* ('his own nature'), and *de zwakheid onzes natuurs* ('the weakness of our nature').[14]

Spinoza causes a certain amount of confusion by his occasional capitalization of *natura*, used in this nonsystematic sense, in expressions referring to God. Thus he sometimes writes *Dei Natura* and *Natura Divina* (cf. Letters 21, 34, 54; V & L, III, pp. 87, 128, 182: *Op. Post.*, 1677, pp. 499, 520, 570). Both of these expressions mean 'the nature of God' and not, as the second of them might suggest, 'godlike Nature'.

IV

(1) Spinoza's systematic and nonsystematic senses of the term *modus* are particularly difficult to distinguish, and that for three reasons: (a) lack of capitalization, except in Letters 10 and 12 (and even there it is not consistent); (b) the uniquely large number of nonsystematic senses, both idiomatic and non-idiomatic, of the term; and (c) the fact that, since a chief nonsystematic sense of *modus* is 'way', and modes in the systematic sense are modifications of substance, i.e. 'ways' in which the one substance is modified, under one or another of its attributes, the semantic boundary between 'mode' and 'way' is sometimes blurred and shifting.[15]

The Dutch (and, for that matter, English) counterparts of *modus* are less ambiguous than the Latin term. In the *Short Treatise* the term *manier* is occasionally used for 'way' or 'manner', e.g. *de vierde manier van kennisse* ('the fourth kind of knowledge'), *op dezelfde manier* ('in the same way') (*KV*, II, 26, app., V & L, IV, pp. 88, 96). On the other hand, the standard word for 'mode' – *wijze* – is also used, in the same confusing manner as *modus*, to mean 'way', e.g. *op deze wijze* ('in this way'), *op een andere wijze* ('in another way'), *op wat wijze* ('in what way'), *in geenerlei wijze* ('in no way)'.

In Letter 12 *Modus* in the systematic sense is capitalized several times; e.g. in the phrase *Substantiae . . . Affectiones Modos voco* ('I call the modifications of substance modes').[16]

(2) *Modus* occurs in a great many Latin idioms, and Spinoza uses most of them. In addition to the expressions already mentioned (p. 337 above), the following compounds include some form of *modus* (in the accusative, ablative, or genitive cause): *admodum* ('very'), *diversimode* ('in different ways'), *dummodo* ('in order that'), *ejusmodi* ('of that kind'), *hujusmodi* ('of this kind'), *quemadmodum* ('like'), *quomodocunque* ('in whatever manner'), *solummodo* and *tantummodo* (both meaning 'only').

Among other idiomatic expressions there are: *aliquo modo* ('to a certain extent') – an expression which can also have the non-idiomatic sense 'in any way' – *modo* ('provided that' and, in another idiomatic sense, 'just now'), *modo . . . modo* ('now . . . now'), and *modus* in the special sense of 'measure' or 'quantity', as in *divitiarum modus* ('measure of wealth') (IV, app. 29).

(3) *Modus* is also unique among Spinoza's terms in its number of homonyms. The ablative absolute *modo* which, as we have seen, has several nonsystematic idiomatic senses, also has the nonsystematic non-idiomatic sense 'in a way'. *Legum modo* means 'in the form of laws'; *modo satis* means 'sufficiently'. Omitting expressions already mentioned (p. 337 above), I note a few of Spinoza's other non-idiomatic uses of *modus*:

One family of expressions uses the ablative plural *modis* ('in . . . ways') with a variety of numerical or quasi-numerical modifiers, e.g. *duobus modis* ('in two ways'), *multis . . .* ('in many . . .'), *plurimis* ('in more than one . . .'), *variis . . .* ('in different . . .'), *omnibus . . .* ('in all . . .'), and *infinitis modis* ('in infinite ways') – an expression to which I shall return in section V.[17] The ablative singular *modo* ('in . . . way') is also modified by *eodem . . .* ('in the same . . .'), *hoc . . .* ('in this . . .'), *hoc aut ullo . . .* ('in this or that . . .'), *ullo . . .* ('in any . . .'), *quocumque . . .* ('in any . . . whatever').

Aliis modis means 'in other ways' and *alio modo* normally means 'in another way', but *alio . . . cogitandi modo* (V, 40, n.) has the systematic sense 'by another . . . mode of thought'. *Certo modo* means 'in a certain way', but *a certis Dei modis attributorum* (II, 11, pr.) has the systematic sense 'by certain modes of God's attributes'.

There is a similar merging of systematic and nonsystematic senses in expressions using *modus* with a genitive gerund. *Modus instituendi* ('way of establishing') is clearly nonsystematic; but *modus imaginandi, . . . percipiendi, . . . contemplandi* ('way of imagining, perceiving, looking at'), though strictly speaking nonsystematic, may easily be assimilated to the systematic expression *modus cogitandi* ('mode [of the attribute] of thought'). Spinoza, after all, follows Descartes in treating *imaginare*, *percipere*, and *contemplare* as forms of *cogitare*; thus a way of imagining or perceiving is, in systematic terms, a mode of thought.

V

In sections II–IV I have presented – perhaps in excessive detail – textual evidence that there is an implicit distinction in Spinoza's writings between the systematic and nonsystematic senses of three important philosophic terms, all of them as it happens nouns. *Absolutum* and *infinitum* are adjectives, and this grammatical status appears to have disqualified them – and their adverbial counterparts *absolutê* and *infinitê* – from being identified by capitalization.[18]

(1) The systematic sense of *absolutum* is close to the first of the two systematic senses of *infinitum* (which I call *infinitum I*), although their nonsystematic senses are quite distinct.

(a) In a passage which refers explicitly to ideas but implies a more general identification, Spinoza writes: *absoluta, sive adaequata et perfecta* ('absolute, or adequate and perfect') (II, 34). In its systematic sense *absolutum* means 'perfect' with the secondary meaning 'unlimited' – as in the expressions *absoluta potestas* ('unlimited power'), *absoluta voluntas* ('perfect will'), *absoluta potentia* ('unlimited capacity'), *ex absoluta natura alicujus attributi Dei* ('from the perfect and unlimited nature of some one of God's attributes') (I, 23 & pr.).

The adverb *absolutê* has two closely related systematic senses: *absolutê I* (as I shall call it) means 'without limitation' and *absolutê II* means 'without exception'. *Absolutê II* functions in place of *infinitê*, which – so far as I can determine – is not used by Spinoza in a systematic sense.[19]

(i) Examples of *absolutê I* include: *absolutê . . . unicuique summo Naturae jure . . . licet* ('everyone is permitted, without any limitation, by the highest right of nature') (IV, app. 8), and *absolutê ea agere, quae firmandis amicitiis inserviunt* ('to do, without limitation, those things which serve to strengthen friendships') (IV, app. 12).

(ii) Examples of *absolutê II* include: *absolutê omnia* ('all things without exception'), *absolutê . . . omnia naturalia* ('all natural things without exception'), and *omnia absolutê Naturae individua* ('all individual things in nature without exception') (IV, pref., V & L, I, p. 184).

But the key phrases are *ens absolutê infinitum* and *substantia absolutê infinita*, to which I shall return shortly (see also note 19 above).

(b) *Absolutum* in the nonsystematic sense of 'total' or 'complete' occurs in such expressions as *absoluta ignorantia* ('total ignorance'), *absoluta privatio* ('absolute privation'), and *imperium absolutum* ('complete mastery'). In this last expression the nonsystematic sense ('complete') approaches the systematic sense ('unlimited'), blurring the distinction between the two.

There are at least three nonsystematic senses of the adverb *absolutê*. I shall list them, beginning with the sense that is most remote from both systematic senses and ending with a sense close to *absolutê I*.

(i) *Absolutê* in the first nonsystematic sense means 'as such' or 'in itself'; it occurs in such expressions as *absolutê considerata* ('considered in itself'), *quatenus absolutê consideratur* ('in so far as it is considered in itself'), and the assertion that God is the cause of an individual idea not as *res absolutê cogitans* ('a thinking being as such' [or 'in itself']) but as affected by another idea of which he is also the cause (II, 9 pr.)

(ii) *Absolutê* in the second nonsystematic sense means 'completely' or 'entirely'; it occurs in such expressions as *absolutê pendere* ('to depend entirely'), *absolutê imperare* ('to master completely'), *absolutê tollit* ('destroys entirely'), and the celebrated: *Mens humana non potest cum Corpore absolutê destrui* ('The human mind cannot be entirely destroyed with the body') (V, 23).

(iii) *Absolutê* in the third nonsystematic sense means 'without qualification', as in the statement that certain propositions *vocantur absolutê aeternae veritates* ('are, without qualification, called eternal truths') (Letter 10), and in the expression *potest absolutê dici* ('it can be said without qualification') (IV, 28, pr. – a passage in which the adjective *absolutum* is used in the systematic sense).

(2) It is a central contention of this paper that the term *infinitum* has two distinct but related systematic senses, which I call *infinitum I* and *infinitum II*. *Infinitum I* means 'perfect without limitation'; *infinitum II* means 'all without exception'. In the first sense the term may be used in either the singular or plural; in the second sense it is limited to the plural. Thus, strictly speaking, it should be written *infinita II*.

(a) I justify my interpretation of *infinitum I* by reference to Spinoza's statement that each of the divine attributes is *infinitum, sive summê perfectum, in suo genere* ('infinite, or supremely perfect, in its kind') (Letter 4, V & L, III, p. 11), and his seeming equation of *absolutê infinito* with *summê perfecto* (I, 11 pr. 2). In the *Short Treatise*, *oneyndelijk* (or *oneyndig*[20]) ('infinite') is regularly conjoined with *volmaakt* ('perfect'); God is described as *oneyndelijk of aldervolmaakst* ('infinite or supremely perfect') (*KV*, I, 9, V & L, IV, p. 34).

Infinitum occurs in this first systematic sense in a number of key expressions: *ens . . . infinitum* ('a being . . . perfect without limitation'), *infinitum in suo genere* ('perfect and without limitation in its kind'), and the assertion that each of the attributes expresses *aeternam et infinitam essentiam* ('an essence which is eternal, perfect, and without limitation').

As we have seen (note 18 above) *infinitas* in its systematic sense is the noun counterpart of *infinitum I*; it could thus be called *infinitas I*, and means 'unlimited perfection'.

(b) I justify my interpretation of *infinita II* as meaning 'all [things] without exception' by reference to several passages in which Spinoza conjoins *infinita* and *omnia*.[21] He asserts that the universal is predicated equally *de uno ac de pluribus, ac de infinitis* [II] *individuis* ('of one [individual], and of more than one [individual], and of all individuals without exception') (II, 49, n., V & L, I, p. 117). In the same passage he states explicitly that *universale . . . de omnibus ideis praedicatur* ('the universal . . . is predicated of all ideas'). It seems clear that *infinita II* is here used synonymously with *omnia*. The term *homo* ('human being'), according to Spinoza, is predicated *de infinitis* [II] *singularibus* ('of all individuals without exception'). This reading is confirmed by Spinoza's reference to a property or set of properties in which *omnes conveniunt* ('all [human beings] agree') (II, 40, n.1, V & L, I, p. 105). In any case, the number of individual human beings is *not* infinite in the nonsystematic sense of 'countless' or 'indefinite'.

Elsewhere Spinoza places *infinita II* in apposition to *absolutê* [II] *. . . omnia naturalia* ('all natural things without exception') (I, 32, cor. 2). And in many passages – e.g. I, 16 & pr., 17, n., V & L, I, p. 53; II, pref., 3, pr. – the phrase *infinita infinitis modis*, i.e. *infinita* [II] *infinitis* [II] *modis* ('all things without exception in all ways without exception') is followed by some such expression as *hoc est, omnia* ('that is, all things'). In the *Short Treatise* God is described as having *alles ofte oneyndelijke eigenschappen* ('all or infinite attributes') (*KV*, I, 2, V & L, IV, p. 7), and, even more explicitly, *oneyndige*[,] *volmaakte, en alle eigenschappen* ('infinite[,] perfect, and all attributes') (*KV*, II, 1 add., V & L, IV, p. 7, n. 1).

But why does Spinoza use *infinita* in the second systematic sense at all; why not just *omnia*? My guess is that (i) he regards *infinita II* as a more emphatic form of *omnia*, since it means 'all [the things] there are' or 'all conceivable [things]', as well as 'all [things] without exception'; and (ii) he uses the single, though equivocal, term *infinitum* in order to assert a systematic connection between the distinct though related concepts 'perfect without limitation' and 'all without exception'.

What the two concepts have in common is the idea of unconditional affirmation,[22] exemption from all negation and limitation.[23] Spinoza does not define the infinite[24] but he characterizes infinite existence as involving the *absoluta affirmatio existentiae alicujus naturae* ('perfect and unlimited affirmation of existence of some kind'). He brings out the connection between what I call *infinitum I* and *infinita II* in the claim that any being which can think *infinita* [II] *infinitis* [II] *modis* ('all things without exception in all ways without exception') must be an *ens cogitans infinitum* [I] ('a thinking being which is perfect without limitation') (II, 1, n.).

The expression *un umex infinitis* [II] *Dei attributis*, in my interpretation, means 'one among all the attributes of God [that there are]'. The adverb *absolutê* in the expression *absolutê infinitum* [I] is the functional equivalent of *infinitê II*; it means '[including all things] without exception'. Thus *substantia absolutê* [II] *infinita* [I] means 'a substance perfect, without limitation, including all things without exception'.

Several key passages of the *Ethics* include both of the systematic senses of *infinitum*, e.g. the claim that from God's *infinita* [I] *natura* there necessarily flow *infinita* [II] *infinitis* [II] *modis*, that is, from God's 'nature, perfect without limitation', there necessarily flow 'all things without exception in all ways without exception' (I, 17, n., V & L. I, p. 53). The phrase *natura divina infinita absolutê attributa habeat* (I, 16 pr.) is *prima facie* puzzling. The Spinozistic attributes are not (distributively) *absolutê* [II] *infinita* [I] (neut. pl.); only the *natura divina* is *absolutê* [II] *infinita* [I] (fem. sing.). Rather, each of them is *infinitum* [I] *in suo genere* ('perfect without limitation in its kind'). But the attributes are (collectively) characterizable as being *absolutê* [II] *infinita* [II] in the sense of *absolutê* [II] *omnia*: 'all [that there are] without exception'. Thus the entire phrase means 'the divine nature has all the attributes [that there are] without exception'.

Both senses, of course, appear in Spinoza's definition of God: *Per Deum intelligo ens absolutê infinitum* [I], *hoc est, substantiam constantem infinitis* [II] *attributis, quorum unumquodque aeternam et infinitam* [I] *essentiam exprimit* ('By God I understand a being perfect without limitation, including all things without exception, that is, a substance consisting of all attributes without exception, each of which expresses an essence eternal and perfect without limitation') (I, def. 6).

(3) *Infinitum* in the nonsystematic sense is a numerical or quasi-numerical term, meaning 'countless' or 'indefinitely many'; it occurs in such expressions as *infinitis exemplis* ('by countless examples') (I, app., V & L I, p. 68), *cum infinitis aliis* ('with countless other things') (Letter 19, V & L, III, p. 63), and *ex infinitis rectangulis* ('from countless right angles') (Letter 60, V & L, III, p. 200). It also occurs in the Letter on the Infinite (Letter 12) and in the discussion of the Paradoxes of the Infinite (I, 15, n.), where it is set in the context of a discussion of quantifiability, comparability, and measurability. *Quantitas infinita* means 'indefinite quantity' and *numerus infinitus* 'indefinite number' (I, 15, n., V & L, I, pp. 48, 49). *Infinitum* in this nonsystematic sense is never used to modify the systematic terms *attributum, ens, substantia,* or *Deus.*

The expression *in infinitum,* which Spinoza uses where we would normally use *ad infinitum,* means 'in countless steps or stages' and refers to what Hegel calls a *schlechte Unendlichkeit.*[25] According to Spinoza, the fact that we can affirm *infinita* ('countless things') or can sense *infinita corpora* ('countless bodies') – in both cases successively rather than simultaneously – does not mean that our capacity to will or sense is *infinita* [I], i.e. 'perfect without limitation' (II, 49, n., V & L, I, p. 116). In contrast to the case of the *ens cogitans infinitum* [I], discussed at p. 343 above, there is no semantic bridge leading from the nonsystematic sense of *infinitum* to either of its systematic senses.

I have discovered only one nonsystematic use of the adverb *infinitê*, in the expression *infinitê superatur* ('is very greatly surpassed') (IV, app. 32). As already noted, Spinoza does not use *infinitê* in a systematic sense, but instead uses *absolutê II* where one might have expected *infinitê II*.

VI

It will be evident to readers familiar with the Spinoza literature that my interpretation of the infinity of the attributes is indebted to a suggestion put forward by H. H. Joachim in 1901. According to Joachim, the term 'infinite', as applied to attribute, means 'complete': 'each Attribute is "infinite" *in suo genere*: it is in itself the full, all-inclusive expression of that character of Reality which it is.'[26] Substance, Joachim claims, is infinite in the sense of complete, all-inclusive, and self-contained; Spinoza's God includes 'all Attributes'. His nature is 'absolutely complete [i.e. *infinitum I*], includes all *infinita II*] essential positive forms of being, and cannot be conceived as in any way limited'.[27]

A generation later A. Wolf – with less consistency and without reference to Joachim – made the parallel claim that by 'infinite' Spinoza means 'complete' or 'all'.[28] However, neither Joachim nor Wolf makes a clear or systematic distinction between 'infinite' in the sense of 'complete' and 'infinite' in the sense of 'all' – my *infinitum I* and *infinita II*, respectively – or between systematic and nonsystematic senses of Spinoza's terms. By making both kinds of distinction, and by providing an organized sampling of Spinoza's usage, I have attempted to refine, develop, and support the Joachim-Wolf interpretation.

That interpretation has the further merit of eliminating the *aporiai* of traditional interpretations of the attributes as *infinita* in the nonsystematic sense of 'countless' or 'indefinitely many'. Joachim makes it clear that the 'infinity' of the attributes has nothing to do with number:[29]

every number [is] finite . . . [and] applicable only to what can be 'pictured' [by *imaginatio*] as well as 'thought' [by *intellectus*]: infinity belongs only to what can be thought and not pictured. . . . The true infinite cannot have its nature expressed in number . . . at all.

If we *will* endeavor to enumerate God's Attributes, we shall find that no number can exhaust them: but this indicates no indefiniteness in God, but simply the absurdity of conceiving him under 'modes of imagination.'

Spinoza himself sharply contrasts the idea of an *ens absolutê infinitum* [I] with that of a being having 'three, four, etc. attributes' (Letter 64, V & L, III, p. 206). He could equally well have said 'three million' or 'four billion'. The point is that *no* possible number of attributes could amount to 'all the attributes without exception'. Elsewhere he states explicitly: *nec Numerum,*

345

nec Mensuram, . . . quandoquidem non nisi auxilia imaginationis sunt, posse esse infinitos [II] ('neither number nor measure. . . ., since they are nothing but aids to the imagination, can be infinite [i.e. include "all without exception"]') (Letter 12, V & L, III, p. 41).[30]

Wolf insists that, although the two known attributes could not be considered 'innumerable' or 'infinitely many', they 'may well be *all* the attributes. . . . Spinoza did not posit innumerable attributes at all'. Rather, he 'posited "infinite or all the attributes", in the sense of "certainly two, possibly more" '.[31] For Spinoza, according to Wolf, 'there *may be*, but there need not be [,] more than two Attributes'.[32]

The key distinction, as Joachim and Wolf seem only dimly to have realized, is not between two and three, or two million and three million, attributes, but between *one, more than one*, and *all* attributes. Spinoza made this distinction – between *unum, plura*, and *infinita* [II] – very clearly in another connection (see II, 49, n., cited at p. 343 above). *One* attribute cannot of course be *infinitum II* (we have seen that in this second systematic sense the term can be used only in the plural); and it is *infinitum I* only in its kind. But *plura attributa* – 'more-than-one attribute' – *can* be *infinita II;* can be 'all the attributes there are without exception'.

The term *unum* has distinct senses parallel to the distinct senses of infinitum.[33] (1) *unum* in the nonsystematic numerical or quasi-numerical sense means 'one as distinct from two, three, etc.'; (2) in the non-numerical systematic sense (*unum* I) the term means 'single without division'; (3) in the 'hierarchical' systematic sense (*unum II*) it means 'one but not more than one'.

The following cases may be distinguished, using the nonexclusive-disjunctive relation expressed by the Latin '. . . *sive* . . .' ('either . . . or, and perhaps both') – in Spinoza's usage this amounts almost to a conjunctive equivalence relation: '. . . that is to say . . .' (as in *Deus sive Natura*) – together with the exclusive-disjunctive relation expressed by *aut . . . aut* ('either . . . or, but not both').

(1) Both *unum* and *infinitum* would be used in the nonsystematic numerical sense in a series made up of exclusive disjunctions: *aut nullum aut unum aut duo aut . . . aut infinita* ('either none or one or two or . . . or indefinitely many').

(2) Both terms would be used in the non-numerical systematic sense in a nonexclusive-disjunctive equivalence relation: *unum* [I] *sive infinitum* [I] (as applied to *ens*) or *una* [I] *sive infinita* [I] (as applied to *substantia*), i.e. '[a being or substance which is] single without division, that is to say, perfect without limitation'.

(3) Both terms would be used in the "hierarchical" systematic sense in a sequence made up of exclusive disjunctions, one disjunct of which is itself a nonexclusive disjunction: *aut unum* [II] *aut plura aut omnia-sive-infinita* [II] ('either one-but-not-more-than-one or more-than one or all, that is to say, all-without-exception').

In Spinoza's sense, the term *plura* functions as the systematic non-numerical counterpart of the entire series of nonsystematic numerical terms: *duo-tres-quattuor* . . . up to but not including *infinita*, the latter term being used in the nonsystematic numerical or quasi-numerical sense of 'indefinitely many'.

A recent commentator, as a result of his failure to distinguish between the nonsystematic numerical sense and the systematic non-numerical sense of *unum*, charges Spinoza with making 'contradictory' claims, namely, that (a) God is one in the sense of single [*unicus*] (I app., V & L, I, p. 66) and (b) whoever 'calls God one or single [*unum vel unicum*] has no true idea of God' (Letter 50, V & L, III, p. 173).[34] In fact, *unicum* in the first claim is used in a systematic non-numerical sense equivalent to *unum I* and means 'single without division', whereas in the second claim – as the context makes clear – the expression *unum vel unicum* has the quite different nonsystematic numerical sense of 'distinct from two, three, etc.' Spinoza is saying that it is a mistake to think of God as one being rather than two or three, since God is 'one' only in the quite different sense of 'single without division'. This claim is perfectly consistent.

None of the Latin phrases given in the three numbered paragraphs above (pp. 346f.) appears verbatim in Spinoza's writings, but I would insist that all of them reflect the spirit of his philosophy.

Spinoza's claim that *plura attributa* can without absurdity be assigned to *uni substantiae* (I, 10, n.) is to be interpreted in this light, as is his related claim: *plus realitatis . . . plura attributa* (I, 9 & 10, n.), which means not 'the more reality . . . the more attributes' – that would imply a grotesque correlation: an entity with reality-quotient 3 would have 3 attributes; an entity with reality-quotient 39 would have 39, etc. – but a non-numerical, non-quantitative hierarchy: entities with the *lowest* degree of reality have *one* attribute; entities with *more than the lowest* degree of reality *have more than one* attribute; the entity with the *highest* degree of reality has *infinita* [II] *attributa* – *all* the attributes there are without exception.

It is Spinoza's conviction that this highest degree of reality belongs to God alone.

NOTES

1 'I know that these words [viz., 'indignation', 'hatred', etc.] have different meanings in common usage. But my aim is to explain not the meaning of words but the character of things, and to refer to things by using words whose customary meanings will not be entirely opposed to the meanings that I want to give them. Let this one notice suffice.' (*Eth.* III, def. of the emotions, 20, expl.) All translations from the Latin – and Dutch – are my own unless otherwise indicated.

2 That a given term has both systematic and nonsystematic senses, or more than one systematic sense, means that it is equivocal. Equivocity, however, is to be distinguished from the consistently special senses, peculiar to a period or an author, of given terms. Spinoza uses several terms in special Cartesian senses, e.g. *imaginatio* ('image-having', which includes sense-perception and memory, as well as imagination in the post-Kantian sense); *objectivum/objectivê* (not 'objective(ly)' but 'conceptual(ly)' or 'subjective(ly)'); *formale/formaliter* (not 'formal(ly)' but 'actual(ly)' or 'objective(ly)').

3 I am grateful to E. M. Curley for having alerted me (in a private communication) to the intricacy and inconsistency of editorial policy regarding capitalization in earlier and later editions of Spinoza's Latin (and Dutch) works. (See note 4 below.)

4 Editorial policy with respect to capitalization differs sharply in the two currently available editions of Spinoza's works. Van Vloten and Land (first ed., 1882, third ed., 1914) regularly capitalize the terms *natura* and *ratio* (but not *modus*) when they are used in systematic senses, regularly using lower case for the nonsystematic senses. They had announced this policy in the preface to the first edition, but without mentioning specific terms or making a distinction between systematic and nonsystematic senses:

> *Interpunctionem, pro nostra necessitate minus idoneam, imo praeposteram,*
> *non ad hodiernum quidem morem exigere, sed una* cum literarum
> majuscularum usu *ita reformare tentavimus, ut verborum contextus et*
> *continuatio hodiernis lectoribus quam certissime appareret.* (We have
> undertaken to reform a [system of] punctuation less suitable, even quite
> inappropriate, to our needs, not requiring it to conform to present
> standards but [reforming it] *through the use of capital letters* so as to make
> the context and continuity of the terms appear as plainly as possible to
> today's readers) (*Opera*, ed. J. van Vloten and J. P. N. Land, 4 vols., third
> edn, The Hague: Nijhoff, 1914, I, p. x; emphasis added.)

Hereafter this edition will be cited – in cases where a given letter, preface, appendix, or note from the *Ethics* covers more than one page, as well as for all references to the *Improvement of the Understanding*, *Short Treatise*, and *Theological-Political Treatise* – as 'V & L' followed by capital roman numerals for volume, and arabic numerals, or lower-case roman numerals (as here), for page. In the 1882 edition the passage quoted appears on p. xi.

Van Vloten and Land's lapses from their stated policy are infrequent. In the *Ethics*, for example, of sixty-six occurrences of *natura* in the systematic sense that are uncapitalized in the *Opera Posthuma* edition, van Vloten and Land capitalize sixty-two, leaving only four in lower case.

In contrast, Gebhardt, in his 1925 Heidelberg Academy edition, regularly retains the capitalization of the 1663, 1670, and 1677 editions. He notes its inconsistency, but merely suggests – not very convincingly – that Spinoza's irregular capitalization of such terms as *natura* may mark varying 'nuances of thought'. Here is his editorial announcement:

> *Dagegen ist das Schwanken in dem Gebrauch der grossen Anfangsbuchstaben*
> *bei Wörtern wie 'Natura', 'Mens', 'Corpus' u. dgl. beizubehalten, weil darin*

*möglicherweise die Schreibung Spinozas wiedergegeben ist und in dieser
stärkeren oder geringeren Hervorhebung eine Nuance des Gedankens sich
zeigen kann* (C. Gebhardt, ed., Spinoza, *Opera*, II, 318).

5 The expression *rerum natura* ('the nature of things'), in which *natura* has the
nonsystematic sense of 'essence' or 'character', is often used as a general
synonym for *natura* in the systematic sense, and sometimes written *rerum
Natura* (cf. Letter 2, V & L, III, p. 6), but never *Rerum Natura* or *Rerum natura*.

6 Spinoza's handwritten copy of Letter No. 6 (*c.* 1661) to Henry Oldenburg,
which was preserved in the archives of the Royal Society of London, contains
remarkably little capitalization. Even *deo* and *dei* appear in lower case. The
passage in which these terms occur – at the end of the letter – was omitted by
Spinoza when he was preparing the letter for publication in the *Opera Posthuma*.
If he had kept this passage, he would doubtless have capitalized *deo* and *dei*,
and perhaps also *natura*, which appears in the systematic sense in the same
sentence (cf. V & L, III, p. 25; Gebhardt, IV, 36; *Opera Posthuma*, p. 416).

7 I base these figures on the Gebhardt edition, which provides a careful collation
of the existing manuscripts, none of them, unfortunately, in Spinoza's own hand.
Natuur in the systematic sense is capitalized four times by Gebhardt in cases
where the term is left uncapitalized – inadvertently, I assume – by van Vloten and
Land. Two occurrences of *natuur* in nonsystematic senses are capitalized by
Gebhardt, following the original edition; here the inadvertence is that of
Spinoza's earliest copyists. Van Vloten and Land, consistently, use lower case.
On the other hand, van Vloten and Land, presumably by inadvertence, capita-
lize *natuur* in nonsystematic senses twice where Gebhardt uses lower case.

8 *Qua ratione* can have the rather different idiomatic sense, 'in what respect' or 'in
what sense' as at II, 35, n., and in Letters 32 (V & L, III, p. 122) and 75 (V & L,
III, p. 228).

9 In political contexts one finds such expressions as *ratione aetatis et virtutis*
('with respect to age and power') (*Tr. Th.-P.*, 17, V & L, II, p. 281).

10 *Recta ratio*, as in the expression *recta vivendi ratio*, is the standard medieval
Latin equivalent of the Greek *orthos logos* ('right rule or formula').

11 The expression *rerum natura* in the sense of 'the nature [or 'character'] of things'
occurs in my epigraph, there contrasted with 'the meaning of words'.

12 Spinoza might have intended 'essence' as a second systematic sense of *natura*,
the first being 'cosmos' or 'universe'; but this would have needlessly duplicated
the available systematic sense of *essentia* and thus is unlikely.

13 In the expression *natura Rationis* ('the nature of reason') (V, 29 pr.) *Ratio* is
used in the systematic sense and *natura* in the second non-idiomatic nonsystematic sense.

14 I have already noted (p. 336) two passages in which *natuur* occurs in both systematic and nonsystematic senses, the first being marked by capitalization. We
also find in a single sentence the expressions *behoord van natuur* ('belongs by
nature') and *zij wezentlijk in de Natuur* ('exists in nature') (*KV*, app. 2, V & L,
IV, p. 94).

15 Wolf, whose version of Spinoza's letters is generally reliable, mistranslates *a
modo quo* (Letter 12: V & L, III, 40) as 'from the *mode* whereby' (A. Wolf,

349

The Correspondence of Spinoza, London, 1928, p. 118; italics added). It should of course be rendered 'from the *way* in which'.

16 It may be that in this case Spinoza is using capitalization to indicate mention of the term *modus* (*Modus voco*: 'I call "modes" ') rather than to mark its systematic sense. (Elsewhere he either capitalizes or italicizes mentioned terms.) But even so, he does capitalize *modus* in three other passages where the term is *not* being mentioned: *Duratio Modorum, Modorum existentia,* and *ipsi Substantiae Modi* (Letter 12, V & L, III, pp. 39, 41: *Op. Post.,* 1677, pp. 466, 468).

17 Wolf mistranslates *infinitis modis variet* (Letter 64, V & L, III, p. 206) as 'varies in infinite *modes*' and *infinitis modis expressa sit* (Letter 66, V & L, III, p. 207) as 'is expressed in infinite *modes*' (*Correspondence,* pp. 308, 310; italics added). In both cases *modis* means 'ways'. Cf. the phrase in the passage of the *Ethics* (II, lem. 7, n.) to which Spinoza refers in Letter 64: *infinitis* modis *variant* ('differ in infinite *ways*') as well as II, 7, n.: *modus extensionis et idea illius modi una eadem est res, sed duobus* modis *expressa* ('a mode of extension and the idea of that mode are one and the same thing expressed in two different *ways*' (Stirling-White versions; emphasis added).

18 I have found the related substantive *infinitas* only in the expressions *Dei infinitas* ('God's infinity') (*Cog. met.*: V & L, IV, p. 207), *infinitatem ... exprimere* ('to express infinity') (I, 23, pr.), and *infinitatem exprimunt* ('[they] express infinity') (I, 10, n. and *De int. em.,* V & L, I, p. 33). In all of these cases *infinitas* means not 'indeterminate number or quantity' but 'quality or character of being infinite' – where 'infinite' corresponds to *infinitum I*, i.e. 'perfect without limitation'. Thus *infinitas* is equivalent to 'unlimited perfection'. But, despite its status as a noun, and its systematic meaning, it is not capitalized.

19 Thus there is some justification for Gueroult's repeated use of the rather odd expression *infiniment infinie*, in place of Spinoza's *absolutê infinita,* as applied to substance. (Cf. M. Gueroult, *Spinoza,* Paris, 1968, vol. I, pp. 69ff, 190ff, and passim.) But Gueroult fails to note that, in my terms, his phrase means *infinitê* [II] *infinita* [I] ('perfect without limitation and including all things without exception'). See below.

20 Although Dutch has two forms of the word for 'infinite' – *oneyndig* and *oneyndelijk* – Spinoza seems to have made no attempt to use them for distinguishing between systematic and nonsystematic senses.

21 I interpret the term *omnia* in the frequently used phrase *Deus, sive omnia Dei attributa* as the equivalent of *infinita II*; thus the phrase means 'God, or all of God's attributes without exception'.

22 In the *Improvement of the Understanding* Spinoza points out that certain positive concepts, among them *infinitum,* are expressed by negative terms, since their contraries, such as *finitum,* arose first in human speech and *nomina positiva usurparunt* ('usurped positive words') (*De int. em.,* V & L, I, p. 28). But, he insists, the finite is a negative or privative form of the infinite, rather than vice versa as the terms would suggest.

As early as the *Metaphysical Thoughts,* Spinoza had insisted that *Dei infinitas, invito vocabulo, sit quid maximê positivum* ('God's infinity, despite the [negative] term, is something wholly positive') involving *summam perfectionem* ('the highest perfection') (*Cog. met.,* II, 3, V & L, IV, p. 207).

23 In Letter 36 Spinoza uses *determinatum* to mean 'limited' and *indeterminatum* (lit. 'unlimited') to mean what *infinitum I* means in the *Ethics* – in such expressions as *indeterminatum et perfectum* and *absolutê* [II] *indeterminatum* (V & L, III, pp. 132, 133). In the *Ethics* he uses *determinatum* and *indeterminatum* in the quite different sense of 'determinate' or 'determined' and 'indeterminate' o 'undetermined', respectively. (Cf. I, 26 & pr., 27, 28 & pr.)

24 Gueroult (*op. cit.*, pp. 70–3), remarks on this absence of definition and its contrast to Spinoza's care in defining *aeternum*, suggesting as its cause the complexity of an adequate ontological theory of infinity.

25 G. W. F. Hegel, *Werke*, Berlin, 1844, XV, 341.

26 H. H. Joachim, *A Study of the Ethics of Spinoza*, Oxford, 1901, p. 23.

27 *Ibid.*, pp. 28, 41.

28 A. Wolf, 'Spinoza's Conception of the Attributes of Substance' (originally in *Proceedings of the Aristotelian Society*, 1927), as reprinted in S. Paul Kashap (ed.), *Studies in Spinoza*, Berkeley, 1972, p. 26.

29 Joachim, *op. cit.*, pp. 34, 35, 41. Siegfried Hessing has made a similar point in terms of the contrast between appearance and reality: 'Die scheinbare *Zwei* sind *Eines*. Das scheinbar *Viele* ist *Eines*.' (Introduction to *Spinoza: Dreihundert Jahre Ewigkeit*, 2nd edn., The Hague, 1962, p. xxvi.)

30 Gueroult, who speaks dramatically of the 'chute foudroyante du nombre, précipité des hauteurs de l'intelligible dans les bas-fonds de l'imagination' – a fall which 'creuse un abîme entre l'arithmétique et la géométrie' – and says flatly that for Spinoza 'l'infini et le nombre s'excluent' (*op. cit.*, pp. 517, 518), himself lapses into a quasi-numerical interpretation of the *infinita attributa* (cf. *ibid.*, pp. 158ff). Not only does Spinoza, in contrast to Descartes, who had declared in the *Meditations*, 'Whether I wake or dream $3+2=5$', dethrone number; he enthrones geometrical figure, raising it almost to the ontological level of the divine attributes. He might plausibly have called a circle *infinitus* [I] *in suo genere* because, among other things, its *infiniti* [II] *radii* are precisely equal. Spinoza does not state this in so many words, but I sense it between his philo-geometric lines, as perhaps Hegel did, when he said: 'so ist "unendlich" [as applied to the attributes] nicht im Sinne des unbestimmten Vielen zu nehmen, sondern positiv, wie ein *Kreis* die vollkommene [i.e. what Hegel elsewhere in this passage calls 'wahrhafte'] Unendlichkeit in sich ist' (*op. cit.*, p. 343; italics added).

31 Wolf's formulation is perhaps a bit cumbersome, but H. F. Hallett's "refutation" is both inept and unfair:

> A suggestion which must certainly be rejected has been made by more than one commentator [presumably, Joachim and Wolf], viz. that since 'infinite' does not mean an indefinitely large number but rather 'complete', the two Attributes that we know are, or may be, *all* the attributes, in that they complete the nature of substance. How 'two' can be 'infinitely many' passes my comprehension (*Aeternitas: A Spinozistic Study*, Oxford, 1930, p. 291, n. 2.).

But of course neither Joachim nor Wolf claimed that "two" can be "infinitely many"; Hallett has, in my terms, substituted an inappropriate nonsystematic sense of *infinitum* ('countless' or 'indefinitely many') for the appropriate systematic sense, *infinita II* ('all without exception'). Two attributes might perfectly well be 'all the attributes [there are] without exception'.

32 Wolf, 'Spinoza's Conception', p. 26.

33 I am indebted to Siegfried Hessing for the suggestion (in a private communication) that Spinoza's uses of *unum* parallel his uses of *infinitum*.

34 David Savan, 'Spinoza and Language', *Philosophical Review*, vol. 67 (1958) as reprinted in Marjorie Grene (ed.) *Spinoza: A Collection of Critical Essays*, New York, 1973, p. 65.

20 Über die Staatslehre Spinozas

Kudo Kisaku, Kanagawa

Die Staatslehre Spinozas wurde durch Hobbes' Gedanken vom Staate großenteils beeinflußt. Aber sie war nicht nur unter dem Einfluß der Theorie dieses Engländers, sondern stand auch mehr noch im Gegensatz zu ihr. Obgleich sie zwar in ihrem Ausgangspunkte miteinander übereinstimmten, so hegten sie doch ganz verschiedene Meinungen über die beste und höchste Staatsform. Das scheint hauptsächlich aus der Verschiedenheit der beiden Denkweisen über die Natur und die Vernunft zu stammen. Diese Schrift handelt über die Stellung der Natur und der Vernunft in der Staatslehre Spinozas und auf welche Weise der Staat durch beide gebildet wird.

I

Nach Hobbes ist das Naturrecht

> the Liberty each man has to use his power as he wills himself, for the preservation of his own Nature, that is to say, of his own Life; and consequently, of doing anything which in his own judgement and Reason, he shall conceive to be the aptest means thereupon.[1]

Daher ist es klar, daß das Naturrecht hier nur dem Menschen zufällt, und zwar scheint seine Ausübung überaus vernunftgemäß. Indem aber jeder so sein Recht vernunftgemäß ausübt, erhebt sich auch eine Frage, warum sich der 'War of every one against every one'[2] ergibt. Wenn die Vernunft auch hier wie bei Spinoza ein Gemeinbegriff wäre, welcher den gemeinsamen Nutzen zwischen sich selbst und andern sucht, so würde kein Streit unter den Menschen entstehen. Wenn sich der Streit trotzdem ergeben würde, so würde die Vernunft hier nur subjektiv oder egozentrisch ausgeübt werden. Insoferne würden die Beziehungen der Menschen zueinander notwendig feindselig werden, besonders wenn keine gemeinsame Macht über die Menschen gestellt würde. Und trotz des Gebrauches der Vernunft würden die Menschen einander feind werden, also Feinde, die von der menschlichen Vernunft selber erobert werden. Sie würden hier eher bloß Dinge als solche sein. Man könnte sehen, daß Bacons Idee von der Eroberung der Natur bis zu den Beziehungen der Menschen zueinander durchgedrungen ist.

Dagegen fällt Spinozas Naturrecht nicht bloß dem Menschen zu. Es heißt eigentlich das Bestreben, womit jedes Ding in seinem Sein zu beharren sucht und ist im allgemeinen die Macht der Selbsterhaltung. Hier kann es sich um keine Bedingung handeln, die Macht rational auszuüben. Das Naturrecht der Menschen spezialisiert die Macht der allen Dingen gemeinsamen Selbsterhaltung. Und zwar besteht die Natur der Menschen nicht in der Vernunft, sondern in der Begierde. Darin liegt das Naturrecht der Menschen, daß sie nach ihrer Begierde die Macht ausüben, was aber bei Hobbes als irrational angesehen würde. Doch nach Spinoza ist es nicht irrational, denn was natürlich ist, ist bei ihm nicht immer irrational. Nur vom menschlichen Standpunkte aus gesehen, wird es zwar als irrational angesehen, aber an sich selber betrachtet, widersetzt es sich dem allgemeinen Naturgesetz, denn das menschliche Naturrecht gehört zu diesem allgemeinen Gesetz. Es fehlt Spinoza am Gedanken, daß was rational ist, auch natürlich ist und was irrational ist, auch widernatürlich ist. Es ist nur ein Ausdruck des Gedankens, der die Lage der Menschen in ihrer Herrschaft über die Natur betont, wenn man von dem, was in der Natur ist als rational oder irrational spricht. Man kann insoferne die Natur nicht erfassen so wie sie ist, sondern nur verzerrt. Die rationale Ausübung der Macht bedeutet hier nicht nur den Gebrauch der Begierde nach der Vernunft, sondern auch die rationale Beherrschung durch dieselbe, was eben nach Spinoza unmöglich und nichts anderes als die Folge aus der falschen Naturanschauung ist. Es ist eine allbekannte Tatsache, daß er von Anfang bis Ende sich negativ gegen diese Beherrschung der Begierde durch die Vernunft verhielt.

Der Mensch kann sich zwar unter allen Umständen seines freien rationalen Urteilsvermögens nicht begeben und wenn er am meisten der Leitung der Vernunft folgen würde, würde er unter seinem eigenen Rechte stehen. Wie aber oben erwähnt, steht er mehr unter der blinden Begierde als unter der Herrschaft der Vernunft. Besonders unter dem Naturzustande wird sein Naturrecht durch die ununterbrochenen Kämpfe der Menschen gegeneinander gleich Null.[3] Man kann also nicht verneinen, daß der rationale Mensch, wie stark er auch als einzelner ist, in diesem Zustande der schwächste wird. Um im Naturzustande zu leben, muß der Mensch, ob Weiser oder Tor, unter der Herrschaft der Begierde oder des Triebs stehen, der ihn zum Handeln treibt und durch den er sich in seinem Sein zu erhalten sucht. Sowohl in den Beziehungen der Menschen zueinander als in ihren Beziehungen zu allen andern Dingen, würden sich die durch den Trieb bestimmten menschlichen Handlungen erst als physisch ausdrücken. Der Naturzustand der Menschen ist derselbe der physischen Kämpfe, die auf den Gegensätzen der Begierden zueinander beruhen. Wenn die Ausübung des Naturrechtes die Bestätigung des menschlichen Seins bedeutet, so sind die Handlungen nach dem Naturrecht für die Menschen notwendig. Indem die Menschen im Naturzustande nach dem Naturrecht handeln, ist es auch notwendig, daß sie als solche zu sein aufhören. Insoferne sie im Naturzustande existieren, können sie nicht sein und um als solche zu leben, sollten sie notwendig diesen Zustand wieder einsetzen und sich selbst zu wirklich frei Seienden machen. Hierin besteht der Zweck des staatlichen Zustandes und die Bildung dieses Zustandes ist nicht von der Vernunft abhängig, die sich ohnmächtig gegen Begierden und Affekte zeigt, sondern von Begierden und Affekten, die über den Naturzustand herrschen. Darin besteht die Eigenartigkeit von Spinozas Staatslehre. Um es kurz zu sagen: der staatliche Zustand ist bei ihm wesentlich natürlich.

II

Ein großer Unterschied zwischen der Staatslehre von Spinoza und von Hobbes mag darin gefunden werden, daß Spinoza das Naturrecht nicht vom Naturgesetz unterscheidet und jenes mit diesem gleichsetzt. Dort gehört das Naturrecht der Menschen zwar zum allgemeinen Naturgesetz und ist mit diesem eigentlich identisch, aber Spinoza behauptet, daß wenn auch der staatliche Zustand die Überwindung des Naturzustandes durch die Macht bedeutet, der Staat selbst doch von der Vernunft als freie Einrichtung begründet werden soll. Dafür sollte dies auch bei Spinoza geben, was dem Naturzustande von Hobbes als 'precept found out by reason' entspricht. In diesem Punkte gibt es auch bei ihm die Vorschrift oder das Gebot der Vernunft, was dem sehr ähnlich ist, das bei Hobbes als 'Precept of Reason' bedeutet. Spinoza sagt in seiner Abhandlung vom Staate:

> Da aber die Vernunft uns lehrt, Frömmigkeit zu üben und ruhigen und guten Sinnes zu sein, was eben nur im Staate möglich ist, und da außerdem nur dann die Menge gleichsam einem Geiste folgte, wie es der Staat erfordert, wenn sie Gesetze hat, die nach der Vorschrift der Vernunft verordnet ... die Gesetze des besten Staates müssen ja auch nach dem Gebote der Vernunft verordnet sein.[4]

Auch in der Ethik gebraucht er die Worte: 'die Vorschrift der Vernunft' und 'das Gebot der Vernunft',[5] die überaus moralisch sind und als Norm des gesellschaftlichen Lebens angesehen werden sollen. In der Abhandlung vom Staate wird die Vorschrift der Vernunft zwar auf das gesellschaftliche Leben beschränkt, aber von ihrem Wesen aus gesehen, würde sie ebenso als moralisch betrachtet werden wie in der Ethik.

Wie oben erwähnt, kann das Vernünftige bei Spinoza natürlich (nicht widernatürlich) sein, aber das Natürliche ist nicht immer rational. In diesem Sinne ist die Vorschrift der Vernunft nicht auch zugleich das Naturgesetz, sondern nur das dem Menschlichen eigentümliche Gesetz. Das Naturrecht kann vielmehr als das allen Dingen Gemeinsame, nach ihm lex naturalis sein. Im Theologisch-Politischen Traktate teilt Spinoza das Gesetz in zwei Teile: das von der Naturnotwendigkeit abhängige Gesetz und das vom menschlichen Belieben abhängige.[6] Dieses Gesetz ist 'nichts anderes als die Lebensweise, welche die Menschen zu irgendeinem Zweck sich oder andern vorschreiben.' Und es wird auch in zwei Teile geteilt: das menschliche Gesetz, das bloß der Sicherung des Lebens und des Staates dient und das göttliche, das sich allein auf das höchste Gut, nämlich die wahre Erkenntnis und Liebe Gottes bezieht.

In der Abhandlung vom Staate würde somit die Vorschrift der Vernunft als zum menschlichen Gesetze gehörig angesehen werden: kurz in diesem menschlichen Gesetze werden die Vorschrift der Vernunft und die von dieser abgeleiteten Gesetze des Staates enthalten sein. Auch das göttliche Gesetz ist bei Spinoza verschieden vom religiösen Gesetze der Offenbarung, und wird besonders das natürlich-göttliche Gesetz genannt. Die wahre Erkenntnis Gottes in diesem Gesetze bedeutet in seiner Philosophie die Erkenntnis Gottes und des Wesens der Dinge sub specie aeternitatis. Dieses Gesetz ist das höchste, das ohne seine Philosophie nicht gedacht wird, und von dem die Vorschrift der Vernunft und die bürgerlichen Gesetze abgeleitet werden.

> Welches aber diese Mittel sind und welches die Lebensweise, die ein
> solcher Zweck erfordert, und wie sich daraus die Grundlagen des besten
> Staates und die Art und Weise der Menschen untereinander
> herleiten, das gehört zur gesamten Ethik.[7]

Daher ist es klar, daß dasjenige was als Mittel zum natürlich-göttlichen Gesetz gilt, die Vorschrift der Vernunft ist. Und zwar ist es in der Ethik, weder im Theologisch-Politischen Traktate noch in der Abhandlung vom Staate, wo es sich um diese Vorschrift handelt. Diese beiden Schriften handeln hauptsächlich vom Naturrechte, aber das bedeutet nicht, daß es in Spinozas Staatslehre an der Vorschrift der Vernunft mangelt. Sie ist vorzüglich in der Ethik vorzufinden wegen der Moralität, die in der Vorschrift selbst enthalten ist.

Im Naturzustande handeln die Menschen nach ihrem Naturrechte und dadurch ergeben sich die Gegensätze der Menschen zueinander. Sich von solchem Kriegszustande zu befreien, sollten sie ihr Naturrecht übertragen, nachdem sie sich gegensätzlich zueinander verhalten. Diese Übertragung wird auch nach der Anleitung der Vernunft ausgeführt, aber die gegensätzlichen menschlichen Begierden können durch die ohnmächtige Vernunft überwunden werden. Wenn auch die Überwindung des Naturrechtes vernunftgemäß sein mag, so läßt sich ihre Wirkung doch insofern kaum erwarten als die Menschen in diesem Fall nur von der Vernunft abhängen. Daher findet Spinoza nicht in der Vernunft das, was die Übertragung des Naturrechts gültig macht, sondern in den Affekten. Um irrationale Affekte, die über den Naturzustand herrschen, zu überwinden, sind die größeren Affekte zu ihrer Überwindung notwendig. Die Überwindung der Affekte folgt nach Spinoza dem Gesetze der gegenseitigen Beziehungen der Mächte. Wie dieses dynamische Gesetz den Naturzustand beherrscht, so läßt sich auch seine Überwindung durch dasselbe möglich machen. Die Affekte, die den Naturzustand überwinden, sind keine einzelne wie Affekte, die überwunden werden. Sie heißen gemeinsame Affekte[8] und diese gemeinsamen Affekte werden nicht von der Vernunft gebildet. Die Menschen lassen sich mehr von den Affekten als von der Vernunft leiten. Daß daher solche Menschen miteinander übereinstimmen und 'gleichsam von einem Geiste geleitet' sind, ist nicht sowohl von der Vernunft als von den Affekten möglich, und zwar von gemeinsamen, nämlich 'durch gemeinsame Hoffnung oder Furcht oder den Wunsch, eine gemeinsam erlittene Unbill zu rächen'.[9]

Durch die Aussicht auf sofortigen Gewinn und die drohende Furcht vor Augen verführt, verzichten die Menschen darauf, nach dem Guten zu streben. Der Affekt strebt viel mehr nach dem bevorstehenden Gewinn als nach dem Guten in der Zukunft. Wenn so der Affekt auf etwas Gegenwärtigem beharrt, die Vernunft dagegen ihre Absicht auf etwas Zukünftiges richtet, und zwar durch die Macht der Affekte, die Leidenschaften heißen, überwältigt wird, so ist die Übertragung des Naturrechts im Naturzustande unmöglich. Niemand kann nur durch die bloße Vorschrift der Vernunft das Naturrecht übertragen, ohne daß die gemeinsamen Affekte die bevorstehende Gefahr, Angst und Furcht überwinden, die allesamt aus den Leidenschaften hervorgehen. Gewiß würden die Gegensätze der Leidenschaften zueinander durch die gemeinsamen Affekte überwunden werden, aber die gemeinsame Furcht und der gemeinsame Wunsch, die erlittene Unbill zu rächen, die Spinoza als die gemeinsamen Affekte ansieht, sind eigentlich passiv, d.h. Leidenschaften. Nach ihm sind die Menschen einander entgegengesetzt soweit sie von Leidenschaften bedrängt werden oder sie stimmen ihrem Vermögen nach miteinander überein, nicht aber ihrem Unvermögen oder ihrer Negation nach, und folglich auch nicht durch die Leidenschaften. So, warum können sie nach den Leidenschaften miteinander übereinstimmen? Zu diesem Punkte sagt Spinoza in der Ethik: 'Sofern die Menschen nach der Leitung der Vernunft leben, und nur insofern, stimmen sie der Natur nach notwendigerweise immer überein.'[10] Aber hier handelt es sich darum, nicht nach der Vernunft, sondern nach den Leidenschaften übereinzustimmen. Wenn die Übereinstimmung nach den Leidenschaften dasselbe bedeutet wie nach dem Unvermögen der Menschen oder nach ihrer Negation und nicht ihrer Natur zufolge, so ist es undenkbar, daß die Affekte die beginnende Ursache für die Bildung staatlichen Zustandes sein können.

Die Ethik Spinozas behandelt zwar die Art und Weise wie der staatliche Zustand von dem Naturzustande gebildet wird, aber hier handelt es sich hauptsächlich um das ethische Leben der Menschen, vorausgesetzt, daß menschliches Leben nur im Staate möglich ist. Dagegen in seiner Abhandlung vom Staate geht es darum, wie der staatliche Zustand vom beginnenden Zustand des menschlichen Seins gebildet wird. Vorausgesetzt, daß die Menschen viel mehr von den Leidenschaften als von der Vernunft beherrscht werden, so wird hier Aufklärung darüber gebracht, daß der staatliche Zustand als Überwindung des Naturzustandes nicht von etwas außerhalb dieses Zustandes, sondern innerhalb desselben durchgeführt wird. Da die Abhandlung vom Staate vorethische Probleme erörtert, scheint auch ihre Behandlungsweise der Leidenschaften von jener in der Ethik völlig abzuweichen.

Wenn Leidenschaften, die einander entgegengesetzt sind, die Menschen nicht untereinander vereinigen können, so würde der staatliche Zustand bei Spinoza nicht entstehen. Über die Veränderung der menschlichen Handlungen sagt Spinoza in der Ethik:

> Wenn in demselben Subjekt zwei entgegengesetzte Handlungen angeregt werden, so muß notwendig entweder in beiden oder in der einen alleine Veränderung vor sich gehen, bis sie aufhören einander entgegengesetzt zu sein.[11]

Das ist ein Grundsatz, der sich auf den Menschen als Einzelwesen anwenden läßt, in dem sich zwei entgegengesetzte Leidenschaften ergeben haben.

Und bei Spinoza wird der Staat in der Analogie mit dem Menschen gedacht und so gedacht, würde 'dasselbe Subjekt' in dem obigen Zitat durch den Naturzustand ersetzt werden. Und zwar folgendermaßen: Wenn zwei entgegengesetzte Leidenschaften oder Mächte in dem Naturzustande angeregt werden, so muß eine Veränderung notwendig entweder in beiden oder in der einen allein vor sich gehen, bis sie aufhören, einander entgegengesetzt zu sein. Vom Standpunkt der dynamischen Beziehung der Affekte zu einander gesehen, bedeutet dies, daß die eine schwächere der zwei entgegengesetzten Leidenschaften durch die andere stärkere überwunden wird und sich dieser anpaßt, bis die beiden nicht mehr einander entgegengesetzt sind. Hier handelt es sich darum, wie diese stärkere Leidenschaft zu bilden?

Zu diesem Punkte sagt Spinoza: 'Von je mehr zusammenwirkenden Ursachen ein Affekt hervorgerufen wird, um so stärker ist er.'[12] Die Affekte der meisten Menschen, Angst und Furcht zu überwinden, die jedem Menschen im Naturzustande innewohnen, werden so viel stärker, daß sie andere Leidenschaften zu überwinden vermögen und hier erst entsteht eine notwendige Veränderung im Naturzustande. Kurz: wenn die meisten Menschen miteinander übereinstimmen, 'um die gemeinsame Furcht zu beseitigen und das gemeinsame Übel abzuwehren',[13] entsteht der staatliche Zustand als notwendig. Insoferne sind diese Affekte nicht passiv, sondern aktiv – und wenn sie auch nicht immer aus der Vernunft entspringen mögen, so haben sie doch nach Spinoza die gleichen Inhalte wie jene, die aus der Vernunft entspringen. Ja, da sie aus der allen Menschen gemeinsamen Beschaffenheit

des Selbsterhaltungsstrebens stammen, so enthalten sie in sich etwas Rationales. Und so werden diese rationalen gemeinsamen Affekte nicht von außerhalb des Naturzustandes gebildet, sondern innerhalb desselben. In diesem
Punkte ist der Naturzustand wie im *Leviathan* und in *De Cive* beschrieben als
außerhalb des staatlichen Zustandes 'out of civil states, extra societatem
civilem[14] angesehen worden. Bei Spinoza aber gibt es keinen solchen
Ausdruck. Wenn auch hier der Naturzustand der vorstaatliche Zustand ist,
so ist jener doch nicht außerhalb dieses. Die Bildung des staatlichen Zustandes
vom Naturzustande ist keine sogenannte räumliche Bewegung oder Ver-
schiebung von Außen in das Innere. Der staatliche Zustand besteht in der Überwindung des Naturzustandes, d.h. der Angst und Furcht vor dem Tode. Wenn
es sich bei Hobbes un die Politik der Ortsbewegung handelt, so handelt es sich
bei Spinoza um jene der sogenannten qualitativen Veränderung. Wenn man
die gemeinsamen Affekte in Frage stellt, so versteht man unter ihnen die
Affekte, nach denen sich die Menschen dadurch zu einer Vereinigung
zusammenschließen, etwas als Moment zu haben. Da – und insofern sie
nichts anderes als Affekte selbst sind, so würde es unausweichlich sein, daß
der staatliche Zustand unsicher ist, weil derselbe von gleichsam gemeinsamen
Affekten gebildet wird. Die Beständigkeit und Sicherheit des staatlichen
Zustandes können nicht nur von den Affekten abhängig sein. Die gemeinsamen Affekte können zwar die wesentliche Bedingung für die Bildung des
staatlichen Zustandes sein, aber keine für dessen Beständigkeit und Sicherheit.[15] Wie oben gesagt, haben die gemeinsamen Affekte die Beseitigung und
Überwindung der gemeinsamen Furcht zum Zwecke. Dazu haben sie Mächte,
die nicht augenblicklich, sondern beständig sein müssen. Daher spricht
Spinozas Abhandlung vom Staate nicht weiter von den gemeinsamen
Affekten wie oben erwähnt. Und von neuem behandelt sie die Übertragung
des Naturrechts durch den Vertrag.

III

Auch bei Hobbes wird behauptet, daß die Möglichkeit, die Menschen vom
Naturzustande zu befreien teils in ihren Leidenschaften und teils in der
Vernunft besteht. Soweit man dies oberflächlich versteht – oder da es sich
hier um die Leidenschaften und die Vernunft handelt – so mag man behaupten,
daß Hobbes und Spinoza in Bezug auf die Bildung des staatlichen Zustandes
miteinander übereinstimmen. Aber nach Hobbes sind diese Leidenschaften
'fear of death, desire of such things as are necessary to commodious living;
and a hope by their industry to obtain them'.[16]
Ließen sich diese Leidenschaften als Mächte äußerlich machen, so wären
die gemeinsamen Affekte Mächte zur Überwindung entgegengesetzter
Affekte und müßten daher etwas Positives haben. In diesem Punkte scheinen
die Leidenschaften notwendig bei Hobbes zur Befreiung vom Naturzustande

verglichen mit den gemeinsamen Affekten Spinozas negativ zu sein. Die Vernunft würde daher bei Hobbes zur Bildung des staatlichen Zustandes eine große Rolle spielen, als ob sie die Negativität der Leidenschaft zu ersetzen imstande wäre, während die Vernunft bei Spinoza nur eine nebensächliche Rolle zu haben scheint.

Auch bei Spinoza ist das Naturrecht, das zur Überwindung des Natur- zustandes oder zur Bildung des staatlichen Zustandes durch den Vertrag übertragen wird, 'rights as being restrained, hinder the peace of mankind',[17] kurz: das Irrationale. Die gemeinsamen Rechte (oder die Rechte der Menge), die durch die Übertragung entstehen, sind nichts anderes als die Rechte oder Mächte, das irrationale Naturrecht zu unterdrücken, nach welchem jeder Mensch willkürlich handelt. Von ihrem Inhalte aus gesehen, würden sie Rechte sein, gemeinsame Affekte gesetzmäßig zu begründen. Und das Gesetz, das über die Übertragung des irrationalen Naturrechts herrscht, ist nicht rational, wie Hobbes es denkt, sondern sehr natürlich. Es ist ein allgemein gültiges Gesetz der menschlichen Natur, daß 'man von zwei Übeln das kleinere wählen solle'[18] und daß

> niemand etwas, das er für gut hält, vernachlässigt, es sei denn aus Hoffnung auf ein größeres Gut oder aus Furcht vor einem größeren Schaden, sowie daß niemand ein Übel erträgt, es sei denn, um ein größeres zu vermeiden oder aus Hoffnung auf ein größeres Gut.[19]

Das ist nach Spinoza das Gesetz der Vernunft. Dieses Gesetz ist darum natürlich, weil 'es der menschlichen Natur so stark eingeprägt ist'.[20] Und daher wird es unter die ewigen Wahrheiten gerechnet, mit andern Worten, es ist vernünftig. Kurz: es ist rational wie natürlich. Durch dieses Gesetz wird es von selber klar, daß der Mensch vor allem seinen Nutzen sucht, aber dieser Nutzen wird auf zwei Weisen gesucht. Auf eine Weise sucht der Mensch aus seinem subjektiven, egoistischen Interesse heraus den Nutzen und klebt dabei an dem bevorstehenden Nutzen. Auf eine andere Weise sucht er vernunftmäßig denselben Nutzen. In jenem Falle stehen die Menschen einander entgegen und geben Anlaß zur Entstehung eines Kriegszustandes. In diesem Falle aber wird der Nutzen, für sich und die andern gemeinsam gesucht und dadurch trägt man zum Friedenszustand bei. Hier ist die Vernunft nicht der Natur entgegengesetzt, sondern an sich natürlich. Und zwar ist der Nutzen, den die Menschen hier suchen, nicht ihnen gegegen- wärtig bevorstehend, sondern steht im Zusammenhang mit einem künftigen Gut. Jedenfalls ist es nach Spinoza natürlich und notwendig, daß der Mensch seinen Nutzen sucht.

Bei Spinoza werden der Vertrag und seine Verwerfung nach dem Natur- rechte geschlossen, welches auf dem allgemein gültigen Gesetze beruht. Wenn auch der Vertrag zwar die Übertragung des Rechtes bedeutet, so darf aber das Naturrecht selbst dadurch nicht verletzt werden, vielmehr zielt der

Mensch eher durch den Vertrag darauf hin, sein Naturrecht zu erhalten und zu vergrößern als im Naturzustande. Die Übertragung des Rechtes ist ein Mittel, dem Menschen seinen größern Nutzen als zuvor zu bringen und ihm ein viel freieres Sein zuteil werden zu lassen. Auch darin ist ein großer Unterschied zwischen Hobbes und Spinoza, daß der Mensch durch den Vertrag sein Naturrecht oder seinen Nutzen zu vergrößern strebt. Bei diesem darf der Mensch zu seinem bevorstehenden Vorteil einen sogenannten trügerischen Vertrag schließen – und wenn die Erfüllung des Vertrages ihm selbst keinen Vorteil zu bringen scheint, so kann er ohne Zögern den Vertrag verwerfen. Es kann sich hier nicht um 'faith, obligation and mutual trust'[21] wie bei Hobbes handeln. Auch im staatlichen Zustande wird der Mensch viel mehr von Begierden und Leidenschaften als von der Vernunft beherrscht wie im Naturzustande. Hier geht es um das Sein des Menschen selbst, nicht um das Sollen. In solchem Gedanken über den Vertrag scheint das ethische Moment ausgeschlossen zu sein. Wenn der Mensch nach seinem Naturrechte den Vertrag verwerfen kann und darf, so ist es anerkannt, daß jeder Mensch derart willkürlich wie im Naturzustand handelt. Insofern ist der Gesellschaftsvertrag unmöglich und wenn er auch geschlossen wird, so wird doch dieser Zustand zum Naturzustand umgeformt, soweit man eben die oben erwähnte Lehre vom Vertrag anerkennt. Wenn man einige Beispiele des Vertrags sieht, welche Spinoza im Theologisch-Politischen Traktat und in der Abhandlung vom Staate gibt,[22] so wird es dann klar, daß sie eben dieselben sind wie Verträge von Privatmännern untereinander in sehr ungewöhnlichen Fällen. Auch der durch Furcht erzwungene oder gegen die Staatsgesetze verstoßende Vertrag, wird für die Zukunft nur unter der Voraussetzung des Bestehenbleibens der vorangegangenen Umstände geschlossen. Wenn sich diese Umstände aber ändern, so ändert sich auch das ganze Verhältnis.[23] Das ist als clausula rebus sic stantibus bekannt.[24] In diesem Punkte lehrt Hobbes, daß ein gegebenes Wort treu gehalten werden soll, aber Spinoza sagt: 'Weder die Vernunft noch die Schrift lehrt, daß man jedes gegebene Versprechen halten müsse'[25] denn der Zweck des Vertrags besteht wie oben erwähnt, bei Spinoza darin, das Naturrecht zu erhalten und zu vergrößern. Es ist hier selbst wider die Vernunft, daß der Vertrag durch und durch getreu befolgt werden sollte. Er soll nach den Umständen befolgt werden, daher ist 'jeder Vertrag nur in Kraft in Anbetracht seiner Nützlichkeit; kommt diese in Wegfall, so wird auch der Vertrag hinfällig und verliert seine Gültigkeit.'[26] Bei Spinoza ist der Mensch 'sein eigener Richter' nach dem Naturrecht, was ihn von Hobbes unterscheidet. Wenn daher dem Menschen aus dem Versprechen mehr Schaden als Nutzen erwächst, dann entscheidet er nach eigenem Ermessen, daß das Versprechen aufzuheben sei, und er hebt es auf Grund des Naturrechtes auf.

Wenn man auch im Vertrag unter Privatmännern großen Wert auf den Privatnutzen legt, so ist es doch notwendig, in Verträgen zwischen Staat und

Bürger den Privatnutzen nicht zu überlegen. Hier kann der Vertrag eher contractum als pactum[27] heißen und der Nutzen wird da als Gemeinwohl und überaus rational angesehen. Um diesen Vertrag zu erfüllen sollte der Staat selber rational systematisiert werden und auch die Bürger sollten rational sein. Wie aber Spinoza sagt: 'Wenn die Menschen von Natur aus so beschaffen wären, daß sie zwar nur das begehrten, worauf die wahre Vernunft sie verweist, dann brauchte sicherlich die Gesellschaft keine Gesetze'[28] und der Vertrag würde nicht notwendig sein, wenn die Menschen rationell handeln würden. Der Vertrag ist aber notwendig, denn die Menschen können auch im staatlichen Zustande lieber irrational als rational sein. Außerdem übergeben die Bürger dem Staate nicht alles, was sie haben. Sie behalten sich viele von ihren Rechten zurück und suchen durch ihre eigenen Rechte, die sie für sich zurückbehalten, nicht das Gemeinwohl, sondern den privaten Nutzen. Wenn der Bestand des Staates auch so von der Treue der Bürger abhängt, so kann der Staat doch von den Bürgern nicht vieles erwarten. Und wenn daher in den Verträgen zwischen Staat und Bürger 'noch etwas anderes zum Versprechen nicht hinzukommt',[29] so kann die Vertragserfüllung nicht sicher sein. Kurz: den Menschen, welche Verträge nicht erfüllen, sollen Strafen auferlegt werden und kein Staat kann ohne Regierung und Gewalt bestehen.

Der Staat soll also den irrationalen Gewalten der Bürger keine bloß ohnmächtige Vernunft gegenüberstellen, welche die Leidenschaften nicht zu kennen vermag, sondern gesetzmäßige Gewalten. Hier wird der Staat zur Gewaltseinrichtung. In der politischen Philosophie Spinozas ist es bemerkenswert, daß die Ohnmacht der Vernunft betont wird und daß im Staate Gewalt um Gewalt notwendig wird. Die Aufhebung des Naturzustandes, über den sich die Gewalten ausbreiten, wird durch die sogenannten gemeinsamen Gewalten als die gemeinsamen Affekte durchgeführt und wie im Naturzustande ist die gegenseitige Beziehung zwischen Staat und Bürger gedacht, wobei eine gewisse Spannung zwischen beiden besteht. Zwar sind die Gewalten oder Mächte, die der Staat den irrationalen Gewalten der Bürger gegenüberstellt, rational, weil sie auf gemeinsamen Affekten beruhen, aber sie sind nicht absolut. Ja, die Gewalten des Staates sind nicht immer rational, weil der Staat 'die gemeinsame Furcht der meisten Bürger in Empörung wandeln kann'.[30]

Wenn der Staat auf den gemeinsamen Affekten der Bürger nicht beruhen kann, so entsteht ein Kriegszustand zwischen Staat und Bürger und selbst wenn auch der staatliche Zustand durch die gemeinsamen menschlichen Affekte gebildet wird, so können diese doch kein wesentliches Attribut des Staates sein. Sie trennen sich vom Staate selbst und können dessen Kritiker sein, aber auch der Staat kann die gemeinsamen Affekte unbeachtet lassen, denn er kann ihretwegen nicht sicher sein und sieht oft seine Unantastbarkeit und Absolutheit verletzt. Wenn sich in meisten Fällen ein Staatsumsturz dadurch ergibt, daß der Staat den Grund seiner Errichtung vernachlässigt, so soll untersucht werden, wie eigentlich der Staat beschaffen sein sollte, nicht in den Sturz zu geraten.

IV

Bei Spinoza wird der Staat, wie schon oben erwähnt, als rational angesehen soweit er auf den natürlichen gemeinsamen Affekten beruht. Nach ihm wird zwar die Vernunft der Natur nicht gegenübergestellt, sondern stimmt mit dieser überein. Wenn nun der Staat von der natürlichen Vernunft systematisiert würde, so würde es keine Trennung zwischen Staat und Bürger jemals geben. Nur derjenige Staat ist der mächtigste, der im übereinstimmenden allgemeinen Nutzen der Menschen die Vernunft mächtig macht, welche doch eigentlich ohnmächtig ist. Der mächtigste Staat ist nicht ein Staat mächtig und gewaltig mit Hilfe der Militärmacht und Androhung von Strafen. In solchem mächtigsten Staate muß die Vernunft als Macht verwirklicht werden und soweit der Vertrag zwischen Staat und Bürger auf den gemeinsamen Affekten der Bürger beruhend geschlossen wird, kann man die Vertragserfüllung als natürlich und notwendig ansehen, nicht als verbindlich. Da die große Majorität der Bürger als irrational betrachtet wird, so soll die Vernunft einsehen, womit eine Menge von irrationalen Menschen übereinstimmt und worin ihr Gemeinwohl gelegen ist. Hier wird die natürliche Vernunft wirklich. Im Theologisch-Politischen Traktat preist Spinoza daher die hebräische Theokratie,[31] weil dieser Staat hauptsächlich auf das Gemeinwohl der Hebräer Rücksicht nimmt. Und der plötzliche Untergang der niederländischen Republik des siebzehnten Jahrhunderts kam ihm zufolge einerseits davon, daß dieser Staat wegen der Oligarchie die natürlichen gemeinsamen Affekte der Bürger nicht verstehen konnte.[32]

Von der Herkunft seiner Entstehung aus gesehen hat der wirkliche Staat nach ihm besondere geschichtliche Umstände. Er sieht im englischen und im römischen Volk Umstände[33] – und sieht in beiden diese Beispiele. Das römische schuf seinen Tyrannen ab und wandelte die Regierungsform um, aber das englische Volk im siebzehnten Jahrhundert schuf den Monarchen ab. Durch den Unabhängigkeitskrieg wandelten die Staaten von Holland die Regierungsform um, wobei diese Beispiele nur den Wechsel der Monarchen (beim englischen und römischen Volk) oder die Wiederaufrichtung der fast schon verlorenen Regierung (bei den holländischen Staaten) zeigen. Jeder Staat hat seine geschichtliche Individualität und wenn auch die Regierungsform eine Umwandlung durchmacht, so kann diese von den gemeinsamen Affekten der Bürger gebildete Staatsindividualität nicht ausgelöscht werden. Also ist die Umwandlung der Regierungsform nach Spinoza bloß formal. Von ihrem Inhalte aus gesehen, ist die Lage wenig verändert. Auch in der politischen Anschauung Machiavellis können wir diese Denkweise vorfinden.[34] Daher kann das Gemeinwohl, worum es sich im Staate doch handelt, von der abstrakten, bloß allgemeinen Vernunft nicht gesucht werden. Das Gemeinwohl soll nur gesucht werden, wenn die geschichtliche Individualität jedes Staates in Betracht gezogen wird, denn die gemeinsamen Affekte der Bürger, auf denen die Individualität beruht, werden nicht gleich behandelt, sondern verschieden zufolge geschichtlicher und geographischer Bedingungen der Staaten. Kurz: das Gemeingut soll von der natürlichen und zugleich auch geschichtlichen Vernunft gefunden werden. Wenn das, worin die Menschen miteinander übereinstimmen natürlicher ist als das, worin sie einander entgegengesetzt sind, so ist der staatliche Zustand ursprünglicher als der Naturzustand, obgleich jener logisch und zeitlich nach dem gebildet wird. In diesem Sinne würde der staatliche Zustand ein natürlicher heißen und auch der Staat würde eine zweite Natur genannt werden können. In der Abhandlung vom Staate handelt es sich um die natürlichen Ursachen und Grundlagen des Staates, welche nicht aus Lehrsätzen der Vernunft abgeleitet werden, sondern aus der allgemeinen Menschennatur[35] und aus dieser Natur wird sowohl der staatliche Zustand als der Naturzustand gebildet. Und Spinoza hält Natur für Macht, daher ist die wechselseitige Beziehung der Menschen dieselbe wie jene der Mächte angesehen worden, die nicht nur im Naturzustand, sondern auch im staatlichen Zustand betrachtet wird. Dies bedeutet, daß bei der Bildung der Staatslehre von Spinoza die dynamische Betrachtung der Affekte als Mächte oder als Naturdynamik eine große Rolle spielt. Hier aber läßt sich nur der Staat als natürlich nicht ansehen, denn selbst der Vertrag, welcher allgemein als rational gehalten wird, ist nicht denkbar ohne auf die Natur oder die Affekte der Menschen Rücksicht zu nehmen. Der Vertrag besteht in der übereinstimmenden Menschennatur, ihren Nutzen zu finden. Die Vertragserfüllung wird nicht als verbindlich angesehen, sondern als notwendig nach der Natur der Menschen, was bei Spinoza Freiheit bedeutet. Der Vertrag soll demnach derart geschlossen werden, daß seine Nichterfüllung als widernatürlich angesehen wird.

Wie oben erwähnt ist nach ihm niemals widernatürlich was vernünftig ist, sondern es ist natürlich. Daher möchte man glauben, daß Spinozas Denkweise stoisch gewesen wäre, aber die Vernunft ist in Spinozas Philosophie nicht immer im Gegensatz zu den Leidenschaften. Vernunft und Leidenschaften kommen aus einem und demselben Ursprung. So gedacht, gibt es nur eine scheinbare Übereinstimmung zwischen der Stoa und Spinoza. Die Staatsmacht darf das Naturrecht oder die Bürgerfreiheit nicht unterdrücken, sondern ist identisch mit dem gemeinsamen Recht der Bürger, das Naturrecht oder die Freiheit zu erhalten und zu vergrößern. Also ist der Staat nicht gewaltsam, denn er versichert den Bürgern Freiheit und Gemeinwohl bis zur äußersten Grenze. Hier handelt es sich um den Staat, wo jeder Bürger dessen Macht – was die Summe der Gesamtmacht aller Bürger bedeutet – als sein

Recht ausüben kann. Die Regierungsform eines solchen Staates nennt er Demokratie. Dieser Staat ist nach Spinoza der beste, welcher der 'Freiheit, die die Natur jedem einzelnen gewährt, am nächsten kommt'.[36] Und nur er heißt auch der Staat mit einer absoluten Regierungsform, wenn er die Bürgerfreiheit am meisten anerkennt. Nach Hobbes heißt der Staat im allgemeinen: mortal God; bei Spinoza aber ist er wegen des Nutzen der Bürger notwendig, d.h. er ist nur Mittel zum Gemeinwohl aller Bürger, niemals der Zweck selbst. Also ist der Staat nicht mortal God, sondern der Bürger selber soll als solcher angesehen werden. Wenn der Zweck des Staats in der Freiheit besteht, so ist diese dann nichts anderes als dieselbe Freiheit der einzelnen Bürger. Der Staat ist nichts als ein rationales Instrument der Menschen.

Im Theologisch-Politischen Traktate führt Spinoza 'all unser Begehren, soweit es berechtigt ist' auf diese drei zurück: 'die Dinge durch ihre ersten Ursachen verstehen, die Leidenschaften zähmen oder den Zustand der Tugend erlangen und endlich sicher und bei gesundem Körper leben'.[37] Und die Mittel, die dem ersten und zweiten Zweck unmittelbar dienen, werden nach ihm in der Menschennatur selbst gefunden. So ist nur das Streben nach der Menschennatur selbst notwendig, um die Menschen vernünftig zu machen und obgleich der Staat, wie zuvor erwähnt, das Instrument zum menschlichen Gemeinwohl ist, so dient es doch nicht als Instrument zur Rationalisierung und Bildung der Menschen an sich. Hier handelt es sich um den Staat, soweit er als Mittel zur Lebenssicherheit und Erhaltung des Körpers betrachtet wird und da dieses Mittel nicht in der menschlichen Natur selber, sondern in äußern Dingen gefunden wird, so wird es öfter als Schicksal angesehen. Das dem Menschen aufgegebene Schicksal kann nach ihm durch Menschenmacht umgebildet werden, wenn es auch nicht vollständig ist. Indem Spinoza behauptet, daß die Menschen das aufgegebene Schicksal zum Zweikampf herausfordern, es überwinden und zum Instrument menschlichen Glücks machen, ist er offenbar ein Nachfolger von Machiavelli.[38]

Der Mensch kann nicht vollends rational werden, wie sehr er auch danach strebt, sonst würde der Staat nicht notwendig sein. Soweit Menschen in aller Welt existieren, kann von einer Aufhebung des staatlichen Zustandes keine Rede sein. Was hier sein wird, ist nur die Staatsumwälzung zum bessern, freien Leben der Bürger. Spinoza sagt: 'Sicherlich ist die Liebe zum Vaterland die höchste Frömmigkeit, die man zeigen kann.'[39] Aber diese Frömmigkeit zielt darauf hin, nicht sowohl die Organisation des gangbaren Staates als den staatlichen Zustand selbst zu erhalten. Wenn die große Mehrheit der Bürger einen Staat zur Revolution auffordern würde, so würde es bei Spinoza als notwendig angesehen werden, denn 'das Wohl des Volkes muß höchstes Gesetz sein, und alle menschlichen wie göttlichen Gesetze müssen sich nach ihm richten'.[40]

NOTES

1 Hobbes, *Leviathan, The English Works of Hobbes* (London, 1939), vol. III, ch. 14, p. 116.
2 *Ibid.*, chap. 13, p. 113.
3 *Tract. Politicus Spinoza Opera* ed. G. Gebhardt (Heidelberg, 1924), vol. II, ch. 2, § 15.
4 *Ibid.*, § 21.
5 *Ethic*, IV, prop. 62.
6 *Tract. Theologico-Politicus*, ch. 4, p. 59.
7 *Ibid.*, p. 60.
8 *Tract. Politicus*, ch. 6, § 1.
9 *Ibid.*
10 *Ethic* IV, prop. 35.
11 *Ethic* V, ax.1.
12 *Ibid.*, prop. 8.
13 *Tract. Politicus*, ch. 3, § 6.
14 Hobbes, *Leviathan*, ch. 14, p. 113; *De Cive*, ch. 1.
15 A. G. Wernham, *B. d. Spinoza, The Political Works* (Oxford, 1958), p. 26.
16 Hobbes, *Leviathan*, ch. 16, p. 116.
17 *Ibid.*, ch. 15, p. 130.
18 *Tract. Politicus*, ch. 3, § 6.
19 *Tract. Theologico-Politicus*, ch. 16, pp. 191–2.
20 *Ibid.*, p. 192.
21 Hobbes, *Leviathan*, ch. 14.
22 *Tract. Theologico-Politicus*, ch. 16, p. 192, *Tract. Politicus*, ch. 3, § 17.
23 *Tract. Politicus*, ch. 3, § 14.
24 C. Belail, *Spinoza's Philosophy of Law* (The Hague, 1971), p. 30.
25 *Tract. Politicus*, ch. 3, § 17.
26 *Tract. Theologico-Politicus*, ch. 16, p. 192.
27 S. Zac, 'État et nature chez Spinoza', *Revue de Métaphysique et de Morale*, 1964, no. 1, pp. 30–1.
28 *Tract. Theologico-Politicus*, ch. 5, p. 73.
29 *Ibid.*, ch. 16, p. 193.
30 *Tract. Politicus*, ch. 4, § 6.
31 Sieh, *Tract. Theologico-Politicus*, ch. 17.
32 *Tract. Politicus*, ch. 9, § 14.
33 *Tract. Theologico-Politicus*, ch. 18, pp. 226ff.
34 N. Machiavelli, *The Discourses* (translated by Leslie J. Walker, London, 1975), Book I, chs. 16 and 17, p. 252ff.
35 *Tract. Politicus*, ch. 1, § 7.
36 *Tract. Theologico-Politicus*, ch. 16, p. 195.
37 *Ibid.*, ch. 3, p. 46.
38 N. Machiavelli, *The Prince* (translated by A. Gilbert, Durham, N. Carolina, 1965), ch. 25.
39 *Tract. Theologico-Politicus*, ch. 19, p. 232.
40 *Ibid.*

ENGLISH SUMMARY: ON SPINOZA'S THEORY OF THE STATE

Though Hobbes and Spinoza agreed with each other in the starting point of their political arguments, they had different opinions as to the best form of state. This difference of opinion seems to emerge from their different ways of thinking about nature and reason. There is the idea of the conquest of nature by the reason at the basis of Hobbes's opinions. Arising from this idea the reason plays an important part in the reasonable exercise of the natural right, the formation of the political order, the laws of nature and the notion of contract. But according to Spinoza the reason is powerless against nature in so far as the latter signifies appetites and passions, and is overwhelmed by them. Therefore the reason is powerless to overcome the state of nature where appetites and passions prevail. The passions are overcome only by themselves. In such a case the overwhelming passions are called common passions. The common passions which are regarded as natural in origin play a decisive part in overcoming the state of nature and in forming the political order. Also in the notion of contract the natural passions of men, who above all look after their own interests, are regarded as more important than the reason, that is, contract without self-interest is entirely invalid.

However, the reason is not only regarded as powerless. While reason is called the common notion in the theory of cognition, it pursues the common interests among men in the field of moral and social practice. Therefore it has a close relation to the common passions and cannot have real significance without them. When Spinoza says that the state ought to be organized by reason, reason is not opposed to nature, but is regarded as united with it. Thus it means that the state is not artificial but natural. In the state the people transfer their natural right by contract. But Spinoza's contract is not to restrain but to restore the natural right which is taken for granted in the state of nature; that is, it aims at the restoration and preservation of the natural right or its enlargement, namely, the freedom of the people. Therefore the fulfilment of the contract is regarded rather as free or necessary than as obligatory. The power of state is thought to be a common right to preserve and to enlarge the natural right of the people. Thus the state must guarantee to the people their freedom and welfare. Such a state is called a democracy by Spinoza. The state is established for the sake of the freedom and welfare of the people. The state is a means to this end, not the end itself. Thus the state is not mortal God, but the people must be regarded as such.

21 Femmes et serviteurs dans la Démocratie spinoziste

Alexandre Matheron, Paris

Il est significatif, dit-on parfois, que la rédaction du *Traité politique* s'interrompe précisément au chapitre XI: tout se passe comme si, écrasé par les apories d'un démocratisme inconséquent, Spinoza avait succombé à la tâche. Et, de fait, nous sommes bien en présence, sinon d'une contradiction, du moins d'un paradoxe apparent. Dans la Monarchie spinoziste idéale, le Conseil du Roi devait comprendre des représentants de toutes les catégories de citoyens,[1] mais il était précisé, sans justification aucune, que certains habitants ne pouvaient appartenir au corps civique: outre les étrangers, les repris de justice, les muets et les fous, s'en voyaient exclus les serviteurs et assimilés.[2] Dans l'Aristocratie idéale, à nouveau sans la moindre justification, les mêmes personnes se trouvaient privées du droit de poser leur candidature à l'Assemblée patricienne;[3] si les muets et les fous n'étaient plus mentionnés, sans doute faut-il admettre qu'il s'agissait là d'un oubli. Quant à la Démocratie idéale, dont on nous dit pourtant qu'elle va être étudiée sous sa forme la *plus large possible*, la seule chose que nous en apprenions finalement, c'est que les mêmes exclusions y sont maintenues à peu près telles quelles;[4] celle des femmes et des enfants vient s'y ajouter, mais il est bien évident qu'elle était implicite dans les deux constitutions précédentes. Spinoza, cette fois, consent enfin à s'expliquer; il fait même assez longuement à propos des femmes.[5] Mais son explication semble au premier abord si faible, si plate, d'un empirisme et d'un conformisme si étrangers à l'inspiration habituelle de la doctrine, que l'on croit comprendre à la fois pourquoi il avait tant tardé à nous la donner et pourquoi il n'a pu poursuivre: mauvaise conscience, pourrait-on penser; sentiment confus d'une irréductible discordance entre ce que les principes permettaient de déduire en toute rigueur et ce que des nécessités extra-philosophiques imposaient l'obligation d'en déduire. Le cas est banal, et beaucoup s'en accommodent; Spinoza, lui, aurait eu l'honnêteté de s'arrêter là et d'en mourir!

Peut-être. Mais peut-être aussi conviendrait-il de ne pas décider trop vite, à la place de Spinoza, de ce qui est impliqué dans les principes de sa Politique. Que celle-ci, en un sens, soit d'inspiration foncièrement démocratique, voilà qui n'est guère contestable; mais toute la question est de savoir *en quel sens*.

368

Que Spinoza, comme tout un chacun, admette et justifie certains 'préjugés' dont la fonction idéologique est manifeste, nul ne saurait en disconvenir; mais il les justifie *par des raisons* qu'il nous expose, et qu'il faudrait d'abord examiner en elles-mêmes et pour elles-mêmes, en les prenant au sérieux, sans affirmer d'emblée leur inconsistance théorique sous prétexte que les motivations pragmatiques en sont flagrantes. Et si ces raisons, après examen, s'avéraient pleinement conformes au sens véritable, attesté par ailleurs, du démocratisme très particulier de Spinoza? Si elles contribuaient, à leur tour, à nous éclairer davantage encore sur ce sens? Le paradoxe, dans ces conditions, disparaîtrait. Non pas, certes, le malaise que l'on peut déceler sous la plume du philosophe; mais il faudrait alors lui assigner une autre origine.

Le problème, à vrai dire, ne se pose guère pour les enfants, les repris de justice, les fous et les étrangers: rien que d'évident sur ces divers points. Admettons, si l'on veut, que l'exclusion des muets est futile; sans doute Spinoza les assimile-t-il à des simples d'esprits. Restent les femmes et les serviteurs: l'enjeu, cette fois, est de taille, car ils constituent tout de même, pris ensemble, la majorité de la population autochtone adulte et 'normale' de n'importe quel État. Commençons par les seconds, dont le cas est théoriquement le plus simple, mais dont l'identification pose un problème.

Justifions, tout d'abord, l'emploi du mot 'serviteurs'. Le terme qui figure au chapitre XI du *Traité Politique* est 'servos'. Mais 'servus', au dix-septième siècle, peut avoir un sens très large: non seulement il désigne indifféremment un esclave ou un serf, mais il s'applique souvent à d'autres catégories encore. Hobbes, dans sa version latine du *Leviathan*, l'utilise pour rendre l'anglais 'servant', qu'il distingue nettement de 'slave', sans pourtant que ce dernier mot reçoive un équivalent latin spécial;[6] dans le *De Cive*, la correspondance était encore plus précise: les 'servi' étaient considérés comme un genre dont les 'ergastuli' (définis exactement de la même façon que les 'slaves' du *Leviathan*) constituaient seulement une espèce, et cette distinction faisait l'objet d'une comparaison avec celle qu'opérait la langue française entre 'un "serviteur", et un "serf", vel un "esclave" '.[7] Grotius, de son côté, pour prendre un autre auteur que connaissait bien Spinoza, tend à ranger sous une même rubrique toutes les formes possibles de 'servitude': à côté de la 'servitude parfaite' qui caractérise les esclaves au sens romain, et qu'il oppose à la condition des 'gens de journée' dont la liberté a pour rançon l'incertitude quant à l'avenir,[8] il rattache pêle-mêle à la 'servitude imparfaite' l'esclavage septennal hébreu, la situation des 'laboureurs qui étaient attachés aux terres qu'on leur donnait', celle des 'gens de mainmorte' et celle des 'mercenaires ou gens à gages';[9] dans ce dernier groupe, précise-t-il pour bien souligner la fluidité des transitions, les apprentis anglais, pendant le temps de leur apprentissage, ne diffèrent guère des esclaves proprement dits.[10] Locke, lui, apercevra un infranchissable fossé entre ces deux sortes de dépendance:[11]

les 'bourgeois' de la fin du siècle commenceront à mettre l'accent sur l'entière liberté de leurs employés; mais ceux des générations précédentes éprouvaient, semble-t-il, un certain orgueil à imaginer entre eux-mêmes et leurs serviteurs une relation de type seigneurial, que leur culture latine les prédisposait à mal distinguer d'un rapport de maîtres à esclaves.[12] Compte tenu de ce contexte, rien n'interdit donc de donner aux 'servi' de Spinoza la même extension qu'à ceux de Hobbes, ou qu'à ses 'servants', ni d'y englober tous ceux qui se trouvent assujettis à l'une ou l'autre des 'servitudes' de Grotius – c'est-à-dire, précisément, tous les 'serviteurs' au sens français.

Rien non plus ne l'impose encore, dira-t-on. Certes. Mais considérons maintenant la terminologie utilisée par Spinoza dans les chapitres consacrés à la Monarchie et à l'Aristocratie. Parmi les adultes autochtones, sains d'esprit, 'honnêtes' et de sexe masculin, deux sortes d'individus y sont privés de toute possibilité de participer au pouvoir. La première catégorie est désignée au chapitre VI par le mot 'famuli',[13] dont nul ne contestera qu'il puisse signifier 'serviteurs', avec assez souvent la nuance de 'domestiques', sans que le statut juridique d'esclave y soit nécessairement impliqué; à ce mot, au chapitre VIII, vient se substituer l'expression 'qui ... serviunt',[14] qui indique aussi bien la 'servitude' en général que l'esclavage en particulier. La seconde catégorie, elle, est caractérisée exactement de la même façon dans les deux chapitres: elle comprend tous ceux qui 'servili aliquo officio vitam sustentant'.[15] Le chapitre VI, à vrai dire, pourrait à la rigueur donner à penser que nous avons là une simple explication de 'famuli'; mais, au chapitre VIII, le mot 'denique' vient lever toute ambiguïté: il s'agit bien d'un autre groupe, composé d'individus qui, sans qu'on puisse absolument dire qu'ils 'servent', vivent néanmoins d'un emploi 'servile'.

Lesquels? Regrettons ici la petite faute d'inattention que se sont pieusement transmise des générations de traducteurs. On s'accorde pour faire dire à Spinoza, au § 14 du chapitre VIII, que les cabaretiers et les brasseurs ('Oenopolae et Cerevisarii') se rangent sous cette seconde rubrique. Si l'on procède ainsi, c'est sans doute que l'on interprète avant de lire: on admet comme allant de soi que Spinoza, à la manière aristotélicienne, entend par 'servili aliquo officio' toute occupation dont la 'bassesse' tend à empêcher ceux qui l'exercent d'accéder aux vertus exigées par la qualité de citoyen, et l'on en conclut assez logiquement qu'il doit refuser cette qualité à ceux qui vivent de l'exploitation d'un vice. Or le texte latin, sans la moindre équivoque, dit exactement le contraire. Spinoza vient de déclarer qu'un Patriciat héréditaire 'en droit' était incompatible avec la forme aristocratique de gouvernement, sous laquelle l'Assemblée suprême doit élire elle-même en toute souveraineté ses propres membres, mais qu'il n'existait aucun moyen d'empêcher les Patriciens de coopter 'en fait' leurs enfants ou leurs consanguins. Il ajoute alors que le régime n'en conservera pas moins sa nature si cet état de fait n'est pas officialisé par la loi et si le reste de la population ('reliqui') n'est pas exclu. Une longue parenthèse indique en même temps *qui* l'on doit entendre exactement par ces 'reliqui': pourront poser leur candidature à l'Assemblée tous ceux, mais ceux-là seuls, qui sont nés dans le pays, en parlent la langue, ne sont pas mariés à des étrangères, ne se sont pas déshonorés ('par quelque crime', ajoutait VI, 114), ne 'servent' pas, et enfin ('denique') ne vivent pas non plus d'une occupation servile; et Spinoza enchaîne aussitôt: '. . . parmi lesquels il faut compter aussi les cabaretiers et les brasseurs'.[16] Les choses sont donc claires: cabaretiers et brasseurs ('oui, même eux', semble vouloir dire Spinoza) figurent, eux aussi, *parmi ceux* qui remplissent les conditions requises; eux aussi, quoi qu'on puisse penser du caractère 'morale- ment' douteux de leur profession, doivent être rangés au nombre de ceux qui *ne vivent pas* d'un emploi servile. Si Spinoza a éprouvé le besoin de le préciser, n'est-ce pas pour souligner que l'expression 'servili aliquo officio' n'avait ici aucune connotation éthique?

Reste à savoir ce qu'elle dénote positivement. Mais, une fois levé cet obstacle à la compréhension du texte, le principe de la solution devient très simple. Un état a quelque chose de 'servile' lorsque, sans se confondre avec l'un ou l'autre des emplois occupés par ceux qui 'servent', il leur ressemble cependant par tel ou tel de ses aspects. Par lequel? Il ne peut s'agir, on vient de le voir, de la *nature de l'activité exercée*, si 'dégradante' soit-elle: si le commerce des boissons alcoolisées ne constitue pas un handicap, à plus forte raison en sera-t-il de même pour la pratique des 'arts mécaniques'. Il ne s'agit pas non plus de la *pauvreté* prise en elle-même; car, dans l'armée de la Monarchie spinoziste, pourtant composée uniquement de citoyens,[17] une solde sera versée en temps de guerre à ceux 'qui quotidiano opere vitam sustentant':[18] cela implique bien l'existence au moins possible de citoyens qui, faute de réserves suffisantes et de serviteurs capables de les remplacer en leur absence, perdent tout moyen de subsister lorsqu'ils cessent de travailler de leurs propres mains au jour le jour. Reste alors un seul critère de ressemblance, et par conséquent d'exclusion: l'état de *dépendance par rapport à un employeur*, quel qu'en soit le degré ou la forme. Sinon, qu'imaginer d'autre?

A partir de là, tous les découpages sont possibles, et finalement indifférents. On pourrait, par exemple, réserver 'famuli' et 'qui . . . serviunt' aux seuls esclaves; non pas aux serfs, bien entendu, car leur existence est impossible aussi bien dans la Monarchie idéale, où le sol est nationalisé et loué aux particuliers par l'État,[19] que dans l'Aristocratie idéale où chaque paysan est propriétaire de sa terre;[20] les emplois 'serviles' seraient alors les emplois salariés: ceux qu'exercent les 'mercenaires ou gens à gages' de Grotius.[21] Mais c'est peu probable si l'on admet que Spinoza envisage des modèles de constitutions applicables à la Hollande, où l'esclavage est interdit. On peut aussi, conformément à un usage assez fréquent de 'famuli', entendre par ce mot et par 'qui . . . serviunt' les domestiques au sens strict; les 'servilia officia', dans ce cas, seraient exercés par les autres salariés.[22] Ou peut encore voir dans 'famuli' et 'qui . . . serviunt' tous ceux, domestiques ou non, qui dépendent de façon stable d'un seul maître, et attribuer les 'servilia officia' aux 'gens de journée' de Grotius, dont il est effectivement difficile de dire si cet auteur assimile ou non leur contrat de 'louage de peine' à une servitude imparfaite.[23] On peut enfin étendre 'famuli' et 'qui . . . serviunt' à la totalité des salariés, journaliers ou non, pourvu qu'ils le soient sans ambiguïté aucune, et faire correspondre les 'servilia officia' à toute la gamme des situations intermédiaires entre celle de serviteur et celle de petit propriétaire: employés qui ont d'autres ressources que leurs gages, artisans tombés sous la coupe du marchand qui leur avance leurs matières premières, travailleurs à domicile, etc. . . . De toute façon, quelle que soit l'extension de la première classe, sa complémentaire sera telle que la classe totale des exclus restera la même dans tous les cas. Un point est donc bien établi: dans la Monarchie et dans l'Aristocratie spinozistes, pourront prétendre à la dignité de citoyens (sans, bien entendu, que cela suffise pour y accéder sous le second de ces deux régimes) tous les propriétaires indépendants, qu'ils soient par ailleurs riches ou pauvres et quelle que soit leur profession; seront légalement exclus, par contre, tous les 'servants' au sens courant du mot anglais, c'est-à-dire tous les travailleurs salariés sans exception,[24] même s'ils ne le sont qu'indirectement ou partiellement.

Cela ne prouve pas encore, dira-t-on à nouveau, qu'il en soit de même dans la Démocratie spinoziste. Ne pourrait-on penser que ce régime, à la différence des deux autres, n'écarte que les esclaves et les serfs? Ce serait, à vrai dire, assez étrange: si le servage est impossible dans la Monarchie et dans l'Aristocratie, on voit mal par quel caractère spécifique la Démocratie se prêterait à sa réapparition; quant à l'esclavage, ce qui a été dit plus haut de son improbabilité s'applique également ici. Mais ne s'agirait-il pas d'une simple hypothèse théorique (à supposer qu'il y ait des esclaves, etc.)? Non, pourtant. Car cette exclusion, au chapitre XI, fait l'objet d'un argument très précis, même s'il est très elliptique; or cet argument, on va le voir, *vaut tout aussi bien pour les serviteurs au sens large*, dont l'élimination sous les deux autres régimes n'avait jusqu'à présent reçu aucune justification. Si les 'servi' de la Démocratie avaient une extension moindre que les 'serviteurs' de la Monarchie et de l'Aristocratie, rien ne viendrait donc rendre compte de cette différence: il faudrait admettre que la raison alléguée au chapitre XI, alors qu'elle nous donne enfin la clef, introuvable partout ailleurs dans le *Traité*, de ce qui a été dit aux chapitres VI et VIII, ne suffit pourtant pas, à cause de sa trop grande généralité, à expliquer ce qu'elle était expressément destinée à expliquer en ce même chapitre XI! Tout devient clair, par contre, si les deux groupes sont identiques. Comment n'en pas conclure que la Démocratie spinoziste, elle aussi, refusera le droit de Cité à l'ensemble des salariés?

L'argument invoqué est en effet on ne peut plus net: seuls peuvent prétendre à la citoyenneté ceux qui, soumis uniquement aux lois de l'Etat, demeurent, pour tout le reste ('in reliquis'), 'sui juris'.[25] Cette dernière expression a-t-elle ici, comme on pourrait le croire tout d'abord, le même sens qu'en droit romain ? S'il en était ainsi, l'explication n'en serait pas une; elle reviendrait à dire qu'il faut refuser tout droit civique à ceux dont le statut légal implique, entre autres choses, qu'ils ne jouissent d'aucun droit civique; rien n'interdirait alors, comme Spinoza le fait remarquer un peu plus loin à propos des femmes,[26] d'admettre n'importe qui: il suffirait de modifier les lois positives. En l'absence d'indication contraire, toutefois, cette interprétation tauto-logique resterait la seule possible, Mais *il y a*, précisément, une indication contraire. Car Spinoza lui-même, au chapitre II, avait pris soin de définir la formule qu'il allait utiliser au chapitre XI: un homme est 'sui juris', déclarait-il, en tant qu'il est capable de repousser ceux qui l'attaquent, de venger à son gré les torts qui lui sont causés, et, absolument parlant, de vivre comme bon lui semble; est 'alterius juris', par contre, quiconque est 'sous la puissance d'autrui'.[27] Et il précisait aussitôt après: avoir quelqu'un sous sa puissance, c'est ou bien le tenir enchaîné ou enfermé (cas particulier des 'slaves' de Hobbes), ou bien lui inspirer de la crainte, ou bien se l'être attaché par des bienfaits qui le disposent à obéir parce qu'il espère en obtenir le renouvelle-ment.[28] Le droit se résolvant en la conjonction du désir et du pouvoir,[29] il était normal de transposer ainsi les notions classiques héritées des juris-consultes romains en termes de puissance effective. Or le décalage est parfois considérable entre ce qu'autorisent formellement les lois positives et ce que le rapport des forces permet vraiment. Dans l'état de nature, où chacun a peur de chacun en permanence, nul ne peut se dire 'sui juris'.[30] Dans la société politique, nul ne l'est jamais entièrement, car la puissance de la collectivité est un instrument de dissuasion irrésistible. Mais, pour tout ce que l'État ne prescrit ni n'interdit ('pour tout le reste', dit ici Spinoza), les situations indi-viduelles peuvent varier du tout au tout: les uns, qui ont les moyens effectifs de prendre des décisions dont le contenu ne leur soit pas dicté par la volonté particulière de quelqu'un d'autre, restent 'sui juris' dans la sphère où la loi commune n'oblige à rien; d'autres, par contre, n'ont pas ces moyens et ne sont 'sui juris' sous aucun rapport. Or les serviteurs, *au sens le plus large du mot*, se trouvent manifestement dans ce dernier cas: dépourvus de propriété personnelle, ils risquent de perdre toute possibilité de subsister s'ils déplaisent à leurs employeurs. Et cela, quel que soit leur statut en droit civil: même si la loi ne prévoit aucun châtiment pour le salarié 'libre' qui désobéit à son patron (ce qui n'est d'ailleurs pas toujours exact au dix-septième siècle), il obéira parce que la crainte et l'espoir l'y contraindront. Du fait de cette dépendance personnelle, on doit donc présumer que les serviteurs se com-porteront toujours, y compris lorsqu'ils exprimeront publiquement une opinion sur la chose publique, comme s'ils n'avaient pas de volonté propre. Et c'est pourquoi, même en Démocratie, ils ne participeront pas au pouvoir:

non qu'ils en soient 'indignes', ni peut-être plus incapables que d'autres par nature; mais, vu leur état, compter leurs voix reviendrait à compter plusieurs fois celles de leurs maîtres – ce qui, précisément, serait anti-démocratique au plus haut point.

Comprenons bien la position de Spinoza. Le démocratisme, chez lui, est le moyen partout présent, y compris dans la Monarchie et dans l'Aristocratie idéales, d'assurer l'auto-régulation du corps social.[31] Mais ce n'est jamais, y compris en Démocratie, une fin en soi. La fin de la Politique en tant que telle, c'est la conservation de l'État. Pour y parvenir, le problème est de mettre au point un système institutionnel qui, en déterminant nécessairement les sujets à accepter les décisions des dirigeants et les dirigeants à prendre des décisions acceptables par les sujets, se reproduira lui-même en permanence.[32] Ce qui implique, entre autres choses, que ce système assure une correspondance assez exacte entre la résultante globale des désirs des gouvernants et celle des désirs de la population dans son ensemble.[33] Cette correspondance s'obtiendra, soit si les gouvernants sont issus de toutes les catégories sociales susceptibles d'agir selon leur volonté propre (Monarchie),[34] soit du moins s'ils sont assez nombreux pour qu'un dénominateur commun rationnel puisse se dégager de leurs débats (Aristocratie).[35] Si tel n'est pas le cas, le mécontentement suscité par les mesures impopulaires[36] que prendra toujours une oligarchie dont les exigences s'opposeront à celles des masses permettra à l'une des factions dont le jeu aura été rendu possible par l'étroitesse même du groupe dirigeant de s'emparer de la totalité du pouvoir.[37] C'est ainsi, et seulement ainsi, que Spinoza envisage la question: l'usage du moyen et les limites de cet usage sont strictement déterminés par la fin.

On voit donc assez bien, dans le cadre de cette problématique, comment apprécier une éventuelle extension du droit de cité à ceux qui ne sont 'sui juris'. Elle serait, tout d'abord, *inutile*:[38] les serviteurs, en tant que tels, ne sont pas à craindre; s'ils s'agitent, c'est parce que leurs maîtres les agitent, mais ils ne constitueront jamais qu'une masse de manœuvre dans les conflits entre propriétaires indépendants; ce sont donc ces derniers, et eux seuls, qu'il faut satisfaire et contenir. Cette mesure, d'autre part, resterait *inefficace*: les serviteurs votant comme leurs maîtres ou pour leurs maîtres, il n'en résulterait aucun élargissement réel de la base populaire du pouvoir. Mais surtout, elle serait *très nuisible* par les conséquences lointaines qu'elle entraînerait. Car elle reviendrait, en donnant 'n + 1' voix à quiconque disposerait de 'n' serviteurs, à introduire l'inégalité parmi les propriétaires eux-mêmes. Non que ce soit 'injuste' en soi, la question n'est pas là; mais l'on aperçoit facilement, dans les deux constitutions proposées par Spinoza, par quel implacable mécanisme ce déséquilibre initial finirait, à la longue, par provoquer l'effondrement du système. Dans la Monarchie, où les members du Conseil sont nommés par le roi à raison de 5 (ou 4, ou 3) par 'familia',[39] seule leur rotation très rapide les empêche, faute de temps, de se laisser corrompre par le souverain;[40] mais il n'en serait plus de même si certains d'entre eux, une fois sortis de charge, se trouvaient remplacés par leurs propres serviteurs: la pression, alors, pourrait s'exercer continûment, et la voie serait ouverte au despotisme – avec l'approbation au moins passive d'un peuple irrité par le mauvais gouvernement de cette oligarchie de fait. Dans l'Aristocratie, les Patriciens doivent être au moins 5,000[41] parce qu'un État de dimensions moyennes a besoin d'être gouverné effectivement par cent hommes au moins et que, dans n'importe quel groupe d'individus pris au hasard, 2 pour-cent seulement ont les aptitudes requises pour devenir de véritables 'leaders';[42] mais si l'Assemblée suprême pouvait accueillir des serviteurs en son sein, chacun s'efforcerait de faire élire les siens pour accroître son influence,[43] et, bientôt, elle n'aurait plus *vraiment* 5,000 membres: les dirigeants réels étant alors en très petit nombre (2 pour-cent de ceux-là seuls qui auraient le plus de salariés à eux parmi leurs propres collègues) leurs rivalités ouvriraient la voie à la monarchie[44] au moment précis où le peuple, mécontent des abus que commettrait inévitablement cette minorité beaucoup trop étroite, serait prêt à soutenir n'importe quel usurpateur. En Démocratie, enfin, il est vraisemblable que le même processus interviendrait: ceux qui auraient le plus de serviteurs finiraient toujours, en toute 'l'égalité' puisqu'ils bénéficieraient d'une majorité automatique, par instaurer une Aristocratie à leur profit. Ainsi le démocratisme de Spinoza, comme celui des 'Levellers' anglais,[45] *exige-t-il*, loin d'y répugner, l'exclusion des salariés.

Cet argument, bien entendu, présuppose l'existence de serviteurs incapables de résister à la pression de leurs employeurs. Mais leur inexistence est-elle concevable? Elle impliquerait, soit une société composée uniquement de petits propriétaires, soit la communauté des biens. Or, si l'État peut en effet agir sur la répartitions des biens, c'est seulement dans certaines limites. Il est entièrement maître de la *propriété foncière*; car, nul n'étant capable de cacher le sol qu'il cultive ni de l'emporter avec soi en case de fuite, nul ne peut non plus l'occuper en sécurité sans la protection des pouvoirs publics;[46] ce que l'État seul rend possible, rien ne l'empêche donc de le modifier à son gré, que ce soit en répartissant également la terre[47] ou en la nationalisant[48] – pourvu, bien entendu, que le système institutionnel tout entier s'accorde avec la solution adoptée.[49] Sur les *biens mobiliers*, par contre, son emprise est beaucoup plus faible: l'argent et les outils se dissimulent facilement, et, si les perquisitions se multipliaient, leurs possesseurs émigreraient en les emmenant dans leurs bagages.[50] Quant à extirper des esprits le désir même de posséder, nulle autorité extérieure n'en est capable, tant que les hommes resteront soumis à leurs passions, ils s'attacheront nécessairement à des choses,[51] l'objet particulier de leur convoitise étant seul à pouvoir changer. S'ils devenaient tous raisonnables, par contre, c'est l'État qui disparaîtrait:[52] les lois du pays d'Utopie ne sont faites que pour ceux qui n'ont plus besoin de lois.[53] Impossible, par conséquent, de supprimer l'économie marchande lorsqu'elle existe; il est même préférable de la stimuler au maximum, car c'est encore le commerce qui unit le mieux les hommes passionnés, alors que la terre, elle, les divise.[54] Mais l'économie marchande a sa rançon: ceux qui auront tout perdu dans la compétition devront 'louer leur peine' pour survivre; et leurs employeurs, aspirant comme tout un chacun à imposer aux autres leurs propres vues,[55] utiliseront à plein les moyens de pression dont ils disposeront à leur égard.

Sans doute la question se fût-elle posée autrement si Spinoza avait prévu la révolution industrielle et ses effets: grandes usines susceptibles d'être enlevées à leurs possesseurs parce qu'indissimulables et intransportables comme la terre, travailleurs plus aptes à résister collectivement en raison de leur concentration. Peut-être, enregistrant ces nouveaux supports de forces, eût-il alors conçu une Monarchie, une Aristocratie et une Démocratie 'prolétariennes'! . . . Mais l'on ne saurait lui reprocher ce manque d'imagination. Ses constitutions sont donc 'bourgeoises'. Il est déjà remarquable, même en Hollande, qu'elles éliminent expressément toute survivance de féodalisme; et que cela se déduise du système.

C'est en fonction de la même problématique qu'est affirmée la nécessité d'exclure les femmes. Mais leur cas, malgré tout, se distingue un peu de celui des serviteurs. Une fois identifiés ces derniers, ce qui n'était pas si facile, et une fois rappelée ensuite la définition des personnes 'sui juris', il en résultait analytiquement qu'elle ne s'appliquerait jamais à eux; quant aux conséquences politiques de leur éventuelle promotion, elles devenaient alors manifestes. L'identification des femmes, au contraire, est immédiate. Mais il n'est nullement évident qu'elles soient condamnées à toujours rester 'alterius juris', même si l'État décide un jour de leur accorder un statut légal identique à celui des hommes.[56] En admettant qu'elles le soient, on voit mal, en pays monogamique, quel déséquilibre grave pourrait entraîner leur admission. Ces deux questions exigent donc un traitement spécial.

La première est examinée dans un contexte polémique. Alors que Grotius, en toute naïveté, affirmait comme allant de soi la supériorité naturelle du sexe masculin,[57] Hobbes, lui, la contestait radicalement: si les femmes, déclarait-il, doivent obéissance à leurs maris dans la plupart de nos sociétés civiles, c'est parce que les lois ont été généralement faites par les hommes; encore n'est-ce pas absolument universel, puisqu'il y eut au moins le royaume des Amazones; mais la nature, de toute façon, n'y est pour rien: aucun des deux sexes, ni physiquement ni mentalement, ne l'emporte vraiment sur l'autre.[58] Spinoza se garde bien de réfuter directement cette thèse par des considérations sur le naturel féminin. Il précise même, renchérissant ainsi sur l'auteur de *Leviathan*, que ces considérations n'auraient aucune pertinence: dans une société hypothétique où les femmes domineraient les hommes, écrit-il, ceux-ci seraient élevés de façon à rester intellectuellement inférieurs ('ita educarentur, ut ingenio minus possent');[59] ce qui sous-entend bien que, dans nos sociétés réelles, l'éducation des femmes est destinée à les adapter au rôle subordonné qu'elles ont à jouer, et que les inégalités traditionnellement attribuées à la nature viennent donc, pour une énorme part, de la culture. Impossible, par conséquent, de prouver quoi que ce soit en se plaçant sur ce terrain là: pour déterminer, parmi les handicaps constatés en fait, quels sont ceux qui tiennent vraiment à l'essence de la femme, il faudrait connaître cette essence, et Spinoza ne la connaît pas. Aussi bien déplace-t-il la question: admettons, semble-t-il dire, que tous les exemples d'infériorité observés soient imputables à un conditionnement culturel imposé par l'homme; mais comment expliquer, précisément, que l'homme, toujours et partout, soit en mesure de l'imposer? Car c'est bien toujours et partout qu'il fait la loi,[60] et non pas, comme le disait Hobbes, la plupart du temps seulement: le cas isolé des Amazones n'est pas significatif, puisqu'elles éliminaient préventivement toute concurrence en assassinant leurs enfants mâles;[61] seuls sont à prendre en compte les groupements humains où les deux sexes coexistent 'concorditer',[62] et aucune exception à cette règle n'y est décelable. D'où cela provient-il donc? Hobbes ne se le demandait pas. Or, selon Spinoza, voilà qui nous renvoie par un autre biais à la nature.

Son raisonnement, ici, relève de la connaissance du second genre, ou plus précisément de celle du 'troisième genre' telle que la définissait le *Traité de la Réforme de l'Entendement*: sans rien connaître de l'essence de la femme, il déduit l'une de ses propriétés par application d'une vérité universelle à un cas particulier; et, dans cette application, il remonte de l'effet à la cause.[63] Toutes choses égales d'ailleurs, nous dit-il, l'"animi fortitudo" et l'"ingenium" constituent très évidemment deux atouts décisifs dans la compétition pour le pouvoir.[64] En réalité, bien entendu, toutes choses ne sont jamais égales d'ailleurs: dans chaque situation concrète, les circonstances accidentelles jouent leur rôle. Mais plus les cas sont nombreux et variés, plus l'influence de ces circonstances tend à s'effacer statistiquement. Si, dans ces conditions, la nature avait également pourvus hommes et femmes en 'fortitudine et ingenio', les multiples sociétés humaines historiquement connues se répartiraient en trois groupes: celles où les hommes domineraient, celles où les deux sexes disposeraient du même pouvoir, celles où les femmes auraient le dessus et éduqueraient les hommes de façon à les maintenir en position d'infériorité.[65] Or, c'est un fait, nous ne connaissons pas un seul exemple de ces deux derniers types de rapports. La fausseté du conséquent entraîne donc celle de l'antécédent: si les femmes sont toujours soumises aux hommes, cela ne peut venir que de leur faiblesse naturelle.[66]

Spinoza, sans nul doute, a pleinement conscience des conditions de validité des limites de son argument. Or, en admettant avec lui que les données historiques dont il dispose soient assez nombreuses et assez indépendantes les unes des autres pour que le recours à l'universalité d'une 'nature' puisse s'imposer, qu'établit-il exactement? Pas grand'chose, en définitive, même si c'est capital pour son propos. Si l''ingenium' dont il parle ici consiste en certaines aptitudes 'intellectuelles', il ne peut s'agir que de celles d'entre elles qui interviennent effectivement dans la lutte pour la domination: aptitude à la ruse, à l'habilité manœuvrière, etc. . . . Quant à la 'fortitudo', elle ne désigne évidemment pas la vertu spinoziste du même nom,[67] qui n'est pas une qualité naturelle; elle signifie plutôt, semble-t-il, une disposition moindre à la crainte et à la pitié: 'larmes de femme',[68] 'pitié de femme',[69] voilà bien qui diminue les chances de succès dans la course à la puissance. A la limite, et comme l'indiquait d'ailleurs le *Traité de la Réforme de l'Entendement*, ce genre de raisonnement ne nous fait connaître de la cause que ce que nous savions déjà de son effet:[70] 'il y a quelque chose',[71] dans la nature des femmes, qui les désavantage dans le jeu des rapports de pouvoir que sont condamnés à entretenir tous les membres du genre humain sous le régime de la passion. C'est peu; et cela n'a rien de particulièrement péjoratif, puisque ces rapports eux-mêmes ne sont en rien valorisés. Mais, de ce 'quelque chose', tout découle: en supposant même une société directement sortie de l'état de nature, sur laquelle aucune institution antérieure n'ait laissé la moindre trace, l'homme y dominerait pourtant la femme dans la majorité des couples, car tout être humain passionné utilise à plein les possibilités qui lui sont données d'imposer aux autres ses propres vues;[72] après quoi, tout aussi nécessairement, le sexe un peu plus fort se servirait de son pouvoir pour amplifier démesurément, par l'intermédiaire de l'éducation dont il se serait rendu maître,[73] la petite inégalité originelle qui aurait rendu possible ce même pouvoir; et ce serait bientôt dans *tous* les couples que la femme se verrait réduite à un état de dépendance irréversible qui l'obligerait à obéir. Aucun espoir d'y échapper, sinon par la régénération philosophique. Jusque là, et quel que soit leur statut légal, les femmes resteront 'alterius juris' comme les serviteurs.

Mais la seconde question se pose alors. L'octroi de la citoyenneté aux femmes serait certainement aussi inutile et aussi inefficace que son octroi aux serviteurs, mais serait-il vraiment aussi nuisible? Car enfin, dans les pays pour lesquels est écrit le *Traité politique*, nul n'a jamais qu'une épouse à la fois: si tout homme disposait de deux voix et non plus d'une seule, aucun changement n'en résulterait dans l'équilibre des forces. La seule conséquence de cette mesure ne serait-elle pas la disparition totale du célibat? Non, répond Spinoza dans les dernières lignes qu'il ait écrites. Et cela, en particulier, pour deux raisons.

En premier lieu, d'une façon générale, tout individu passionné surestime nécessairement ce qu'il aime.[74] Or, sous le régime de la passion, c'est par leur seule beauté que les femmes attirent les hommes:[75] le beau n'étant rien d'autre que ce dont la vue provoque, dans une partie au moins de notre organisme,[76] des réactions physiologiques favorables pour un instant au

378

moins à la santé,[77] cette proposition peut être considérée comme analytique, voire tautologique. Tout homme passionné tend donc à attribuer aux personnes de l'autre sexe une intelligence proportionnelle à leur beauté.[78] On voit ce qui en résulterait sur le plan politique, bien que Spinoza ne le précise pas. Dans une Assemblée où siègeraient les femmes, les plus belles d'entre elles recueilleraient tous les suffrages masculins; et aussi, bien entendu, ceux des épouses de leurs admirateurs, qui devraient voter bon gré mal gré comme l'exigeraient leurs seigneurs et maîtres. Ces séductrices étant elles-mêmes sous la dépendance de leurs maris, tout homme dont la femme aurait 'n' adorateurs disposerait ainsi de '2(n + 1)' voix qu'il utiliserait à sa guise, et le mécanisme décrit plus haut se déclencherait: la Démocratie finirait par se transformer en une aristocratie des possesseurs de jolies femmes (ceux-là mêmes, sans doute, qui auraient *aussi* le plus de serviteurs), l'Aristocratie en une monarchie, et la Monarchie en une despotisme ordinaire.

Mais il y a plus. Car, en second lieu, les hommes supportent mal que les femmes qu'ils aiment accordent la moindre faveur à quelqu'un d'autre.[79] Sans doute la jalousie se manifeste-t-elle également dans les relations de pouvoir entre membres du même sexe: quiconque s'attache a l'un de ses semblables, quelle qu'en soit la raison, exige de lui un attachement réciproque et exclusif; si celui ou celle qui fait l'objet de notre affection se lie d'une amitié trop étroite avec un tiers, nous les haïrons donc l'un et l'autre.[80] Mais dans le cas de la jalousie sexuelle, une cause supplémentaire vient s'ajouter à la précédente: nous associons l'image de la femme aimée à celle des 'pudenda' et des 'excrementa' de notre rival,[81] et, dans la mesure où cette dernière nous faisait déjà horreur par elle-même,[82] notre haine envers l'infidèle et son complice s'en trouve renforcée jusqu'au délire.[83] Sans tenter de psychanalyser Spinoza, on peut au moins comprendre la façon dont il justifierait lui-même cette affirmation bizarre: si nous imaginons que quelqu'un tire de la joie d'une chose qu'un seul peut posséder, a-t-il démontré auparavant, nous ferons tout pour qu'il ne la possède pas;[84] or la femme, physiquement parlant, ne peut être possédée que par un seul homme à la fois; si, par conséquent, un mâle imagine un autre mâle se livrant à une activité sexuelle, alors même que la partenaire de ce dernier ne l'intéressait absolument pas auparavant, cette représentation l'attristera parce qu'elle impliquera celle d'une jouissance dont il se verra exclu; ainsi, pour tout homme, l'idée de l'organe sexuel de n'importe quel autre homme aura-t-elle quelque chose d'odieux; on voit donc comment, lorsque nous soupçonnons l'existence d'un commerce physique entre la femme que nous aimons et quelqu'un d'autre, la haine que tous deux nous inspirent peut se lier à celle qu'éveillait déjà en nous cette image générique insupportable, et quel est l'effet cumulatif de cette conjonction. D'où le paradoxe: si les femmes siègent à l'Assemblée des citoyens, la séduction deviendra l'instrument politique par excellence, mais ceux-là mêmes qui en bénéficieront, et qui voudront nécessairement en bénéficier par ambition, mettront tout en œuvre pour se venger avec une extrême férocité de ceux à qui ils devront leur victoire;[85] quant à ces derniers, pour la même raison, ils ne cesseront de s'entre-déchirer. Non seulement l'État dégénérera, mais le processus se déroulera dans des conditions plus affreuses que partout ailleurs, avec une violence anarchique où l'état de nature transparaîtra. Si les hommes, nulle part, n'ont jamais accepté d'accorder aux femmes un statut légal formellement identique au leur, sans doute cela vient-il de ce qu'ils pressentaient confusément cette conséquence.

Les femmes, contrairement à ce que l'on dit souvent, n'inspirent à Spinoza aucune répugnance particulière. Mais ce qui l'épouvante, c'est l'âpreté des conflits sexuels entre mâles humains. Pour empêcher ces antagonismes de rendre la Cité ingouvernable, le seul moyen qu'il aperçoive, et ce n'est certainement pas de gaîté de coeur qu'il le préconise, est d'exclure de la vie publique celles qui, bien malgré elles parfois, en sont ou peuvent en être l'objet. Il eût exclu les hommes, pour la même raison, s'ils avaient été les plus faibles; et si les deux sexes s'étaient trouvés à égalité, ou si les homosexuels n'avaient pas constitué une minorité insignifiante, sans doute eût-il pensé que cela compliquait singulièrement la question! Tel est son dernier mot en matière de politique.

Mais la Politique, elle, n'a jamais été le dernier mot de Spinoza: elle n'est qu'un moment de son projet philosophique. Par delà l'État, par delà même l'État le plus démocratique possible, le modèle idéal qu'il se fixe[86] en matière de relations interhumaines est une communauté de sages libérée de toute contrainte, où chacun, sous la conduite de sa seule raison, agirait spontanément en accord avec tous[87] sans être soumis à aucune autorité extérieure.[88] Alors, mais alors seulement, disparaîtrait toute relation de dépendance: l'ambition une fois transmuée en désir de faire connaître la vérité,[89] nul ne chercherait plus à dominer qui que ce soit; la propriété privée perdant tout sens pour des amis entre lesquels 'tout est commun',[90] nul n'aurait plus besoin de se plier aux conditions d'autrui pour assurer sa subsistance. Sans doute l'entrée dans une telle communauté implique-t-elle l'accès individuel de chacun de ses membres au règne de la Raison: processus lent et complexe, qui exige un développement considérable de la connaissance. Mais rien ne permet de penser que les serviteurs en soient plus incapables que leurs maîtres: leur infériorité tient à leur situation, non à leur nature. Quant aux femmes, leur handicap naturel est tout relatif: elles sont désavantagées dans la lutte pour le pouvoir comme les boîteux dans une course à pied, mais cela ne préjuge en rien des aptitudes qu'elles ont peut-être pour d'autres choses (y compris, puisque là est toute la question, pour la spéculation intellectuelle), et qui se manifesteraient peut-être lorsque cette lutte viendrait à cesser. Si Spinoza envisage la possibilité d'un amour sexuel fondé principalement, chez l'homme comme chez la femme ('utriusque, viri scilicet et foeminae'), sur la liberté de l'esprit,[91] c'est bien qu'il n'exclut pas la présence de femmes parmi les 'hommes libres' de l'*Ethique*.

Et pourtant, il faut en passer par la médiation politique: la mise en place d'un État spinoziste, qui supprimerait les causes de tous les antagonismes de type féodal (lutte pour la possession de la terre, intolérance religieuse, oppression politique), est la condition *nécessaire* de l'accès du plus grand nombre au règne de la Raison.[92] Or un tel État, obligatoirement 'démocratique' au sens indiqué plus haut, n'en resterait pas moins répressif par définition. Son unique fonction serait d'instaurer un équilibre de forces entre des individus qui, en attendant la libération authentique à laquelle il ne pourrait que les préparer par le conditionnement extérieur auquel il les soumettrait, ne seraient jamais, dans le meilleur des cas, à supposer même que toute survivance féodale ait été vraiment éliminée des lois et des moeurs, que des 'bourgeois' et des 'phallocrates': horizon indépassable, aussi longtemps du moins que l'aliénation passionnelle subsistera. D'où l'indispensable mise à l'écart de plus de la moitié de la population adulte. Mais rien ne garantit que la condition nécessaire soit *suffisante*: on ne peut qu'espérer,[93] sans en être sûr, que le sacrifice ne sera pas vain. La gêne manifeste de Spinoza dans les dernières lignes du *Traité* ne vient donc pas de ce qu'il assume des préjugés sans rapport avec ses principes, mais de ce que, sur ce point précis, les conséquences de ses principes sont cruelles.... Peut-être, en définitive, y avait-il bien là de quoi s'arrêter et de quoi mourir!

NOTES

1 Spinoza, *Le Traité politique*, VII, 4.

2 *Ibid.*, VI, 11.

3 *Ibid.*, VIII, 14.

4 *Ibid.*, XI, 3.

5 *Ibid.*, XI, 4.

6 Hobbes, *Leviathan*, ch. 20 (cf. note 58).

7 Hobbes, *De Cive*, VIII, 2. Le découpage anglais et le découpage latin, chez Hobbes, ne se recouvrent donc pas exactement. Dans l'un et l'autre texte, 'ergastuli' et 'slaves' designent les esclaves enfermés ou enchaînés. 'Servants', qui s'oppose à 'slaves', doit donc englober à la fois les esclaves romains physiquement 'libres', les serfs, et ceux que l'on appelle couramment 'servants' dans l'Angleterre du dix-septième siècle, c'est-à-dire les travailleurs salariés en général (cf. note 24): le chapitre 20 du *Leviathan*, qui étudie uniquement l'origine de la situation des 'servants' à l'état de nature, laisse entièrement intacte la question de leur statut dans la société civile, qui peut être infiniment varié dans la mesure où il dépend de la volonté du souverain; et il est difficile de penser que Hobbes n'a pas choisi ce mot intentionnellement. 'Servi', au contraire, est le genre commun à 'servants' et à 'slaves'. Quant au découpage français tel que l'interprête Hobbes, la seule chose certaine est qu'il ressemble au découpage latin par la distinction qu'il établit entre un terme générique et deux termes spécifiques; 'serviteur', en tout cas, semble bien être l'équivalent de 'servus'.

8 Grotius, *Le Droit de la guerre et de la paix*, II, ch. V, 27 (traduction Barbeyrac, Bâle, 1746).

9 *Ibid.*, II, ch. V, 30. Alors que la servitude parfaite est perpétuelle et limitée seulement par la loi naturelle (si l'on y entre à la suite d'un pacte celui-ci n'impose aucune restriction au pouvoir du maître), la servitude imparfaite est celle qui n'est que 'pour un temps, ou sous certaines conditions, ou pour certaines choses' (*Ibid.*); mais, à l'intérieur de ces limites, c'est tout de même une servitude, car elle implique bien l'obligation d'obéir sans discussion à tous les ordres que pourra donner ultérieurement le maître. L'esclavage en général a une extension plus grande que la servitude parfaite (cf. les esclaves hébreux), mais moindre que la servitude imparfaite; il caractérise ceux qui, en échange de leur travail, ne reçoivent rien d'autre que 'la nourriture et les autres choses nécessaires à la vie' (II, ch. V, 27): ni terre, contrairement aux serfs et aux mainmortables, ni argent, contrairement aux 'mercenaires'. Mais cette différence dans le mode de rémunération est secondaire: ce n'est pas sur elle que Grotius fonde sa classification. Quant à la condition des 'gens de journée', Grotius ne précise pas si elle se rattache ou non à la servitude imparfaite: les journaliers sont bien, semble-t-il, des 'mercenaires', liés par un contrat de 'louage de peine' (cf. II, ch. XII, 18–19); mais peut-être s'en distinguent-ils par le fait qu'ils sont engagés pour un travail si limité, non seulement dans le temps, mais même dans son contenu, que leur contrat ne laisse place à aucune indétermination susceptible de donner lieu à des ordres ultérieurs; dans ce cas, effectivement, ils n'obéiraient pas plus à leurs employeurs qu'un débiteur n'obéit à son créancier en s'acquittant. Mais la transition est vraiment floue.

10 *Ibid.*, II, ch. V, p. 30, note de Grotius.

11 Locke, *Second Treatise of Civil Government*, IV, 24.

12 Sans doute est-ce cela qui avait permis à Charron, par exemple, d'écrire d'abord que l'esclavage, presque entièrement éliminé de nos pays vers l'an 1200, y réapparaissait aujourd'hui massivement dans la mesure où un nombre sans cesse croissant de mendiants et de vagabonds étaient obligés de se vendre pour survivre (*De la Sagesse*, I, ch. XLIII, 6–8: édition de 1601), puis d'affirmer plus loin que 'les serviteurs' étaient 'principalement de trois sortes': les esclaves, dont il nous apprenait alors qu'ils n'existaient pratiquement plus aujourd'hui dans nos pays, les 'valets et serviteurs' (*sic*), et enfin les 'mercenaires' (*ibid.*, III, ch. XV)! . . . D'un chapitre à l'autre, on le voit, le terme générique et le terme spécifique permutaient: et, dans chacun de ces deux chapitres, le terme générique gardait en même temps son sens spécifique.

13 *Le Traité politique*, VI, 11.

14 *Ibid.*, VIII, 14.

15 Cf. les deux notes précédentes.

16 'Verum, modo id nullo expresso jure obtineant, nec reliqui (qui scilicet in imperio nati sunt, et patrio sermone utuntur, nec uxorem peregrinam habent, nec infames sunt, nec serviunt, nec denique servili aliquo officio vitam sustentant, inter quos etiam Oenopolae et Cerevisarii numerandi sunt) excludantur, retinebitur nihilominus imperii forma . . .' (*Le Traité politique*, VIII, 14). Le 'quos' de 'inter quos', étant au masculin pluriel, ne peut avoir d'autre antécédent que 'reliqui'; ou, si l'on préfère, que l'expression 'qui scilicet . . . vitam

sustentant', qui en est l'explication. La traduction habituelle, qui est en réalité une rectification de la lettre du texte au nom de ce que l'on *suppose* en être le sens véritable (Spinoza se serait alors mal exprimé), revient au contraire à donner pour antécédent à ce 'quos' le neutre singulier 'servili aliquo officio'.

17 *Le Traité politique*, VI, 10.

18 *Ibid.*, VI, 31.

19 *Ibid.*, VI, 12.

20 *Ibid.*, VIII, 10.

21 Cf. note 9.

22 On retrouverait ainsi la distinction que faisait Charron entre 'valets et serviteurs' et 'mercenaires' (cf. note 12).

23 Cf. note 9.

24 'The term servant in seventeenth-century England meant anyone who worked for an employer for wages, whether the wages were by piece-rates or time-rates, and whether hired by the day or week or by the year.' (C. B. Macpherson, *The Political Theory of Possessive Individualism: Hobbes to Locke*, Oxford University Press, 1962, Appendix, p. 282.)

25 *Le Traité politique*, XI, 3.

26 *Ibid.*, XI, 4, 2ᵉ phrase.

27 *Ibid.*, II, 9.

28 *Ibid.*, II, 10.

29 *Ibid.*, II, 4, 5, 8. Ce point est précisément rappelé en XI, 4.

30 *Ibid.*, II, 15.

31 Sur cette 'cybernétique' politique de Spinoza, cf. A. Matheron, *Individu et communauté chez Spinoza* (Paris, Editions de Minuit, 1969), 3ᵉ partie.

32 *Le Traité politique*, I, 6; V, 2; VI, 3, etc.

33 *Ibid.*, VII, 4.

34 *Ibid.*

35 *Ibid.*, VIII, 6. En Démocratie, les deux méthodes coïncideraient par définition.

36 *Ibid.*, III, 9; IV, 4.

37 *Ibid.*, VIII, 12. Et, bien entendu, cela recommencera avec le nouveau pouvoir, quelle qu'en soit la forme: une monarchie dite 'absolue' n'est jamais qu'une oligarchie déguisée (*Ibid.*, VI, 5).

38 'Inutile, inefficace, nuisible': c'est ainsi que Spinoza caractérise souvent les mesures dont il préconise le rejet (cf. *Tractatus theologico-politicus*, tout le chapitre XX; *Le Traité politique*, X, 5).

39 *Le Traité politique*, VI, 15.

40 *Ibid.*, VII, 13.

41 *Ibid.*, VIII, 2.

42 *Ibid.*

43 Cf. *ibid.*, VIII, 4, 'in fine'; XI, 2, 'in fine'.

44 Cf. *ibid.*, VIII, 12.

45 Cf. sur ce point C. B. Macpherson, *op. cit.*, III, pp. 107–59.

46 *Le Traité politique*, VIII, 19.

47 Comme en Théocratie (cf. *Tractatus theologico-politicus*, ch. XVII; éd. Gebhardt, III, p. 216).

48 Cf. note 19.

49 Ce qui exclut ces deux mesures pour l'Aristocratie, où la propriété du sol devant être à la fois privée et aliénable, le maintien de l'égalité n'est pas absolument garanti (cf. note 20).

50 Cf. *Le Traité politique*, VIII, 10.

51 Cf. *Ethique*, III, 12; III, 13, scolie.

52 Cf. *Tractatus theologico-politicus*, ch. V (éd. Gebhardt, III, p. 73).

53 *Le Traité politique*, I, 1.

54 *Ibid.*, VII, 8.

55 *Ethique*, III, 31, avec coroll. et scolie.

56 *Le Traité politique*, XI, 4, les 2 premières phrases.

57 Grotius, *op. cit.*, II, ch. V, 1 et 8.

58 *Leviathan*, ch. 20. Spinoza, rappelons-le, pouvait lire cet ouvrage dans son édition latine de 1668 ou dans celle de 1670, ainsi que dans sa traduction néerlandaise de 1667.

59 *Le Traité politique*, XI, 4.

60 *Ibid.*

61 *Ibid.* Hobbes avait dit que les Amazones abandonnaient par contrat leurs enfants mâles aux peuples voisins (*op. cit.*, ch. 20). Spinoza 'rectifie' au passage!

62 *Le Traité politique*, XI, 4.

63 Cf. *De Intellectus Emendatione* éd. Gebhardt, II, p. 10.

64 *Le Traité politique*, XI, 4.

65 *Ibid.*

66 *Ibid.*

67 *Ethique*, III, 59, scolie.

68 '. . . lacrimis muliebribus' (*Tracticus theologico-politicus*, Préface; éd. Gebhardt, III, p. 5). Il est précisé que ces larmes viennent de la crainte.

69 '. . . muliebri misericordia' (*Ethique*, IV, 37, scolie 1). Si cette 'pitié de femme', comme le dit ici Spinoza, empêche de tuer les animaux, elle doit empêcher bien davantage encore de tuer les hommes. Et c'est un handicap dans la lutte!

70 Cf. *De Intellectus Emendatione*, éd. Gebhardt, II, p. 10, note *f*.

71 'Ergo datur aliquid' (*ibid.*).

72 *Ethique*, III, 31 avec coroll. et scolie.

73 Cf. note 59.

74 *Ethique*, III, 26 et scolie.

75 *Le Traité politique*, XI, 4. cf. *Ethique*, IV, Appendice, 19.

76 Cf. *Ethique* III, 11 scolie (sur la 'titillatio').

77 *Ibid.*, I, Appendice (éd. Gebhardt, II, p. 82).

78 *Le Traité politique*, XI, 4. On peut évidemment sourire de l' importance politique qu'attribue Spinoza à ce fait; mais sans doute généralisait-il ce qu'il avait entendu dire du rôle des femmes dans les intrigues de cour.

79 *Ibid.*, cf. note précédent.

80 *Ethique*, III, 33–5.

81 *Ibid.*, 35 scolie.

82 *Ibid.*

83 *Ibid.*

84 *Ibid.*, 32.

85 Sur cette contradiction interne de l'ambition passionnelle, sous sa forme la plus générale, cf. *Ibid.*, III, 31, coroll. (citation d'Ovide); *Ibid.*, IV, 37, scolie 8 (2ᵉ phrase).

86 Cf. *Ibid.*, IV, Préface (éd. Gebhardt, II, p. 208).

87 *Ibid.*, IV, 18 scolie.

88 Cf. note 52.

89 Cf. *Ethique*, V, 4 scolie (De l'*Ambitio* à la *Pietas*).

90 Lettre 44 (éd. Gebhardt, IV, p. 228).

91 *Ethique* IV, Appendice, 20.

92 Cf. A. Matheron, *op. cit.*, ch. XI, pp. 505–14.

93 Sur le rôle 'hors système' de cet espoir chez Spinoza, cf. A. Matheron, *Le Christ et le salut des ignorants chez Spinoza* (Paris, Aubier, 1971), ch. V; ch. VII, p. 276.

ENGLISH SUMMARY: WOMEN AND SERVANTS IN
SPINOZISTIC DEMOCRACY

The only thing we know about Spinozistic Democracy is that it excludes women and 'servos' from citizenship. Several considerations seem to make clear that 'servos', here, does not mean 'slaves' in particular, but, as in Hobbes's terminology, 'servants' in the most general meaning of the word: people working for an employer, all kinds of wage-earners included. This exclusion of women and servants, far from being grounded on a mere 'prejudice', is a logical consequence of Spinoza's own 'democratism'. For if democratism, according to Spinoza, is the only possible way (in Monarchy and Aristocracy as well as in Democracy) to achieve a perfectly self-regulated political system, it is never (not even in Democracy) an end in itself: beyond the limits of this function, it becomes, not only useless, but even harmful. In order to fix these limits, one has to consider nothing more than real power relations. Servants, then, ought to be excluded because, even if legally 'free', they are actually dependent: if they were citizens, their objective situation would oblige them to vote according to their masters' will; which would involve inequality amongst the employers themselves and, sooner or later, change Democracy into Aristocracy, Aristocracy into a narrow oligarchy leading to Monarchy, Monarchy into despotism. Women, in the same way, ought to be excluded because, as far as we may conclude from effect to cause, there must be 'something' in their nature (Spinoza does not really assert that he knows what, and his statement is not particularly depreciative) that makes them unable to overcome men in competition for power: if they were citizens, the only part they could play in political assemblies would be that of recruiting supporters for their ambitious husbands, with an efficiency proportional to their attractiveness; which would lead both to inequality and to additional conflicts between men, with the same final result again. Democracy, though the most perfect state, is but a state, the function of which is still to regulate power relations between ignorant people; and ignorant people, even in the best case, will remain 'bourgeois' and 'phallocrates': political science has to take this inescapable datum into account. It is only in a Spinozistic community of 'free men' (and certainly women too) that, competition for domination and riches having ceased, there would be room for everybody.

22 Spinoza and Christian thought: a challenge

Robert Misrahi, Paris

INTRODUCTION

Now and again commentators venture Christian interpretations of Spinoza's thought with a view to 'recuperating' – as French terminology would put it – the atheist philosopher. Some emphasize his professed admiration for Christ, others rely for evidence on his excommunication from the synagogue, while the part played by charity and love in his doctrine of true piety is vindicated by quite a few. But all feel entitled to see in Spinoza's philosophy a twofold intimation: it is considered as betraying sympathy for the Christian doctrine and at the same time acknowledging its debt to Christian thought for what is best in its own spiritualist inspiration.

This clearly appears to us as a vain attempt to distort the meaning of Spinoza's philosophy and – once its explosive power is thus muffled – to make it instrumental to Christian spiritualist idealism, that is to a doctrine which, in the seventeenth century, was both the dominant doctrine and the doctrine 'establishing' moral order in the Ancien Régime monarchic society. Yet in this use of Spinoza's philosophy to meet the needs of Christian apologists are accumulated errors which, in the eyes of the contemporary philosopher, are much more detrimental in so far as they jeopardize the very truth of a doctrine and falsify it, than in what they betray of a moral practice as widespread as it is disreputable.

Our present study aims to unmask such Christian interpretations of Spinoza's philosophy, our purpose being to restore, in the face of such distortions, the genuine features of Spinozism – that is indeed of a practical atheism and of an ethical and political doctrine which was at that time subversive.

I SPINOZA'S PHILOSOPHY: A NON-CHRISTIAN DOCTRINE (NEITHER CATHOLIC NOR PROTESTANT)

A *Against the 'divinity' of Christ*

Obviously the first question to examine is that of Christ's ontological status. But unlike the commentators whose approach as a rule is naïve, we mean to be critical in our reading of Spinoza's writings (whether from the *TTP* or from the *Ethics*). This inevitably entails bearing in mind the radical criticism of language that Spinoza himself evolved throughout his writings as well as the necessarily two-tiered reading of the *Ethics*, since Spinoza, both as a Marrano and as a critic of language, was in fact led to resort to a twofold use of language, or, to put it more accurately, to give apparently identical phrasing different meanings. This use of language is not unprincipled but original; besides, it contains the key to its own meaning: it consists in using familiar words but with a new imputation, itself made clear by Spinoza's own definitions (see *Ethics*, III, gen. def. of the emotions, XX, Expl.).[1]

From this standpoint, our reading of Spinoza's writings will unequivocally rely on internal evidence, as Spinoza himself bids us read the Scriptures: elucidation must come from the Scriptures themselves, not from super-imposed external interpretation. In the same line, we shall only interpret Spinoza's statements on Christ by putting them into context (that is the *TTP*) and by linking them to *Spinoza's* purpose (and not the commentator's) which is to *interpret* the very letter of the Scriptures.

As regards Christ, two points will be examined: first, the 'revelation' through Christ, and subsequently of Christ. Each of these points will provide an opportunity to point out that Spinoza's conception of Christ was un-equivocally heretical and humanist, and that the high moral regard and intellectual respect he had for his person in no sense betrayed a Christian attitude, but merely elicited an attempt at comprehension by a philosopher living in a Christian environment and striving to elucidate the dominant faith of his contemporaries.

(i) Against divine 'revelation' through Christ and Christ alone

Spinoza deals with the question of revelation through Christ in chap. IV of the *TTP*. It is significant that this chapter is the most frequently quoted in support of the theory of a pseudo-Christian inspiration in Spinoza.

But in this case, the test is plainly misinterpreted if not falsified, since the very title of the chapter remains unquoted as well as the main aim and conclusions being neglected. This chapter is in fact entitled 'Of the Divine Law' and it aims to determine the relation between scripture and the concept of Divine Law, that is, in this instance, of authoritative legislation.

This leads to an obvious conclusion: in itself, a divine law is a divine decree, which means an everlasting law of nature bearing evidence to the identity, in God, of 'Understanding' and 'Will'. In the opening pages of this fourth chapter, Spinoza reminds us of his doctrine which is, indeed, the one he developed in the *Ethics*. 'Divine Law' is only a convenient expression; in fact it intimates the necessary and universal order of Nature.

But if this is obvious *to us* (Spinoza and his reader) it is not so *in the Scriptures*. There we are compelled to make an indirect interpretation which is what Spinoza does. He points out that for the *Hebrews* (quoting the text will be sufficient) God's 'revelations' are viewed as 'laws': '[Moses] thus conceived all his discoveries, not as eternal truths, but as precepts and ordinances, and commanded them as God's laws' (Wernham, p. 79).[2] Spinoza can hardly be expected to accept this interpretation which is prompted by obedience; and indeed, two pages later he writes: 'I conclude then that the stupidity of the masses and their failure to think is the only reason why God is described as a legislator or King, and called just, merciful, and so on. . . .' (*ibid.*, p. 83).

Christ on the contrary 'perceived things truly and adequately' (*ibid.*, p. 79) to quote Spinoza, who only devotes two of the fourteen pages of this chapter to Christ. Spinoza then goes on with a description which, being faithful to the word of the Scriptures, is self-evident: 'in saying that God revealed himself to Christ or to Christ's mind directly and not through words and images' (*ibid.*, p. 81). Then he proceeds to an interpretation of the texts and concludes: 'We can only mean that Christ truly perceived, that is intellectually understood, what was revealed to him.'

Accordingly the conclusion, in our eyes, is clear: the purpose of chapter IV is in no sense to establish whether Christ was or was not divine. It is to oppose the two possible ways (in the Scriptures) of receiving God's 'decrees': either as 'laws', that is compulsory legislation (which is the way the Hebrews received them, especially the prophets who had 'visions' and delivered edicts), or as 'eternal truths' (which is the case for Christ and the Apostles who are more like 'doctors', who know and teach, than 'prophets' who see and prescribe).

Indeed Spinoza favours comprehension rather than obedience; hence his regard for Christ. But would having respect and admiration for Buddha, in Buddhist countries, necessarily entail being a worshipper of Buddha, especially if this traditional meaning was given new implications?

What Spinoza does is to replace the word Christ by the phrase 'Christ's mind' which is as good as a definition; let us consider the meaning of this phrase, that is the ontological status of Christ. To construe the sense of this status, we need to refer to the concept of 'eternal Truth' that is essential to what was 'revealed' to Christ, in fact 'understood' by Christ. What Spinoza calls 'eternal truths' is in fact what reason apprehends of the data of nature. For this reason, '[The] essence [of the Apostles' religion] which is chiefly moral, like the whole of Christ's doctrine, can readily be apprehended by the natural faculties of all' (Elwes, *TTP*, ch. XI). Therefore, that Christ should apprehend eternal truth instead of civil legislation (like Moses) means that Christ's *mind* understands by means of natural light the Truth of a natural or moral kind: when Spinoza writes the phrase 'Christ's mind' he merely implies the ability to understand which is inherent in each man (the third kind of knowledge) and not the actual divinity of an individual being.

We shall leave it to Spinoza to conclude: after speaking of Christ, i.e. at the close of § 5 of this same chapter IV (*TTP*), he writes:

> that in fact God acts and directs everything by the necessity of his own nature and perfection alone; and finally, that his decrees and volitions are eternal truths, and always involve necessity. This was the first point which I proposed to explain and prove (Wernham, p. 83).

Now the question is quite clear: Spinoza has merely intended to criticise and counteract a relation to God the foundation of which had been prescription and obedience, and instead advocate a relation to God the foundation of which would be knowledge and understanding. Of this relation to God (that is, we must not overlook it, to nature) through intellectual understanding, Christ often (but not always, as we have seen) provides a good example. But it is an illustration only, a sort of didactic model; Christ is a 'doctor' (why not a Rabbi?) and teaches as such. But his teaching is mostly conveyed by his exemplary life. This made clear, which incidentally implies a radical departure from Christianity and its mysteries, Spinoza *in this same chapter IV*, recapitulates the basic points of his doctrine: God and Nature are identical since

> [if] nothing can either be or be conceived without God, it necessarily follows that everything in nature involves and expresses the concept of God in proportion to its essence and perfection; so that the more we learn of things in nature, the greater and more perfect is the knowledge of God we acquire (ibid., p. 71).

Clearly it is the very doctrine of the *Ethics*: let us keep in mind that for Spinoza, God being the substance, that is nature, or again an infinite number of infinite attributes which find expression in each singular aspect, it is impossible (not to say absurd) to restrict God to being merely one of these singular aspects which constitute nature. This is precisely the reason why Spinoza speaks of Christ's mind and not of Christ. Addressing Christian readers, he refers to the ethical model which is theirs, but without ever making his their doctrine of the divine essence of Christ.

For that reason, Spinoza carefully makes it clear again, in the following chapter, that *Christ in no way invalidates Judaism*:

> From this it is easily seen that Christ in no way abolished the law of Moses, for Christ has no wish to introduce any new laws into the state, his main object being to teach moral precepts and to distinguish them from civil law (ibid., p. 91).

Moses is a civil lawgiver, whereas Christ restricts his teaching to what can be founded on universal law, not on ceremonies (*TTP*, chap. V). Therefore Christ is merely a righteous man, no God incarnate or a new legislator.

There is no trace of mystery or mystical inclination in all this, least of all of any Christian trend of thought. The closing lines of *TTP*, chap. V, speak for themselves:

> and if they [those who invalidate natural light] boast of having some supra-rational faculty, it is a mere figment, and far inferior to reason. . . . I shall merely add that we can know men only from their works; so that if a man is rich in such fruits of the spirit as love, joy, peace, long-suffering, kindness, goodness, faithfulness, meekness and temperance against which there is no law (as Paul says in the Epistle to the Galatians, chapter 5, verse 23), then whether he has been taught solely by reason or solely by scripture, he has in truth been taught by God, and is wholly blessed. I have now dealt with all the questions I proposed to discuss in connection with the divine law (ibid., p. 107).

Thus for Spinoza 'divineness' lies in the knowledge of nature and commendable moral conduct, and not at all in worship or in imitation of Christ, least of all in his being made divine. Christian 'revelation' is no more than natural light, or rational understanding in that it is the very source of moral sense. *In fact*, Christ falls under the common law. It may sound provocative; but Spinoza arouses indignation. What he achieves, *by using familiar words but put to own use*, is adequation to his contemporaries, speaking to them in their own language: but only to bring them round gently to read *his own ideas*.

A passage from the *Ethics* will corroborate this point – the scholium to prop. 68, part IV (we shall deal with it more extensively later on). In this scholium, Spinoza poses the identity of the mind of Christ with the idea of God. To begin with the God mentioned, needless to say, is the God of the *Ethics* as we have already pointed out, that is to say the substance, undetermined and impersonal. As for the 'idea of God', it can only be what we apprehend of God through what is made explicit of him in the attribute of thought; but the inevitable consequence is that this idea of God must be necessary and eternal like the attribute of thought itself (*Ethics*, I, 21), and as such is stamped in *every human mind* in as much as the human mind constitutes a part of thought.

Consequently the mind of Christ is nothing other than the idea of God (*Ethics*, IV, 68, sch.) namely the idea of God partaking of thought (*Ethics*, I, 21, proof), that is to say a universal consequence to the attribute thought itself (*ibid*). So that the phrase 'the mind of Christ' illustrates an intellectual truth of universal application without ever having either to contradict Judaic law or to refer to an individual soul in Christ. Spinoza's doctrinal position is unambiguous and all the more provocative in its lack of ambiguity as it does not preclude but on the contrary asserts a genuine sense of fellowship with the true Christian, that is the man of virtue: the mind of Christ is the idea of God, *that is to say the knowledge* that each being may acquire through the second and third kinds of knowledge. From a dogmatic and doctrinal standpoint (or even an ecclesiastical and pastoral one) no strictly Christian element can be traced.

Moreover, this doctrine in no way contradicts Judaic law. Curiously enough, and this point has been totally overlooked by all the commentators, Spinoza almost always quotes from Hebrew writings whenever he quotes from Christ or the Apostles. In *Ethics*, IV, 68, he quotes Moses, then the Patriarchs and Christ; in *TTP*, IV, Moses and Christ; Solomon and Paul (end of chapter IV); again Christ and Moses (chapter V); and Jeremiah and Christ (chapter VII) 'the very doctrine inculcated here by Christ just before the destruction of the city was also taught by Jeremiah before the first destruction of Jerusalem, that is, in similar circumstances'. Through pairing these authors, Spinoza makes it clear that for him Christ and Hebrew writers have identical status; the difference between the Torah and the Gospel lies in the functional specificities of each of these *foundational texts* and not in the divine essence of a Messiah whose coming is prophesied in one text and recorded in the other. *The Old Testament is political, the New Testament is ethical* there is nothing more to it.

In addition, Spinoza makes it plain that *he does not understand* the assertions of the Church concerning the divine essence of Christ – a polite way of suggesting that they are absurd. He writes in Chapter I of the *TTP*:

> the voice of Christ, like the voice which Moses heard, may be called the voice of God. I must at this juncture declare that those doctrines which certain churches put forward concerning Christ, I neither affirm nor deny, for I freely confess that I do not understand them (Elwes, p. 19, *TTP*, I).

In the light of these qualifications expressly made by Spinoza; it is easier to assess the tremendous bearing of this other statement: 'Christ in no way abolished the law of Moses, for Christ had no wish to introduce any new laws into the State, his main object being to teach moral precepts and to distinguish them from the Civil law' (Wernham, p. 91)

Revelation through Christ, is not a new law; it is not of a supernatural order; and Spinoza 'does not understand' its meaning in the same way as the Church: the path is clear now for further discussion of the dogmas of incarnation and resurrection.

(ii) Against the incarnation and the resurrection of Christ

In this respect, Letter LXXII to Oldenburg is particularly illuminating and leaves no room for doubt. Spinoza reminds his correspondent that 'knowledge of Christ in the flesh is in no way necessary for the attainment of salvation'. Since Spinoza can hardly be expected to think of reaching salvation outside the knowledge of God, the above statement necessarily entails negation of a divine essence in Christ's material being, i.e. of an incarnation of God in the body of Christ. The rest of the letter confirms this interpretation; in the indirect and coded style so typical of this philosopher, out of friendship for his correspondent, Spinoza grants him that to Christ in the flesh may be opposed what is commonly referred to as 'God's eternal son', a phrase which will be received as 'Christ in the spirit' by this same correspondent. This ambiguity of language is in no way intentionally misleading (Spinoza always gives the key to his code) but is due to sheer benevolence. Christian commentators, however, most often leave out full quotation or interpretation of the paragraphs dealing with Christ. As regards our purpose, which we intend to be both more painstaking and more honest, we shall read Spinoza's writings in an exhaustive and objective manner without ever censuring passages inconsistent with our demonstration. Here is what Spinoza writes to Oldenburg, following his polite denial of Christ in the flesh (Letter LXXIII):

> but it goes differently with God's Eternal Son who appears in *everything*, *especially in the human mind*, and more specifically in Jesus-Christ. No one indeed is able to reach blessedness unless he possesses this wisdom, since this wisdom only enables to tell truth from error, good from evil. And because this wisdom, as I already said, finds its *best* expression in Christ, his disciples taught it as if it had been revealed by God, and they derived from Christ's mind a greater glory than the others. When some Churches add that God had taken a human shape, I have expressly warned that *I did not understand what they mean*: indeed, to tell the truth, to assert this is no less absurd than to suggest that a circle has taken the shape of a square . . . you will know better than I which of these interpretations are suitable for those Christians you know.

The length of the quotation is justified since it contains the references most often supplied by the Christian commentators, though, it must be said, in curtailed form. Spinoza's doctrine appears in full light: there is no need to believe in Christ in the flesh, for the metamorphosis of God into man (the incarnation of God in Christ), if carefully scrutinized, is sheer absurdity, and incoherent irrelevance, not to say an unintelligible assertion. ('I do not understand what they mean.')

That this doctrine should echo some of the polemics which were rife among the Christian sects of Holland (Collegiantes v. Calvinists, Socinians v. Orthodox) is to be expected, and historical criticism daily finds new proofs of Spinoza's connections with Christian heretics whether oppositional or liberal. But systematic and unbiased criticism also reveals Spinoza's connections with oppositional Judaism (e.g. Daniel de Prado) or Spinoza's cultural debt to the Chief Rabbi Manasseh ben Israel or to the progressive humanist Van den Enden.

The fact is that, even once *all* critical sources have been scanned, the basic problem resides not in which cultural elements Spinoza was steeped in but in the exact scope of the original doctrine which he derived from these elements at the same time as he went far beyond them.

For all these reasons, the rejection of incarnation must be placed within the context of Spinoza's system taken as a whole. Now, Spinoza himself recentres on the system thanks to the expression 'God's eternal Son' since he defines it as 'God's eternal wisdom', a wisdom which 'revealed itself in everything'. Now, this wisdom of God, in the Spinozist context, is none other than the rational power in every being, i.e. of Nature as a whole. Besides, the notion of expression is central here: the world expresses God since, viewed under the aspect of his essential permanence, God is the world itself.

More specifically, 'God's wisdom', besides being eventually the rational power of nature, also refers to the *idea* of God and the *understanding* of God which are infinite activities of the thinking power, and activities which gather existence and scope *in and through the human mind itself*, however paradoxical this may sound to a reader superficially skimming through Spinoza. Here is what Spinoza writes:

> From this and from prop. 21, part I, and other propositions, it is
> apparent that our mind, in so far as it understands, is an eternal mode of
> thinking, which is determined by another eternal mode of thinking, and
> this one again by another, and so on to infinity: so that they all
> constitute at the same time the eternal and infinite intellect of God
> (*Ethics*, V, 40, sch., tr. A. Boyle).

Thus Christ, even though in the spirit, cannot be God alone for Spinoza since this man (Christ) only expresses what is given to every human mind to express as part of the attribute thought; the man Christ, by means of the example of his virtue and his living moral teaching, only expresses with full force this universal truth which tells that blessedness will be reached thanks to the knowledge which leads to joy, charity and justice.

If the reader (in this instance Oldenburg) thinks that any adherence to traditional Christian dogma may be traced in all this, he alone bears the responsibility of this misunderstanding and debars himself from progress on the way to real freedom. To Oldenburg, the faithful friend on whom he refuses to impose his own ideas, Spinoza only proposes a means of freeing himself and his Christian friends (by meditating on his definitions). But when addressing young Albert Burgh, a former Protestant recently turned Catholic, Spinoza is far more brutal and straightforward. In his Letter LXXVI, the philosopher writes:

> all that is used to distinguish the Roman Catholic Church from the
> other Churches is utterly superfluous and founded on superstition only.
> [And further on] young fool, who practised upon you that you were led

into the belief that you have indeed swallowed the Eternal and Supreme Being and sheltered him in your entrails?

Spinoza, who again in this letter alludes to the Spirit of Christ (no more than a spirit of equity and justice), thus resolutely challenges this privilege of Roman Catholicism which Albert Burgh would like to see as the only Church on account of the greater number of its followers; firmly opposing the primacy of Catholicism, Spinoza does not recoil from more outspoken criticism: he blames the Church for its 'superstition', its tendency towards idolatry and even its political intolerance (Letter LXXVI). In the same letter, he writes:

I do assess at its full value the advantage of the political order set up by this Roman Church which you praise so high; I would grant you that no other church is more cunning in outwitting the people or ruling the souls, were it not for the Moslem Church which, under this respect, far supersedes all the others; ever since its origin, no schism so far has even split this church.

This criticism of the Roman Catholic Church's authoritarian attitude in political matters may also, indirectly, be aimed at the theocratic authoritarian attitude of the Calvinists and Ancient Hebrews; and it is precisely because this criticism is for him of such momentous importance (*Spinoza is the founder of democratic thought in Europe*) that Spinoza merely assigns the Christian religion a moral function without ever linking it to any political or social system of legislation. The Roman Catholicism which is concerned here stands worlds apart from the true religion, which cannot, in Spinoza's eyes, be anything other than the full recognition of the rights of reason. He says so explicitly in his letter to A. Burgh:

Shall I be taxed of arrogance and pride only because I resort to reason and rely on the Word of God only which is in the mind and can never be either misshaped or corrupted? ... Leave aside this evil superstition, acknowledge the reason that God granted you and cultivate it if you do not want to reckon yourself among beasts (Letter LXXVI).

If Christ is in no shape whatsoever the incarnation of God, and if, leaving aside the Roman Catholic superstitions, Spinoza thinks fit to define Christian doctrine by the mind of Christ, that is the cosmic wisdom present in every human mind in the shape of reason, the necessary conclusion must be as follows: for Spinoza, 'Christian doctrine' serves only as a referential sign to connote, so to speak in coded form, what stands, in his eyes, as best in the ethical foundations of Protestant society. Even so, there must be no equivocation on the meaning of this permanent praise which exclusively concerns Christian doctrine in so far as it represents the ethics of charity and justice:

Oss

Spinoza praises not a man-God but a mind, i.e. a universal thinking power and a very rarefied cultural stand. Ultimately for Spinoza the mind of Christ is in fact none other than the spirit of Christianity at its best, that is Christianity understood as an ethical culture without either boundaries or legislation.

As to Christ's *resurrection*, it cannot be expected any more than Christ's incarnation to be accepted at face value, or even to be actually integrated into Spinoza's system. Spinoza himself leaves no room for any such literal interpretation when, in Letter LXXV to Oldenburg, he plainly states:

> my conclusion is that Christ's resurrection was indeed of entirely
> spiritual nature and revealed exclusively to the faithful in the shape best
> befitting them: Christ was given eternity and rose from the Dead in that
> his exceptionally saintly behaviour taught the example of his life and
> death; and he raises his disciples from the dead in that they follow his
> example.

Thus in the same way as Christ should not be said to be the material incarnation of God, he should not be said to have resuscitated either.

Thus Spinoza rejects all the dogmas which, as no one will deny, are the very foundations of the Christian doctrine; since, besides incarnation and resurrection, he also discards the ritual of communion and the dogma of transubstantiation, only retaining for his definition of Christian doctrine the spirit of justice and of charity.

Such conclusions should satisfy a reader inclined to sympathize with Christian doctrine: it would then be possible to reconcile Spinoza's doctrine with the doctrine of Christianity in its authentic, purely spiritual form, freed from all rites and superstitions; such a form of the Christian doctrine might even gather strength from Spinoza's authority at the same time as Spinoza's system might gather strength from this same Christian doctrine from which he supposedly derived the best of his inspiration.

With such an approach, endeavouring to shed light on Spinoza's system by means of Christian doctrine, however elevated his reflexion and his dignity, such a reader would be committing not merely a fault, but a grave intellectual error. He would be leaving aside what doctrinal exactitude requires: that the dogmas which define Christian doctrine be taken literally, and that, besides, this same Christian doctrine should stand for no more than a simple moral claim for virtue instead of a rich and highly complex *Weltanschauung*.

Now, Spinoza appears most reserved when confronted with Christian doctrine as a global entity, even though he deals with this question in a highly discreet and respectful way. In Letter LXXV to Oldenburg already quoted, Spinoza insists that 'the Christians understand at spiritual level what the Jews understand at material level'. What is involved here is the justification and interpretation of Spinoza's *own approach*: since the Christians (because they disown themselves as Jews) interpret at spiritual level what the Jews (because they own themselves as Jews) interpret at material level, Spinoza (who neither acknowledges nor owns himself as Christian) interprets at spiritual level what the Christians (because they own themselves as Christians) interpret at material level (incarnation, resurrection, transubstantiation).

Indeed, some will object that Spinoza does not wish to appear a Roman Catholic, but what about his being a liberal reformed Christian? The answer, unequivocally, is that it cannot be, precisely because of the texts already quoted and more particularly the last letter to Oldenburg. All the same, in letter LXXVI to Albert Burgh, Spinoza praises 'the perfectly pure among men who worship God by means of their justice and their charity: among them, Lutherans, Menonites, Enthusiasts. . . .' Here we are: Spinoza mentions the righteous men of the Protestant Church, but only after reminding us that such men are to be found in *all* churches, and by referring, to define such righteousness not to a well-knit doctrine, but to moral qualities which exist as well in the Levitians, as we shall prove later.

In all this, neither Christ nor Christian doctrine is ever gauged in relation to a totality of qualities, and yet this totality alone would allow their essence to be determined or Spinoza to be fully committed. Now, Spinoza is a philosopher, and to forget it in this context would be imprudent. Therefore, once fully acquainted with the moral tribute of sympathy and admiration paid by Spinoza to the spirit of Christianity, and if our purpose is truly to determine Spinoza's position in relation to Christian doctrine and the *complete meaning of this relation*, we must see it as our duty to sound *the very foundations* of Spinoza's doctrine regarding the basic concepts that go to make up the Christian doctrine *qua* doctrine and not only as an undefined body of purely moral precepts; in other words, Spinoza's doctrine and Christian doctrine will have to be compared and contrasted in regard to the basic aspects which give Christian thought the full organic structure of a doctrine. En route, we shall realize that in fact it is radical criticism which we are faced with: but this criticism is directed at philosophers who as such are likely to *decipher* a coded and unobtrusive way of saying things and who besides do not seek novelty for the sake of novelty or criticism for the sake of criticizing. In addition, Spinoza's critical approach remains indirect, being neither polemical nor aimed at individuals, and it can without inconsistency go along with an exaltation of Christ's high moral distinction.

Let us now consider in more detail this indirect but none the less relentless criticism of the doctrinal foundations of Christian thought.

B *Against Christian doctrine and against Calvinism*

(i) Against the beginning of the world and against creation

As far as ontology is concerned, Spinoza's system definitely stands in radical opposition to a duality of God and the world, and consequently to the idea of a world created by a transcendent being. Judaism indeed is as much affected by this refusal of creational dualism as Christian doctrine. The obvious conclusion in that case is that Spinoza's doctrine, adverse to both Judaic ontology and Christian ontology, can hardly be likened to the Christian conception of the world which we mean to examine here.

Among the commentators, it is true, one can trace endeavours to reintroduce duality at the very heart of Spinozist ontology; in their endeavours, the commentators rely on the notion of naturing nature, supposedly antagonistic with natured nature; or else they postulate an idea of infinite substance as contrasted with attributes or modes which are only infinite within their kind, or with singular modes which are always finite whichever way they are considered. These endeavours prove in fact unjust towards Spinoza and his original conception of the world, unitarian and eternitarian. From the *Short Treatise* down to the *TTP*, the *Correspondence* and the *Ethics*, Spinoza continually insists on the unity of the being: the attributes are not distinct and separate beings, the substance is present in each attribute but also in each mode, and God, who is nature in its infinite totality, is no more than a permanent disposition in real and singular beings to unite.

Spinoza's doctrine of Man (anthropology) best illustrates, explains, and supports this unitarian ontology. Man is one. Extension and thought, i.e. Body and Mind, are ways of naming a single reality. For this reason, neither body nor mind can influence each other: their existence is simultaneous and their action elicits but one single event. Moreover the mind being the idea of the body it can only be through better knowledge of the body that simultaneously, body and mind reach a higher level of perfection.

An examination of Spinoza's doctrine of desire would, in this respect, be illuminating, but this concept will have to be considered when we deal with the *Ethics*.

None the less we shall meet again on the ontological level the same oneness we found on the anthropological level: the attributes are the multiform and simultaneous aspects of the one substance, i.e. nature (extension, thinking power, etc.), i.e. the world itself (this very world as Hebrew terminology puts it: ha olam ha zé). The fact that we only know two of these attributes in no way means that the other attributes are actually transcendent: substance is *wholly* expressed in every attribute and therefore also in extension and thinking power. Monism and immanence cannot possibly be extenuated only because of the difference between the cognizable and the uncognizable (the other attributes).

Immanentist and monist, such is Spinoza's philosophy, but this in no way allows us to deem it materialistic and therefore to oppose it as such to Christian doctrine: in fact, Spinoza's system is *neither idealistic nor materialistic* since each attribute necessarily finds its meaning by reference to itself and to the whole and not by reference to one selectively isolated attribute which might be either extension or thought. What matters here is not the labels we attach to different concepts, but the consequences, and the consequences only, of this strict monism and of the eternity of this world: in Spinoza's system there can be no creation of the world hence no divine creator of this world, God being none other than the world itself in its essence and its eternity.

References to all these problems will be found in the Appendix to the *Ethics*, Part I, in which Spinoza denounces the superstitions, frantic fantasies and anthropomorphic imagination of traditional religious ontologies, or in Letter XLIII to Jacob Osten in which Spinoza, against the accusations launched by Lambert of Velthuysen, denies his being an atheist but maintains all the same his doctrine of the oneness of the world and holds it impossible for God to be a legislator, a king, a judge, or a creator. Of course, Spinoza continues to use traditional words like morality, salvation, creation, but he endows them with a *totally different meaning*.

If 'God' indeed is neither a creator nor a judge, the moral consequences for men are far-reaching, and necessarily lead to the elaboration of a system which *unequivocally turns its back on Christianity*.

We shall assess these consequences in each of the following sections.

(ii) Against the immortality of the soul

As regards immortality more specifically, we need to be aware of the ambiguity of the terminology, so as not to credit Spinoza with a belief which is not his as might happen through gambling on the proximity and apparent likeness of such concepts as eternity and the immortality of the soul. Spinoza as is well known, heavily stresses this eternity which is ours (*Ethics* V, 23 and scholium). But at the same time (*Ethics*, V, 21) he carefully rejects any conception of an immortality related to the substance, a conception which would profess personal permanence for an individual endowed with self-recollection and imagination.

We must equally insist that Spinoza established (in Part II) that man is not a substance, and that the concept defining man inasmuch as he is not a body is not the concept of the soul (*anima*) but of the mind (*mens*).

Under these conditions, what Spinoza entirely dismisses is the ethical function that is assigned to the immortality of the soul by Christian doctrine; and he even discards it as purely imaginary and contingent on the knowledge of the first kind. Kant's philosophical system would provide an illuminating counter-example. At non-dogmatic level (that is posing an axiom and no longer a dogma) Kant, like Descartes before him, makes his the basic elements of the Christian doctrine on the immortality of the soul along with the 'ethical' function of this immortality: it allows for indefinitely possible moral improvement, leaving room for a potential synthesis between happiness and virtue; in a word, it makes punishments and rewards possible, i.e. post-mortem sanctions depending on the 'moral' or 'immoral' conduct during life. These sanctions of course surmise the extension in after-life of the permanences of an individual endowed with self-remembrance, all this being incompatible with Spinoza's conception of eternity. Since, for Spinoza, the 'human mind' (with its individual memory and individual characteristics) only *lasts* as long as the body (of which it is the idea) itself.

Witness Letter LXXV to Oldenburg: Spinoza here refers to Christ's death as real but to his resurrection as entirely 'spiritual'. The apostles 'rose from the Dead' only in so far as their lives were led on the model of Christ's life and 'Christ's death', being thus lifted, as Christ himself had been, to a higher degree of virtue.

This letter is instructive in several respects: if Christ himself never rose from the dead, no man ever will, except 'spiritually'; besides, this letter clearly shows that eternity stands for immortality; and this concept of eternity rises in full force. For Christ, for his disciples, but also for every human being, eternity is indeed real and not to be discarded, but at the same time it is no more than the spiritual and permanent enduring *in the mind of every living human being* of that memory and recollection of Christ, of his disciples, or indeed of any other man.

It then becomes easier to understand what the eternity of the *Ethics* V, 23, scholium, actually means: it has nothing to do with the immortality of the imagining power or of the substance, and it does not merely concern the recollection of one being by another; it also affects the very truth and validity of a being outside time, and independently from his individual ephemeral existence. Now, this validity stems from an extra-temporal and eternal truth but it also stems from an ethical system of values as is shown by Spinoza's interpretation of Christ's resurrection.

The closing paragraphs of the *Ethics* V, in fact, support this 'mental' interpretation of man's eternity. To be eternal consists in the way one is, the way one exists in relation to the true 'virtue', that is rational power and intellectual understanding. Here is what Spinoza writes in the *Ethics*, V, 38: 'the more the mind understands things by the second and third kinds of knowledge, the less it will be passive to emotions that are evil, and the less it will fear death' (Boyle). And the scholium insists that thanks to the third kind of knowledge 'it follows that the human mind may be of such a nature that that part of it which we showed to perish with the body may be of no moment to it in respect to what remains'.

When Spinoza states that 'we feel and experience our being eternal', he implies *only part* of the human mind, that part which is defined by reason and intellectual intuition, i.e. the understanding *activity*. This leaves no room for ambiguity; this eternal part of the human mind, although independent from duration, is none the less dependent upon our bodily existence and coeval with this existence. In the *Ethics*, V, 39, Spinoza writes 'he who has a body capable of many things has a mind of which the greater part is eternal' (*ibid.*) The scholium reminds us that such bodies are related to minds which know little fear of death and which are eternal for their main part. And Spinoza goes on:

> In this life then, we principally endeavour to change the body of an infant, in so far as its nature allows and is conducive there to so that it is capable of many things and so that it is referred to a mind which is most conscious of God, itself and other things: or so that all that which has reference to its memory or imagination should be scarcely of any moment, whatever with respect to its intellect as I said in the Note, prev. Prop. (*ibid*).

The *Ethics* therefore ends not on the immortality of the soul but on the authentic victory over the fear of death, and this victory leads to eternity. But eternity only affects one part of the mind namely understanding. Moreover this eternal understanding is linked to a body with manifold abilities; it will indeed survive this body but as an extra-temporal truth recorded *in fact* in the memory of other men or by *right* and potentially in a picture aiming at comprehending as much as it can of what has constituted and is combining to constitute 'the complete features of the universe'.

As a victory over the fear of death, an accession to what is best in man, Spinoza's eternity clearly gives itself as an ethical concept; but inserted within an ethical context which stands worlds apart from Christian ethics.

(iii) Against an ethical doctrine based on fear and punishment

If there is no after-life for man beyond death, it is for the reason that 'true philosophy' (Letter to A. Burgh) for Spinoza should never be grounded in fear or hope. Spinoza's 'virtue' must rest on a strictly self-sufficient principle of autonomy (which is, as we know, action adequate to its own essence and finding in itself, and itself only whenever possible its own justification). And therefore Spinoza's 'God' can in no sense be a legislator or a judge, no more than eternity can be an after-life in which would be granted rewards and punishments, or any kind of permanence of the individual.

In Spinoza's system, it is by proceeding *a contrario* that validation and direct foundation are secured: freed from divine transcendence and immortality for the individual, ethics can only rest on ethical grounds. It necessarily implies that, first and foremost, it must free itself from fear and the imaginary sanctions which occasion this fear.

Scholium to the *Ethics*, V, 41 is particularly illuminating on this question and the doctrine expressed there (all the more forceful as it is thus situated *at the close* of the *Ethics*, immediately following the last proposition (V, 42)) on blessedness which is not the reward of virtue, but virtue itself. In the *Ethics*, V, 41, scholium, Spinoza asserts the general notion of the vulgar seems to be quite the contrary. . . . They think that piety, religion and all things which have reference to fortitude of mind are burdens which after life they will lay aside, and hope to receive a reward for their servitude, that is their piety and religion. Not by this hope alone, but also, and principally, by the fear of suffering dreadful punishments after death, are they induced to live, as far as their feebleness and weak-mindedness allows them, according to the divine laws; and if this fear and hope were not in men, but on the other hand if they thought that their minds were buried with their bodies, and that there did not remain for the wretches worn out with the burden of piety the hope of longer life, they would return to life according to their own ideas, and would direct everything according to their lust, and obey fortune rather than themselves (*ibid.*).

This theory is fundamental to Spinoza's system and close to his heart since it is also to be found in the *Preface* to *TTP* (where he condemns fear as the source of all religious superstitions and political bondage) as well as in Letter LXIII to Jacob Osten where he answers the attacks launched by Lambert of Velthuysen:

In truth, I think I can see in what quicksands this man is foundering. . . . He fears punishment. . . . In return for his bondage, he expects God to honour him with rewards that are sweeter to him than the very love of God.

And Velthuysen might have had good reason to object that, in the seventeenth century, any ethical approaches based on nature as a monist whole and on an absence of sanctions after death, and entirely resting on the self-sufficiency of a free mind, were indeed atheist doctrines. That Spinoza should deny the accusation in no way modifies the issues; his doctrine is clearly a system doing away with a personal God, with the immortality of the soul, and with either reward or punishment ensuing righteous or criminal conduct.

In any case, none of these points can be deemed Christian. Moreover, none can be said to be either Protestant or reformed. For if Spinoza consistently keeps away from polemics against religion, the fact remains that this 'religion' of his is to a large degree original and extraordinary since it is neither Judaic (Spinoza refuses Mosaic law for Holland, it being only valid for a Hebrew State) nor Catholic (Spinoza rejects the superstitions and the authoritarian ways of Rome) nor Protestant either (Spinoza refuses the divinity and incarnation of God in Christ and Christ's genuine resurrection, but also predestination).

We feel entitled to go even further and say that the doctrine of Spinoza is perhaps best accounted for precisely when taken as a virulent and relentless challenge of Calvinism.

(iv) Against predestination and against the signs of election

It is indeed Calvinism (and not only orthodox Judaism) which is concerned by the repeated assaults of Spinoza on dogmatism and superstition. Having been formed before all other Protestant sects, Calvinism was in the Holland of the seventeenth century the dominant faith of the majority.

This aspect of Calvinism is most appropriately developed and compounded in the 'confession of Westminster'³ drawn up during the Synod of 1647 and with which Spinoza may well have been acquainted. This doctrine is equally presented in almost official form in Hoorbeek's book, *Theologica practica* (Utrecht, 1663), the organization of which is worth noting: immediately below the title to Book II, 'De Deo', follows the title of the first chapter: 'De predestinatione'. And indeed, what lies at the very heart of Calvinism is the doctrine of predestination, which is accurately described in chapter III of the *Confession of Westminster*, this chapter being entitled 'Of the eternal decrees of God' (not to mention Calvin's *Institutio Christianae Religionis*).

Spinoza uses the very same expression ('the decrees of God') in Part I of the *TTP*, and he refers to a 'decree of the mind' in Part II of the *Ethics* when he carries out the examination of free will. But it is clear that Spinoza uses the Calvinist word 'decree' in a sense altogether different from its use in Protestant tradition: in the *TTP*, the 'decrees of God' mean no more than 'the eternal laws of nature'. Which is hardly surprising since God does not act out of free choice (*Ethics*, II, 3, sch.) and since his power does not compare with the will of a King (*ibid.*). For 'things could not have been produced by God in any other manner or order than that in which they were produced' (*Ethics*, I, 33). Thus, when Spinoza deals with necessity in the world but also when he deals with the determination of human actions (e.g. *Ethics*, I, 28), he takes the opposite stand towards Calvinist doctrine which posits free will (utterly useless, as we shall see) in man, and almighty free will in God. The use of identical words (decree, free will) for antithetical notions places Spinozism within the cultural background of the period; but at the same time, each term used by Spinoza sounds antagonistic to this background through systematic subversion of the Calvinist senses of these terms.

If we take a closer look at the implications of predestination, this time not from an ontological standpoint but from an ethical one, we shall be better able to assess the determination of Spinoza as a systematic opponent to the doctrine.

The wording of the *Confession of Westminster* is as follows:

THE CONFESSION OF FAITH, AND THE LARGER AND SHORTER CATECHISM.

First agreed upon by the Assembly of Divines, at Westminster, 1647.

Chap. III. Of God's eternal decree.

Nº 3. By the decree of God for the manifestation of his glory, some men

and angels are predestinated unto everlasting life and others
fore-ordained to everlasting death.

Nº 5. Those of mankind that are predestinated unto life, God, before
the foundation of the world was said, according to his eternal and
immutable purpose, and the secret counsel and good pleasure of his will,
hath chosen in Christ unto everlasting glory, out of his mere free grace
and love, without any foresight of faith and good works, or perseverance
in either of them, or any other thing in the creature, as conditions or
causes moving him thereunto, and all to the praise of his glorious grace.

Chap. IX. Of free will.

Nº 3. Man by his fall into the state of sin hath wholly lost all ability of
will to any spiritual good accompanying salvation so as a natural man
being averse from that good, and death in sin, is not able by his own
strength to convert himself or to prepare himself thereunto.

If we carefully examine the basic concepts expressed in this text, then
Spinoza's writings appear as systematic refutation of these concepts. To
begin with, we must note that 'predestination' is for the Calvinist theologian
a divine 'decree', i.e. *an act* by which the created being is granted an inescapable future in after-life; and that this 'decree' comes from *deliberate* ('secret
counsel') and *discretionary* ('good pleasure of his will') as well as contingent
decision. Besides, this decree is never relevant to the creature ('without any
foresight of faith and good works') and yet, for the very reason that it is
election, it elicits the *love* of God for man and his *freedom* ('out of his mere
grace and free love').

It appears clearly that these descriptions which constitute the very essence
of predestination are precisely *the ones that Spinoza will explicitly contradict*
when he exposes how he conceives of God first, then of the relation of this
'God' to man, and lastly of the ethics of life and salvation. For the God, nature
is a total system of necessary determinations and not a power to act
deliberately. Nature eternal and not finite is to itself its own causation and the
unfolding of its own power. No deliberate or personal or transcendent action
whatsoever may exist in such a system of nature. And this is true not only of
the *Ethics* but also of the *TTP*: for, as Spinoza says in *TTP*, VI, § 5, one can
'show from scripture that the decrees and mandates of God, and consequently
his providence, are merely the order of Nature' (Elwes).

It would have been most unlikely indeed to come across anything more or
less akin to the doctrine of predestination in a philosophical system like
Spinoza's which challenges the notion of a transcendent being as well as the
possibility for the Cosmos to be contingent or for miracles or grace to take
place.

Spinoza's God, moreover, is explicitly defined as free from all emotions and
consequently of love towards men. 'God is free from passions, nor is he

affected by any emotion of pleasure or pain' (*Ethics*, V, 17). It comes to saying that 'God, to speak strictly, loves no one nor hates any one' (*ibid.*, cor.). He can hardly be expected in these conditions to predestinate and accordingly elect an individual as a proof of his love.

Even though predestination is everlasting and unchanging, it can in no way compare with the determinism of nature according to Spinoza, since this determinism cannot be the result of an isolated and transcendent act taking place outside the comprehensive whole of nature, nor can it be regarded as a free, that is contingent, action, or an action out of grace or love. It stands to reason, then, that the whole system of Spinoza's philosophy, denying the possibility of an act of predestination, inevitably also denies the very concept of election.

Neither individuals nor nations are liable to 'election' according to Spinoza who, thus, simultaneously discards the Hebrew doctrine of an elected people and the Calvinist doctrine of a possible election for the individual. As far as the Hebrews are concerned, 'their election and vocation consisted simply in the temporal prosperity and advantages of their state' (*TTP*, III, Wernham, p. 57). And to account for what is recorded in Scripture, one need only resort to 'God's outward help'. Of course, for Spinoza 'outward help' is a figure of speech; for in this same chapter III, as in other passages, he again vehemently asserts: 'It is all one whether we say that all things come to pass in accordance with the laws of nature, or that they are governed by God's decree and guidance' (*ibid.*, § 2, p. 53).

We must needs bear in mind this last definition if we are to understand the exact sense and implication of Spinoza's critical examination of individual election, a criticism to be found in this same chapter and therefore concerning both Jews and Calvinists: in this critical approach, the use of traditional terminology should not undermine our interpretation, since we shall always keep in mind the previous definitions.

> since the power of everything in nature is simply the power of God, by which alone all things come to pass and are determined, and since man too is a part of nature, it follows that everything a man procures for himself,[4] gets from nature without any effort of his own, is given him by God's power alone, working either through human nature or through things external to it. Thus, all that human nature can do by its own unaided power . . . we can rightly call the inward help of God; and everything else that turns out to its advantage through the power of external causes, the outward help of God. From these same premises we can readily discover the true meaning of God's election. For if everything a man does is governed by the predetermined order of nature, i.e. by God's eternal guidance and decree, then no one chooses any way of life for himself, or does anything whatsoever, unless he has been specially

called and chosen by God before all others to perform that task or to live that manner of life (*ibid.*, p. 55).

Acquainted as we are with Spinoza's method, we are not surprised at his investing traditional terminology with a meaning altogether different from the one currently in use; thus 'election' means to Spinoza nothing other than the very action of nature and the individuals, since 'inward help' and 'outward help' only refer to 'God's guidance' that is, as made clear by now, *Nature itself and its laws*. Besides, this election understood as purely natural determinism is *universal* in spite of its being called *singular*: *every* individual, through particular vocation, is led to behave or act in a way which is unique.

To be quite explicit: Spinoza politely but firmly rejects the Calvinist concepts of predestination and election, and it is in unambiguous relation to this Calvinist context that he works out his own doctrine through a complete reversal which indeed deserves to be called dialectic: 'Man's true happiness and blessedness lies solely in the enjoyment of good. Not in feeling elated because such enjoyment is his alone' (these being the very words by which Spinoza begins chapter III on the 'Vocation of the Hebrews').

By what and by what *signs* is a man known to be elected? This notion of a 'sign of election', so often invoked in Scriptures, plays an especially important part in Calvinist doctrine: all Protestant anxiety is rooted in this uncertainty of the faithful belief as to how God will decide of his own salvation as ruin; and the pre-eminent Calvinist 'sign' of election, i.e. material and worldly success, essentially serves to overcome this anxiety.

Spinoza clearly refuses as invalid any outward sign of election, starting with any sign of prophetic calling: 'In this respect prophetic knowledge is inferior to natural knowledge which needs no sign, and in itself implies certitude' (Elwes, *TTP*, II, Cf. Prophets).

The ethical and non-religious bearing of Spinoza's doctrine of truth thus appears in full light. To say that truth is to itself 'its own sign' (*index sui*) does not only provide an epistemological definition of what it is to be true by rejecting any criterion placed outside self-reflecting evidence; it also implies, through radically new use of the old theological term 'sign', a complete rejection of religious and especially Calvinist approach in the quest of truth and in the ethical consequences of this quest; for the denial of all outward sign opens on to a new doctrine of salvation contemplated as inward self-sufficiency. We shall have to consider this point again. For the moment, let us only remark that salvation and access to truth meet: 'A man's true happiness and blessedness lies simply in his wisdom and knowledge of truth, and not in the belief that he is wiser than others or that others lack true knowledge' (Wernham, p. 51).

And just as there is no outward sign of truth, there is no outward sign of election and salvation, since this sign would be outside salvation itself. In Spinoza's view, election and the sign of election are in no way objective realities but only manners of speaking. For the true election being in fact accession to truth (in its self-evidence and inward sign) and *any man* being endowed with the ability to reach knowledge, it must follow that for Spinoza *any man* is liable to be elected and saved. And this universal liability to reach blessedness, with what it implies of interiority by self-awareness, is therefore the negation indeed of election and predestination, as well as the rejection of this selection and metaphysical segregation that Calvinism necessarily entails and which is so contrary to the true inspiration of Spinoza's philosophy.

Shall we say then that all men are automatically 'saved' or that all men are alike? Certainly not. But for Spinoza, the only sound difference worth noticing (besides the uniqueness of each individual) is the contrast between *the wise man and the ignorant man* granted that *any man* at any time is able to reach knowledge, since the mind can at any time form an idea of one's emotions, i.e. an idea of the idea of the way one's body is affected. In cases when this endeavour to reach knowledge has not been made by all, then the wise man alone reaches liberty (another name for salvation or blessedness: *Ethics*, V, 36, sch.) and the difference between the ignorant man and the wise man is then immense, although this difference in no way results from former election. This is particularly important for understanding the full implications of Spinoza's position since it provides the very conclusion to the *Ethics* (*Ethics*, V, 42, sch.).

Now it is perfectly clear that everything goes as if the actual purpose of the *Ethics* were to oppose to the Calvinist doctrine of salvation another doctrine *altogether different* in which salvation would appear not as the decision of a transcendent, arbitrary and predetermined selection but as the result, always within reach, of an effort to understand through reflexion the only way to reach complete fulfilment and actual eternity.

All men are able to be wise men, but few make the necessary effort; and for this reason they are but few who reach this 'true and supreme good' mentioned in the *Treatise on the Correction of the Understanding*. If, then, the men who are to reach liberty are in restricted numbers, it is not because of an arbitrary, restrictive and divine grace at work but because of the nature of liberty and salvation themselves, strictly immanent and human, a nature which necessarily entails that they should seldom be reached and only with difficulties.

But another reason, equally fundamental, warrants potential liability to reach universal salvation: there is no mention of original sin or of the fall, two concepts which are granted even more fundamental and awe-inspiring functions in Calvinism than they are in any other monotheist religion.

(v) Against original sin

Spinoza's ethical position as a doctrine in itself denies validity of the notion of sin itself and consequently of original sin. If ordinary moral notions are no more in Spinoza's philosophy than extrinsic denominations to describe the nature of our imagination but in no sense the qualities of the things themselves, it already appears that the idea of sin for Spinoza is little more than a manner of speaking. We may even go further. If the basis of virtue is the endeavour to preserve one's being (*Ethics*, IV, 18, sch.), then to be good is in fact nothing more, when it is viewed and defined according to reason (and not according to imagination), than to be enjoyed as appropriately useful (*Ethics*, IV, 18, sch.). Whereas evil is none other than what prevents us from enjoying self-sufficiency and the efficiency we derive from knowledge. Ultimately 'if men were born free they would form no conception of good and evil as long as they are free' (*Ethics*, IV, 68). For, as Spinoza's demonstration points out, the free man is the one who is directed by reason, and as such has no ideas except adequate. Now the concepts of good and evil are only the expressions of our emotions and not at all objective truths: 'good' and 'evil' mean nothing to the free man or to Spinoza.

For these reasons, Spinoza's system leaves out even more definitely the idea of original sin, as the scholium to IV, prop. 68 makes clear. In this note, Spinoza interprets the text of Genesis in the perspective of the *Ethics*:

> And this and the other points seem to have been meant by Moses in his history of the first man. . . . Thus it is related that God prohibited free man from eating of the tree of knowledge of good and evil, and that as soon as he ate of it, at once he began to fear death rather than to desire to live (Boyle).

In Spinoza's eyes, this narration is a fiction since man cannot be born free, and consequently the first man (if ever there was a first man) could not have been born free either. But Spinoza gives his own interpretation of this fiction from Scripture: when, fictitiously, Moses posits that *man is free* (in the sense that man would enjoy pure volition and free will) he necessarily, *ipso facto,* posits that he knows of neither good nor evil (and that *he forms no ideas* of either).

In the context of this fiction, one might be expected to explain original sin as consisting in the loss of freedom in consequence of the knowledge of good and evil, and in the fear of death. Now it is precisely this interpretation of the Fall that prop. 68 intends to refute: man was not born free and consequently he *spontaneously forms* the ideas of good and evil, that is to say behaves and thinks according to imagination. First, there is no room left for *any fall,* since, from the very outset, man has been living under the three-dimensional limitation of imaginary affectivity, of lack of freedom and of morality (i.e. of 'good' opposed to 'evil'), whereas in the myth of the Fall man only loses his freedom and knows the limits of morality *as a consequence* of a free act. Second, we must point out that in Spinoza's system, this imaginary and fake life lived according to 'good' and 'evil' does not result from a metaphysical evil nor elicit its existence, for this concept of evil has no objective correlative, it being no more than an inadequate idea. Finally, in Spinoza's view, this 'evil' can be resisted since the inclination towards joy is strong enough to incite us to seek freedom by the means of knowledge. And all men, by right, may seek freedom.

Thus to the Calvinist idea of essential and absolute evil (an idea to be taken up again by Kant) Spinoza opposes the idea of a fictitious evil, a mere inadequate endeavour to describe our own impotency and ignorance.

Losing its metaphysical and dogmatic status, evil is no longer the ontological cataclysm which was to launch the whole mysterious catenation of punishments and forgiveness, of saving grace and doom. 'Evil' is none other, from the viewpoint of the imagination, than what we name as such (i.e. inadequate knowledge and non-being); or else, from the rational standpoint, it is what prevents our fully being, our enjoying freedom, our knowing joy. That is indeed what prevents our being 'saved' but in an intrinsic and unnecessary, that is finally contingent, manner.

For, as we have seen, any man may endeavour to know himself and by so doing leave aside the inadequate concepts of good and evil and consequently the false ideas of sin, punishment and reward, doom and salvation. By knowing himself, on the contrary, man is able to gain for himself his own blessedness and liberty, i.e. his own salvation which no disqualifying metaphysical inhibition, no essential or original hindrance would prevent. The truth is that Spinoza contradicts the Calvinist idea of sin not only by means of the cogency of his system, but also by means of the far-reaching inspiration of his *wisdom*: this inspiration is optimistic and humanist; not at all, as in Calvinism, inhuman and ascetic.

(vi) Against asceticism and austerity

Without necessarily reconsidering here the whole of Spinoza's ethical system, one may assert that the central concern of Spinoza's philosophy is the definition of the 'true good' as being the enduring enjoyment of a supreme and perfect joy (*Treatise on the Correction of the Understanding*). This because, in the very heart of a Christian and Calvinist seventeenth century, Spinoza resolutely defines man by desire: 'Desire is the very essence of man' (*Ethics*, III, definitions of the emotions, 1). Now this extension of the capability to exist, named desire, though this extension be obtained by means of knowledge, contains joy itself.

For this reason the question of ethics, in Spinoza, cannot consist in finding the means to counteract desire; for that would mean to combat life itself. More relevant is the concern to delimit the conditions in which desire may actualize in self-sufficiency, and not merely deploy itself in passive servitude and alienation. The aim in view remains this joy by which the potentialities of existence take increase: but good will be only the active joy, i.e. the joy which finds in itself its own justification. The means, as we know, to enjoy this active joy is mainly through the third kind of knowledge. The 'true good' that is reached then is blessedness itself, which actually means freedom and mental satisfaction (*Ethics*, V, 36, note).

Yet this joy (also called 'glory' or 'mental intellectual love towards God'), though it can be opposed, as active and enduring, to the passive pleasures of ordinary emotions, cannot be opposed to existential fulfilment or to the concrete actualization of desire, provided this desire is aware of its own self and adequate to its own self, i.e. self-sufficient. Here indeed lies the originality and audacity of this doctrine of Spinoza who thus challenges and shatters the whole Calvinist cultural system.

The *Ethics*, V, echoes in fact the *Ethics*, IV, 21: 'No one can desire to be blessed, to act well or to live well who at the same time does not desire to be, to act, and to live, that is actually to exist.' It is important in this context to admit that the blessedness – freedom – contemplated in Part V in no way removes or invalidates this foundation of *all joy*: actual existence. But this individual and joyful desire actually existing and founded by means of self-sufficiency on its own awareness is the very opposite of Calvinist asceticism and austerity. Now we shall be better prepared to understand the full implications of this other fundamental statement of Part IV (*Ethics*, IV, 45, sch.):

> My reason is this, and I have convinced myself of it: no deity, nor any one save the envious, is pleased with my want of power or my misfortune, nor imputes to our virtue, tears, sobs, fear, and other things of this kind which are significant of a weak man; but on the contrary, the more we are affected with pleasure, thus we pass to a greater perfection, that is we necessarily participate of the divine nature. To make use of things and take delight in them as much as possible (not indeed to satiety, for that is not to take delight) is the part of the wise man. . . . To feed himself with moderate pleasant food and drink, and to take pleasure with perfumes, with the beauty of growing plants, dress, music, sports, and theatres, and other places of this kind which man may use without any hurt to his fellows.

Joy, temperate and happy enjoyment of the commodities of life, inward freedom and 'blessedness' by means of knowledge of oneself and the efficient activity of one's mind, such are the plainly tangible determinations to meet a 'salvation' which has nothing in common (except the name, much as the constellation of the Dog is named after the animal, without any other resemblance) with Calvinist salvation which is to be reached only by means of anxiety and fasting and which logically led to the indirectly suicidal asceticism of a Schopenhauer.

But asceticism does not exclusively consist in shunning pleasure and condemning desire, with the distressing prospect of the permanent possibility of doom. It also consists in an infatuation for these conducts or actions that Spinoza would call 'sad': whether it be by general praise of *suffering*, or by regarding *pity* or *remorse* as moral values, Christian asceticism can be best defined as a general inclination for the negative values of life, to resort to almost Nietzschean terminology. Now it is also these negative values of 'life on the decline' that Spinoza firmly and relentlessly denounces: from strictly axiomatic point of view, Spinozism is equally and totally an anti-Calvinism.

Opposed as he is to Calvin, and by anticipation to Kant and Schopenhauer, Spinoza is none the less different from Nietzsche. For there is in Spinoza this philosophical intuition of reflexive self-control, of freedom and this criticism of religion. Although his whole being, his whole doctrine shrank from Calvinism as arbitrary predestination, mortifying asceticism and retributive morals, Spinoza did not yield to an easy dialectic reversal which would have induced him to approve of anarchism, hedonism and violence. On the contrary, Spinoza opposed uncontrolled folly as strongly as asceticism; Spinoza's relentless opposition to Calvinism does not rise from a difference in faith, but from his being the philosopher of clear reason, of the joy of actually existing, of the possibility for every one to be 'saved'.

II SPINOZA, A JEWISH AND ATHEIST PHILOSOPHER, ADMIRING CHRIST AND SOLOMON

As we have seen, it is impossible to assimilate Spinozism to Christian doctrine in general and Calvinism in particular. Whether dealing with the creation of the world, the immortality of the soul, the ethics of retribution, or predestination, or original sin, or asceticism, Spinoza explicitly refutes each of the six concepts that fundamentally go to make up Christian doctrine and particularly Calvinism. And Spinoza's doctrine is indeed so remote from these metaphysical ontologies that it can be said to have formed in *opposition* to them.

But the analysis of doctrines to which we have devoted the previous pages does not entirely clarify the relation of Spinoza to Calvinist Christian doctrine. We must add a few remarks to account for one or two facts which it is difficult to overlook: first, the undeniable admiration that Spinoza felt and professed for the man Christ, and subsequently the profound identity of the leading ideas of Spinoza's doctrine with the traditional inspiration of Jewish thought. *Neither of these two facts* can possibly be overlooked if one is to analyse the relation of Spinoza to Christianity, though the commentators systematically omit one out of the two facts, whichever one they choose to consider.

Concerning Spinoza's admiration for Jesus Christ, we are able by now (after our detailed study) to understand it for what it is: Spinoza is in no sense Christian, his doctrine is even downright opposed to Calvinism and Christian thought, therefore his praise of the person of Christ is the praise by the philosopher of the man who possesses virtue and knowledge.

Are there no other men possessing virtue and knowledge? Why should it be Christ? Our interpretation is as follows. Spinoza is a philosopher without religion, and even, we think, an atheist. Therefore he is not compelled to submit to the discriminating articles of a faith which would have been his, had he been a pious Jew. Thus he is enabled to think freely as a *universalist philosopher*, and this in the precise historical environment in which he was given to live and think, i.e. the society of Calvinist Holland, unsettled by democratic risings in political matters, and oppositional dissidence in religious matters. In these circumstances, his attitude towards Christ and Christianity is perfectly logical and not unexpected. As a universalist philosopher *alert to the language of a social group*, Spinoza is entitled to admire in the man-Christ the most pregnant symbol, *for this social group*, of the ethics of justice and love which were also Spinoza's ethics. Our philosopher therefore feels admiration for the most admired man in this social group first because he indeed regards Christ as *a righteous man* and also because it allows Spinoza to gain the hearing of his readers and disciples. For as we know Spinoza holds that the philosopher must speak the ordinary language of the community.

There is another motivation to this eulogy of Christ as a man: by combating Calvinist doctrine as a system and admiring Christ as a person, Spinoza does not sever himself from his social environment and, more important, he sides with his Protestant disciples, all genuine Christians but practically all opposed to Calvinism. For it is *with them* that Spinoza fights for freedom of thought. Since it is indeed dogmatic predestination and asceticism which stunts freedom and not the human quality and universality of Christ.

In this respect it must be acknowledged that Spinoza's eulogy is ambiguous enough to compel one to be extremely careful in his interpretation of the true significance of this admiration. When Spinoza speaks of Christ, he means the 'man': but cursory reading will see in the name of Christ a mention of his divinity without further checking of the exact and complete bearing of Spinoza's doctrine of nature.

Our interpretation is not imperilled by this ambiguity since we never use Spinoza's terms unless we have read their definitions.

Thus Spinoza's eulogy of Christ is of more restricted bearing than usually believed: opposed as he is to Catholicism and Calvinism, Spinoza admires Christ the man and the man only, which is his way of paying his tribute not only to the generosity of the best among Christians but moreover to the courage and clear-sightedness of the dissident Protestant sects in their fight for freedom.

Spinoza's eulogy of Christ as man and man only can be even further restricted.

Let us consider the second fact mentioned above: the intimate link of Spinoza's thought to Jewish thought. No detailed exposition of the proximity of Spinozism and Judaism taken as a doctrine and as a philosophy can be made here. We shall only refer to the presence in both Judaic and Spinozist thoughts of the love of life, the commendation of joy, the rejection of the immortality of the soul, the encomium of knowledge.

Our concern is to know whether this proximity of the two systems will have repercussions on Spinoza's universalist doctrine. We shall in no sense consider a possible conformity of Spinoza's doctrine with Judaic religion as such: hostile to Calvinism for some reasons (more particularly his love of joy and freedom), Spinoza is no less hostile to Judaism for other reasons (more particularly his loathing of the spirit of obedience and imaginary ideation). So that if Spinoza proves close to Judaic thought, it will be in an altogether different manner: refusing it as a religion, he will preserve it as a deep source of inspiration and as an ethical disposition.

This Jewish inspiration does not only enable Spinoza to be exceptionally open to far-reaching meditation on joy; it also accounts for the fact that, out of *a certain kind of faithfulness* (a certain kind of eternity . . .) towards this Jewish society which was rejecting him out of fear and incomprehension, Spinoza should have chosen to refer to Christ inasmuch as he was a Jew (in this respect, Christ *and* Spinoza will have to be regarded, *quatenus*, as Jews, as we shall demonstrate).

For it is only in so far as he was a Jew that Spinoza could avoid being lured into the belief in Christ's divinity, and as a Jew again that, in a Christian country, Spinoza could admire in Christ the Jewish man, full of wisdom and virtue.

We have already considered this aspect of Christ at the beginning of our study; Spinoza always calls our attention to the fact that Christ never contemplated overthrowing Judaic legislation (*TTP*, IV). For Spinoza, Christ (who cannot be God: how could a finite mode be the substance?) is a man, and this man is a Jew: a Rabbi. Now, if we remember, Spinoza often quotes Christ along with other great Jewish figures, among them Jeremiah: 'this precept of Christ and Jeremiah concerning submission to injuries was only valid in places where justice is neglected, and in a time of oppression, but does not hold good in a well-ordered state' (*TTP*, VII, Elwes).

Here is an indirect criticism of humility as a permanent injunction (Spinoza is not Christian); and also an indirect statement that Christ and Jeremiah are *equivalent*: in similar circumstances, other men than Christ can deliver similar teaching of similar virtues. But we know of this already: 'the essence [of the religion of the Apostles] . . . is chiefly moral, like the whole of Christ's doctrine' (*TTP*, XI, Elwes).

Therefore Christ's exceptional status does not consist in his moral essence (since he shares it with the Apostles and with the Prophets) no more than in the 'Spirit of God' which, simply means besides God's thought in man, *charity*: 'From the premises which he (John) there accepted as his own he concludes that the man who has love (*charitas*) has in truth the spirit of God' (*TTP*, XIV, Wernham, p. 115).[5]

Christ's exceptional status must be sought elsewhere: in his preaching a *Jewish virtue* (charity) on a *universal* plane after, and as a consequence of, the destruction of the particular Hebrew State. In effect, after reminding us that Levitian (chap. XIX, V. 17. 18) urged the Hebrews to love one another, but within the limits and with respect of the institutions of the Hebrew State, Spinoza again illustrates his idea (respect of the laws of the country where the Jews happen to live and submission of all worship to the civil laws) by means of the example of Jeremiah urging the Jews to seek the safety of the city where they were led as captives. Then he proceeds:

> and after Christ saw that they were going to be scattered over the whole world, he taught them to practise piety to all men without exception: which obviously shows that their religion was always adapted to the public good (*TTP*, XIX, Wernham, p. 215).

It is clear that Christ's exceptional status essentially consists in being a *Jew* who, for the time when they are scattered, preaches the only acceptable form of religion for the Jews following the destruction of the State and consequently the uselessness of any particular legislation; and this new form of Judaic religion, which remains Judaic, is none other than the moral teaching known now as Christian doctrine.

Now Spinoza's position is easier to understand: a Jew himself, remaining faithful to his community yet freed from either religion or faith, Spinoza can admire in Christ not a deity but a man, and it so happens that this admirable man is a Jew; Christ, according to Spinoza, does not invalidate Mosaic Law but, after the destruction of the Hebrew State and the Diaspora, he brings Judaism to the only universal form that allows it to be both reflexive and worth teaching as a doctrine: the ethical form. In Christ, Spinoza admires a Jewish Rabbi extending to the whole of mankind that part of the teaching of the Torah which is purely ethical.

For Spinoza Christ's teaching is only worthwhile in so far as it is an ethical teaching (as far as we are able to comprehend or to define properly Spinozist moral doctrine). But if we are to consider Christian doctrine in so far as it is a metaphysical doctrine and a system, then it is essentially represented by Calvinism in Spinoza's view; and we know that, far from making it his, Spinoza worked out the most exact and relentless criticism of it; *it also happens that* our philosopher seems partly to have made up his own system after the reverse of Calvinism. We are made to watch the invasion of the negative into the positive, to watch *the first steps of the modern dialectics of liberty and so to speak the true beginning of these dialectics.*

An admirer of a man, an enemy to a doctrine: Spinoza makes a distinction between the man Christ and the doctrine (Calvinist, or at times Catholic): this same divided position repeats itself as a basic and logical pattern as concerns the Jews: Spinoza acknowledges and betrays the highest consideration for a man Solomon at the same time as he strongly opposes a doctrine the Judaic dedication to obedience. Here is what our philosopher says:

> No one in the whole of the Old Testament speaks more rationally of God than Solomon, who in fact surpassed all the men of his time in natural ability. . . . He taught . . . that humanity has no nobler gift than wisdom, and no greater punishment than folly (see proverbs XVI, 22. 23) (*TTP*, II, Elwes).

and further down: 'Solomon says (Prov. XXI, 15) "It is a joy to the just to do judgement" but the wicked fear' (*TTP*, IV, *ibid.*). It is worth noting that in the paragraph immediately following, Spinoza expatiates on one the fundamental ideas of his doctrine and of the *Ethics*, i.e. on the priority of understanding:

> In as much as the intellect is the best part of our being, it is evident that we should make every effort to perfect it as far as possible if we desire to search for what is really profitable to us. For in intellectual perfections the highest good should consist (*TTP*, IV, *ibid.*).

This comes from chapter IV of the *TTP* ('Of the Divine Law') and it exactly anticipates the doctrine of the *Ethics*. If we go further in this same chapter IV, Spinoza, after reminding us of his theory of understanding, i.e. of natural light (and this *after* referring to Solomon), comes back to Solomon and *repeats his statement*:

> him, who speaks with all the strength of his natural understanding in which he surpassed all his contemporaries. . . . I mean Solomon, whose prudence and wisdom are commended in Scripture rather than his piety and gift of prophecy. He in his proverbs calls the human intellect the well-spring of true life, and declares that misfortune is made up of folly. 'Understanding is a well-spring of life to him that hath it; but the instruction of fools is folly' (Prov. XVI, 22). Life being taken to mean the true life (as is evident from Deut. XXX, 19), the fruit of the understanding consists only in the true life, and its absence constitutes

punishment. All this absolutely agrees with what was set out in our fourth point concerning natural law. Moreover our position that it is the well-spring of life, and that the intellect alone lays down laws for the wise, is plainly taught by the sage, for he says (Prov. XIII, 14): 'The law of the wise is a fountain of life' – that is . . . the understanding. In chapter III, 13, he expressly teaches that the understanding renders man blessed and happy, and gives him true peace of mind. 'Happy is the man that findeth wisdom, and the man that getteth understanding' (*TTP*, IV, *ibid.*).

I shall be forgiven this long final quotation since I have only made use of Spinoza's authority to make clear the *very sense* of my conclusions: our philosopher rejects Jewish religion as legislation and ceremonies, but he is far from rejecting its philosophical implications. For, unlike Christ, who represents only the universal Jew endowed with moral virtue and charity in Spinoza's eyes, Solomon is regarded by our Dutch philosopher as the most enlightened Jew of the Old Testament, i.e. a true sage and a man of understanding. That is to say that Spinoza's doctrine of salvation, i.e. Spinoza's *doctrine of blessedness through knowledge*, precisely springs and wells *from Solomon* 'A well-spring of life' such is understanding (and not charity only, unaccompanied by knowledge) for Solomon and Spinoza. Besides, for Solomon and Spinoza, blessedness, reached through knowledge, finds in itself its own reward and folly its own punishment.

This in no way entails for Spinoza Jewish citizenship; it is neither possible nor desirable in the Diaspora and for this reason Spinoza rejects Moses's law which was only valid for the Ancient Hebrew State. Solomon, on the contrary, is more than a legislator who rules – he is a philosopher who endeavours to understand, and it is as such that he may be said to be, from the doctrinal standpoint, the true source of Spinoza's inspiration, he Solomon the sage, and not Christ the righteous.

Now we can see clearly that the Dutch philosopher, the citizen of the United Provinces, is neither 'Jew' nor 'Christian'. Hostile to Moses's doctrine (as authoritarian and juridical) and to Calvin's (as coercive and awe-inspiring) Spinoza none the less shows admiration for Christ the righteous man and Solomon the righteous and wise man.

Granted the foundations of this wisdom, there remained however to work out a doctrine which would be both audacious and original, particular and universal, the doctrine of God-Nature which alone was to allow for the existence of a truly free man, was to allow man to be a God for man. This doctrine, systematic and immanent as it is, of course nowhere appears in Solomon: for this reason, Spinozism may be said to have been to itself indeed its own foundation and its own beginning. And for this reason it may still be, everywhere and for everyone, like a well-spring of true joy and a perpetually renewed birth (*Ethics*, V., 35, scholium).

NOTES

1 See my essay 'Le Désir et la Réflexion dans la Philosophie de Spinoza', Paris-London, Gordon & Breach, 1972, as well as my book *Spinoza*, Paris, Seghers, 1964, and the footnotes to my translation of the *TTP*, Paris, Gallimard, Bibliothèque de la Pléiade, 1954.

2 Quotations from the *TTP* are from the translation by A. G. Wernham, *Spinoza, The Political Works*, Oxford, 1958, and from the tranlation by R. H. M. Elwes, Spinoza, *A Theologico-Political Treatise and a Political Treatise*, New York, Dover Publications, 1951. For the *Ethics* I have used the translation by A. Boyle, *Spinoza's Ethics* and *On the Correction of the Understanding*, London, Dent, 1959.

3 S. Leonard, *Histoire du Protestantisme*, vol. II, pp. 266–9.

4 In this context see Max Weber, *L'Ethique Protestante et l'Esprit du Capitalisme* (English edition, London, Allen & Unwin, 1967), and the notion of hard work as a sign of election.

5 It must not be inferred from this quotation that Charity is pivotal in Spinoza's doctrine. Here is what Spinoza writes in the *Ethics*, IV, Appendix XVII:

> However, to give aid to every poor man is far beyond the reach of the wealth and power of every private man. For the riches of a private man are far too little for such a thing. Moreover the ability and facility of approach of every man are far too limited for him to be able to unite all men to himself in friendship: for which reason the care of the poor is incumbent on society as a whole, and relates to the general advantage only.

23 Spinoza and ecology

Arne Naess, Oslo

In what follows I do not try to prove anything. I invite the reader to consider a set of hypothetical connections between Spinozist and ecological thought. Most of them seem obvious to me, but every one needs to be carefully scrutinized. They are (of course) built upon a set of definite interpretations of ecology and of the texts of Spinoza.

The industrial states adopt policies which to some extent limit pollution and conserve non-renewable resources. There is also a slight recognition of over-population in the sense of too great a consumption *per capita*. In short, there is in the industrial states a shallow movement in favour of protection of the environment, or better, the ecosystems. But there is also a deeper, international movement which tries to modify attitudes towards nature and the whole conception of the relations of culture to nature. It has deep social and political implications.

Rachel Carson, who started this international movement fifteen years ago, found man's arrogance or indifference towards nature ethically unacceptable. The driving force of the movement was and is still philosophical and religious. The field bio-ecologists, who work in nature, are on the whole manifesting attitudes of love and respect that have made an impact upon millions of people.

There is a deep convergence in metaphysics, ethics and life styles among the people inspired by field ecological thinking. The issues of pollution, resource depletion and over-population are not neglected within the deep ecological movement, but they are integrated in a vastly more comprehensive frame of reference. This frame includes the study of non-industrial cultures, some of them showing a remarkable ecological equilibrium combined with affluence.[1]

History is littered with the remains of cultures that upset the equilibrium. There is a growing understanding that even if we cannot and will not imitate any of the original affluent cultures, we shall have to establish post-industrial societies in equilibrium. Spinoza may turn out to be an important source of inspiration in this quest.

In what follows I accordingly invite friends of Spinoza to consider the many

418

aspects of his philosophy that seem to accord with basic strivings within the deep ecological movement. I do not think it important to get a final conclusion about exactly which concepts or aspects accord best with which concepts or aspects of that movement. There is room for different interpretations. I offer only one.

The interpretation made use of in this article is elaborated in more detail in A. Naess, *Freedom, Emotion and Self-subsistence*, Oslo: Universitets-forlaget, 1975. Notes will refer mainly to that work (abbreviation: FES).

1 The nature conceived by field ecologists is not the passive, dead, value-neutral nature of mechanistic science, but akin to the *Deus sive Natura* of Spinoza. All-inclusive, creative (*as natura naturans*), infinitely diverse, and alive in the broad sense of pan-psychism, but also manifesting a structure, the so-called laws of nature. There are always causes to be found, but extremely complex and difficult to unearth. Nature with a capital N is intuitively conceived as perfect in a sense that Spinoza and out-door ecologists have more or less in common: it is not a narrowly moral, utilitarian or aesthetic perfection. Nature is perfect 'in itself'.

Perfection can only mean completeness of some sort when applied in general, and not to specifically human achievements. In the latter case it means reaching what has been consciously intended.[2]

2 The value-dualism spirit/matter, soul/body does not hold in Spinoza nor is it of any use in field ecology. The two aspects of Nature, those of extension and thought (better: non-extension), are both complete aspects of one single reality, and *perfection characterizes both.*

In view of the tendency to look upon the body as something more crude than spirit, both field ecologists and Spinoza oppose most forms of idealism and spiritualism – and, of course, moralism. (I am not sure these -ism-words deserve to be used in this connection.)

3 Nature (with a capital N) according to Spinoza, and the universe according to modern physics, are not *in* time. As an *absolutely* all-embracing reality, Nature has no purpose, aim or goal. If it had a purpose, it would have to be part of something still greater, for instance a grand design. Time is only definable *within* the network of relations of Nature, therefore Nature as a whole cannot have aims or goals which refer to time.

There is, in ecological thought, a marked reaction against facile finalism, especially in sophisticated research. The development of 'higher' forms of life does not make field ecologists less impressed with the 'lower' forms, some of which have flourished for countless millions of years and still 'are going strong'. (Too strong, some will say, thinking of recent epidemics of flu!) There is no 'purpose' in time such that the bacteria do not have any function or value when 'higher' forms have developed.

4 There is no established moral world-order. Human justice is not a law of nature. There are, on the other hand, no natural laws limiting the endeavour

to extend the realm of justice as conceived in a society of free human beings. These Spinozist thoughts are important for striking the balance between a submissive, amoral attitude towards all kinds of life struggle, and a shallow moralistic and antagonistic attitude. Future societies in ecological equilibrium presuppose such a 'third way'.

5 Good and evil must be defined in relation to beings for which something is good or evil, useful or detrimental. The terms are meaningless when not thus related.[3]

This accords well with the effort of field ecologists in general and social anthropologists in particular, to understand each culture 'from within'. It contrasts with explaining or moralizing on the basis of a definite value code dominant within particular (mostly industrial) societies.

6 Every thing is connected with every other. There is a network of cause-effect relations connecting everything with everything. Nothing is causally inactive, nothing wholly without an essence which it expresses through being a cause. The ecologist Barry Commoner has called 'All things are connected' the first principle of ecology. Intimate interconnectedness in the sense of internal rather than external relations characterizes ecological ontology.

7 Every being strives to preserve and develop its specific essence of nature. Every essence is a manifestation of God or Nature. There are infinite ways in which Nature thus expresses itself. And there are infinite kinds of beings expressing God or Nature.

The pervasive basic *striving* is no mere effort to adapt to stimuli from the outside. It is an active shaping of the environment. Successful acts create new wider units of organism/environment. The basic urge is to gain in extent and intensity of self-causing. The term 'self-realization' is therefore better than 'self-preservation', the first suggesting activeness and creativity, the latter a passive conservative or defensive attitude.[4]

8 Another name for the ability to act out one's nature or essence is 'power', *potentia,* the substantivation of the verb 'to be able', *posse.* It is not the same as to coerce others.

The power of each thing is part of God's power. God or Nature has no other power than ours.

Each and every existing thing expresses God's nature or essence in a certain determinate way ... that is ... each and every thing expresses God's power ... (*Ethics,* I, proof of proposition 36).

All beings strive to maintain *and gain* power. This need not be a striving to dominate, subdue or terrorize. The establishment of symbiosis, 'living together', rather than cut-throat competition marks a gain in power. At higher levels of self-realization, the self encompasses others in a state of increasing intensity and extension of 'symbiosis'.[5] The freedom of the individual ultimately requires that of the collectivity.

420

9 If one insists upon using the term 'rights', every being may be said to have the right to do what is in its power. It is a 'right' to express its own nature as clearly and extensively as natural conditions permit.

That right which they [the animals] have in relation to us, we have in relation to them (*Ethics*, Part IV, first scholium to proposition 37).

That rights are a part of a separate moral world order is a fiction.[6]

Field ecologists tend to accept a general 'right to live and blossom'. Humans have no special right to kill and injure, Nature does not belong to them.

10 There is nothing in human nature or essence, according to Spinoza, which can *only* manifest or express itself through injury of others. That is, the striving for expression of one's own nature does not inevitably imply an attitude of hostile domination over other beings, human or non-human. Violence, in the sense of violent activity, is not the same as violence as injury to others.

The human attitude of violence and hostility towards some species of animals have made it impossible to study realistically their life and function within the whole. The field ecologist who deeply identifies with the species studied is able to live peacefully with any kind of wild animal. This attitude harmonizes with the view of Spinoza concerning free man (*homo liber*). Spinoza has a kind of doctrine about the development of affects (Parts III and IV of the *Ethics*), and makes the field ecologist's symbiotic attitude inevitable if the development proceeds far enough.

In what follows other Spinozist thoughts are mentioned which harmonize with those of field ecologists even if the latter do not often develop them consciously.

11 Every being has its unique direction of self-realization, its particular essence, but 'the greatest good' is the

understanding realization of the union [*cognitio unionis*] of our mind with the whole Nature (*On The Improvement of the Understanding*, Paragraphs 13–14).

12 The realization of union with the whole Nature is made through the understanding of the particular things as a manifold of expressions or manifestations of Nature (God). But Nature or God is nothing apart from the manifestations.

Spinoza rejects the kind of *unio mystica* which results in a turning away from particulars and from nature.

The more we understand the particular things [*res singulares*], the more we understand God (*Ethics*, Part V, proposition 24).

Spinoza's concept of Nature and its manifestations lack the features which make nature (in the more common connotations) something inferior to spirit or to God.

Ecological thinking presumes an identification with particulars in their internal relations to each other. The identification process leads deeper into Nature as a whole, but also deeper into unique features of particular beings. It does not lead away from the singular and finite. It does not lend itself to abstract thinking or contemplation, but to *conscious, intuitive, intimate interaction*.

13 'Rationality' is wise conduct maximizing self-realization. It cannot be separated from perfection, virtue and freedom.

Since reason does not demand anything contrary to Nature, it demands that everyone loves himself, looks for what is useful, . . . and that he strives to obtain all which really leads man to greater perfection (*Ethics*, Part IV, proposition 18, scholium).

Since self-realization implies acts of understanding with increasing perspective, rationality and virtue increases with the development of understanding. The greatest understanding is 'an understanding love of Nature', *amor intellectualis Dei*. This implies acts of understanding performed with the maximum perspective possible, or loving immersion and interaction in Nature.[7]

14 Interacting with things and understanding things cannot be separated. The units of understanding are not propositions, but acts. To the content of ideas in the 'attribute of non-extension' there corresponds an act in the 'attribute of extension'. Ultimately these attributes are attributes of the same, but the human way of understanding is such that we have to treat them separately.

Increase of rationality and freedom is proportional to increase of activeness; each action having the aspects of understanding and of a behaviour or inter-action. Not all acts need be overt.

15 Since a gain in understanding expresses itself as an act, it is in its totality a process within the extended aspect of Nature and can be studied as such.

This point is of prime importance to the methodology of etiology. The 'world' of a living being is investigated through study of its manifest ('molar' not 'molecular') behaviour. Spinoza furnishes etiology with a frame of reference completely devoid of the kind of 'mentalism' and 'introspectionism' that has often obstructed the study of cognition in animals and men.

The framework of Spinoza and of general etiology is also well suited to counteract the tendency to conceive human knowledge as something existing independent of acts of particular human beings in particular situations – and stored wholesale in libraries.

The formulation of Spinoza does not point to any definite form of 'behaviourism'. We are free to inspect critically any contemporary version.

There is no reason to identify the concepts of 'behaviour' with that of Watson or Skinner.

16 Most of the basic concepts used in the *Ethics* when characterizing the human predicament are such as can be used whatever the cultural context. They are furthermore adapted to general characterizations covering smaller or greater parts of the animal, plant and mineral kingdoms. Some of these concepts have already been mentioned.

Spinoza rarely touches upon questions concerning animals, but where he does, he shows that his main concepts are not only intended to apply to humans.[8] He warns, however, against thinking that the joys of insects are the same as those of humans. Each kind of living being is content with and delights in what corresponds to its nature or essence.

Among the important concepts which have a wider application than to the human species one may note the following:

perfection (cf. point 2)
good and evil (cf. points 4 and 5)
striving to express one's nature or essence (cf. points 7 and 8)
self-preservation, self-realization (cf. points 7, 11 and 13)
power (cf. points 8, 9 and 10)
rationality (cf. points 13 and 14)
virtue (cf. point 13, cp. the expression *potentia seu virtus*)
freedom (cf. points 13 and 14)
understanding (cf. points 14 and 15)
feeling (3P57sch.)
emotion (cf. 3P57sch. The passive ones are confused ideas, cf. *Ethics*, 3aff. gen. df.)
confused idea

For all these terms it holds that Spinoza's definitions are open as regards their exact range.[9]

Some are clearly intended to be applicable at least to a major part of the kingdom of animals. Because of equivalences holding between many of them the range of all of them can, without doing violence to Spinoza's texts, be made as large as suitable within ecology and theory of evolution.

The comparatively wide applicability of Spinoza's basic *concepts* does not imply uncritical *statements* about similarities between humans and other living beings. It ensures a broad continuity of outlook and the possibility of fighting human arrogance and cruelty.

Ecological thought typical of active field ecologists is not entirely homogeneous. And Spinoza's texts are of course open to various interpretations. In spite of this my conclusion is positive: No great philosopher has so much to offer in the way of clarification and articulation of basic ecological attitudes as Baruch Spinoza.

NOTES

1 Highly readable: Marshall Sahlins, *Stone Age Economics*, London, Tavistock, 1974.
2 'Perfection' is not a term which is introduced in the *Ethics* by means of separate definition, and it is something admitting of degrees. Joy is an emotion through which the mind is said to *become more* perfect (Part III, scholium to proposition 11). Whatever its connotation, 'more perfect' cannot be separated in denotation from 'more powerful'. Compare Part IV, proof of proposition 41: 'Joy . . . is the emotion through which the power of the body/and therefore also of the mind/to act, increases or is furthered.' The relation to action, and therefore to understanding, is intimate. The more perfect, the more active and the less passive, according to Part V, proposition 40. In short, 'more perfect than cannot in denotation be separated from a number of other basic relations. The application of the term to Nature or God clearly is on a par with the application of terms like 'love' (*amor*), 'rationality', 'mind', that is, it cannot be taken in any precise sense known from phenomena *in* Nature.
3 The concurrence of the words *bonus* and *malus* in the *Ethics* admits of various conceptualizations. According to Part IV, definition 1, in the *Ethics*, '*x* is good for *y*' does not mean more than '*x* is useful for *y*' or '*x* is known by *y* to be useful for *y*'. The expression '*x* is useful for *y*' is equivalent to '*x* causes an increase in *y*'s power', '*x* causes an increase of *y*'s freedom' and '*x* causes an increase of *y*'s perfection'. More about these equivalences in *FES*, pp. 107–9.
4 According to Part III, proposition 6, *every* thing, as far as it is in itself, strives to preserve in its being. The term *perseverare* I take to mean something much more active than just to survive. Therefore I accept as equivalent '*x* increases in power' and '*x* increases in level of *self-preservation*' (*FES*, p. 97).
5 Good relations to others are obtained according to Part IV, propositions 46, 50 (scholium), 72, a.o. through generosity and other forms of non-injury (ahimsa). According to Part IV, proposition 45, 'Hatred can never be good', that is, according to Part IV, definition 1, it can never be useful to us. Therefore it cannot cause an increase in power or understanding.
6 It must be conceded that Spinoza holds that we cannot be friends of animals or include them in our society. Only humans can be friends of humans and be members of our societies (see Part IV, appendix, chapter 26). And because we are more powerful than animals, we have more rights. We may *use* animals as we see fit, and one cannot issue laws against molesting them (Cf. Part IV, scholium 1 to proposition 37, and appendix, chapter 26).
7 The basic position of 'understanding', *intelligere*, in Spinoza's system, is seen from its intimate relation to 'causing'. If something is caused adequately through something else, it is adequately understood through this something, *and* vice versa. (*FES*, p. 40, cf. Part III, first part of first definition). Activeness is intimately related to understanding because the specific activity of the mind *is* understanding. It is also related to power and freedom in so far as increased activeness is internally related to increase in power and freedom. In this way not only intuitive understanding of the highest (third) kind but also the understanding of the laws of nature is promoting power, freedom, joy and perfection.

8 The pan-psychism of Spinoza is expressed in the scholium to proposition 13 in Part II (of the *Ethics*). Other individuals than humans are animated, *animata*, but in different degrees, *diversis gradibus*. He even (in the proof of proposition 1, Part III) uses the expression 'the minds of other things' *aliarum rerum mentes*. About the difference in appetites and joys between various kinds of animals, see scholium to proposition 57, Part III.

9 Spinoza does not directly say so, but I think he would deny rationality of any kind to other beings than humans. He speaks, however, about 'virtue or power' of animals, and he more or less identifies virtue and rationality. 'To act virtuously is nothing else than to act according to reason; . . .' (Part IV, proof of proposition 56).

Spinoza may evidently be interpreted in various ways as regards the relation of animals to man. We have been interested in the main trend of his reasoning and the main features of his terminology.

24 Letter from Spinoza to Lodewijk Meyer, 26 July 1663

A. K. Offenberg, Amsterdam*

INTRODUCTION

The forty-nine letters of Spinoza hitherto known to us[1] have now been supplemented by a fiftieth, recently purchased by the Library of the University of Amsterdam. However, only twelve of these forty-nine letters have been preserved as originals, so that the new acquisition constitutes the thirteenth currently known letter in Spinoza's own hand.

In 1903, the twelve letters then accessible were brilliantly published by Willem Meyer in a facsimile edition with transcriptions, annotations and translations into Dutch, English and German.[2]

The subject matter of the new letter[3] is related to a portion of a communication from Spinoza to Henry Oldenburg dated 17/27 July 1663 and to a letter from Spinoza to Lodewijk Meyer of 3 August of the same year.[4] These letters deal with the publication of Descartes's *Principia Philosophiae*, expounded geometrically by Spinoza and supplemented by the *Cogitata Metaphysica*.[5] Urged by his Amsterdam friends, Spinoza had prepared this text for publication, and it was the only work to appear under his name during his lifetime.[6] The two known letters provide some rather useful background on the motives for this edition and the preface by Lodewijk Meyer, which is itself quite exceptional; the new letter has supplied us with additional data, especially on the *Cogitata Metaphysica*.

The consensus on this particular work has not been altogether favourable; it is nevertheless of particular significance in understanding the evolution of Spinoza's philosophy. A well-known commentator, Dunin-Borkowski, feels 'ill at ease'[7] even at the beginning of the *Cogitata Metaphysica*: in his view, Spinoza's ideas were at least eighty years behind the times. It should be borne in mind, however, that it is not his own ideas that Spinoza expounds, but those of Descartes, with whom he did not always agree, as is clear, *inter alia*, from Lodewijk Meyer's preface.

The work is based on what may be termed the 'lecture notes' of Spinoza's young student, Johannes Casearius, whom Spinoza felt to be too immature to

* Bibliotheca Rosenthaliana, University of Amsterdam.

understand his ideas, so that he had objectively explained to him those of Descartes.[8] The measure of this objectivity, however, is open to argument; according to Kuno Fischer[9] the *Cogitata Metaphysica* constitutes a direct attack on the *Principia Philosophiae*, but this is disputed by such authors as J. Freudenthal[10] and Ch. Appuhn.[11]

I do not intend – nor do I feel sufficiently competent – to assess the significance of this letter within the framework of our knowledge of Spinoza's work. After a facsimile of the letter, a transcription and an English translation of the text,[12] I shall endeavour to shed some light on a few aspects of the newly discovered document. It is my hope that others, more knowledgable than myself, will undertake to subject its many other facets of interest to a more profound analysis.

Amyn heer
Myn her Lodovijk Myer
Doctor in de medecyn, L.A.M.*
tot
Amsterdam
per cuvert.

Amice Suavissime
    epistolam tuam gratissimam heri accepi; in qua
    quaeris an recte [-citaveris] indicaveris cap. 2. p. 1. appendicis omnes
    prop. etc.[a] quae ibi ex parte i princ. citantur. deinde
    an non delendum sit id quod in 2[a] parte assero. [-filium]
    nempe filium dej esse ipsum patrem. denique an non
    mutandum sit, quod ajo me nescire quid vocabulo
    personalitatis intelligant theologi. quibus Dico 1°.
    te omnia quae cap. 2. appendicis indicavisti; recte
    a te indicata esse. Sed capite 1° dicti appendicis pag.
    1. indicasti scholium prop. 4. et tamen mallem ut scholium
    prop. 15 indicasses, ubi ex professo, de omnibus modis
    cogitandi dissero. deinde pag. 2 ejusdem capitis in
    margine scripsisti haec verba. *negationes cur non*
    sint ideae ubi loco hujus verbi *negationes* ponen-
    dum *entia rationis* nam de enti ratione in gene-
    re loquor, quod nempe non sit idea, 2° quod [-quae]
    dixi filium dej esse ipsum patrem puto clarissime sequi
    ex hoc ax. nempe, quae in uno tertio conveniunt
    ea inter se conveniunt. Verum quia res apud me
    nullius est momenti, si hoc quosdam theologos posse

---

* Liberatium Artium Magister (Master of Liberal Arts).

13 *Facsimile of letter from Spinoza to Lodewijk Meyer, 26 July 1663*

offendere putas: fac prout tibi melius videbitur. 3º denique me fugit quid vocabulo personalitatis intelligant
theologi, non vero quid per id vocabulum critici intelligant. interim, quia exemplar penes te est, ipse haec
melius videre potes, si tibi videntur mutanda, fac ut
lubet. Vale amice Singularis mejque memor vive
qui sum   tibi addictissimus
Datum Vorburgi, 26 Julii   B. d^e. Spinoza.
   1663

To
   Lodovijk Myer, Esq.
      Doctor of Medicine, L.A.M.
         at
            Amsterdam
               Per post

Most amiable Friend,
   Your very welcome letter reached me yesterday. You ask me whether
you have correctly indicated in Chapter 2 of the first part of the
Appendix all propositions etc. cited there from Part 1 of the *Principia*.
Moreover, whether or not my assertion in the second chapter, i.e. that
the Son of God is the Father himself, should be deleted. Finally,
whether a modification should be made where I state that I do not know
what the theologians mean by the word 'personalitas.' To this I say:
   1. That everything indicated by you in Chapter 2 of the Appendix is
indeed indicated correctly. In the first chapter of this Appendix, however,
on the first page, you refer to the scholium on prop. 4, whereas I would
have preferred you to refer to the scholium on prop. 15, where I
particularly discuss all manners of thought. Then, on page 2 of the
same chapter, you have written these words in the margin: 'Why the
"*negationes*" are no "*ideae*",' where the word '*negationes*' should be
replaced by '*entia rationis*,' since I am discussing an '*ens rationis*'
generally, and am saying that this is not an '*idea*'.
   2. That the Son of God is the Father himself, as I have said, follows
very clearly, I believe, from the axiom that those things which coincide
with a third thing also coincide with one another. However, this question
is of no importance at all to me; therefore, if you believe that this
might give offence to some theologians, please do whatever you think is
best.
   3. Finally, it eludes me what the theologians mean by the word
'*personalitas*', but I am aware of the meaning attached to it by the

philologists. In the meantime, since the copy is available to you, it would be better if you were to decide on these things yourself; if you feel this should be changed, please follow your own judgment.

Farewell, my dear friend, and continue to think of me, who am,

Most devotedly yours,

B. de Spinoza

Voorburg, 26 July 1663

COMMENTS

This Spinoza letter allows several new inferences which are relevant to the original history of the printed text of the *Principia Philosophiae* and the appended *Cogitata Metaphysica*, and leads to certain conclusions which, in turn, raise new questions.

The systematic manner in which Spinoza summarizes the preceding letter from Meyer conveys moreover a fairly clear picture of the contents of that hitherto unknown letter.

At the time of Spinoza's reply, 26 July 1663, at least the first part of the *Cogitata Metaphysica* had already been typeset, and possibly the rest of the book as well (except for Meyer's preface, as evidenced by the letter which Spinoza wrote to him on 3 August). Meyer nevertheless asked whether anything had to be changed or even omitted, and it does seem that changes must indeed have been made in the text. Spinoza states in his letter that the 'exemplar' is accessible to Meyer, thus referring most probably to the manuscript submitted for typesetting.[13] It is unlikely that Meyer sent proof sheets to Spinoza, it being uncommon in those days to leave so much text standing in type while waiting for the outcome of a correspondence conducted with an author residing far from the place where the book was being set in type and printed. Since Meyer lived in Amsterdam, the copy was accessible to him, i.e. he could check and consult it at the printer's, and was in a position to make changes. It is more likely that specimen sheets of the typeset pages were sent to Spinoza, and the minor changes which he wanted were eventually included in the list of errata printed after Meyer's preface, in the final phase of the publishing operation. Major changes could be made only by 'cancelling', i.e. by resetting the pages involved, while discarding and replacing the leaves that had already been printed. The letter of 3 August indicates, among other things, that at that time Spinoza required a change as well as an addition in the text of the *Principia Philosophiae*, which entailed the resetting of four printed pages (the leaves K2 and K3).[14]

The new letter also establishes that Meyer's contribution to the definitive text of the *Principia Philosophiae* and the *Cogitata Metaphysica* actually amounted to more than a mere polishing of the Latin style (as had been the impression conveyed to Oldenburg in Spinoza's aforementioned letter of

17/27 July 1663), since Spinoza states in his answer to Meyer that the latter has provided all references correctly – and these references are part of the text. Spinoza furthermore notes that Meyer had written something erroneous in the latter's marginal annotations, which would seem to indicate that the marginalia are in Meyer's hand. In most of the modern translations, these marginal notes are incorporated in the continuous text, without the translators or editors having been aware that they were not authored by Spinoza.

The following remarks may be offered on the final changes in the printed text as a result of this letter. First of all, Spinoza suggests that the reference to the scholium on proposition 4 appearing on the first page of the *Cogitata Metaphysica* – a part to which he refers as the Appendix – be changed to a reference to the scholium on proposition 15. This first page is p. 93 of the definitive edition.[15] The change was eventually included in the list of errata, and was clearly identified and justified by Gebhardt in the text as established by him. However, an examination of a fairly random number of translations of this text published in the course of the past century[16] shows that Spinoza's request was not in any way implemented; the reference to the scholium on proposition 4 was retained in all cases.

On the next page, the word *'negationes'* in the margin was to be changed to *'entia rationis'*.[17] This correction was likewise included in the errata, but, strangely enough, not justified by Gebhardt,[18] whereas the translations cited above consistently give the version here specified by Spinoza. How are we to explain this discrepancy? My original surmise of textual corrections having been on the press for part of the edition appears to be untenable. This is corroborated by a personal inspection of some twenty copies (largely in the form of photographic reproductions).[19] The more likely explanation is to be found in the edition of the text preceding Gebhardt's, i.e. the one edited by J. van Vloten and J. P. N. Land,[20] on which the translations are evidently based. The second erratum was corrected in this 1895 edition, while the first was allowed to persist through some inadvertence or oversight.

The two other possible changes are harder to trace. They relate to Meyer's suggestion, cited by Spinoza in the first paragraph of his letter, to delete the assertion that 'the Son of God is the Father himself', and to Spinoza's intimation that he does not know what meaning the theologians assign to the concept of *'personalitas'*. The background and implications of these questions in terms of the philosophy of religion will have to be expounded and interpreted by authorities in this field; suffice it here to surmise that Meyer did indeed do what he intended to, and to some extent modified – with Spinoza's consent – the original text.

The remark that 'the Son of God is the Father himself' occurs in chapter X of Part II of the *Cogitata Metaphysica*. In the printed text, however, it is merely stated that the Father shared his own eternity with the Son,[21] which does not accord with the phrase cited by Spinoza. The axiom which Spinoza cites in the letter in support of his proposition is axiom 15 in Part II of the *Principia Philosophiae*.[22] His comment on the '*personalitas*' occurs at the beginning of chapter VIII in Part II of the *Cogitata Metaphysica*.[23]

Comparison of the printed text with Spinoza's answer in the letter definitely suggests that the text was adapted in accordance with Spinoza's response. Had these changes been made after completion of the actual printing, one would expect the pertinent passages to have been cancelled, but no certain evidence that this was the case has come to my knowledge.[24] Conceivably, however, the second part of the *Cogitata Metaphysica* had not yet been set and printed when Meyer consulted Spinoza; this possibility assumes even greater significance in the light of Spinoza's remark that Meyer might as well decide for himself, since the copy was accessible to him.

In conclusion, I may be permitted some remarks about Spinoza's personal attitude with regard to the publication of his book. His real intentions, especially with the *Cogitata Metaphysica*, have often elicited wonderment. This work has alternately been regarded as a modification of scholasticism, an unconscious expression of pantheistic ideas and, conversely, an ingenious demonstration that the philosophy of Descartes had now been superseded.[25] Spinoza makes it clear in his letter to Oldenburg that he also wished to use this publication to draw the attention of those in high places in the Republic to his person and work; then, in case his opus were favourably received, he would be allowed to continue publishing unmolested, and thus be in a better position to express his personal views.[26] Spinoza here evidently alludes to the brothers De Witt, and according to Willem Meyer he did indeed attain his aim.[27] The work was translated into Dutch by Pieter Balling[28] within the next year, and it probably also contributed – along with the impression created by his *Tractatus Theologico-Politicus*, which was already widely circulated by that time – to the honorific invitation of 1673 to occupy the Chair of Philosophy at Heidelberg, although he had to decline this offer.[29]

It seems plausible, however, that Vloemans was correct in 1931, when he suspected intuitively that Spinoza in 1663 did indeed hope to earn a professorate with his book. Vloemans writes (translated from the original passage):[30] 'What can Spinoza possibly have intended or hoped to convey with all these expositions about which, at heart, he couldn't have cared less, since the convictions he held differed fundamentally from the ones here written down?'

And now we read for the first time how Spinoza himself felt about a certain question in his book: '. . . *res apud me nullius est momenti* . . .'!

NOTES

1 Carl Gebhardt wrote in 1924 (passage translated from the German): 'The search made by W. Meyer for further Spinoza letters has unfortunately remained unsuccessful; my own efforts to enrich our knowledge of Spinoza's correspondence have likewise all failed.' (Spinoza, *Opera*, edited by Carl Gehardt under

the auspices of the Heidelberg Academy of Sciences (1925), vol. IV, p. 381. Hereafter cited as *Opera*.)

2 *Nachbildung der im Jahre 1902 noch erhaltenen eigenhändigen Briefe des Benedictus Despinoza*, edited by W. Meyer, The Hague, 1903. (Limited edition of 200 copies.) This edition actually reproduces facsimiles of only eleven originals. Two other letters (XII and LXIX) were still extant in the nineteenth century, but had disappeared when Meyer prepared his facsimile edition. There is, however, a lithographic reproduction of Letter LXIX, published by H. W. Tydeman in the *Utrechtsche Volks-Almanak* for 1844, between pages 160 and 161. Meyer regarded this lithography as a quasi-original and included it in facsimile as the twelfth Spinoza autograph. (Cf. W. Meyer, *op. cit.*, 'Erläuterungen zu den facsimilierten Briefen des Benedictus Spinoza; A: Allgemeine Bemerkungen', p. 1.) A communication from F. Akkerman, Groningen, indicates that of the two originals known to have been privately owned in Berlin prior to the two world wars one (Letter XXIII) is now preserved in the State Library for Prussian Cultural Heritage, West Berlin; the other (Letter LXXII), auctioned in 1917, cannot be traced at this time.

3 The letter is in the Manuscript Department (under call number G x 18) of the Library of the University of Amsterdam.

4 *Opera*, IV, Letter XIII (pp. 63–9) and Letter XV (pp. 72–3).

5 *RENATI DES CARTES* / PRINCIPIORUM / PHILOSOPHIÆ / Pars I, & II, / *More Geometrico demonſtratæ* / PER / BENEDICTUM de SPINOZA *Amſtelodamenſem*. / *Acceſſerunt Ejuſdem* / COGITATA METAPHYSICA, / *in quibus difficiliores, quæ tam in parte Metaphyſices generali, quàm / ſpeciali occurrunt, quæſtiones breviter explicantur*. / [Fig.] / AMSTELODAMI, / *Apud* JOHANNEM RIEWERTS, *in vico vulgò dicto*, de Dirk / van Aſſen-ſteeg, *ſub ſigno Martyrologii*. 1663. 4°.

6 C. Louise Thijssen-Schoute, *Lodewijk Meyer en diens verhouding tot Descartes en Spinoza* (with summary in French), Leiden, 1954, pp. 8–9. (Mededelingen vanwege het Spinozahuis (Bulletin of the The Spinoza House Society), no. 11.)

7 Stanislaus von Dunin-Borkowski, *Spinoza*, vol. 3: *Aus den Tagen Spinozas*, Part 2: 'Das neue Leben', Münster, 1935, p. 98.

8 See Spinoza's letter to Simon de Vries of late February 1663 (Letter IX, *Opera*, IV, p. 142): 'Nec est quod Caseario invideas. Nullus nempe mihi magis odiosus, nec a quo magis cavere curavi quam ab ipso quamobrem te omnesque notos monitos vellem ne ipsi meas opiniones communicetis nisi ubi ad maturiorem aetatem pervenerit ...' (You have no cause to envy Casearius. Really, he causes me a great deal of unpleasantness, and never have I taken more care to be heedful than in his case, so that I would like you and all acquaintances to be cautioned not to communicate to him my views until such time as he will have reached a more mature age.) Also see the aforementioned letter to Oldenburg (cf. note 4): 'quem ego cuidam juveni, quem meas opiniones apertē docere nolebam, antehac dictaveram' which I had dictated earlier to a young man to whom I did not wish to teach my views).

9 Kuno Fischer, *Geschichte der neueren Philoſophie*, vol. 2: *Spinozas Leben, Werke und Lehre*, 4th ed, rev. Heidelberg, 1898. (In this edition, Fischer deals in detail with Freudenthal's reaction; see note on pp. 306–10.)

10 J. Freudenthal, 'Spinoza und die Scholastik', in *Philosophische Aufsätze, E. Zeller gewidmet*, Leipzig, 1887, pp. 98–9.

11 Spinoza, *Oeuvres*, translation, comments and notes by Ch. Appuhn, New ed, rev., Paris, 1964, vol. I, p. 227, note 4.

12 My sincere appreciation goes to Dr F. F. Blok, Institute of Neophilology and Neo-Latin, Amsterdam, who has been most helpful in establishing the text and with the translation from Latin.

13 When preparing the Dutch edition of this paper (*Brief van Spinoza aan Lodewijk Meyer, 26 juli 1663*, Amsterdam: University Library, 1975), I hesitated about the meaning of 'exemplar' and supposed at first that Spinoza might have seen proofs. Having since had the pleasure of receiving a communication with detailed documentation from Mr F. A. Janssen, Krommenie – who has strongly influenced my opinions in this respect – I am now satisfied that the term 'exemplar' can only refer to the manuscript copy submitted to the printer for typesetting, it being most unlikely that proofs were sent to Spinoza. It is difficult to communicate the evidence within the scope of this contribution. For a contemporary reference to the meaning of 'exemplar" cf. J. A. Comenius, *Orbis sensualium pictus. Hoc est omnium fundamentalium in mundo rerum et in vita actionum pictura et nomenclatura./Die sichtbare Welt. Das ist aller vornemsten Welt-Dinge und Lebens-Verrichtungen Vorbildung und Benahmung*, Nuremberg, 1658, p. 190 (leaf M7, verso). For the question of proofs, cf. L. Voet, *The Golden Compasses. A History and Evaluation of the Printing and Publishing Activities of the Officina Plantiniana at Antwerp*, vol. II, Amsterdam, 1972, pp. 300–1.

14 Cf. Gebhardt, 'Textgestaltung', *Opera*, I, p. 610.

15 *Opera*, I, p. 233, line 33.

16 Examples of translations examined:

(a) *René Descartes' Prinzipien der Philosophie, erster und zweiter Theil, in geometrischer Weise begründet durch Benedict von Spinoza aus Amsterdam. Mit einem Anhang: Metaphysische Gedanken des Letztern . . .* , translated and annotated by J. J. Kirchmann, Berlin, 1871, p. 100. (*Philosophische Bibliothek*, vol. 41.)

(b) *B. de Spinoza's sämmtliche Werke, aus dem Lateinischen, mit einer Lebensgeschichte*, by Berthold Auerbach, vol. I, 2nd ed, Stuttgart, 1871, p. 88.

(c) *The Principles of Descartes Philosophy by Benedictus de Spinoza* (*The Philosopher's Earliest Work*), translated from the Latin with an introduction by Halbert Hains Britan, La Salle, Ill., 1961, p. 116. (Reprint of the 1905 edition.)

(d) Baruch Spinoza, *Earlier Philosophical Writings: The Cartesian Principles and Thoughts on Metaphysics*, translated by Frank A. Hayes with an introduction by David Bidney, Indianapolis, 1963, p. 108. (The Library of Liberal Arts, no. 163).

(e) Spinoza, *Oeuvres*, translation, comments and notes by Ch. Appuhn, New ed, rev., vol. I, Paris, 1964, p. 337. (Originally published in 1905.)

17 *Opera*, I, p. 234, line 28.

18 This also applies to the change from *Ei* to *Si*, *Opera*, I, p. 236, line 16.

19 Amsterdam, University Library (2 copies); The Hague, Royal Library (3 copies); Leeuwarden, Provincial Library; Rijnsburg, Library of The Spinoza

House Society; Baarn, private collection of Menno Hertzberger; Nieuwkoop, Messrs De Graaf, antiquarian booksellers; Paris, Bibliothèque Nationale (3 copies); Bonn, University Library; Munich, Municipal Library (2 copies); Hanover, State Library of Lower Saxony; Göttingen, Municipal and University Library; Jerusalem, University Library; Washington, D.C., Library of Congress (2 copies). Not examined: London, British Library (2 copies); Cincinnati, Hebrew Union College Library; East Berlin, German City Library; Tübingen, University Library.

20 *Benedicti de Spinoza Opera quotquot reperta sunt*, edited by J. van Vloten and J. P. N. Land, 2nd edn, vol. III, The Hague, 1895, pp. 192–3.

21 *Opera*, I, p. 271, lines 29–30. It is of interest to note the remark of Dunin-Borkowski, *op. cit.*, p. 136, on the reaction of Professor A. Heereboort, of Leiden, to the theories of the Spanish philosopher Benedict Pereyra on this question. Here we may possibly have the background to explain Meyer's reluctance to publish this assertion.

22 *Opera*, I, p. 185, lines 4–5.

23 *Opera*, I, p. 264, lines 10–13.

24 Only in the copy No. 1815 B36 of the Amsterdam University Library are the leaves Q1 and Q4, R1, R2, R3 and R4 pasted on strips. These leaves cover part of the text of chapters VIII and X. Remarkably, however, the text is printed from the same type as the other copies examined by me, where there is no question of any cancellations.

25 B. Wielenga, *Spinoza's 'Cogitata Metaphysica' als Anhang zu seiner Darstellung der cartesianischen Prinzipienlehre*, Heidelberg, 1899, p. 8. (Doctoral thesis.)

26 Letter XIII: 'Hac nempe occasione forte aliqui, qui in mea patria partas tenent, reperientur, qui caetera, quae scripsi, atque pro meis agnosco, desiderabunt videre; adeoque curabunt, ut ea extra omne incommodi periculum communis juris facere possim.' (For perhaps on this occasion persons will be found who in my native country hold the highest offices, and who will wish to see the other things which I have written and acknowledge as my own work; and who will then see that I can publish them without any risk of inconvenience.)

27 *Brieven van en aan Benedictus de Spinoza benevens des schrijvers Betoog over het zuivere denken*, translated from the Latin by W. Meyer, Amsterdam, 1897, p. 82. (*Klassieke Schrijvers*, vol. 44; Spinoza's Works, vol. III.)

28 This translation actually offers more than the original; Spinoza corrected, changed and expanded the text in many places. Cf. Gebhardt, 'Textgestaltung', *Opera*, I, pp. 611–12. The two minor changes on pp. 93 and 94 of the Latin edition are indeed incorporated in this translation; the more influential changes which Meyer had proposed in chapters VIII and X of the *Cogitata Metaphysica* were evidently approved by Spinoza: the Latin text is translated literally in these instances.

29 See the letter from J. Ludwig Fabritius to Spinoza of 16 February 1673 and Spinoza's reply of 30 March 1673, Letter XLVII and Letter XLVIII, respectively, *Opera*, IV, pp. 234–6.

30 A. Vloemans, *Spinoza. De mensch, het leven en het werk*, The Hague, 1931, p. 273.

25 Spinoza et la révélation philosophique

Jean Preposiet, Besançon

> Tu ne te feras point d'image taillée, de représentation quelconque des choses qui sont en haut dans les cieux, qui sont en bas sur la terre, et qui sont dans les eaux plus bas que la terre.
>
> *Deutéronome*, V, 8

Le projet spinoziste se présente sous un double aspect. Philosophie de type rationaliste en même temps que recherche de la béatitude, le spinozisme allie l'esprit critique à la ferveur religieuse. A ce titre, Spinoza marque une étape importante dans la longue histoire des rapports de la Raison et de la Foi. Un simple coup d'oeil sur cette histoire laisse apparaître, à l'observateur le moins averti, un accroissement irréversible de la connaissance positive au détriment de la croyance. Profaner le monde, afin de l'expliquer, de manière à mieux le dominer, telle aura été la vocation de l'Occident chrétien. L'Histoire a parfois son ironie. Traquant partout le mystère, les héritiers d'Athènes et de Jérusalem ont voulu transformer la Nature en Intelligence, le monde des choses en monde des signes. Le savoir donnant le pouvoir, et la puissance multipliant les moyens de connaître, cette transformation devait aboutir à une désacralisation totale de la réalité naturelle. Au prix d'une technique subtile de réduction de l'Être et d'une ascèse savante face à la Vie, l'homme a fini par faire de la Nature un pur objet, le monde étant de plus en plus considéré comme le très prosaïque terrain de ses prouesses technologiques. Evolution heurtée, comportant ça et là des arrêts, des bifurcations imprévues et quelques retours en arrière, mais qui n'a cessé de se préciser inexorablement, depuis les origines de notre civilisation intellectuelle jusqu'au nihilisme contemporain annoncé pathétiquement au siècle dernier par Nietzsche.

Il semble intéressant d'examiner le rôle qu'un philosophe comme Spinoza a pu jouer dans cette métamorphose.

On sait que Spinoza admet l'existence de deux voies parallèles vers le salut: la Foi et la Philosophie. La foi vise le Dieu-Personne, celui des Écritures, lequel s'est révélé aux hommes par sa Parole, perçue et transmise au moyen de la sensibilité et de l'imagination des Prophètes, ensuite connue 'immédiatement' par le Christ. La foi entraîne l'obéissance à l'Être. La philosophie, quant à elle, donne la connaissance de l'Être. A partir d'une seule idée vraie: la définition du Dieu-Substance, le Sage, échappant à la passivité et à l'inconscience de l'ignorant, 'ne cesse jamais d'être' mais devient au contraire 'conscient de lui-même, de Dieu et des choses'.

On rejoint ici les principes traditionnels de la *Gnose*. Les simples fidèles, les ignorants, voués à l'obéissance, ne pourront être sauvés que par la croyance, tandis que le salut par la connaissance complète, 'per ardua via', restera l'apanage de quelques-uns seulement.

Toutefois, la gnose spinoziste se complique du fait que, dans le système, la relation de l'homme au divin prend, non plus simplement deux formes distinctes, comme cela se produit dans la tradition dualiste du gnosticisme, où l'on oppose la 'gnôsis' à la 'pistis', mais comporte trois degrés successifs de perfection, chaque type de lien religieux correspondant à l'un des trois genres de connaissance: 'imaginatio, ratio, scientia intuitiva'.

D'après Spinoza, le prophétisme ne fait que traduire la phase historique du primat de l'imagination. Les 'primitifs' savent peu. Ils doivent beaucoup imaginer. Les Prophètes ayant perçu et enseigné le message divin par l'intermédiaire des images ou bien à l'aide de signes extérieurs, la connaissance prophétique reste 'extrinsèque' et inadéquate. Elle n'enveloppe, par elle-même, aucune certitude.

Le Christ, en revanche, personnifie le second moment de la religion: celui de l'universalité. En effet, dépassant le particularisme de l'Ancien Testament qui marqua l'Alliance de l'Eternel et du Peuple élu, le message du Christ s'adresse au genre humain tout entier. Jésus, d'après Spinoza, a été la bouche de Dieu ('Os Dei'). Lui seul a connu les choses d'une façon 'intrinsèque', 'vere et adaequate', puisque Dieu s'est révélé à lui directement, intellectuelle-ment, par la pensée pure, et non plus par le détour des représentations sen-sibles ou des figures imaginaires. Le Prophète était l'homme des apparences. Le Christ, qui a apporté au monde une vérité religieuse pour tous, au moyen des simples notions communes de la raison objective, est l'homme de l'essence. On comprend que, selon le témoignage de Tschirnhaus, Spinoza ait pu considérer Jésus-Christ comme 'le plus grand des philosophes'.[1]

Le troisième moment, celui de la connaissance concrète et singulière de l'essence de Dieu, défini comme substance, connaissance philosophique devant entraîner la libération et le salut des hommes, ouvre l'accès du sujet au savoir qui transfigure. Dans cette phase ultime, Dieu se révèle enfin dans sa vérité pure, par une coïncidence mystérieuse de l'intelligence humaine avec l'infinité de l'Être éternel.[2]

Cette révélation philosophique de l'essence-existence de Dieu, vécue personnellement et dont Spinoza témoigne à travers son oeuvre tout entière, appelle un certain nombre de remarques.

D'un point de vue général, on notera en premier lieu que le système spinoziste contient les germes d'une philosophie de l'histoire. Le strict parallélisme de la logique et de l'existence, attesté par la fameuse proposition 7 de la seconde partie de l'*Ethique*, où Spinoza pose explicitement l'identité de l'"ordo rerum' et de l'"ordo idearum', postule l'unité absolue de l'Être. Le monde réel et la conscience des hommes étant de même nature, on peut dire qu'il existe une cohérence de l'ensemble des déterminations, des pratiques et des significations humaines, constituant ce que l'on nommera plus tard la Raison historique. D'ailleurs, cette égalité ontologique absolue, cette identité rigide, sous l'effet de l'espèce de fatalité qui pousse les contraires à s'attirer réciproquement, ne pouvait manquer d'aboutir un jour à la mise en mouvement de la Substance éternelle infinie. Hegel, dont la dette envers Spinoza est immense, sera l'auteur de la 'chiquenaude' qui fera basculer l'éternité spinoziste dans l'historicité dialectique. Quoi qu'il en soit – et bien que le spinozisme puisse se définir essentiellement comme une philosophie de l'éternel – Spinoza, renouant par-delà les siècles et les cultures avec la tradition joachimite des trois âges de l'humanité,[3] vision eschatologique dont on retrouverait facilement des prolongements chez Vico ou chez Comte, envisage manifestement les grands traits d'un développement historique de la nature humaine. Trois moments sont perceptibles aux différents plans de son système: 1e sur le plan religieux, avec la triple révélation: prophétique, christologique et philosophique, 2e sur le plan politique, avec le cycle des régimes monarchique, aristocratique et démocratique, 3e sur le plan gnoséologique, avec les trois degrés de la connaissance.

Contrairement à ce qu'on pourrait croire, Spinoza ne fait pas disparaître entièrement le facteur temps de son univers. Et même, selon l'auteur de l'*Ethique*, toute conception du monde et des choses reflète certaines conditions historiques déterminées, collectives ou individuelles, cependant que les hommes *sont*, en un certain sens, ce qu'ils *pensent*. La vie et le savoir, les choses et les idées s'organisent à l'intérieur de trois moments essentiels qui, tout en traduisant une seule et même réalité fondamentale, se succèdent historiquement.

Au stade final du processus épistémologique et ontologique: la 'Scientia intuitiva' de l'*Ethique*, Spinoza a reçu une véritable illumination. Son entendement, vivifié par le désir de Dieu, 'Amor Dei intellectualis', a aperçu dans un éclair la signification de l'Être. La nature divine s'étant révélée à lui, Spinoza a voulu extérioriser et transmettre à ses lecteurs son expérience philosophico-religieuse. Pour cela, il a été conduit à 'prophétiser' à sa façon. Seulement, au lieu d'agir, à la manière des anciens Prophètes, par les voies affectives et émotionnelles de l''imaginatio', il s'est efforcé de démontrer objectivement son Dieu. Si bien que, chez lui, l'enseignement religieux anthropomorphique cède la place à un messianisme géométrique qui vise l'essence du Dieu-Substance. Il va sans dire que l'objet de ce nouveau prophétisme nous entraîne très loin du Dieu de la tradition monothéiste. L'Être suprême perd ici son visage. Transformé en pur concept, l'Absolu devient non-figuratif. Ne possédant plus aucune forme représentative déterminable, Dieu cesse alors nécessairement d'être sujet et toute transcendance s'évanouit. Un transfert du sacré commence à s'opérer avec Spinoza: 'Homo homini deus'. Le panthéisme spinoziste annonce la mort de Dieu et l'humanisme athée du dix-neuvième siècle. Bien entendu, du fait de son ontologie de l'individuel, l'auteur de l'*Ethique* ne pouvait encore considérer l'essence générique de l'homme que comme un simple être de raison.[4] Mais plus tard, lorsque l'anthropologie aura définitivement supplanté la théologie, rien ne pourra plus empêcher la divinisation du genre humain de s'accomplir dans les esprits. Ce sera l'avènement de l'humanitarisme abstrait et du totalitarisme sociolâtrique, jusqu'à ce que cette auto-déification de l'homme finisse par être dénoncée à son tour comme l'aliénation extrême, notamment par les adversaires de l'humanisme feuerbachien, considéré comme une simple sécularisation du christianisme. Stirner et Nietzsche ont bien vu que la nécessité de dépasser l'homme est une conséquence inéluctable de la mort de Dieu. Malheureusement, en attendant la venue du *Surhumain* nietzschéen[5] ou de l'*Unique* stirnérien,[6] c'est l'inhumain qui triomphe sur la terre. Orphelin métaphysique, depuis qu'il a perdu la figure et le regard de Dieu, l'homme cherche en vain son propre visage, dans un monde où il reste désormais tout seul avec le mal.

Spinoza, quant à lui, parvient à rapporter notre connaissance naturelle à Dieu, la Nature et Dieu étant confondus. En effet, la compréhension de l'essence de Dieu par la lumière naturelle lui semble tout aussi 'divine' que la révélation dite surnaturelle, 'puisque c'est la nature de Dieu en tant que nous en participons ("quatenus de ea participamus") et les décrets divins qui nous la dictent en quelque sorte'.[7]

Dieu et la Nature sont identiques. On peut en déduire que tout ce qui existe dans la nature est divin. Or, quoi de plus divin que l'Entendement?[8]

Par conséquent, l'entendement humain possède, chez Spinoza, en plus de sa valeur formelle, instrumentale et logique, un contenu ontologique objectif qui permet à l'esprit de l'homme de 'reproduire parfaitement la Nature ('maxime referet Naturam'), puisqu'il existe un Être dont l'essence objective est aussi la cause de toutes nos représentations, ce qui permet à notre connaissance de posséder objectivement l'essence, l'ordre et l'unité de la Nature'.[9]

Ainsi, à la suite des Prophètes et du Christ, le Philosophe, homme de l'entendement, est appelé à devenir l'agent d'une forme nouvelle de révélation religieuse. Mais, cette fois, Dieu ne se révèlera pas lui-même aux hommes, s'adressant à eux en personne ou leur envoyant son fils pour annoncer son Royaume, comme ce fut le cas au temps des Prophètes, lors de l'ancienne Alliance, ou à l'époque de Jésus. Désormais, le rapport de Dieu et des hommes est renversé. La révélation philosophique, issue de la connaissance du troisième genre, procède de la seule force de l'entendement humain ('potentia intellectus'), lequel participe de l'infini. Pur objet d'une révélation transcendante dans le théisme judéo-chrétien, l'homme en devient ici au contraire le sujet actif, grâce au pouvoir de sa pensée.

Une autre incarnation du Verbe – incarnation purement intellectuelle, si l'on peut dire – va s'accomplir par le seul effet de la puissance de l'entendement des hommes. La Religion se trouve alors dépossédée au profit de la Philosophie, appelée désormais à dévoiler, par ses propres ressources, en plus de la réalité essentielle du monde, le chemin de la béatitude. C'est par le Philosophe que Dieu existe dans sa vérité. Selon les conceptions chrétiennes, le Verbe s'est fait chair pour sauver la Nature corrompue par le péché. Dans le spinozisme, l'homme spirituel devra naître de l'homme charnel, sans aucun appui extérieur. La Nature ne sera sauvée que par la Nature, parce que la Nature est Dieu.

Etrange destin que celui de Spinoza. Le plus religieux des penseurs occidentaux devait réaliser malgré lui l'athéisme des temps modernes. Cherchant à diviniser la Nature, il n'a pu que naturaliser Dieu. Posant l'identité du savoir et de la béatitude, il allait ouvrir la porte à la déification de l'intelligence, devenue fin en soi.

NOTES

1 Cf. Charles Appuhn, *Spinoza*, Paris, Delpeuch, 1927, p. 100.
2 *Ethique*, V. 23: 'Amor Dei intellectualis, qui ex tertio genere oritur, est aeternus'.
3 Joachim de Flore, *Concordia*, Livre V, ch. 48: 'Le premier temps a été celui de la connaissance, le second celui de la sagesse, le troisième celui de la pleine intelligence ... Le premier âge se rapporte donc au Père qui est l'auteur de toutes choses, le second au Fils qui a daigné revêtir notre limon, le troisième âge sera l'âge du Saint-Esprit, dont l'Apôtre dit: *Là où est l'esprit du Seigneur, là est la liberté.*'
4 Cf. *Ethique*, II, 40, scolie 1.
5 Cf. *Zarathoustra*, Prologue, 3, 4, tr. H. Albert, Paris, Mercure de France, 1948: 'Je vous enseigne le Surhumain. L'homme est quelque chose qui doit être surmonté. ... Le Surhumain est le sens de la terre. ... Ce qu'il y a de grand dans l'homme, c'est qu'il est un pont et non un but: ce que l'on peut aimer en l'homme, c'est qu'il est un *passage* et un *déclin*.'
6 Cf. *L'Unique et sa propriété*, tr. Reclaire, Paris, J. J. Pauvert, 1960, 2e partie: *Moi*: 'A l'aube des temps nouveaux se dresse l'Homme-Dieu. A leur déclin, le Dieu seul se sera-t-il évanoui et l'Homme-Dieu peut-il vraiment mourir si le Dieu seul meurt en lui? On ne s'est pas posé cette question; on a cru avoir tout fait lorsqu'on eut de nos jours victorieusement mené à bout l'oeuvre de lumière et vaincu le Dieu; on ne remarqua pas que l'Homme n'a tué le Dieu que pour devenir à son tour *le seul Dieu qui règne dans les cieux*. L'*au-delà extérieur* est balayé et l'oeuvre colossale de la philosophie est accomplie; mais l'*au-delà intérieur* est devenu un nouveau Ciel et nous appelle à de nouveaux assauts: le Dieu a dû faire place à l'Homme et non à Nous. Comment pouvez-vous croire

que l'Homme-Dieu soit mort, aussi longtemps qu'en lui, outre le Dieu, l'Homme ne sera pas mort aussi ?'

7 *Tractatus theologico-politicus*, ch. I.
8 Cf. *Ethique*, V, 36.
9 *Tractatus de Intellectus Emendatione*, 99.

ENGLISH SUMMARY: SPINOZA AND PHILOSOPHICAL REVELATION

Fired by thirst for truth and by the search for eternal beatitude, Spinoza worked out a religious philosophy closely linked to his theory of knowledge and his ontology. Spinozism, coming after prophetic and messianic revelation, proposes a third form of revelation, the philosopher being the one true intercessor with the Absolute, in a pantheistic system in which traditional religious concepts no longer have their accepted meanings.

26 Spinozism and Japan

Hiroshi Saito, Kanagawa

C. Gebhardt says: 'hundert Jahre nach seinem Tode finden wir wirkliches Verständnis für seine Lehre in der europäischen Welt'.[1] But it is really 'wirkliches Verständnis für seine Lehre'? If it is really so, what is the 'wirkliches Verständnis für seine Lehre in der europäischen Welt'? And is there any possibility to find 'wirkliches Verständnis für seine Lehre in der anderen – nicht-europäischen – Welt'?

In this paper I dare to propose a new horizon from which it will be able to draw a hidden facet of Spinoza's philosophy, for Spinozism has to unfold itself by encountering not only the European world, which could not accept Spinozism for about a century after his death, but also the non-European world. Re-examination of Spinozism from a non-European viewpoint, for example through a Japanese prisma, will probably develop a phase of Spinozistic studies different from that of European ones.

I think that the situation of Japanese Spinozistic studies after the Second World War has been one of stepping into the original phase where Spinozism has been digested in the Japanese spiritual climate, while the Spinozistic studies in Japan in the early stage had been mainly carried out by importing Spinozistic studies from Europe as such. Now if we are aware that Spinozism has been unfolded manifoldly in accordance with encountering different worlds, namely European and non-European, it may be said that Spinozism should be understood as a philosophy which has concealed its true structure in depth. In other words Spinozism has not yet revealed its real and concrete structure by encountering only the European world. The system of Spinozism hides such diversified elements and different streams of thought that it would reveal itself only by a worldwide encounter.

Thus in order to deepen understanding of the philosophy of Spinoza I think that it would be indispensable to ask from outside Europe how Spinozism has been accepted as a leading philosophy in the main philosophical stream of the modern European world against strong censure of the *atheistic* aspects of Spinozism. To ask anticipates an answer. Asking about the reconciliation of Spinozism with the European world presupposes already a certain answer, from which we can expect the conspicuous figure of Spinozism in the light of a non-European viewpoint.

442

I

In order to clarify the effects of Spinozism on the European world I dare to simplify the development of Spinozism by reviewing the history of modern philosophy. It is a historical fact that it took almost a century after his death before Spinoza's philosophy was accepted by Europe.[2] What prevented his acceptance? He was not a lonely stranger wandering about the European world. Nevertheless, it seems to me that a deep gulf lies between Spinoza and the philosophical world around him. It was at the end of the eighteenth century that Spinoza was taken into the mainstream of modern European philosophy that began with the philosophy of Descartes and Leibniz and develops into German idealism. It might be said that a drastic change has been produced in the attitude toward the philosophy of Spinoza since the end of the eighteenth century.

Gebhardt pointed out,

Nichts ist deshalb unrichtiger als die oft gehörte Behauptung, während der ersten achtzig Jahre des achtzehnten Jahrhunderts sei Spinoza *vergessen und unbeachtet gewesen*. Spinoza war niemals weniger vergessen als während der Zeit, da sein Name mit Schimpf und Schande bedeckt war und die Majorität nur ein verächtliches Lächeln für seine Lehre hatte.[3]

On the other hand we cannot simply judge that such a disgraceful and insulting attitude toward Spinoza was due directly to misunderstanding or misreading his works. The acceptance of Spinoza was impossible without his reconciliation with the European world. In other words the European world changed itself through encountering the philosophy of Spinoza, and this caused the drastic change of attitude toward the philosophy of Spinoza.

What, however, caused this change? It was not the philosophical world that gave 'professional and theological obloquy' to Spinoza as the author of the *Tractatus Theologico-Politicus* and *Ethica*, etc. At that time his works were thought of as typically atheistic and godless, and the word 'Spinozistic' produced only a negative response. We have to pay attention to the fact that the European philosophical world which accepted Spinoza had already become tolerant and Spinozistic, namely atheistic, within about a century.

Accordingly the acceptance of the philosophy of Spinoza at the end of the eighteenth century in Europe would not have happened unless the European world had itself experienced a fundamental change in the spiritual field. Europe accepted the philosophy of Spinoza in the self-denying process, which provided good soil for the seed of Spinozism to fall on. Under this complexity the philosophy of Spinoza was identified with the mainstream of modern European philosophy, and simultaneously his contradiction to the traditional

443

philosophy of Europe became evident. There is a continuity and at the same time a discontinuity between the philosophy of Spinoza and the European world. Therefore the assumption that there lies a lineal continuation in the development of philosophy from Descartes and Spinoza to Leibniz in the seventeenth century is only one of the possible ways of approaching Spinoza, though it has grown almost into an established theory. Since the Spinoza renaissance at the end of the eighteenth century it has been taken for granted that the philosophy of Spinoza is just such a lineal continuation.

But the ground for this assumption must be closely examined. Before the European world encountered the philosophy of Spinoza, he himself had encountered European philosophy. By encountering the European world the philosophy of Spinoza became invested with the air of modern philosophy which had penetrated seventeenth-century Europe. From then on Spinoza had to reconcile himself to the thoughts which dominated the philosophical world with which he began to communicate. Spinozism has been regarded by many writers as the logical development of Cartesian philosophy; however, it was not with Cartesian philosophy that he became familiar at the outset.

The philosophic literature which had nourished the young mind of Spinoza was not philosophy in Latin, but Hebrew philosophic literature. His nascent philosophic doubt arose as reaction to the philosophy which he read in Hebrew,[4] as we shall see. Accordingly we do not argue that Spinozism should be represented as reflecting or reproducing the mystical theosophy of the Kabbalah, or the ideas of Maimonides and other medieval Jewish philosophers, or the revived Platonism of Giordano Bruno and other writers of the fifteenth and sixteenth centuries.[5]

It is not an easy task to trace the thoughts which influenced him to present the philosophy of Spinoza as a systematic whole. In the history of Spinozistic studies we can reckon up a variety of contradictory epithets which are used to describe the characteristics of his philosophy. On this point Hallett writes:

> Probably no philosopher of repute has been worse served by his
> expositors and commentators than Spinoza. Monist, pantheist, atheist,
> acosmist, ethical nihilist, mechanist, mystic, and even dialectical
> materialist, are among the epithets more or less commonly used to
> describe and pigeon-hole a doctrine which, nevertheless, though
> neglected, misinterpreted, and deplored has never been despised as a
> mere curiosity of philosophical history.

Are such diversities of interpretation supposed to depend solely on the inconsistencies within the philosophy of Spinoza or on misreading his system? We may rather insist that the possibility of various interpretations has been concealed deeply in the metaphysics of Spinoza. In other words, the metaphysics of Spinoza survives, and can only survive, as a true *philosophia perennis*, as the catalyst of scepsis and schism.[6]

Though the philosophy of Spinoza itself is to be thought such a meta-physics as *philosophia perennis* that survives in itself, the historical studies on the system of Spinoza have been destined to a path which leads to the deep gulf almost impossible to bridge and where Spinozism finds itself on the other side.

II

How is it possible to get to a proper and thorough appreciation of the philosophy of Spinoza? What is the originality of his philosophy? Is it possible to discern the purely Spinozistic among the full variety of inter-pretations? It is true that much ingenuity has been spent, perhaps we might say misspent, in tracing the supposed 'sources' of Spinozism in the historical studies of his philosophy:[7] and of course, as Caird further suggests, it is to be considered that the originality of a philosophical writer is not to be determined simply by the measure in which his ideas are traceable to earlier sources, or by the suggestions he has caught up from other minds.[8] The necessary thing is not to scrutinize the complex origin of his system but to try to change the point of view which has dominated many writers for these three hundred years. According to that point of view the system of Spinoza played an important and indispensable part in the formation of the mainstream of European philosophy, namely 'la route royale de la philosophie'.

What is the 'route royale de la philosophie'? I think it becomes clear when we show the relationship of the philosophy of Spinoza with that of the European world, which many writers used to decide his position in European philosophy. For instance, Brunschvicg argues, 'c'est de Kant même, que surgissent, aux dernières années du XVIIIᵉ siècle, le rajeunissement et le renouvellement du rationalisme de l'Ethique.'[9] What enables him to presume that Spinozism casts its shadow on Kantian criticism? If any influence of Spinozistic philosophy is traceable in the system of Kant, he must have accepted it unconsciously, for it was not from Kant but in the circles of the post-Kantian idealists that the tide of Spinoza's renaissance occurred, and moreover, Kant himself did not appreciate the philosophy of Spinoza.

Brunschvicg, by taking the system of Spinoza as a centre for the under-standing of the metaphysical movement which starts with the revolution of Cartesian philosophy and ends in the system of Leibniz's *Theodicy*, gives grounds for the presumption that Spinoza's philosophy survived in Kantian criticism.[10] He continues, 'la foi traditionelle d'un Pascal, le rationalisme intégral d'un Spinoza, se rapprochent dans la doctrine de Leibniz, et se réconcilient.'[11] In like manner the system of Leibniz is considered as an integration of full variety of thoughts in the seventeenth century. The signi-ficance of Spinozism in the 'route royale' of European philosophy is to be recognized not only in the logical development of Cartesian philosophy but

445

also in the religious continuity which is deeply rooted in the ideas of European history.

It is not so difficult to discern a similar interpretation that places the system of Spinoza in the 'route royale' of modern European philosophy. For instance, Gebhardt says 'seine [Spinoza] Philosophie wurde die Seele der großen spekulativen Systeme, die in Deutschland auf dem Boden des kantischen Kritizismus entstanden. Fichte, Schelling, Schleiermacher, Hegel . . . alle waren sie Schüler Spinozas.[12] And we may suppose this as a typical presumption hidden in the interpretation of Spinoza's philosophy, a presumption which we can, more or less, trace in modern philosophical history, and which has been strongly taken for granted as the definite course of the philosophical development in modern Europe. This is what Brunschvicg means by the 'route royale de la philosophie'.

But we cannot fail to observe that there is hidden a formula or hypothesis from which this conventional interpretation in regard to Spinozism has arisen. If we examine the conventional judgment that there is one unitary development in European philosophy from Descartes through Spinoza and Leibniz to Kant, by standing on the point that the metaphysical background of Spinoza is completely different from that of Descartes, Leibniz and Kant, whose position in the philosophical history has already become definite, then a different perspective of Spinoza's philosophy will open before us.

It might be said, as Roth pointed out, that Descartes and Spinoza represent two distinct poles of thought, and the essential conflict between Descartes and Spinoza is found already clearly and definitely developed in the *Guide for the Perplexed* by Maimonides. But to gain the proper appreciation we have had to wait until the peculiar position of Spinoza in the history of European thought was acknowledged by readers. Certainly we cannot understand the historical place of a thinker unless we can determine not only his 'reading but also his 'readers'.[13] According to Roth, we have to see in the basis of Spinoza's system a monistic metaphysic which is a direct derivative of the philosophy of Maimonides.[14]

We may add one more thing in regard to the problems from which Spinoza began to philosophize. The general bearing of his system becomes more intelligible when we give a close consideration to what the nascent philosophic doubt for him was, and how different the metaphysic background of young Spinoza was from that of Descartes. In respect of that there have been built various hypotheses in order to explain the breaking with the Synagogue and the genesis of Spinoza's philosophy; Révah makes a profound contribution in deepening the conclusion which Gebhardt has built up.[15]

We cannot deny, of course, the coincidence of terminology between both philosophers and a logical development from Descartes to Spinoza; nevertheless, this fact does not provide the key for demonstrating that a young Spinoza awoke in the spiritual climate of Cartesian philosophy. At the same time

Révah, excluding a plausible explanation that Spinoza had experienced a Christian phase in the development of his philosophy, writes: 'Spinoza s'est éveillé à la réflexion philosophique sous l'influence du déisme de certains Marranes d'Amsterdam, Uriel da Costa et surtout Juan de Prado.' And Prado was the person who was excommunicated from the Synagogue in 1657 about a year after Spinoza's excommunication. Révah continues further that 'le déisme des hétérodoxes sefardim, variété du déisme européen XVIIᵉ siècle, avait fourni à Spinoza le climat où devait s'opérer son propre développement spirituel.'[16]

In the light of the foregoing we can conclude that Spinozism comprises in the depth of its system the esoteric field of oriental wisdom, with which he was familiar: He started his philosophy in a climate of outlandish heresy, and not from the atmosphere of Cartesian philosophy. Thus a considerable emphasis is to be laid upon the metaphysical background with which his philosophy started out, while Descartes began with his philosophy from the Christian tradition, even though we might say that 'die neuzeitliche Philosophie von Descartes an hat diesen christlichen Gott ja negiert'. It is impossible, or at least dubious, to assert that Spinozism originated under Christian influence.

Schulz suggests a remarkable point in regard to the 'ganze neuzeitliche Metaphysik' in *Der Gott der neuzeitlichen Metaphysik*. He says:

In der Tat: die ganze neuzeitliche Metaphysik entstammt dem Christentum. Sie hat dankbar, sich in ihrer geschichtlichen Herkunft erkennend, dies Erbe anzuerkennen. Aber – und dies ist die andere Seite – die ganze neuzeitliche Metaphysik entspringt dem Christentum, indem sie es zu Ende denkt. Die neuzeitliche Metaphysik beginnt mit dem Abschied nehmenden Aufstand gegen den christlichen Gott.[17]

In this sense it is also problematic to say that 'Spinozismus beginnt mit dem Abschied nehmenden Aufstand gegen den christlichen Gott', because Spinoza began his philosophy independent of the influence of Christianity. In spite of the proposition's separation from the Christian tradition Descartes was destined to philosophize God as the last ground for metaphysical certainty of scientific knowledge. He could not thoroughly separate himself from the Christian tradition where God as a creator, a governor, a law-giver, acts by will and design. Supposing two kinds of *substantia*, *infinita* and *finita*, he tried to explain the 'Verhältnis von Gott und Welt', and for the sake of this attitude he could not get out of the thick wall of Christian belief.

On the other hand, as Schulz says, 'Von Spinoza her gesehen stellt die christliche Lehre den unsinnigen Versuch dar, Gott einerseits als allmächtig anzusetzen und anderseits ihm gegenüber den Menschen als ein Wesen zu bestimmen, das bei aller Abhängigkeit doch relativ selbständig ist.'[18] So far as the 'Verhältnis von Gott und Welt' is concerned, the break between Descartes and Spinoza, namely the discontinuity between the 'route royale de la philosophie' and Spinoza, is too deep and definite to explain them consistently. Even though we can assert with Schulz that 'die neuzeitliche Philosophie von Descartes an hat diesen christlichen Gott ja negiert', still something discontinuous, which occupies a decisive meaning in dealing with the 'Verhältnis von Gott und Welt', is concealed between both systems.[19] I do agree with Heidegger, of course, that Cartesian philosophy comprises 'eine zu innerst gründende Verwandtschaft', but it seems impossible to make a proper room for Spinoza's system in this 'Verwandtschaft' between Descartes and Heidegger.

What is, then, this negative phase of Spinoza's philosophy? For the sake of this negative phase Spinoza had to be excluded from the 'route royale de la philosophie' as a godless person declaring 'mauvaises opinions' and 'horribles hérésies'.[20] This was his encounter with the European world.

Our consideration is to be focused upon the heresy of Spinoza, which has given rise to profuse characterizing of Spinoza's God.

III

In the light of the foregoing it becomes clear that the deepest concern in the development of modern philosophy was how to reconcile its own system with the Christian God. For this reason the connection drawn between Descartes and Spinoza can similarly be traceable in the philosophical development from Spinoza to Leibniz.

To what extent did Leibniz accept the monistic philosophy of Spinoza, including its outlandish heresy? The following lines in a letter sent from Leibniz to l'Abbé Nicaise are suggestive of how he understood the relation between Descartes and Spinoza and its development. He writes:

> il s'ensuit qu'il n'y a ni choix ni providence: que ce qui n'arrive point, est impossible, et que ce qui arrive, est nécessaire. Justement comme Hobbes et Spinoza le disent en termes plus clairs. Aussi peut-on dire, que Spinoza n'a fait que cultiver certaines semences de la Philosophie de M. Descartes, de sorte que je crois qu'il importe effectivement pour la Religion, et pour la piété, que cette philosophie soit châtiée par le retranchement des erreurs qui sont mêlées avec la vérité.[21]

As for the logical connection, in the systems of both Spinoza and Leibniz much similarity has been pointed out. In fact it is rather true to say that, in spite of a deep concern in the system of Spinoza, Leibniz himself does not seem to have appreciated Spinozistic philosophy so far as we can judge from his expressed attitude upon Spinozism. He writes to Bourget:

> c'est justement par ces Monades que le Spinozisme est détruit. Car il y a autant de substances véritables, en pour ainsi dire, de miroirs vivans de l'Univers toujours subsistans, ou d'Univers concentrés, qu'il y a de Monades, au lieu que, selon Spinoza, il n'y a qu'une seule substance. Il

auroit raison, s'il n'y avoit de Monades; et alors tout, hors de Dieu, seroit passager et s'evanouiroit en simples accidens ou modifications, puisqu'il n'y auroit point la base des substances dans les choses, laquelle consiste dans l'existence de Monades.[22]

Now what is that which Leibniz had to 'détruire' in the system of Spinoza, if the logical development can be precisely recognized in both systems, namely one-substance doctrine and monadology? As we have already insisted, the prevailing philosophical problem since Descartes in modern Europe was how to reconcile the traditional Christian God with the philosophers' God inside their own system. By identifying God with nature in the system, Spinoza's God differs conspicuously from the God of other philosophers; by this is meant his denial of the traditional God.

Leibniz's definition of a 'necessary being', or *Ens a se*, is, according to Parkinson, the same as what Spinoza calls *causa sui*, on the definition of which he bases his first proof of the existence of God in the *Ethics*. It can be further pointed out that no doubt Leibniz follows Spinoza in what he says about the eternity of God. For Leibniz, as for Spinoza, eternity has nothing to do with duration at all but differs from it in nature.[23] But what is important is that any similarity between them is chiefly confined to the logical treatment of God: as Russell insists keenly, Leibniz fell into Spinozism whenever he allowed himself to be logical.[24] Again it is even logically inappropriate to take Spinoza in the main philosophical stream from Descartes through Leibniz to Kant, without taking into account the religious backgrounds which gave the decisive influence, positive or negative, to the growth of each system. In fact, the great difference between Spinoza and Leibniz is that Leibniz emphatically reaffirms the doctrine of final causes,[25] which proves Leibniz's concept of God to be strongly bound up with traditional belief.

The origin of the concept of Spinoza's God, however, belongs to his exotic background wherein varieties of heresy may originate. The fundamental idea of Spinoza's metaphysics manifests itself in the principle *Deus est natura*, or *Deus sive natura*, with which Spinozistic concepts are thoroughly imbued. The characteristic conceptions such as freedom, necessity, causality, duration, eternity, finite and infinite, etc., although all had been borrowed from the traditional terminology of European philosophy, should be grasped under the principle of *Deus sive natura*. Such treatment of God, namely the idea of his depersonalized God as it were, is impossible to find at least in the traditional beliefs of Christianity.

Hence it follows that rationalism in the Spinozistic system, in so far as concerning the philosophical idea of God, is far from that of the Cartesian and Leibnizian systems which shaped themselves inside the framework of traditional belief. The distance which existed not on the cogency of their logical form but in their religious bearings has produced different figures of rationalism. Rationalism in a sense is the attempt to give rational grounds for religious belief. In this respect we can declare that rationalism itself consists in presupposing the relation between God and man, wherein the intuitive faculty of man to grasp the existence of God is regarded as lying in himself. It is impossible to seek grounds for rationalism in itself, since it is based only on an irrational 'Spannung von Gott und Mensch'. Spinozistic rationalism, presupposing its own relation between God and man, consequently derives its direction independent from other rationalistic systems. In this sense Wolfson's insistence is true: the *Ethics* is not a communication to the world; it is Spinoza's communication with himself.

The outstanding symptom of the rationalistic system of Spinoza can be observed most conspicuously in his theory of affects. As Fromm pointed out, Spinoza saw that affects, like thought, can be *both* rational and irrational and that the full development of man requires the rational evolution of both thought and affect. It is unthinkable for Spinoza to split man's thinking and feeling, since his theory of affects is the result of his principle of the homogeneity of nature.[26] Thus Spinozistic rationalism develops a different scope of knowledge which implies some heterogeneous elements incompatible with the knowledge of modern science.

The tension of God and man, which was of great concern to the philosophers related to the Christian tradition, disappears in the Spinozistic system through man's intellectual love of God, which is nothing but a rational affect, in so far as it belongs to man. According to Spinoza, the intellectual love of the mind toward God is that very love of God whereby God loves Himself, not in so far as He is infinite, but in so far as He can be explained through the essence of the human mind regarded under the form of eternity; in other words, the intellectual love of the mind toward God is part of the infinite love wherewith God loves Himself.[27]

Hence it follows that God, in so far as He loves Himself, loves man, and consequently, that the love of God toward man, and the intellectual love of the mind toward God, are identical.[28]

Now it becomes clear from what has been quoted that the depersonalized concept of God in the Spinozistic system is rooted in the world independent from Christian tradition: he deals with the relation between God and man in the non-Christian field. Accordingly if we compare two rationalistic systems such as Spinozistic and Leibnizian, regarded as based on the independent metaphysical world, then however we may string them together as unitary rationalism in the logical development, still we cannot but discern the split between them in the depth of their religious consciousness.

Now we proceed to the problem of godlessness in the Spinozistic system, by examining whether he was really godless or God-intoxicated, as Novalis declared. Spinoza's theology might be compared to that of Aristotle, with its conception of an impersonal deity devoid of will and acting by necessity, against which medieval thinkers constantly argued. But the similarity recognized in both theologies is never to be thought of only as a return to Aristotle or as applying his impersonal unmoved mover. Indeed Spinozism marked a radical departure from the traditional theologies of the three revealed religions – Judaism, Christianity and Mohammedanism. In the traditional conceptions of God in these three religions, however differently stated, there was one common element which was considered essential. It was the element of the personality of God, by which was meant the existence of a certain reciprocal relation between the conduct of man toward God and the conduct of God toward man.[29]

It is true that Spinoza himself was not fully conscious of his own radical departure and that not only the common people but also the learned accused him as a horrible atheist; nevertheless he never considered accommodating himself to the insulting oppositions against him. He was concerned most profoundly in concentrating upon the systematic and yet endless pursuit of the study of his own philosophy, not upon reconciling himself with various untrue accusations. Despite his eager desire that philosophy should be pacifying in its essence, the existence of his philosophy itself had stirred up not only curiosity but also bitter obloquy against him in almost every Christian nation. Nowadays, however, it has been taken for granted as a fixed interpretation of his philosophy that Spinozism occupies an important role in developing the unitary stream of European philosophy.

Hence we may declare that the European world, by accepting Spinoza's philosophy which, in fact, it had continuously been refusing, was forced to realize how profound and radical the Spinozistic departure from European tradition had been. This is the fatal course through which the European world has progressed in encountering Spinoza's philosophy, the existence of which always deprived the European world of its religious background, and on the basis of which many varieties of thought have been developed. Keen accusation and theological obloquy had to be brought against Spinozism because of the urgent need of the European world to protect itself against dangerous heresy.

According to the fixed, established interpretation, as it were, which might be said to be dominant in Japanese Spinozistic studies, a long study of Spinoza has reached the theory that there is a unitary development from Descartes through Spinoza and Leibniz to German idealism; in other words that Spinozism *is* to be reconciled with the 'route royale de la philosophie'. Against this I feel a little hesitation: this quasi-fixed interpretation of placing Spinozism into the mainstream of European philosophy is nothing but a result of reconciliation between the Spinozistic heresy and Christianity in the spiritual climate of modern Europe. Without having repeated such reconciliations Spinozism would not have unfolded itself in the development of European philosophy any longer. In spite of it, here should be emphasized that

451

such a reconciliation must be a phenomenon typical of the European world whose cultural unity is based upon Christianity. In other words such reconciliations are necessary because they have occurred inside the realm of the Christian world.

Here in concluding this paper we have to think of the fact that Spinoza was excluded from the European world because of his heresy, not only during his lifetime but also for more than a century after his death, and after that his philosophy has revived as admirable and God-intoxicated in the same European world where he was branded as one of the most wicked atheists. This means the hermeneutic revolution in philosophical history and a drastic change of attitude towards Spinozism in the modern European world. Nevertheless this hermeneutic revolution is a result of reconciling Spinoza's philosophy to the European world in the development of philosophical studies. This has made it clear that Spinozism conceals something contradictory to the philosophical tradition of Europe which goes back to Christianity, namely the background of the European religious tradition.

Through the hermeneutic revolution of Spinozism there have clearly emerged two faces of Spinoza, and at the same time two contradictory attitudes toward Spinozism have come into the self-consciousness in the development of modern European philosophy.

What is contradictory to the European tradition in Spinoza's philosophy is not always contradictory to the non-European world. Hence one may assert that although Spinozism had been brought up in the European world, nevertheless it is a philosophy which contains something transcending the boundary of Europe.

It is worthwhile to pay attention to the fact that the strong censure of Spinozistic atheism raised in Europe has disappeared in accordance with a philosophical movement of philosophizing without God, which is clearly traceable in the development of modern European thought from Descartes and Leibniz through German idealism to Heidegger. This movement made it possible to reconcile Spinozism to the European world, but this movement, I might say, developed fundamentally without having to do with the religiosity of Spinoza's philosophy. Spinoza's God had already intended for something trans-European which could call forth a sincere response from the Japanese religious and philosophical background.

If Spinozism had been read from the non-European standpoint, a characteristic proposition, *Deus sive natura*, would never have been inconsistent with Spinoza as a God-intoxicated philosopher. Now in Japan one may expect to read Spinozism in a different context from the European world whose cultural background is deeply characterized with Christianity. These hermeneutic considerations proposed here are precisely those which have been developed according to a non-European point of view, namely through the encounter between Spinozism and Japan.

NOTES

1 Gebhardt, *Die Lehre Spinozas*, auf Grund des Nachlasses von J. Freudenthal, 1927, S. 209.
2 Während Spinoza so durch Mendelssohn, Lessing, Jacobi, Goethe und Herder aus dem Grabe befreit wurde, und der so oft für tot erklärte Denker von neuem ein Lebendiger unter Lebenden dastand, erhob sich seine Lehre zu einer Stellung von weltgeschichtlicher Bedeutung. Der *unverschämte, elende, gottlose Spinoza* wurde nun *der heilige, der göttliche Spinoza*. Verehrung schlechthin wurde seinem Denken dargebracht (J. Freudenthal, *Spinoza Leben und Lehre*, Zweiter Teil, bearbeitet von C. Gebhardt, S. 236).
   And L. Brunschvicg says also: l'*Éthique* de Spinoza eut la réputation d'une machine de guerre contre les dogmes officiels. Aujourd'hui nous y verrions tout autre chose . . . l'idéal de la vérité philosophique', *Spinoza et ses contemporains*, Paris, 1951, p. 281.
3 Gebhardt, *op. cit.*, S. 217.
4 See H. A. Wolfson, *The Philosophy of Spinoza*, New York, 1970, p. 13.
5 See John Caird, *Spinoza*, Philadelphia, 1888, pp. 36f.
6 Hallett continues: 'It is to this essentially catalytic character that we may attribute the persistence of the broad appeal of Spinozism after nearly three hundred years of professional neglect and theological obloquy' (H. F. Hallett, *Creation, Emanation and Salvation*, The Hague, 1962, preface).
7 Caird, *op. cit.*, p. 36.
8 *Ibid.*, p. 37.
9 Brunschvicg, *op. cit.*, p. 307.
10 *Ibid.*, p. 308.
11 *Ibid.*
12 Gebhardt, *op. cit.*, S. 236.
13 See Leon Roth, *Spinoza, Descartes and Maimonides*, New York, 1963, pp. 143f.
14 Cf. *ibid.*, p. 145.
15 Cf. I. S. Révah, *Spinoza et Juan de Prado*, Paris, 1959, pp. 11f.
16 *Ibid.*, p. 53.
17 W. Schulz, *Der Gott der neuzeitlichen Metaphysik*, Neske, 1959, S. 55.
18 *Ibid.*, S. 66.
19 Schulz points out:

Vergleichen wir die Inhalte der Philosophie Descartes mit den Inhalten der Philosophie Heideggers, so könnte ein solcher Versuch nur künstlich und wenig überzeugend ausfallen. Achten wir dagegen auf das *Grundgeschehen*, das die Philosophie beider Denker darstellt, dann zeigt sich eine zu innerst gründende Verwandschaft. Descartes und Heidegger wollen beide den Menschen als Wesen der Endlichkeit erweisen. Descartes geht dabei so vor, dass er in einem ersten Schritt die Welt durch seinen methodischen Zweifel fraglich macht, dabei auf das Ich stösst, und erst in einem zweiten Schritt dieses Ich als endliches herausstellt, indem er es abhebt gegen den vollkommenen Gott. Heidegger dagegen vollzieht den Nachweis der

Endlichkeit des Daseins, indem er zeigt, dass das Dasein im Nichts steht (*ibid.*, S. 50).

20 These words are read in the sentence of Spinoza's excommunication from the Synagogue in Amsterdam. It was on 27 July 1656, when he was twenty-four years old.

21 G. W. Leibniz, *Opera Philosophica Omnia*, J. E. Erdmann, Scientia Aalen, 1959, S. 139.

22 *Ibid.*, S. 720.

23 G. H. R. Parkinson, *Logic and Reality in Leibniz's Metaphysics*, London, 1965, pp. 77ff.

24 B. Russell, *A Critical Exposition of the Philosophy of Leibniz*, London, 1975, p. vii.

25 Cf. R. G. Collingwood, *The Idea of Nature*, London, 1965, p. 110.

26 Erich Fromm, *Sigmund Freud's Mission*, London, 1957, p. 7.

27 B. Spinoza, *Ethica*, V, prop. 36 (trans. by Elwes, London, 1883).

28 *Ibid.*, V, corol. prop. 36.

29 Cf. H. A. Wolfson, *op. cit.*, pp. 346ff.

27 La Méthode et le donné

Reiko Shimizu, Tokyo

I

Le *Tractatus de Intellectus Emendatione* (que nous appellerons désormais la *Réforme*), seul écrit où Spinoza parle de la méthode, est peu volumineux; il n'occupe que trente-six pages dans ses *Oeuvres Complètes* éditées par C. Gebhardt à Heidelberg.[1] Du point de vue de sa structure, en tête se place une introduction qu'on appelle couramment 'préliminaire moral' où il est question du but général de la philosophie. Ensuite viennent trois règles de la vie quotidienne; Spinoza semble tenir compte de la 'Morale provisoire' cartésienne. Et puis une classification et un examen de plusieurs modes de connaissance, dont on trouve d'équivalents dans deux autres de ses ouvrages aussi (le *Court Traité*[2] et l'*Ethique*)[3], déterminent quel est le meilleur. Ce n'est qu'après toutes ces démarches préalables qu'il aborde enfin le problème de la méthode. Malgré l'importante différence du *Court Traité* à la *Réforme*, quant à la description et à l'appréciation de divers modes de connaissance, il nous suffira, pour le moment, de faire deux remarques. Premièrement la *Réforme* analyse en détail et recommande la connaissance discursive ou raisonnement, second genre de connaissance dans l'*Ethique*, qui était presque ignorée dans le *Court Traité*, jugée inutile à l'union ('Vereeninginge') avec l'extérieur à cause de son caractère indirect. Deuxièmement la meilleure connaissance, qui, dans le *Court Traité*, n'était rien d'autre que l'intuition, capable de l'union et de la jouissance ('Genietinge'), cumule, dans la *Réforme*, la fonction de la déduction aussi bien que celle de l'intuition, tout comme l''intellectus' dans les 'Regulae' de Descartes.

II

Voici, en résumé, la méthode décrite par Spinoza dans la *Réforme*: l'entendement humain est pourvu de la 'vis nativa' avant même de procéder à l'activité intellectuelle et complexe, de la même manière que l'homme est né muni des 'instrumenta innata' avant d'accomplir une tâche difficile à l'aide des instruments complexes. L'entendement se forge par cette 'vis' des 'instrumenta intellectualia', par lesquels il acquiert de nouveaux outils et de nouvelles puissances; ainsi nous arrivons au 'sapientiae culmen' (*DIE*, II, 13–14). Or, selon Spinoza, ces outils intellectuels, c'est l'idée vraie ('idea vera'); la méthode qu'il faut suivre consiste donc, au début, à obtenir une idée de plus en plus parfaite en prenant pour norme une quelconque idée vraie donnée ('cujuscunque data idea vera', *DIE*, II, 18). Mais ce n'est encore qu'une moitié de la méthode, car la direction ainsi recommandée est qualifiée de 'prima via' de la connaissance (*DIE*, II, 18). Le rapport entre deux idées est, selon Spinoza, le même qu'entre leurs essences formelles ('essentia formalis') respectives, ou leurs objects ('ideatum', *DIE*, II, 14).

Il suit que, dit-il, la connaissance réflexive de l'idée de l'Être le plus parfait sera supérieure à la connaissance réflexive de toutes les autres idées, c'est-à-dire que la méthode la plus parfaite sera celle qui montre comment l'esprit doit être dirigé selon la norme de l'idée de l'Être le plus parfait ('data idea Entis perfectissimi', *DIE*, II, 16).

Autrement dit, la connaissance doit partir, à sa dernière phase, de l'idée de l'Être le plus parfait, c'est-à-dire de celle de Dieu, et en déduire toutes les autres. Mais notons ici que l'idée de Dieu n'est pas encore *donnée*. L'idée *donnée* de Dieu n'est pas l'idée d'une chose particulière *donnée*. Ce petit mot *donné* revient, en tant qu'épithète de l'idée considérée comme le point de départ de la méthode, sept fois au total (sans compter les deux cas où il est employé vers la fin du livre, en parlant des définitions, *DIE*, II, 34–5) dans les trois seules pages concernant l'idée, minime passage d'une esquisse rapide de la méthode, dans une des parties du peu gros livre. D'où vient cette déconcertante fréquence? De plus, ce mot n'est utilisé, dans ces trois pages, qu'une seule fois en parlant de l'idée de Dieu (*DIE*, II, 16); et six autres fois il se rapporte à l'idée d'une chose particulière. Que tout cela signifie-t-il? Nous essaierons d'éclaircir un problème suggéré, nous semble-t-il, par ce mot et son emploi.

Nous pensons que déjà le début du livre implique en herbe la difficulté qui empêchera plus tard la bonne continuation de l'ouvrage. Il va sans dire que l'auteur n'est pas conscient de tout cela, et il ne le sera pas dans le cadre de la *Réforme*. C'est précisément pour cela que le livre restera document d'un échec.

D'ailleurs, quoi qu'il entende par là, Spinoza sait assez clairement que l'idée de Dieu n'est pas encore *donnée*, car tout à la fin du résumé de la méthode, il dit qu'il nous faudra veiller à arriver le plus vite possible ('quanto ocius pervenire', *DIE*, II, 19) à l'idée de Dieu, et par ailleurs dans un contexte quelque peu différent, il fait remarquer la nécessité de ramener ('redigere', *DIE*, II, 34) toute idée à celle de Dieu. Bref, la méthode comporte dans son ensemble en postulat l'idée *donnée* de Dieu et c'est par rapport à ce postulat que la première voie est tracée à partir de l'idée quelconque d'une chose particulière. Aussi peut-on dire schématiquement que Spinoza considère comme une sorte de pis-aller la possibilité d'ascension partant de l'idée d'une chose particulière qui nous est familière, tandis qu'il recherche la meilleure méthode dans la descente, c'est-à-dire la voie partant de l'ultime idée, celle de Dieu. On y voit aisément une analogie avec F. Bacon, Hegel, Heidegger.

III

En tout cas la méthode de Spinoza se fonde sur l'idée, et par cela même elle partage la même inspiration avec celles de Hobbes, de Descartes et de Locke. Maintenant, il s'agit de rechercher le signe de l'idée vraie, agente même de la méthode.

D'abord, l'idée doit être claire et distincte comme chez Descartes. Selon notre auteur, toute idée fausse provient de la connaissance vague et confuse. La confusion est due à la manière de considérer dans sa totalité un problème composé de multiples parties sans le diviser en de simples éléments. Par contre, une idée vraie est ou bien très simple elle-même ou bien composée d'éléments simples d'une manière précise. Puisqu'une idée simple ne peut qu'être vraie et qu'elle nous est forcément claire et distincte, toute idée claire et distincte est vraie ('clara et distincta ac proinde vera', *DIE*, II, 25).

Mais si une idée est claire et distincte, ce n'est pas le seul signe de sa vérité; ou plutôt une autre condition s'impose pour qu'une idée puisse être acceptée par nous de manière claire et distincte. Spinoza pense qu'une idée vraie se distingue d'une fausse surtout par un caractère intrinsèque ('denominatio intrinseca', *DIE*, II, 26) et en donne un exemple: l'idée d'un ouvrage conçu par un ouvrier selon la bonne technique est vraie même si cet ouvrage n'existe pas réellement. Dans ce cas, la vérité de l'idée ne dépend en aucune façon de l'existence de la chose extérieure ni de la concordance de l'idée avec elle. Elle ne dépend pas seulement de la conscience claire de l'idée, mais aussi et surtout elle est garantie par une connexion ordonnée des idées qui soutiennent cette conscience claire et distincte. Nous arrivons ainsi au signe de la vérité que Wolfson appellera 'self-consistency'[4] et que Roth qualifiera de 'coherence'.[5] On peut savoir facilement, selon Spinoza, la vérité ou la fausseté d'une idée par une connexion des idées nées de cette idée. Et il dit:

> l'esprit, s'il s'applique à la fiction . . . pour . . . déduire à partir d'elle ce qui peut l'être dans un ordre convenable, en dénoncera aisément la fausseté. Et si l'objet de la fiction est vrai par sa nature, et que l'esprit s'y applique pour le comprendre et commence à en tirer des déductions dans un ordre convenable, alors il avancera avec bonheur et sans être interrompu (*DIE*, II, 23–4).

Ici il voit la garantie de la vérité dans une connexion convenable des idées. Autrement dit, l'idée vraie peut être reconnue claire et distincte, donc vraie, comme nous montre l'exemple d'un ouvrage cité plus haut, par sa conception cohérente, ou par la possibilité d'en déduire d'autres idées sans interruption.

IV

Dans le *Court Traité*, la connaissance fut considérée comme la perception d'une chose extérieure:

> le comprendre est un pur pâtir ('een pure lydinge') – c'est-à-dire une perception, dans l'âme, de l'essence et de l'existence; de sorte que ce n'est pas nous qui affirmons ou nions jamais rien d'une chose, mais c'est elle-même qui en nous affirme ou nie quelque chose d'elle-même (*KV*, I, 83).

C'est pourquoi, dans le *Court Traité*, la voie de connaissance commençait à partir d'une chose extérieure, soutenue par sa manifestation ('vertoning', *KV*, I, 100) dans l'esprit. Donc la réception plus ou moins extatique pour ainsi dire de la chose par l'esprit distinguait une idée vraie d'une idée fausse. C'est dans la *Réforme* qu'apparaît une autre voie ou façon de voir. Une connaissance doit se donner la preuve de sa véracité. Une idée doit se montrer vraie surtout par son caractère intrinsèque.

> Elle ne reconnaît pas un objet extérieur à la pensée comme cause, mais elle doit dépendre de la puissance et de la nature même de l'entendement. . . . Aussi la forme de la pensée vraie doit-elle être recherchée dans cette pensée même et déduite de la nature de l'entendement (*DIE*, II, 27).

C'est ainsi que la vérité d'une idée est établie par rapport à, ou s'appuyant sur, une série d'idées comprenant l'idée en question: comme porteur et garant de la vérité, l'idée ou la connexion des idées prennent place de la rassurante existence de la chose extérieure du *Court Traité*.

Pourtant la vérité d'une idée ainsi établie, garantie dans l'idée elle-même ou dans la connexion des idées, et sans aide de la chose extérieure, est méthodologiquement valable mais philosophiquement insuffisante, car, sans éclaircir à l'avance les rapports entre l'idée immanente et la chose extérieure, la transcendence de l'idée qui *ne reconnaît pas un objet extérieur comme cause*, risque d'être totalement vide de sens. Ni dans la *Réforme* ni ailleurs, Spinoza ne cherche spécialement, à la différence de Descartes, à trouver le fondement ontologique à sa méthode; ce qui ne veut naturellement pas dire que sa méthode n'ait aucune prémisse ontologique. Elle est présentée ici sur la base d'une réflexion ontologique, formulée plus tard, comme on sait, dans l'*Éthique*: 'l'ordre et la connexion des idées sont les mêmes que l'ordre et la connexion des choses' (*E.*, II, 89).

On est permis de voir dans cette prémisse ontologique, comme le font assez grand nombre de spinozistes dont, récemment, Wolfson,[6] une correspondance réelle et macrocosmique de la nature toute entière et réelle d'une part, avec le domaine tout entier des idées réelles d'autre part. Toutefois cette interprétation une fois admise, il ne faut pas en cloncure que la connaissance humaine retombe dans une acceptance impuissante par cette correspondance de la nature avec l'idée, ni que l'esprit humain, privé d'activité devant l'ordre des idées indépendante, se transforme en une *Schau* purement passive, puisque, dans la *Réforme*, l'ordre des idées n'est pas considéré comme quelque chose qui impose une pure *Schau* à l'esprit humain, quelque chose qui nous est extérieure ou étrangère. Au contraire, l'ordre des idées, quand en parle Spinoza, est toujours entouré et pénétré de la connaissance humaine. Tandis que la pensée développée suivant le bon ordre est aussi vraie que l'idée d'un ouvrage conçu par un ouvrier selon la bonne technique, le doute vient du désordre des idées. De là, nous concluons que si l'ordre des idées est mentionné toujours par rapport à la connaissance humaine, c'est que cet ordre est immanent à l'esprit humain aussi, malgré la possibilité d'y supposer un ordre macrocosmique du domaine des idées indépendante. Disons mieux: il n'y a d'ordre que celui qui est pénétré par l'esprit humain. Spinoza écrit à Bowmeester:[7]

> Les perceptions claires et distinctes que nous formons dépendent de notre seule nature et de ses lois déterminées et permanentes, c'est-à-dire de notre puissance absolument nôtre: elles ne dépendent pas du tout du hasard, c'est-à-dire de causes agissant selon des lois déterminées et permanentes, mais inconnues de nous et étrangères à notre nature et à notre puissance (*Ep.*, IV, 188).

La connaissance dépend de la 'nature de notre propre entendement', des 'lois de l'entendement'; elle ne peut être autre chose que 'la connexion [des idées] par l'entendement'. L'ordre des idées n'est jamais une transcendance, imposée de l'extérieur, que l'on ne puisse qu'accepter et à laquelle on doive obéir. Il est immanent à l'esprit humain, auquel il appartient. Il n'est pas lui-même un objet de contemplation, comme chez Platon ou Saint Augustin; les idées n'abolissent pas la nécessité de l'activité intellectuelle humaine en se développant. C'est pourquoi, à la différence du *Court Traité*, Spinoza envisage ici la connaissance discursive comme un important élément de la méthode. Nous devons nous-mêmes déduire les idées une à une en accomplissant l'activité intellectuelle du raisonnement.

Aussi n'est-il pas nécessaire, nous semble-t-il, d'imaginer la correspondance quelque peu mystique en tant que fondement de la méthode spinoziste. Les principes de sa méthode sont d'abord la volonté de se procurer l'objet en général maniable, ensuite la certitude que maniable est ce qui est immanent à l'entendement, enfin une ontologie peu originale de ne voir l'objet ni la chose que tant que l'entendement peut les saisir. Conséquence logique des deux principes précédents, elle implique une affirmation, non plus originale, que le sujet du savoir se situe du côté de l'esprit humain, et non pas du côté de l'objet. C'est précisément elle qui fonde la méthode spinoziste: l'esprit humain apparaît, par son propre ordre intellectuel, comme raison de l'articulation des êtres réels; l'homme procède à la connaissance selon son propre ordre intellectuel, conformément aux règles du cohérent et du *clair et distinct*, en développant a priori les idées. Par conséquent, pour estimer l'ontologie spinoziste à sa juste valeur, nous devrions avoir toujours à l'esprit que dans sa lettre citée à Bowmeester, Spinoza exclut du domaine philosophique tout ce qui n'est pas maniable par l'entendement; que dans le texte de la *Réforme* le mot 'ideatum' est employé exprès en parlant de l'objet.

v

Ce n'est pas dans le sens péjoratif que nous disions que l'ontologie spinoziste est peu originale. Elle l'est dans ce sens qu'elle partage la volonté et la certitude fondamentales avec la plupart de grands philosophes contemporains. Cette volonté et cette certitude, nous les voyons par exemple chez Hobbes, considérant la philosophie comme une 'computatio', n'adopte, en tant que ses éléments, que ce qui est conçu de quelque manière que ce soit.[8] Nous les voyons aussi chez Descartes qui traite 'des choses autant qu'elles sont perçues par l'entendement' dans les 'Regulae' et définit la 'natura simplex', élément fondamental de la méthode, comme choses simples 'respectu nostri intellectus'.[9] Nous les voyons enfin chez Locke qui, se gardant de libérer la pensée sur 'the vast ocean of Being', propose une 'New Way of Ideas'.[10] Voilà l'attitude philosophique fondamentale de l'époque.

Interdisant à l'esprit d'appareiller au large du vaste océan de l'Être et lui recommandant de tout regarder 'respectu nostri intellectus', cette attitude, apparemment timide et défensive, se révèle ne point l'être au cours de l'histoire de la pensée moderne, où elle va affirmer sa prépondérance. Elle portera plus tard ses fruits, comme on sait, dans le développement des sciences naturelles et dans la maîtrise de la nature. Kepler qui mesura l'exactitude de la connaissance en prenant pour critère les 'nudae quantitates' et Galilée qui voulut 'mesurer tout ce qui est mesurable et rendre mesurable tout ce qui ne l'est pas encore', ne l'annonçaient-ils pas par leur intention de réduire la nature à sa définition quantitative et maniable? En sorte que voir cette même attitude philosophique derrière la méthode de Spinoza, cela peut bien être simpliste mais non humiliant. D'un autre point de vue, ce qui importe ici, c'est notre prise de position. Puisque nous sommes, pour le bien ou pour le mal, ses enfants, il nous paraît plus fructueux, pour maintenir la philosophie spinoziste en tant qu'objet maniable par nous, de supposer une telle ontologie dans la méthode spinoziste, que d'y voir une ontologie mystique qui dépasserait notre entendement.

VI

La *Réforme* consacre ses dernières pages au problème de la définition, où, après avoir traité la connaissance des choses particulières qui doit être faite 'per seriem', Spinoza écrit à peu près comme suit: si les choses particulières doivent être connues par série, la série ne veut pas dire ici telle ou telle connexion des choses extérieures; il serait impossible et d'ailleurs oiseux de suivre la connexion; la connaissance des choses particulières est obtenue surtout dans la série des connaissances partant de Dieu, etc. (*DIE*, II, 36–8).

Premièrement Spinoza semble vouloir dire par là que la connaissance véritable ou utile nous est refusée tant que nous nous bornons à invoquer le monde des choses comme tel, qui pourrait bien inspirer notre imagination et nous inciter à exprimer des pensées fragmentaires, mais la connaissance proprement dite, connaissance savante, n'est jamais fragmentaire; elle n'est possible qu'en ensemble organique et dans cet ensemble; c'est alors seulement que nous sommes en état de parler de sa vérité et que par conséquent elle devient maniable par nous. Une telle interprétation tirée de la description plutôt brève de la connaissance des choses particulières est cohérente avec l'esprit de sa méthode traité plus haut; elle s'accorde aussi avec son mépris de l''experientia vaga' (*DIE*, II, 13) naïvement soumise aux choses telles qu'elles arrivent; elle participe enfin du même ordre, en ce qui concerne la négation du savoir fragmentaire, que la critique de F. Bacon dans la seconde lettre à Oldenburg (*EP.*, IV, 8).

Quant au deuxième point aussi, c'est-à-dire les rapports entre la connaissance des choses particulières et celle de Dieu, ils rentrent naturellement dans le cadre de la méthode de Spinoza. Toutefois, si quelque chose nous arrête ici, c'est que la série mentionnée et exigée se limite à celle qui commence à partir de Dieu. Autrement dit, la première voie à laquelle Spinoza reconnaissait un certain rôle et un certain droit lorsqu'il a parlé de la méthode concernant l'idée, disparaît complètement de la scène lorsqu'il parle de la définition. Cette fois, il s'agit seulement de rendre plus ample ('ampliorem reddere', *DIE*, II, 34) la connaissance de Dieu, c'est-à-dire la voie d'en descendre (*DIE*, II, 34). Cela tient naturellement, du point de vue directement formel, de la distinction qu'il fait, au début du passage concernant la définition, entre le créé et l'incréé. Mais l'introduction de cette nouvelle distinction, qui n'est pas sans rapport, nous semble-t-il, avec la fréquence soudaine, dans le même passage, des mots comme 'vero' ou 'revera', nous fait sentir une certaine coïncidence, même indirecte, avec l'emploi particulier du mot *donné*, que nous avons étudié plus haut. En tout cas, la première voie va prendre bientôt sa revanche sur la définition qui l'a rejetée.

VII

Dans la *Réforme*, comme le montre l'expression: 'essentia particulari, affirmativa, sive vera et legitima definitio' (*DIE*, II, 34), résumant ainsi l'esprit de la méthode, l'essence est considérée comme équivalente à la définition. C'est-à-dire, de même que ce qui est qui est 'ideatum' par l'entendement constitue l'objet, seul ce qui peut se définir en définition constitue l'essence. Ici, l'essence, ou définition, de Dieu devrait être clairement présentée, si la connaissance essentielle n'est vérifiée que dans la série partant de Dieu. Or certains passages concernant la définition nous montrent que la définition de Dieu reste ce que l'on doit faire effort pour atteindre aussitôt que possible ('quamprimum', *DIE*, II, 36). Elle est à acquérir, elle n'est pas encore acquise.

C'est ainsi que Spinoza déclare la nécessité de 'quelque principe' ('aliquod fundamentum', *DIE*, II, 38) pour conduire notre pensée à la définition de Dieu, et prescrit d'une manière concrète que ce principe, c'est la connaissance de la nature de l'entendement qui connaît, c'est-à-dire sa définition. Ici comme là, la définition de l'entendement, une chose particulière parmi d'autres, est exigée avant celle de Dieu. Cependant, le raisonnement de Spinoza commence à tourner en rond; pour définir l'entendement, il faut avoir défini l'entendement, car c'est le sujet de la définition tout aussi bien que son objet. Ainsi Spinoza s'arrête pour trouver la méthode de découvrir la définition en général et en déduire la définition de l'entendement. Là aussi, c'est un impasse puisque c'est toujours l'entendement qui essaie de se découvrir la définition et qu'il lui fait d'abord se définir. Ensuite Spinoza songe un moment que la définition de l'entendement soit claire par elle-même ('per se clara'), chance à laquelle il renonce en disant: 'Definitio intellectus tamen per se clara non est' (*DIE*, II, 38). Mais il n'y a aucune autre issue pour lui que de recourir à cette expérience qu'il reniait toujours et qu'il continue à considérer comme impropre: espérant encore que la définition de l'entendement *s'éclaircira*, il essaie de décrire, en se fondant sur l'expérience, les propriétés de l'entendement en huit paragraphes. Or, rien ne s'éclaircit par soi-même; la *Réforme* est interrompue, n'ayant pu proposer aucune définition, dans une douleureuse confusion et une répétition sans fin.

VIII

Rappelons-nous que Spinoza écrit, relativement tôt, dans la *Réforme*:

remarquons d'abord qu'il ne sera pas ici question d'une recherche à l'infini; je veux dire que, pour découvrir la meilleure des recherches du vrai, il n'est pas besoin d'une autre méthode pour rechercher la première et pour trouver la seconde, nul besoin d'une troisième, et ainsi à l'infini: car, de cette façon, on ne pourrait jamais parvenir à la connaissance du vrai ni même à aucune connaissance (*DIE*, II, 13).

Selon lui, il en est de même des instruments matériels : s'il est vrai qu'il faut un marteau pour forger, et que pour avoir un marteau, il faut forger et ainsi de suite, cela ne veut pas dire que les hommes sont incapables de forger. Car dans la réalité les hommes ont commencé par fabriquer des outils simples, à leur portée, avec lesquels ils ont réussi à en fabriquer de plus perfectionnés, en élargissant de cette manière leur fabrication. Pour revenir au problème de la connaissance, on peut procéder de la même manière : l'entendement se forge, au début, des outils intellectuels ou idées, dans la mesure du possible, par sa propre force innée, grâce auxquels il acquiert d'autres forces pour la recherche plus avancée, afin de parvenir ainsi au faîte de la sagesse, etc. (*DIE*, II, 14).

Or, les dernières pages de la *Réforme* décrivant la définition ne nous donnent-elles pas précisément un exemple typique de la 'recherche à l'infini' ? Chercher la définition de l'entendement qui définit, n'est-ce pas la même aberration que de chercher un marteau pour fabriquer un autre marteau qui n'existe pas ? L'unique moyen qu'a proposé Spinoza de ne pas tomber dans cette régression à l'infini fut, quand il s'agissait des idées, un outil intellectuel très simple, c'est-à-dire 'une quelconque idée donnée', à partir de laquelle la première voie s'ouvre dans la direction de l'idée de Dieu. Pourquoi, cette fois-ci, lorsqu'il est question des définitions, équivalentes des idées dans le système fondamental spinoziste, est-il tombé dans le bourbier de la régression à l'infini dont il se gardait bien ? Il aurait pu trouver en effet dans la définition de l'entendement un appui, très familier dans un sens ; loin d'être la clef de voûte, elle déclenche la régression à l'infini et finit par interrompre l'ouvrage même.

IX

Essayons de trouver la réponse d'abord en analysant le texte de la *Réforme*. Nous pouvons tout de suite dire qu'ici deux méthodes sont proposées sans que leur rapport ou leur différence ne soient précisés. Bien qu'en prenant l'exemple du marteau, Spinoza semble nier l'existence de la seconde ou la troisième méthode, il propose en réalité deux méthodes à la fois, ou plutôt une méthode à deux temps, et non pas une méthode unique et unilatérale : il admet d'une part, en parlant des définitions aussi bien que des idées, la méthode qui consiste à partir d'une idée *donnée*, d'une définition *donnée*, pour arriver jusqu'à l'idée et définition de Dieu, alors que, d'autre part, il prêche comme ultime méthode la déduction à partir de l'idée et définition de l'Être le plus parfait. Puisque la seconde voie commence là où aboutit la première, elles ne sont pas tout à fait pareilles ; an moins il doit y avoir une certaine différence de caractère ou d'ordre quant aux idées et définitions qu'on obtient sur l'une ou l'autre. La connaissance ne peut qu'être provisoire par la première voie, étant donné qu'elle part des idées et définitions disponibles sur place et pour l'heure, tandis que par la seconde, chemin de retour à partir de l'ultime principe, la vérité d'une connaissance se situe sur un ordre tout à fait différent. D'ailleurs le point de retour, jonction du 'terminus ad quem' d'une voie et du 'terminus a quo' de l'autre, implique sans doute des difficultés de fait qu'éprouvent également F. Bacon, Heidegger et, fondamentalement sinon formellement, Hegel. Pourtant par eux, les différences des deux voies sont plus clairement saisies et, surtout la première voie, dont le caractère provisoire ne leur échappe point, est habilitée comme telle. C'est pourquoi elle peut être formulée matériellement dans la deuxième partie de *Novum Organum*, dans la première partie de *Sein und Zeit* et dans *Phänomenologie des Geistes*. Quant à Spinoza, par contre, on se demande s'il a l'intention précise de présenter la première voie comme une propédeutique et, comme nous le montre l'addition, souvent désinvolte, du mot *vrai* à 'une idée quelconque donnée', point de départ de la première voie, les deux voies ne sont pas clairement différenciées pour leur caractère respectif; ce qui a pour résultat la même certitude exigée à la première voie qu'à la seconde. Si la régression à l'infini apparaît justement là où l'entendement cherche à se définir, c'est que l'auteur commet l'erreur d'exiger à la première voie la certitude qui lui est impossible, dont est capable seule la voie de retour après la connaissance de Dieu. Si bien que derrière la confusion des définitions, nous entrevoyons la revanche de la première voie, esquissée dès le début et négligée par la suite.

Ainsi l'ambiguité des rapports entre les deux voies avait en fait sa source dans les considérations sur les idées; l'idée inaugurant la première voie était tantôt comparée à un outil imparfait et primitif, tantôt prise tout simplement pour vraie, alors que l'on ne savait pas encore à quel niveau et à quel titre elle pouvait l'être. Si, malgré cela, le problème restait latent, c'est que, premièrement, la distinction du *crée* et de l'*incréé* n'intervenait pas encore et que, deuxièmement, il ne s'agissait pas de présenter la méthode d'une façon concrète mais de montrer sa structure générale.

Quand il aborde la définition, au contraire, comme si la première voie n'existait pas, Spinoza met l'accent sur la seule voie de descente, déduction à partir de Dieu, et demande la définition concrète, puisque ce ne serait qu'une répétition que de montrer la structure de la méthode déjà établie sous une forme générale par rapport aux idées. De plus, la définition est une idée formulée par exemple sous forme verbale, matière et instrument immanents à la conscience qui philosophe, donc l'équipement indispensable de la Philosophie *formulée*, si bien qu'il est urgent de donner les définitions très concrètes, puisque la *Réforme* a été projetée afin de servir du préliminaire.

C'est pourquoi il reconnaît d'abord, contredisant le cas des idées, la déduction directe à partir de Dieu comme unique méthode valable; ensuite comme le cas précédent, sans définir directement Dieu, il rappelle brusquement la voie qui part pour Dieu; et enfin, contre le cas des idées encore une fois, il s'efforce de définir concrètement l'entendement. Mais cette fois, avant d'essayer de définir l'entendement, le *créé* est malencontreusement distingué de l'*incréé*, et Spinoza insiste un peu trop sur le fait que le premier ne peut se définir en soi mais par l'intermédiaire des définitions précédentes dans la série qui part de Dieu. Et l'existence et la signification de la première voie étant, nous répétons, complètement ignorées du point de vue formel, il est d'ailleurs impossible de définir, et avec une certitude absolue, une chose créée qu'est l'entendement. Dans ces conditions-là, la régression à l'infini de la définition n'a rien d'étonnant.

X

Cependant pour quelles raisons Spinoza, pour qui la méthode idéale est la déduction à partir de Dieu, a-t-il essayé plus d'une fois de partir de l'idée ou définition particulière? Nous venons de voir la raison, formelle, pour laquelle cet essai finit par un échec. Mais si c'est ainsi, on peut toujours se demander pourquoi alors il n'a pas voulu commencer tout simplement par l'idée ou définition de Dieu et ce qu'il demande à la première voie.

Ici il nous faut retourner au mot *donné*. Comme nous avons vu, Spinoza propose de partir de l'idée particulière pour obtenir l'idée *donnée* de Dieu et rapporte cette épithète presque uniquement à la seconde.

L'article *donné* du *Vocabulaire technique et critique de la Philosophie* de Lalande – ouvrage très commode en ce sens qu'il décide souvent tout net sur un problème qui n'est pas toujours simple – définit le mot comme 'ce qui est immédiatement présenté à l'esprit avant que celui-ci y applique ses procédés d'élaboration', définition rencorcée par une citation de V. Egger:

> J'emploie ce mot comme synonyme d'immédiat, de premier, de conscient. Le *donné* s'oppose à l'inféré, au construit, à l'hypothétique, donc à tout *objet* en tant qu'objet, à tout non-moi, à l'espace en tant que construit, à l'avenir en tant qu'hypothétique. Une philosophie qui commence par la psychologie prend pour base le *donné*.[11]

Dans les premières étapes de la philosophie où elle cherchait sa *base* dans le psychique, la définition est sans doute justifiée prenant le *donné* pour base de la philosophie. Car, dans ces étapes-là, il s'agissait surtout d'intérioriser la base du savoir, et l'on croyait naïvement que la base, psychique et par conséquent immédiate à l'esprit, ne pouvait qu'être nécessaire et maniable. On s'arrêtait là sans plus se demander si le psychique, à seul titre d'être tel, peut vraiment fournir la base au savoir. Par exemple – comme remarqueront Aaron et Gibson[12] – tout en reconnaissant l'idée, clef de sa philosophie, comme objet 'in the mind', Locke ne parlait qu'en passant de sa manière d'être 'in the mind' et de la signification de l'objet;[13] Descartes présenta le gage de la nécessité de la 'natura simplex' en disant:

il n'y a que peu ce natures pures et simples, dont, de prime abord et par elles-mêmes, nous puissions avoir l'intuition, indépendamment de toutes les autres, soit par des expériences, soit par cette lumière qui est en nous.[14]

Chez eux, ce qu'ils considèrent comme la base du savoir reste, *donné* ou non, en l'état non encore purifié, immédiat et amorphe, puisqu'aucune attention n'est payée pour savoir si cela est maniable ou non. Mais toute philosophie qui a pour point de départ la réflexion sur l'esprit humain, dans l'intention d'atteindre le maniable, ne finit-elle pas nécessairement, si elle se garde de la mauvaise foi ou du mysticisme, par reconnaître l'action constructive de l'esprit, exclue par Lalande et Egger, comme élément intégral du *donné*, précisément à cause de son intention initiale, une fois qu'elle exige la base du savoir du côté de l'esprit et non du côté du monde des choses? Et nous pensons que l'*idée donnée* est conçue par Spinoza à ce haut niveau auquel sa réflexion philosophique est parvenue, dépassant ainsi celui dont d'autres philosophes étaient satisfaits, parce qu'il a suivi, fidèle, jusqu'au bout l'intention vers le maniable, partagée et non pas toujours suivie par la plupart de ses contemporains. Par conséquent, dans la *Réforme*, le *donné* ne peut se définir simplement comme ce qui est immédiatement présenté à l'esprit, étant donné que l'auteur l'emploie par rapport à l'action de l'esprit plus purifiée, après avoir examiné de divers modes de connaissance, voire même après avoir rejeté l'expérience, tout en y voyant une certaine utilité, puisqu' elle 'n'est pas déterminée par l'entendement' (*DIE*, II, 10); et que les exemples de l'ouvrage ou du marteau sont donnés comme pour confirmer ce mot. Enfin, chez lui, le mot *donné* est lié à la fonction de *fabriquer* ('formare', *DIE*, II, 27–8), à l'action de *se forger* ('facire' *DIE*, II, 13–14) de l'esprit humain, comme le montre l'exemple du marteau et, comme le montre aussi l'exemple de l'ouvrage, se fonde, bien qu'implicitement, sur la capacité et nature de l'entendement. Le *donné* exige la participation constructive de l'entendement pour se réaliser, et pour cette raison implique le refus de tout ce qui se présente à l'esprit sans être construit par l'entendement, en y voyant 'quelque chose de vague, que l'âme y est passive' (*DIE*, II, 32). C'est pourquoi on peut affirmer qu'il *décolle* de cette notion simpliste du *donné* en tant que base du savoir, definie par Lalande et Egger et dont on a un exemple typique chez Locke.

Ainsi le mot *donné* une fois pris dans ce sens-là dans la *Réforme*, il nous devient possible de considérer l'idée *donnée* comme formée avec la part constructive de l'entendement, ou plus exactement, comme une idée maniable. En effet, Spinoza emploie souvent l'image d'un outil en parlant de l'idée *donnée*, à laquelle il demande avant tout d'être 'intelligibilis', expression favorite au dix-septième siècle, est celle qui, 'en tant qu'essence formelle de l'objet, peut être l'objet d'une autre essence objective' (*DIE*, II, 14); cela veut dire qu'il est possible de rendre 'ideatum' l'idée elle-même suivant l'intention vers le maniable.

Vouloir arriver à l'idée de Dieu en partant de l'idée *donnée* considérée sous cet aspect, c'est donc vouloir étendre le domaine du maniable jusqu'à Dieu; c'est viser à se procurer l'idée de Dieu en tant que *donnée*; celle-ci ne se constitue le but d'arrivée qu'ainsi entendu. Cette volonté fait partie intégrale de l'intention d'intérioriser l'ensemble des déductions à partir de l'idée de Dieu, c'est-à-dire la Philosophie; elle est cohérente et conséquente avec l'attitude philosophique de Spinoza que nous avons vue plus haut.

XI

La première voie, celle d'ascension vers l'idée de Dieu à partir d'une idée *donnée*, a pour toute mission d'amplifier ainsi le *donné*. Mais s'il en est ainsi, d'où vient cette curieuse persistance qu'il montre à la garder jusqu'à vouloir la rappeler plus tard, en dépit de ses propres principes, en parlant des définitions? Ne nous suggère-t-elle pas un autre problème?

Dans une page de la *Réforme*, Spinoza dit, après avoir défini la sphère comme formée par un demi-cercle qui tourne autour de son centre:

> Cette idée est vraie avec certitude et, bien que nous sachions qu'aucune sphère de la nature n'a jamais été ainsi engendrée, . . . (*DIE*, II, 27).

Dans ce cas précis, l'homme, sans tenir compte de la sphère qui existe 'revera' dans la nature, doit rechercher les idées ou définitions maniables de la sphère en se référant toujours à ce qui est clair, distinct et cohérent; il ne faut pas reconnaître un objet extérieur comme cause, il ne faut dépendre que de la puissance et de la nature même de l'entendement. Or, Spinoza ne suit pas cette ligne de conduite quand il s'agit directement de l'idée ou définition de Dieu: il a recours de nouveau à la première voie; il prend le parti d'amplifier la maniabilité des moyens de bord, c'est-à-dire des idées ou définitions déjà acquises. Pourtant cela ne signifie pas l'absence, chez Spinoza, de la conscience de Dieu, matière première de son idée ou définition; cela signifie au contraire ceci: il existe une conscience de Dieu, telle qu'elle exigerait, étant amorphe, une trop grande force et un trop grand courage pour se faire 'facire' d'un seul coup comme idée ou définition; Spinoza le sait vaguement. Une telle conscience de Dieu n'est pas, nous semble-t-il, sans rapport avec le Dieu du *Court Traité* – celui qui apparaît à l'entendement qui ne peut se mettre en relation avec lui que d'une façon ecstatique; celui dont on voudrait être 'liés dans les chaînes aimables de l'amour' (*KV*, I, 108) et 'être les serviteurs ou même les esclaves' (*KV*, I, 87), puisque c'est là le bonheur même des hommes. En tout cas, l'attitude particulière de Spinoza qu'il prend, dans la *Réforme*, vis-à-vis de l'idée et définition de Dieu ne s'explique, quelle que soit sa propre intention, qu'en tenant compte de la conscience de Dieu.

Par conséquent, la conscience de Dieu ainsi entendue, il n'est plus difficile de comprendre, par rapport à celle-ci, le problème des deux méthodes, qui entraîne l'interruption de la *Réforme* comme le retour du mot *donné*: primo la confusion concernant la méthode vient de la première voie même, rappelée brusquement, qui n'est pas facile, pour plusieurs raisons, à joindre à l'ultime méthode; secundo, si l'auteur insiste sur la première voie, c'est que la conscience de Dieu est difficile à manier toute seule; tertio, puisque la manière d'être de celle-ci lui est sans doute embarrassante, il penche à insister sur une autre manière, c'est-à-dire *donnée*.

Si un ouvrage philosophique achevé peut se qualifier plus heureux qu'inachevé, cette conscience de Dieu n'est rien d'autre qu'une cause de malheur pour la *Réforme*. Mais cette cause de malheur invite l'auteur à approfondir la réflexion sur ce que peut être la base de la philosophie et permet ainsi la notion du *donné*, en tant que base, de *décoller* cessant d'être directe et amorphe, tout simplement présentée à l'esprit. L'expression 'cause de malheur' est donc injuste.

XII

Le décollage est un acte grandiose; c'est quitter la solide terre, contre la gravitation, pour s'exposer au risque dans un espace sans soutien. Pleinement contre nature, il engendre de l'inquiétude, de la peur et parfois même de la douleur. Si c'est une des preuves de la grandeur humaine et une *expérience* par excellence dans ce sens qu'il s'agit d'entrer dans une situation instable et périlleuse et d'en sortir, il ne constitue nullement un point d'arrivée; il ne vous procure pas cette paix qui permette désormais l'arrêt de tout fonctionnement de l'appareil. Mais au contraire, il constitue lui-même un point de départ vers une nouvelle expérience sans doute dangereuse; c'est le commencement du possible qui vous demande un plus grand courage et inflige une plus grande souffrance.

En ce qui concerne la notion du *donné*, l'aventure de Spinoza dans la *Réforme* pourrait être comparée avec raison au décollage. Une autre aventure intellectuelle précédente, celle de la transition d'une philosophie dépendant de l'objet à l'immanentisme dans le *Court Traité*, avait encore un certain soutien dans l'esprit du temps. Par contre, entre la position, courante avant Kant, d'accepter, d'une manière naïve, indistincte et généreuse, comme *donné* tout ce qui se présente à l'esprit d'une part, et la nouvelle position, celle de Spinoza, de penser que le *donné*, s'il se veut vraiment intelligible et maniable par l'esprit, est construit par la participation de l'entendement et à travers une réflexion sur sa manière d'être *donné*, d'autre part, il existe une telle différence qu'on ne peut pas ne pas penser au décollage d'un avion, bien que toutes les deux s'accordent à voir le sujet du savoir dans l'esprit humain et le *donné* du savoir dans le psychique. Dans le cas de la seconde position, qui suppose, si l'on reprend l'expression chère à Wittgenstein, un 'Netz' muni d'une certaine 'Masche,[15] la solution de continuité du *donné* d'avec la nature proprement dite est plus accusée et permet moins librement à l'entendement de prendre une posture confortable, 'historical' ou 'plain' comme chez Locke. Et notre philosophe qui exige la détermination du *donné* par l'entendement et qui compare une idée ainsi *donnée* à un outil ou à un ouvrage ('opera'), s'élève jusqu'à cette hauteur où il y a sûrement moins de paix pour le sujet du savoir (est-on permis d'y voir sa trop bonne foi?), en laissant se reposer au sol ses collègues contemporains dont Locke à la tête, exactement du même âge que lui. S'il n'était pas de si bonne foi, il pourrait éviter, comme le font les autres, un mot tel que le *donné* qui n'a guère de chance de s'arranger; même s'il ne peut le faire, il pourrait passer à la Philosophie, en donnant quelques exemples tout faits de la définition, soit d'une chose particulière, soit de Dieu, après avoir décrit sommairement la structure de la méthode; et ainsi la *Réforme* aurait été bien achevée en tant que préliminaire de la Philosophie, alors qu'en réalité elle reste un échantillon de confusion et d'échec. C'est pour le malheur de Spinoza qu'il n'a pas pu s'attacher au sol.

XIII

Avant Kant ce *décollage*, même implicite, demande sans doute une certaine audace, mais il laisse un problème irrésolu; ou plus exactement, puisqu'il a pour cause la bonne foi intellectuelle, disons qu'en ce moment même apparaît un nouveau problème. D'ailleurs, Spinoza ne faisant pas explicitement du *donné* un thème central de discussion, notre interprétation ne dépasse guère une simple conjecture et dans un sens le problème est même plutôt le nôtre que le sien: celui de savoir si le *donné* devient par lui-même ou bien il est rendu tel par nous. Le *donné*, lorsqu'il devient tel, 'déterminé par l'entendement' ou plus généralement selon ce qu'on appelle les formes subjectives et les catégories, est certes construit par l'action de l'esprit humain et distingué par cela même du direct et amorphe; mais il reste, en tant que tel, le *donné* général. Et, lorsqu'on se figure par exemple un historien qui promène ses yeux attentivement sur des amas de chiffres et de documents qu'il considère tous comme *donnés* puisque faits par les hommes, sans pouvoir en produire aucune considération, aucune description historique, n'est-il pas trop évident que la philosophie ne peut prendre départ avec le *donné* général, qui n'est pas encore tout à fait *donné* au philosophe en tant que base utilisable de sa science? Tout comme la pensée historique, impossible si les matériaux ne sont choisis et déterminés par la décision subjective de l'historien, le *donné* général ne raconte rien de lui-même au philosophe; il n'a une certaine signification d'ensemble que si déterminé a priori par le philosophe à qui il appartient de décider quoi et comment. Et cette sélection fait tel ou tel *donné* significatif pour le philosophe, ou plus généralement, pour le sujet du savoir. Nous le voyons clairement dans le cas de Rickert qui aborde de front la question du *donné*; malgré son insistance qui va jusqu'à distinguer la 'Gegebenheit' d'avec d'autres formes de connaissance et à la nommer 'Kategorie des Diesseins',[16] il finit par assurer que la nécessité du jugement porté à travers cette catégorie n'est pas celle du 'Müssen' ni du 'Psychischer "Zwang" ' mais celle du 'Sollen';[17] que la catégorie constructive de la 'Gegebenheit' n'a de sens que lorsqu'elle est précédée par la décision subjective de valeur. L'action constructive du sujet, même forte et précise, ne fait pas encore de *donné*; le *donné* devient tel, ou plutôt il est rendu tel, par la décision subjective a priori de prendre pour tel précisément *ce donné*. Il n'y a pas de *donné* sans décision ou sélection subjective. 'A selective system of cognitive orientations to reality', expression de Talcott Parsons désignant la science,[18] caractérise en effet, non seulement la science, mais toute activité intellectuelle qui ne peut pas rester indifférente des rapports entre le sujet du savoir et son objet.

Or Spinoza, lui aussi, semble rencontrer dans la *Réforme* le problème de déterminer le *donné* général, après avoir *décollé* à cette position de le considérer comme le résultat de l'intervention constructive de l'entendement. C'est ainsi qu'à propos des axiomes indistinctement généraux, il les rejette en disant qu'ils 'ne déterminent pas l'entendement à considérer une chose singulière plutôt qu'une autre' (*DIE*, II, 34). Et puis, le voeu qu'il exprime deux fois, en finissant de parler des définitions, que celle de l'entendement 'soit claire par elle-même', ne montre-t-il pas paradoxalement que Spinoza pense à une autre façon de l'obtenir que celle d'attente passive; c'est-à-dire elle pourrait être claire, non pas par elle-même, mais par la décision subjective a priori. Toutefois il n'adopte pas, comme on sait, cette autre façon et même évite de faire face à sa possibilité.

La *Réforme* est abondamment annotée par l'auteur. La note sur la 'vis nativa', éclairant ses rapports avec l'extérieur, est simple et banale: 'Per vim nativam intelligo illud, quod in nobis a causis externis *non* causatur' (*DIE*, II, 14 – nos italiques), dans l'édition de C. Gebhardt. Or chose curieuse, ce *non* manque dans les 'Opera Posthuma', publiés en latin au lendemain de la mort de notre philosophe, tout aussi bien dans ses *Oeuvres Posthumes* en hollandais (*De Nagelate Schriften*), traduites directement de son manuscrit: 'dat in ons door uitterlijke oorsaken veröorzaakt word.'[19] Cette omission de *non* (ou de *niet*) dans les deux éditions indépendantes prouve clairement que ce n'est pas là une faute d'impression ou de transcription, que le manuscrit même ne comportait pas ce mot. Mais C. Gebhardt avait raison de l'ajouter, comme l'exige le contexte, en attribuant la faute à l'inattention de l'auteur. Toutefois, s'il nous est permis de voir dans l'acte manqué, comme Freud, une résistance des désirs et des inquiétudes refoulés, l'inattention de Spinoza correspond à un secret souhait de retourner là où il pourrait se reposer sur quelque chose d'autre, puisque lui pèse déja lourd ce *décollage* de l'entendement qui construit. Si déjà il a de la crainte et peur à propos du fardeau que l'intériorisation va imposer au sujet, il est naturel que, après le *décollage* entrepris quand même, Spinoza évite de faire face à une plus grande exigence, vaguement entrevue, qu'est la décision subjective a priori. Le retour fréquent des mots comme 'etiam', 'enim', 'nimirum', 'necessario', en plus de 'vero' ou 'revera' dont nous avons parlé plus haut, dans la seconde moitié du passage concernant les définitions, et dans un contexte qui n'est pas toujours évident, s'explique relativement à l'état d'âme de l'auteur que nous venons de décrire.

Tout bien considéré, cependant, exiger la décision subjective a priori à nous-mêmes, en tant que fondement ultime du *donné*, c'est entreprendre presque l'impossible surtout avant que Kant n'établisse la notion de la construction subjective. A un philosophe qui, en face de la réalité toute entière, prétend *donner* vraiment le *donné*, et non pas en décrire la structure et la propriété, cette exigence de plus demande sans doute trop de courage et de force. Du reste, tant que le fondement du *donné* est perçu comme décision ou choix, le point d'Archimède soulevant cette gigantesque sphère de l'ensemble du *donnée* qu'est la réalité elle-même, ce n'est même plus le *nous*, ce doit être le *moi*; la Philosophie ne peut commencer que comme une sorte de formulation avec le sujet de la première personne du singulier. Même si, devant cet état de choses, Spinoza rebroussait chemin, il ne saurait être accusé de lâche ou de mauvaise foi, car ne peut rebrousser chemin que celui qui en a fait, surmontant la crainte et peur. D'ailleurs Spinoza ne rebrousse pas: la Philosophie, actuelle *Ethique*, commencée après l'interruption de la *Réforme*, présente tout au début la définition de Dieu à la première personne du singulier; et presque toutes des vingt-six définitions sont données de la même manière, c'est-à-dire par le *moi* à mains nues;[20] ce qui signifie rien de moins que Spinoza se choisit comme sujet de la décision, comme point d'Archimède. On pourrait donc dire que la *Réforme* sert de préliminaire à l'*Ethique*, avec le *décollage* de la notion du *donné*, avec la nouvelle exigence qu'il provoque, avec hésitation devant sa gravité, enfin avec l'échec où conduit cette hésitation; du point de vue de la conscience qui philosophe, elle n'est pas inachevée, elle est sans aucun doute finie et parfaite d'une manière la plus heureuse.

Ce qui nous importe pourtant, ce n'est pas la *Réforme* elle-même, achevée ou non, ni ses rapports avec l'*Ethique*, mais ce qu'elle nous apprend à nous qui vivons notre vie actuelle, par l'attitude que l'auteur y prend vis-à-vis du *donné* en particulier et du Problème en général; celle de voir le Problème là où personne n'en aperçoit, d'en rechercher la solution par telle voie jusqu'au bout, de retourner au point de départ chaque fois que la voie s'avère impasse et de toujours recommencer sans reculer devant la difficulté de la tâche. Appelons 'Mut der Wahrheit', reprenant Hegel, cette attitude, intellectuellement courageuse et sincère. Elle continue aujourd'hui à nous être utile en démystificatrice, malgré la distance temporelle qui nous sépare de Spinoza; elle nous invite à remettre en question plusieurs notions fondamentales sur lesquelles nous nous reposons sans nous douter de rien et en nous référant auxquelles nous portons des jugements. Celle de l'Expérience, par exemple, est-elle aussi évidente qu-on ne le pense?

Trois cents ans se sont écoulés depuis la mort de Spinoza. Si par le recul du temps nous sentons parfois mystérieuses ou étranges certaines de ses préoccupations et de ses expressions, nous devons lui reconnaître, vu son attitude envers le Problème, un plus grand 'Mut der Wahrheit', qu'à ceux qui acceptent l'Expérience ou le *donné* sans y voir aucun problème, tout en se prétendant empiristes et qui renient toute philosophie classique (y compris le spinozisme) en la traitant de métaphysique, épithète qu'ils voudraient péjorative.

NOTES

1 Benedictus de Spinoza, *Tractatus de Intellectus Emendatione, et de Via, qua optime veram rerum Cognitionem dirigitur, Spinoza Opera*, herausgegeben von Carl Gebhardt, Heidelberg, Carl Winter, vol. II, pp. 1–40. Pour les oeuvres et la correspondance de Spinoza, nous donnons seulement l'abréviation (*DIE* pour la *Réforme*), le tome et la page de cette édition.

2 Benedictus de Spinoza, *Korte Verhandeling van God, de Mensch en deszelfs Welstand, Spinoza Opera*, vol. I, pp. 1–121 (siglum: *KV*).

3 Benedictus de Spinoza, *Ethica, ordine geometrico demonstrata, Spinoza Opera*, vol. II, pp. 41–308 (siglum: *E.*).

4 Harry Austryn Wolfson, *The Philosophy of Spinoza*, New York, Meridian Books, 1958, vol. II, p. 99ff.

5 Leon Roth, *Spinoza*, London, Allen & Unwin, 1954, p. 27.

6 Wolfson, *op cit.*, p. 23ff.

7 Benedictus de Spinoza, *Epistolae, Spinoza Opera*, vol. IV, pp. 1–342 (sigle: *Ep.*).

8 Thomas Hobbs, *Elementa Philosophica, Sectio Prima, De Corpore*, in *Opera Philosophica quae Latine scripsit Omnia*, studio et labore G. Molesworth, vol. I, Scientia Aalen, 1961, pp. 1–11.

9 René Descartes, *Regulae ad Directionem Ingenii, Oeuvres de Descartes*, publiées par P. Adam et Ch. Tannery, tome X, Paris, Librairie Philosophique J. Vrin, 1966, p. 418.

10 John Locke, *An Essay concerning Human Understanding*, collated and annotated by A. C. Fraser, New York, Dover Publications, 1959, pp. 26–7, 31.

11 André Lalande, *Vocabulaire technique et critique de la philosophie*, Paris, PUF, 1951, 6e éd., pp. 247–8.

12 E.g. Richard Aaron, *John Locke*, Oxford, Clarendon Press, 1963, p. 97ff.; James Gibson, *Locke's Theory of Knowledge and its Historical Relations*, Cambridge University Press, 1960, p. 18ff.

13 Locke, *op. cit.*, pp. 32–4.

14 Descartes, *op. cit.*, pp. 383–4.

15 Ludwig Wittgenstein, *Tractatus Logico-Philosophicus*, London, Routledge & Kegan Paul, 1963, pp. 136–8.

16 Heinrich Rickert, *Der Gegenstand der Erkenntnis*, Tübingen, Verlag von J. C. B. Mohr (Paul Siebeck), 1921, S. 331.

17 *Ibid.*, S. 178ff.

18 T. Parsons and E. Shils, *Towards a General Theory of Action*, Harvard University Press, 1954, p. 167.

19 *Spinoza Opera*, II, p. 324 (Textgestaltung).

20 Les 26 définitions placées au début de chacune des 4 premières parties de l'*Éthique* comprennent 23 verbes à la première personne du singulier: 14 'intelligo', 4 'intelligam', 2 'dico', 2 'voco' et 1 'apello'. En outre il y a 2 'dicitur' (Définitions II et VII de la première partie) et 1 'est' (Définition V de la seconde partie), mais ceux-là supposent le *moi* comme sujet de 'dicere' et celui-ci devient 'dico' dans l'*Explication* suivante. Ainsi, toutes les définitions sont, de fait, données avec le sujet de la première personne du singulier.

ENGLISH SUMMARY: THE METHOD AND THE GIVEN

(A) From the first part of *Tractatus de Intellectus Emendatione* (DIE), Spinoza of those days seems to have had two thoughts in relation to his future work:

1 True philosophy should start from the 'given' idea or definition of God, origin of the universe, and by deducing ideas or definitions of other beings should reproduce the whole Nature *objectively*.

2 It is difficult to meet at once the idea of God; therefore this should be reached step by step from the 'given' ideas or definitions of more familiar and particular things, and the preliminary work tracing back to 'series causarum' is needed. Ideas or definitions will, if familiar and particular, be easily 'given', therefore, if the nature of the 'given' is amplified, the idea or definition of God must appear in the horizon of the 'given'. At that time the preliminary work will fulfil its mission, and just then, the main task or true philosophy, whose 'terminus a quo' is the 'given' idea or definition of God will arise with enough reason. Most of the footnotes in *DIE* seem to mean that Spinoza intended to finish the preliminary work, which is named 'prima via' by him, and he transferred the work of (1) to 'mea Philosophia' which would have been written.

(B) Spinoza deals with definitions in the last part of *DIE*, and tries there to define intellect concretely as 'fundamentum' in order to arrive at the definition of God. That is, he chooses the definition of intellect as a starting point of 'prima via', then from that point he tries to define God. He stopped, however, without defining even one of the most familiar and particular things, intellect, because he was driven out towards the direction of 'regressus in infinitum' in that *DIE* should define intellect but which needs the definition of intellect in order to achieve this.

473

In this thesis I study the adjective 'given' which comes across with curious frequency in *DIE*. This adjective is used in a particular idea or definition which is a starting point of 'prima via' except one case. With this clue to work upon, I would also like to study the reason why *DIE* was not completed, and the relationship between the reality of a frustration of *DIE* and the establishment of a final system of *Ethica*.

28 The Spinoza houses at Rijnsburg and The Hague

Guido van Suchtelen, Amsterdam

I THE HOUSE AT RIJNSBURG

Benedict de Spinoza (1632–77) was excommunicated in Amsterdam, in July 1656; yet he continued his residence in that city and its surroundings (the village of Ouderkerk) for a considerable time. Not until the autumn of 1660, at the age of twenty-seven, did he settle at Rijnsburg. This prosperous village was the centre, from 1621 to 1801, of the Brotherhood of Collegiants, a Protestant sect which had abolished certain special Calvinist theses and rites. Spinoza had already met some prominent Collegiants in Amsterdam. It is probable that the surgeon Herman Hooman, with whom he lodged, was also a member of this Baptist brotherhood.

There are no documents predating 1677 about Spinoza's home on the Katwijkerlaan at Rijnsburg. According to notes made by the seventeenth-century Amsterdam surgeon Monnikhoff, however, the façade of this house bore an inscription consisting of four lines from *Maysche Morgenstondt* (May Morning), a poem by Dirck Camphuysen, who was an adherent of the Collegiants:

Ach! waren alle Menschen wijs/   [Alas! If all Men were wise,
  En wilden daarbij wel!   and were benign as well—
De Aard waar haar een Paradijs/   the Earth would then be Paradise,
  Nu isse meest een Hel.   whereas now it often is a Hell!]

After the death of Spinoza's landlord, the house gradually became dilapidated. By 1896 it was occupied by two working-class families. The gable was then still intact, allowing the house to be identified. When it was offered for sale, Dr Willem Meyer, an eminent Spinozan scholar and translator, used the opportunity to form a society (28 April 1897) for purchasing the house and thus perpetuating the memory of the philosopher's life and work.

The house was carefully restored as a museum, in the style of the seventeenth century. The room believed to have been used by Spinoza was furnished with items listed in the notarial inventory drawn up after his death and recovered by A. L. Servaas van Rooijen in 1888. A wooden workbench of the type used in the late seventeenth century for grinding lenses was set up in the adjoining smaller room (although Spinoza followed a different procedure, as we now know).

The principal feature of the museum is its library. First of all, it comprises a virtually complete reconstruction of Spinoza's personal collection as it must have been in 1677, according to the aforementioned notarial itemization. While the volumes are not the actual ones he owned, they all represent editions which he must have used. Moreover, there are many seventeenth- and eighteenth-century books dealing with Spinoza and his philosophy. According to the custom of the day, the volumes are arranged by size rather than by subject. Most of them were acquired with the financial aid of G. Rosenthal, whose generosity also made it possible for The Spinoza House Society [Vereniging Het Spinozahuis] to purchase the house itself (1897). The Society has since kept the museum in good repair and organized annual lectures which are published in its Bulletin ('Mededelingen').

The six-hundred-odd volumes were seized by the German occupation forces in 1941 and removed. Following the liberation of the Netherlands (May 1945), the library holdings were recovered almost complete in Germany and restored to the museum. During the war years, the house was the property of a private individual who was able to keep it out of the hands of the Germans and eventually returned it to the Society; he also had a small bust of the philosopher, by the sculptor Oscar Wenckebach, erected in the back garden (1945).

Spinoza lived here in his frugal way from the autumn of 1660 to April 1663. Johannes Casearius, a student of theology at the University of Leiden, is believed to have stayed with him for some time during that period; he was instructed by Spinoza, who wrote about him to his friend Simon Joosten de Vries.

It was in this house that Spinoza wrote his adaptations of Descartes's *Principia Philosophiae* (the only texts to appear under his own name during his lifetime), and also worked on the *Short Treatise* and probably on the plan for his *Ethica*. It was also here, in July 1661, that he received a visit from Henry Oldenburg which was to usher in a most important correspondence on the physics of the period (the saltpetre discussion with Boyle). Spinoza's Rijnsburg years were among the most fertile of his life.

II DOMUS SPINOZANA AT THE HAGUE

According to Johann Köhler (Colerus), Benedict de Spinoza lived from 1670 until his death on 21 February 1677 in a small boarding room at the home of the house painter Hendrick van der Spijck. This is corroborated by the notarial inventory of the philosopher's possessions, traced by A. J. Servaas van Rooijen in 1888, which indicates that Spinoza died at the house of van der Spijck. An investigation of the records relating to the house of Spinoza's landlord was carried out by M. Campbell at the time of the erection of the Spinoza statue by F. Hexamer (1880); a further search of old deeds and titles was conducted by Dr C. Gebhardt in 1923. The results of both studies definitely establish the premises known as 72–4 Paviljoensgracht as Spinoza's last place of residence.

The house was built in 1646. Its first owner was Jan van Goyen, the famous landscape painter and real-estate speculator, who let it. It was ultimately bought from his heirs by Havick Steen – a son of the painter Jan Steen – who in turn sold it on 13 June 1669 to the father of Spinoza's landlord, from whom Spinoza rented a room for 80 Dutch guilders a year. This was most likely a garret which faced the street and where, according to his biographers, he spent most of his time.

It was here that Spinoza had his discussions with Leibniz on Descartes's laws of motion and here that he showed him the manuscript of his *Ethica* (1676), which he had just then completed. Here he lived near the residence of his protectors, the famous statesmen Jan and Cornelis de Witt, whose brutal massacre (1672) caused him to exclaim: 'Ultimi barbarorum!' From this house, too, the philosopher undertook his never-explained trip to Condé's winter quarters near Utrecht. Here also he wrote many of the letters which are of prime importance for a proper understanding of his doctrine. And it was from here that, on 25 February 1677, his funeral train proceeded to the New Church on the Spui, inside which church he was buried in rented grave No. 162; this grave was emptied after twelve years. It is not known, therefore, where the earthly remains of Spinoza were deposited or what happened to them. However, a memorial slab (1927) and a small upright monument (1968) can now be seen outside the church.

In 1923 Dr Carl Gebhardt, the Frankfurt Spinozist, made plans to buy the house where Spinoza died. It was then being used as a public house and brothel. With the assistance of his friend Professor A. S. Oko (Hebrew Union College, Cincinnati), he was able to raise most of the purchase money, which was later supplemented by a mortgage. On 4 January 1927, Gebhardt established a foundation named *Domus Spinozana*, which acquired the house a few weeks later (25 January). Two of the aims of Domus Spinozana were to collect objects and books relating to Spinoza and to organize meetings of Spinozists from all over the world. It also became the seat of the international *Societas Spinozana*, which had already been established in 1920, and the Dutch chapter of which operated from here between 1933 and 1940. (The international Societas Spinozana became inactive after mid-1940, when the Netherlands was overrun by the Germans.)

In February 1927, after its provisional restoration, Domus Spinozana was ceremoniously inaugurated during a congress in memory of the 250th anniversary of the philosopher's death. It then served as a centre of *living*

Spinozist thought, inspired by Dr Carl Gebhardt and Dr J. H. Carp, now referred to as the 'Hague School', and largely characterized by a mystical interpretation of the philosopher's works. The house preserved and performed this function until 21 October 1940, when the Rosenberg 'Einsatzstab', or raiding commando, seized the building and sequestered everything in it.

After the German occupation, at the end of 1945, Domus Spinozana was re-established, but the Board at that time had no better use for the house than to let it. Eventually, however, in 1971, the property was transferred to The Spinoza House Society [Vereniging Het Spinozahuis], which has owned the other Spinoza house, the one at Rijnsburg, since 1897.

In March 1976, the *Stichting Monumentenfonds* (a foundation for the preservation of architectural monuments in The Hague) took over the Domus Spinozana; this institution carried out the urgently needed restoration of the neglected building, allowing at least part of the philosopher's last abode to become again accessible to the public as a museum, on the occasion of the 300th anniversary of his death (21 February 1977).

29 Body awareness as a gateway to eternity: a note on the mysticism of Spinoza and its affinity to Buddhist meditation

Jon Wetlesen, Oslo

DOES SPINOZA'S PHILOSOPHY REQUIRE A 'MYSTICAL EXPERIENCE' IN ORDER TO BE UNDERSTOOD?

Now and again the question is raised whether the philosophy of Spinoza is a kind of mysticism or not. In Holland, for instance, this question was formerly debated between members of 'The Hague School', who argued for a mystical interpretation, and members of 'The Rijnsburg School', who argued against it, since they were more in favour of a rationalistic point of view.

Recently this old discussion has been revived by Professor Hubbeling at the University of Groningen. In an article on 'Logic and Experience in Spinoza's Mysticism', he takes sides with the rationalists.[1] He argues that although Spinoza's philosophy has a mystical structure, in the sense that it defends certain doctrines which are often adhered to by typical mystics, this can be explained without assuming that Spinoza himself was a mystic or had any mystical experiences. It can be explained on the basis of logic and rational thinking alone, especially those logical rules which may be established on the basis of axioms 1 and 4 in Part 1 of the *Ethics*.

By way of implication, I suppose that Professor Hubbeling would also hold that in order to reach an adequate understanding of the doctrines of Spinoza, it is sufficient to read his definitions, axioms, postulates, and so forth carefully, and to follow his reasoning as he deduces his propositions. This is sufficient in the sense that it does not require any particular 'mystical experience' in order to grasp the meaning of what Spinoza has to say.

As an example of such a doctrine which has a mystical structure without presupposing any mystical experience, either on the part of Spinoza or his readers, Professor Hubbeling mentions: 'seeing the world and the human self in one great all including vision, i.e. seeing things *sub specie aeternitatis* (from the viewpoint of eternity).'[2]

On this score, however, I believe that Professor Hubbeling's interpretation is not entirely correct. In my opinion, he exaggerates the importance of the second kind of cognition, or reason, at the expense of the third, which is

479

intuition. In fact, Professor Hubbeling seems to admit this to some extent himself when he remarks that he is 'inclined to say that Spinoza's mysticism is, generally speaking, founded on the second way of knowledge and not on the third way.'[3]

I am aware that this is a controversial field of investigation, and that it is bristling with difficulties of interpretation. It has lately taken Professor Gueroult at Paris some 600 pages of well-packed discussion to clarify Part 2 of the *Ethics*, where Spinoza's theory of knowledge is developed.[4] I shall draw on his investigations in the following, and attempt to bring out some of their implications for the questions at hand.

Contrary to Professor Hubbeling, I will argue that the mystical structure of Spinoza's philosophy can not be adequately cognized without presupposing a certain kind of mystical experience, and I see no reason to doubt that Spinoza himself had this kind of experience in rich measure. Moreover, I hold that this experience is first of all related to a certain kind of body awareness, quite similar to that which is cultivated in Buddhist meditation, and that it may very well be considered a kind of mystical experience.

WAS SPINOZA A MYSTIC?

As far as Spinoza himself is concerned, I think we may safely characterize him as a mystic in the sense that he had penetrated deeply into the field of mystical experience; at least a certain kind of mystical experience. I shall postpone for the moment how this kind of experience should be defined. Suffice it to say here that Spinoza appears to refer to such a *unio mystica* in his auto-biographical sketch at the beginning of the *Treatise on the Improvement of the Understanding*. Here he describes his initial enlightenment as 'a cognition of the union which the mind has with the whole of nature' (§ 13).

Moreover, this experience, which Spinoza went through at some early point in his career, was crucial for the reorientation of his way of living. It gave him an internal motivation and power to liberate himself from the enslaving passions of everyday life, so as to give priority to eternal ends before temporal (§ 10), and to reintegrate the latter within the framework of those values and norms which follow from the former (§§ 4, 11). From Spinoza's own account, we may gather that this was a kind of meditative experience (§ 7). These moments of illumination were 'at first rare, and of very short duration, yet afterwards, as the true good became more discernible, they became more frequent and more lasting' (§ 11).[5]

According to Spinoza's mature conceptions in the *Ethics*, this union of the mind with the whole of nature must have reference to nature in so far as it is conceived under the attribute of thinking. In so far as nature is conceived under the attribute of extension, there must be a parallel union of the body with the whole of nature. This follows from Spinoza's theory of a structural and functional isomorphy between the attributes, and from his conception of the mind as the idea of the body. Now, the body can be conceived in two ways, either from the viewpoint of abstract duration and time, or from the viewpoint of eternity. Accordingly, the mind, which is the idea of the body, will be differently conceived in each case. I take it that when Spinoza writes about the union of the mind (or the body) with the whole of nature, this must be understood as equivalent with conceiving the mind (or body) from the viewpoint of eternity.

TO CONCEIVE THE ESSENCE OF THE BODY FROM THE VIEWPOINT OF ETERNITY

This is a main point in Spinoza's mysticism. In the *Ethics* the cognition of things from the viewpoint of eternity is identified with the third kind of cognition, as can be seen from 5P31Dem.[6] However, in 5P29Dem, which is referred to in 5P31Dem, Spinoza states that a person cannot cognize anything from the viewpoint of eternity, except in so far as he conceives the essence of his own body in this way. Since this passage is crucial for the mystical interpretation adduced here, I shall quote Spinoza's own words:

> therefore this power of conceiving things from the viewpoint of eternity does not pertain to the mind except in so far as it conceives the essence of the body from the viewpoint of eternity (5P29Dem).

My argument for holding that this statement supports a mystical interpretation is briefly as follows: in order to conceive anything else from the viewpoint of eternity, a person must be able to conceive the essence of his own body in this way. Now, the essence of the body, as well as of the mind, is here supposed to be a singular essence, while the three kinds of cognition are all general. From this it would seem to follow that the singular essence cannot be an object of cognition. Therefore, if it is perceived at all, it must be perceived in another manner. And this is what Spinoza affirms, I believe, when he states that we may feel and experience that we are eternal. In that case, the cognizing subject, who actually *is* this eternal and singular essence, feels and experiences that he is existentially engaged in the act of cognition while attending to its general contents. This must be a highly personal experience, and if it be granted that it is a mystical experience, we may conclude that such a mystical experience is a precondition for an adequate understanding of the philosophy of Spinoza by the third kind of cognition.

I shall first attempt to substantiate this argument, and then draw out some further implications as to its existential contents. To conceive the essence of the body from the viewpoint of eternity is to be aware of its effort to persevere in its being in a concrete and continuous duration. The power of the body,

481

by which it conserves its existence, is the very power of God, or his active essence, in so far as it is the immanent cause of the singular essence and existence of the body. To be aware of this is to be aware that one's own life participates in the life of God, which, once again, points to the conception of a *unio mystica*. This kind of body awareness involves not only concrete duration, but also the viewpoint of eternity. And this insight generates wisdom, which is the main condition for freedom. At this point Spinoza's theory, and especially the practice which it entails, has a close affinity to certain kinds of Buddhist meditation, which I shall also show.

THE ESSENCE OF THE BODY (AND THE MIND) IS A SINGULAR ESSENCE

The first premise in my argument for a mystical interpretation of 5P29Dem is that Spinoza is here referring to the singular essence of the body, and hence to the singular essence of the mind, which is its idea. This can be established, I believe, from Spinoza's own reference in 5P29Dem to 5P23. If we read 5P23 together with its demonstration, which refers to 5P22, we see that Spinoza is writing about 'the essence of this or that human body' of which there is necessarily given in God an idea from the viewpoint of eternity. In his essay, Professor Hubbeling agrees that 5P22 should be interpreted in this way. He too believes that Spinoza is writing about an *essentia particularis* in this context.[7]

IT IS ALSO AN ETERNAL ESSENCE

This singular essence is not only conceived from the viewpoint of eternity; according to 5P23Sch it is eternal by itself: 'This idea which expresses the essence of the body from the viewpoint of eternity is . . . a certain mode of thinking which pertains to the essence of the mind, and is necessarily eternal.' That is to say, the singular essence of the body is an eternal essence, and the idea of this essence constitutes the singular essence of the mind, which is also eternal.

THE THREE KINDS OF COGNITION ARE ALL GENERAL

The second premise of my argument is that each of the three kinds of cognition are general in character. That is to say, they employ general categories in their attempt to understand things, even when these things are singular entities.

I base this interpretation on 2P40Sch2, where Spinoza introduces the three kinds of cognition as three ways of forming 'universal notions' (*notiones universales*), as he calls them. It should be noticed, however, that his use of the term 'universal notion' in 2P40Sch2 differs from his use of it in 2P40Sch1. In the second scholium it is used neutrally with regard to the distinction between the three kinds of cognition, and thus equivalently with what I call a general category, which may be either a general concept or proposition, or a general image. In the first scholium, on the other hand, it is used for notions belonging to the first kind of cognition only. Moreover, the general categories belonging to the second kind of cognition are called common notions (or common and specific notions), while those belonging to the third kind of cognition are called 'the essence of things'. Following Professor Gueroult, I interpret this expression as 'the general essence of singular things'.[8]

THEREFORE THE SINGULAR ESSENCE OF THE BODY IS NOT AN OBJECT OF COGNITION

If this interpretation is correct, it follows that when Spinoza in 5P29 Dem writes about the mind's conceiving the essence of the body from the viewpoint of eternity, he does not mean that the mind cognizes the singular essence of the body, for this cannot be cognized by the general categories of any of the three kinds of cognition, not even the third.

In this connection we should not forget that according to Spinoza's ontology, only singular essences are real, while general essences as well as other general concepts, propositions, images, and so forth, are not real except in so far as they are modes of cognition.[9] They are either entities of reason or entities of imagination. If this be so, then one should think that Spinoza's system of philosophy as a whole must have the status of an entity of reason, since all its definitions, axioms, propositions, demonstrations, and so forth, purport to express either general essences or general truths. In that case, the reality which this system seeks to account for must be something beyond the general categories of the system itself, and belong to that which is singular, and not to be grasped by the categories of thinking. On this interpretation, Spinoza's philosophy is congenial to mysticism indeed.

NEVERTHELESS, THIS SINGULAR ESSENCE CAN BE FELT AND EXPERIENCED IN A HIGHLY PERSONAL MANNER

Shall we conclude, then, that the mind can in no way perceive the singular essence of the body? Not at all. For, as Spinoza goes on to say in 5P23Sch:

> Nevertheless, we feel and experience (*sentimus, experimurque*) that we are eternal. . . . We feel that our mind, in so far as it involves the essence of the body from the viewpoint of eternity, is eternal, and that its existence cannot be defined by time or explained by duration.

483

In other words, although a person may not be able to cognize his singular essence by any of the three kinds of cognition, he may, nevertheless, feel and experience it in a direct manner. It follows that this must be an extremely personal experience, since it has nothing general about it; it is a peculiar involvement of the person, who actually is this singular essence, in his acts of cognition while he attends to the general contents of the cognition. It is this personal experience which is required, according to 5P29Dem, in order to understand anything from the viewpoint of eternity, or by the third kind of cognition.[10] And we may add that this experience is a special way of being conscious of oneself, of God, and of things, as Spinoza says in 5P31Sch, 39Sch, and 42Sch.

AN EXISTENTIAL DIFFERENCE BETWEEN THE SECOND AND THIRD KINDS OF COGNITION

The difference between the second and third kinds of cognition, therefore, is not that the second cognizes a general entity and the third a singular; both cognize a general entity. Nor is the difference to be found in this, that the second kind of cognition is deductive, while the third is not. Both are deductive, although in two different ways. The difference is first of all an ontological, or existential, difference. The third kind of cognition requires an existential participation on the part of the cognizing subject himself. If this personal experience is lacking, his cognition will only be of the second kind, at best, or of the first, at worst.

The second kind of cognition proceeds by an external and formal deduction, whereby the general properties of singular things are established by subsuming them under properties which are common to all things under a certain attribute, or common and specific to certain classes of things. The third kind of cognition, on the other hand, proceeds by an internal and genetic deduction, proceeding 'from an adequate idea of the formal essence of certain attributes of God to the adequate cognition of the essence of things' (2P40Sch2). This cognition is adequate because it proceeds genetically and understands the essence of things through their first cause, or God, who in a certain sense is the adequate cause of each thing, since he is the immanent cause of all causes.

However, as Professor Gueroult argues, there need not be any difference in the cognitive content between the common and specific notion of a thing and the idea of its general formal essence. The difference arises from the way this content is cognized. The crucial condition which must be met, if a person is going to transform his cognition of a property into a cognition of an essence, is that he be able to cognize it from the viewpoint of eternity.[11] From 1D8 and 5P30Dem we see that this is the same as cognizing the thing through the existence of God; for eternity is the existence of God in so far as it is implied by his essence. But this, according to 5P29Dem, requires first of all that the cognizing person be able to cognize the essence of his own body from the viewpoint of eternity.

This interpretation fits remarkably well with Spinoza's way of contrasting the second and third kinds of cognition in 5P36Sch, although in this scholium he mentions only the essence (and existence) of the mind. But the same observations may be transferred to the essence (and existence) of the body.

According to Professor Gueroult's reading of this passage, the first line in its second half should be divided in two.[12] When Spinoza writes: 'Again, since the essence of our mind consists in cognition alone, the beginning and foundation of which is God' (1P15, 2P47Sch), he is writing about the general essence of the mind, as genetically defined through God as its immanent cause, and hence as an object of the third kind of cognition. However, when he goes on to write that: 'It is clear to us in what manner and for what reason our mind follows with regard to essence and existence from the divine nature and continually depends on God', he is writing about the singular essence of the cognizing person. The singular essence of the cognizing person is existentially engaged in the very act of cognition, whereby he cognizes the general essence of the mind (or body), as stated in the first half of the sentence.

It is by this existential involvement that we 'feel and experience that we are eternal' (5P23Sch), and this feeling adds a clarity (5P36Sch) and certainty (2P43Sch, 49Sch) to our cognition, which makes the third kind of cognition 'much more powerful' than the second kind, as Spinoza remarks later on in 5P36Sch. He continues:

> For although I have shown generally in the First Part [of the *Ethics*] that all things (and consequently also the human mind) depend on God with regard to essence and existence, yet that demonstration, although legitimate and beyond the reach of doubt, does not, nevertheless, affect the mind as much as when the same is concluded from the essence itself of some singular thing which we say depends on God.

This singular involvement, moreover, is a main condition for Spinoza's ethics of liberation; for it is only through the power which it releases that a person can effectively counteract the strength of the passions and thereby gain freedom.

TWO WAYS OF CONCEIVING THINGS AS ACTUALLY EXISTING

I would like to add here some further considerations in support of this view. These considerations may serve, at the same time, as a concretion of what it means to conceive the essence of the body (or mind) from the viewpoint of eternity. There are especially two passages which may be helpful in this connection, the one following immediately after 5P29Dem, namely 5P29Sch, and the one referred to in this scholium, namely 2P45Sch.

> Things are conceived by us as actual in two ways, either in so far as we conceive them to exist with relation to a certain time and place, or in so far as we conceive them to be contained in God and to follow from the necessity of the divine nature. But those things which are conceived in this second manner as true or real, we conceive from the viewpoint of eternity, and their ideas involve the eternal and infinite essence of God, as we have shown in 2P45, to the Scholium of which the reader is also referred (5P29Sch).

This passage may be interpreted either as drawing a distinction between two ways of conceiving this as actual, or between two ways of conceiving this as existing. I quite agree with Professor Gueroult that the latter interpretation has the stronger textual support, for instance when it is read in the light of 2P8Cor, 45Sch, 5P23Sch, and 30&Dem.[13] Let me also quote from 2P45Sch:

> By existence I do not mean here duration, that is, existence in so far as it is conceived abstractly and as a certain form of quantity. I speak of the very nature of existence, which is attributed to singular things because they follow from the eternal necessity of the nature of God, infinite in number and in infinite ways (1P16). I speak, I say, of the very existence of singular things in so far as they are in God. For although each one is determined by another singular thing to exist in a certain manner, yet the force by which each of them perseveres in its existence follows from the eternal necessity of the nature of God (see (1P24Cor) (2P45Sch).

When 5P29Sch is read together with 2P45Sch, we can say that things are conceived by us as actual or as existing in two ways. If we adopt an 'existentialist' terminology, we may call the first one 'authentic existence' and the second 'inauthentic existence'. The first one gives us 'the very nature of existence', and by this alone do we see things 'as true or real'.

THE ACTUAL ESSENCE OF THE BODY (AND MIND), WHICH IS ITS REAL EXISTENCE, IS THE VERY FORCE, OR CONATION, BY WHICH IT CONSERVES ITS BEING

Applying this terminology to 5P29Dem, we may say that when the mind conceives the essence of the body from the viewpoint of eternity, it conceives this essence as actually existing. It is close to hand to identify this with the 'actual essence' of which Spinoza writes in 3P7. I shall return to this presently.

The essence and existence of the body is then conceived to be contained in God and to follow from the necessity of the divine nature; and the idea of the body will then involve the eternal and infinite essence of God, as Spinoza says in 5P29Sch.

Let us follow his reference to 2P45Sch at this point. When the essence of the body is viewed as authentically existing in this way, it is viewed as the very existence of the singular thing, in so far as it is in God and follows from the eternal necessity of the nature of God. And, most important of all, it is seen that the force by which the body (and mind) perseveres in its existence follows from the eternal necessity of the nature of God.

From this we may conclude that when the singular and eternal essence of the body is seen by the mind as actually existing in this authentic way, it is conceived as an actual essence. In 2P45Sch, this is called 'force', which is nothing else than the conation of the body (or mind) to persevere in its being. This part of Spinoza's theory is developed in 3P6&Dem and 7&Dem.[14]

THE MYSTICAL UNION OF GOD'S POWER AND MAN'S

When we follow Spinoza's own references in 3P6 and 7, together with those in 2P45Sch, we may gather that the conation or power of each singular thing, that is, its actual essence, is nothing else than the actual power of God (cf. 1P34, 4P4Dem), or his active essence (cf. 2P3Sch), not in so far as it is infinite, but in so far as it can be explained by the actual essence of man (4P4Dem). Since God is absolutely infinite (1D6), it follows that he must be indivisible (1D12, 13&Sch). Therefore his essence and existence are one and the same (1P20), as are also his essence and power (1P34). Furthermore, since God is the immanent cause of all things (1P18), it follows from his indivisibility that he must be present in all his effects, and equally present in parts and wholes (2P45, 46&Dem). As a consequence, the power of God must be present in the conation of each singular mode, and be so in its totality. This is what the person feels, experiences, and is conscious of when he conceives the essence of his body (or mind) from the viewpoint of eternity.

When the term 'active essence' is used about the power of God, it is traditionally taken as equivalent with the term 'the life of God'.[15] When a person is aware how his singular essence, or actual essence, follows from the active essence of God, he may be said to be conscious of participating in the very life of God, and to be united with God in a mystical union. And this is a most intimate personal experience.

However, at the same time we must take care to point out that this union does not amount to an identification of the essence and existence of man with the essence and existence of God, as some critics of Spinoza will have it (cf. 2D2, 10Sch). The two remain distinct, or rather, incommensurable; since God, or *natura naturans*, is the immanent cause of all modes, or *natura naturata* (1P29Sch), and incommensurable with his effects with regard to both essence and existence (1P17Sch). For this reason Spinoza's philosophy should not be considered as pantheistic, as much as panentheistic.

CONCRETE DURATION FROM THE VIEWPOINT OF ETERNITY

There is another implication of 2P45Sch to which I will also draw attention. This is concerned with the relation between the viewpoint of eternity and duration. As Professor Gueroult has made clear, the viewpoint of eternity does not entail an abolition of duration, but only of duration in so far as it is abstractly conceived by the imagination.[16] Then it is conceived as something measurable in relation to a temporal framework. To the extent that a person goes into the cognition of himself or other things from the viewpoint of eternity, his imaginations concerning abstract duration in time will cease to be experienced as an external reality. He will be reflectively aware that his ordinary conceptions concerning external things, for instance of things past or things future, or of things existing at other places, are nothing more than inadequate projections of his own imagination (cf. 2P17Sch, 49Sch, 5P2). This reflective self-awareness involves a new kind of consciousness (cf. 5P31Sch, 39Sch), which has 'no when nor before nor after' (cf. 1P33Sch2). All the same, this cognition has duration. But this duration is nothing else than the experience of the conation of the body (and mind). The only difference is that now the duration of the body is experienced in a concrete way, as flowing from the life force of the person himself, which is the very life of God. This conception of concrete duration is very close to the 'living duration' (*durée vécue*) of Henri Bergson, although Spinoza's apprehension of its eternal ground is much more profound than his.[17]

One of the properties of this duration is its continuity. This is brought out in Spinoza's remark in 5P36Sch, quoted above, where he says that the person who cognizes something by the third kind of cognition sees how it 'continually depends on God'. The continuity of modal duration follows with necessity from the indivisibility of God's essence or power, which is its immanent cause.

It is true that Spinoza does not use the term 'concrete duration' in 2P45Sch. In that context it seems rather that he uses the term 'duration' as if it were equivalent with 'abstract duration', or 'duration which can be determined in time', as he also calls it in 5P29Dem. However, his definition of duration in *Thoughts on Metaphysics* clearly shows that he would agree to the terminology used above. In Part 1, Chapter 4, § 2 of that work Spinoza writes that

Duration is an attribute under which we conceive the existence of created things according as they endure in their own actuality. From this it clearly follows that duration is not to be distinguished from the totality of a thing's existence except in thought.

TRANSCENDENTAL BODY AWARENESS

It should also be noted that when a person is aware of the essence or conation of his body from the viewpoint of eternity, he has a kind of transcendental awareness which is quite different from, or incommensurable with, an empirical cognition of the body. It is concerned with the body which he *is*, and not the body which he *has*. The empirical cognition belongs to the first kind of cognition. When the body is perceived in that way, it is seen from the viewpoint of an external observer. This observer may be another person or oneself. In either case the body is perceived in an external way together with other external things in the common order of nature; and related to those mental constructs which help us to define the positions of things in time and space. The body is seen as part of the 'life space' of a person, as the phenomenologists would call it. But this entire life space is constituted through the imagination, which remains an abstract and inadequate cognition, as can be seen from Spinoza's summary of this part of his theory in 2P29Cor. This pertains both to the ordinary cognition of everyday life, and to the cognitions within the framework of the various empirical and formal sciences, such as the natural and social sciences and in the humanities.

On the other hand we have the body of which a person is aware in the third kind of cognition. This is felt and experienced from the participant's point of view. Now, since whatever is cognized in the empirical way, within the framework of time and space, belongs to that which is constituted by the imagination, it follows that the constituting body itself cannot belong to time and space. In this sense it is not an empirical body, but a transcendental body; that is to say, it is a necessary condition for generating the constituted body which is conceived by the imagination.

The transcendental body has its being in concrete duration, but not in time and space. However, this can be understood either in a weak sense, in so far as it is understood by the second kind of cognition, or in a strong sense, in so far as it is understood by the third kind of cognition. When it is understood by the second kind of cognition, it is merely understood 'from a certain viewpoint of eternity' (*sub quadam aeternitatis specie*) (2P44Cor&Dem). In this perspective the body may be said to be timeless and spaceless. But when it is understood by the third kind of cognition, it is seen from the viewpoint of eternity (*sub specie aeternitatis*) in the full sense, which is also to see it from the viewpoint of infinity. It is here alone that it is seen to follow from the power of God.[18]

A GATEWAY TO ETERNITY

When a person is reflectively aware of his body and its affections and affects in this way, he no longer mistakes the products of his imagination for external things (5P2), but screens off the tendency to hypostasize the products of the imagination. In this way error and false consciousness are counteracted by adequate cognition; and as a consequence, the passions are counteracted by the active affects. According to 5P4Sch, this is the chief remedy against ignorance and the passions, and therefore, we may add, the foremost strategy of liberation in Spinoza's ethics of freedom.

Through this awareness 'the mind can cause all the affections of the body or the images of things to be related to the idea of God', as Spinoza states in 5P14. In 5P15 and 16 he goes on to say that the more a person understands himself and his affects in this way, the more he loves God. From the references in 5P39Dem, we see that this implies that such a person will have a body which is fit for many things, and therefore a mind of which the greatest part is eternal. In other words, this kind of body awareness is a gateway to eternity, so to say.

AN AFFINITY TO BUDDHIST INSIGHT MEDITATION

It is really curious that when Spinoza comments on this in 5P16Dem, he says that 'this love [of God] is connected (*junctus*) with all the affections of the body (5P14), by all of which it is cherished (5P15), and therefore (5P11) above everything else ought to occupy the mind.' The Latin term *junctus*, or *jungere*, is etymologically related to the Sanskrit term *yoga*, which derives from the root *yuj*, 'to bind together', 'hold fast', 'yoke', French *joug*, Norwegian *åk*, etc.[19] In the Indian cultural area, the term *yoga* serves, in general, to designate any ascetic technique and any method of meditation. In its 'mystical' acceptation, the emphasis is on man's effort to break away from the dispersion and automatism that characterize profane consciousness, and to gain a state of integration which may be characterized as a union with God. It is by 'identifying' himself with Divinity that the yogi attains this integration and internal freedom, which consists in a return from a fragmentary to a total way of being.[20]

I do not mean to suggest that Spinoza used the term *jungere* here in order to allude to *yoga* in its Brāhmanic or non-Brāhmanic forms. I doubt that Spinoza had any direct knowledge about these Indian techniques at all. And yet, it is very interesting that he uses exactly this term in exactly this connection. At least it is interesting from the point of view of a 'perennial philosophy'.[21]

The kind of *yoga* that I would attribute to Spinoza appears to have an especial affinity to certain forms of Buddhist meditation. I use the term 'meditation' in a wide sense here which includes also 'contemplation'. According to a classification of different kinds of meditation or mental culture (*bhāvanā*) which is current within the southern branch of Buddhism, there are two main types of meditation; mental concentration (*samātha bhāvanā*) and insight meditation (*vipassanā bhāvanā*).[22]

Mental concentration in this connection consists in an increasing intro-version, achieved by progressively diminishing the impact of external stimuli. This type of meditation is not so typically Buddhist, but is held in common with Hindu yogic practices. It appears that Spinoza would not have evaluated this kind of meditation so highly, at least not if his statement in 4P18Sch may be taken as an indication of his attitude: 'Indeed, so far as the mind is concerned, our intellect would be less perfect if the mind were alone and understood nothing but itself.' It may be correct to say, perhaps, that in so far as Spinoza was a mystic, he was not of the extremely introvertive type.[23] This attitude on the part of Spinoza is shared by several schools of Buddhism in the Far East, especially among the Ch'an, or Zen Buddhists.[24]

Insight meditation, on the other hand, is a more specifically Buddhist form of meditation. It is based on the principle of Right Mindfulness (*Sammā sati*), as explained in the *Satipaṭṭhāna Sutta*,[25] and consists in an awareness of the body, including its postures and breathing; of the feelings, the mental processes and of mental objects. This fourfold way of mindfulness or aware-ness (*sati*) is first of all a kind of bare attention,[26] which appears to be very close in character to the feeling, experience and consciousness which Spinoza presupposes in connection with the third kind of cognition. Accord-ing to the Buddhists, this mindfulness leads to insight (*vipassanā*) concerning bodily and mental processes, much along the lines which Spinoza clarifies in 5P2–4&Sch, when he writes about having a clear and distinct conception of the affections and affects of the body (and mind). Moreover, according to the Buddhists, the fruition of this insight is nothing less than wisdom (*paññā*).

For the Buddhists, as much as for Spinoza, there is a necessary connection between ignorance and bondage under the passions, and between wisdom and freedom (cp. 3P1, 3). The ignorant person will falsely hypostasize the entities of his imagination, thus believing in the substantiality of egos and things. By this his suffering (*dukka*) is caused. The sage will be aware of the true status of these things, seeing the non-substantiality of egos (*annattā*, cf. 2P10) and of things (*anicca*).[27] They are nothing but *dharmas*, as the Buddhists would say, or modes, as Spinoza would say. They are modes of cognition, constituted through the imagination of the person, arising from the modifications or affections of his body. Through the body awareness described above, the natural attitude of everyday life, which unduly onto-logizes these things, is bracketed.

In the northern branch of Buddhism the different kinds of meditation are classified in a similar manner. In Tibetan Tantric Buddhism, for instance, the 'mind yoga' (or *Mahamudra*) forms a close parallel to the insight medita-tion referred to above, as does also the so-called 'cultivation of the innate mind' in Chinese Ch'an Buddhism and Japanese Zen Buddhism.[28]

It is a strong point in these Eastern traditions that they emphasize the practice of meditation. On this score Western philosophers and others have much to learn. Nevertheless, one finds also among Western mystics a variety of meditative techniques, and if I am not mistaken, Spinoza's way to freedom, through an awareness of the body from the viewpoint of eternity, is remarkably similar to the way of the Buddha.

IS THIS A MYSTICAL EXPERIENCE?

I conclude, then, that Spinoza's philosophy can not be adequately understood by the third kind of cognition, unless the cognizer becomes existentially involved in his act of cognition in a way that amounts to a very personal experience.

However, it may still be asked whether it is well founded to call this a mystical experience? Whether it is, depends, among other things, on how we define the term 'mystical experience'. Considering the literature in this field, there seems to be a fairly high consensus that one should include both cognitive and affective elements in the concept of a mystical experience.[29] Among the cognitive characteristics there is the cognition of God, or of something which is recognized to be the absolute reality; and the emphasis must be on the immediate and intimate awareness of one's own relation with this divine presence. Among the affective characteristics there is first of all the pure attitude of love, both towards God and towards one's fellow-beings in nature. There are also other affects included, such as pure joy or blessedness, and tranquillity.

It seems to me that in so far as the third kind of cognition involves a personal experience, it satisfies these requirements of a mystical experience. On the cognitive side this is an intimate cognition of God (4P28), or rather, of singular modes through God (5P24, 27Dem); involving a highly personal feeling and experience (5P23Sch) of the essence of one's own body from the viewpoint of eternity (5P29Dem). That is to say, the person who is engaged in this kind of cognition must clearly experience how his own essence and existence follows from the essence and existence of God, and how it continually depends on it (5P36Sch).

On the affective side, moreover, this third kind of cognition generates active joy, which is also called blessedness or felicity (5P32Dem, 33Sch, 36Sch); active love, which is also called repose in oneself (5P27, 32Dem, 36Sch, 42Sch) and intellectual love of God (5P32Cor, 33, 35, 36&Cor). Besides, these affects generate active desire, or fortitude, which has reference to the well-being of others as much as of oneself (3P59Sch, 4P73Sch, 5P41).

MYSTICAL EXPERIENCE; A PRECONDITION FOR SPINOZA'S ETHICS OF LIBERATION

This cognition and the affects which it generates constitute the source of the basic values and norms of Spinoza's ethics, just as they do in the ethics of wisdom and love which may be found among most mystics in the world.[30] Without the experiential basis of the third kind of cognition, I am afraid that it could not be a motivating source for this kind of ethics at all. Reason alone is not enough (4P17Sch). So I cannot see that anything is gained by purging the element of mystical experience from the philosophy of Spinoza, and reducing it to the rational element alone.

On the contrary, it seems to me that when we approach the philosophy of Spinoza, there is always a certain danger of becoming overly involved in its technical apparatus of definitions, axioms, propositions, demonstrations and so forth. Our approach may easily become more intellectualistic or academic than was intended by Spinoza himself. However, if we desire to avoid this, it may be helpful to ask what is the living experience which served Spinoza as a source of his philosophy? If we suppose that there is a mystical experience at the bottom of it, we may perhaps also ask if Spinoza's reflections may be of any help to us in order to penetrate somewhat deeper into this experience, and to see its implications somewhat clearer, both in theory and in the practice of our own lives.

NOTES

1 H. G. Hubbeling, 'Logic and Experience in Spinoza's Mysticism' in J. G. van der Bend (ed.), *Spinoza on Knowing, Being and Freedom*, Assen, 1974, pp. 126–43.
2 *Ibid.*, p. 126.
3 *Ibid.*, p. 139.
4 M. Gueroult, *Spinoza, i. Dieu (Éthique, 1)* Paris, 1968; *ii. L'Âme (Éthique, 2)*, Paris, 1974.
5 For supplementary evidence concerning Spinoza's early experiences of mystical union, see his *Short Treatise on God, Man and his Well-Being*, tr. A. Wolf (1910), New York, 1963, pp. 78–80, 100, 115, 116, 147, 149, and especially pp. 123, 133, 135.
6 To be read as follows: *Ethics*, Part 5, Proposition 31, Demonstration. Other abbreviations which I also use are: Corr – Corollary, D – Definition and Sch – Scholium.
7 Hubbeling, *op. cit.*, pp. 133, 137–8.
8 Gueroult, *op. cit.*, ii, pp. 429ff., 459–66, 547–51.
9 *Ibid.*, p. 463.
10 *Ibid.*, pp. 440, 464–66.
11 *Ibid.*, p. 343, and also pp. 377, 390, 453–6.
12 *Ibid.*, p. 549, and also pp. 120, 454ff.
13 *Ibid.*, pp. 616–18, and also pp. 296ff., 422–4, 439, 586, 609–15.
14 *Ibid.*, pp. 422, 447.
15 Cf. Gueroult, *op. cit.*, i, p. 381, concerning the traditional equivalence between the term 'active essence' (*essentia actuosa*) and the term 'life of God' (*Vita Dei*). See also Gueroult's remarks on the mysticism of Spinoza in i, p. 9; ii, pp. 464, 534.

16 Cf. *Ibid.*, ii, p. 613.
17 Cf. *Ibid.*, i, p. 504.
18 Cf. *Ibid.*, ii, pp. 409ff., 415, 416, 609–15.
19 Cf. M. Eliade, *Yoga, Immortality and Freedom*, New Jersey, 1958, pp. 4–5.
20 Cf. A. Daniélou, *Yoga, The Method of Re-Integration*, London, 1949, p. 16. On Spinoza's theory of liberation through identification with God, see Gueroult, *op. cit.*, i, pp. 82, 83, 128, 129, 346; ii, p. 128.
21 Cf. A. Huxley, *The Perennial Philosophy* (1946), London, 1959, p. 9.
22 W. Rahula, *What the Buddha Taught*, New York, 1959, p. 68.
23 Cf. W. T. Stace, *The Teaching of the Mystics*, New York, 1960, p. 17, concerning this and other types of mysticism.
24 Cf. D. T. Suzuki, *Essays in Zen Buddhism*, i (1927), London, 1973, pp. 79ff., 85, 233, 237, 260, 262; ii (1953), 1972, pp. 25, 26, 109, 127, 331; iii (1953), 1973, pp. 17, 73; and also *The Zen Doctrine of No Mind* (1949), London, 1972, pp. 18, 25–7, 32–7, 43–50.
25 Tr. by Soma Thera, *The Way of Mindfulness*, Kandy, 1941.
26 Cf. Nyanaponika Thera, *The Heart of Buddhist Meditation*, London, 1962, pp. 29, 30ff., 89, 102.
27 Cf. Nyanatiloka, *Buddhist Dictionary. Manual of Buddhist Terms and Doctrines* (1952), rev. ed by Nyanaponika, Colombo, 1972: 'Ti-lakkhana, the three Characteristics of existence; Impermanence (*anicca*), Suffering (*dukkha*), Not-Self (*anattā*)'.
28 Cf. C. C. Chang, 'Yogic Commentary', in W. Y. Evans-Wentz (ed.), *Tibetan Yoga and Secret Doctrines*, (1935), London, 1965, pp. xxvii-xlii. See also his book, *The Practice of Zen* (1959), New York, 1970, pp. 204–19, 'The Seven Different Types of Meditation Practice', esp. pp. 214–15. On the importance of body awareness in Zen, see T. Deshimaru, *Vrai Zen*, Paris, 1969, and even more, his pupil, H. Hof, *Mer Människa, Meditation och Terapi enligt Zen-Metoden*, Stockhom, 1975.
29 I have consulted for instance, R. M. Jones, 'Mysticism' in D. D. Runes (ed.), *Dictionary of Philosophy*, New York, 1962; D. Knowles, *What is Mysticism?* London, 1967, pp. 13, 30, 122, 126, 128; W. T. Stace, *op. cit.*, pp. 9ff., 14–18; E. Underhill, *Mysticism*, (1911 rev. edn, 1930), London, 1960, pp. 72ff., 81ff.
30 This theme is further explored in my book, *The Sage and the Way. Studies in Spinoza's Ethics of Freedom* (forthcoming).

30　On translating Spinoza

Paul Wienpahl, Santa Barbara

This paper concerns a few problems, principles and insights encountered in translating the writings of Spinoza into English. It stems from six years of work, during which time everything that Spinoza wrote has been translated, re-translated and commented on. The translations have been made from Carl Gebhardt's Heidelberg edition of the works, with reference to the *Opera Posthuma* (1677), the *Nagelate Schriften* (1677), and Pieter Balling's translation into Dutch of *Descartes' Principles of Philosophy* (1664). Every sentence of the translations has been compared with standard Dutch, English, French and German translations of Spinoza, of which there are uncommonly few that are complete and by a single hand.[1]

I should also mention that there is a particular source for the translations in my personal life. In 1959 I began the practice of Zen or Ch'an Buddhism, known in Japanese as *zazen*. I hasten to add that this has not resulted in a Buddhistic interpretation of Spinoza. Indeed I have done all I can to avoid interpretation, including making a translation which depends on having the Latin of Spinoza on facing pages, and which is rather to make that understandable than to be substitute for it in English. The practice of *zazen* has, however, been a vital source for my understanding of what Spinoza said. For example, the notion of egolessness in Zen Buddhism, as well as some experience of egolessness, albeit very small, resulted in seeing that Spinoza's description of God in the *Ethica* may well be taken as a description of egolessness.[2] This in turn is of help with his idea of human freedom.

I will note, finally, that I early adopted a principle of translation which had often to be violated, but led thereby to important results – or so they seem to me. This principle is that of translating a Latin word wherever possible by an English word with a Latin root. English is a mixture of words of Anglo-Saxon origin with words of Latin origin. The proportion of the latter is far higher than that of the former (four-fifths), though on any given page in English in the twentieth century 60 to 90 per cent of the words are of Anglo-Saxon provenance. Thus, users of my translations (students) often get the impression that it is not a translation. It constantly turns them to a dictionary. On the other hand, as I have said and as we shall see, the principle leads at least to interesting results. It need scarcely be mentioned that this principle is related to another: wherever necessary, sacrifice style to literalness.

I

The basic insight of the *Ethica*, and the insight underlying all of Spinoza's writings including *Descartes' Principles*, is set forth in the first fourteen propositions of Part I. Propositions 1 to 8 are about 'substance', propositions 9 and 10 are about 'attribute', proposition 11 asserts that 'God exists . . . necessarily', and proposition 14 that besides God no substance can be given or conceived. The insight, that is, is that there are not *substances*.

The consequences of this insight are momentous. Spinoza immediately draws two of them in the corollaries to proposition 14. The first is that God is uniquely (*Deum esse unicum*), that is, that in the nature of things only one substance is given, and it is absolutely infinitely (*absolute infinitam esse*). The second is that the extended thing (*rem extensam*) and the thinking thing (*rem cogitantem*) are either God's attributes, or affections of attributes of God.

A third consequence lurks more deeply than the first two and surfaces best in the context of translating Spinoza. The Scholastics and Descartes had said that God is unique, and all were agreed that there is only one material substance (though they talked of material *things*). They did this, however, in the Aristotelian atmosphere. That is to say, they talked and thought in terms of things and their properties, and the actions they perform. Put grammatically, they used the verb 'to be' (*sum, esse*) as a copula more often than they did as an active verb. When they wanted to express the activity of being, they tended to employ the unclassical verb 'to exist' (*exsto*, or *ex(s)isto*, *existere*). The third consequence of Spinoza's insight is that 'to be' should never be used as a copula, but only as an active verb. Thus, instead of 'the house is brown', given Spinoza, we should say, 'the house is brownly'. Hence we have 'God is uniquely' and substance is 'absolutely infinitely' in the first translation of the first corollary above.

Given this, one sees that the concept of property is similarly and correspondingly altered. Property-words become adverbs. Not only is 'is' active, but even the subjects of sentences become verbal forms. The best example of this is in the main word for what we commonly call 'God': *Being*. God is perfectly or infinitely. Modes are finitely or imperfectly. They exist. That the concept of property is altered follows from seeing that there are not substances, since it depends on the notion of substance.

Greek thought received the fullest expression of one of its aspects in the so-called 'substance-attribute metaphysics'. This metaphysics is reflected in the grammar of the common Western languages. Discourse is measured in paragraphs, paragraphs are composed of sentences. Sentences either attribute a property to a subject or express an action performed by a subject. A common notion or axiom of Descartes's day was: no attributes, or no properties or qualities are of nothing (*nihili nulla sint attributa, nullaeve proprietas aut qualitates*, Principles, I, 52, and its very form suggests that it is a grammatical requirement). In seeing that *substances* (the things of which properties, etc., are) cannot be given, Spinoza was seeing, grammatically speaking, that the forms of ordinary speech must be violated if he was to express himself properly; and 'properly speaking' was a favourite phrase of his. We should, for example, say, 'properly speaking "the house is brownly," *not* "the house is brown".'

Before taking a look at some instances of what his insight involves in translating him, I call attention to three examples of Spinoza's own acute and explicit awareness of the fact that the common grammar required violation if he was to make himself understood. I will add to these cases which he himself used an adjective where one would expect an adverb, and where he used an adjective as well as an adverb to modify a verb.

In the appendix to *Descartes' Principles*, in writing of God's immensity, Spinoza says, 'From which it follows that God's *Infinity*, an unwilling noun-substantive, is something maximally positive'. Gebhardt, vol. I, p. 253, ll. 30–1: *Ex quo sequitur, quod Dei* Infinitas, *invito vocabulo, sit quid maxime positivum*. Frank A. Hayes in a recent translation of the book in the Library of Liberal Arts, 1963, has: 'From this it follows that the infinity of God, despite the form of the word. . . .' In the EU, p. 33, Spinoza has a discussion of negative terms.[3]

Again, writing in Letter 12 of his fundamental distinction between eternity and duration, Spinoza says that we should explicate modes's existing by means of *Duration*, 'but in fact that of Substance by means of *Eternity*, that is, infinite fruition of to be existing or, in unwilling latinity, *essendi* [of to be be-ing].' '*Substantiae vero per Aeternitatem, hoc est, infinitam existendi, sive, invita latinitate, essendi fruitionem*' (p. 55, ll. 2–3).

A few remarks should be interposed here. Abraham Wolf in his translation of the *Correspondence* renders the line: 'but we can only explain the existence of Substance by means of Eternity, that is, the infinite enjoyment of existence or (in awkward Latin) *essendi*,' leaving the last untranslated. Appuhn, the best French translator, has 'joyousness of existence or being' and omits the important and revealing '*invita latinitate*'. In his German translation Gebhardt includes the phrase but omits the verb, making little sense; '*der Existenz oder (dem Latein zum Trotz) Seins*' (existence or (in defiance of the Latin) being). The reader, of course, is left in the dark about the defiant verb, which Elwes notes is an unclassical form. 'The Latin verb of being is, as the ancients themselves admitted, defective in a most inconvenient degree' (vol. II, p. 319).

The example also requires some explanation, which will be amplified later.

497

The 'ancients' made little or no distinction between 'be' and 'exist'. For instance the nominal form of 'to exist', that is, 'existence' was given by '*esse*'. Spinoza had at his disposal '*sum, esse*', '*exsto*', and the participles or gerunds '*essentia*', '*ens*', '*existentia*', and '*existendum*'. '*Essentia*' is commonly translated with '*essence*', which we will see is philosophically unsound. I translate it with 'being' (and analogously '*existentia*' with 'existing' instead of 'existence'). Then to distinguish '*esse*' (when used nominally), '*ens*', and '*essentia*' I use 'be-ing', '*being*', and 'being'. This becomes important because '*Ens*' is the proper name of what we commonly call 'God' or 'Nature', the latter being appellatives; see Preface, Part IV *Ethica*, where the famous '*Deus sive Natura*' occurs on p. 206. See also pp. 169–70 in Ch. 13 of the TTP; p. 177 in Elwes's translation.

Next, attention should be called to the TTP, p. 38, ll. 24–5 where Spinoza explains the Biblical name for God '*Jehova*', 'which in Hebrew expresses these three tenses of *to be existing*'. The three tenses are the future, the present, and the past; and the Latin here is: '*quod Hebraice haec tria tempora existendi exprimit*'. One should also recall that Spinoza wrote a Grammar of Hebrew (unfinished) in which he calls attention to the fact that originally all words in Hebrew except interjections and conjunctions were verbs.

Finally, I use italics in the English, where they do not occur in the Latin, when Spinoza is mentioning rather than using a word; a practice he himself often employs (either that or that of capitalizing the word).[4] As for the somewhat barbarous 'to be existing', it has the merit of combining 'be' and 'exist' which for Spinoza in the case of God have the same use (*Ethica*, Part I, prop. 20); although he commonly used 'exist necessariously' to distinguish the 'exist' used for modes from that used with 'God' (see p. 496, where prop. 11 is quoted).

The third example of Spinoza's attention to grammatical issues comes from Letter 75, p. 315, ll. 13–17, where, in the course of a discussion about the TTP, he remarks:

> Finally you believe that the places in the Gospel of John & in the Epistle to the Hebrews are repugnant to what I have said, because you measure the phrases of oriental Languages by European modes of speaking, & although John wrote his Gospel in Greek, nevertheless he Hebraized.

One should not forget that, although Spinoza spoke Portuguese in his home and wrote his apology for excommunication in Spanish, his language of learning and instruction was Hebrew. Furthermore, as was just noted, he spent much time on a grammar of Hebrew, and, as he tells us, not simply of Scriptural Hebrew (which is true of so many grammars of Hebrew) but of the Hebrew language. It is also of interest that contemporary authorities on Scripture entertain the view that John's Gospel was not written originally in

Greek. Spinoza's remark, therefore, is also a sign of the care and linguistic awareness with which he read John.

Turning now to cases where an adverb is clearly indicated, although Spinoza used an adjective, let us look at props 8 and 22, Part I, *Ethica*. These are also cases where 'is' occurs as an active verb; although it seems to be, and is taken by translators to be, a copula. Prop. 8 reads: '*Omnis substantia est necessario infinita*.' I read this as 'Every substance necessarily is infinitely.' Elwes (for example, but all the other translations have the same in their respective languages) reads: 'Every substance is necessarily infinite.' However, 'to be infinitely' seems clearly indicated, for in the demonstration we have: '*Erit ergo de ipsius naturae, vel, finita, vel infinita existere*' (since by prop.7 to exist pertains to the nature of a substance). This should come into English by: 'It will therefore be of its nature to exist either finitely or infinitely.' Elwes, the French, and the German translations nevertheless read something like: 'It will therefore be of its nature to exist either as finite or as infinite.' Here the NS, translated, reads: 'It will then be of its nature to exist either finite or infinite.'

Prop. 22, in which both an adverb and an adjective modify a verb, reads: '*Quicquid ex aliquo Dei attributo, quatenus affectum est tali modo, qui & necessario, & infinita per idem existit, sequitur, debet quoque & necessario & infinitum existere*.'[5] This comes sensibly, if not grammatically correctly, into English as: 'Whatever follows from some attribute of God, in so far as it is affected by such a mode that it exists both necessarily & infinitely by means of that attribute, is also bound to exist both necessarily, & infinitely.' Using 'modified' and 'modification', Elwes in the relevant portions reads: 'exists necessarily and as infinite.' Appuhn, using 'affected' and 'modification', has '*existe nécessairement et est infinie*' (exists necessarily and is infinite).

This second case also embodies the confusion between 'to be' and 'to exist' which Spinoza tried vainly to undo (see Letter 34 at the end, for example). 'Is' in the languages I know is fundamentally ambiguous between 'to be' and 'to exist'. In seventeenth-century Dutch the verb for 'to exist' (*wezentlijk zijn*) did not even have a root different from the verbs for 'to be' (*wezen* and *zijn*). (This may be why Gebhardt did not notice the change in the NS to 'must be' from 'must exist', see note 5.) The ambiguity is of enormous philosophical importance, another of the insights which comes with translating Spinoza. It is one of the reasons men like Anselm, Descartes, and Spinoza were convinced by the so-called 'ontological argument', and men like Gaunilon, Hume, and Kant found it unsatisfactory.[6]

II

We have noted two important consequences of the insight that there are not substances which were immediately stated by Spinoza himself: the corollaries to prop. 14 (p. 496 above). The third consequence, which we have stated, that properly speaking 'is' should not be used as a copula, results in the translation of corol. I on p. 496: (*Deum esse unicum*) God is *uniquely*, and that the one substance is absolutely *infinitely* (not 'is infinite').[7] However, I am concerned here with Spinoza's own second consequence: that the extended thing and the thinking thing are either God's attributes, or affections of attributes of God.[8] Having seen that there are not substances, Spinoza had, of course, to account for the talk in the 'new' philosophy (Descartes's) of the two substances, mind and matter (*res cogitans* and *res extensa*). The solution to his problem came in the concept of the attribute. In the *Ethics*, Part III, explication of def. XX, p. 195, Spinoza expresses his awareness of another problem, that of introducing new terminology. We have, he says in effect, to do the best we can with current terminology. Else we run the risk of not being understood at all. In his day the words 'attribute' and 'property' were used almost interchangeably (see the common notion on p. 496); although Descartes tended to reserve 'attribute' for the most important property of a thing, that or those that essentially make it what it is. Spinoza proceeded to employ the term as a means of talking about what were then being called 'mind' and 'body' or 'matter'. His idea was to speak adjectively or attributively of these 'things', not substantively.[9]

Accordingly Spinoza defines an attribute (def. 4, Part I) as follows: 'By means of *attribute* I understand that which understanding perceives concerning a substance, as if constituting its being' (*tanquam ejusdem essentiam constituens*, of which the conventional English translation (that is, the Aristotelian translation) is: 'as constituting its essence'. (Elwes, for example, also has 'as' instead of 'as if' for '*tanquam*'.) Spinoza then specifies (prop. 9) that a substance can have more than one attribute (Descartes had specified one each for mind and matter); and that (prop. 10) an attribute is bound to be conceived by means of itself. He adds in the scholium to prop. 10 that just because we can conceive of two attributes as really distinct (a real distinction is one between two substances, for Spinoza, or between two substances or a substance and its attribute for Descartes) – just because we can conceive of two attributes as really distinct, we can nevertheless not conclude thence that 'they constitute two *beings* [*entia*] or two diverse substances.'

When you turn to his definition of 'substance' (3, Part I) you find that it includes this, that a substance can be conceived solely by means of itself (*per se*). That is to say, 'attribute' and 'substance' are to be used in virtually the same ways; or attribute-words ('mind', 'body') and substance-words ('God', 'Nature', '*Being*') are to be used in virtually the same way; that is, as subjects of sentences. The difference is that the first are adjectives and the second 'proper' nouns (in fact, of course, they are proper names). Spinoza explicitly states this in Letter 9, where he specifies what he means by 'substance' (p. 46) and adds: 'I understand the same by *attribute*, except that it is called *attribute* with respect to understanding when attributing a certain such nature to a substance.'[10]

It follows, then, that when Spinoza uses the word '*mens*' (mind), he is using it adjectively, even when it appears as the subject of a sentence. Properly speaking there is only one subject for all sentences: 'God' or its alternates 'Nature' and '*Being*'. Since our subject is translating Spinoza, we turn next to the problem of translating '*mens*' in the *Ethica*. The problem, incidentally, would also appear in *writing* the *Ethica*. It applies equally to translating a letter by Spinoza. Since his correspondents failed to understand him (though Hudde, Balling, Meyer and Tschirnhaus were close to it), there is no problem in translating '*mens*' in letters not by Spinoza. There is, however, the problem of consistency in the translation in the whole correspondence. One solution to it is what has just been done: simply to call attention to it.

In the first edition of the *Ethica*, that is, in the OP, the problem is given, or was given, a singularly elegant solution: a distinctive use of capital letters. Unfortunately the solution does not appear in the NS, the companion to the OP which appeared simultaneously with it in 1677. Thus, we cannot be sure of the identity of the author of the solution. Glazemaker, who produced the NS, used a different manuscript from that used for printing the OP, and the solution may not have been in his manuscript. On the other hand, it may also not have been in the manuscript used for the OP, presumably the one left by Spinoza at his death. (There are no extant manuscripts of the *Ethica*.) Surely on such an important issue the solution to the problem would have been communicated to Glazemaker by the printer – if by no one else. Still, if the solution were not in the manuscript, but was devised by one of the editors of the OP, would not the same have been true?

The matter remains a mystery to me. However, the identity of the actual author of the solution is not important. Whoever it was, and my own guess is Lodewijk Meyer, it was someone who understood Spinoza very well indeed.[11] This has not been true of subsequent editors. For after the second edition of the *Opera* (Paulus, Jena, 1802–3) and the third (Gefroerer, Stuttgart, 1830), the solution was dropped from the printings of the *Ethica*; namely in Bruder's text of 1843, probably the most widely read of all the editions in Latin. It appears in none of the English translations of the *Ethica*. It is in none of the German translations due to the nature of that language, in which all nouns are capitalized; though it could have occurred with another device had its importance been recognized. It does appear in Appuhn's French translation, though it is dropped in the later and most recent French translation by R. Caillois, Paris, 1967. It was, finally, restored by Gebhardt in the Heidelberg edition of the complete writings.[12]

Specifically, the device consists in capitalizing the initial letters of '*mens*' and '*corpus*' when they appear as attribute-words. The device is also used elsewhere throughout the *Ethica* when Spinoza uses a common word in an important special way, as he does when he is using 'Mind' and 'Body'. Thus, *'Natura'* is capitalized when it equals 'God', very often *'Ens'*, 'Individual', and all the names of the Affections.

That Spinoza uses *'natura'* in a special way is evident in the *Ethica*. However, it is actually stated in Letter 73, p. 307, where Spinoza says that he does not at all mean by 'God' and 'Nature' what is ordinarily meant. Nature for him, of course, is animate (schol., prop. 13, Part II). *'Ens'* is often a proper name and therefore to be capitalized. 'Individual' (*Individuum*) is Spinoza's word for what has been called 'atom', the basic corporeal unit, though its definition is profoundly different from that of 'atom' (see section on bodies after prop. 13, Part II). Finally, the Affections for Spinoza are kinds of behaviour rather than states of character or dispositions to kinds of behaviour.

The device changes the sense, if you will, of the word. 'Really' for example, has a different sense from 'really!'. So too is 'Mind' different from 'mind' and 'Body' from 'body'.[13] The difference in sense in the *Ethica* betokens the difference between the use of an adjective and the use of a noun. One has only to read the *Ethica* with 'Mind' and 'Body' in it in the proper places to feel the power of the device. Gebhardt quite understates the effect. It is far more than a difference of nuance. The device reflects an entire difference in philosophical outlook – the shift from the Aristotelian to the Spinozistic, or, it might be said, from the ancient to the modern. A good place in the *Ethica* to notice in brief compass the interplay between 'Mind' and 'mind' and 'Body' and 'body' is in the scholium to prop. 2, Part III.

The concept of attribute (and with it the change in the sense of 'mind' and 'body') dissolves the strange and vexing problem of the nature of the union of mind and body. Spinoza brings this out explicitly in the scholium to prop. 13, Part II. We now see, he says, what is to be understood by means of 'the union of the human Mind and Body'. The union is only a problem when mind and body are *thought* of as substances. When we think of a union, we think of something taking place between two *things*. If these things are conceived as really distinct, their union becomes inconceivable. When, however, they are thought of as aspects or attributes of the same thing, there is not even a question of their union. There is no question about the manner in which the two sides of a coin function together. As I say, the problem of the union is not solved. It dissolves with this other way of thinking. One comes with it to see, as Spinoza continues in this scholium, that every thing in nature is animate ('minded').[14] This vision gives the experience of what Spinoza called 'the union of the mind with the whole of Nature' in the EU (p. 8, ll. 26–7; the capitalizing is not consistent in the EU, increasing its mystery in the *Ethica*). Talk of this experience leads naturally to another matter: Spinoza's distinction between imagination and understanding.

III

Given that there are not *substances* (notice the impropriety of 'there are no substances', since God is), it follows that there are no faculties, such as *the* understanding, the imagination, the will, etc. (see, for example, schol., prop. 48, Part II). There are actions of understanding, imagining, willing, etc. Thus, in the following we shall omit 'the' before 'understanding', etc. Another great problem in translating the *Ethica* is the use of articles. The problem is especially acute because Latin does not have a definite or an indefinite article – a fact that has led to much reification, as well as unnecessary abstraction, in Western thought. The matter is pursued further, on p. 511 below.

If the formal structure of the *Ethica* has one fault, a possibility which I am reluctant to admit, it is that the term 'understanding' is nowhere explicitly discussed. It is instead widely used throughout and receives its meaning from the whole context – which is in its way fitting. (Spinoza himself remarks in the scholium to prop. 11, Part II that we must read him all the way through. See note 5 on the absence of a definition of 'Mind'. 'Imagination' *is* defined (schol., prop. 17, Part II), as well as used throughout. Furthermore, it is explicitly treated in the EU (pp. 32, 33) and in several letters, notably 12 and 37. However, it is treated almost in passing in the scholium in question, and this reader was not alerted to the importance of its relation to understanding until he had thoroughly digested the EU, the letters and, importantly, the TTP.

Before discussing the distinction between imagining and understanding, I want to set forth an opinion without justifying it textually. It is that Spinoza attempted in the EU, among other things, to clarify what he meant by understanding. The word he was using in those days was 'perception.' For example, where he specified the genera of knowledge (as he called them in the *Ethica*, schol. II, prop. 40, Part II) he called them the four modes of perceiving (p. 10). Furthermore, when one compares the OP with the NS or Balling's translation of Descartes's *Principles* with the Latin version, it is often found that where the Latin text has '*percipere*' the Dutch has '*verstaan*' (understand). The opinion also has it that Spinoza failed in this task; and that this is the reason why the EU remained unfinished, though he constantly tinkered with the *Ethica* and the letters until his death. The fact seems to be that the EU could not be finished because it was couched in such terms that this was impossible; for example, the full-blown notion of the attribute had not yet been developed. (In the ST the Dutch for 'property' is used instead of that for 'attribute'.) A fresh start had to be made. This became Part II of the *Ethica*, and when it was accomplished the important notion of understanding was defined, not explicitly, but in context.

There probably was, however, another reason than the terminological for the failure of the EU – as well as the later failure, if it is a failure, to treat explicitly of the distinction between imagination and understanding in the *Ethica*. The reason is that Spinoza's notion of understanding was so different from any such notion current in his day. This reason has to do with his seeing that there is no real distinction between Mind and Body, for he had to clarify a way of knowing, understanding, in which *both* Mind and Body play a role (see note 5 again).

Well, then, as Spinoza defines imagination in schol. prop. 17 it includes what we ordinarily call imagining (for which he employs the word '*fingo*', also '*affingo*', '*feign*', which gives him 'fiction' and 'fictitious'), *and* what we ordinarily call perceiving and sensing (hearing, visually seeing, etc.). Literally it is the having of any images, or imaging (auditory, etc., as well as visual). For him we take any thing we experience, including fictions, to exist external to us until we find a reason for not doing so. In the section on imagination in the EU all this is extended to the use of words. In Letter 12 we find that this implies a further extension. The activity of the physicists and the mathematicians (for example, in dealing with the infinite) is an activity of imagination, although we can also understand the infinite. In Letter 37 the extension is even greater. There the distinction between understanding and imagination is stated as that 'between true ideas, and the rest, namely the fictitious, the false, the doubtful, and absolutely all those which depend solely on memory.'[15]

Given this extremely broad notion of imagination, we are in a position to see that the second and third genera of knowledge specified in schol. II, prop. 40, Part II, even though the second is *called* 'opinion' or 'imagination' and the third 'reason', are in fact the work of imagination. And it is significant that Spinoza goes on in the scholium to say that '*Besides* these two genera of knowledge . . . there is another third, which we shall call knowing intuitively ['*scientia intuitiva*'],' (emphasis added). The third is, in fact, an aspect of understanding. It is also really the fourth genus because there is a first genus: knowledge by vague experience (or wandering experience, experience as it wanders without the conduct of reason). Intuitive knowing is knowledge of singular things, or, as Spinoza puts it, 'adequate knowledge of the being of things'. It is unmediated by concepts, universal notions, common notions (axioms) and what we ordinarily call 'ideas' (the false, the fictitious, the doubtful and absolutely all those of memory).

This is the having of true or adequate *ideas*. Given the lack of a real distinction between Mind and Body, it is a kind of awareness in which the distinction between subject and object disappears. It is probably best exemplified in activities which we *know how* to perform. Before we know how to perform them we can be told or we can think *about* them. In *learning* to perform them we may also do these things. When we can perform them, however, the knowing and the acting blend into a single performance. Knowing how to swim, then, and how to play tennis, come close to exemplifying this kind of knowing. They do not, however, complete the job. For Spinoza also says that this genus of knowing 'proceeds from an adequate idea of the formal being of certain of God's attributes to an adequate knowledge of the being of things'. Since God and his attributes are one and the same thing, this kind of knowing proceeds from an adequate idea (i.e. total experience) of God. At first glance it would seem that we can learn to swim without having had what might be called a religious experience. However, as will be seen in the sequel, this glimpse has to be extended by several others.[16]

We observed in note 8 that Spinoza himself used 'is' as a copula, although we have said that a consequence of seeing that there are not substances is that 'is' should not be used as a copula (p. 496). We have seen that this may be qualified by 'properly speaking'. We are now in a position to see that it may also be qualified by turning to the distinction between imagination and understanding. When the activity is imaginative (as all ordinary use of words and, hence, exposition are) the use of 'is' as a copula is (sic) justifiable. For such activity the substance-attribute metaphysics, or the distinction between knower and known, is at work. Most, if not all of the *Ethica* itself, then, is a work of imagination; though it can effect understanding.

There are, therefore, numerous examples which are not simply grammatical in Spinoza's writings in which he himself seems to violate fundamental implications of his insight that there are not substances. One of these is particularly apt with respect both to the insight and to the distinction between imagination and understanding. It occurs in connection with a crucial difference between Descartes's and Spinoza's definitions of 'substance' (the former's is given explicitly in def. 5 at the end of the Second Response to the Objections to the *Meditations*, and in *Principia* I, 51 and 52; the latter's in def. 3, Part I, *Ethica*). Both men have it that a substance is a self-existent thing. At least Descartes does in *Principia* 51, where he also says that there can really only be a unique substance, namely God. However, in def. 5 *and* in *Principia* 52 (where he defines 'created substance') Descartes employs the common notion referred to on p. 497 above: no properties or attributes are of nothing.[17] It is the absence of this notion in Spinoza's idea of a substance which distinguishes him from Descartes and its absence is part and parcel of the view that two or plural substances are not given (from which it follows that 'is' should not properly be used as a copula). Put slightly differently, Spinoza rejects this common notion in his metaphysical thinking; or, as far as understanding is concerned, the notion is dropped.

However, in Letter 13 (p. 65, l. 29) Spinoza *uses* the notion in the form: no properties are of nothing, to support the view of the impossibility of a vacuum. He is being critical of Boyle in the letter. The context, therefore, is science, in this case chemistry. When we have in mind, therefore, Spinoza's broad conception of imagination we see that it is quite proper that he should use a common notion which as a matter of understanding he would abandon.

The example also brings out or helps to make clear the fact that scientific thinking or reason, in Spinoza's term, is an activity of imagination, again in his sense. It further, incidentally, calls attention to another problem in translating the *Ethica*: the questions of textual reliability and whether Spinoza completed the writing of the *Ethica*. Reason, or the third genus of knowledge, is defined (schol. II, prop. 40) in terms of 'universal notions' (Dog, Horse, Human being) and 'adequate ideas of the properties of things'. The latter turn out, with the help of props. 38 and 39, to be the common notions, and Spinoza himself says at the beginning of schol. I: 'With these things [i.e. props 38, 39, and 40] I have explicated the cause of notions, which are called *Common*, and which are the foundations of our reasoning.' Our example of Spinoza's use of the common notion in Letter 13 brings out or helps to make clear the fact that reason is an activity of imagination by implication. That is, we can see that Spinoza's basic insight or understanding leads him to abandon a crucial common notion, as far as understanding things is concerned. On the other hand, he is willing to use that common notion in a scientific or rational context. The inference is that he can do this as an activity of imagination.[18]

The matter of textual reliability appears in the foregoing as follows. I have it that reason is based on 'universal notions' and 'common notions', inferring that 'adequate ideas of the properties of things' refers to common notions. In fact in the OP, Gebhardt's, and the other Latin texts, the first phrase is not 'universal notions' (*notiones universales*). It is '*notiones communes*' or common notions. However, if 'adequate ideas of the properties of things' equals 'common notions,' and the line quoted from schol. I certainly indicates that it does, then '*notiones communes*' renders 'adequate ideas of the properties of things' redundant. Furthermore, Spinoza has taken great care to define 'universal notions' in schol. I. Thus, one would expect that '*notiones communes*' is a textual mistake. And when we turn to the NS we find that, although the Dutch in the place in question is '*gemene kundig-heden*' (common notions), the Latin being translated is indicated in the margin as '*Notiones universales*'. Only understanding Spinoza's definition of the fourth genus of knowledge can settle this matter of textual unreliability, and introduce the proper sense here.[19]

IV

I have referred to the ambiguity in 'is' between 'to be' and 'to exist' (p. 498). Since a consequence of Spinoza's insight is that 'is' should not, at least in the context of understanding, be used as a copula, it is to be expected that one of the crucial words in Spinoza's vocabulary would be '*sum, esse*' (I am, to be), together with its various forms, '*ens*' and '*essentia*' especially. And, indeed,

'God' is defined by means of 'ens absolute infinitum'. We may next look at translating these words.

The first thing that strikes one making a translation of Spinoza is the handling which 'essentia' has received (the word is not only of crucial importance, it occurs in the first line of the *Ethica*). It has almost invariably come into English as 'essence', or with a variant of it like 'essentiality'.[20] The French translators have used 'essence'. The Germans and the Dutch with great, though not as great, regularity have used '*Wesen*' (sometimes '*Wesenheit*' and occasionally '*Sein*'), and '*wezentheit*' (sometimes '*wezen*'). Thereon, as I shall suggest, hangs enormous philosophic confusion, not only about Spinoza but generally. In the case of Spinoza the confusion has been abetted by the rendering of 'existentia' with 'existence', and the translation of another verb involved with 'is' (a cognate of 'exsto') 'consto'.

Properly speaking, rendering 'essentia' (a participial form of 'esse') with 'essence' is not translating. It is a kind of transliterating, as is, of course, the result of my principle of translation: find an English word with a Latin root wherever possible. However, whether it be translating or transliterating, it would be all right, were it not for strange difficulties with the word 'essence'. It would be all right, because a meaning of 'essence' is 'being'. However, it has always had a suspicion of another meaning and now virtually only has this other meaning. This according to the *Oxford English Dictionary*, which lists 'being, existence' as obsolete for 'essence', is: 'the connotation of the class-name' which turns an essence into something very like a Platonic entity, or did until Wittgenstein helped us out with: look for the use, not the meaning.

We can, I think, best and most briefly get into what is involved here by quoting a paragraph from Spinoza, together with a commentary on it by Charles Appuhn, his devoted French translator. The paragraph is from Ch. 2, Part I of the Appendix to *Descartes' Principles*, p. 238 in Gebhardt. Appuhn's remarks occur on pp. 434–5, vol. 1 of his translation.

> And thus from these things what is to be understood from these four [uses of 'esse'] is clearly seen. For the first *be-ing* [*esse*] to wit of *Being* [*Essentia*] is nothing other than that mode in which created things are comprehended in the attributes of God; *be-ing*, next of *Idea*, is said, according as all things are contained objectively in the idea of God; *be-ing*, further, of *Potency* [*Potentia*] is said only in respect of the potency of God by which he could create all things not yet existing from absolute freedom of will; *be-ing*, finally, of *Existing* [*Existentia*] is the being itself of things external to God, and considered in themselves, and is attributed to things after they are created by God.[21]

Of the paragraph Appuhn notes that these distinctions are of Peripatetic and Thomist provenance, and

507

are clarified, says Freudenthal, by relating them to scholastic authors such as Suarez, Scheibler, and in particular Heereboord, who in his *Meletemata* (p. 343) teaches that the essences of things [*essences des choses*] have existed for all eternity in the form of ideas in the divine understanding; that things are said to exist in their causes in so far as they are contained in the active potency [*puissance*] of the latter: as the rose is in the active potency of the sun, the essences of the things have existed for all eternity in the active potency of God; the essences of things are said to exist in themselves outside of their causes when they have been produced; finally, when the be-ing of essence [*l'être de l'essence*] which formerly existed in potency [*en puissance*] comes to exist in act, we have the be-ing of existence.

Appuhn's remarks exemplify the confusion in the term 'essence' when it is used to translate '*essentia*'. We have it here that the essence of a thing before it is created exists as an *idea* in the mind of God. That is to say that it is something like the connotation of a class-name. In fact what seems to be meant by Heereboord, as well as by Spinoza in the paragraph in question, is that *things* exist in the mind of God before he creates them. They have their being, or reality if you will, in God's mind before they exist outside it. See the definition of 'Being' in lines 2–4 of the paragraph from Spinoza.

Throughout the commentary on my translation I have occasion to observe that the being of a thing (*essentia rei*) or a thing's being (*rei essentia*) for Spinoza is the thing, since for him all the so-called 'properties *of* a thing' are essential to it. For Descartes, on the other hand, as well as for the Peripatetics and Scholastics, the being of a thing is its defining property (the property necessary for it to be what it is). The rest of its properties are accidents.[22] That notion of the defining property is in part responsible for the confusion in 'essence'. It results in coming to identify the being of a thing, i.e. a thing, with its definition. Thus do ideas of things become confused with things.[23]

In the context of Aristotelianism and the Western tradition generally the rendition of '*essentia*' with 'essence' makes some sense because in that tradition when we speak of a thing's essence (being) we are referring to that which makes it essentially what it is. In the context of Spinoza's thought 'essence' simply will not do. What makes a thing what it is includes all of its properties (to use an Aristotelianism); that is, it is the thing itself.

In this connection we understand Spinoza's so-called 'determinism' better than we do when we speak simply of determinism. When Spinoza says that all things necessarily are as they are (for example, prop. 29, Part I *Ethica*), he at least has in mind the notion that all the properties of a thing are necessary properties. In terms of the distinction between necessary properties and accidents, he is saying that there are no accidents. In this respect it is misleading to think of Spinoza's 'determinism' as a causal determinism; though he certainly accepts the proposition that every thing has a cause (for example, prop. 28, Part I). Wienpahl is what he is because of the colour of his hair as well as because he is a rational animal. For certain purposes we can think of him, while ignoring the colour of his hair; but considered in himself, the colour of his hair is as important as is his rationality.

It follows from this, of course, that any thing is constantly changing. It is improper to speak of God as the sum total of things. The notion of whole and part is infelicitous in a view in which the notion of substance (particularly as Descartes, say, held it) is in effect rejected, or is as far as understanding is concerned. Nevertheless, when we do consider God imaginatively as the collection of individual things, since every thing constantly changes, it follows that God constantly changes. Although Spinoza does not say in Part I that God is immutably, props. 17 (God is constrained by no one) and 19 (God is eternally) show that Spinoza would accept it. Although it seems to be, it is not, however, in conflict with the realization that God constantly changes. For all that is meant by God's immutability is that fact that his decrees, to use the language of the TTP, could not be otherwise. That is to say, things could not happen other than they do (prop. 33, Part I).

We could go on citing facets of this view indefinitely. The foregoing, however, should be sufficient to help us realize that '*essentia*' in the *Ethica* can only come into English with the participle of the English verb for being, namely 'being'.[24] When we return, then, to thinking of Descartes or the Scholastics, we see that to render the word with 'being' in those contexts is also perfectly all right. A thing's essence (being) is what makes it what it is. For these other philosophers it happens that what makes a thing what it is is one or more of its many properties instead of all its properties. Still it is in a sense the thing's being that we are talking about when we speak of its essence.

It may be remarked here, as it could have been remarked earlier, that when the concept of substance (particularly as Descartes held it) is abandoned, or rather seen through,[25] the notion of a property is radically altered. The concepts of substance and property are correlative. Each depends on the other for its definition. Seeing that one of them can be abandoned results in seeing that the other can. Then the distinction between properties and actions breaks down. In Spinoza's terminology the distinction is seen to be a distinction of reason, not a real distinction. You find that you can view your world as a kind of fluidity. The ocean is a suitable simile. There is Being and the modes of being constantly rising up from it, and just as constantly subsiding into it.

We can see here why Spinoza wanted to establish the distinction between 'being' and 'existing'.[26] In the Latin as well as in the English the two words have different roots. The root of '*essentia*' is '*esse*' (to be), that of '*existentia*' '*sto, stare*' (to stand). With the preposition '*ex*' (from) the word means 'to stand out from' God *is*. Modes of being *exist*. They stand out from being. We may also say that they have their reality in or by existing. God has his reality by being. However, as both Spinoza (prop. 20, Part I) and Descartes (*Meditations* V) have seen, being and existing are the same for God. This is probably a reason why Spinoza could not make the distinction between 'being' and 'existing' firm. Another, as we have noted, and as the citation from the *Oxford English Dictionary* quoted on p. 507, the quotation from Letter 12 on p. 497, and the quotation from the TTP, p. 498, about '*Jehova*' show, is that 'is' is fundamentally ambiguous in our languages between 'to be' and 'to exist'.

The linking of 'God' with 'substance' may now be seen to be less than fortuitous. For the root of 'substance' is also in '*sto*'. A substance is that which *is* under (*sub*) what stands out. 'Substance' and 'Being' are, consequently, terms, despite their difference in roots, which easily refer to the same 'thing' (a frequent German translation of '*Ens*' (*Being*) is '*Ding*' or '*das Ding*'). The so-called 'ontological argument' is much clearer with 'substance' than it is with 'God' or 'Being'. The 'argument' is that God by definition (or by very conception) involves existence. With 'substance' and in the formal mode of speech, the point is perfectly clear: ' "sub*stance*" involves "exi*stence*".' There is only a prepositional, not a substantive, difference between the two.[27]

Let us move now to another important verb, which like '*ens*' and '*essentia*' (as well as '*existentia*' when you see the relation between 'substance' and 'existence'), is involved in Spinoza's definition of God. I refer to '*consto*'. Def. 6, Part I, *Ethica* is: '*Per* Deum *intelligo ens absolute infinitum, hoc est, substantiam constantem infinitis attributis, quorum unumquodque aeternam, & infinitam essentiam exprimit*' (emphasis added). '*Consto*' appears here in the participle '*constans, constantis, constantem*'. It is another verb rooted in '*sto*' and can mean, for example, 'exist', 'consist', 'stand firm', 'be clear', etc. In English in this definition it has thrice been rendered by 'consist' and once by 'constitute'. Appuhn has '*constituée*'. The Germans have used '*bestehen*' and the Dutch '*bestaan*', each of which can mean pretty much what the Latin word means, with 'consist' quite common. What we get commonly, then, is that God 'consists of (or is constituted by) infinite attributes . . .'. In effect, we get it that God has infinite attributes in much the same sense as that chairs have legs; where 'attribute' is confused with 'property' despite the extraordinary use of 'attribute' which Spinoza introduced.[28]

Fortunately, in the TTP we have Spinoza's own explicit comment on the use of '*consto*'. There on p. 20, ll. 25–7 he quotes Deut. 34, v. 10 in Hebrew which he renders into Latin by: '*et non constitit* (proprie surrexit) *unquam Israeli propheta sicut Moses*. . . .' This comes into English as: 'and there has never been established (properly risen up) in Israel a prophet like Moses. . . .'[29] We have here, that is, Spinoza's own view on the translation of a verb in Hebrew. He uses '*consto*' (*constitit*), which was customary in his day, but adds a parenthesis to indicate that *'surrexit'* (risen up) is preferable. When this is used in def. 6 we have it that God is substance rising up in infinite attributes. This is certainly quite different from 'constituted by' or 'consisting of' infinite attributes. However, *'consto'* also allows, see above, 'standing firm in infinite attributes' or 'being clear in infinite attributes' (one might say, 'being apparent to us in infinite attributes').

Given what has been said up to this point, let us now get the definition into English: 'By means of *God* I understand *being* absolutely infinitely, that is, substance being established in infinite attributes, each of which expresses being eternally and infinitely.' Contrast this with, for example, Elwes's translation: 'By *God* I mean a being absolutely infinite – that is, a substance consisting in infinite attributes each of which expresses eternal and infinite essentiality.' And contrast that with Hale White's: 'By God I understand Being absolutely infinite, that is to say, substance consisting of infinite attributes, each of which expresses eternal and infinite essence.' Elwes's version has the merit of using 'consisting in', in which *'consist'* may have the now archaic meaning: 'to exist in a fixed or permanent state' (*Webster Second International*); in which case it is much better than White's 'consisting of', though neither it nor the latter can be used in other contexts where *'consto'* occurs. White's version, on the other hand, has the merit of using 'Being' instead of 'a being' and 'substance' instead of 'a substance'. However, neither of the definitions treat *'ens'* and *'essentia'* verbally, as we do by employing adverbs as modifiers. Let us get further into this, bearing in mind the active use of 'is'.[30]

Take first the matter of the articles 'a' and 'the' (see the opening paragraph of section III, p. 503 above). The Dutch, German, and French translations also have them (the Dutch and French have 'a being', the German *'das'* which could be omitted when the expression comes into English). In this connection I will remark that White quite properly capitalizes 'Being' even though it is not in the original text (*ens*). Usually in the *Ethica* (in the OP) where Spinoza uses *'ens'* and *'Deus'* it is capitalized (for convenient examples, see the Prefaces to Parts II and IV). However, despite the relative consistency with which *'mens'* and *'corpus'* are capitalized where they should be, the capitalization of *'ens'* is not strictly followed. Proof-reading in the seventeenth century does not seem to have been what it is today.

White properly uses 'Being' because *'ens'* used with *'Deus'* is, strictly speaking, a proper name. This has much to do with the use of articles. In fact they should appear in def. 6. This is related to the fact of God's unity or the fact that he is uniquely. He is Being in the philosophy of Spinoza. Plural Gods are not given. There are not substances. Two or plural substances are not given. God is not *a* being (among beings). The Cartesian qualification that he is an infinite being as distinct from finite beings (uncreated as distinct from created substances) hints at this, may even be a confused way of putting

511

it. Perceived clearly and distinctly, God is Being. The great distinction between Spinoza and his immediate predecessors may be put this way: for him God is Being, not *a* Being. 'A Being' is not only confused, it is grammatically unsound. Further, as is implied in note 23, the ontological 'argument' works for Being. It does not work for a being.[31]

Let us now move further afield, out of the *Ethica* into other things that Spinoza wrote, such as the TTP and the letters. The value of the letters for understanding the *Ethica* has been realized, but too often the TTP has been regarded as a *'livre d'occasion'*, a kind of political tract for the day. It is in fact, in my judgement, a fitting companion for the *Ethica*, written every bit as much *sub specie aeternitatis* as the latter. It may be regarded as Spinoza's account of God as the latter occurs in imagination, the *Ethica* as that account as he is with understanding. That it is of God as he is imagined may have helped the impression that the TTP is of a time and not eternal. Such, as I say I believe, is not the case. We have already seen its use in the matter of *'Jehova'*.[32] We have also just noticed its use in the matter of translating the definition of 'God' as far as *'consto'* is concerned. Turn now to its use with other aspects of that definition. First, however, consider a remark in one of the letters.

In Letter 73, the same in which he tells us that he does not mean by 'nature' what people ordinarily mean (see above p. 502), Spinoza writes about the use of the word 'God' in the TTP.

> I foment [he says (p. 307)], a sentiment concerning God, & Nature widely diverse from that which Modern Christians are accustomed to defend. For I state that God is the immanent cause of all things *not*, as they say, the transient. I affirm, I say, with Paul, & perhaps also with all the ancient Philosophers, even although in another mode, that all things are in God, & are moved in God; & I would dare also to say with the ancient Hebrews, in so far as it is permitted to conjecture from traditions even if these are adulterated.

The God, to speak improperly, of the TTP is the God of the *Ethica*. The idea of God in the TTP is that of the ancient Hebrews, '& perhaps' that also of 'all the ancient Philosophers'. In the *Ethica* that idea is deepened, but not otherwise changed, until it is the idea of Being instead of a being. It is, as will become clear, God's idea instead of an idea of God.

In the TTP Spinoza frequently illuminates the idea of God as it affected the ancient Hebrews. He does so especially in the first chapter which is about prophecy (see pp. 24 ff.). There we find his opinion that the ancient Hebrews often tended to use the word 'God' (or one of God's appellatives) as an adjective or adverb rather than as a noun. Thus, for example, we are told that they used 'God' 'for expressing a thing in the superlative degree'. God's mountains or the mountains of God were the highest mountains. God's subversion of a city was the maximum destruction that could come to it. 'The cedars of God' was used for expressing the trees' unusual size. When the ancient Hebrews wanted to say that a *great* fear fell over the people, they might say 'and the fear of God fell over the people'. Solomon's natural knowing was called 'God's knowing' (*Dei scientia*) to signify that it was divine or above the common. The phrase, then, 'the knowledge of God', which suggests so inevitably to the dualist that God is the object of that knowledge, as perhaps even will 'God's knowledge', can mean simply the highest degree of knowledge, or understanding. Given that Mind and Body are aspects of the same thing, or given the 'union which the mind has with the whole of Nature' (EU, p. 8, ll. 26–7), this kind of knowing could be that in which there is no real distinction between subject and object, or in which the distinction is not made (for there is not a real one); a kind of knowing that is neither subjective nor objective. Before this is unfolded further, let us return to the letters.

Towards the end of his life Spinoza became involved in a correspondence with Tschirnhaus about the issue of accounting for the variety of things. Tschirnhaus had written that Descartes cannot possibly deduce this from extension without supposing that God is the cause of motion, for extension is inert (Letter 82). He asks Spinoza's opinion about the matter; indicating that he knows that Spinoza has other views, which he may have been unwilling to make manifest for some reason or other.[33] Spinoza replies in what is the last letter in the OP, Letter 83. The reply is possibly poignant, for in what we have as the first paragraph he wonders whether life will suffice for clearing these matters up and indicates that up till then it has not been permitted him to dispose them in order. He could have been anticipating his death seven months later, or he could simply have been saying that these matters take a devil of a long time to get clear on (see note 36). Be this as it may, in the same paragraph he provides Tschirnhaus with, it seems to me, an answer of extraordinary clarity (see note 31). It is:

> As for your question, whether the variety of things can be deduced at the outset [*a priori*] solely from a conceiving of Extension, I believe I have already shown sufficiently clearly that it is impossible; and on that account matter is ill-defined by Descartes by means of *Extension*; but that it is necessarily bound to be explicated by means of an attribute which expresses being eternally, & infinitely [*quod aeternam, & infinitam essentiam exprimat*] (emphasis added).

This, of course, comes out in earlier translations as: 'which expresses eternal and infinite essence'; but what it says to me is that extension in Spinoza's view is an expression of *being*; that is, an activity, living when both attributes are considered, motion when only extension is. For Descartes matter was inert and, therefore, motion needed a cause. For Spinoza matter, or Being looked at materially, was active. As an expression of Being, it had to be. Thus Spinoza did not require a *Deus ex machina* to account for motion in the physical expression of reality. For some time I thought that the activity of reality was accounted for in Spinoza by his seeing that every thing is animate (schol. prop. 13, Part II); that is to say, that the attribute of *thinking* extended, so to speak, throughout reality. Letter 83 made it clear that, while this is true (thinking extends through reality, it is an infinite attribute), the activity of the world, corporeally considered, does not have to be accounted for by this means. The other attribute, extension, is also active, an expression of being. Reality, if you will, is both animate and in motion. Extension, as well as Thinking, is being eternally, and infinitely.[34]

God, then, is *being* absolutely infinitely, that is, substance being established in infinite attributes, each of which expresses being eternally and infinitely. We have noticed that 'being established' (*constantem*) might be rendered with 'rising up'. It may also be noticed that '*substantia*', like '*existentia*', is basically a participial form. In its case the root is '*substo*', which gives '*substans*' and thus '*substantia*'. Thus, we might have it that God is *being* absolutely infinitely, that is, substancing rising up in infinite attributes, each of which expresses being eternally and infinitely. However, we do not have to resort to obsolete verbs, which 'to substance' is, to get to the point.

The point is that knowledge of God is knowledge of *being* absolutely infinitely. In prop. 11, Part I God's existing is shown. Prop. 12 states that no attribute of a substance can be truly conceived, from which it would follow that a substance can be divided. We arrive, thence, at Prop. 13, which is that a substance absolutely infinite is indivisibly. In *Descartes' Principles* this appears as prop. 17, Part I: '*Deus est ens simplicissimus.*' God is *being* most simply. Knowledge of God is knowledge of *being* most simply.

Let us put it slightly differently, employing the preposing of the genitive case which is common in Spinoza and, except in the early Dutch translations, uncommon in later versions of him. God's knowledge is knowledge of *being* absolutely infinitely. God's knowledge is knowledge of *being* most simply. Introducing what we have been told by Spinoza of the ancient Hebrew's use of 'God', this becomes: the highest or best knowledge is knowledge of *being* most simply. Knowing in the highest degree is knowing of *being* most simply. In the vernacular, we find that the best knowledge is knowledge of living most simply.

When we move from imagining God to understanding him, we have God's knowledge. The idea *of* God becomes God's knowledge. This is the highest or best knowledge. It is knowledge in which the distinction between mind and body is seen for what it is: a distinction of reason.[35] It is consequently knowledge, or, better, knowing which is equally of Mind and Body. Imagination is more of Body than of Mind. Understanding is equally of both. In it the subject knowing and the object known merge. Knowing God is knowing how to be most simply. Understanding God is a state of being, in Spinoza's language, a mode of being.

Part V of the *Ethica* from prop. 21 to the end deals with this mode of being or being freely – it is human freedom. (Props 1 to 20 deal with remedies for the passive Affections, or what Spinoza calls human servitude.) There is no need to recapitulate what is written there, but I would note that Spinoza says in the next to last scholium that 'the common persuasion of the vulgar seems to be' other than his (prop. 41). He believes, for example, that 'Beatitude is not virtue's reward, but virtue itself' (prop. 42). What he has also seen and stated in his own way (see Part V) is that knowledge of or understanding God is knowing in which 'God' does not appear, except adjectively or adverbially. Knowing God is simply being.

The common persuasion of the crowd is indeed otherwise. Despite the injunction of the second commandment they employ images of God. They cling to the idea *of* God and this keeps them from God's idea. In a letter Leibniz remarked of Spinoza that 'He has a strange Metaphysic, full of paradoxes.'[36] Recall Spinoza's advice to Bouwmeester (see above, p. 504). To understand 'it is necessary before all things to distinguish between understanding, & imagination, or between true ideas, & the rest, namely the feigned, the false, the dubious, and absolutely all those which depend solely on memory.' 'A true idea is bound to agree with its ideate' (*Idea vera debet cum suo ideato convenire*, Ax 6, Part I). This is one of the paradoxes. A true idea is bound to come together (*convenire*) with its ideate. With a true idea of God one is simply, that is, one simply is.

We must be careful here, however. We have likened Spinoza's intuitive knowledge to knowing how to swim (p. 505), because it is an activity of knowing in which Mind and Body play an equal part. We also know, on the other hand, that intuitive knowing proceeds from an adequate idea of God's attributes (i.e. of God, prop. 40, Part II, schol. 2) to an adequate knowledge of things. Thus it would seem that a person cannot know how to swim without having had a religious experience. In the practice of Zen Buddhism the question arises: is a child taught to sit in the lotus position and to do this quietly for a half-hour enlightened (for Dogen had said that *zazen is enlightenment*)? The answer is clearly, no. Yet what is the difference between an adult and a child sitting quietly in the lotus position?

Surely simply to be is not enough. A dog is simply, and simply is. It does not worry. Its mind is not full of plans and memories, but we would not say that it has Spinoza's understanding Love of God. All things are animate, though in different degree (*Ethica* III, schol., prop. 13). Spinoza answers the question himself in the scholium to prop. 39, Part V (He who has a Body apt for a great many things, has a Mind of which the maximum part is eternally). The answer is given by means of a comparison between a child 'who has a Body apt for very few things, & maximally depending on external causes' and consequently 'has a Mind which, considered solely in itself, is almost *not* conscious of itself, or of God, or of things'; and an adult 'who has a Body apt for a great many things' and consequently 'a Mind which, considered solely in itself, is very conscious of itself, & of God, & of things'.

There are ways of simply being: the way of the child and the way of the sapient. Time strikes a difference between them. The child who sits quietly in the lotus position for a half-hour on the first occasion is not doing *zazen*. The adult who has repeatedly done this may be. And it may not be. For there is another difference, which Spinoza strikes in that scholium. It has to do with the degree of consciousness of oneself, of God, and of things, which an individual has. Simply to be takes time, and it involves awareness of oneself and of things.[37] It is being in the highest degree consciously.

V

I wish to close with a final and quite different remark. Once some of the foregoing things and others like them are seen, it makes no difference whether we say, for example, 'God's being is uniquely' or 'the essence of God is unique'. Though we seem to have been dealing with grammatical facts, either the matter with which we have been concerned, or grammar is far deeper than meets the eye. Our languages are not dualistic or non-dualistic. We are, and consequently the languages as we use them are or are not. It may help us to think for a time adverbially and adjectivally instead of nominally. Once we have, however, the device, like the Buddhist's raft for getting to the other shore, can be left behind. Mystics have long used our languages as they are with as much or as little success as scientists. This may be a reason why, if he did not, Spinoza did not invent the device of 'Mind' and 'Body', and why he only occasionally mixed adverbs with adjectives as modifiers of verbs.

NOTES

1 So far as I know only Charles Appuhn's (Paris, 1904 and 1934) and Berthold Auerbach's (Germany, 1841 and 1870), and these men did not translate the Hebrew Grammar. There has never been a complete translation in English. The sole approximation is Elwes's *The Chief Works of Benedick de Spinoza*, translated from the Latin with an introduction by R. H. M. Elwes, 2 vols, George Bell, London, 1883. This was issued later in the USA by Dover Publications, New York, 1951. Elwes lacks many of the letters and the Hebrew Grammar. The translation of the *Political Treatise* in it is not by Elwes, but a friend, A. H. Gosset. There have been four complete translations of the *Ethica* in English; Daniel Drake Smith's (Van Nostrand, New York, 1876 and 1888); W. H. White's in 1883 (rev. edn 1894); A. Boyle's in 1910 (now in *Everyman's Library*, No. 481); and Elwes's.

2 See my *The Matter of Zen; Zen Diary*; 'Spinoza and Wang Yang-Ming' (*Religious Studies*, Oct. 1969); 'Ch'an Buddhism, Western Thought, and the Concept of Substance' (*Inquiry*, Summer 1971); and 'Spinoza and Mental Health' (*Inquiry*, Summer 1972).

3 Abbreviations are as follows: *Treatise on the Emendation of Understanding* = EU; *A Theological-Political Treatise* = TTP; *Political Treatise* = TP; *The Short Treatise* = ST. Page references are to the appropriate volume in Gebhardt and are duplicated in the English of my translation. OP and NS stand for *Opera Posthuma* and *Nagelate Schriften*.

4 Standards of printing in the seventeenth century were not what they are today, nor were such rules as that about mention and use as consistently followed. The context often sufficed for the latter. It is of interest that, in the NS and Pieter Balling's Dutch translation of the book on Descartes, the printer, Jan Rieuwertz, sometimes used 'vv' for 'w'.

5 Bruder (1834 edition of the *Opera*) and Gebhardt, following the OP, have '*modificatum*' and '*modificatione*' for '*affectum*' and '*modo*'. I make the change because in the NS the Dutch for 'affected' and 'mode' are used, and '*affectum*' and '*modus*' are listed in the margin as the Latin words being translated. In his *Textgestaltung* Gebhardt does not notice this important difference, though he does observe that the NS has '*is*' (is) for '*existit*'. He also does not note that the NS has 'must be' (*moet wezen*) for '*debet existere*' (is bound to exist). The Dutch for 'exist' in the seventeenth-century translations of Spinoza was '*wezentlijk zijn*'.

In the early days, as some of the letters show, Spinoza used '*modifico*' and '*modificatio*' for which he later substituted '*afficio*' (to affect) and '*modus*' (mode). This destroyed the relation between '*modifico*' (modify) and '*modificatio*' (modification). However, it provided him with '*affectio*', and '*affectus*', the word which Elwes translated by 'emotion'. The advantage gained more than paid the price for the loss of the other relation. For Spinoza then had basically the same word for discussing human behaviour (the emotions, or better the topic of Part III) that he had for discussing any thing whatever. Thus, 'modes' def. 4, Part I) are defined in terms of affections (*affectiones*) of a substance; '*bodies*' (def. 1, Part II) are defined in terms of modes (of God's being); and Affections ('*affectus*', def. 3, Part III) are defined in terms of affections of the Body. I capitalize 'Affection' to distinguish it from 'affection', that is, to distinguish '*affectus*' from '*affectio*'. The unity of thought Spinoza attained by the move to '*afficio*' from '*modifico*' is enormous. It is sustained in English by the use of 'Affection' and entirely lost by the use of 'emotion'. Appuhn retained it by using '*affection*' for both '*affectus*' and '*affectio*'. However, because he employs no device to distinguish 'Affection' from 'affection', the result is sometimes confusing.

It may be noted on an analogy between '*affectus*' and '*conceptum*' (see note 34), that Spinoza's word for the Affections (or active and passive action) is in fact a verbal form. Thus, just as he chose 'conceiving' rather than 'perception' to treat the mind as active, so did he select a word which is a participle for talking about the so-called emotions. He had a marked penchant for verbal forms.

517

It should be observed, too, that '*mens*' (mind) is not defined in the *Ethics*. 'God', 'substance', 'mode', 'body', etc. are, but not 'mind'. The significance of this will appear later.

I note finally that prop. 22 reads basically differently in the NS and in the OP. This is not, however, the place to enter into that detail. The proposition may, taking this and the differences noted above into account, have read: 'Whatever follows from some attribute of God, in so far as it is affected in such a mode that it is both necessarily, and infinitely by means of that attribute, is also bound to be both necessarily, and infinitely.' The proposition is one of those about the infinite modes, which have caused much speculation. '*Modifico*' may have lingered in these propositions (see also 23) because of this, to which the variant readings may also be due. Cf. note 6.

6 Prop. 22 (cf. note 5) is one of those concerning the infinite modes, which have caused so much puzzlement in readers of Spinoza. This may be why one early version of the *Ethics* had '*modificatio*' instead of 'modus', etc. in prop. 22 and another the reverse (the translator of the NS, Glazemaker, used a different manuscript from that which went into the printing of the OP). As noted, Spinoza gradually moved away from the term '*modificatio*' and its verb in favour of '*affectio*' and its verb. It is possible that he thought of preserving the first set for the discussion of the infinite modes.

The notion of infinite mode is explained, and made simple, I think, by Spinoza himself in Letter 64 with the reference to the section on bodies after prop. 13, Part II. There he explains that we can conceive of combining one body with another, or one individual with another to get a third individual, etc., until we can think of the whole world as one huge individual. So we can think of the modes of one attribute taken all together as one huge (infinite) mode of that attribute. Getting rid of the notion that there are substances led Spinoza in the area of physics to change the notion of the atom to that of the individual (which is in fact infinitely divisible, see the definition of 'individual' in the section on bodies). It is an extension of this insight, I believe, which led him to speak of infinite as well as finite modes. Otherwise the notion of infinite modes is relatively inconsequential.

7 Corol. I also says that in the nature of things only one substance is given. Again properly speaking, we should not speak of *one* substance or say that there is only one God. If God is uniquely, then, properly speaking, the concept of number does not apply to him. Spinoza calls explicit attention to this in Letter 50. Having pointed out that we can only speak of *two* coins, say, if we have the universal idea of 'coin', Spinoza says that we only therefore improperly speak of God as one (we can have no universal idea of God because he is uniquely; see schol. I, prop. 40, Part II, *Ethica* on the origin of universal notions like dog and human being). Or rather, we either speak of God improperly as one or we 'have no true idea concerning God' (p. 240). Thus to say that only one substance is given is to speak improperly. Spinoza somewhat mollifies this in the corollary, for he has it that only one substance 'is given' (*dari*). When he uses the phrase 'in the nature of things' (*in rerum natura*) and speaks of something as being given (instead of 'is'), he is not talking about nature, but how we talk about nature. The impropriety of speaking of one substance accounts in part for the

curious phrase in the highly important prop. 5 of Part I: '*duae, aut plures*'. 'In the nature of things two or plural substances ... are not given.' In English this has usually been translated 'two or more', but the point is that two or more than one (i.e. plural) substances cannot be given. It is not multiplicity that counts, but plurality. For the same reason Spinoza is improperly referred to as a monist. More strictly speaking, he is a non-dualist.

8 The reader will immediately observe that 'are', the plural of 'is', is used here as a copula. We will return to this in the next section.

9 The reader may recall here p. 1 in the *Blue Book* where Wittgenstein indicates that a chief source of philosophical bewilderment is the tendency to think that there is a thing corresponding to it when we come across a substantive. The reader may also consult requisite III, p. 35, EU, for which see note 10.

10 It follows that only proper names would appear in the 'definition' of what Spinoza in the EU calls an 'uncreated thing'. The third requisite for such a definition is: it should have no substantives which can be turned into adjectives (p. 35). It is interesting to read the definition (6) of God in Part I in this light. This notion of an attribute, by the way, resolves the question over which there has been much debate: does God 'have' infinite attributes (i.e. countless attributes) or only two? (Properly speaking God does not *have* attributes. He is established or clear (*constans*) in attributes. Def. 6.) The answer is that, properly speaking, the question of number no more applies to attributes than it does to God or Substance. This, because Spinoza understands the same by the two words. Thus, the question of the number of the attributes, properly speaking, is meaningless. Improperly speaking there are two: the mental and corporeal. Spinoza nowhere speaks explicitly of another, i.e. specifies it. If, furthermore, the attributes are countless (infinite in that sense), why can no one even *think* of a third? Cf. note 28.

11 I guess Meyer because his preface to Spinoza's book on Descartes shows great understanding of the author of the *Ethica*. Furthermore, Wolf reports (translation of the *Correspondence*, p. 51) that Meyer was addicted to capitalization.

12 Actually the device appears only in the *Ethica* with consistency. In the other writings, such as the EU, it does not. It is not in the works published while Spinoza was alive: the TTP and *Descartes' Principles*. Gebhardt restored it with but a single comment (p. 318, vol. II): 'because possibly Spinoza's writing is therein reproduced, and in this stronger or weaker relief (*Hervorhebung*) a nuance of the thought can show itself.'

13 The difference between the sense and the meaning of a word in this manner is discussed in P. Wienpahl, 'Frege's *Sinn und Bedeutung*,' *Mind*, October 1950. The theme of the paper is: the sense of a word is the physical properties of its tokens.

14 It is most significant that the section on bodies follows this scholium. We cannot, says Spinoza, go on further to understand the nature of a Mind without first talking about that of a body.

15 P. 189. Spinoza here is writing to a friend, Johann Bouwmeester, who has asked about a method for understanding. Spinoza's advice is that there is such a method. It includes getting rid of all ideas of the memory. St John of the Cross (*Ascent of Mount Carmel*, Image Edition, p. 265ff.) and the author of *The*

Cloud of Unknowing (trans. by Clifton Wolters, Penguin Books, p. 58 ff.), for example, give precisely this advice for attaining the mystical experience of the union with God. The Zen Buddhist advises us to empty our minds, to attain no-mind, in order to achieve enlightenment or awakening (Buddhahood).

This is as good a place as any to note a delightful feature of Spinoza's names for reality, that is, for God. For a while I thought it helpful to refer to God with 'it' instead of 'he' ('*Deus*' is masculine). This finally became unnecessary. 'God' (*Deus*) is masculine, 'Nature' (*Natura*) is feminine, and 'Being' (*Ens*) is neuter. Gender is a temporal matter not an eternal one. It is an affair of imagination not understanding.

16 This notion of intuitive knowing may be compared to Wang Yang-Ming's principle that knowledge and action are one and the same. See 'Spinoza and Wang Yang-Ming' (note 2), or *Instructions for Practical Living*, Columbia University Press, 1963.

The distinction between imagination and understanding has led to another problem in translation, related as it is to the broad notion of imagination. Elwes particularly noticed this problem. In a great many of the propositions in Part III and in the definition of the Affections, Spinoza uses the word 'imagination' where it does not seem to make sense if we think of it as we usually do. Elwes solved the problem by translating the Latin word (verb or noun) with 'conceive' and 'conception'.

17 Hobbes, by the way, uses this common notion in his objections to the *Meditations*, and in a manner which shows that he finds it not only unobjectionable, but in fact indispensable. His version of it is: 'we cannot conceive any act whatever without its subject' (E. S. Haldane and G. R. T. Ross, *Philosophical Works of René Descartes*, London and New York, 1967, vol. II, p. 65; Ch. Adam and P. Tannery, *Oeuvres de Descartes*, Paris, 1966, vol. VII, p. 175). Descartes's def. 5 is in fact still another version of the notion which he employs to explicate the definition. Spinoza states def. 5 in *Descartes' Principles* as: 'Everything in which something is immediately, as in a subject, or by means of which something which we perceive exists, that is, some property or quality or attribute of which there is in us a real idea, is called *Substance*.' He then quite properly omits use of the common notion in his explication of the definition. To include it, as Descartes did, is in effect redundant.

18 Should the reader want further evidence here, please consult Footnote Y, p. 22 in the EU, where Spinoza indicates that there is an indefinite number of hypotheses which will explain successfully the motions of the heavenly bodies. See also Letter 12. Cf. note 25.

19 Much has been written about the common notions (see, for example, Wolf's translation of the *Correspondence*, p. 377). Some have thought and said that they can be expressed by a single word, that is, that they are like what Spinoza calls 'universal notions'. They are, in fact (at least in Spinoza and Descartes), what were also called 'Axioms'. See, for example, *Ethica*, p. 50, ll. 2–3, where Spinoza says of a proposition that it is an axiom and may be enumerated among the common notions. See also Descartes's heading for the section on axioms at the end of the Second Response. It is '*Axiomata sive Communes Notiones*'.

On the matter of whether Spinoza ever completed the *Ethica* it may be said that, although he actually engaged in the work of getting the *Ethica* printed in August or September of 1675 (see Letter 68), a project he abandoned, there is plenty of evidence in the *Ethica* as it was first printed in the OP, that it remained to the end of his life an unpolished work. For example, on p. 136 in Gebhardt's text, at the end of Part II, we read that Spinoza will show us something in 'the Fourth Part' of the work. This is a result of Gebhardt's editing, as he notes. For in the OP the reference is to 'the Third part'. Originally the *Ethica*, as the title of the ST indicates, was probably a three-part work, the present Parts III, IV, and V forming one part. There is also evidence that the Appendix to Part IV was written some time after Part IV and simply tacked on to it. With more time it might have been incorporated into Part IV. We have already also noticed the occurrences of '*modifico*' instead of '*afficio*' in props. 22 and 23, Part I.

20 There are one or two exceptions in, for example, Wolf's translation of the *Correspondence*. However, they occur in Letter 20 by Blyenberg who wrote in Dutch, and used '*wezen*' instead of '*wezenheit*'. Sometimes where he has '*wezen*' '*essentia*' occurs in the Latin translation in the OP. Wolf indicates that he followed the Dutch version and he sometimes translated '*wezen*' as 'essence' and sometimes as 'being'.

21 It is to be remembered that the Appendix, 'Metaphysical Thoughts', deals with Descartes in terms used by the neo-Scholastics and that Spinoza tells us in Letter 13 that the views in the book are often the contrary of his own. However, Spinoza also frequently expresses dissatisfaction with the Scholastic definitions of certain terms. That he does not in this case probably indicates that these definitions were acceptable; given, of course, that he profoundly deepened the Scholastic idea of God and in such wise that God was no longer seen as an anthropomorphic creator.

22 In the closing lines of the Appendix Spinoza says that he will not bother with real accidents and other qualities, as they have been sufficiently exploded (*satis illa explosa sunt*).

In relation to Appuhn's remarks about Heereboord in the preceding paragraph it may be added that both the latter and Spinoza had a term and a distinction which introduce a further clarification into the 'essence' of a thing. The term is 'objective' and the distinction is that between the objective and the formal reality of a thing. The objective reality of a thing is the idea of it in someone's Mind. Its formal reality is constituted by the thing itself. Thus Heereboord could have thought of things as having their *objective reality* before their existence in the mind of God. In the case of Spinoza, or rather in the light of Spinoza, we can see that the objective reality of a thing corresponds to its existing according to the attribute of thinking. Its formal reality corresponds to its existing both according to the attribute of thinking *and* according to that of extension, for the *idea* of a thing can be either its form or a psychological occurrence in some Mind. (In the first case 'idea' has its Greek meaning, as when we speak of Plato's Ideas or forms.) Spinoza's non-dualism is implicit in the notion of the objective and formal reality of a thing. With this we see that Spinoza's non-dualism may be regarded as the result of a clarification of notions in neo-Scholasticism. Without that clarification Descartes remained a dualist and made dualism more explicit in his view that there are two kinds of created substance. The reader should now re-read the paragraph from Spinoza on p. 21. In defining the be-ing of an idea Spinoza used the notion of objective reality.

23 Hence Kant's criticism of the ontological argument: you cannot prove the existence of a thing from the idea of it. Correct. You can, however, prove the thing's existence from the thing, that is, from the thing's being. The ontological argument has seemed valid to some, invalid to others, because of the confusion about '*essentia*'. Hence, too, Spinoza's desire to distinguish 'being' and 'existing'. In Letter 34, as noted above, he says that he formerly proved God's unity on the basis of the distinction between 'being' and 'existing'. The letter was written in 1666. In the book on Descartes (1663) he uses this method. By 'God's unity' Spinoza is referring to the fact that God is uniquely, which is the same as to say that God exists necessarily; that is, that there cannot be plural Gods, which is prop. 11, Part I of *Descartes' Principles*. Compare note 23 with the last paragraph of Sec. I, p. 502 above.

We have, incidentally, to be careful with what is said at the outset of the foregoing paragraph, that you cannot deduce the existence of a thing from the idea of it. With Spinoza's distinction between imagination and understanding as given in Letter 37 (p. 503 above) this is not true. There he distinguishes between a *true* idea and all the rest. We can 'deduce' the existence of a thing from its true idea. Axiom 6, Part I, *Ethica*: 'A true idea is bound to agree with its ideate.' Confusion about the ontological 'argument' is thus seen to depend also on not making Spinoza's distinction between understanding and imagination. As long as we are imagining things (in Spinoza's use of the term) Kant's critique of the 'argument' is valid.

24 The principle of using English words with Latin roots played a perverse part in this rendition. It, so to speak, *forced* it through. Spinoza's work required violation of the principle. The same is true, though to a lesser extent, for the important word 'understanding' (*intellectus*, the past participle of the verb '*intelligo*', cf. notes 5 and 34). The tendency to translate this with 'the intellect' is tempting, and it has been often but not always yielded to in other translations.

25 It may be retained for certain purposes. Indeed, until recently in science, for example, in atomic physics, it has been a most useful concept – perhaps the most important of concepts for the origin and development of science Cf. p. 506 above where Spinoza's use of a certain common notion is discussed.

26 When you have decided to translate '*essentia*' with 'being', it is a natural move to render '*existentia*' with 'existing' instead of the more nominal 'existence'.

27 Spinoza has this form of the 'argument' in Letter 12, p. 54, ll. 1–3, though not, of course, in the formal mode. Cf. note 31.

28 Appuhn, possibly because of this confusion, perpetuates the notion that there is an infinite *number* of attributes (instead of the notion that the attributes are infinite) by reading 'constituted by an infinity of attributes'. His cohort, Caillois, does the same thing, but with a different verb: 'consisting in an infinity of attributes'. Both render the other occurrences of '*infinitus, a, um*' in the definition with 'infinite'. D. D. Smith also has it thus in his translation into English. See note 30. Compare notes 28 and 30 with note 10.

29 'Being established' is the compromise I have arrived at for '*constantem*'. It has

the '*sto*' in it, with a different preposition, and it fits every other occurrence of '*consto*' in Spinoza's writings.

30 The two other English translations, or translations into English, are as follows. Boyle's is the same as White's, except for 'a being' and 'a substance'. Smith's reads ' "I understand by God the Absolutely infinite Being" that is to say, substance constituted by an infinity of attributes, each of which expresses an eternal and infinite essence.'

31 It may be observed here that the 'argument' is not strictly speaking an argument. Descartes distinguished between analytic and synthetic methods, or '*a priori*' and '*a posteriori*' reasoning. This meant (which is not clear when these phrases are not translated, as they customarily are not), looking at an issue *at first* or at the outset, and looking at it later (posteriorily). Looking at it at first was to see the issue as it clearly is, by itself. Looking at it later was to expound it by chains of reasoning, so as to make it clear. The perspicuity required for the first method is rare. Most people require the exposition, even as they do in the demonstration of a theorem in geometry. Such demonstrations are not proofs, really, they are showings, so that what is clear in itself, but hard to see, can become clear – by being exposed, so to speak, in detail. Thus the 'ontological argument' is not an argument. Spinoza makes this clear in the scholium to prop. 11, Part I, *Ethica*, where God's existing necessarily is set forth. Descartes makes it clear in postulate 5 in the Second Response. Cf. note 27.

32 A tenseless form of the verb 'to be' or 'to exist', which shows that the Hebrews as well as the Greeks were working on the concept of being or what is – the first in the manner of the Hebrews, the second in the manner of the Greeks.

33 At first Spinoza seems to have accepted Descartes's laws of motion (Letter 32). Later he had indicated that he was thinking of others (Letter 60).

34 Another matter of translation. In his explication of the definition of 'idea' in Part II, Spinoza says that he uses '*conceptum*' rather than '*perceptio*', because the noun *perceptio* seems to indicate that the Mind is passive with respect to the object. '*Conceptum*', on the other hand, seems to express an action of the Mind. What is involved here is that '*perceptio*' is a nominal form; whereas '*conceptum*' is a past participle, i.e. a verbal form. I have accordingly translated it with 'conceiving' (see l. 2 of the letter quoted). Now consider '*res extensa*' and '*res cogitans*'. '*Cogitans*' is a present participle and '*extensa*' a past participle, hence probably 'the extended thing' and 'the thinking thing'. However, with Spinoza's explication in Part II, and with his statement about Extension as an expression of being infinitely, we may at least think of 'the extending thing'. The vagaries of grammar are large and notable.

35 Spinoza uses this notion in the *Ethica*, but does not define it there. See ch. 1, Part I of the Appendix of *Descartes' Principles* for his definition of 'real distinction' and 'distinction of reason'. See p. 504 above for 'real distinction'. A distinction of reason is one we make for a certain purpose. Spinoza's insight can be put as: there are no real distinctions.

36 Quoted in Freudenthal's *Die Lebensgeschichte Spinozas*, Leipzig, 1899, p. 206. '*Il a une étrange Métaphysique, pleine de paradoxes.*' Leibniz went on to criticize some of Spinoza's demonstrations, but concluded: 'It is not as easy as one thinks to give veritable demonstrations in metaphysic.' (In those days

'metaphysics' came close to meaning the study of God and the soul. See Letter 70, p. 303; the full title of the *Meditations*; and p. 1 of its Dedication.)

37 I have spoken of religious experiences. So-called religious or mystical experiences are not essential for God's knowledge. They occur in connection with knowledge of God, and in so far as we are at the level of imagination. As such they may precede God's knowledge, but they need not. God's knowledge is not an experience *of* God. It is a way or mode of living. According to Spinoza it is accompanied by Joy. It may not involve ecstasy. The latter is rather a property of mystical experiences. I think it unlikely that Spinoza had such experiences. He seems to have been temperamentally unsuited for them. One should, I think, rather say that he lived a mystical life. He was a mystic in this sense, not in the usual sense of one who has mystical experiences. These are temporal affairs. He lived *sub specie aeternitatis*. This may be why people think of him as a rationalist (actually he was a radical empiricist): his life was so measured, so *untemperamental*.

31 Spinoza – the outsider

Colin Wilson, Cornwall

Spinoza has the curious distinction of being the least influential of the great philosophers.

To someone approaching Spinoza for the first time, this is the most obvious and puzzling thing about him. Every history of philosophy devotes a chapter to Spinoza, and no one seems to doubt his right to so much space. But why is he so important? What other great philosophers did he influence? Where can we find any trace of his ideas – no matter how diluted – in the modern world? There are still plenty of traces of Platonism and Aristotelianism and Cartesianism – even Hegelianism. By comparison, Spinozism seems to have been a kind of dead end – his ideas influenced a few eighteenth-century Deists, and a few nineteenth-century atheists, then seemed to fade away. History has played the same trick on a number of other philosophers who seemed highly significant in their own time – Reid, Lotze and Eucken, to name a few at random. So by what right does Spinoza continue to occupy his position in the histories of philosophy?

Of course, the *Ethics* is obviously a philosophical masterpiece. But even this only underlines the problem. For it is essentially a closed system. And in philosophy, closed systems are at a disadvantage. Nietzsche continues to exercise more influence than Schopenhauer, not because he is a better writer – he is not – but because he left most of his questions unanswered. The same goes for Kierkegaard and Husserl and Wittgenstein. The great systematizers – Hegel, Lotze, Whitehead – are somehow too impressive; they kill all desire to take up where they left off. Spinoza's *Ethics* is considerably shorter than Lotze's *Macrocosmos* or Whitehead's *Process and Reality*, but its geometrical propositions make it look even more impregnable. Goethe used to read it in Latin, but I can think of few modern poets who would attempt it even in English.

Nietzsche made the same point about Spinoza in *Beyond Good and Evil*, in a scornfully hostile passage. And, oddly enough, came close to putting his finger on the reason for Spinoza's fascination for other thinkers. He attacks the 'tartuffery' of Kant, then turns his fire on Spinoza, the hocus pocus in mathematical form, by means of which Spinoza has clad his philosophy in armour and visor – in fact, the 'love of *his* wisdom', to translate the term fairly and squarely – in order to strike terror into the heart of the assailant who would dare to cast a glance on that invincible maiden, that Pallas Athene; how much personal timidity and vulnerability does this masquerade of a sickly recluse betray.

And then he goes on to make one of his most celebrated statements:

It has gradually become clear to me what every great philosophy up till now has consisted of – namely, the confession of its inventor, and a sort of involuntary and subconscious autobiography.

Now Nietzsche is not entirely wrong to look askance at Spinoza's 'armour'; his own polemical and dramatic methods are certainly more striking. But when he suggests, in effect, that we forget the philosophy and look at the philosopher, he immediately provides the answer to his own attack. Anyone who knows the slightest amount about the life of Spinoza knows that it is nonsense to speak of his personal timidity and vulnerability. Like Nietzsche – another sickly recluse – he revealed remarkable courage and inner strength. His greatness lay, to a large extent, in his capacity for 'outsiderism', in standing alone, apart from society, in renouncing the pleasures that make life tolerable for most of us, and transcending personal needs in pure creativity. Once we have come to admire this courage and inner strength, we can also see how it is reflected in the 'impersonal' form of the *Ethics*. Like Plotinus, Spinoza believed that a philosopher should leave the personal behind. He began a semi-autobiographical treatise – *On the Improvement of the Understanding* – but seems to have left it unfinished. But his major work was an assertion, both in form and content, of the transcendental nature of philosophy. Nietzsche is defiantly polemical. Spinoza is defiantly scientific.

Now those of us who know something of the history of philosophical logic since Leibniz will be inclined to shake our heads. Russell and Whitehead pursued a related dream; so did Hilbert; Frege and Gödel brought their edifices crashing. I am inclined to believe that Spinoza's work is vulnerable to the same sort of criticism. But before I consider this possibility, I would like to follow Nietzsche's prescription, and examine the philosophy as part of the personal development of the philosopher.

For a contemporary Englishman, the background to Spinoza's philosophy is almost impossible to grasp. This is partly because the battles Spinoza fought were won two centuries ago. There is still plenty of religious – and racial – intolerance in the world; but now no intelligent person accepts it as norm. We find it almost impossible to imagine a time, for example, when the majority of people approved of the Inquisition – or at least, took it for granted. (As an imaginative exercise, we might try it in reverse, and envisage a completely vegetarian society that regards our meat-eating as a horrible, grisly remnant of the Dark Ages.)

So to even begin to understand Spinoza, we have to make an effort to understand the long-standing persecution of the Jews in Spain and Portugal – an effort that is aided by our proximity in time to the Nazis. In 1492, three hundred thousand Jews were expelled from Spain, and thousands died of starvation or in shipwrecks. Some took refuge in Portugal; they were made to pay a high price in exchange for a limited period of time there; those who were unable to leave when their time was up were enslaved. The others moved on to further sufferings.

The Spanish atrocities against the Protestants in the Netherlands are an equally brutal and horrifying story. So when the Dutch revolted and threw off the Spanish yoke, Jews and Protestants felt they were united by a certain common cause. This is why Spinoza's grandfather – a Portuguese Jew who had been forcibly 'converted' to Christianity – came to Amsterdam. The Jewish community found religious freedom in Holland.

All of this may enable us to understand – even if we fail to sympathize with – the religious bigotry of Spinoza's co-religionists. From Voltaire to H. G. Wells, rationalists have shaken their heads over Jewish religious fanaticism, and suggested that it is an unfortunate reaction to centuries of persecution. (This argument is hardly convincing; intense devotion to their religion has been a Jewish characteristic since long before the Diaspora.) Whatever the reason, it seems clear that Jews – like Christians and Moham-medans – have been capable of a pretty high degree of bigotry and intolerance in matters of religion. Spinoza wrote:

> The love of the Hebrews for their country was not only patriotism, but also piety, and was cherished and nurtured by daily rites till, like the hatred of other nations, it must have passed into their nature. Their daily worship was not only different from that of other nations (as it might well be, considering that they were a peculiar people, and entirely apart from the rest), it was absolutely contrary. Such daily reprobation naturally gave rise to a lasting hatred deeply implanted in the heart: for of all hatreds, none is more deep and tenacious than that which springs from devoutness or piety, and is itself cherished as pious (*Tractatus Theologico-Politicus*, 17).

From which we may infer that Spinoza would have thoroughly approved the 'forecast' made by H. G. Wells in *The Shape of Things to Come:*

> And yet . . . in little more than a century, this antiquated obdurate [Jewish] culture disappeared. It and its Zionist state, its kosher food, its

Law and the rest of its paraphernalia, were completely merged in the human community. The Jews were not suppressed; there was no extermination . . . yet they were educated out of their oddity and racial egotism in little more than three generations.

In his early teens, Spinoza had a chance to observe this 'antiquated and obdurate' bigotry at first hand. Uriel Acosta was a Portuguese Jew of considerable eminence; in Lisbon, he had permitted himself to be forcibly converted, and risen to an important position in the service of the State. Preferring freedom, he moved to Amsterdam and reverted to the religion of his fathers. Acosta had a passionate belief in reason, which he carried to aggressive extremes. A treatise pointing out that the traditions of the Pharisees were at variance with written Law was taken as an unfriendly act by the Jewish community, while another work questioning the immortality of the soul provoked bitter fury. He was twice excommunicated from the religious community, and the sentence was lifted only when he grovelled in the dust on the threshold of the synagogue, allowing the congregation to walk over him. Being a man of spirit and intelligence, he was soon excommunicated a second time, and the 'retraction' was repeated. When he rebelled a third time, the community united to force him into submission; he wrote a violent denunciation of the elders, and shot himself. The story aroused enough controversy to be turned into a popular drama by Gutzkov. Spinoza was fifteen when Acosta killed himself in 1647. By that time, he was already aware that his own temperament was basically rational and scientific, and must have anticipated a similar fate.

Spinoza lacked Acosta's hot-headedness; his motto was *Caute* (caution). There were many pressures on him to conform; his father and grandfather were prosperous merchants; in the small, closed Jewish community of Amsterdam, the highly intelligent youth was inevitably a person of some prominence. He showed considerable distinction as a student of the Talmud; from this he passed on to Jewish philosophy and Cabbalistic mysticism. Unlike the empirical Anglo-Saxons, Jewish communities are inclined to take a certain pride in their more brilliant sons. Spinoza's father probably had every reason to assume that he would, in due course, become the religious and intellectual leader of the community.

It would be fascinating to know at which point Spinoza himself realized that this was out of the question – that his commitment to reason would inevitably sunder him from the society of his co-religionists. Possibly it happened as a consequence of the suicide of Acosta. It must certainly have taken many years to develop into a powerful and settled conviction, sufficiently strong to enable him to bear the shock of total rejection when it came. Dates are unfortunately lacking in the biographical materials, so it is not clear when he first began to abandon his attendance at the synagogue. Nor

do we know how soon thereafter he abandoned caution and allowed himself
to express his increasing scepticism to other young men. But common sense
suggests that it was fairly close to his twenty-fourth year – when he was
excommunicated. As Nietzsche's Zarathustra points out, separating oneself
from the herd is a painful and exhausting process. Nietzsche was the son of a
Protestant clergyman, and went through the same experience. His letters and
autobiographical fragments make clear the spiritual agonies he suffered;
yet nineteenth-century Germany was an entirely different matter from
seventeenth-century Amsterdam; to begin with, there were educators like
Schopenhauer to turn to. Spinoza's equivalent of Schopenhauer was
Giordano Bruno, and Bruno was burnt alive for his freethinking. Spinoza's
agony must have been even greater than Nietzsche's. Logic suggests that he
kept his rebellion to himself for as long as possible.

Neither do we know how much pain the break finally cost him. We are
told only that he was summoned before the Rabbins and elders of the synagogue in 1656 and accused of 'rationalistic' views, such as that angels do not
exist, that the soul might simply be another name for life, and that the Old
Testament says nothing of immortality (the opinion that had caused Acosta's
downfall). We are told that Spinoza stood his ground, declined an offer of
an annuity if he would continue to conform to the external practices of his
religion, and that when he still refused, there were violent threats of excommunication. The struggle may have continued for days or weeks. Finally,
on 27 July 1656, there was a solemn ceremony of excommunication, which
was, in effect, a spiritual execution. G. H. Lewes describes it:

> High above, the chanter rose and chanted forth, in loud lugubrious
> tones, the words of execration; while from the opposite side another
> mingled with these curses the thrilling sounds of the trumpet; and now
> black candles were reversed, and were made to melt drop by drop into
> a huge tub filled with blood. This made the whole assembly shudder;
> and when the final *Anathema Maranatha!* were uttered, and the lights all
> suddenly immersed in the blood, a cry of religious horror and execration
> burst from all; and in that solemn darkness, and to those solemn curses,
> they shouted Amen, Amen!

How far this description is accurate is open to question; but the actual
formula of excommunication, published by van Vloten, makes it clear that it
comes fairly close to the actual spirit of the ceremony. The aim was to break
Spinoza and throw him into the outer darkness, to make him feel that his
wickedness had led to his total rejection by every decent man and woman.

Shortly thereafter, to emphasize that he was now some kind of human
offal, a fanatic attempted to stab him to death in the street. The blow missed
and tore his coat. Lewes says he 'walked home thoughtful' – a statement that
reveals his inability to imagine himself into the situation. Spinoza must have

529

walked home shattered and traumatized, realizing that there was now no point in trying to salvage a little security and normality from the situation. He had to turn his back on the world of his childhood and accept solitude and exile. When he left to live outside Amsterdam, he must have felt like some wounded creature dragging itself away to die. All of which sounds melodramatic; but then, Spinoza's situation *was* a subject for melodrama.

It is interesting, and by no means entirely futile, to ask: What sort of philosopher might Spinoza have become if he had been born into a non-Jewish community – perhaps in England or France? We know that his philosophy was deeply influenced by his studies of the Talmud, and by the peculiarly intense nature of Jewish Theism. But then, he had also read certain mystics – like Ibn Gebirol, Moses of Cordova and Bruno himself. As an Englishman or Frenchman, he might have been equally influenced by Plato and Plotinus.

I am willing to be corrected, but it seems to me that Spinoza's temperament was scientific and logical rather than religious. Under different circumstances, he might have been another Descartes, or Newton, or even Shelley, a 'beautiful and ineffectual angel'. By temperament he was a Platonist and something of a Stoic. (Significantly, Goethe used to travel with the *Ethics* and the *Meditations of Marcus Aurelius*.) That is to say, he was an idealist in the Platonic sense, one who agrees that our human purpose is to lift the mind beyond desires and trivialities, beyond merely incidental beauties, to contemplate the truth and beauty of the universe itself – as Socrates explains in the *Symposium*. In a sense, it is quite inevitable that a great philosopher should be a Platonist, since the basic aim of philosophy is to rise beyond the 'triviality of everydayness' to a bird's-eye vision of broad generalities. Einstein compared the scientist to a town dweller who enjoys getting into the country, to contemplate mountains and lakes instead of endless bustle and chatter. Individual scientists and philosophers may differ in a thousand ways; but all share this common impulse to achieve a 'bird's-eye view'.

The evidence of his book on Descartes suggests that Spinoza was basically a rationalist who, under different circumstances, might have learned to accept some modified form of Judaism (as Descartes and Leibniz accepted Catholicism), while his main interests were directed towards a kind of critical philosophy. In which case, we might only know his name as an obscure commentator on other philosophers, a minor disciple of Descartes, like Geulincx (Spinoza's fellow countryman).

Whatever else the effect of the excommunication, it must have driven all tendency to amateurism and dilettantism out of his system. It faced him squarely with the question of what he really believed, and whether his belief was worth the discomfort and loneliness he had to endure. At least the bigotry of his fellow Jews accomplished one important result: it prevented him from ever taking intellectual freedom for granted as some basic human right, like the air we breathe. Having paid such a price for it, freedom of thought became a positive ideal, a kind of religious conviction.

But then, reason itself seems a feeble battle cry. On its most familiar human level, it is little more than the ability to add up a column of figures correctly. Descartes's radical doubt only led to a self-contradictory Dualism. (If the world is mind and matter, how do they interact?) If Spinoza was to justify his sacrifice, his freedom had to lead to something a little more inspiring than that.

It led, of course, to that gigantic philosophical counterpart to *Paradise Lost*, Spinoza's own Promethean effort to justify the ways of God to man, the *Ethics*. In the meantime, as an intermediate step, there came the *Theologico-Political Treatise*, a seminal work of rationalist criticism of the Bible. Issued anonymously in 1670, it caused widespread controversy and ran through many editions. When his identity became known the book was denounced as an instrument 'forged in Hell by a renegade Jew and the devil'. It is, of course, a remarkable work; but if Spinoza's reputation rested on this alone, he would be classified with Voltaire and Tom Paine as a moral rebel rather than a philosopher. It was the *Ethics* for which Spinoza spent his life preparing, the great Hegelian synthesis, the Ultimate System. (In fact, Spinoza never wrote the projected work: the book we have is no more than an outline.) The *Ethics* was his answer to his old master Morteira and the other elders who had expelled him.

In his two-volume work on the philosophy of Spinoza, Harry Austryn Wolfson has pointed out the dozens of influences that went to make up the *Ethics*, from Plato and St Anselm to Bruno and Descartes. Yet it was White-head who remarked that Western philosophy could be regarded as a series of footnotes to Plato, and it would not be inaccurate to regard the *Ethics* as an enormous commentary on the *Symposium*, with its view that man's highest aim is contemplation of universal truth. From the modern point of view, the *Ethics* has been written back to front. The final Part (V) deals with man's aims and purposes, Parts III and IV with the emotions, Part II with the mind, Part I with God and the universe. The last three Parts are an attempt at a phenomenological psychology of man, the first two at a metaphysics.

I shall not attempt a summary of the *Ethics* – which would take far more space than I have available – but confine myself to some general comments. This is basically an immense and static System, based on the mystical notion that God *is* the universe, and vice versa. One commentator remarks that Spinoza does not assert the existence of God; he asserts that existence *is* God.

That sounds the kind of meaningless and irritating proposition that makes logical positivists reach for their revolvers. But, in fact, Spinoza is prepared to argue his way towards it step by step, starting from man and his problems. The first and most basic question is obviously: why, if God is the universe, is there such a thing as evil? To which Spinoza replies that there isn't. All creatures have their own trivial, personal view of evil and good, based on their desires and needs. A cold wind seems bad to a man who has just fallen in the canal; itself, the wind is neither good nor bad – just air in motion, according to natural laws.

Man himself is merely a fragment of the whole – a leaf on a tree, a blade of grass in a field. His basic aim is self-preservation, and this governs his notions of good and evil. His powers are obviously very limited indeed. He is not body *and* soul, as Descartes taught; the mind is the mirror of the body. Here we seem to be fairly close to the psychology of Hume and the empiricists – and possibly of Gilbert Ryle – in which mind is a product of the body as smoke is a product of fire. But it is also worth bearing in mind the view of Whitman and D. H. Lawrence that man is a living unity, and that 'mind' and 'body' are two sides of the same coin, so to speak. Spinoza's basic feeling seems to come closer to this attitude.

The emotions cause man to be a slave to nature and its forces; under-standing and self-control can free him from this slavery. Maugham borrowed the title of Part IV – *Of Human Bondage* – for his novel about an intelligent man's irrational slavery to a worthless woman, and the book is a fairly accurate reflection of Spinoza's view of the emotions. 'Evil' is basically ignorance. Man achieves freedom by using his understanding to dispel it. Selflessness is not a virtue; all of us are self-seeking, but the wise man seeks things of permanent value; the stupid man is misled by his emotions to strive for unworthy aims and objects.

All this sounds drearily deterministic; it is certainly thoroughly naturalistic, only one step away from the naturalism of Hume or the total materialism of nineteenth-century thinkers like Büchner. Religious people will object that it denies human freedom; idealists that it denies transcendental values; evolu-tionists that it offers a static universe. Aware of these objections, Spinoza takes a bold leap into theology, and leaves all his opponents startled and bewildered. The world consists of shadow and substance – Plato's 'form' and 'idea', Schopenhauer's 'Will' and 'illusion'. Spinoza calls them 'mode' and 'substance'. 'Modes' are the temporary forms of the basic underlying reality. This reality is God. God is infinite and incomprehensible; in our worm-like state (at one point, Spinoza compares man to a worm living in the blood-stream of the universe), we can only see two of God's attributes – thought and extension. There are millions more which are beyond our comprehension.

All the same, because we are fragments of God, we possess the ability to rise above our mere humanity and glimpse the essential nature of the universe and of God. So the aim of life is clear: to increase the understanding.

It becomes possible to see why Spinoza ceased to exercise any profound influence in philosophy after the seventeenth century. His 'improvement' of the Cartesian dualism is not really acceptable on any practical level. To accept it as satisfactory, you have to rise to Spinoza's idea of God as one with nature, then transfer this mystical idea to the human realm. It is very hard – in fact, it requires a kind of mental sleight of hand – to see mind and body as somehow inseparable – at least, without slipping into the materialist viewpoint that mind is merely a product of body. The trouble is that human experience keeps making us aware of ourselves as mind *and* body. We say 'The spirit is willing but the flesh is weak'. Every day of our lives we become aware of ourselves as two conflicting forces. So monist solutions, no matter how logically satisfying, fail to appeal to our common sense.

But all this is far from the whole story of Spinoza's declining influence. Altogether more serious is the kind of criticism implied in Nietzsche's comments about 'unconscious autobiography'. Apart from the accusation of 'timidity and vulnerability' – which we have seen to be unfounded – Nietzsche is accusing Spinoza of being a kind of liar, or at least, a self-deceiver.

Admirers of Spinoza may shrug and ask why Nietzsche deserves to be taken so seriously. The answer is that Nietzsche's attitude has become, to a greater or lesser extent, the attitude of modern philosophy. And not merely 'existential philosophy' – the school with which Nietzsche's name is usually associated. Kierkegaard – the founder of existentialism – criticized metaphysical 'Systems' on the grounds that trying to shape your conduct according to one of these systems is like trying to find your way round Copenhagen using a map of the world on which Denmark is the size of a pinhead. In short, that a System is too much of a 'bird's-eye view' from whose dizzy altitude the real world becomes practically invisible. And this is a matter in which logical positivists find themselves in total agreement with existentialists. Both agree that philosophy ought to deal with reality as we actually know it, not with some idealistic abstraction. And so, for practical purposes, we may regard Nietzsche as the spokesman of the whole anti-metaphysical point of view. Let us, therefore, try to grasp the essence of Nietzsche's objection to Spinoza, and the existentialist viewpoint from which it sprang.

Interestingly enough, most of Nietzsche's references to Spinoza – they can easily be tracked down through the index to his Collected Works – indicate his sense of kinship; he speaks of him as 'the most upright of sages', and praises his stoicism and self-sufficiency. And Nietzsche was too self-analytical not to be aware of the parallels between himself and the Jewish philosopher. Both were 'sickly recluses'; both were 'outsiders', rejected by their own community, living in rented rooms on a low income, devoting themselves to the life of the mind. Neither were celibate by choice; both had fallen in love and been rejected; both shrugged off the disappointment and turned back to the serious business of creating a 'revaluation of values'. Both were men who, in the words of Husserl, had had 'the misfortune to fall in love with philosophy'. Both were obsessed with truth. Clearly, then, Nietzsche's rejection of Spinoza was no sudden flash of irritation. There were two other major figures towards whom Nietzsche's attitude was equally ambiguous and ambivalent: Socrates and Wagner. It was where Nietzsche felt most attracted that he felt the need to reject most violently.

The attraction is easy enough to explain. Spinoza *is* an immensely attractive figure. Goethe regarded him as a kind of saint. 'None had spoken so like the Saviour concerning God as he,' he told Lavater. And Bertrand Russell, who is predictably hostile to Spinoza's metaphysics, nevertheless describes him as 'the noblest and most lovable of the great philosophers'.

All of which makes us aware that the truth about Spinoza – as we intimated at the beginning of this essay – is that any attempt to judge him must start from Spinoza the human being. Judged *in vacuo*, the *Ethics* may be 'noble', but it is rather repellent. And as speculative philosophy – according to Moore the art of arousing thought in other philosophers – it has been a great deal less fruitful than Hume's *Essay*, Kant's *Critique* or Husserl's *Ideas*; in appearance, at least, it is a little too inhumanly perfect. It is when we have come to know Spinoza the man that we are in a position to appreciate him as the author of the *Ethics*.

What we admire is the man of incredibly tough moral fibre who stood up against the whole age, the 'prophet who contradicted the Prophets', as Goethe called him. Apart from Nietzsche, the other 'outsider' he most resembles is the mystic William Blake, another intransigent visionary who lived a life of neglect (although Blake at least had a wife to share it with him). Spinoza's enemies drew strength from bigotry and the opinion of 'the herd'. Spinoza not only stood alone; he refused to be embittered or prejudiced. Yet in spite of his mystical love of God – which he equated with knowledge – we feel that Spinoza saw the world through natural eyes. If he is a martyr, it is to reason, not religion.

And reason is simply the intellectual form of freedom. In the *Tractatus Theologico-Politicus* he is concerned with religious and political freedom. In the *Ethics*, be becomes concerned with the freedom of the spirit itself, man's longing to escape all the limitations of the earth and of his own weakness. He avoids the usual snare of religious pietism. He has little use for pity, and none for humility, which he regards as hypocrisy or weakness. He dismisses the usual notions of good and evil; for Spinoza, as for Nietzsche, virtue is based on power and ability. Neither does he have any use for the view of Socrates, that since the philosopher spends his life trying to escape his body, death is some kind of consummation. Altogether, he seems to have escaped most of the fallacies that Nietzsche most detested.

And yet it is at precisely this point that Nietzsche and Spinoza part company. Nietzsche was physically sickly, but he carried his gospel of power to its logical conclusion. When he conceived the idea of Zarathustra, the preacher of the Superman – he was above the lake of Silvaplana at the time – he wrote on a slip of paper: 'Six thousand feet above men and time.' The idea that came to him was that all religions and philosophies have so far been mistaken about the highest good. It does not lie in moral virtue, or in self-restraint, or even in self-knowledge, but in the idea of *great health and strength*. This, says Nietzsche, is the fundamental constituent of freedom. Once man has these the others will follow, for most of his evils – and his intellectual confusions – spring from weakness.

It follows that the philosopher should recognize man as inadequate – 'human, all too human' – and strive to bring about the advent of the super-man. For Nietzsche, reason is a manifestation of strength. Man's chief duty is to nurture his strength and his optimism, and to teach men to strive to evolve.

Now Spinoza quite definitely sets his face against evolutionism – or teleology – in the appendix to Part I. Since God is perfect, he asks, how can he have mere purposes? Admittedly, he seems to risk self-contradiction at this point. For he admits that God is 'partly' personal, and that will and thought are among His attributes. Nevertheless, we would be mistaken to think of God as sharing such personal qualities as desire and purpose. For a moment, we seem to glimpse Spinoza's mental picture of God; some unthinkable gigantic creature, like nature itself, breathing quietly in its sleep, unconsciously producing all the activity we see around us as a mere by-product of its tremendous breathing. . . .

For Spinoza, man's ultimate perfection is to achieve 'cosmic consciousness', to transcend all his mere emotions, and to rise on wings of reason to the contemplation of this vast indifferent godhead.

Now at a fairly early stage in his career, Nietzsche had admired Socrates above all other philosophers; it seemed to him that the ultimate good was Thought. Then, in *Human, All too Human*, he turned against his old masters and ideals; he comes to feel that thought is trivial and unimportant compared to life. He ceased to believe in thought or reason as the vehicle that would transport man to the infinite. The thinkers, from Socrates to Kant, are deniers of the body and of life. And Spinoza, he feels is, unrealistic; he scornfully dismisses 'the no-more-laughing and no-more-weeping of Spinoza, the destruction of the emotions by their analysis and vivisection, which he recommended so naively'.

And so his indictment of Spinoza amounts to this: that the philosopher, rejected by society, withdrew into solitude and sought consolation in thought. He 'transcended' his humanity by rejecting it, dismissing the emotions as trivial. Now Nietzsche, like Blake, believed that the right way to transcend the emotions is to outgrow them; *not* by starving them to death. Zarathustra loves life; he loves nature; he loves to see pretty girls laughing and dancing. Spinoza's solution smacked to him of sour grapes.

This is not to say that Nietzsche did not believe in thought, or in self-discipline. But he believed they were only part of the answer. If a man is

535

hungry, he cannot satisfy his belly by thinking about food. But he can use his intelligence to find ways of obtaining food. And it is better to find food than to talk yourself into believing you are not hungry. It is better to have a wife – or mistress – than to find ascetic reasons for condemning sex. To over-indulge the emotions is disastrous for the philosopher; to starve them in the name of reason is just as bad.

Basically, then, Nietzsche is accusing Spinoza of producing a false solution to the problem of the philosopher. Nietzsche created a new concept of the philosopher; not merely Rodin's thinker, sitting with his chin in his hand, but a whole and complete human being – something like Plato's philosopher-king. In *Man and Superman*, Shaw has a thoroughly Nietzschean definition of the philosopher: 'he who seeks in contemplation to discover the inner will of the world, in invention to discover the means of fulfilling that will, and in action to do that will by the so discovered means.' Obviously, Spinoza fulfils the first clause triumphantly. But he erected this activity of contemplation into the whole duty of the philosopher, his ultimate aim and purpose. His only 'action' was to write and think, and he attempted to give his ideas an air of icy self-sufficiency by casting them in the form of Euclidean propositions. It could be argued that his book justifies inaction, withdrawal from the world.

Since Nietzsche, this notion of the philosopher as the complete human being has become an integral part of the twentieth-century philosophical tradition – and not only for existentialists. A. N. Whitehead expressed it forcefully in his last book *Modes of Thought*:

Nothing can be omitted, experience drunk and experience sober, experience sleeping and experience waking, experience drowsy and experience wide-awake, experience self-conscious and experience self-forgetful, experience intellectual and experience physical, experience religious and experience sceptical, experience anxious and experience carefree, experience anticipatory and experience retrospective, experience happy and experience grieving, experience dominated by emotion and experience under self-restraint, experience in the light and experience in the dark, experience normal and experience abnormal.

It is true that few philosophers measure up to this standard; but most existentialists nevertheless take care to bear it in mind.

At which point I must 'declare my interest', and explain the nature of my own approach to the problem. My first book, *The Outsider*, was concerned with such men as Spinoza and Nietzsche – men whose inner development demanded a rejection of society – and often their own rejection *by* society. Whitehead defined religion as 'what a man does with his solitude': and since such inner-development usually demands a withdrawal into solitude, it would probably be true to say that most 'outsiders' are concerned with religion – although often of a highly personal and mystical kind.

In the great ages of religion, such men could usually find refuge in the Church. They might still be 'outsiders' – like Eckhart and Savonarola and St Francis and St John of the Cross – but they could nevertheless find in the Church a creative outlet for their energies. Outsiderism – the sense of not belonging to society – could be justified as a need to belong to a still higher society – of saints and god-seekers. So, in a paradoxical sense, there *was* a place for 'outsiders' in society.

Then, for better or for worse, the Church ceased to be the dominant intellectual force in society, even if it could still bully Descartes into suppressing his major work on the universe. Modes of thought were 'secularized'. The man with a powerful urge to inner development now had to find his own way to self-realization. Spinoza was one of the first of these 'outsider' figures. Two centuries after this death, 'outsiderism' had become the intellectual disease of the West. My own interest in the subject arose from the fact that so many of the great Romantics of the nineteenth century died tragically – either through insanity or disease or suicide.

But because the sickness had become so widespread, it was easier to reach a diagnosis. Many of the Romantics, from Shelley and Kleist to Van Gogh and Stefan George, were inclined to believe that life is fundamentally tragic. Man has brief glimpses of god-like intensity, but they vanish and leave him trapped in 'this dim vast vale of tears'. Yet other 'outsiders' took a less pessimistic view. William Blake insisted that man consists of three components: body, emotions and intellect. When intellect – which he called Urizen – is allowed to dominate, it becomes a force for evil, and the Fall occurs. In a healthy human being it must combine with intellect and body; these then give birth to a fourth component, imagination (Los). Half a century later, Dostoevsky – another seminal existentialist thinker – expressed the same view symbolically in the three brothers Karamazov. Ivan, the intellectual, comes close to insanity by suppressing emotions and body in the name of intellect.

Nietzsche, we have seen, reached the same position; but only after he had purged his system of the pessimism of Schopenhauer, which had totally dominated his early thinking. And having achieved optimism at the price of ruthless self-vivisection, he became violently intolerant of thinkers like Socrates and Spinoza, whom he regarded as 'life-deniers', glorifiers of 'Urizen'.

We may feel that, in the case of Socrates, this is hardly fair. Socrates was a soldier as well as a thinker; he could apparently out-drink and out-march his friends as well as out-think them. He held love to be as important as reason, and seems to have regarded the health of the body as equally important (as did Spinoza). Nevertheless, Nietzsche condemns him as an arid rationalist who allowed reason to dominate his life. The citizens of Athens who condemned Socrates to death seemed to believe that he was primarily a sceptic – a sneerer. Nietzsche seems to feel they were not entirely wrong.

And what of Spinoza? I would suggest that, while Nietzsche's 'existential criticisms' were, to a large extent, justified, there are nevertheless elements in Spinoza's temperament that Nietzsche left out of account because he was unable to understand them. His criticisms apply to the naturalistic part of Spinoza – Spinoza the sceptic – not to Spinoza the mystic.

Now to a modern reader, Spinoza's psychology seems as inadequate as John Stuart Mill's. Here we feel most strongly that Spinoza's insight was limited by the strength of his reaction against contemporary 'unreason'. He begins Part III by stating aggressively that most writers on the emotions have treated them as if they belonged to the realm of the 'soul'; he, Spinoza, proposes to treat them as if they obeyed the usual laws of nature – which he proceeds to do in a manner worthy of Somerset Maugham. No doubt his method was a salutary shock to most of his readers. But after three centuries, it has ceased to be shocking. Freud went much further in 'reducing' man to a bundle of uncontrolled impulses. And there are modern behavioural psychologists who have gone even further. Now the reaction is setting in. Many of us feel that the naturalistic view of man leaves out more than it puts in. The philosopher St Martin pointed out that the kind of 'humility' that insists that man is a mere grain of sand on some universal beach leads to laziness and cowardice. It is easy enough to demonstrate that every man suffers from the delusion that he is the most important being in the universe (what Robert Ardrey calls 'the fallacy of central position'), but it is too easy to slip into the opposite assumption – that he is the least important being in the universe. Even Freud's naturalistic psychology opened up all kinds of strange possibilities – for once we have admitted the existence of the subconscious, we have taken a long step away from naturalism. (This is why some behaviourists have refused to acknowledge its existence.) We find ourselves having to decide on the possibility of a 'collective unconscious', which in turn may lead to questions about telepathy and psychokinesis, and whether the subconscious mind may be responsible for poltergeist phenomena. Spinoza would have dismissed all these as superstitions.

Probably the closest modern equivalent to Spinoza's psychology is the 'existential psychology' of Sartre. Sartre's first book, *A Theory of the Emotions*, stated the thoroughly Spinozist doctrine that an emotion is simply another name for frustration; when we want something and we act, we feel no emotion; it is when we want something and are frustrated that we feel emotion. The more elaborate psychology of *Being and Nothingness* is constructed on this foundation. Emotion is basically an attempt to deceive ourselves. But for Sartre, there is no God, so the trivial drama of human stupidity and self-deception is played out against a background of universal emptiness.

On the other hand, comparison of Spinoza with Sartre makes us realize that Sartre is in one respect immensely more sophisticated; he had grasped Husserl's insight that all consciousness is *intentional* – that each perception is fired towards its object like a grappling hook. This in turn led Husserl (though not Sartre) to the notion of a 'transcendental ego' presiding over consciousness and ultimately responsible for intentionality; he came to see philosophy as the task of uncovering the secrets and mysteries of the transcendental ego. We might say that Husserl counterbalanced the Freudian Unconscious with the notion of a Superconscious mind.

Again, many non-naturalistic psychologists have felt that the most basic and interesting fact about human consciousness is that *there seems to be something wrong with it*. Pascal and Newman chose to call it 'original sin'. But it was also recognized by Gurdjieff, who said that our problem is that 'ordinary consciousness' is a form of sleep. While we are asleep, says Gurdjieff, we are little more than machines. He would have said that Spinoza's psychology is simply the psychology of the machine. What interested Gurdjieff was the possibility of awakening from sleep and utilizing some of the hidden potentialities of consciousness. Again, we are close to Husserl and the 'secrets of the transcendental ego'.

So Spinoza's psychology, while brilliant and full of insights, will strike most modern readers as simplistic, not to say mechanistic. It is perhaps significant that he called his Part IV 'Of Human Bondage', while Pascal wanted to call the equivalent book of his own psychology 'The Greatness and Misery of Man'. One feels sometimes that Shaw's remark about Shakespeare applies equally to Spinoza: that he understands human weakness, but not human strength.

But then, the essence of Spinoza lies not in his vision of man, but in his vision of God. And here we see why Nietzsche found it impossible to come to grips with this aspect of his thought. In this respect, Nietzsche was a thoroughgoing nineteenth-century rationalist, like Tennyson and Emerson and Carlyle; he might have an idealistic hankering after the transcendental or the absolute, but in his heart of hearts he believed God to be a crude superstition, a hangover from the ages of unreason. Spinoza, on the other hand, felt himself at home in a great mystical tradition that can be traced back in ancient India, China and the Middle East. In all natural things – practical things – he felt himself to be a reasonable, natural human being. But he felt that a point came where human knowledge had to recognize its own inadequacy. G. K. Chesterton once pointed out that mystics should not be considered less rational and practical than other people; on the contrary, they are often more rational and practical because they know precisely where their knowledge begins and ends. One of the oddest things about mystics is that they often seem to have very precise insights into the nature of God. As they struggle to express these insights, with immense clumsiness, you feel that this is not romantic verbalizing; they are struggling for precision, but language defeats them.

I do not know whether Spinoza knew anything about the mystics of China or India, or even about the Sufis; what is quite certain is that he would have felt perfectly at home in their tradition, as he did in the tradition of Cabbalism. For these mystics, God was not an idea, but a reality. They experienced God in moments of deep insight or of sudden intense ecstasy. A hungry man is not more certain of the existence of hot soup than the mystic is of God.

In this sense, God is an insight, a 'bird's-eye view' of the universe. I should say, perhaps, that God is *experienced* as an insight. Man is confined in the narrowness of personal existence, and all his habits seem determined to keep him trapped, like some prisoner chained to the floor of his cell by an iron collar. The philosopher observes with pity and irony the triviality that wastes the lives of most men. He feels that they are stuck in the present like flies on flypaper. His aim is freedom, and he knows that the first step is to avoid the flypaper. So the two parts of the *Ethics* on human bondage should not be regarded as a comprehensive psychology so much as a series of moralistic observations on human nature, of the kind that can be found so abundantly in the writings of the religious philosophers, from Boethius to Loyola.

What is perhaps most difficult to understand from the 'natural standpoint' is that once a man has clearly grasped the nature 'of human bondage', he may quite suddenly experience a deep intuition of the nature of freedom. The Hindu saint Ramakrishna was about to kill himself with a sword when the 'Divine Mother' revealed herself, overwhelming him with a tremendous vision of *meaning* – of some vast torrent of universal energy that drives nature like a giant dynamo. Nietzsche himself experienced this vision on at least two occasions, and felt that it transcended all human ideas of good and evil. And Bertrand Russell – another 'sceptic' – once identified the source of his own scientific inspiration as 'the very breath of life, fierce and coming from far away, bringing into human life the vastness and fearful passionless force of non-human things.'

This is the mystic's basic realization, and to some extent, it is accessible to all of us, at least by analogy. I may *say* that I know what a rose smells like, yet when I first smell a rose bush in spring, I realize how much I had forgotten. The reality is somehow so much more real and rich than anything I could conjure up mentally in midwinter. And the same goes for all the meaning of the universe. We are cut off from meaning as a prisoner in the deepest and dampest dungeon in the Bastille is cut off from the sunlight. The prisoner may imagine the sunlight; he may even dream he is outside; but when he actually feels the sun and breathes in the air, he realizes that the mind is absurdly inexpert in conjuring up absent realities. The mystic 'knows' a little of the nature of God by pursuing this analogy – by imagining a reality a thousand times as great, and a thousand times as real and startling, as a spring morning. Of course, the imagination is totally inadequate; yet it *can* catch a glimpse of this vision of meaning. And this is enough to make him aware that all our human 'knowledge' is crude and absurd and totally inadequate. The reality is so infinitely rich that it is absurd to speak about 'evolution'. In believing that the universe could 'evolve', we are merely projecting our human inadequacy on the ultimate reality. . . .

And now, perhaps, we can begin to see the paradox of Nietzsche's criticism of Spinoza. In effect, he read the last four parts of the *Ethics* and accused Spinoza of mistaking his intellectual concepts for reality. If Spinoza had been alive, he would have pointed to the first part of the *Ethics*, and accused Nietzsche of using the word 'reality' without the faintest insight into its meaning. Yet this, too, would have been unfair. Nietzsche also had his glimpses of that 'breath of life', fierce and blowing from far away. The two great philosophers approached the same basic concepts from opposite points of view. Both had glimpsed the reality, but they called it by different names.

And ultimately, Spinoza had the last word. For ultimately, Nietzsche became a Spinozist. That may sound absurd; yet how otherwise can we interpret the idea of Eternal Recurrence? It makes no sense in the context of Nietzsche's evolutionary philosophy. Yet it makes sense to a mystic. Nietzsche began his life as a disciple of Socrates and the stoic philosophers. He swallowed Schopenhauer's Buddhistic pessimism. Then came the 'visions', the glimpses of 'bliss rising from the depths of nature' (as he expressed it in *The Birth of Tragedy*). Nietzsche transcended good and evil – and Socratic 'reason'. He came to feel that man owes allegiance only to that 'fearful passionless force of non-human things'. He preached the superman. And then, as his imagination grasped for a moment the concept of the super-human, he saw that ultimate force as something too vast to be contained in such a mere human concept as evolution. In the angels' chorus at the beginning of *Faust*, Goethe had written:

Es schaümt das Meer in breiten Flüssen
Am tiefen Grund der Felsen auf,
Und Fels und Meer wird fortgerissen
In ewig schnellen Sphärenlauf.
(Against the cliffs with roaring song
In mighty torrents foams the ocean
And cliffs and sea are whirled along
With circling orbs in ceaseless motion.)

Imagine this vision multiplied a thousandfold and you have an approximation to Spinoza's vision of God – and Nietzsche's vision of that mighty ultimate force behind the universe. 'Circling orbs in ceaseless motion' – eternal recurrence. It became Zarathustra's ultimate affirmation, beyond the superman. And so, in the end, the vision of Spinoza and the vision of Nietzsche blend into a kind of unity.

From our point of view, it is fortunate it happened so late in the day. Philosophers are never so entertaining – or so instructive – as when they are beating one another over the head.

32 Spinoza et l'état des Hébreux

Sylvain Zac, Paris

Dans l'*Ethique*, démontrée 'more gemetrico', la philosophie de Spinoza dénonce par la puissance du vrai qui lui est immanente les présupposés philosophiques de toutes les religions d'inspiration biblique: idées de la transcendance de Dieu, de sa spiritualité absolue, de sa liberté de choix et de création, de ses desseins cachés ou déchiffrables qui présideraient au gouvernement du monde et, enfin, l'idée de sa puissance royale et judiciaire qu'il exercerait sur les hommes, liée elle-même à la croyance au libre-arbitre de l'homme. Dans le *Traité théologico-politique*, livre de combat pour la liberté de penser, Spinoza s'attaque directement aux dogmes qui sont propres au judaïsme: dogme de la vocation des Hébreux, profitant d'un don spirituel qui leur est réservé, dogme de la divinité de la loi mosaïque dont ils sont les destinataires et les dépositaires, dogme de la valeur inconditionnée de leurs cérémonies de culte mises au même rang que les enseignements éthiques de Moïse et des prophètes.[1]

Spinoza tâche de démontrer, d'un côté, que ces dogmes sont infirmés par les textes même de l'Écriture, interprétés correctement, et, d'autre part, qu'ils sont à rejeter, à partir de certaines considérations tirés de sa propre philosophie. Ce sont surtout ces dernières qui retiendront notre attention.

Le dogme de l'élection de Dieu a un sens philosophique, lorsqu'il s'agit des individus humains. On peut dire, en effet, que tout individu humain – comme d'ailleurs toute chose – profite du 'secours interne de Dieu', dans la mesure où le 'conatus', aspect dynamique de son être, expression de la puissance de Dieu à un degré déterminé, lui permet de vivre et de vivre aussi bien que possible en égard à l'ordre nécessaire des choses.[2] Autrement dit, lorsqu'un individu augmente sa propre perfection grâce à la connaissance adéquate des choses, de soi-même et de Dieu, il participe davantage de la nature de Dieu. Aussi, tout en dissociant l'idée de vocation de celle d'un appel adressé par Dieu, tout en admettant que l'augmentation chez cet individu du stock des idées adéquates relève de l'ordre prédéterminé de la nature, on s'exprimerait correctement en disant qu'il doit sa perfection à une vocation singulière de Dieu, que Dieu l'a élu de préférence aux autres.[3] Mais ce qui est vrai pour les individus, envisagés dans leurs essences individuelles, est totalement faux pour les peuples. En effet la nature crée des individus et non des peuples. L'idée de peuple est liée à celle d'une communauté politique qui consiste dans une association de 'conatus'. L'appartenance d'un individu à tel ou tel peuple se reconnaît seulement à sa langue, à ses moeurs et à ses institutions dont il porte la marque.[4] Aussi l'idée de la supériorité spirituelle d'un peuple par rapport aux autres peuples est vide de sens: un peuple peut-être supérieur aux autres seulement par son esprit civique; et cela dépend de la nature des lois et des institutions de l'État où il vit.[5] En tout cas il ne faut pas confondre le salut politique et le salut philosophique. Il y a d'ailleurs une incompatibilité d'essence entre l'idée d'élection, prise à la lettre, relevant du désir de se glorifier au détriment des autres et l'idée de béatitude, état d'un homme uni à Dieu par la connaissance adéquate. Quiconque connaît l'état de béatitude s'unit aussi aux autres hommes en s'unissant à Dieu: sa joie veut se communiquer et se communique universellement comme la connaissance adéquate dont elle est l'expression affective. Bien communicable et partageable, elle alimente la générosité et non l'orgueil et la haine qui en est la conséquence.[6]

Mais Paul ne dit-il pas que si l'avantage des Juifs est grand, c'est que les paroles de Dieu lui ont été confiées? Ne sont-ils pas les détenteurs légitimes de la loi? Mais en quel sens la loi de Moïse est-elle divine? Elle l'est bien sûr, en tant que les Hébreux la rapportent à Dieu depuis sa donation au mont Sinaï. Mais elle ne l'est pas si, en se plaçant au point de vue de la vérité de la chose, on qualifie de 'divine' seulement la règle de vie réclamée par le souverain bien, connaissance et amour de Dieu, découlant nécessairement de l'idée de Dieu contenue objectivement dans notre entendement.[7]

A vrai dire, cette règle de vie, conçue comme une vérité éternelle et comportant la nécessité d'une vérité mathématique n'a pas le statut d'un commandement. Mais comme chez Spinoza, en vertu du principe de l'identité de la connaissance et de l'amour, ce qui relève de la pure pensée se traduit nécessairement par un mode d'existence bien déterminés, on doit dire que la loi divine est aussi prescriptive, et que les maximes qui en découlent peuvent être considérés en quelque sorte comme des commandements de Dieu ('jussa Dei').[8] Mais l'emploi de ce vocabulaire anthropomorphique ne doit pas nous empêcher de souligner qu'elle comporte des caractères qu'on ne saurait attribuer à aucune loi proprement humaine, telle que la loi juridique, prescrite par un homme ou certains hommes à d'autres hommes. En effet, découlant de la connaissance adéquate, fondée, en dernier lieu sur des notions communes, elle est 1e une, car il n'y a qu'un seul souverain bien, 2e universelle, car l'essence infinie de Dieu et son éternité, fondement de cette loi, sont connues de tous, à condition que notre esprit soit délivré des préjugés de la tradition et des pièges du langage, 3e indépendante de toute foi historique, relevant du témoignage et, en dernier lieu, de la connaissance par ouï-dire et, enfin, 4e excluant tout culte extérieur et trouvant en elle-même sa propre récompense, elle ne nous invite nullement à rechercher par des moyens mécaniques les faveurs de Dieu.[9] Or la loi de Moïse – du moins si l'on se réfère à l'Écriture elle même, ne se présente pas comme une seule règle de vie, mais comme un ensemble de prescriptions dictées par un Dieu, souverain, législateur et juge, et s'imposant aux Hébreux comme des ordres dont ils ne comprennent pas bien l'utilité. Elle est réservée à un seul peuple et adaptée à la mentalité d'un seul groupe d'hommes. Fondée sur des témoignages historiques souvent contradictoires d'ailleurs, elle ne répond pas aux conditions de la normativité intrinsèque du vrai. Enfin, ne dissociant pas le culte extérieur du culte intérieur, elle énonce en même temps, comme toute législation positive, des sanctions matérielles, conditions de son application.[10] Or, s'il en est ainsi, on comprend bien que la loi de Moïse ne peut nous procurer la béatitude qui consiste dans la seule connaissance de Dieu et ne saurait nous apporter la tranquillité absolue de l'âme solidaire del' amour et de la moralité. L'obéissance à la loi de Moïse, qu'on l'envisage dans ce qu'elle commande ou interdit, n'exclut pas les conflits intérieurs, la tentation de la transgresser et la transgression elle-même. C'est la vérité de l'enseignement de Paul: 'ceux qui vivent sous la loi ne peuvent pas être justifiés par la loi'.[11]

Quant aux cérémonies du culte, indifférentes au Souverain bien, elles ne concernent en rien – nous venons de l'entrevoir – la tranquillité et la béatitude des individus. Elles sont de pures ombres par rapport aux actions qui découlent de notre nature seule. Elles sont bonnes seulement par commandement en tant qu'elles constituent des adjuvants précieux à la bonne marche d'une communauté politique: elles constituent chez les Hébreux, des signes extérieurs d'une foi de type national dont la fonction est de leur servir comme moyen de se reconnaître réciproquement en tant que fervents serviteurs d'un État lui-même sacralisé et proclamé royaume de Dieu. Les cérémonies sont de l'ordre de l'institution et tout ce qui est institutionnel relève du politique au sens général; tout Église, du moment qu'elle est statutaire, comporte un aspect politique et constitue, pour ainsi dire, un État dans un État. Il en est ainsi également des Juifs depuis leur dispersion. Mais dans l'État des Hébreux, où la religion et l'État sont indissolublement liées, les cérémonies sont des lois de l'État lui-même. Le Christ a-t-il aboli la loi de Moïse ou est-il venu l'accomplir, sans chercher de rien y ajouter ni de rien en retrancher? La réponse de Spinoza est nuancée. L'enseignement moral du Christ est un enseignement universel, détaché de toute exigence politique particulière, car, contrairement à Moïse il a connu les commandements eux-mêmes non comme lois voulues par Dieu, mais comme des vérités éternelles connues adéquatement; aussi, du moins ceux qui ont compris son enseignement sont libérés de la loi mosaïque, bien que désormais la loi divine, au sens fort du terme, soit inscrite à jamais dans leur coeur.[12] Mais d'autre part puisque toutes les prescriptions culturelles aussi bien que les lois juridiques contenues dans la *Torah* concernent la vie de l'État, il n'en a abrogé aucune. Le Christ n'a pas voulu introduire de nouvelles lois dans l'État. Ce qu'il a reclamé, c'est qu'on apprenne à distinguer les enseignements moraux des lois de l'État, les uns exigeant le consentement intérieur de l'âme, alors que les autres réglementant seulement l'action externe.[13] A vrai dire le Christ – Spinoza le reconnaît – n'est pas le premier d'avoir dénoncé la subversion de l'éthique par le statutaire au sein de l'État des Hébreux. Un des thèmes les plus fréquents des prophètes d'Israël est que les cérémonies ne peuvent remplacer la purification de l'âme, l'usage constant des vertus et, enfin, les secours apportés aux pauvres et aux opprimés. Mais Spinoza ne nie nullement le sens éthique des juifs et la vocation d'universalité des prophètes. Ce qu'il veut établir c'est que la loi de Moïse n'a égard qu'au bien de l'État et que, pour vivre dans la béatitude, il ne suffit pas de respecter la législation d'un État, si parfaite qu'elle soit.

Une telle thèse aboutit nécessairement à une condamnation sans appel du judaïsme rabbinique, celui des juifs de la seconde dispersion. Puisque toutes les ordonnances de la *Torah* sont des lois de l'État, Spinoza en conclut logiquement que depuis la disparition de l'État des Hébreux, les juifs ne sont pas plus tenus par la loi de Moïse qu'ils ne l'étaient avant la fondation de leur État. C'est de la seule législation de l'État que la religion des Hébreux tire sa force de loi. Une fois leur État détruit, la religion aurait dû se ramener chez eux à un enseignement universel de la raison ('catholicum rationis documentum'). Citant Jérémie à l'appui de sa thèse, Spinoza soutient que celui-ci aurait écrit aux juifs de Babylone qu'étant désormais sous le dépendance d'un roi étranger, leur pacte avec Dieu, fondement de leur propre État est 'ipso facto' annulé et qu'ils auraient désormais à se conformer en tous points aux lois de leur nouveau pays. Il ne semble pas que la référence à Jérémie soit légitime.[14] Mais en tout cas la thèse même de Spinoza est nette: le judaïsme religion liée à la vie d'un État ne survit plus à lui-même depuis la dispersion que par la force de la tradition; c'est la tradition qui favorise ce qu'on appelle la séparatisme juif et, par contrecoup, la haine des peuples dont ils sont entourés, renforce chez les juifs leur résistance à leur intégration totale dans les pays de la diaspora.[15]

Mais laissons de côté le problème de l'attitude de Spinoza à l'égard du judaïsme de son temps, et relisons attentivement les chapitres III, IV, V du *Traité théologico-politique*. Nous nous apercevrons que si l'on envisage uniquement l'État des Hébreux, le dogme de la vocation des Hébreux répond selon lui à une réalité historique, du moins à une certaine période de son histoire, Spinoza enseigne, en outre, que la loi de Moïse qui a assuré long-temps la stabilité de l'État et, enfin, que les cérémonies du culte ont contribué à développer le sentiment civique des Hébreux, en transformant, par la vertu de l'accoutumance, le sentiment de l'obéissance à la loi civile en un sentiment de liberté.

Si l'élection des Hébreux n'a pas trait, comme nous l'avons vu, à leur supériorité dans la spéculation et dans ce qui touche la 'vraie vie', elle concerne effectivement la félicité temporelle de leur État, sa prospérité matérielle et son aptitude à faire face au cours de son histoire aux dangers de toute sorte. Ce qui a fait la supériorité du peuple hébraïque par rapport aux autres peuples ce furent son régime social, ses institutions, ses lois et aussi la 'fortune' qui a présidé à la fondation et à la conservation de son État pendant tant d'années.[16] Non pas que la 'fortune' ait selon Spinoza un fondement ontologique; elle est, au contraire, exclue par ce que Spinoza appelle la 'direction de Dieu', c'est-à-dire par l'enchaînement des choses naturelles.[17] Mais si le philosophe sait qu'il y a un ordre de la nature fixe et immuable, il est vrai aussi qu'en raison de l'enchevêtrement des séries des choses il ne sait pas toujours lui-même comment les parties s'accordent avec le tout. Aussi lorsqu'il se trouve en présence d'évènements, qui relèvent du 'secours extérieur de Dieu', causes extérieures dont nous ne comprenons pas le lien et la nécessité, bien plus que du 'secours intérieur de Dieu' se manifestant particulièrement dans notre pouvoir de comprendre, il lui est permis de dire que Dieu dirige les choses par des causes inattendues et d'employer le mot 'fortune'.[18] Est-ce à dire que, selon Spinoza, l'existence d'un État sain et prospère relève toujours de la fortune? Sans admettre l'idée platonicienne du philosophe-roi, Spinoza conçoit cependant un État fondé sur les exigences de la raison qui devrait sa stabilité et sa durée à la seule vigilance et à la seule prudence de ses gouvernants. Sans être une communauté de sages – car alors l'existence même de l'État ne serait pas indispensable – un tel État releverait cependant surtout des aptitudes et de l'efficacité des mesures prises à bon escient par des hommes.[19] Mais nous partons de ce fait que les Hébreux, sortis de l'Egypte, manquaient de toute culture politique et de toute éducation civique. Aussi leur sort politique, soumis en raison de leur ignorance, aux fluctuations de la fortune, devait être misérable. Or, malgré tout, l'État des Hébreux a subsisté et prospéré. Le peuple ne peut expliquer cet état de choses qu'en faisant intervenir une direction étrangère, celle de Dieu, non tel qu'il se déploie dans l'activité de l'entendement humain, absolument autonome, mais tel qu'il agit par des causes extérieures, connues et imprévisibles. Ils voient dans la bonne marche de leurs institutions la main de Dieu et attribuent leur chance à une providence particulière qu'ils appellent leur élection par Dieu.[20]

D'autre part, bien qu'au sens fort du terme, la loi de Moïse est une loi humaine – une règle de vie servant seulement à la vie de l'État – elle est aussi une loi divine d'abord parce qu'elle a été établie par la révélation, c'est-à-dire par voie prophétique et, ensuite, parce qu'en raison de ses effets bienfaisants, on pouvait la rapporter à Dieu. On sait que, selon Maïmonide, Moïse, prince des prophètes, était à la fois législateur, homme d'état et philosophe: le véritable prophète est celui dont le coeur est plein de sagesse et qui l'emporte sur les autres hommes par sa connaissance spéculative.[21] Spinoza, au contraire, ne cesse de protester contre tout rapprochement entre le prophète et le philosophe, même lorsqu'il s'agit de Moïse. D'abord Moïse n'a pas connu la vraie nature de Dieu, puisqu'il accorde à Dieu, considéré comme roi et législateur, des attributs moraux, tels que, par exemple la justice et la miséricorde, qui n'appartiennent qu'à la nature humaine. D'autre part, ayant perçu les commandements seulement, imaginativement et non intellectuellement, il n'a pas compris pourquoi le régime politique que les Hébreux auront édifié sur ses instructions sera le meilleur et pourquoi de cette façon le but poursuivi par ce peuple sera vraiment atteint.[22]

Il reste cependant qu'un des thèmes majeurs du *Traité théologico-politique* est que, sans compter avec un défaut grave de la législation mosaïque, base de l'État des Hébreux, qui a fini à la longue par vicier les institutions – nous y reviendrons – celle-ci aurait pu assurer la perpétuité de l'État. Spinoza insiste certes sur la caducité de la loi mosaïque depuis la dispersion du peuple juif, mais il admet qu'en raison de son origine, elle a été considérée comme intangible au cours de l'existence de l'État des Hébreux. Certes toutes les mesures devant être prises au cours de l'histoire d'un État n'ont pas pu être prévues dans cette législation: d'où l'importance des pontifes et des prophètes chargés de consulter Dieu et de transmettre au peuple et à ses gouvernants les vouloirs divins. Mais aucun oracle ni aucun message prophétique ne devait être accepté s'il n'était pas conforme à la loi mosaïque, loi de la patrie.[23]

D'autre part la fidélité ou l'infidélité à la loi mosaïque est au cours de l'histoire de l'État des Hébreux une des causes de sa splendeur, dans le premier cas, ou de sa décadence, dans le second cas. Le Christ lui-même nous l'avons vu, n'a pas voulu détruire la loi de Moïse comme loi de l'État. Certes il semble y avoir contradiction entre le précepte évangélique de la non-résistance à la violence et la loi mosaïque qui prescrit à chacun de réclamer au juge des dommages pour un tort subi par lui, non certes par vengeance, mais pour défendre sincèrement le loi de la patrie contre les assauts des méchants. On ne résout pas cette contradiction en disant que le Christ a voulu corriger des dispositions internes de l'âme et non des actions externes qui relèvent de l'autorité du législateur. En effet, une des conséquences de l'interprétation spinoziste de l'Écriture est que dans l'*Ancien* comme dans le *Nouveau Testament* on ne sépare pas l'intérieur de l'extérieur, la foi des oeuvres. Aussi, même dans le cas de la loi civile les motifs de l'obéissance comptent autant que l'obéissance, du moins en ce qui concerne la garantie de son efficacité. L'explication est toute autre: une loi est en elle-même abstraite; on ne saurait l'appliquer sans tenir compte du 'où' et du 'quand'. Il y a même des circonstances où elle est entièrement inapplicable. Il faut remarquer d'abord que le principe de la non-résistance à la violence se trouve déjà chez Jérémie. Or Jérémie a vécu lors de la première dévastation du Temple, dans une époque où le pays, en état de perdition, ne jouit plus de l'autorité et de l'arbitrage d'un État digne de ce nom. Le Christ a vécu dans une époque semblable à la fin du régime du second temple. D'ailleurs chez le Christ comme chez Jérémie il s'agit d'un enseignement, d'une prédication et non pas d'une nouvelle loi susceptible de remplacer la loi de Moïse qui condamne l'acceptation de l'injustice qu'on en soit victime soi-même ou un autre. Dans un État sain c'est l'État seul qui détient le monopole de la vengeance. C'est le devoir de chaque citoyen de l'y aider et la loi du Talion, à condition qu'on l'applique dans le seul intérêt de l'État, est entièrement valable.[24]

Enfin si Spinoza affirme que les cérémonies du culte doivent être exclus du contenu de la parole de Dieu nous prescrivant seulement la pratique de la justice et de la charité, il montre aussi qu'elles remplissent un rôle exemplaire dans le développement de l'esprit civique des citoyens. Leur rôle essentiel est d'intégrer les lois dans le rythme de l'existence des citoyens et d'en faire, pour ainsi dire, une 'seconde nature'. Les lois constituent l'âme de l'État, mais dans la mesure où elles prennent forme de commandements, elles comportent toujours un caractère de précarité. Même si l'on ne pense pas que la loi excite la convoitise, en tant qu'elle est interdiction en même temps que commandement, il reste cependant qu'il est dans sa nature d'être transgressée et, par conséquent, d'être étrangère à notre nature. C'est en ce sens qu'on peut opposer – du moins si l'on se fie à une première approximation – la contingence de la loi civile à la nécessité de la loi physique. Aussi pour éliminer les aléas dans l'application de la loi, on utilise dans toutes les formes de l'État – que le pouvoir appartienne à un seul, à quelques'uns ou à la collectivité toute entière – les lois naturelles de la dynamique des passions afin de la renforcer par un recours à des sanctions. Mais si la crainte du châtiment est, au sein de l'État un mobile qui empêche souvent la transgression de la loi, elle finit, cependant même si elle ne dégénère pas en terreur, par nous ôter toute ardeur dans l'accomplissement du devoir. Aussi dans tout État digne de ce nom on devrait établir des lois telles que les citoyens soient contenus moins par la crainte que par l'espoir.[25] Nous verrons que ce fut notamment le cas des Hébreux au cours d'une certaine époque de leur histoire. Mais il y a plus: l'obéissance elle-même, en tant qu'elle consiste à exécuter des commandements par soumission à la seule autorité d'un chef, semble exclure une adhésion fervente à la loi, condition indispensable au fonctionnement de la société politique. On peut concevoir bien sûr, une société où les hommes, étant guidés par la seule raison, chacun accomplirait d'une âme libre ce qui est utile à tous. Mais dans une telle société on n'aurait pas besoin de lois, c'est-à-dire que le politique y cèderait la place à l'éthique. Mais tel ne fut pas le cas des Hébreux, sans culture et pétris de superstitions. Comment faire que tout en obéissant à loi de la patrie, ils aient le sentiment de s'appartenir à eux-mêmes et d'accomplir leur devoir avec plaisir et joie? La loi est certes un joug, mais comment faire que ce joug soit doux? Nous verrons que ce problème est résolu dans l'État des Hébreux par l'introduction de la religion dans l'État de sorte que le peuple accomplisse son devoir par dévotion, par enthousiasme religieux. Mais pour que la dévotion elle ne soit pas affectée, les cérémonies du culte comportaient chez les Hébreux un caractère de régularité et de quotidienneté et donnaient à tous les citoyens le même rythme de l'existence; elles avaient trait, en outre, à la vie profane – régimes alimentaires, techniques agricoles, soins du corps, habitudes vestimentaires, etc. – aussi bien qu'à la vie sacrée, culte du temple, par exemple. Autrement dit, les cérémonies du culte étaient des habitudes collectives. Or une habitude, une fois enracinée dans notre être, prend une apparence de liberté. L'obéissance nous coûte, lorsque pour obéir, on doit constamment lutter contre la tentation de la désobéissance. Mais, en raison de l'incorporation des rites dans la vie des Hébreux, leur pratique-ci devient elle-même une pratique continuelle de l'obéissance ('continuus obedientiae cultus'). Or comme les Hébreux mettent les lois et les cérémonies au même rang, leur comportement civique est canalisé par un rythme régulier analogue à celui des rites. D'où il résultait que c'est la chose commandée et non la chose défendue qui suscitait leur désirs.[26] C'est pourquoi sans pouvoir dire qu'ils accomplissaient leurs devoirs envers Dieu spontanément – car ce ne seraient plus alors des devoirs – on s'exprimerait correctement en affirmant que c'est de plein consentement qu'ils obéissaient à Dieu.[27]

Il résulte de toutes ces considérations que la loi de Moïse, étant une loi de l'État, elle ne lie pas les juifs à perpétuité. Aussi la vraie religion, dont Spinoza reconnait l'unité et l'universalité, repose sur une alliance éternelle de connaissance et d'amour et non sur une alliance d'un Dieu-roi avec son peuple. Mais, d'autre part, il faut selon lui reconnaître la supériorité de régime politique ('praestantia ejus') des Hébreux du moins au cours d'une longue période de son existence.[28] Aussi Spinoza va-t-il se demander quel est le fondement et la nature de cet État, quelles étaient ses institutions, quel fut la cause de sa décadence et de sa chute et, enfin quels enseignements politiques on peut tirer de l'histoire des Hébreux.

Spinoza apporte une réponse à questions dans les chapitres XVII, XVIII et XIX du *Traité théologico-politique*, où il décrit la succession des événements de l'Histoire des Hébreux et détermine leurs causes en suivant les textes de l'Écriture et en employant son vocabulaire. Faut-il dire alors que les notions de révélation, de prophétie, d'oracle, etc. peuvant être, selon Spinoza, des catégories historiques? Il est vrai que pour Spinoza la science politique est une science appliqueé: liée intimement à l'art de gouverner, elle ne saurait se réduire à un enchaînement de concepts, sans se référer à l'expérience historique. Il est même impossible selon lui, de concevoir une solution efficace à un moment donné dans une société déterminée, sans en trouver un exemple plus ou moins approchant dans le passé.[29] Mais, en abordant l'étude, l'histoire des Hébreux, où du moins, selon la thèse de Spinoza, le miraculeux joue un grand rôle, ne rejette-t-il pas le principe du déterminisme, fondement de toute reconstitution du passé ? Il ne le semble pas. D'abord Spinoza précise que dans ses investigations historiques, il se préoccupe seulement des causes prochaines, en se bornant à la détermination des rapports de l'avant et de l'après. Ensuite les opinions, celles des gouvernants comme des gouvernés, même si elles sont fausses, même si elles sont des causes moins importantes que les causes économiques, par exemple, elles interviennent aussi dans l'explication des institutions et des évènements. Or, parmi les opinions, les croyances religieuses ont une 'efficace' tout à fait particulière : même l'histoire profane nous donne une quantité d'exemples de rois qui cherchent à se diviniser ou du moins à se sacraliser eux-mêmes afin de pouvoir régner sur les coeurs comme sur les corps, en justifiant leur autorité politique au nom de Dieu dont ils seraient les lieutenants sur terre. C'est ainsi qu'ils cherchent à assurer leur pouvoir par la force de la superstition susceptible non seulement de réaliser la convergence des idées et des coeurs autour du trône, mais encore de développer le sens du sacrifice.[30] Certes on peut concevoir un État fondé seulement sur le suffrage réfléchi et l'accord des hommes, c'est-à-dire uniquement sur des critères raisonnables. Mais d'abord un État où l'autorité politique serait justifiable de la raison seule, ne correspond à aucune réalité historique. Tous les États dont l'histoire nous donne des exemples reposent sur une dynamique des passions et c'est pourquoi la connaissance des passions et des lois qui les régissent est indispensable à la science politique, tantôt pour les dompter, tantôr pour les canaliser, tantôt, enfin, pour en faire les stimulants d'une action utile à l'État. Or les opinions, surtout religieuses, dans la mesure où elles ont directement ou indirectement une signification politique, sont inséparables, selon Spinoza, des passions. Elles sont des idées inadéquates qui alimentent certes des affections telles que l'intolérance et la haine sous toutes ses formes, mais aussi les illusions de la liberté, l'espoir d'une vie digne d'être vécue dans la concorde intérieure et extérieure, et, enfin, l'héroïsme et l'esprit de sacrifice. Or pour saisir la signification des opinions religieuses chez les Hébreux, il faut se référer à leur propre vocabulaire. Ce que fait Spinoza et nous suivrons son exemple, en reprenant la reconstitution spinoziste de l'histoire des institutions politiques de l'État des Hébreux, des causes de leur bon fonctionnement et de leur décadence.

D'ailleurs le *Traité théologico-politique* n'est pas un ouvrage de pure spéculation philosophique comme, par exemple l'*Ethique*. C'est un plaidoyer pour la liberté de penser et contre l'immixtion du Clergé de toutes les Églises et surtout de l'Église dominante dans la vie de l'État. Les chapitres consacrés à l'État des Hébreux constituent une des pièces maîtresses de sa démonstration. Mais si sa démonstration peut avoir la moindre chance de convaincre les théologiens au service du cléricalisme, même s'il s'adresse à ceux dont l'esprit n'est pas encore obnubilé par les superstitions, elle doit employer leur propre vocabulaire, celui de la Bible. C'est d'autant plus nécessaire que ces théologiens se réfèrent eux aussi à l'histoire des Hébreux pour justifier leur droit d'intervenir dans la vie de l'État de s'ériger en censeurs permanents des actes de la souveraine puissance et en gardiens fidèles de l'orthodoxie des opinions religieuses et philosophiques. Toutefois on ne saurait d'avantage tirer de l'histoire de l'État des Hébreux des enseignements politiques – ce qui est l'objet de l'histoire selon Spinoza – sans utiliser des concepts d'ordre politique, dont l'application est universelle et que le philosophe peut déterminer à partir de la 'philosophie vraie'. L'utilisation de ces concepts permet à Spinoza, d'une part d'aller au devant des évènements recueillis dans l'Écriture pour en saisir la signification et de déterminer leur enchaînement causal, et d'autre part, de conceptualiser les résultats obtenus, de façon à les intégrer dans une science politique, philosophiquement fondée.[31]

Dans le chapitre XVI du *Traité théologico-politique* qui sert d'introduction aux chapitres consacrés à l'État des Hébreux, Spinoza délimite les concepts nécessaires à l'intelligence du problème des fondements de l'État, en les présentant de telle façon qu'ils permettent une nouvelle lecture de l'histoire de l'État des Hébreux, en découvrant la signification universelle des problèmes qu'elle pose. Nous voulons avant de passer à l'interprétation spinoziste de l'histoire de l'État des Hébreux, analyser quelques concepts politiques tirés du ch. XVI, susceptibles d'en éclairer le sens exact:

(a) *Droit naturel et droit positif.* Le droit naturel ('jus naturalis') d'un individu humain, abstraction faite de l'organisation politique et de la religion, est une règle de conduite qui ne diffère guère des lois physiques que suivent toutes les choses naturelles avec une nécessité inéluctable. Il se mesure au degré de la puissance de chacun, au succès ou à l'échec de son effort pour se conserver, cet effort étant une expression à un degré déterminé de la puissance de Dieu ou de la Nature, envisagée dans sa totalité et dans son aspect dynamique. Quel que soit le degré de perfection d'un individu, il suit la loi de sa nature définie par son essence singulière, sans tenir compte des intérêts d'autrui, sans éprouver un sentiment d'obligation. Aussi, en se plaçant au point de vue droit naturel les valeurs juridiques et éthiques sont dépourvues de sens. Ceux qui vivent selon la loi de la convoitise vivent, selon la même nécessité naturelle que ceux qui vivent selon la loi de la raison, sans qu'il y ait ni une règle normative pour leur indiquer une autre façon de vivre ni des moyens coercitifs et persuasifs pour les obliger à la suivre. Des chances identiques, dit le roi Salomon, se présentent à l'état de nature au juste et à l'impie, au pur et à l'impur. L'état de société est au contraire un état où les hommes au lieu de s'entre-déchirer et de se condamner ainsi à la solitude, à l'insécurité et à la misère, nouent entre eux des relations d'assistance réciproque, en associant leur 'conatus' afin de découvrir les moyens les plus sûrs pour chacun de favoriser le deploiement de son propre 'conatus'. Il naît alors une 'volonté commune', qui, précisément parce qu'elle réunit toutes les forces des individus, est capable de fixer le légitime et l'illégitime, le juste et l'injuste. L'histoire de l'État des Hébreux nous apportera un exemple du passage de l'état de nature à l'état de société et de la façon dont se délimitent les pouvoirs au sein de la société.[32]

(b) *L'idée de pacte social.* C'est par une décision ferme et par un engagement que les individus humains constituent un lien social afin de ne plus vivre sous le régime de l'appétit qui les entraîne dans des directions divergentes et à se laisser guider désormais par le seul commandement de la raison, principe d'accord et de convergence entre les hommes.[33] Au point du départ de la communauté politique il y a engagement, promesse donné, pacte, fidélité à la foi jurée, droit de prendre des sanctions au cas d'une rupture d'alliance. Il est vrai que Spinoza dit que ce pacte ne peut avoir aucune force si les contractants qui, à l'état de nature, ont le souverain droit de prescrire à eux-mêmes leur loi et de l'abroger, ne trouvent pas en lui et dans ses effets un moyen de satisfaire leurs intérêts. Autrement, frappé de nullité, il disparaît du même coup. Dire qu'il est fait selon les suggestions de la raison, c'est dire simplement qu'il repose sur un calcul réfléchi des intérêts, et que, dans certaines conditions, comme, par exemple, dans le cas d'une tyrannie, il est dissous 'ipso facto' par la résistance que les individus y opposent. Aussi est-ce un problème de savoir pourquoi Spinoza met en relief l'idée de pacte dans notre texte bien plus que dans les autres textes politiques? Les notions d'engagement, de libre décision, de la vertu liante des mots, etc., n'ont en effet, rien de spinoziste; elles sont incompatibles avec l'idée spinoziste de la nécessité universelle des choses et avec sa théorie du langage qui réduit les mots à des images qui, loin d'exprimer notre pensée véritable, nous indiquent seulement les choses à travers les modifications du corps. Mais Spinoza explique lorsqu'il s'agit de l'usage de la vie, il est préférable et même nécessaire de considérer les choses comme possibles et non comme nécessaires.[34] C'est ainsi que nous parlons de 'lois humaines' dans le sens de prescriptions ou de consignes qu'un homme ou un groupement humain donnent à un autre homme, ce dernier n'en comprenant pas la nécéssité. C'est avec le même droit qu'il emploie le mot 'pacte'. En tout cas, nous en savons jamais parfaitement de quelle manière les choses sont ordonnées et enchaînées. Par conséquent, dans l'usage de la vie, il est légitime de considérer l'homme comme un 'empire dans un empire'. Mais en se référant aux chapîtres suivants, on s'aperçoit que l'emploi du mot 'pacte' s'imposait ici par la matière qu'il élabore. En effet l'idée d'alliance est dans les Écritures une idée fondatrice, alliance inscrite sur des pierres ou inscrite dans le coeur et les esprits, fidélité ou infidélité au pacte du Sinaï, rupture possible du pacte du côté de Dieu ou du côté des Hébreux. Que la notion de pacte soit dans le *Traité théologico-politique* une notion opératoire; la meilleure preuve est le contenu que Spinoza y donne au pacte fondateur de la société: tous s'engagent à organiser leurs rapports réciproques de façon que chacun d'eux 'réfrène son appetit dans la mesure où il nous pousse à faire du tort à autrui, de ne faire à personne ce qu'il ne voudrait pas qu'il lui fût fait et enfin de défendre le droit d'autrui comme le sien propre'.[35] Texte déconcertant dans un ouvrage de Spinoza, car il pourrait signifier que des principes éthiques président déjà à la constitution du pacte. Or Spinoza ne cesse de répéter que c'est la souveraine puissance et elle seule qui est la source des valeurs éthico-sociales. En tout cas ce que Spinoza présente comme cause fondamentale du pacte fondateur n'est rien d'autre que le principe formulé à la fois par Hillel et par le Christ comme étant le fondement de la loi de Moïse. Hillel dit: 'ce que tu détestes pour toi-même, ne le fais pas à ton prochain. C'est là toute la loi: le reste se borne à la commenter'.[36] Le Christ reprend l'enseignement de Hillel: 'Ainsi ce que vous désirez que les autres fassent pour vous, faites le vous-même pour eux: voilà la loi et les prophètes'.[37] Mais qui est l'autre? Qui est mon prochain? C'est ce que Spinoza se demandera en réfléchissant sur ce qu'il considère comme étant la législation nationale des Hébreux.

(c) *La démocratie comme essence de l'État.* Sans distinguer le problème du fondement de l'État et celui de la forme du gouvernement, Spinoza affirme que la société où le pacte social est toujours respecté sans porter atteinte au droit naturel, c'est-à-dire à la puissance de chacun, est un État démocratique, où les individus transfèrent leur pouvoir ni à un autre individu, ni à quelques individus mais à une assemblée générale de tous les individus jouissant d'un droit souverain sur tout ce qui est en leur pouvoir.[38] Non pas que Spinoza nie l'existence du régime monarchique ou aristocratique. L'histoire en donne des exemples nombreux, alors que le régime démocratique, dans la pureté de son essence, est un régime rare. Mais Spinoza déclare que s'il a préféré prendre le régime démocratique comme système de référence dans l'étude des fondements de l'État, c'est qu'il semble être le 'régime le plus naturel ('qui maxime naturale videbatur') et s'approcher davantage de la liberté que la nature accorde à chacun ('maxime ad libertatem quam natura unicuique concedit, accedere').[39] Mais en quoi consiste la liberté naturelle? Dans la non-dépendance d'un homme par rapport à un autre homme. Non-dépendance du moins théorique. Sous le régime démocratique, soumis au principe de l'unanimité ou de la majorité, chacun transfère ses pouvoirs non pas à tel ou tel individu mais à lui-même, considéré, selon une expression de Rousseau dans son 'existence relative'. Or toute l'argumentation de Spinoza consiste à montrer que la supériorité du régime théocratique des Hébreux provient de ce qu'il exclut la dépendance d'un homme par rapport à un autre homme et que le régime des rois, où l'obéissance se transforme en servitude, est le commencement de sa décadence.

(d) *État de nature et état de religion.* A l'état de nature, les notions de droit positif, c'est-à-dire de droit par institution, et de péché sont, nous l'avons vu, dépourvus de sens. Par contre, par état de religion ('status religionis') on entend un état où les hommes sont soumis à un droit positif, communiqué par Dieu, générateur d'obligations et donnant lieu à des péchés. On pourrait certes concevoir une religion fondée sur la connaissance adéquate, où l'obéissance, signe de l'hétéronomie de la volonté, se transforme en amour. Une telle religion est dite naturelle à juste titre: elle est fondée sur la lumière naturelle, accessible à tout entendement humain, indépendemment de telle ou telle organisation politique. Mais à l'état de nature il n'y aucune chance que les hommes parviennent à la connaissance adéquate. Ne connaissant pas les causes des commandements par la lumière naturelle, les hommes ont dû concevoir d'abord la religion comme un code donné aux hommes directement ou indirectement par Dieu. Or un tel Dieu ne peut-être conçu que comme un Dieu governant et législateur, c'est-à-dire à partir des catégories politiques. D'où cette conclusion que l'état de nature est antérieur en nature et dans le temps à l'état de religion. La meilleure preuve que les hommes ne sont pas tenus à l'état de nature de suivre un droit divin révélé, c'est que Dieu ait trouvé nécessaire de conclure avec les Hébreux un contrat et qu'il les oblige de le respecter par un engagement solennel. Le pacte de Dieu avec les Hébreux ne diffère guère du moins dans sa forme du pacte qui dans les différentes formes d'État marque le passage de l'état de nature à l'état de culture: en renonçant à leur liberté naturelle, les Hébreux ont transféré leurs droits à Dieu et promis de lui obéir en tout. Le droit positif révélé y devient ainsi le droit positif de l'État.[40]

Ces remarques faites, nous pouvons étudier les circonstances de la formation de l'État des Hébreux, le fondement que ceux-ci lui ont donné et les conditions du bon et mauvais fonctionnement de leurs institutions au cours de leur histoire.

L'état de nature a-t-il effectivement existé ou n'est-il qu'un concept opératoire? On trouve chez Spinoza des affirmations en faveur de la première thèse: l'état de nature précède non seulement logiquement, mais encore chronologiquement à l'état de société. Mais, d'autre part, comme il soutient que l'union des hommes en société résulte d'une nécessité naturelle et répond à leurs intérêts vitaux, on peut aussi en conclure que l'état de nature est, selon Spinoza, un état-limité dont nous pouvons avoir une expérience au cours de l'histoire, lors de la décomposition d'un État, lors de son retour à l'état de nature au moment de la dissolution de ses institutions.[41] Mais nous avons surtout un exemple typique de l'état de nature dans celui où se trouvaient les Hébreux, à leur sortie de l'Egypte, où n'étant plus sous la juridiction d'aucune autre nation, ils sont abandonnés à eux mêmes, libres de se donner une législation nouvelle et de fonder leur propre état en se choisissant un territoire, base matérielle de cet État.[42]

Ils auraient pu évidemment établir eux-mêmes leurs lois et exercer le pouvoir collectivement: ce qui se passe lorsqu'on adopte le régime démocratique, le plus ancien et le plus naturel des régimes politiques. Mais des anciens esclaves, qui au cours de leur séjour en Egypte n'ont pas participé à la vie de l'État – les esclaves, en effet, ne sont pas des sujets – et qui, en outre, n'ont jamais joui des loisirs indispensables à l'éducation de leur esprit, sont incapables de se gouverner eux-mêmes.[43] Aussi pour ne pas confier leur destin politique à un seul homme – ce qui aurait pu représenter la cause d'une nouvelle forme d'esclavage – ils ont décidé sur le conseil de Moïse de transférer leur droit à Dieu, et à Dieu seul. Autrement dit, les Hébreux ont décidé de renoncer à leur droits naturels au profit de Dieu, en s'engageant de lui obéir et de mettre en pratique tout ce qu'il leur aura prescrit.[44]

Pour bien comprendre la vraie signification du pacte des Hébreux avec Dieu, il convient d'apporter les précisions suivantes:

1 Le Dieu des Hébreux est celui qu'on désigne dans l'Écriture par le nom Jehova (Yod; Hé, VaV, Hé). Il ne désigne pas, selon Spinoza, l'idée de l'existence nécessaire de l'Être suprême – idée philosophique étrangère évidemment aux Hébreux – mais l'idée d'un Être qui existe dans les trois temps. Dieu est l'être qui a toujours existé, existe et existera. Mais le mot être signifie en Hébreu non seulement 'exister', mais encore 'être auprès', 'se trouver près'.[45] D'où un nouveau sens du mot Jehova: il est celui qui se désigne comme devant être auprès de son peuple d'une façon permanente, dans l'avenir comme dans le passé. Si les Hébreux aliènent donc leurs droit au profit de Dieu, c'est qu'il est leur protecteur et qu'il est susceptible de réaliser les conditions nécessaires au déploiement de leurs 'conatus'.

2 Dieu n'a trouvé bon de conclure son alliance avec les Hébreux, qu'après leur avoir manifesté auparavant sa puissance surprenante par les miracles qu'il a accomplis en leur faveur afin de les délivrer de l'esclavage.[46] Les miracles de Dieu lors de la sortie de l'Egypte, dit le psalmiste, sont les puissances de Dieu: se trouvant dans une situation périlleuse, Dieu a ouvert aux Hébreux d'une façon inattendue et imprévisible la voie du salut. Le motif de l'engagement des Hébreux est donc l'espoir: espoir en la puissance de Dieu qui les conservera dans l'avenir comme dans le passé.[47]

3 Le pacte est conclu librement, sans céder à la violence ou une menace quelconque. L'État des Hébreux est ainsi fondé par une multitude libre qui s'efforce de vivre pour elle-même et d'entretenir sa vie. État entièrement opposé à celui dont ils ont été victimes en Egypte où ils s'efforçaient surtout d'éviter la mort.[48]

4 Il a été conclu à l'unanimité ('nec diu cunctati, omnes aeque une clamore promiserunt').[49] L'expression 'una clamore' exprime d'une part, l'idée d'enthousiasme, et, d'autre part, l'idee que dans un 'pacte social' quel que soit la façon dont on le conçoive, l'unanimité est requise: en effet l'obéissance totale et sans réserve au souverain – dans notre cas à Dieu – n'est concevable que si personne ne tâche de garder ses droits naturels afin d'en profiter, une fois l'État constitué, pour ravir aux autres leur liberté et de les tenir à sa merci.

5 Le régime politique ainsi formé est un régime théocratique, dont Dieu est à la fois souverain, législateur et gouvernant. La religion et le droit

positif s'y confondent. Mais, d'autre part, cette théocratie ressemble curieusement à une démocratie. D'abord les Hébreux ont transféré leurs droits non pas à une personne en particulier, mais à Dieu seulement, la dépendance de tous, sans exception, vis-à-vis de Dieu signifiant, en réalité, la non-dépendance de l'homme vis-à-vis de l'homme.[50] D'autre part, au terme de ce pacte, ils avaient tous le même droit de participer à l'administration de l'État, de consulter Dieu, de recevoir et d'interpréter les lois.[51]

Mais un État peut-il être gouverné directement par Dieu sans la médiation d'un mortel? C'est avec enthousiasme que les Hébreux se rendirent à la montagne de Dieu afin de l'écouter et de recevoir ses ordres. Mais dès la première rencontre et après avoir entendu la voix de Dieu, ils furent pris par la terreur et l'épouvante. Aussi ont-ils décidé de rompre le premier pacte avec Dieu, et de transférer à Moïse leur droit de consulter Dieu, et d'interpréter les lois. Désormais ils obéiront seulement aux communications que Moïse aura reçues de Dieu, lui seul ayant désormais le droit de prophétiser.[52]

On peut se demander quelle est la signification de l'épouvante dont les Hébreux furent pris lors de leur contact direct avec Dieu? En partant des textes que de l'*Exode* et du *Deuteronome* que Spinoza cite, on dira que c'est la grandeur inaccessible de Dieu et sa majesté redoutable qui leur ont fait peur. Malgré la distance qui sépare les gouvernants des gouvernés, il doit malgré tout y avoir entre eux une commune mesure. Autrement la communication devient impossible.

Mais au chapitre XIX, Spinoza affirme qu'au fond la distinction qu'il fait entre les deux pactes ne correspond dans l'Écriture qu'à une façon d'exposer les choses. En réalité les Hébreux ont transféré leurs droits à Dieu seulement par la pensée, c'est-à-dire théoriquement, et non pas en fait.[53] En réalité, jusqu'à la conclusion du pacte avec Moïse qui a assumé en plein accord avec le peuple tous les droits d'un roi, ils gardèrent pour eux-même le droit de commander. C'est que la religion, qu'elle soit révélée par la lumière naturelle ou par la voie prophétique ne peut prendre force de commandement que par la médiation des hommes capables d'appliquer des sanctions. En l'absence d'une médiation des hommes ayant le droit de gouverner et de prendre des décrets dans des situations particulières, il est impossible de dire que Dieu régit les affairs humaines avec justice et équité. C'est seulement dans les pays où les justes détiennent le pouvoir qu'il y a des chances de découvrir des traces de la justice divine.[54] La signification du premier pacte avec Dieu serait donc que, Moïse, devenu chef suprême, seul porteur et interprète des lois divines, juge suprême, investi à lui seul du don prophétique, ne règne pas arbitrairement. A la fois homme d'État et prophète, il l'emportait sur les autres par sa vertu divine. Sa popularité, malgré les reproches qu'on a pu lui faire, il l'a obtenue non pas par des moyens frauduleux mais par des oeuvres où le peuple reconnaît la marque du divin.[55]

Ce n'est pas sans raison, d'ailleurs, que les Hébreux divinisaient Moïse.

*Tss

Tout se passe comme s'il n'avait pas comme les autres rois l'ambition du pouvoir et que las de la charge du pouvoir il aurait préféré que le règne fut assumé par le peuple lui-même. C'est ce qui résulte notamment d'un récit qu'on lit dans le livre des *Nombres* (ch. X, vers 2–30). Moïse se faisant assister par soixante-dix anciens pour remplir ses fonctions de gouvernement et de justice, ces derniers placés autour de sa tente commencèrent à leur tour à prophétiser. Ce qui signifie évidemment que c'est par l'investissement de Moïse qu'ils éxécutaient leurs tâches. Or deux hommes, Eldad et Medad, se mirent à prophétiser dans le camp, sans aucune initiative de la part de Moïse. Etant donné que selon le pacte que le peuple a conclu avec lui, il avait seul le droit de communiquer au peuple les oracles et les réponses de Dieu, ces deux hommes ne commettent-ils pas un crime de lèse-majesté? Personne, du vivant de Moïse, fut-il un vrai prophète, n'avait le droit de prêcher quoi que ce soit au nom de Dieu, sans un ordre préalable venant de Dieu. Josué estimait que ces deux hommes devaient être punis. En quoi il avait parfaitement raison. Mais Moïse préféra pardonner aux coupables et reprocha même à Josué de vouloir le persuader d'exercer dans toute sa rigueur son droit de monarque, alors que ce n'est pas par esprit de domination et par ambition qu'il règne sur son peuple. Non seulement l'exercice du pouvoir en tant que tel ne l'exalte pas, mais il le décourage plutôt. D'où cette déclaration: 'voudrais-tu qu'il n'y eût que moi pour régner; pour moi je souhaiterais que le peuple tout entier prophétisât.' Autrement dit Moïse préférerait que chaque Hébreu comme lors de ce que Spinoza appelle le premier pacte avec Dieu, ait le droit de s'adresser directement à Dieu et qu'ainsi chacun détienne lui-même son pouvoir spirituel.[56]

Moïse avait tous les pouvoirs d'un monarque ordinaire: il détenait à la fois le pouvoir législatif, exécutif et judiciaire. On sait que déjà, du vivant de Moïse, le grand pontife, Aron, frère de Moïse, était chargé de l'interprétation des décrets de Dieu et de l'administration du droit sacré. Mais il ne remplissait sa fonction que par un mandat express de Moïse que celui-ci aurait pu d'ailleurs lui retirer.[57] Aussi l'autorité de Moïse aurait pu être même plus pesante que celle d'un monarque qui règne en vertu des 'forces réunies' qu'il détient du peuple et non en vertu d'un droit relevé. Mais Moïse ne l'oublions pas, était un monarque prophète, dont on reconnaît l'authenticité non seulement par les signes et les miracles qu'il a accomplis, mais encore et surtout par la pureté des moeurs. Aussi a-t-il pris toutes les dispositions pour que le peuple accomplisse son devoir non tant par la crainte que par un élan spontané.[58]

Une preuve supplémentaire en faveur du comportement désintéressé de Moïse, c'est qu'il n'a pas fondé ni voulu fonder une monarchie héréditaire.[59] Le roi, selon Spinoa, n'est, en réalité, que l'expression symbolique de la 'volonté commune'.[60] Il en conclut que la communauté politique meurt en quelque sorte en même temps que le roi: à la mort du roi le pouvoir souverain revient naturellement à la multitude qui peut décider à bâtir l'État sur des bases nouvelles. Mais la dissolution de l'État après la mort de Moïse par le retour du pouvoir au peuple n'avait pas un caractère de légitimité: c'est qu'à travers le pacte avec Moïse, les Hébreux ont confirmé leur alliance avec Dieu pour l'éternité. Les Hébreux ont renoncé à leur droit ainsi d'élire un succésseur à Moïse. Mais d'autre part, Moïse lui-même, élu à cause de sa vertu divine, aurait trahi sa mission en transmettant son pouvoir en vertu du droit de sang. Aussi pour que le peuple soit gouverné, pour que la 'communauté de Jehova' ne soit pas comme un troupeau sans pasteur, il a désigné Josué comme successeur, après avoir consulté Dieu et après lui avoir imposé la main. Ce qui signifie selon le cérémonial rituel de l'époque qu'il était confirmé dans ses charges futures et investi d'une autorité légitime et reconnue comme telle par Dieu par la voie prophétique.[61]

Mais la désignation de Josué comme chef politique et militaire du peuple répondait à une situation exceptionnelle, celle d'un peuple nomade à la recherche d'un territoire. Moïse cependant n'a prévu ni le mode de désignation ni le mode de succession des futurs chefs politiques, une fois le pays de Canaan occupé. Il a prévu des dispositions telles que cet État, une fois enraciné en un territoire ne soit ni populaire – ce qui signifierait une rupture d'alliance avec Dieu – ni monarchique – car il serait dangereux qu'après la mort de Moïse un chef jouît d'autant de pouvoir que lui-même – ni enfin aristocratique – car le principe de l'égalité des citoyens exclut l'idée de noblesse, qu'il s'agisse de noblesse de sang ou de noblesse élective.[62] Il a fallu que le régime reste théocratique.[63] Mais la notion de théocratie doit prendre un sens nouveau. La suprême autorité n'appartiendra plus à un homme vêtu d'une majesté divine: les chefs ne seront plus, en réalité, que des fonctionnaires, des administrateurs de l'État.[64] Elle appartient à la loi de Moïse gardée avec le soin le plus religieux dans le saint des saints. L'expression 'loi de Moïse' – Spinoza le montre dans un texte célèbre – s'emploie souvent pour l'esprit de Dieu parce qu'elle exprime la pensée de Dieu. Suivre les prescriptions de la *Torah*, c'est gouverner au nom de Dieu.[65] La fidélité à la loi de Moïse est la vraie piété du côté des gouvernants et du côté des gouvernés.

Etant donné les principes généraux de l'administration prévus par Moïse, voyons maintenant comment ils ont été appliqués après l'occupation du pays de Canaan par les 'phalanges de Dieu' sous le haut commandement de Josué.

Le pays une fois conquis, partagé entre toutes les tribus à l'exception de la tribu des Lévites, vouée à Dieu et n'ayant pas le droit de posséder en propre une part du sol, il ne constituait pas à vrai dire un seul État. Chaque tribu formait un État autonome, son autonomie étant à la fois interne et externe. Les tribus étaient, en réalité, les membres d'une fédération de la même façon que leurs hautes puissances des États confédérés de Hollande.[66] Cependant elles sont toutes liées par un lien commun, à savoir le lien de la religion, se réduisant, comme nous l'avons vu, à l'unité d'un code révélé. C'est ce respect de la religion qui constitue la vraie garantie de leur alliance, de leur désir de vivre les uns à côté des autres et avec les autres. Aussi lorsque l'une d'elles foulait du pieds un des principes sacrés de la législation divine, elle cessait par là même d'être puissance alliée pour devenir une puissance ennemie. C'est ainsi que s'explique la guerre menée contre les Benjaminites qui par leur conduite inhumaine ont offensé toutes les autres tribus et rompu les liens éthiques qui les réunissaient à elles.[67]

On appelle juges les chefs des tribus. Cette appellation se justifie, car ils n'avaient aucun pouvoir législatif. La loi de Moïse ne doit être modifiée en aucun cas: on ne doit rien y ajouter ni rien en retrancher. Leur rôle unique c'est de trancher les litiges et d'administrer le territoire qui leur est confié selon les principes de la législation révélée.[68] Comment ont-ils été désignés? On ne trouve la-dessus – dit Spinoza – rien de certain dans l'Écriture. Ceux qui après la mort de Josué assumèrent l'administration de l'État, on les appelle 'vieillard' dans l'Écriture. D'autre part, comme on le sait, les Hébreux emploient souvent le mot 'vieillard' pour désigner un juge. Aussi peut-on conjecturer que les juges étaient choisis en raison de leur âge et aussi de leurs qualités personnelles.[69] Mais ce qui est sûr c'est que l'administration d'une tribu était à la fois hiérarchisée et centralisée: lorsque les juges subalternes étaient embarassés par un cas délicat, ils devaient s'adresser au juge hiérarchiquement supérieur, qui, à son tour, s'il trouve que le point en question n'est pas prévu par le droit révélé, devait consulter un troisième juge jusqu'à ce qu'on remonte au juge suprême.[70] Mais celui-ci n'avait pas davantage le droit de prononcer une sentence selon son bon plaisir. Ce juge suprême, qui était en même temps un chef de tribu, était alors dans l'obligation de consulter le pontife, qui, selon les instructions de Moïse, avait seul le droit, une fois interrogé par le représentant du pouvoir politique, de s'adresser à Dieu et de lui apporter une réponse, qui, d'ailleurs, afin d'éviter que le pouvoir sacerdotal ne s'empare pas du pouvoir suprême, devait être considéré comme un simple conseil et ne prenait force de décret, qu'après avoir été examinée et ratifiée par le juge. Le pouvoir politique et le pouvoir sacerdotal s'équilibrant réciproquement.[71]

Les principes de l'administration étant tels, on comprend qu'il y avait peu de risque, pour que le pouvoir des chefs politiques ne dégénère en tyrannie. D'abord il y avait – nous venons de le voir – le contrepoids du grand pontife ne fût-ce que dans l'obligation ou l'on se trouvait de le consulter. Ensuite les chefs, ne pouvaient ne pas prendre en considération la venue possible d'un prophète, qui après avoir confirmé par des signes eux-mêmes prévus par la loi l'authenticité de son oracle, incarnait, comme Moïse lui-même, le droit de censurer leurs actes et de leur transmettre des ordres révélés et précis au nom de Dieu.[72] Les fonctions du prophète sont multiples mais en tant que personnage politique son rôle consiste à permettre aux chefs politiques de se 'réemparer du pouvoir', pour employer une célèbre expression de Machiavel, c'est-à-dire de ramener l'État à ses propres fondements, conditions de sa stabilité originelle dont il tend à s'éloigner par la force des choses.[73] C'est surtout le contrôle du peuple qui était le meilleur antidote contre l'abus du pouvoir. En effet, il ne fut pas loisible à quiconque, fût-il un chef, de déformer le sens exact d'une loi inscrite dans la *Torah* pour justifier une mesure tyrannique, car, selon une prescription de Moïse, la loi devait être connue de tous: pour que les paroles de Dieu restent gravées dans les coeurs de tous les Hébreux, le pontife devait réunir le peuple tous les sept ans dans un lieu déterminé afin qu'il les réentende et les réapprenne, chaque individu étant obligé de lire et de relire personnellement la loi de façon qu'il n'y ait dans son esprit aucune méprise. Aussi si les chefs transgressaient sciemment la loi, ils s'exposaient inévitablement à la haine du peuple, haine d'autant plus impitoyable qu'elle était une haine théologique ('odium theologicum').[74]

Ajoutons que l'organisation militaire de l'État des Hébreux était telle que tout en développant chez eux des vertus guérrières, elle était aménagée de telle façon que le militarisme, danger redoutable pour la liberté du peuple, ne puisse pas se développer. En effet le danger du militarisme consiste d'abord en ce qu'une armée peut devenir, en temps de paix comme en temps de guerre, un instrument de domination politique d'un chef ou d'un gouvernement, ensuite, en ce que des chefs militaires, profitant du prestige obtenu par les victoires auxquelles ils ont présidé, s'emparent eux-mêmes du pouvoir sous les acclamations des foules et, enfin, que la guerre elle-même soit érigée enfin en soi ou qu'en tout cas elle soit plus tentante que la paix. Mais, d'abord, l'armée des Hébreux, était une armée de citoyens, enrôlés sous les drapeaux tous sans exception de vingt jusqu'à soixante ans – au cas d'un danger pour le pays évidemment – et non pas une armée de mercenaires. Or rien n'est plus redoutable pour un apprenti-tyran qu'une armée de citoyens libres qui, ayant prêté serment non à un chef politique ou militaire mais à Dieu lui-même, attribue sa victoire ni à la vaillance du chef ni même à sa propre vaillance mais à son Dieu, Dieu des armées, qui intervient directement dans toutes les péripéties de leur histoire pour défendre la loi mosaïque, âme de leur État.[75] D'autre part il n'y avait pas à craindre que dans une situation grave, pris d'une terreur, le peuple ne cherche le salut auprès d'un chef militaire prestigieux et ne le plaçat au dessus de la loi. On ne désignait un général en chef ou un général d'armée que pour une année en maximum, sans que celui-ci ait le droit à une prolongation ni à une nouvelle désignation.[76] D'ailleurs dans une situation exceptionnelle seul Dieu choisissait – où du moins les Hébreux croyaient qu'il en était ainsi – un commandant militaire unique pour la population entière, comme ce fut le cas de la désignation de Gédéon, de Samson et de Samuel.[77] Enfin étant donné que l'armée des Hébreux était, à l'époque des juges, la 'nation armée' elle-même, les aventures guérrières dont les armées des mercenaires se rendent coupables si souvent sont presque inconcevables. En effet, ce sont les mêmes hommes qui participent aux différentes activités du pays en temps de paix et assurent la défense du sol sacré de la patrie en temps de guerre: le chef d'une armée de tribu est, en temps de paix, son chef politique; l'officier est dans le civil juge au tribunal et le soldat y est simple citoyen.[78] Tous sont des citoyens en uniforme. Or un citoyen – c'est là une conséquence de clauses du pacte social – cherche dans l'existence même de l'État les conditions de sa propre vie et même d'une 'vie vraie', et non pas – ce qui est contraire à la nature et à la raison – un moyen glorieux pour se suicider. Sous le règne du peuple, il y a eu peu de guerres intérieures et extérieures: on ne s'y bat que pour ses autels et foyers et on évite des guerres de conquête d'où on ne peut rapporter dans le meilleur des cas que des cicatrices gratuites.

Quant au peuple lui-même, tout y contribuait, le sentiment comme l'intérêt, pour entretenir chez lui le patriotisme et l'obéissance civique D'abord, puisque servir l'État, c'est pour eux, servir Dieu et que leur sol était sacré à leurs yeux au sens propre du mot, rien ne leur eût paru plus infamant qu'une trahison, une expatriation ou un exil forcé. D'autre part, les institutions proprement économiques dans l'État des Hébreux, étaient telles que ceux-ci ne pouvaient nulle part trouver des conditions de vie meilleures. Tous, sans différence entre les gouvernants et les gouvernés, jouissaient d'un même droit de propriété sur une part égale du sol: le pays est la propriété de Dieu, les Hébreux en sont les hôtes et ceux-ci sont reçus tous avec les mêmes égards. D'autre part, pour empêcher que les uns n'accaparent les terres et les biens de ceux qui, pressés par le besoin, étaient contraints de les vendre, on a établi une juridiction au sujet de l'année du Jubilée, comportant tous les cinquante ans un affranchissement général des biens, des terres, qui retrouvent le patrimoine de leur premier possesseur.[79] D'autre part, la pauvreté elle-même était supportable à cette époque, car à partir du principe fondamental de ce régime suivant lequel aucun citoyen ne doit être soumis à un autre, la charité envers le prochain, c'est-à-dire envers le concitoyen, érigé en devoir religieux, rigoureusement règlementé, comportait une force d'obligation. Ajoutons enfin que les loisirs et les fêtes – tels que le Sabbat et les trois grandes fêtes de l'année – étaient également règlementés, chaque fête avec un cérémonial qui lui est propre, pour que le service de Dieu, rigoureusement identique au service de la patrie, s'effectue dans la joie et ne se transforme pas dans une morne habitude.[80]

Avec le régime des rois commence malheureusement la décadence de l'État des Hébreux. Avec Machiavel avant lui et J. J. Rousseau après lui, Spinoza épouse la tendance antiroyaliste de Samuel: vouloir un roi mortel, c'est rompre l'alliance conclue avec Dieu dans le désert; vouloir transférer la souveraineté de l'État du temple à la cour, c'est changer, en réalité, le fondement de l'organisation de l'État. Certes les rois, eux-mêmes, reconnaissent, en principe l'autorité suprême de Dieu et de sa loi. D'ailleurs comme de nombreux juges, ils étaient désignés par des prophètes. Mais, c'est une illusion de penser qu'un roi, conscient de son pouvoir absolu, puisse se résoudre à se soumettre sans arrière-pensée à une législation, fût-elle d'origine divine, sans y apporter aucune modification. C'est aussi évidemment contraire à l'idée qu'un roi se fait de soi-même que de consulter sur des points précis les pontifes et surtout d'accepter sans rechigner les reprimandes, les invectives et les ordres des prophètes. D'où l'infidélité des rois à la loi mosaïque, refus de courber la tête devant Dieu, dont les interventions par la bouche des prêtres et des prophètes, constituent une menace perpétuelle pour leur droit de souveraineté. D'où la tendance à l'idolâtrie, la pire des trahisons envers Dieu, car elle consiste à construire d'autres temples à d'autres Dieux afin que ces temples soient des émanations de la cour, alors qu'en réalité la cour, là où elle existe, doit être justiciable des exigences du seul temple, seule demeure de la souveraineté de l'État. D'où la lutte contre les prophètes, qui se multiplient au temps des rois, ne cessant de mordre sur les prérogatives royales (non seulement dans tout ce qui touche l'administration de la justice et la protection des pauvres, mais encore les problèmes de la paix et de la guerre et celui même de la succession des rois). D'où souvent la destruction physique des prophètes et surtout la tentative de susciter de faux prophètes capables de contrebalancer le prestige spirituel des vrais prophètes aux yeux des masses et de les rallier frauduleusement à ses propres vues. Ajoutons que comme dans toutes les monarchies ordinaires, le pouvoir des rois d'Israël, pouvoir précaire s'il y en a, ne cesse d'être contesté par les sujets eux-mêmes.[81]

La meilleure preuve de la décadence de l'État des Hébreux sous le régime des rois, c'est la multiplication des guerres intérieures d'une cruauté inhumaine, entre le royaume de Juda et celui d'Israël et des guerres extérieures, commandées souvent non pas par la nécessité de la défense, mais par le désir des rois d'assurer grâce à leur victoire la stabilité de leur trône.[82] Dans ces conditions, on comprend que les deux royaumes hébreux ont fini par succomber l'un après l'autre à l'assaut des ennemis extérieurs.

Spinoza consacre un petit nombre de lignes au second État des Hébreux qui n'est, selon lui, que l'ombre du premier. En effet, l'histoire du second État comporte deux périodes, celle où les Hébreux sont soumis aux rois des Perses et des Seleucides, celle où les pontifes, de la famille des Maccabées, usurpent les droits des chefs de tribus et exercent pour leur propre compte l'autorité absolue. Il est caractéristique que Spinoza ne souffle pas un mot de la première période, où s'élabore un judaïsme qui ne se présente plus comme lié aux grandeurs et aux misères d'un État, mais comme une sorte d'Église. Mais il met l'accent surtout sur la seconde période, où les pontifes s'emparent simultanément du pouvoir sacerdotal et du pouvoir politique. D'où une totale dégénérescence du 'royaume de Dieu'. Le régime théocratique des

Hébreux fondé sur le principe de l'égalité civique et spirituelle des citoyens devant Dieu cède la place à un régime clérical, où sous le prétexte d'une vocation singulière qui leur serait accordée par Dieu, les uns cherchaient à s'élever aux plus hautes dignités en s'emparant du pouvoir.

Mais ce n'est pas par un simple hasard que les pontifes sont arrivés au pouvoir sous le second temple. On peut en découvrir la vraie cause dans un vice des institutions politiques de l'État des Hébreux qui, depuis leur premier établissement, n'a cessé de les ronger. Ce mal, où Spinoza voit l'effet d'une vengeance divine contre son peuple, c'est l'instauration d'un sacerdoce réservé exclusivement à la tribu de Lévi seule habilitée d'interpréter les lois et d'administrer le culte, déchargée de tout travail et reconnue comme une sorte de noblesse de sang. Le ministère sacré devait être réservé initialement aux premiers-nés sans exception et c'est ainsi que toutes les tribus eussent restées égales en droit et en dignité. Mais comme tous les Israélites à l'exception des Lévites, ont adoré le veau d'or, les premiers-nés ont été écartés et remplacés par les lévites. L'existence d'un pouvoir sacerdotal indépendant est certes sans inconvénients majeurs, lorsque les détenteurs du pouvoir politique, entourés eux-mêmes d'une auréole divine, ont les moyens nécessaires pour les soumettre à leur propre contrôle; elle est, au contraire, d'une gravité suprême, lorsque le pouvoir de l'État est divisé en un pouvoir proprement politique et en un pouvoir sacerdotal, en conflit l'un avec l'autre ou pire encore lorsque le pouvoir sacerdotal s'empare du pouvoir politique et s'arroge le droit de l'égiférer dans tous les domaines, dans celui de la spéculation comme dans celui de l'action.[83]

On pourrait montrer que l'histoire des Hébreux que Spinoza parcourt rapidement dans un seul chapitre ne comporte pas toute l'objectivité requise. C'est ainsi, par exemple que le texte cité du livre d'Ezéchiel sur les effets désastreux de l'instauration du sacerdoce des Lévites est détaché de son contexte et n'a pas le sens que Spinoza lui donne. Spinoza – nous l'avons montré ailleurs – n'est pas toujours fidèle au principe de l'interprétation de l'Écriture par elle-même, qu'il a pourtant formulé lui-même.[84] Mais, il faut remarquer à sa décharge qu'il ne s'intéresse pas à l'histoire des Hébreux pour elle-même. Le but du *Traité théologico-politique*, c'est la défense de liberté de penser, en général, et de la liberté de philosopher en particulier. Ce plaidoyer, étant donné le public auquel Spinoza s'adresse, s'appuie sur les conséquences d'une nouvelle interprétation de l'Écriture. En se demandant ce qu'il faut entendre, selon l'Écriture elle-même, par la 'parole de Dieu', par la notion de 'foi' etc., Spinoza tâche, d'abord, d'établir le principe de la séparation totale de la philosophie et de la foi, condition indispensable de la liberté de philosopher. D'un autre côté, en reconstituant à partir de l'Écriture l'histoire des Hébreux et de l'organisation de leur État, il s'interroge si on ne peut pas en tirer des enseignements politiques utiles pour l'aménagement d'un État moderne, tel que celui des Pays-Bas, par exemple, dont il connaissait les institutions et les problèmes, afin qu'on puisse y développer les conditions les plus favorables à la liberté de philosopher, etc., par conséquent, à la vie philosophique elle-même.

Il faut d'abord remarquer, que même abstraction faite du vice interne de l'État des Hébreux, à savoir l'institutionalisation d'une caste sacerdotale, on ne saurait le prendre comme modèle dans les conditions historiques actuelles. Le régime théocratique des Hébreux, fondé sur un pacte conclu par eux avec Dieu, est un régime révolu. En effet, les chrétiens eux-même affirment que, selon l'Evangile, Dieu a remplacé le pacte conclu avec un seul peuple, inscrit sur des tables de pierre, par un nouveau pacte inscrit dans le coeur et l'esprit de tous les hommes. La 'religion du citoyen' a cédé ainsi la place à la 'religion de l'homme'. Aussi comme un État est toujours particulier, c'est-à-dire qu'il est l'organisation politique d'un groupement particulier et non de l'humanité toute entière, on ne voit pas comment on peut tirer des arguments de l'*Ancien Testament* en faveur d'une théocratie moderne. D'ailleurs, on ne saurait séparer la vie d'un État moderne de ses relations commerciales avec les autres États. C'est particulièrement vrai pour un pays comme les Pays-Bas, où l'échange des richesses et des idées est la règle. Or un État théocratique comme celui des Hébreux, en raison même de sa religion purement nationale qui, par ailleurs, règle le rythme d'existence de chaque individu, est condamné à vivre replié sur lui-même et sans relations avec l'extérieur.

Aussi le clergé calviniste aurait-il tort de vouloir, comme les pontifes papistes dans d'autres pays, invoquer la théocratie hébraïque pour justifier leur influence politique au sein de l'État. Dans le monde chrétien, le fondement de l'État ne saurait être le même que chez les Hébreux.[85] Toutefois on peut tirer de l'histoire des Hébreux un certain nombre d'enseignements politiques.

(a) Il est dangereux à la fois pour l'État et pour la religion d'accorder aux ministres du culte un pouvoir exécutif au sein de l'État. Sauf sous le second temple, les pontifes n'avaient dans l'État des Hébreux qu'un pouvoir consultatif: ils pouvaient donner des conseils aux gouvernants, mais à condition expresse qu'ils les leur demandent et que l'initiative ne vienne pas d'eux-mêmes. C'est que d'un côté, le pouvoir politique étant indivisible, laisser au clergé, celui de l'État papiste, ou celui d'une église nationale, un pouvoir effectif dans la direction de l'État, c'est en réalité ruiner ce dernier. D'un autre côté, étant donné que les prêtres sont des hommes comme les autres et n'hésitent pas d'user de moyens démagogiques pour affirmer leur influence sur les foules, ils interprètent les lois non dans le sens de la rigueur spirituelle, mais selon les *intérêts fluctuants des hommes*. C'est ainsi, comme le dit le prophète Malachie, ils font de la loi un objet de scandale.[86]

(b) Si les représentants des Eglises statutaires se mêlent aux affaires politiques, c'est qu'ils prétendent qu'il leur revient à eux seuls d'interpréter la loi divine et d'oeuvrer à la réalisation ici-bas de la parole de Dieu. Mais ce que l'histoire sacrée nous apprend, c'est que le grand pontife, chargé de l'administration du droit sacré et de l'interprétation des décrets de Dieu n'a rempli ses fonctions que par un mandat exprès de Moïse, chef politique. Il est vrai que peu à peu le sacerdoce se transmettait chez les Hébreux héréditairement. Mais dans un pays chrétien personne n'admet plus le principe de la transmission héréditaire de la prêtrise. Aussi les ministres de la parole de Dieu doivent se soumettre dans leurs enseignements et dans l'administration du culte aux indications décisives de la souveraine puissance.[87] La vraie parole de Dieu, ne consiste pas dans les vues spéculatives des théologiens, simples inventions humaines, au nom desquelles ceux-ci sèment la discorde au sein de l'État. Elle se ramène – c'est un des thèmes majeurs du *Traité théologico-politique* – à la prescription du principe de la pratique de la justice et de la charité. Or l'application de ce principe ne peut se faire au cours de l'histoire que par l'intermédiaire des autorités politiques.

(c) Spinoza ne croit pas à une efficacité durable des coups d'états et de révolutions. Renverser un tyran, ce n'est pas pour autant se débarrasser de la tyrannie en tant que telle: le nouveau pouvoir est certes nouveau, mais il est aussi un pouvoir et, pour échapper à la contestation du peuple, il emploiera les mêmes moyens que le pouvoir qu'il vient de renverser. Aussi Spinoza ne préconise nullement l'abolition de la monarchie. Dans un pays comme l'Angleterre, par exemple, ou il y a une vieille tradition monarchique, l'arrivée au pouvoir de Cromwell et les conséquences qui en ont résulté sont considérés à juste titre comme des évènements fâcheux. Mais ce ne fut pas le cas des Hébreux: s'ils n'ont pas pu s'adapter, comme nous l'avons vu, au régime monarchique, c'est qu'en raison de leur religion, ils ont vécu pendant de nombreux siècles sous un régime à la fois théocratique et populaire. Or la Hollande, de son côté, n'a pas davantage, un passé monarchique. Les Hollandais ont eu seulement des Comtes et non des Rois. Rien ne prouve d'ailleurs qu'ils ont transféré à leurs Comtes leurs propres droits. C'est même le contraire qui est vrai: l'assemblée des États de Hollande s'est réservé le droit de rappeler les Comtes à leur devoir, lorsqu'ils portaient atteinte au prestige de l'assemblée et à la liberté des citoyens. Aussi depuis la reconquête de son indépendance, l'exercice du pouvoir, fondé sur le principe des assemblées souveraines, a retrouvé en Hollande, tous ses droits.[88] C'est au nom de l'Écriture que Spinoza combat la tentative du clergé calviniste d'établir que la monarchie est le seul régime politique voulu par Dieu.

(d) Si les théologiens calvinistes sont en Hollande des partisans du régime monarchique, c'est qu'ils pensent que c'est le régime le plus favorable pour la propagation de leurs vues spéculatives qu'ils attribuent faussement à l'Écriture elle-même. En présentant comme faisant partie de la parole de Dieu des idées philosophiques qui ne sont en réalité que des inventions de

566

leur esprit, ils traitent ceux qui ne les partagent pas d'hérétiques et de schismatiques. La liberté de philosopher serait-elle donc condamnée par les Saintes Écritures dont ils se réclament?

Certes la cohérence et la solidité de l'État des Hébreux reposait – nous l'avons vu – sur l'unité de la foi. Mais la foi des Hébreux se réduisant uniquement à l'obéissance, laissait de côté les opinions sur l'essence de Dieu et de ses propriétés, adaptées à la compréhension de chacun, qu'il soit prophète ou simple particulier. Des choses purement spéculatives ne relevaient pas chez les Hébreux du droit révélé. C'est seulement sous le second temple que se sont développées des sectes religieuses, celles des pharisiens et des saducéens qui soulevaient des controverses d'ordre spéculatif sur des points tels que la résurrection des corps, la prédestination et la liberté des hommes etc. Autant de causes de la rupture de l'unité idéologique de l'État, de la persécution d'hommes d'une grande probité intellectuelle, accusés d'impiété et de schismatisme, et de la disparition de l'autorité de l'État, qui, inféodé à la secte la plus nombreuse et la plus populaire, celle des pharisiens, devient lui-même un État sectaire et par là-même cesse d'être un État vrai. Pour éviter toutes ces calamités, un seul moyen: admettre que la piété et le vrai culte de la religion consistent seulement dans les oeuvres, c'est-à-dire dans la pratique de la justice et de la charité, et, pour le reste, accorder à chacun la liberté de juger.

NOTES

1 Spinoza, *Opera*, ed. Gebhardt, *Tractatus theologico-politicus*, chs. III, IV,V.
2 *Ibid.*, p. 46, ll. 4–16.
3 *Ibid.*, p. 46, ll. 16–23.
4 *Ibid.*, ch. XVII, p. 217, ll. 17–24.
5 *Tractatus politicus*, ch. V, p. 311.
6 *Tractatus theologico-politicus*, ch. III, p. 44, ll. 14–27.
7 *Ibid.*, ch. IV, p. 60, ll. 20, 28.
8 *Ibid.*, ch. IV, p. 60, l. 22.
9 *Ibid.*, p. 61.
10 *Ibid.*, p. 62.
11 *Ibid.*, p. 59, l. 18.
12 *Ibid.*, pp. 64–5.
13 *Ibid.*, p. 65.
14 Spinoza cite trop librement le passage de Jérémie dont il s'inspire. Le texte hébreu dit: Recherchez la paix de la ville où je vous ai déportés; priez pour elle à Dieu, car de sa prospérité dépendra la vôtre (Jérémie, ch. XXIX, 7). Et lorsqu'on place ce verset dans son contexte il n'a pas du tout le sens que Spinoza lui attribue. Le prophète s'adresse aux juifs déportés par Nabuchodonosor, alors que Sédécias siégeait encore sur le trône de David. Encouragés par de faux prophètes, les déportés espéraient en leur retour prochain dans leur patrie. Jérémie, sûr de la défaite du royaume de Juda, prévient ses compatriotes au nom

de Dieu qu'ils y resteront soixante-dix ans et que, par conséquent, ils doivent en attendant coopérer à la prospérité de leur nouveau pays et de prier pour lui. Si toutefois ils gardent au cours de leur exil leur fidélité à Dieu, il les ramènera au pays de leur ancêtres (Jérémie, ch. XXIX, p. 1–16.) Jérémie ne dit nulle part qu'il suffit d'être déporté par un ennemi pour que, sans même être citoyen libre et avant la défaite définitive de notre propre pays on ait le droit de rompre le pacte conclu avec le Dieu d'Israël (*ibid.*, ch. XXIX, p. 6–17).

15 *Ibid.*, ch. III, pp. 56–7.

16 *Ibid.*, ch. III, p. 47, ll. 26–30.

17 *Ibid.*, p. 45, ll. 32–4.

18 *Ibid.*, p. 46, ll. 22–4.

19 *Ibid.*, p. 47, ll. 7–17.

20 *Ibid.*, p. 47, ll. 17–25.

21 Maïmonide, *Guide des Egarés*, trad. Munk, II, ch. XXXVIII, p. 300.

22 *Tractatus theologico-politicus*, ch. IV, p. 64, ll. 1–10.

23 *Ibid.*, ch. XVIII, p. 218, ll. 23–30.

24 *Ibid.*, ch. VII, p. 103.

25 *Ibid.*, ch. V, pp. 75–115.

26 *Ibid.*, ch. XVII, p. 216.

27 'Quare eidem omno assuefactis ipsa non amplius servitus, sed libertas videri debuit: unde sequi etiam debuit, ut nemo negata, sed mandata cuperet; ad quod etiam non parum conduxisse videtur, quod certis annis temporibus otio et laetitiae se dare tenebantur, non ut animo, sed ut deo ex animo obtemperarent. *Ibid.*, ch. XVII, p. 216, ll. 24–9.

28 *Ibid.*, ch. XVII, p. 201, l. 4.

29 *Tractatus politicus*, ch. I, §. 3.

30 *Tractatus theologico-politicus*, ch. XVII, pp. 203–4.

31 *Ibid.*, ch. XVI, p. 189.

32 *Ibid.*, p. 196, *Ethique*, IV, p. XXXVII, Scolie II, p. 32.

33 *Tractatus theologico-politicus*, ch. XVI, p. 191, ll. 28, 31.

34 *Ibid.*, p. 192, ll. 25, 26; ch. III, p. 58, ll. 23–7.

35 'omnia dirigere et appetitum, quatenus in damnum alterius aliquid suadet, fraenare, neminique facere, quod sibi fieri non vult, jusque denique alterius tanquam suum defendere. *Ibid.*, ch. XVI, p. 191, ll. 30–5.

36 Talmud, ch. 31, a.

37 Evangile selon Matthieu, ch. 7, v. 12.

38 *Tractatus theologico-politicus*, ch. VII, p. 103, ll. 19–27.

39 *Ibid.*, ch. XVI, p. 195, ll. 14–17.

40 *Ibid.*, ch. XVI, p. 198, ll. 20–35.

41 *Tractatus politicus*, chs. II, XV.

42 *Tractatus theologico-politicus*, ch. V, p. 74–5; ch. XVII, p. 205.

43 *Ibid.*, ch. V, p. 75.

44 *Ibid.*, ch. XVII, p. 205, ll. 24–5.

45 Rabbi Jehouda Halevy, *Sefer Hacuzari*, en hébreu, 1947, Tel-Aviv, ch. IV, p. 233.

46 'Vous avez vu vous-même comment j'ai traité les Egyptiens, comment je vous ai emportés sur les ailes du vautour et amenés vers moi,' *L'Exode*, 19,4; *Tractatus theologico-politicus*, ch. XVII, p. 205, ll. 35–7.

47 *Ibid.*, ch. I, p. 23, ll. 30–5.
48 *Tractatus politicus*, chs. VI, VI.
49 *Tractacus theologico-politicus*, ch. XVII, p. 205, ll. 25–6.
50 *Ibid.*, ch. XVII, p. 206, ll. 23–5.
51 Le droit de consulter Dieu et d'interpréter la loi fut réservé ultérieurement aux membres de la tribu de Lévi, tribu de Moïse et d'Aron. Nous verrons que, selon Spinoza, les privilèges spirituels accordés à une seule tribu, ont fini par développer chez les Hébreux le cléricalisme et l'anticléricalisme, causes de la décadence de l'État. Dans sa constitution primitive tous les premiers nés de tous les Hébreux devaient être consacrés à Dieu. *Nombres*, VIII, 17. *Tractatus theologico-politicus*, p. 218, ll.1–3.
52 *Ibid.*, ch. XVII, p. 207.
53 *Ibid.*, ch. XXI, p. 250, l. 25.
54 *Ibid.*, p. 231, l. 30.
55 *Ibid.*, p. 239, l. 18.
56 *Ibid.*, ch. XVII, Adnotation XXXVI, p. 265.
57 *Ibid.*, ch. XVII, p. 209.
58 *Ibid.*, ch. XX, p. 239, ll. 25–33.
59 *Nombres*, 27, 22.
60 *Tractatus politicus*, ch. VII, p. 25.
61 *Tractatus theologico-politicus*, ch. XVIII Adn XXXVIII, p. 265.
62 *Ibid.*, ch. XVII, p. 208, ll. 1–4.
63 *Ibid.*
64 *Ibid.*, p. 209, ll. 14–15.
65 *Ibid.*, ch. I, p. 26.
66 *Ibid.*
67 *Ibid.*, ch. XVII, p. 211.
68 *Ibid.*, Adn XXXVIII, pp. 266–7.
69 *Ibid.*, p. 211.
70 *Ibid.*, Adn XXXVIII, pp. 266–7.
71 *Ibid.*, p. 209, l. 26.
72 *Ibid.*, pp. 313–14.
73 *Tractatus politicus*, ch. X, §. 1.
74 *Tractatus theologico-politicus*, ch. XVII, p. 212, l. 30.
75 *Ibid.*, ch. XVII, p. 213.
76 *Tractatus politicus*, chs. VII, XVII.
77 *Tractatus theologico-politicus*, ch. XVII, pp. 211–12.
78 *Ibid.*, p. 200.
79 *Ibid.*, p. 216.
80 *Ibid.*, pp. 202, 29.
81 *Ibid.*, ch. XVII, pp. 219–20.
82 *Ibid.*, ch. XVIII, p. 224.
83 *Ibid.*, ch. XVII, pp. 217–21.
84 S. Zac, *Spinoza et l'interprétation de l'Écriture*, Presses Universitaires de France, 1965.
85 *Tractatus theologico-politicus*, ch. XVIII, pp. 221–2.
86 *Ibid.*, ch. XVIII, p. 223.
87 *Ibid.*, ch. XIX, p. 234.
88 *Ibid.*, ch. XVIII, pp. 206–88.

Sylvain Zac

ENGLISH SUMMARY: SPINOZA AND THE HEBREW STATE

The Hebrews as the chosen people – this is one of the propositions of the *Tractatus theologico-politicus* – do not have a spiritual meaning. They have, rather, an historical and political meaning. What are the foundations and the institutions of the Hebrew State? What was, in spite of its excellence, the primary cause of its decline and fall? In answering these questions, Spinoza draws lessons which throw a new light on the aims he pursues in his political works.

In *Tractatus theologico-politicus*, Spinoza disproves the Jewish dogmas of the Hebrews' spiritual vocation, of the divine character of the Mosaic Law, and of the absolute worth of the religious ritual.

Nevertheless, he argues that the dogma of the Hebrews' vocation is closely related to the excellence of the political institutions of the Hebrew State; he insists upon the beneficial consequences of the Mosaic Law considered as Law of the State, and observes the part taken by religious ritual in the development of the consciousness of freedom through submission to law.

There is more: using concepts borrowed from his own political philosophy (concepts of natural law, positive law, social contract, democracy, religious state) Spinoza endeavours to prove directly that the Hebrew State owes its superiority to the bases they give to it: (a) the pact concluded with God Himself, in consequence of which the equal dependence of all men to God excludes the dependence of man to man; (b) the pact concluded with Moses, intercessor between God and His people, whose part was to give 'God's Word' an historical reality.

Especially in *Judges* period, one can see that the Hebrews' theocratic system works in a democratic manner: principle of federalism inside the State; political sovereignty incarnated only in Mosaic Law; precise measures in order to avoid tyranny; principle of the 'armed nation', permitting conciliation of patriotism and antimilitarism; social institutions of great originality (jubilee, anti-slavery laws, periodical management of leisure-time, juridically organized solidarity).

The Golden Age, for the Hebrew State, came to an end with the arrival of the Kings. Transition of the sovereignty from 'Temple' to 'Court' ended in breaking off the equilibrium of the State: perpetual tensions between kings and their subjects, on one hand, between kings and prophets on the other; internal wars of an unhuman cruelty; growing number of external wars, which finally ended in the ruin of the State.

Besides, Spinoza's antiroyalism is indissolubly bound up with his anti-clericalism: it is the installation of a sacerdotal, independent power, hereditarily owned by Levi's tribe, which was, according to Spinoza, the chief cause of the advent of monarchy, and consequently of the Hebrew State's decay.

570

Finally, Spinoza, being a supporter of a pragmatic conception of history, points to political consequences of his analysis of the causes of greatness and decline of the Hebrew State: (1) the dangers of the interference of the clergy in the State's affairs, for State as well as for religion; (2) the principle of supremacy of political power, only able to insert the Divine Law in history; (3) the principle of superiority of the popular way of government over the monarchical one; (4) the respect of the freedom of thought in all that concerns speculative ideas, because Hebrew faith excludes every dogma concerning God's essence and His relation to World and Man.

Epilogue – ban invalid after death

Siegfried Hessing, London

I have already hinted before in this book (pp. 32ff.) at certain intentions of 'tinting' Spinoza and Spinozism in order to match accordingly the universalism usually accepted as a facet of Christianity and only then to accept Spinoza *orbi sed non urbi*. While doing this the very truth would be neglected that this universalism of Christ (Jewish in fact!) attracted Spinoza, and is the very same Jewish universality proclaimed by our prophets long, long ago. Robert Misrahi, in his excellent contribution to this book (p. 387ff.): 'Spinoza and Christian thought – a challenge', has admirably unmasked this trend in a keen and daring way to show how (Christian) scholars have quoted from the whole context only the particular parts which support their claim to Christianize Spinoza. A re-Judaization has already begun to dawn and gain momentum for him as for Jeshu, who would also appear over-paganized, when all organic traces of Jewish kernel and shell are removed altogether.

Shall we join Henry Mechoulan in saying with Victor Cousin, 'Spinoza was more of a Jew than he thought himself'?

These introductory words will fully explain why it is so convenient for Christian Spinozists to appear as defenders of Spinoza against his Jewish background, especially when pointing today as three hundred years ago, at the ban – as if such excommunication would still be valid, just as in Catholic eyes an anathema remains for ever and ever! I have already heard rumours that the document exhibited in the Library Ets Haim of the Portuguese Synagogue in Amsterdam, shows (regrettably?) no signatures as expected. When attending the Spinoza celebrations in The Hague, in February 1977, I recalled that Heinrich Heine, an ardent lover of Spinoza, urges the visitor of Amsterdam not to overlook that marvellous synagogue. So I visited it with my wife, and we had a chance to see then that questionable document with no signatures on it, which made me continue pondering on the enigma. There I was warmly received by D. da Silva Solis, with whom I later entered into an inspiring correspondence confirming a certain common affinity, which I quote:

> Ets Haim will be obliged to receive a copy of *Speculum Spinozanum*. As we consider that Baruch de Espinoza is a genius which belongs to the *world* just as Einstein, we did not organize as a religious Yeshiva a

special exhibition leaving this to the University of Amsterdam (Section Rosenthaliana) and the City of The Hague, where 300 years ago the great philosopher was buried in the New Church. However, we put all the material from our library and archives relative to Spinoza at the disposal of the Exhibition in Amsterdam, Paris and Buenos Aires (Museo Judio). Thanking you for your friendly feelings, shalom u berachah, yours, etc.

In the meantime I collected opinions about the ban, signed or unsigned, to throw more light on such a dark affair, kept dark, on purpose as it were . . . And the first encouraging words I received were from Edgar Samuel:

> I am afraid that suggestions that the ban on Spinoza should be lifted are based on the misconception that such a Cherem, like a Roman Catholic ban, persists beyond the grave, which I believe is not the Halachic view. You are in good company because David ben Gurion made the same suggestion. Historic events cannot be readjusted, only their effect on the present can be altered.

And just *this* was and still is the purpose of my present third collective homage to Spinoza, not only to present again new admiration and interpretation about his perennial teaching but also to clarify the significance of the Cherem, to be regarded as a life sentence for a living human being with the aim of ex-communicating him from his living community and banning him into an individual 'exile'. It was to please the authorities of the Dutch host-country, offering a new homeland and freedom for Jews in those turbulent times. . . .

> The ban against Spinoza was the due paid to Caesar rather than to the God of Israel!

But it was not, as Christian scholars want us to believe, that the ban is still valid beyond the grave which covers everything earthly and, that the Jews are still 'banning' Spinoza today as they are 'crucifying' Christ in their wishful thinking!

When we have in mind that even a personality like Menasse ben Israel, Spinoza's teacher, was once banned himself for twenty-four hours because he displeased his superiors, then our approach will take a less rigid consideration today. At the time of the pronouncement of the Cherem, Manasseh ben Israel was not in Amsterdam, otherwise – as some Spinoza scholars advance an opinion today – he would surely have softened to a certain extent the harshness of the excommunication, which anyhow appears for us softened by the (intended?) lack of signatures for posterity, as if limiting this rigidity for the short lifespan of man only.

The first authentic attitude of the Secretary of the Vereniging Het Spinoza-huis, Guido van Suchtelen, whom I had the pleasure to know and esteem for a long time, brings like an official echo from the wardens of the posthumous continuity of the humous existence of the man who was Baruch de Spinoza. This attitude deserves an undivided attention.

If you want to know it absolutely precisely:

1 The manuscript of the ban is no longer in the Library de Montezimos, but in the Municipal Archives of Amsterdam. I have held it several times in my hands.
2 The protocol is not signed by anybody (as also other protocols in the book are not signed). Absolute conclusions could *only* be deduced from it by leaders of the Portuguese-Israelitic Community in Amsterdam.
3 The ban is irrevocable and has been pronounced for ever and ever. Eternities do not end in 1977. . . .
4 The eternal validity of the ban is the exclusive concern (i.e. under the liability) of the Portuguese-Israeli Community in Amsterdam.

MY PERSONAL OPINION

Spinoza at that time provoked very consciously the ban. For him – and for others as well, banned at nearly the same time – it was an honour and a confirmation of his independence as a thinker. Without any ban he would have remained for ever the insignificant merchant as he was before 1656!

Thus: lifting the ban however (as already said) impossible, would say as much as: Bento, you are now again annexed by the orthodox believers, you have lost your sagacity (*caute!*) and you have become worthless, only good to be forgotten. . . . And then, who are we properly speaking, that we want to 'rehabilitate' once again the great thinker of Holland after three centuries? Do we perhaps do the same for Uriel da Costa, who lived in Spinoza's neighbourhood? For Johannes Koerbagh, his best pupil? For those approximately ten or twenty other Portuguese Israelites, who were banned at nearly the same time? Or, for Rabbi S. Lorincz, who was still excommunicated in 1975 in Jerusalem? For Spinoza himself and his friends and disciples, the ban had little or no significance at all. Why after three hundred years do we rather suddenly speak of 'stain'? Mr J. Klausner, as you know, has also exclaimed: 'Lifted is the ban!' In whose name actually? And hereby he falsified, in his translation, Spinoza's own words in order to bring the philosopher again into line. Spinoza experts will not join here. Absolutely not.

Not satisfied with such 'personal' and un-Spinozistic an outburst, I continued to wait for more unbiased and authentic information which came from the Municipal Archives in Amsterdam:

In 1940 and later years the old Archives of the Portuguese-Israelitic Congregation were transferred to the Municipal Archives. The copy enclosed with this letter and the copy in your possession are probably made from the same text. There are no signatures.

Another letter soon hoped to answer my query regarding the validity of the ban after death and the implications for the man excommunicated:

There are various sorts of Jewish excommunications: cherem is one of them. There are even various sorts of cherem: in the more severe form it was pronounced in the synagogue, with some accompanying ritual. No doubt Spinoza's cherem came into effect by such proclamation (from the teba), not by registering a note about it, signed or unsigned. There is no reason to doubt that this proclamation was really made. About the question of the validity of this cherem after Spinoza's death, I feel not entitled to give an opinion.

But I was still tireless in my efforts to get access to the official text of the Jewish law (Halacha) and understanding Jewish scholars like Louis Jacobs gave me their help gladly. Before I come to this, I still feel pleasantly obliged to the echo received from other Spinoza admirers who shared or did not share my mission in clarifying Spinoza's contemporaries via his posterity and now our contemporaries indeed. So I give priority to D. da Silva Solis in his noble position, when timelessly linking a quasi-past with another quasi-present:

I thank you for your very interesting letter of 17th March. Your view on the Herem is very interesting. I confess I did not know that a Herem expires with one's death. So a reason the more to ignore the claim to cancel the Herem against Spinoza since it was never *pronounced* [his Italics] by a Beth Din. We organized in Ets Haim an exhibition to commemorate that 350 years ago the first Hebrew book was printed in Holland and edited on the printing press of Haham Menasse ben Israel. Enclosed find please a photocopy of an article I wrote on Menasse ben Israel. Wishing you and your dear wife a happy Pessah, yours etc. . . . .

Certain prejudices are still prevalent among Jews, and non-Jews as well, against a so-called re-Judaization of Spinoza, but when considering that the ban ceased when the ephemeral life of Spinoza ceased in the eyes of other ephemeral men, then people will stop thinking and speaking of an annulment of a non-existing or fictitious ban. Instead they will rather think of how such an 'heretical' philosopher in a quasi-self-contradiction predicted, with a prophetic and historic vision, the re-erection of the Jewish state after the karmic dispersion among other nations to become again a nation like them and to manifest at the same time their universality which needs no Christianization to be recognized as such.

Sylvain Zac responded to my mission soon:

I thank you vividly for your letter which has interested me much. I congratulate you equally of having contributed for a third time to the diffusion of Spinoza's thought in the world. A remarkable work! I had

575

the occasion during my career to reflect on the conditions of Spinoza's excommunication. The biographies at our disposal are vague and themselves a little bit antisemitic. . . . There was a danger of considering Holland an asylum for atheism. I agree with you, that Spinoza has contributed more than others to the knowledge of treatises essential for the Jewish thought.

There is still a tendency to exploit the 'Christianization' of Spinoza's ideas grafted on him against his wish (as grafted on Jeshu against his wish later!) to justify Misrahi's warning, while too many pose as well-wishing protectors and 'sole agents' of a Jew, who does not need re-Judaization but only acceptance *pro forma*, not *de jure*. Authentic circles fear to 'loose' the monopolized grip in such an international affair and would rather prefer to keep the cherem still valid *ad absurdum* in spite of the standing Jewish Law as Tract. Berachot, ch. 3 (p. 19A) fully backed by Shulchan Aruch, Yorde De'ah, ch. 334, paragraphs 3 and 4. The spirit of such law wills

that the tombstone not only covers the body of a sinner, but buries the sin itself, which on the cemetery as beth olam (eternal world) has no (eternal) value anymore as the body itself in its ephemerousness has not . . . Sic!

No better could I finish this epilogue than by putting emphasis on my friend Robert Misrahi's introduction to his article in this book (p. 387):

Now and again commentators venture Christian interpretations of Spinoza's thought with a view to 'recuperate' – as French terminology would put it – the atheist philosopher. Some emphasize his professed admiration for Christ, others rely on his excommunication from the synagogue, while the part played by charity and love in his doctrine of true piety is vindicated by quite a few. But all feel entitled to see in Spinoza's philosophy a twofold intimation: it is considered as betraying sympathy for the Christian doctrine and at the same time acknowledging its debt to Christian thought for what is best in its own spiritual inspiration. This clearly appears to us as a vain attempt to distort the meaning of Spinoza's philosophy and – once its explosive power is thus muffled – to make it instrumental to Christian spiritualist idealism . . . Our present study aims to unmask such Christian interpretations of Spinoza's philosophy, our purpose being to restore, in the face of such distortions the genuine features of Spinozism.

I am glad to add – in the last moment – some ultra-important opinions about the Herem:

Gerschom Scholem, in his recent letter of 8 August 1977:

It seems to me that the question of the validity of the Herem after the death and the relevant prescriptions about treating the coffin, was already raised by several people after Ben-Gurion put up his suggestion. There was much controversy about this in the Hebrew Press at that time, but I do not recall the details. But I *distinctly* recall having been present when Klausner made his speech in 1927 and when we left the hall, some people laughed at his emotional performance (Our brother are you! . . .) and said that under Jewish Law it was sheer nonsense and proved only that Klausner was ignorant of the Law. *I do not know whether they were right* (my Italics, Ed.).

Asa Kasher (editor of *Philosophia*, Bar-Ilan University, Ramat Gan), in his letter of 14 August 1977:

My general point of view is that the ban is an institutional product and its validity and consequences should be considered only within the confines of that institution which produced it, namely the particular community of Amsterdam. Not being a member of the community, not being an observing Jew, not considering the trial – if there was one – fair enough – all these are sufficient conditions for one to disregard the ban. On the other hand, any formal step taken with regard to the ban should be valid within the same institution, otherwise it would be pointless or at least not strong enough for rendering it absolutely invalid. I know that the community of Amsterdam is not willing to render the ban invalid and to my mind they are right – for them to render it invalid means that they will carry out a formal process of considering the ban, its background, etc., but since no files about Spinoza's ban are available to them or to anyone else, they cannot initiate the required process, even if they were willing to do it. May I remark that the only item in the ban which has seemed to apply in our times as well is the ban on reading the books Spinoza wrote, but this is a mistaken impression, based on a wrong translation of the ban. The last line of the ban concerns MSS which Spinoza *had* written or copied before the ban was produced. None of the books we have (excluding, perhaps, some parts of the *Tractatus*) had already been written then.

Isaiah Berlin expressed some doubts in his letter of 3 March 1976:

I fear that Ben-Gurion's re-admission of Spinoza to the bosom of the Jewish community would be accepted neither by the holders to religious Orthodoxy within it nor by Spinoza himself, who would not have regarded Ben-Gurion as the embodiment of the rationality which he consistently advocated.

Kasher thus re-confirms an opinion of the community as I mentioned before, very unmistakably, when quoting the 'sincere' attitude of the noble-minded pillar D. da Silva Solis. I, therefore, reiterate my viewpoint that the full text of the ban so often quoted and misquoted contains only (justifiable or not) a stern warning to every living member of the community with the imperative to abstain from any contact with this ex-'communicated' person all his life. Thus: the ban with its punishing effect, can refer with harm only to the then con-temporary living heretic but expires with the expiration of his life. I see *'sheer nonsense'* claiming now after Spinoza's death the revocation of a now non-existing ban with a pseudo-phantom importance only for certain minds. . . .

CONCLUSION

The phenomeno-'logical' aspect of Baruch de Spinoza, with evidential existence from 24 November 1632 to 21 February 1677, has been the nailing target for excommunication whose purpose was to ban any communication with his community at such turbulent times, even more turbulent for such a little, ant-size and ant-industrious nation 'exiled' and dispersed among other giant nations, especially when considering their few rebellious nationals. Spinoza's nation has now in our present time and in Spinoza's posterity been granted absolution from its collective existential and historical exile, and Spinoza himself already a long time ago, although then an individual and being existentially exiled within his exiled scattered nation, has wisely and with no hate foreseen such an event centuries ahead. . . .

We thus have the mission to consider, respect and recognize the trans-existential invalidity of such a ban concerning only the radius of proper existence with existential com- and implications from cradle to grave and its marvellous radiation into perennial essence so to speak! We have then to ponder how Spinoza himself was heralding the gospel of freedom for all individuals on this globe from illusive bondage within self-imposed boundaries of any existential burden already considered an exile in itself. His aim was to become and to make us become conscious of self, God and world not as three separate ental elements but rather as the same one elementary wholeness and individuation to identify with. Then – we will not fail to 'feel and experience' with Spinoza together 'that we are eternal'; in the phenomenological shell of existential striving for completion via our essential kernel in the spirit of the eternal and eternalizing equation of a quasi-seemingly unequalness: *rupam-arupam, forma sive essentia* (i.e. form or formlessness, *existentia = essentia*), allness or no-thingness as the very same enigmatic circle: 0, i.e. zero (of *ratio sive causa sive de-terminatio*!), void, sunya, ayin . . .

Baruch, you need no defenders now and especially no defenders or protectors against such paradoxically perennial-contemporaries: short-sighted and short-living in temporary time and place. You need no defenders beyond the existential realm (or rather aspect) of life when transcending into the essential (aspect of) beyondness of the very same otherless life; perennial as the philo-sophia and phil-ousia which is its true mirror indeed. Hence: what has been once exiled was valid only once within the onceness of the walls of phenomena and phenomenological concerns. Huang-Po seconds Spinoza: 'The ignorant eschew phenomena but not thought, the wise eschew thought but not phenomena.'

Whatsoever the mind understands under the form of eternity, it does not understand by virtue of conceiving the (so-called) present actual *existence* of the body but by virtue of conceiving the *essence* of the body under the form of eternity.

In Spinoza's tradition 'this world' as here and now is called 'the world of lies' – maya – while YHWH said to Israel to hear it and to take it into their hearts (not heads!): 'I AM (is) YOUR ELOHIM IN TRUTH! YHWH IS THE ELOHIM! YHWH IS ECHAD! *Deus sive natura: vel deificans et deificatus vel naturans et naturatus via omnia animata sumus ...*

Are such thoughts aiming to universalize, omnialize and oceanize the single, isolated desperately lonely drop *heresy* when able to extend, expand drop-consciousness into divine-cosmic omni-consciousness while including self, God and world with universal, divine, oceanic feeling as otherless one? Are they heresy? And is a thinker like Spinoza still punishable with unending *exile* or cherem when leading to liberation from any *existential exile* under the tyranny of the phantom of heterophobia? Liberation from fear of para-otherness *per se* imprisoned in a pseudo-exile itself 'as if' beginning with birth and ending with death? Spinoza opened daringly the rusty gates into our immense and unknown beyondness, while still quasi on 'this side' of siding thoughts to help introspecting omnidentity, all-oneness or one-allness in the evangelium of:

YHWH IS ELOHIM, OUR ELOHIM! YHWH IS ECHAD!

The sole zoharic (trans-)mission of man in this world is 'to know that YHWH is ELOHIM' (and no-'thing' else: no elseness, eitherness and no otherness *per se*)! Knowledge was lifeless, sinful since the first encounter and brought our all expulsion from Eden, because dichotomizing, splitting the way, truth and life which 'I am' myself, namely into knower (a who) versus a pseudo-other as known (a what). We cannot know such whatness but feel and experience '*that* we know that we know': *cognitio sui, ratio sui, causa sui*, indeterminacy of true otherlessness. ....

Unknowable sinless life could repatriate all mankind again from the universal exile in outer-Eden while knowledge-hunting like Münchhausen for a phantomized quasi-otherness with the aim of destroying such pseudo-otherness in self-alienation and this has brought us now on the very brink of our own self-destruction: the greatest menace of mankind and its farcical man-kindness indeed. ....

Spinoza was eager to lift such a universal ban from mankind leading from self-bondage to self-salvation and thus fully unconcerned himself with the fate of his individual excommunication during his forty-five years of feeling and experiencing timeless eternity which has nothing to do with a so-called 'duration' of existential strife estranging man from essential omni-awareness.

We have not to worry at all about Spinoza (this he did already for himself successfully!) but about ourselves to vote and devote our longing for lifting the ban from 'knowing' (a separating quasi-otherness) with the urge and aim to re-turn to the otherless magic of unknowable life in Eden:

sentimus experimurque nos omnes aeternos
quia omnia animata esse.
LE CHAYIM!

Index